Hanoverian Britain and Empire

The domestic and colonial history of Britain in the period between the Hanoverian succession and the early nineteenth century is the subject of the new essays collected in this volume, presented in memory of the distinguished historian Philip Lawson. Beginning with two historiographical surveys, the contributions go on to illuminate many of the issues which are at the forefront of historical research and controversy, including the aristocracy, the British problem, the political role of women, British identity, and the problems of empire in both India and America.

Philip Lawson at the Lewis-Walpole Library, Farmington, Connecticut

Hanoverian Britain and Empire

Essays in Memory of Philip Lawson

EDITED BY

Stephen Taylor
Richard Connors
AND
Clyve Jones

THE BOYDELL PRESS

First published 1998
The Boydell Press, Woodbridge

ISBN 0 85115 720 3

The Boydell Press is an imprint of Boydell & Brewer Ltd
PO Box 9, Woodbridge, Suffolk IP12 3DF, UK
and of Boydell & Brewer Inc.
PO Box 41026, Rochester, NY 14604–4126, USA

A catalogue record for this book is available
from the British Library

Library of Congress Cataloging-in-Publication Data
Hanoverian Britain and empire : essays in memory of Philip Lawson /
edited by Stephen Taylor, Richard Connors, and Clyve Jones.
    p. cm.
"Philip Lawson – a bibliography": p.
Includes bibliographical references and index.
ISBN 0–85115–720–3 (alk. paper)
    1. Great Britain – History – 1714–1837.   2. Great Britain – Colonies
– History – 18th century.   3. Great Britain – Colonies – History – 19th
century.   4. Imperialism – History – 18th century.   5. Imperialism –
History – 19th century.   6. Hanover, House of.   I. Taylor, Stephen,
1960– .   II. Connors, Richard, 1964– .   III. Jones, Clyve, 1944– .
IV. Lawson, Philip.
DA480.H25   1998
941.07 – dc21   98–34196

This publication is printed on acid-free paper

Printed in Great Britain by
Antony Rowe Ltd, Chippenham, Wiltshire

Contents

Acknowledgments

The editors are grateful to the Department of History at the University of Alberta for a grant to cover the cost of indexing, to Mr Alasdair Hawkyard for compiling the index, and to Mrs Carol Mackay and Mrs Elizabeth Berry in the Department of History at the University of Reading for typing it. Professor Edward James provided invaluable advice and assistance on computing matters. We would also like to acknowledge the assistance of Mrs Eileen Lawson, Mrs Corinne Connors, Dr David Marples, Dr Kenneth Monroe, Mr Roy Wolfe, Mrs Linda Bridges of the Department of History, University of Alberta, and the Institute of Historical Research, University of London.

Abbreviations

Add. MS	Additional Manuscript
B.L.	British Library
Bodl.	Bodleian Library
Cobbett, *Parl. Hist.*	*The Parliamentary History of England from the Earliest Period to the Year 1803* (36 vols., 1806–20)
D.N.B.	*Dictionary of National Biography*
H.L.R.O.	House of Lords Record Office
H.M.C.	Historical Manuscripts Commission
I.O.L.	India Office Library
L.J.	*Journals of the House of Lords*
P.R.O.	Public Record Office
P.R.O.N.I.	Public Record Office of Northern Ireland
R.O.	Record Office
S.P.	State Papers
U.L.	University Library

The place of publication is London, except where otherwise stated.

Contributors

H. V. Bowen is Senior Lecturer in Economic and Social History at the University of Leicester. He is author of *Revenue and Reform. The Indian Problem in British Politics, 1757–1773* (Cambridge, 1991), *Elites, Enterprise and the Making of the British Overseas Empire, 1688–1775* (Basingstoke, 1996), and *War and British Society, 1688–1815* (Cambridge, 1998). He is currently writing an economic history of the East India Company between 1756 and 1813.

John L. Bullion is Professor of History at the University of Missouri-Columbia. He has written *A Great and Necessary Measure. George Grenville and the Genesis of the Stamp Act, 1763–1765* (Columbia, Mo., 1982) and several articles on British politics and imperial policy during the 1750s and 1760s. He is presently completing a collection of essays on King George III, the earl of Bute and the American revolution.

David Cannadine is Director of the Institute of Historical Research and Professor of History at the University of London, having previously been Moore Collegiate Professor of History at Columbia University, New York. Among his many books are *The Pleasures of the Past* (1989), *The Decline and Fall of the British Aristocracy* (1990), *G. M. Trevelyan. A Life in History* (1992), *Aspects of Aristocracy. Grandeur and Decline in Modern Britain* (1994) and *The Rise and Fall of Class in Great Britain* (1998).

Elaine Chalus, who gained her Oxford D.Phil. in 1998, tutors students in modern British history at the University of Oxford and sub-edits *Past and Present*. Her interest in women's involvement in eighteenth-century political life dates back to her studies with Philip Lawson when a Master's student at the University of Alberta. Her most recent publication (edited with Hannah Barker) is *Gender in Eighteenth-Century England. Roles, Representation and Responsibilities* (1997).

R. E. Close was a student of Philip Lawson and is now working on a Ph.D. at the University of Cambridge under the supervision of C. A. Bayly. Her doctoral dissertation examines the political and social dynamics of missionary communities that fostered aboriginal resistance to British colonial rule in Upper Canada and South Africa in the early nineteenth century. She is currently employed as a lecturer in European intellectual and social history at the Faculté Saint-Jean, the University of Alberta.

Richard Connors completed an M.A. thesis under the supervision of Philip Lawson in 1989. He then undertook doctoral research at Cambridge University. He was a Social Sciences and Humanities Research Council of Canada Postdoctoral Fellow 1993–5, and is now an Adjunct Professor at the University of Alberta. He has published a number of articles on eighteenth-century British and imperial history, and is in the process of editing the Commons' journal of Philip Yorke, 1743–51, for the Parliamentary History Record Series. He is also completing a book for the Macmillan Press, which examines social policy and state formation in Hanoverian Britain.

D. W. Hayton was educated at the University of Manchester (where he played in the same undergraduate departmental football team as Philip Lawson) and New College, Oxford. For many years he served on the research staff at the *History of Parliament* and remains a consultant editor of the 1690–1715 section. Since 1994 he has lectured in modern history at Queen's University, Belfast. The author of numerous papers on British and Irish history in the late seventeenth and early eighteenth centuries, he has also edited several volumes, the latest of which is *The Parliamentary Diary of Sir Richard Cocks, 1698–1702* (Oxford, 1996). He is joint-editor of *Irish Historical Studies*.

Clyve Jones, Assistant Librarian at the Institute of Historical Research, University of London, and editor of the journal *Parliamentary History* (where he worked with Philip Lawson), has published widely on the early eighteenth-century house of lords and the peerage for which he was awarded a D.Litt. in 1995. He has edited several sources, including *The London Diaries of William Nicolson, Bishop of Carlisle, 1702–1718* (Oxford, 1985) with the late Geoffrey Holmes, and *Tory and Whig. The Parliamentary Papers of Edward Harley, 3rd Earl of Oxford, and William Hay, M.P. for Seaford, 1716–1753* (Woodbridge, 1998), with Stephen Taylor, as well as several collections of essays, including *Britain in the First Age of Party, 1680–1750. Essays Presented to Geoffrey Holmes* (1987).

Linda Kerr completed her University of Alberta Ph.D., 'Quebec: The Making of an Imperial Mercantile Community, 1760–1768', under Philip Lawson in 1992. She was Philip's only doctoral student. She is Assistant Visiting Professor at the University of Alberta and a Lecturer for Athabasca University. Her research interests are in transatlantic trade and the impact of politics upon the success of British merchants in Quebec, and in First Nations educational history.

P. J. Marshall, former Rhodes Professor of Imperial History at King's College, London, is President of the Royal Historical Society. He has been associate editor of *The Writings and Speeches of Edmund Burke* (editor, Oxford, vols. V and VI); a member of the editorial committee of *The Correspondence of Edmund Burke* (joint-editor, Cambridge, vols. VII and X); and editor of *The Cambridge Illustrated History of the British Empire* (Cambridge, 1996), and *The Oxford History of the British Empire. Vol. II: The Eighteenth Century* (Oxford, 1988). His other books include *East India Fortunes. The British in Bengal* (Oxford, 1976), and *Bengal and the British Bridgehead. Eastern India 1740 to 1828* (Cambridge, 1987).

David Milobar is Visiting Assistant Professor at Simon Fraser University. His work has concentrated on Quebec and the British Atlantic in the long eighteenth century. He has written articles on that subject and is completing a monograph on Quebec and the British empire. He is also engaged in a research project on aboriginal peoples and popular prints in eighteenth-century Britain.

Frank O'Gorman has been Professor of History at the University of Manchester since 1992. His publications include *The Whig Parts and the French Revolution* (1967), *Edmund Burke. His Political Philosophy* (1973), *The Rise of Party in England, 1760–1782* (1975), *The Emergence of the British Two-Party System, 1760–1832* (1982), *British Conservatism. Conservative Thought from Burke to Thatcher* (1986), and *Voters, Patrons and Parties. The Unreformed Electorate of Hanoverian England, 1734–1832* (Oxford, 1989). Recently, he has turned his attention to ritual and symbolic forms of popular prints.

Karl Schweizer is a Ph.D. graduate of the University of Cambridge, where he worked with the late Sir Herbert Butterfield. In addition to many articles, he has published among other books: *The Devonshire Diary* (1982), *Lord Bute. Essays in Reinterpretation* (1988), *Cobbett and his Times* (1993), *England, Prussia and the Seven Years War* (1991), *William Pitt, Earl of Chatham* (1993), and *François de Callieres. Diplomat and Man of Letters* (1995). He is currently Professor in the Department of Humanities and Social Sciences, New Jersey Institute of Technology, and a member of the Graduate School, Rutgers University.

Ian K. Steele, Professor of History in the University of Western Ontario, is a Killam Senior Fellow and author of several books on early American and British imperial history. These include: *The Politics of Colonial Policy. The Board of Trade in Colonial Administration, 1696–1720* (1968), *Guerillas and Grenadiers. The Struggle for Canada, 1689–1760* (1969), *The English Atlantic, 1675–1740. An Exploration of Communication and Community* (1986), *Betrayals. Fort William Henry and the 'Massacre'* (1990), and *Warpaths. Invasions of North America* (1994).

Stephen Taylor is Lecturer in History at the University of Reading. He has written numerous articles on politics and religion in the early eighteenth century, edited *The*

Church of England c.1689–c.1833 (Cambridge, 1993) with John Walsh and Colin Haydon and *Tory and Whig* (Woodbridge, 1998) with Clyve Jones, and is reviews' editor of *Parliamentary History*.

Peter D. G. Thomas was Professor of History at the University of Wales, Aberystwyth, from 1976 to 1997. His nine books include five on the American revolution and biographies of Lord North and John Wilkes. He was the supervisor of Philip Lawson's doctoral thesis.

Keith Wrightson is Reader in English Social History at the University of Cambridge, and a Fellow of Jesus College. His is the author of *English Society, 1580–1680* (1982), and co-author with David Levine of *Poverty and Piety in an English Village. Terling, 1525–1700* (1979 and 1995) and *The Making of an Industrial Society. Wickham, 1560–1765* (Oxford, 1991). He was a colleague of Philip Lawson at the University of St Andrews in 1981.

Philip Lawson: An Appreciation

RICHARD CONNORS

The aims of this collection of essays are twofold: first, it is a memorial tribute by friends, colleagues and former students of Philip Lawson, a noted scholar of Hanoverian and imperial British history. Secondly, these articles seek to elaborate upon the subjects and areas of research which Philip explored in his all too brief, but impressive and inspirational, academic life. The essays consider a wide variety of topics and are in themselves a testament to the breadth of Lawson's own historical interests and publications. The two broad themes which preoccupied him, and upon which he conducted his research, were domestic and imperial British history during the long eighteenth century. Phil spent most of his career seeking to integrate thoroughly the domestic and the imperial for he felt that they were inextricably linked in the minds of Hanoverian Britons and that historians had done the study of British history a disservice by exploring each in isolation. Lawson's books and articles were shot through with this guiding imperative and skilfully revealed the value of such an approach for the writing of eighteenth-century British history. Those toiling in the Hanoverian field will be aware of these aspects of Philip Lawson's work, but few were fortunate enough to have known him personally.

Next to his wife Eileen, and daughters Elizabeth and Caroline, and save perhaps Manchester United, Philip Lawson's greatest love was history. Born in Morecombe he spent most of his youth in Lancashire, England. Historians are fortunate that Phil chose to study history rather than to pursue a potential career in professional football. He subsequently earned a B.A. and M.A. from Manchester before going on to complete a Ph.D. at the University College of Wales at Aberystwyth in 1980. He then took up a temporary lectureship at the University of St Andrews in Scotland. This experience was followed by a Killam Teaching Fellowship in the History Department at Dalhousie University in Nova Scotia. In 1983, Phil was offered a prestigious Mactaggart Fellowship which took him across Canada to the University of Alberta. The award was designed to attract promising young scholars to Edmonton to await permanent teaching positions at the university. This was but one of numerous awards he attained as a student and professional historian, the last of which was his election in January 1995 as a Fellow of the Royal Historical Society. Philip remained at the University of Alberta for the rest of his career and, from the time he was hired permanently in 1986, he rose quickly up the academic ladder to become a full professor in 1994. At the prime of his life Philip Lawson was diagnosed with lymphoma, the illness against which he struggled courageously for two years until it took his life in October 1995.

From the outset of his academic career Philip Lawson pursued knowledge relentlessly. He believed a scholar's duty was to teach, publish and play an active part in his community. As a university professor, Phil took his teaching responsibilities very seriously. He was extremely kind and generous with his time and intellectual energy. Uniquely, he combined rigorous and uncompromising scholarship with a relaxed and practical approach to lecturing and graduate supervision. As a result, he became a mentor, not only to his own honours, M.A. and Ph.D. students, but also to others who regularly sought his advice. This owes much to the fact that Phil brought to the teaching, research and writing of history the same enthusiasm he had for life. Yet, he was a demanding supervisor and instructor who continually pushed students to better themselves and the discipline. His students were encouraged to pursue their own historical interests and given considerable latitude to do so, since he demanded neither that they study particular topics nor that they rely upon particular historical methods. What he did insist upon, from his students and his colleagues, was that good history required boldly conceived themes which were rigorously researched and written in a clear and simple prose. His essays and books were not only object lessons in concision, but they also reveal the technical skills which he possessed, and which he expected of other historians.

Philip Lawson's research interests were matched by the range of subjects upon which he lectured. This was, in part, a reflexion of the undergraduate teaching requirements of North American universities, but was also a result of Lawson's abiding interest in Britain and its world in the long eighteenth century. He was convinced that the tensions which existed between the centre and periphery – broadly conceived to include not only the Americas but Asia as well – were of paramount importance in the political, social and cultural development of Britain and its colonies. As a result, he offered courses which covered the history of early modern and modern Britain, British constitutional history, the British empire, the American revolution, American colonial history and research seminars upon various aspects of Hanoverian history. His ability to teach these subjects owed something to the fact that he was intimately familiar with their historiographies, and because he fully integrated his research into his teaching. As his research interests broadened to include the Americas and later India, so too did his lecturing. This development also reflected Lawson's conviction that the best lecturers were those historians who were also active research scholars.

Philip Lawson's changing research interests were also mirrored by those of his research students. In the decade that he was at the University of Alberta (1986–95), Phil supervised nearly two dozen research students, the majority of whom were M.A. students, few of whom had ever given serious thought to eighteenth-century Britain before meeting him. Lawson's earliest research students considered topics such as the Falklands crisis in the 1770s, the role of the Bedford faction in the 1760s, or of the attitudes of parliamentarians to dearth during the same period. Drawing upon the wisdom of a supervisor who had recently completed a political biography of George

Grenville, these students researched subjects which were primarily political in content and proudly Namierite in approach. Phil's increasing interest in the history of his adopted country, Canada, and of the colonial experience culminated in a number of articles on the Americas and Britain in the later eighteenth century, upon attitudes towards Canada, and upon the relationship between Quebec and Britain. While he was working on these topics, his graduate students wrote theses upon the Hudson's Bay Company, upon the mercantile classes in post-conquest Quebec, and upon the iconography of James Wolfe. As Lawson became interested in India and the cultural contexts of empire, so too did his students by considering research topics which concentrated upon such themes as ritual and political culture in various parts of the British empire, the politics of music in Hanoverian Britain, and the popular and political culture of the Spitalfields silkweavers. This complementary research pattern owed much to the fact that Philip was deeply committed to history and that he possessed a powerful intellectual honesty which his inspired and enthusiastic students sought to emulate. While he never chose specific research topics for his research students to study, many picked upon one of the innumerable suggestions or ideas which he mentioned in lectures, seminars or his thought-provoking publications. He instilled in his students the desire to tackle historiographically important subjects which they found interesting, and, in over a dozen cases, the confidence to go on to conduct and complete doctoral research at universities in other parts of Canada, in Britain and in the United States. Moreover, he always devoted enormous time and effort to his students. Chapters and manuscripts were read with care and annotated with wit, perception and constructive criticism. Letters and queries were answered immediately and not only were the academic responsibilities of a supervisor conducted efficiently and meticulously, so too were the time-consuming chores of mediating on behalf of his students with university administrators and funding agencies by doing such things as writing scholarship and employment references. He took great pleasure in, though little credit for, the accomplishments of his research students.

The last few years were some of the most exciting in Philip Lawson's career. His open-mindedness and enthusiasm for history were exemplified by the fact that his scholarly interests were continuing to expand, even after he was no longer physically able to lecture or conduct research. His books – *George Grenville. A Political Life*, *The Imperial Challenge. Britain and Quebec in the Age of the American Revolution*, *The East India Company. A History* – and his edited works – *Parliament and the Atlantic Empire* and *A Taste for Empire and Glory* – reflect the various paths his research and writing took throughout his career. Never dropping his interests in eighteenth-century British and imperial history, he had most recently added the study of culture to his research. At the time of his death, Phil was concerned with the effects of empire on Britain, and especially the influence of empire on British culture in the eighteenth century as seen through the empire of tea. It is truly tragic that this ambitious research project, titled 'The Empire Within', was not completed for it would, no doubt, have altered radically our perceptions of the nature of the imperial experience on Hanoverian society. On this subject, he was far more sensitive to ritual and ceremony and their pictorial representations than in his earlier work, but his vision of Hanoverian history remained constant because of his generous view of both sides of the imperial coin – that of the colonizer and the colonized and their effects on each other.

With fond memories of Philip Lawson's life and with his publications and academic legacy to inspire us, we must now take up the challenge of researching, writing and teaching history without him. Philip Lawson will be terribly missed by this friends and by the profession.

Imperial Odyssey:
Philip Lawson the Historian

H. V. BOWEN

During the 15 years or so of his all-too brief academic career, Phil Lawson travelled a very long way, literally and metaphorically, as a scholar and historian. His journey from Britain to Canada – from Aberystwyth to Edmonton, via St Andrews and Halifax, Nova Scotia – took him from the core to the periphery of the old empire, and this migration was parallelled by a similar relocation of his scholarly energies and interests. By the end of his life, Phil had in some ways moved a very long way from beginnings that were rooted very firmly in the world of eighteenth-century British parliamentary politics. Over time, he developed a deep interest in the problems of empire, and in the relationship between imperialism and the development of metropolitan politics, society, and culture. This gradual broadening of horizons can be traced through the changing nature of the publications he produced, and through the several impassioned appeals he made for the empire and imperialism to be written back into mainstream eighteenth-century British history.

As a postgraduate student, Phil was fortunate in his choice of both supervisor and subject. A member of the small army of students inspired and supervised by Peter D. G. Thomas at the University College of Wales, Aberystwyth, he was encouraged to explore hitherto neglected areas of national politics during the tumultuous decade of the 1760s. His foray into the archives gave him a firm grasp of the wide-ranging issues and debates that preoccupied the politicians of the day, and he adopted an extremely rigorous and methodical approach to his source material which stood him in good stead in later years when he endeavoured to write very different types of history. An initial decision to focus attention on George Grenville proved to be fortunate and well-informed for two different, though related, reasons. First, Grenville had not been subjected to systematic treatment by any modern biographer, and hence there was a golden opportunity for Phil's Ph.D. thesis to be extended into a full-length study of that important, yet misunderstood and much-maligned, first minister and politician. This opportunity was seized when much of the material in 'Faction in Politics: George Grenville and his Followers 1765–1770' (University of Wales Ph.D., 1980) was expanded considerably and published as *George Grenville. A Political Life* (Oxford, 1984). Second, and perhaps more significantly, because Grenville in office and opposition had been preoccupied with the problems arising from the post-1756 expansion of Britain's overseas empire, detailed research work had revealed several hitherto unexplored areas of study which demanded, and were to receive, separate treatment. As 'spin-offs' from his main Grenville project, Phil produced two early articles on North America and the East India Company which demonstrated the central importance of imperial issues to politics during the mid- and late-1760s. As far as Grenville was concerned, historians had long believed that, like many of his contemporaries, his approach to the American empire was determined by a narrow, unwavering preoccupation with taxation. Phil, however, demonstrated that after the repeal of the Stamp Act Grenville could not be considered as a 'hard-liner'; rather, he had deplored the use of force in North America, repeatedly advocating moderation, and had developed a broad view of Britain's relationship with the colonies which was based upon a root and branch reform of trade and imperial finance.[1] Similarly, Phil set the first East India parliamentary inquiry of 1767 in a wider political context than had hitherto been the case with historians such as Dame Lucy Sutherland and John Brooke. While not denying that the crude assault of the Chatham ministry upon the Company was based upon short-term, short-sighted motives, Phil recognised that the inquiry of 1767 opened up important issues related to sovereignty and territorial rights in India, and crown-Company relations in general, that were often to dominate parliamentary politics in the years that followed.[2] Phil's perspective on these issues suggests that, if only in passing at this stage, he was already beginning to define the 'imperial problem' ever more widely, and this general broadening of outlook became clear in the next phase of his work as he began to examine different aspects of Britain's relations with her expanding empire.

As the first part of his career ended, changing circumstances and the forging of new scholarly relationships dictated that Phil move beyond the narrow study of parliamentary politics. He always dismissed in characteristically cheerful and robust fashion the ill-informed charge that he was a third generation scholar of the Namier 'school', or a 'crypto-Namierite' as he often mischievously put it, but there is little doubt that at this time, during the mid-1980s, he felt the need to engage the empire outside the parliamentary arena and through a range of different types of sources. This is not to suggest that he entirely turned his back on parliamentary history, for he continued to publish specialist items on that subject and 'high' politics in general,[3] but with close collaborators such as Jim Philips and Bruce Lenman he began to explore two different, though related, dimensions of the imperial experience. Some articles examined the effects, especially the corrupting effect, that possession of an empire had upon Britain itself, while others, based upon detailed examinations of newspapers

1   'Grenville and America: The Years of Opposition 1765–70', *William and Mary Quarterly*, 3rd ser., XXXVII (1980), 561–76. Many of Phil's essays have been collected together by David Cannadine, Linda Colley, and Ken Munro and published in Philip Lawson, *A Taste for Empire and Glory. Studies in British Overseas Expansion, 1660–1800* (Aldershot, 1997).
2   'Parliament and the First East India Inquiry, 1767', *Parliamentary History*, I (1983), 99–114.
3   See, e.g., 'Further Reflections on the Cabinet in the Early Years of George III's Reign', *Bulletin of the Institute of Historical Research*, LVII (1984), 237–40; 'Parliament, Corn and the Constitution: The Embargo Crisis of 1766', *Parliamentary History*, V (1986), 17–37; and (with Karl Schweizer) 'A Political Diary of Charles Jenkinson, 13 May – 29 June 1765', *Historical Research*, LXV (1992), 349–58.

and pamphlet literature, considered changing British perceptions of the expanding world in which they lived. At first, the focus of this work remained on familiar subjects and areas, with continuing interest in India and the East India Company giving rise to important articles on the neglected political dimension of Robert Clive's colourful career, and on attitudes towards the 'nabobs', or returned East India Company servants, who were widely believed to be undermining British society.[4] Later, though, as personal circumstances changed, Phil switched his attention to Canada, a development which paved the way for detailed studies of the British relationship with Quebec.[5]

Phil's great enthusiasm for these subjects was sustained by his strong belief that modern historians had failed fully to integrate the empire into their general work on Hanoverian Britain. Moreover, he argued that when *the* empire was invoked by eighteenth-century scholars it was all-too often an empire narrowly defined by the 13 North American colonies, which meant that India and Canada, not to mention the West Indies, were even further marginalized. In a brief, deliberately provocative, plea for Britain's eighteenth-century empire to be set within the widest possible terms of scholarly and geographical reference, Phil asked if the 'American obsession' was to continue, and suggested that 'The time has surely come to appreciate what was obvious to every eighteenth-century mariner, that Britain's imperial interests and responsibilities could be found at more than one (westerly) point of the compass.'[6] As far as the effects of empire upon Britain were concerned, though, Phil was swimming with, not against, a strong scholarly tide which in the last decade or so has seen a considerable amount of attention devoted to the British imperial experience in a variety of different economic, social, cultural, and political contexts. It remained a source of enduring frustration to him, however, that much of the 'new' imperial history, thought-provoking and ground-breaking though it was, remained preoccupied with forms of imperialism shaped by the British presence in the Atlantic world. Because of this, he always argued that a fuller understanding of the dynamics and representations of eighteenth-century imperialism would evade the grasp of historians until they were more prepared to adopt a much broader view of British interests. This view needed to embrace Africa, South Asia, the Pacific region and the Far East, and to incorporate forms of organization and development based upon, and emerging from, the conquest and administration of 'alien', non-protestant people of the type

4 With Bruce Lenman, 'Clive and the "Black Jagir": The East India Company in Eighteenth-Century Politics', *Historical Journal*, XXVI (1983), 801–29; with Jim Philips, '"Our Execrable Banditti": Perceptions of Nabobs in the Late Eighteenth Century', *Albion*, XVI (1984), 225–41.

5 '"The Irishman's Prize": Views of Canada from the British Press, 1760–1775', *Historical Journal*, XXVIII (1985), 575–96; 'A Perspective on British History and the Treatment of the Conquest of Quebec', *Journal of Historical Sociology*, III (1990), 252–71; '"Sapped by Corruption": British Governance of Quebec and the Breakdown of Anglo-American Relations on the Eve of Revolution', *Canadian Review of American Studies*, XXII (1991), 301–23.

6 'The Missing Link: The Imperial Dimension in Understanding Hanoverian Britain', *Historical Journal*, XXIX (1986), 747–51 (quotations from pp. 748 and 751).

to be found in Canada and Bengal. The newly acquired parts of the empire thus posed a challenge not only to eighteenth-century politicians and administrators but also to modern historians, and Phil remained convinced, rightly or wrongly, that it was a challenge that was not being properly taken up by his contemporaries. While men such as Grenville, Chatham and Lord North dealt simultaneously with the problems of different parts of the empire, historians, increasingly slaves to case-study and narrow specialization, were still tending to treat overseas territories, not as parts of a greater whole but as discrete, self-standing units which had generated their own unique historiographical agendas. The mental map of eighteenth-century imperial administrators and politicians had become much broader during the 1760s, but this was not appreciated by many modern scholars, especially historians of colonial America, and it was often reflected in their inability to make meaningful connexions between different forms and types of British overseas activity.

In taking up the imperial challenge himself, first in a book with that title devoted to the making of the Quebec Act of 1774, and then in a general survey of the East India Company, Phil endeavoured to practise what he preached and, drawing together the threads of his articles, he considered the wide-ranging implications, for metropolis and empire alike, of the growing British presence in Canada and South Asia. The two books are very different: one is a detailed study of the metropolitan response to the conquest of Quebec in 1759–60; the other offers an overview, based on secondary sources, of the rise and fall of the East India Company between 1600 and 1858.[7] Yet for all the differences of ambition, scope, and method that are evident in these two works, both attempt to throw light upon how Britain, and Britons, endeavoured to bring new territories and peoples into the imperial fold in the face of external threats and the deep-seated anxieties about the empire that were repeatedly given expression in debate about the value and worth of different overseas possessions and trends. This was the essence of the 'imperial problem' as Phil saw it. Less concerned with the causes than the consequences of imperial expansion, he painted pictures of a nation, especially during his favoured decade of the 1760s, which could do little to dictate the pace and direction of overseas activity, but which devoted a great deal of energy and thought to the organization and integration of an increasingly polyglot and far-flung empire. Yet, as the book on the East India Company emphasises, the expansion of empire also had profound economic and social consequences upon Britain itself, influencing consumption, taste, manners, art, behaviour and the like. As trade and commerce developed, the empire ceased to be a distant, unimagined object for most Britons. Instead, it shaped everyday experiences, and this helped to embed the empire into the national consciousness in ways which ensured that the imperial experience took on a multi-dimensional form.

---

7 *The Imperial Challenge. Quebec and Britain in the Age of the American Revolution* (Montreal and Kingston, 1989); *The East India Company. A History* (1993).

As if to demonstrate how far he had travelled during his career, Phil's last years were spent exploring the cultural and social manifestations of British imperialism that were associated with material culture, and given particular expression and form through the growth of the tea trade and the addictive habit of tea-drinking. His 'empire of tea' provided him with an organizational framework within which his views about Britain's imperial experience, and the relationships between cores and peripheries, could further be developed and refined. The study of tea allowed him to draw together, through the East India Company, the empires of the east and the west; to examine the effects of empire upon behavioural patterns in British society; and to explore the projection of metropolitan values and habits into the wider empire. This work was in its infancy at the time of Phil's untimely death, but papers published posthumously illustrate how broad his vision of Britain's eighteenth-century empire had become.[8]

Unlike many historians of his generation, Phil increasingly became freed from the scholarly constraints imposed by narrow specialization and a limited geographical range of interests. He roamed widely over the eighteenth-century British world, and his willingness to make connexions between different parts of the empire and the imperial experience characterize the important contribution that he made to Hanoverian historiography. Above all, perhaps, Phil's great enthusiasm for his ever-changing subject transmitted itself in straightforward language to colleagues, friends, and students, and such was the widely felt effect of this that his most lasting scholarly legacy will be the one which inspires others to explore the eighteenth-century empire with the same sort of restless pioneering spirit that he possessed in great abundance.

8 'Tea, Vice and the English State, 1660–1784' and 'Women and the Empire of Tea: Image and Counter-Image in Hanoverian England', both of which are published in *A Taste for Empire and Glory*.

Philip Lawson: A Bibliography

compiled by

RICHARD CONNORS AND CLYVE JONES

Essays reprinted in *A Taste for Empire and Glory. Studies in British Overseas Expansion, 1660–1800* (1997) are marked with an asterisk.

1980

'Grenville's Election Act, 1770', *Bulletin of the Institute of Historical Research*, LIII, 218–28.

'Grenville and America: The Years of Opposition, 1765–70', *William and Mary Quarterly*, 3rd ser., XXXVII, 561–76. *

1983

With Bruce Lenman, 'Clive and the Black Jagir: The East India Company in Eighteenth-Century Politics', *Historical Journal*, XXVI, 801–29. *

'British Traditions and Revolutionary America', *Canadian Review of American Studies*, XIV, 165–73. *

'The British Popular Press and American Revolution', *University Avenues*, no. 1, pp. 20–7.

'Parliament and the First East India Inquiry, 1767', *Parliamentary History*, I, 99–114. *

1984

George Grenville. A Political Life (Oxford: Clarendon Press).

With Jim Phillips, '"Our Execrable Banditti": Perceptions of Nabobs in the Late Eighteenth Century', *Albion*, XVI, 225–41. *

'Further Reflections on the Cabinet in the Early Years of George III's Reign', *Bulletin of the Institute of Historical Research*, LVII, 237–40.

Review of John L. Bullion, *A Great and Necessary Measure. George Grenville and the Genesis of the Stamp Act, 1763–1765* (Columbia, Mo., 1982), in *British Journal for Eighteenth-Century Studies*, VII, 105–6.

1985

'"The Irishman's Prize": Views of Canada from the British Press, 1760–1775', *Historical Journal*, XXVIII, 575–96. *

1986

'The Missing Link: The Imperial Dimension in Understanding Hanoverian Britain', *Historical Journal*, XXIX, 747–51. *

'Parliament, Corn and the Constitution: The Embargo Crisis of 1766', *Parliamentary History*, V, 17–37.

1988

'Reassessing Peterloo', *History Today*, XXXVIII, 24–9.

'Hanoverian Studies: The Impact of Recent Trends on Parliamentary History', *Parliamentary History*, VII, 24–9. *

1989

The Imperial Challenge. Quebec and Britain in the Age of the American Revolution (Montreal and Kingston: McGill-Queen's University Press). [Published in paperback in 1994.]

'"Arts and Empire Equally Extend": Tradition, Prejudice and Assumption in Eighteenth-Century Press Coverage of Empire', *Studies in History and Politics*, VII, 119–47. *

'A Constable's Eye View Re-assessed', *Manchester Regional History Review*, III, 39–42.

'Anatomy of a Civil War: New Perspectives on England in the Age of the American Revolution, 1767–82', *Parliamentary History*, VIII, 145–52. *

Review of Edward Royle, *Modern Britain. A Social History, 1750–1985* (New York, 1988), in *History: Reviews of New Books*, XVIII, 18–19.

1990

'A Perspective on British History and the Treatment of the Conquest of Quebec', *Journal of Historical Sociology*, III, 253–71. *

Review of *Lord Bute. Essays in Reinterpretation*, ed. K. Schweizer (Leicester, 1988), in *Parliamentary History*, IX, 218–19.

1991

'"Sapped by Corruption": British Governance of Quebec and the Breakdown of Anglo-American Relations on the Eve of Revolution', *Canadian Review of American Studies*, XXII, 301–23. *

Review of *The Transformation of Political Culture. England and Germany in the Late Eighteenth Century*, ed. E. Hellmuth (Oxford, 1990), in *Albion*, XXIII, 557–9.

1992

With Karl Schwiezer, 'A Political Diary by Charles Jenkinson, 31 May–29 June 1765', *Historical Research*, LXV, 349–58.

Review of H. W. Bowen, *Revenue and Reform. The Indian Problem in British Politics, 1757–1773* (Cambridge, 1991), in *Albion*, XXIV, 507–8.

Review of Peter Linebaugh, *The London Hanged. Crime and Civil Society in the Eighteenth Century* (1991), in *History: Reviews of New Books*, XXI, 15–16.

1993

The East India Company. A History (London: Longmans). [Hardback and paperback editions published simultaneously.]

Review of *The Blackwell Encyclopedia of the American Revolution*, ed. J. P. Greene and J. R. Pole (Oxford, 1991), in *William and Mary Quarterly*, 3rd ser., L, 221–4.

1994

Review of Geoffrey Holmes, *The Making of a Great Power. Late Stuart and Early Hanoverian Britain, 1660–1722* (1993), in *History: Reviews of New Books*, XXIII, 73–4.

1995

Edited *Parliament and the Atlantic Empire* (Edinburgh: Edinburgh University Press). [A special issue of the journal *Parliamentary History*, XIV, pt. 1, also published as a paperback book.]

'Sources, Schools and Separation: The Many Faces of Parliament's Role in Anglo-American History to 1783', in *Parliament and the Atlantic Empire*, pp. 4–27. *

1997

A Taste for Empire and Glory. Studies in British Overseas Expansion, 1660–1800 (Aldershot: Variorum). [Posthumous reprint of 13 of his published articles, with two previously unpublished papers.]

'Tea, Vice and the English State, 1660–1784', in *Taste for Empire and Glory*, part 5, item xiv, pp. 1–21. *

'Women and the Empire of Tea: Image and Counter-Image in Hanoverian England', in *Taste for Empire and Glory*, part 5, item xv, pp. 1–19. *

1

The Family in Early Modern England:
Continuity and Change[*]

KEITH WRIGHTSON

Historians of the family in early modern England seem to have stopped bickering. The unseemly rows which were once such a source of alarm and disturbance seem to have subsided into the kind of distanced civility characteristic of a spent passion. However, if the present climate is one of what sixteenth- and seventeenth-century commentators on domestic relations would have termed 'living quietly together', this is not to say that the old tensions which wracked the formative years of the subject have actually been resolved. Far from it. To remind ourselves of some of them, and to encourage their discussion, is therefore to take a risk – the risk of promoting one of those family reunions which end in tears.

It is, none the less, a risk that has to be taken sooner or later by anyone seriously concerned with the history of the family in this period, for the simple reason that, to quote Patrick Collinson, 'in no other branch of historical study are such dubious statements so confidently made, such flatly contradictory claims staked out'.[1] Specialists in particular branches of research on the history of the family might well prefer to cultivate their own gardens in peace and to observe the comparable efforts of the neighbours with no more than polite acknowledgment. Yet sooner or later readers, colleagues and, above all, students are liable to ask embarrassing questions about the ultimate purposes of horticulture. Philip Lawson – who had a lively, if often rather sceptical, interest in these matters – sometimes asked me such questions in response to my own forays into the history of family relationships. He never received a really satisfactory answer. This essay is not likely to provide one either. I have no single line to argue. Nor, in reviewing critically some aspects of the historiography of the family in England, do I exempt my own work from stricture. Rather, it represents an attempt by a fretful teacher of the subject, still wrestling with a plethora of competing and often contradictory views and their relationship to larger historical contexts, to try to characterize the state of things, to direct attention to some

* This essay is based upon a paper delivered at the E.S.R.C. Cambridge Group for the History of Population and Social Structure in March 1996.
1 P. Collinson, *The Birthpangs of Protestant England. Religious and Cultural Change in the Sixteenth and Seventeenth Centuries* (1988), p. 81. Collinson was referring specifically to the debate over the 'protestant family' in this period, but his comment has a broader relevance.

outstanding problems of interpretation and to suggest some possible ways of exploring them. It is, then, a discussion paper; written in furtherance of an interrupted conversation with a friend, which, in a sense, continues still.

I

Things seemed so simple once. Forty years ago it could hardly be said that a proper history of the family existed. Nevertheless, it was widely presumed that the principal features of 'the modern western family' were well known and that they were of relatively recent origin. Functionally, it was the basic unit of residence, consumption, procreation, childrearing, and the provision of care and emotional support. Structurally, it was small in size and simple in composition, the 'conjugal' or 'nuclear' family being the predominant household form. Relations with non-resident kin were of limited practical significance and of a somewhat optional nature beyond the closest ties to the nuclear families of origin of the parental generation. The keystones of domestic relationships were a close conjugal bond, based upon the free choice of marriage partners by young adults, and a dominant preoccupation with the nurturing and early socialization of children – both sets of relationships contributing to the emotional intensity of the family. All this was taken to be well-adapted to the realities of an urbanized, industrialized, commercialized, socio-economic order and an individualistic culture, and was generally held to have emerged in the course of the structural 'modernization' of western societies since the nineteenth century.[2]

Prior to that immense, though vaguely defined, historical watershed, it was assumed that a very different set of realities had prevailed. The 'traditional', or 'pre-industrial' family, in contrast, was much more extensive in its functions – which included, for example, a role as the basic unit of production in agriculture and manufactures and a role in education, training, and the provision of social security subsequently transferred to other agencies. It was believed to have been larger in size and more complex in its internal structure, various forms of co-resident 'extended' or 'joint' family being more commonplace. Individual households were located within denser networks of locally-available kin and subject to more powerful kinship obligations. They were permeable also to the powerful controlling influence of community norms and sanctions. Marriage took place at a relatively young age and was subject to arrangement, or at least ultimate control, by parents and kin. Both conjugal and parent-child relations were authoritarian and rigidly patriarchal and the

---

2   For the 'ideal type' of the western family, its 'fit' with industrial society, and trends in the earlier twentieth century, see W. J. Goode, *World Revolution and Family Patterns* (New York and London, 1963), pp. 7–22, and ch. 2. Cf. M. Anderson, 'The Relevance of Family History', in *Sociology of the Family. Selected Readings*, ed. M. Anderson (2nd edn., Harmondsworth, 1980), p. 34.

emotional climate of the family was marked by respect and obligation rather than by warmth or intimacy.[3]

Given such assumptions, change from the 'traditional' to the 'modern' family can be said to have been conceptualized in terms of three essential processes. First, the family was deemed to have undergone a process of *nuclearization* in terms of its composition and residential arrangements, the loosening of kin and community ties, and the emotional focusing of the conjugal family unit. Secondly, relationships of authority within the family were transformed by the growth of *individualism*, a process involving greater recognition of individual needs and aspirations, and the concession of greater personal autonomy to family members. Third, there was the development of a more intense *emotionalism* in family relationships, most notably those of husband and wife and of parents and children. All of this involved a narrowing or contracting of the functions of the family and a more pronounced emphasis upon the cultivation of personal relationships within the nuclear core.

To sketch all this so briefly is, of course, to produce something of a caricature. But it does represent, I think, the essentials of what might be termed the old master narrative of family history – a set of pervasive expectations about the nature and direction of change, derived initially from the evolutionary speculations of the founding fathers of the social sciences, which became deeply embedded in the sociology of the family as it was (and sometimes, surprisingly, still is). And it deserves stressing as a prolegomenon to the discussion of continuity and change in English family life between the sixteenth and the eighteenth centuries for two reasons. First, because to be reminded of this conjectured history of the family serves to underline how great an impact research on the family in the early modern period has now had. Secondly, because its categories and dynamics retain, I think, considerable relevance for thinking about the history of the family in the early modern period.

The past 30 years have, of course, seen a massive growth of interest in the history of the family, as historians have endeavoured to employ the surviving evidence to reconstruct, rather than simply to imagine, the nature of family relationships in the past. In 1980 Michael Anderson attempted to impose some order on what was already a fairly substantial body of published work on the subject, by categorizing it into three distinguishable approaches to the history of the western family: the demographic approach; the household economics approach; and what he called the

3 For 'the classical family of western nostalgia', see Goode, *World Revolution*, pp. 6–7. Cf. the account of 'traditional English family life' in B. Bailyn, *Education in the Forming of American Society* (Williamsburg, 1960), pp. 15–17. Goode showed a degree of scepticism about this model and was aware that change had earlier antecedents, but was not in a position to challenge prevailing assumptions in any fundamental way: see his *The Family* (Englewood Cliffs, 1964), p. 114. Confronting their legacy in the light of recent historical research, primarily on France, is one of the recurrent themes of M. Segalen, *Historical Anthropology of the Family*, trans. J. C. Whitehouse and S. Mathews (Cambridge, 1986).

'sentiments' approach.[4] In doing so, he was also identifying the three roots of the history of the family as we now have it: historical demography, with its concern with household size and structure and vital rates; economic history, insofar as it was concerned with the domestic dimensions of economic structures and change; and the 'new' social and cultural histories, with their focus upon the history of social relationships and the cultural meanings with which they are informed. As Anderson was at pains to stress, each approach had already yielded a formidable body of accumulated knowledge. Each also had contributed much to the 'demythologizing' of the history of the family by revealing unanticipated realities often disconcertingly at odds with prior expectations.[5] Yet, as his critical survey indicated, the cumulative research achievement which had done much to revise specific misconceptions about the nature of the family in earlier centuries, did not yet add up to a constructive reassessment of the course of change in the family over time. A field previously dominated by confident ignorance had become one in which the meaning of new knowledge was hotly contested. He implied that the subject was in a bit of a mess, tried to tidy it up a little, and counselled restraint among participants in its controversies.

Seventeen years later the historical literature is even bigger and more diverse – notably as a result of the elaboration of Anderson's three approaches by a further wave of concern with the history of gender roles and relationships. Yet we are not necessarily much better off as regards agreement about the implications and larger interpretative significance of what we now know, or think we know, about the history of the family. It is possible, however, to claim that we have at least a new set of interpretative alternatives to what I have called the old master narrative of family history. These are exceptionally well-illustrated by the historiography of the family in early modern England.

Essentially, the collision between prior expectations and rapidly accumulating knowledge led to two interpretative challenges to established presumptions about the history of the family, both of these challenges deriving principally from work on the early modern period. First, in the 1970s, came a challenge to the *chronology* of the old master narrative. Many historians retained their basic conception of the nature and direction of the historical transformation of the family – with its emphasis on nuclearization, individualism and emotionalism – but pushed the chronology of change back in time. They thus detached it from the processes of industrialization and urbanization and elaborated its central themes by emphasizing instead the contribution of developments peculiar to the early modern period – above all of the seventeenth and eighteenth centuries. Secondly, and more radically, some historians (notably in the 1980s) began to call into question the very *nature* of the alleged transition. They

4   M. Anderson, *Approaches to the History of the Western Family, 1500–1914* (1980).
5   The 'demythologizing' role of the history of the family has been much stressed. See, e.g., Anderson, 'Relevance', p. 39; Segalen, *Historical Anthropology*, p. 5.

rejected the familiar characterization of the pre-industrial, pre-capitalist, pre-modern family as little more than a sociological myth, and directed attention to certain long-term structural continuities in family attitudes and behaviour – a shift of emphasis which led some to reject the whole notion of a fundamental transition in the nature of family forms and affective relationships.

The first of these challenges is now widely represented in the historiography of the western family. It has, for example, French, American, English and German variants, some of which involve the staking of claims that one or another country or cultural zone was first to breast the tape of modernity in a curious kind of historical olympiad.[6] The second challenge is peculiarly evident in the historiography of early modern England.[7] Both can be considered more closely in their English context.

II

The outstanding English exponent of the first form of interpretative revisionism – the chronological challenge – is, of course, Professor Lawrence Stone. In his *Crisis of the Aristocracy* (1965) Stone was one of the earliest English historians to address seriously the history of the family in the early modern period, and in his *The Family, Sex and Marriage* (1977) he was the first to present a full-dress interpretation of the transition from 'medieval' to 'modern' family forms in England. In the latter work, Stone is concerned not so much to question the nature of the transition in family life as to relocate it into the early modern period. Accordingly, he argues for a tripartite shift in family relationships: a decline in the influence of kin and community over the conjugal family unit; the emergence of more freely chosen and emotionally rich marriages; the development of less authoritarian and more empathetic parent-child relationships. The first of these developments clearly involves a form of nuclearization. The second and third are attributed to the rise of individualism and the growth of emotional 'affect': developments fused in Stone's concept of 'affective individualism'. These 'vast and elusive cultural changes' are traced through a series

---

6   Among the most notable pioneering works of interpretation of this kind were: P. Aries, *Centuries of Childhood* (originally Paris, 1960), trans. R. Baldick (1962); Bailyn, *Education in the Forming of American Society*, pp. 15–25; E. Shorter, *The Making of the Modern Family* (Glasgow, 1976); J.-L. Flandrin, *Families in Former Times. Kinship, Household and Sexuality* (originally Paris, 1976), trans. R. Southern (Cambridge, 1979); L. Stone, *The Family, Sex and Marriage in England 1500–1800* (1977); M. Mitterauer and R. Sieder, *The European Family. Patriarchy to Partnership from the Middle Ages to the Present* (originally Munich, 1977), trans. K. Oosterveen and M. Horzinger (Oxford, 1982).

7   The most forthright statements of such views can be found in Alan Macfarlane's *The Origins of English Individualism. The Family, Property and Social Transition* (Oxford, 1978) and *Marriage and Love in England. Modes of Reproduction 1300–1840* (Oxford, 1986). A preoccupation with continuity, however, exerts a more general influence on recent English writing on the subject. The implications of some of the early work of this kind were first brought out in a vigorously polemical form, linked to a political agenda, in F. Mount, *The Subversive Family. An Alternative History of Love and Marriage* (1982).

of overlapping phases of development from what Stone terms the Open Lineage Family of the medieval period – characterized as 'an open-ended, low-keyed, unemotional, authoritarian institution'; through the Restricted Patriarchal Nuclear Family of the later sixteenth and earlier seventeenth centuries – an entity more closed to external influences but internally powerfully authoritarian; to the Closed Domesticated Nuclear Family of the late-seventeenth and eighteenth centuries – infused by a new spirit of affective individualism expressed in companionate marriage and the permitting of greater personal autonomy to wives and children. During the critical stages of this process of transition the pacemakers of change are the 'upper bourgeoisie and squirarchy' of England, from whom new patterns of behaviour spread up and down the social scale in a process of 'stratified diffusion' – the societal triumph of the Closed Domesticated Nuclear Family being achieved (after a period of Victorian reaction) in the late nineteenth and early twentieth centuries.[8]

Stone's argument thus relocated the essential points of transition in the familiar pattern of change into the early modern period, but with his own conceptualization of the stages and social dynamics of change and a novel emphasis on England's innovatory role. Initially his argument was welcomed and found some support – notably in the work of Randolph Trumbach.[9] Yet whilst general interpretative arguments of this nature remain fairly influential in the historiography of continental Europe, in the English case they reached their apogee with the work of Stone and have subsequently crumbled. Why has this mode of interpretation proved so unconvincing in England?

Essentially, the reason was that, even while Stone was preparing his massive intervention in the subject, other historians of early modern England were independently coming to conclusions about the nature of family life in the sixteenth and seventeenth centuries which seemed to raise more fundamental questions about both the stereotype of the 'pre-industrial' family and the previously assumed transition from 'traditional' to 'modern' family forms. This was the genesis of the second interpretative challenge to established expectations in the history of the family – one which was as inimical to Stone's model of change as to the old conjectural histories of the sociologists.

Already, Peter Laslett had argued, on the basis of his analysis of early census-type listings, that the nuclear family household had been the predominant family form in

England since at least the late sixteenth century.[10] Already Alan Macfarlane, in his pathbreaking analysis of the diary of Ralph Josselin, had argued that Josselin's marriage was based on individual choice and love; that it was companionate in its nature; that he and his wife Jane were centrally preoccupied with the needs of their children and that the extended kinship group was of little practical significance in their lives.[11] These works were not necessarily damaging to Stone's case. The statistical predominance of nuclear family households from an early date could be compatible with his emphasis on the growing psychological nuclearity of the family and the changing emotional quality of domestic relationships. The family life of Josselin, lived out in the years 1640–83, could be taken as an excellent early example of Stone's Closed Domesticated Nuclear Family. As a clergyman Josselin belonged to the right social milieu, and his diary covers the earlier part of what Stone regards as a critical period of transition. What was perhaps far more subversive of Stone's position, and of the new interpretative tradition which it represented, was that these works had set a precedent in English historiography for a demythologizing interpretative stance with regard to several aspects of the old master narrative which continued to influence Stone's model. Moreover, it was one backed up, where possible, with quantitative evidence, or at least a much more systematic analysis of qualitative evidence than had been the case in the tradition of anecdotal exposition to which Stone still adhered in his work on the family.[12] This interpretative preference was not always fully justified – as Jack Goody and E. P. Thompson cautioned at an early stage in comments on the work of Laslett and Macfarlane respectively.[13] But it was enormously attractive to, and influential upon, the generation of research students who had followed the lead set by Laslett and Macfarlane in the early 1970s: self-consciously clearing new paths; seeking out and exploring the potential of new sources – above all for the period c.1560–c.1640 and in relation to the lives of the 'middling and poorer sorts of people' dealt with relatively cursorily by Stone and his predecessors.

As a result, Stone's work was scarcely in print before it was challenged by a whole wave of studies presenting the evidence for arguments about the nature of family relationships between the mid-sixteenth and late seventeenth centuries which have now become familiar to any student of the subject. It was suggested that the

---

10 P. Laslett, 'Mean Household Size in England Since the Sixteenth Century', in *Household and Family in Past Time*, ed. P. Laslett and R. Wall (Cambridge, 1972), pp. 125–58.

11 A. Macfarlane, *The Family Life of Ralph Josselin. A Seventeenth-Century Clergyman. An Essay in Historical Anthropology* (Cambridge, 1970). Macfarlane's findings were complemented in several respects by those of J. Demos, *A Little Commonwealth. Family Life in Plymouth Colony* (New York, 1970), which also includes, in its final chapter, a thoughtful discussion of the differences between the seventeenth-century family and its modern counterpart.

12 Though in his work on other issues Stone was one of the pioneers of the quantitative social history of this period.

13 J. Goody, 'The Evolution of the Family', in *Household and Family*, ed. Laslett and Wall, pp. 103–24; E. P. Thompson, 'Anthropology and the Discipline of Historical Context', *Midland History*, I (1971–2), 41–55.

nuclear family household was not only the statistical norm, but also culturally preferred; that economic independence was regarded as a prerequisite for the formation of new households; that such norms were underpinned by the institutions of service and apprenticeship for young adults, and that the mobility of the young prior to marriage meant that within local communities kinship networks between such households were relatively loose and relations with members of the extended kin of limited practical significance. Straightforward arrangement of marriages by the parental generation was comparatively rare, even among the gentry and aristocracy. In most families the initiative in matchmaking could come from either parent or child, but most commonly came from the young people concerned, with subsequent seeking of parental approval and support. Matches were expected to observe a rough parity in economic and social terms, but were not based upon crude pursuit of economic and social advantage and were expected to involve personal attraction (on a continuum from 'liking' to 'love'). Again, it was emphasized that contemporary moralists from at least the early sixteenth century consistently stressed not only patriarchal authority in the family, but also mutuality between man and wife. Marital love and companionship was strongly endorsed, as was marital sexuality. Nor was this merely prescriptive rhetoric, for independent evidence existed of a strongly companionate ethos in particularly well-documented marriages from the Pastons of the fifteenth century to the diarists of the later seventeenth century. The rigidities of patriarchy were heavily qualified by such expectations and frank recognition was given to the reality of marital conflict and female insubordination; an indication that women were not repressed to the degree that might be inferred from statements of patriarchal authority. As for the relations of parents and children, it was argued that this was a subject dominated by absurd myths of parental indifference and neglect. People in the sixteenth and early seventeenth centuries, no less than in the later seventeenth and eighteenth centuries were powerfully bonded to their children; aware of their distinctive needs and of the stages of their development; preoccupied with providing adequately for them, and perfectly aware of the distinction between parental discipline and abuse. They were also intensely aware of their fragile mortality, yet repeated experience of infant and child deaths bred anxiety rather than a numbed indifference and did nothing to dull the desperate grief occasioned by the loss of a child.[14] And so

14 Among the more significant publications on these themes in what rapidly became a large literature
    were, in chronological order: D. Levine, *Family Formation in an Age of Nascent Capitalism* (New
    York, San Francisco and London, 1977); K. Davies, ' "The Sacred Condition of Equality" – How
    Original were Puritan Doctrines of Marriage?', *Social History*, v (1977), 563–80; Macfarlane,
    Origins of English Individualism; S. Heller Mendelson, 'Debate: The Weightiest Business: Marriage
    in an Upper Gentry Family in Seventeenth-Century England', *Past and Present*, 85 (1979), 126–35;
    K. Wrightson and D. Levine, *Poverty and Piety in an English Village. Terling 1525–1700* (New
    York, San Francisco and London, 1979); *Bastardy and its Comparative History* , ed. P. Laslett, K.
    Oosterveen and R. M. Smith (1980); *Marriage and Society. Studies in the Social History of
    Marriage*, ed. R. B. Outhwaite (1981), esp. chapters by Ingram, Davies and Brodsky Elliott; M.
    Macdonald, *Mystical Bedlam. Madness, Anxiety, and Healing in Seventeenth-Century England*

one could go on.

Such findings and arguments would doubtless have appeared regardless of the publication of Stone's interpretation of the development of the English family, and they were not conceived solely in opposition to his ideas. Yet coming as they did in the immediate aftermath of his apparently authoritative and highly publicized statement, they almost inevitably took on a distinctly negative tone. Stone bestrode the field. He could not be ignored. Accordingly, the arguments of those who did not share his views were repeatedly directed at the demolition of both his characterization of English family life at different points in time, and his periodization of its alleged phases of development. It could scarcely have been otherwise. Yet in retrospect this negativity was not only unfortunate, but ultimately counter-productive. It had the effect of diverting into a sometimes unseemly polemic, energies which might have been better spent on a more constructive reappraisal of the nature of the family in early modern England. It encouraged a gladiatorial interpretative polarization. Above all, in the effort made to clear away what was generally regarded as a premature and over-schematized conceptualization of change in the early modern family, it led to a very damaging neglect of the problem of change itself.

Some of the consequences of that neglect became fully apparent in 1986 with the publication of what remains the only full-scale alternative interpretation to that of Stone (as distinct from critical textbook guides to the state of debate): Alan Macfarlane's *Marriage and Love in England, 1300–1800*. As is well-known, Macfarlane's central theme is the exploration of the nature and implications of what he terms the 'Malthusian marriage system' in England. Marriage in this system was neither universal nor automatic: rather it was chosen (or avoided) on the basis of what amounted to a cost/benefit analysis of its consequences for the individuals involved. Marriage required economic independence and physical and social maturity. It depended upon freedom of choice by the individuals concerned rather than the pressure of parents, kin or community norms. Partners were selected by individual choice, with parents and kin acting only as 'counterbalancing forces'. The principal attractions of marriage were personal companionship and emotional and sexual satisfaction, and it was preceded by romantic courtship. The conjugal relationship was strongly companionate, based on 'a deep bond between husband and wife' and relatively egalitarian in practice, despite the patriarchal assumptions of male authority

---

(Cambridge, 1981), ch. 3; A. Kussmaul, *Servants in Husbandry in Early Modern England* (Cambridge, 1981); E. A. Wrigley and R. S. Schofield, *The Population History of England, 1541–1871. A Reconstruction* (1981); L. Pollock, *Forgotten Children. Parent-Child Relations in England, 1500 to 1900* (Cambridge, 1983). Several of these works were preceded by widely-read doctoral theses. Martin Ingram's important Oxford thesis of 1977, for example, was influential long before its publication in expanded form as *Church Courts, Sex and Marriage in England, 1570–1640* (Cambridge, 1987). By the early 1980s this alternative history of the family in early modern England was being consolidated in such general works as K. Wrightson, *English Society 1580–1680* (1982), chs. 2–4, and R. Houlbrooke, *The English Family 1450–1700* (1984).

embodied in law. The children born to such unions were deeply desired, not so much as heirs to the patrimony, or for their labour, or for insurance against insecurity in old age, but for their own sake, as 'non-utilitarian goods'. Wealth and resources in fact flowed downwards from parent to child and children were valued primarily as sources of emotional satisfaction – counterbalanced by a realistic awareness of the cares and costs of parenthood. Faced with these dominant realities, people had to make their choices. They usually chose to marry if they could, but they married relatively late, having first achieved the wherewithal to sustain the responsibilities of household independence. And this characteristic of prudent family formation was a vital element in the achievement of a degree of demographic control – through its restriction of the reproductive potential of the population – and in the accumulation of economic resources by households.[15]

Much (though not necessarily all) of Macfarlane's characterization of English family relations in the seventeenth and eighteenth centuries – the period providing his best evidence – might command widespread agreement as an account of the social and cultural underpinning of a late-marrying regime among at least parts of the population, at least some of the time. Macfarlane's radicalism, however, lay in generalizing his model to characterize the English as a whole, and above all in contending that by the eighteenth century this was already a centuries-old cultural complex – the counterpart in domestic relations of the weak kinship obligations and individualistic property rights which he had earlier examined in his controversial *Origins of English Individualism* (1978).[16] For Macfarlane, crucially, there was no fundamental transition in English family life in the early modern period to be explained. Rather 'it is possible that between the sixteenth and the nineteenth centuries, and possibly earlier, we are looking at a framework of decision-making, a set of rules and customs, which remain broadly the same'.[17]

Macfarlane thus presents the most forthright statement of the second challenge to the old master narrative. The characteristics of the English family system were not the product of the transition to a capitalistic, industrial, urban, individualistic, social order, whether that transition be dated to the years after 1800 or deemed to have deeper roots. On the contrary, they already existed. They were prominent among the preconditions which made such development possible; part of a long-established cultural complex conducive to economic development and the emergence of a capitalist economy. That is Macfarlane's ultimate message: the old master narrative standing on its head.

15 Macfarlane, *Marriage and Love, passim*, quoting pp. 55, 124, 154.
16 Macfarlane, *Origins of English Individualism*, esp. chs. 3–6.
17 Macfarlane, *Marriage and Love*, p. 30.

III

With the publication of Macfarlane's *Marriage and Love*, the history of the family in early modern England was left in an interpretative quandary. On the one hand, we have an ambitious model of massive cultural change which has been largely discredited as either an adequate depiction of the complex realities of the English family at particular points in time or a convincing account of change across the early modern period. On the other hand, we have a reading of the implications of some of the alternative evidence so audacious in its assertion of an essential cultural homogeneity and massive stability as to leave the reader dumbfounded.

And there we seem to be stuck. Excellent new work continues to appear on particular issues within the broad remit of the history of the family in early modern England – on particular phases of the life-cycle, for example, notably childhood, youth and old age, or on aspects of the domestic economy, notably work, welfare and consumption.[18] Yet in the main there is a marked reluctance to engage with the interpretative dilemma created by the interventions of Stone and Macfarlane, beyond a generally overt rejection of the one and a kind of diffuse scepticism about the full interpretative implications of the other. The loose alliance which opposed the threatened hegemony of Stone in the late 1970s and early 1980s has largely dispersed; but its members have not rallied behind Macfarlane's banner. Rather, they and their successors, have gone off foraging along paths of their own.

The single most important development of the last 15 years has been the emergence of an explicitly gendered account of family relationships, rooted in a feminist critique of the earlier agenda of family history.[19] This has focused attention

18 Particularly stimulating recent works on these themes include H. Cunningham, 'The Employment and Unemployment of Children in England *c*.1680–1851', *Past and Present*, 126 (1990), 115–50; I. Krausman Ben-Amos, *Adolescence and Youth in Early Modern England* (New Haven and London, 1994); P. Griffiths, *Youth and Authority. Formative Experiences in England 1560–1640* (Oxford, 1996); *Land, Kinship and Life-Cycle*, ed. R. M. Smith (Cambridge, 1984); *Life, Death and the Elderly. Historical Perspectives*, ed. M. Pelling and R. M. Smith (1991); K. D. M. Snell, *Annals of the Labouring Poor. Social Change and Agrarian England, 1660–1900* (Cambridge, 1985); D. Woodward, *Men at Work. Labourers and Building Craftsmen in the Towns of Northern England, 1450–1750* (Cambridge, 1995), esp. ch. 7; L. Weatherill, *Consumer Behaviour and Material Culture in Britain 1660–1760* (1988); P. Earle, *The Making of the English Middle Class. Business, Society and Family Life in London 1660–1730* (1989); *Consumption and the World of Goods*, ed. J. Brewer and R. Porter (1993).

19 See, e.g., R. E. Pahl, *Divisions of Labour* (Oxford, 1984), chs. 1–2; *Women in English Society, 1500–1800*, ed. M. Prior (1985); *Women and Work in Pre-Industrial England*, ed. L. Charles and L. Duffin (1985); S. Amussen, *An Ordered Society. Gender and Class in Early Modern England* (Oxford, 1988); L. Pollock, '"Teach Her to Live Under Obedience": The Making of Women in the Upper Ranks of Early Modern England', *Continuity and Change*, IV (1989), 231–58; *Women as Mothers in Pre-Industrial England*, ed. V. Fildes (1990); J. Goldberg, *Women, Work and Life Cycle in a Medieval Economy. Women in York and Yorkshire c.1300–1520* (Oxford, 1992); A. L. Erickson, *Women and Property in Early Modern England* (1993); A. Fletcher, *Gender, Sex and Subordination in England, 1500–1800* (New Haven and London, 1995); L. Gowing, *Domestic Dangers. Women, Words and Sex in Early Modern London* (Oxford, 1996).

sharply upon the realities of power relations within the family and the manner in
which they were sustained and contested. It provides an alternative perspective on
each of the established avenues of approach to the history of family relationships;
exposes and rejects the assumption, buried in the old master narrative, that the
'modern family' represents any kind of crowning achievement; and poses at the very
least an implicit challenge to the interpretative positions of Stone and Macfarlane
alike. It powerfully reaffirms the vital importance of the history of the family and has
done much to recast priorities in the discussion of the subject. Yet it has done
surprisingly little to resolve the larger impasse in the subject regarding continuity and
change in family relationships. Indeed historians of gender appear themselves to be
beset by uncertainties about the extent to which the experience and opportunities of
women between the sixteenth and the eighteenth centuries were characterized by
elements of amelioration, general deterioration, or simply the perpetuation, in
changing ways, of a restrictive and oppressive subordination.[20]

Taken as a whole, it is certainly the case that we know far more than ever before
about the realities of family relationships in the period. When asked to adjudicate on
what it all means, however, the response of historians of the period is commonly one
of mild embarrassment. This essay cannot provide a neat answer to that question. But
perhaps a start can be made on re-addressing the outstanding issues of meaning by
attempting to diagnose the problems of interpretation more clearly. Looking at the
competing alternatives, it seems to me that it is possible to detect three sets of
problems bedevilling attempts to interpret the history (or non-history) of family
relationships in early modern England. These can be summarized as problems of
conceptualization, problems of *verification*, and problems of *credibility*.

To begin with problems of *conceptualization*. It seems evident that attempts to
conceptualize long-term change in the family have continued to be powerfully
influenced by notions of evolutionary development, or of 'modernization', which
carry buried within them the assumption that the distant past is likely to represent a
kind of inversion of 'modernity' (however that concept is defined). This breeds in
turn a tendency to conceive family relationships in terms of polar opposites:
complex as against simple household structures; arranged as against free marriage;
powerful as against weak or optional kinship obligations; authoritarian as against
egalitarian domestic relations; cool and distanced as against warm and intense
emotional climates, etc. etc. Useful as such categories might be as a guide to the
range of possibilities in any historical period, the experience of the historiography of
the family seems to be that time and again interpretative generalizations fall back

20 For discussions of the interpretative difficulties in women's history, see: J. M. Bennett, 'Medieval
Women, Modern Women: Across the Great Divide', in *Culture and History 1350–1600. Essays on
English Communities, Identities and Writing*, ed. D. Aers (1992), and A. Vickery, 'Golden Age to
Separate Spheres? A Review of the Categories and Chronology of English Women's History',
Historical Journal, XXXVI (1993), 383–414.

upon these distinctions as the primary points of reference in an evolutionary development *from* one polarity and *towards* the other. And in expounding such schemes of change many of the complexities and variations of past realities are in effect suppressed or at least accorded insufficient interpretative consideration.

In contrast, those who lay their interpretative emphasis upon continuity tend to focus attention upon elements of apparent structural similarity over time and on short-term adaptations within enduring structures, the respiration of an essentially enduring system. This perspective can produce a tendency to over-modernize the distant past, by privileging these similarities at the expense of differences of mentality, behaviour and context. The alienness of some aspects of past experience is played down and, with them, its variability. The contours of the historical landscape are flattened out. Professor Collinson has likened this habit to a carpenter's plane 'busily removing the knots and other rugosities from a plank of wood, the irregularities which make the subject interesting and a suitable case for historical treatment'.[21] In consequence, change gradually ceases to be a problem – which can certainly lighten the historian's workload, but is hardly an adequate discharge of his or her intellectual responsibilities. Besides which, the practice too rarely includes a recognition that where there is indeed continuity, it too should be regarded not simply as a given fact, but as a problem to be explained.

Secondly, these problems of conceptualization are compounded by problems of *verification* deriving from the enormous difficulties imposed by the inadequate nature of the evidence available to historians for the reconstruction of many dimensions of family life.

Statistical evidence is generally regarded as the most authoritative. Yet it remains the case that the statistics available to us are very often the product of efforts to turn a documentary sow's ear into a silk purse, or at least 'a passable imitation of silk'.[22] Such possibility will depend, of course, on the plausibility of the methodology employed, with all the assumptions buried within it, and its appropriateness to the particular purpose in hand. And such judgments may involve interpretative acts of faith regarding, for example, the representativeness of the 'reconstitutable minority' in family reconstitution studies; the legitimacy of constructing aggregate figures which massage away local, regional and social variation; or the extent to which kinship networks can be adequately reconstructed. Firmly ranked numbers look powerful, and have a habit of taking on a life of their own independent of the interpretative decisions which go into their making. But they can conceal as much as they reveal, and they remain open to alternative readings.

The problem of verification can also be acute in the case of attempts to employ qualitative evidence to explore questions of characteristic behaviour, sentiments and

21 Collinson, *Birthpangs*, p. 83.
22 Wrigley and Schofield, *Population History*, p. 154.

motivations in domestic relations. Very often the best evidence is biassed towards the prescriptive norms of the age (for example in didactic conduct books and sermons); or is the product of sanctions marking the outer boundaries of permitted behaviour (for example, court records); or was generated within relatively restricted social milieux (for example, gentry letter books or the diaries and early autobiographies produced primarily for spiritual purposes by pious members of the professional and trading 'middling sort'). It is no easy task to characterize the large range of behaviour falling between what is revealed by the first two categories of evidence. Was wife-beating regarded with abhorrence, for example, or tacitly tolerated if it remained within the bounds of what the law took to be 'reasonable correction'? Nor is it any easier to assess the representativeness of personal records kept by few people, often for relatively brief periods of a life, usually for reasons other than that of recording family affairs, and sometimes subject to retrospective selection and suppression.

Again, the evidence available to us is often chronologically patchy and uneven. The records of the ecclesiastical courts are at their best between c. 1580 and c. 1640. Personal records like letterbooks, diaries and autobiographies survive in greater numbers from the later seventeenth century. As a result, it is not easy to sustain analysis of particular issues over the whole period. Matchmaking among villagers is best studied before 1640. Kinship networks can best be reconstructed after 1660. Historians concerned with long-term problems of continuity and change can rarely be quite confident that they are comparing like with like. Moreover, the nature of the sources throughout the period is such that many issues, such as marital sexuality or the domestic relations of the poor, are scarcely visible in the records at all if the truth be told.

Difficulties of these kinds can lead to even more unconscious selectivity, argument from silence and interpretative sleight of hand than is usual among historians grappling with the professional imperative of presenting a persuasive case under difficult circumstances – with subsequent squabbling over the significance of example and counter-example. It can encourage a tendency to find what one is intellectually and temperamentally pre-disposed to find in evidence which is all too often thin, highly ambiguous and amenable to a wide variety of possible readings. And the prevailing polarization of interpretation can compound this with an unwillingness to face the implications of those deficiencies and ambiguities. If Stone has been accused of selectivity in his use of evidence to illustrate a preconceived set of interpretative expectations, some of his critics are also vulnerable to the charge of homing-in on material to support their counter-case and playing down both the ambiguities of the evidence and the areas of silence in the records. If Stone allegedly straitjacketed whimpering sources into an over-schematized model of change, more than a few proponents of continuity in family relations have practised a kind of chronological elision, gathering their counter-evidence here and there within an elastically-defined 'early modern' period, with too limited a concern for its changing nature and context, to create an illusion of continuity and deflect attention from the possibility of change. If Stone notoriously seized upon apparent shifts of behaviour within a highly visible, socially prominent, group and made them the touchstone of English experience, an English norm, Macfarlane – and many others, myself included – can be said to have done much the same for the middle ranks of society, the literate professionals and small property owners who generated so much of the available evidence. All these problems are familiar. Yet in the debate over the family in early modern England, it is rare for supporters of either side to take full account – or to recognize that perhaps we never can take full account – of the range of experience which might be anticipated in such a highly stratified and regionally varied society. There has been a very limited willingness to confront openly the limits – socially, thematically and chronologically – of what we actually know, or indeed of what we can ever hope to know.

Thirdly, these various problems of conceptualization and verification add up, in the final analysis, to serious problems of *credibility* for both of the competing interpretative stances. Arguments for massive change in patterns of family life in early modern England seem to rest upon too many 'vast and elusive' shifts to be credible. They evince too little sense of what Peter Laslett calls 'social structural time' – the kind of period necessary, under given historical conditions, to accomplish any such fundamental social change.[23] They have difficulty in providing really convincing demonstrations of alleged changes in attitudes and behaviour, or satisfying explanations of why such major social and cultural changes should have taken place – a great deal usually being left to vague assertions about changes in mentality. In consequence, there is a good deal of skating fast over thin ice, relying upon rhetorical momentum to sustain arguments of a teleological neatness that strains belief. Continuity arguments, on the other hand, seem insensitive to variations of experience both within particular sub-periods and across time. They are too ready to dismiss such changes as can be detected in the larger contexts within which family life was lived as having had no significant impact upon a fundamental structural stability. They play down differences of degree, of context and of meaning which might be of cumulative significance. They do not attempt to explain stability. In sum, they tend to acquire a distinctly ahistorical quality which itself lacks credibility.

These are, I think, some of the essential problems which underlie the diffuse scepticism which has greeted Macfarlane's interpretation no less than the more vocal assaults made upon Stone's position. Given this situation, one might sometimes despair of the subject and conclude that despite the manifest achievements of a generation of historians in exploring particular dimensions of family relationships in the period, there remains overall a sad lack of the kind of constructive thinking that can transcend these interpretative dilemmas and restore a larger sense of direction. The boldness – perhaps recklessness – of the pioneers of the subject might be said to

---

23 P. Laslett, 'The Character of Familial History, its Limitations and the Conditions for its Proper Pursuit', *Journal of Family History*, XII (1987), 273.

have given way to a kind of collective failure of historiographical nerve. If so, the prospect for the subject would be bleak indeed; for, in the words of one critical observer, 'if the family has no significant developmental history, historical interest of a serious kind will not be sustained'.[24]

IV

That, however, would be going much too far. As the dust settles at last on the debates of the 1970s and 1980s, it may be that the prospects are good for a fresh approach to both the history of family relationships between the sixteenth and the eighteenth centuries and the manner in which it connects to other processes of historical change. What might that involve?

In the first place it could involve the paying of more serious attention to the implications of the variability which existed in family life at any given point in time and which is revealed to us in the sources despite their limitations. One such implication is that there is in fact no such thing as *the* history of *the* English family. Rather than paying lip-service to the existence of variation before going on to assert the significance of a dominant English norm – which on past showing is most likely to turn out to be the history of a single class – we might do better to disaggregate the notion of 'the English family' and focus attention upon the range of variation observable in family relationships in England. And having tried to establish that range, we might attempt to characterize and to explain it.

To a considerable extent the first of these tasks – establishing the range of variation – is already under way, though how deliberately it is being pursued is perhaps open to debate. Success in the second task means above all the framing of generalizations in terms of descriptive concepts which are flexible enough to encompass the range of variation, rather than in terms which threaten to obliterate it. Some examples already lie to hand, though their potential is perhaps not always fully realized.

In his work on courtship and marriage in Wiltshire, for example, Martin Ingram has characterized English practice in the late sixteenth and early seventeenth centuries as involving neither unilateral parental arrangement of marriages, nor unilateral freedom of choice on the part of the young, but rather what he terms the 'multilateral consent' of all interested parties. He sees matches as being based upon neither coolly calculated social and economic advantage nor romantic personal attraction, but upon a rough and ready 'parity' between the contracting parties which involved varying configurations of an identifiable range of significant criteria. 'Instead of any clear-cut pattern of "arranged" or "free" marriages, a more subtle system prevailed in which love had a part to play in combination with prudential considerations, the pressure of

24 Collinson, *Birthpangs*, p. 83.

community values and (at middling- and upper-class levels) the interests of parents and sometimes other family members'.[25] *Multilateral consent* and *parity*, as defined by Ingram, are good examples of the kind of flexible descriptive concept with which I am concerned. These notions can encompass a variety of specific experiences in different contexts, ranging from parental acquiescence in the approved initiatives of young couples, to the exercise of a whole range of forms of pressure within families in accordance with the demands of their stations in life and the contingencies of their particular circumstances. They have a general applicability, but also lend themselves to the exploration and explanation of difference in any given generation or over time.

To take another example: in her work on concepts of the family in eighteenth-century England, Naomi Tadmor has demonstrated admirably that to contemporaries the very term 'family' implied not a group of co-resident kinsfolk linked by ties of blood and marriage, but rather a household unit – a group of persons (related or not) living under the same roof and under the authority of a household head. This concept of the 'household-family', as she terms it, describes a structured but highly flexible framework which encompassed both households of different composition and the changing membership of individual households (which might include spouses, children, servants, apprentices, sojourners or any combination of these). The point of this is not to slight the usefulness of analyses of household composition which employ the familiar categories of historical sociology (nuclear, extended, stem, multiple, etc). Rather, it is to re-direct attention to the fact that to contemporaries such differentiation, with its focus on the conjugal core and marginalization of other co-residents, had no real meaning. 'Nuclearity' or 'extension' mattered less than co-residence under a householder's authority. The distinction between them was not one of different family systems, but of responses to different household needs and other contingent circumstances. Tadmor's notion of the 'household-family', then, facilitates a fresh understanding of the structure and dynamics of households in the early modern period, the explanation of variants in household size and composition, and the manner in which the very concept of the family has changed over time.[26]

There seems no good reason why such useful concepts might not be developed for other dimensions of family life in the period. We already have an extensive descriptive literature on, for example, various forms of household economy, kinship relations, marital roles, parent-child relationships and the experience of youth. What is most needed is the creative effort to provide a range of descriptive concepts that can free interpretative thinking from the rigidities of both the old and some new stereotypes of the nature of family relationships in the early modern period.

Given that effort, it is not impossible to imagine the putting together of a more flexible and differentiated characterization of the nature of familial attitudes and

---

25 Ingram, *Church Courts*, pp. 134–42, quotation from p. 142.
26 N. Tadmor, 'The Concept of the Household-Family in Eighteenth-Century England', *Past and Present*, 151 (1996), 111–40.

behaviour in a particular sub-period – say, the extensively-studied later sixteenth and early seventeenth centuries. Such chronological specificity might then provide a more secure foundation for the consideration of processes of change in a more disciplined and informed manner. It could provide a reference point in time for the assessment of the significance of both earlier and later findings – thereby avoiding both the kind of essentially conjectural *status quo ante* represented by Stone's Open Lineage Family, and the more general chronological slipperiness which attends attempts to characterize family life for the period as a whole. It might also identify those central axes of family relationships likely to be crucial to the understanding of processes of both continuity and change.[27]

Secondly, in suggesting a fresh approach to the problem of change, I have in mind a number of points arising from the cautionary experience of the fate of earlier attempts to describe and account for change. The history of the family has done a good deal to undermine the credibility of over-simplified and over-schematic models of change based upon a succession of 'ideal types' which are introduced as an aid to interpretative conceptualization, but have a habit of turning into what purport to be literal descriptions of successive stages of development. If we are to do any better, we need in the first place to pay more attention to the uneven and partial nature of historical change. We are, after all, dealing with not one, but a whole bundle of family histories in such a complex and highly differentiated society. 'Family life' was a mixture of forms. Change is unlikely to have proceeded at an even pace, or in a uniform manner, to have been linear, or unidirectional, or monocausal. Rather it is likely to have involved shifts in the relative salience of particular forms and in their relationships to one another. Moreover, it is likely to have been channelled and qualified by elements of inertia and persistence which were themselves unevenly distributed in social space. We need to incorporate such considerations into any account of change, and in doing so to trace developments over time in a manner which involves what has been termed a 'less heroic and more provisional chronology'.[28]

We also need to pay closer attention to the precise mechanisms of the ways in which family experiences and broader processes of historical change intersect. Historians have perhaps been excessively concerned with the ways in which macro-historical processes – the Reformation; the 'rise of individualism'; urbanization; industrialization – impact *on* families and insufficiently sensitive to the *agency* of families historically. Tamara Harevan, through her work on life-course transitions and the processes of decision-making which these involve, has stressed the ways in which families initiate and resist as well as respond to various forces for change: their strategies and forms of adaptation in changing circumstances; their roles as both

27 As is suggested in P. Rushton, 'Property, Power, and Family Networks: The Problem of Disputed Marriage in Early Modern England', *Journal of Family History*, XI (1986), 215.
28 Vickery, 'Golden Age to Separate Spheres?', p. 413.

custodians of established ways and agents of transition; the importance of the selectiveness of their responses.[29] Given the fact that social and cultural change so often involves less pure innovation than selection from among a range of existing options, such responses and decisions could be crucial, cumulatively, in edging the course of change in one direction, rather than another. Yet as Harevan observes, 'much of this interaction still awaits thorough examination'.[30] The early modern period surely provides enormous scope for the study of such social processes over time.

Whether the task is that of characterizing flexibly and inclusively the recoverable patterns of family relations in a particular generation, or of tracing processes of change, a simple rule of thumb which can be used to good effect is that of remaining sensitive to the interrelationships of *contexts* and *options*. Imperfect as our evidence often is, it is surely sufficient to enable us to go a good way towards delineating the various contexts within which people lived their lives – ideological; legal; economic; demographic; social-structural; material and cultural. Moreover, the recorded incidents of family life – above all those involving the making of decisions – enable us to explore the options which these permitted people in the past: the constraints with which they were obliged to cope; the opportunities afforded them to exercise preferences; the strategies which they adopted in response. Closer consideration of these matters can help us to understand continuities and the processes involved in continuity. It can also provide a point of entry to the discussion and evaluation of change. Shifts in the contexts of family life – severally, or in various combinations – could have the effect of broadening, or of narrowing, the range of options in personal behaviour open to individuals and members of social groups: influencing their life-chances and opportunities; their aspirations and expectations; the range of possibilities of which they were aware, and on which they might act.

In the case of early modern England, we might well consider, or reconsider, the implications of developments in a whole variety of such contexts. In the realm of ideology, for example, there is reason to readdress the question of the social and cultural influence of the moralistic conduct books written between the 1520s and the eighteenth century to define and re-define household roles, and now attracting fresh attention as either sources of novel familial ideals or purveyors of stale platitudes which were subverted by their own contradictions.[31] In that of law, there is much to

---

29 T. Harevan, 'The History of the Family and the Complexity of Social Change', *American Historical Review*, XCVI (1991), 111ff.

30 *Ibid.*, p. 111.

31 For some stimulating recent discussions, see, e.g., Collinson, *Birthpangs*, ch. 3, esp. pp. 90–2; S. D. Amussen, '"The Part of a Christian Man": The Cultural Politics of Manhood in Early Modern England', in *Political Culture and Cultural Politics in Early Modern England*, ed. S. D. Amussen and M. A. Kishlansky (Manchester, 1994), esp. pp. 216–17; A. J. Fletcher, 'The Protestant Idea of Marriage in Early Modern England', in *Religion, Culture and Society in Early Modern Britain*, ed. A. J. Fletcher and P. R. Roberts (Cambridge, 1994), pp. 161–81.

be learned from the complex and contradictory course of change in women's legal rights, status and access to redress: enhanced by the development of equity; diminished by the decline of customary law; threatened by the triumph of common law – an excellent example of change which was both multidirectional and variable in its impact socially and chronologically.[32] In the economic sphere, we might consider the shifts in familial aspirations and strategies implied by such phenomena as the massive inflation of dowry values in sixteenth-century Kent demonstrated by Diana O'Hara, or the redeployment of household labour resources characterized by Jan de Vries as an 'industrious revolution'.[33] Demographically, it seems likely that declining fertility and rising mortality in the mid-to-late seventeenth century, together with population mobility, reduced the pool of living kinsfolk in many local communities – a development with potentially significant consequences for kinship relations.[34] Social-structurally, the growth of the wage-labouring sector of the population must surely have had an impact on the nature of domestic economies, the roles of men, women and children within them and the life-cycles and life-course decisions of the poor.[35] In the sphere of material culture, we might consider the implications of changing standards of housing and domestic comfort and the reallocation of space in households of the middling and upper ranks – developments which John Smail's study of Halifax, for example, links to processes of class differentiation, and shifts in gender roles within a newly defined private sphere complemented by novel patterns of public sociability.[36] This in turn raises the question of the influence of new forms of *élite* sociability, above all the urban season of the late seventeenth and early eighteenth centuries, upon the independent courtship opportunities of the children of the rich.[37] And one might ask also how far the growth of popular literacy and the elaboration of print culture provided access, for at least some, to alternative models of behaviour and more elaborate forms of personal

---

32 See, e.g., Erickson, *Women and Property*, p. 230ff; T. Stretton, 'Women and Litigation in the Elizabethan Court of Requests', University of Cambridge Ph.D., 1993, chs. 2 and 7.

33 D. O'Hara, 'Sixteenth-Century Courtship in the Diocese of Canterbury', University of Kent Ph.D., 1995, ch. 6; J. de Vries, 'Between Purchasing Power and the World of Goods: Understanding the Household Economy in Early Modern Europe', in *Consumption*, ed. Brewer and Porter, pp. 85–132.

34 P. Laslett, 'La parenté en chiffres', *Annales E. S. C.* XLIII (1988), 5–24; D. Cressy, 'Kinship and Kin Interaction in Early Modern England', *Past and Present*, 113 (1986), 58–9. Cf. Z. Razi, 'The Myth of the Immutable English Family', *Past and Present*, 140 (1993), 31–3.

35 See, e.g., T. Wales, 'Poverty, Poor Relief and the Life-Cycle: Some Evidence from Seventeenth-Century Norfolk', in *Land, Kinship and Life-Cycle*, ed. Smith, pp. 351–404; J. Walter, 'The Social Economy of Dearth in Early Modern England', in *Famine, Disease and the Social Order in Early Modern Society*, ed. J. Walter and R. Schofield (Cambridge, 1989), pp. 75–128; D. Levine and K. Wrightson, *The Making of an Industrial Society. Whickham 1560–1765* (Oxford, 1991), chs. 3 and 4; B. Stapleton, 'Inherited Poverty and Life-Cycle Poverty: Odiham, Hampshire, 1650–1850', *Social History*, XVIII (1993), 339–55.

36 J. Smail, *The Origins of Middle-Class Culture. Halifax, Yorkshire, 1660–1780* (Ithaca and London, 1994), ch. 6; M. Johnson, *An Archaeology of Capitalism* (Oxford, 1996), ch. 7.

37 Mendelson, 'Debate: The Weightiest Business', p. 130; P. Borsay, *The English Urban Renaissance. Culture and Society in the Provincial Town, 1660–1760* (Oxford, 1989), esp. part IV.

expression – be they derived from chapbook romances, published autobiographies, the novels of Defoe or Richardson, or the questions and answers on familial matters in John Dunton's *Athenian Mercury*.[38]

These are only a few examples of the opportunities which exist for the investigation of change in family relationships in early modern England; for the recovery of the complex configurations of cause and effect which may have added up, incrementally, to significant shifts in familial attitudes and behaviour and in the range of variation in English family life. Some of them, to be sure, raise possibilities reminiscent of the disparaged arguments of Lawrence Stone (a number of which may yet bear re-appraisal). But they do so in a rather more specific and firmly-based manner, inviting the exploration of comprehensible mechanisms and processes of change, rather than positing 'vast and elusive' cultural shifts. And they imply piecemeal, uneven, multicausal, multidirectional, modifications of the range of experience, rather than neatly definable evolutionary stages on the road to modernity.

V

Change there surely was, then: change which operated in a variety of contexts and directions, which was everywhere inflected by differences of class, age and gender, and which brought different consequences for different people – new opportunities for some; new forms of personal containment for others. And, of course, there was continuity too, what Segalen calls that element of permanence about some of the most elemental dimensions of family experience which 'seems to offer many forms of resistance to social change'; reproducing established patterns; replicating aspects of the experience of successive generations.[39]

Closer attention to the interaction of forces of continuity and change in specific contexts might bring us closer to a convincing history of family relationships in early modern England. It seems unlikely, however, that such work would either resurrect the notion of a fundamental transition in family relations, or endorse the notion of the precocious 'modernity' and massive stability of English family structures over three or more centuries. Perhaps in the final analysis both of these positions derive from an excessive preoccupation with the three central themes of the old master narrative – nuclearity, individualism and emotionalism or 'affect' – leading to an arguably misguided interpretative emphasis upon the significance of their contested absence, presence or emergence. All three were present in the early modern period. All three

---

38 The historical literature on print culture is enormous, but much remains to be discovered about its possible influence in the domestic sphere. For some recent suggestions see, e.g., B. J. Todd, 'Demographic Determinism and Female Agency: The Remarrying Widow Reconsidered ... again', *Continuity and Change*, IX (1994), 425–6; M. Mascuch, *Origins of the Individualist Self: Autobiography and Self-Identity in England, 1591–1791* (Cambridge, 1997). Dunton's *Athenian Mercury* is the subject of the doctoral research of Helen Berry of Jesus College, Cambridge.

39 Segalen, *Historical Anthropology*, p. 293.

also have a history. But perhaps it is a history of their relative salience, adaptation and mode of expression in different contexts, rather than one of either their discovery or their timeless perdurance.

The early modern period may have much to reveal about that. But it does not hold the key to the making of that elusive entity 'the modern family'. If we wish to discuss the origins of some of the central characteristics of contemporary family relationships – in all their present diversity and plasticity – we surely need to look elsewhere: to other times and other criteria. Early modern England witnessed no economic and social upheaval as fundamental as industrialization and urbanization; no demographic change on a par with the introduction of effective contraception; no institutional change – despite the significance of the poor laws – truly comparable to the emergence of the welfare state. It saw no legal change as significant as the married women's property or divorce acts; no educational change as far-reaching as compulsory primary and secondary education and the prolongation of dependency that they entail; no cultural shifts to match secularization, or the emergence and popularization of psychoanalytical ideas; no ideological change so corrosive of established attitudes as the growth of democratic ideologies, the extension of new political and social rights to women and children, the gradual (painfully gradual) erosion of 'patriarchal' assumptions and powers, and the recasting of gender roles.

Such considerations help provide some perspective on the debate over the family in early modern England, and by doing so, to liberate the present generation of historians of family life in the period from the burden of the polarizing interpretative hyperbole of their predecessors. They serve as a reminder that in more than a few respects family relationships as we presently know them were shaped not in the seventeenth and eighteenth, but in the nineteenth and twentieth centuries. What the history of the family in early modern England does show, however, is that 'the making of modern family life' did not involve the *un*making of all that went before. The contexts have changed dramatically. The options have changed fundamentally. The dynamic of change in the family continues, often in unanticipated directions. But culturally, no less than genetically, some family resemblances endure.

2

Eighteenth-Century England as an *Ancien Régime*

FRANK O'GORMAN

As the whig interpretation of the long eighteenth century in English history recedes into the graveyard of historical explanations it may be replaced by a 'revisionist' alternative, first announced by Jonathan Clark in 1985 in his influential *English Society, 1688–1832*. The whigs had described a unique society based on constitutional traditions, not least those of parliamentary government, the rule of law, religious toleration and freedom of speech. The revisionist alternative depicts 'an alternative model of English society under the ancien regime, built now around the subjects which the received methodology has typically excluded from the agenda, or relegated to a minor place: religion and politics, the Church and the social elite of aristocracy and gentry'.[1] England was presented less as a liberal society than as an *ancien régime*, indeed, as a 'confessional state'. The issues at stake in these competing models of eighteenth-century England are momentous. They encompass the nature of eighteenth-century society, the trajectory of English historical development, the possible development of constitutional forms of politics and, not least, the comparable status of English state and society with those of her European neighbours. These are of such overwhelming significance that they demand extended analysis and consideration.

The test of any historical explanation must lie, in part at least, in the effectiveness with which it answers the questions put to it and the extent to which it illuminates the historical period involved. The revisionist argument begins with the assumption that English history in the long eighteenth century was unquestionably a series of sustained and glorious achievement. It seeks to explain the sensational financial and economic advances of the period, the much-lauded establishment of parliamentary government and limited monarchy, the repeated military victories against the national enemy, France, the spectacular expansion of the British empire and, not least, after the Acts of Union of 1707 and 1800, the emergence of a united body politic. As Jonathan Clark puts it: 'We are clearly dealing with a society which improved its position greatly over two centuries from 1660, strengthening its political institutions, its economic base, its strategic position, its colonial presence.' Traditional explanations for this improved strength are to be discarded. These include 'the spurious

---

1   J. C. D. Clark, *English Society 1688–1832. Ideology, Social Structure and Political Practice during the Ancien Regime* (Cambridge, 1985), p. 1.

notions of a bourgeois revolution, of a constitutionalist ideology and an issueless political stability, of an industrial revolution, of a proletariat without belief or dignity, exploited to finance a bleak new world of possessive individualism'.[2] In the place of these discarded explanations we should give weight to the idea of England as an *ancien régime*.

To do so, according to Clark, liberates us from the anachronistic presentation of England in the long eighteenth century as a preparation for the emergence of England as a 'modern' state in the nineteenth. It allows us to portray this period in English history in its own terms. Revisionists thus maintain that it is misleading to incorporate the long eighteenth century within a nineteenth-century paradigm of 'modernity' (which downgrades traditional social and political elements), of industrialization (which had, in truth, made little impact before the early years of the nineteenth century), of secularism (at the expense of a powerful, enduring anglicanism) and of class (in an age of hierarchy and patriarchalism).

To conceive of eighteenth-century England as an *ancien régime* had a further advantage. It lent historiographical unity to a lengthy period (1660–1832), which had been in danger of both fragmentation and serious misinterpretation. It provided a coherent and consistent thematic unity for two very different periods, the superficially tranquil and placid early decades of the eighteenth century, so often presented as 'an unpleasant hangover after the euphoric revolution of the 1640s'[3] and the much more dynamic era of reform and industrialization in the late eighteenth and early nineteenth centuries. Now, the long eighteenth century acquired an identity and a continuity of its own. 'The theoretic formulation of English society between the Restoration and the Reform Bill may best be understood as a mutually-reinforcing system of three main components: monarchy, patrician elite, clerical intelligentsia. The particular form taken by this alliance distinguishes the period markedly from what came before and after.'[4]

To present the history of England in this way offered a yet further, important advantage: it allowed the revisionist historian to emphasize the common features which England shared with her European neighbours and to avoid the mythology of England's 'exceptionalism', the idea that she pursued a unique and independent path to constitutional government, economic revolution and imperial greatness. In other words, England was an *ancien régime* society, in many ways like those of the European continent. 'Only the concept of an ancien regime', argues Clark 'offers

---

2   J. C. D. Clark, 'On Hitting the Buffers: The Historiography of England's Ancien Regime. A Response', *Past and Present*, 117 (1987), 202.

3   J. C. D. Clark, *Revolution and Rebellion. State and Society in England in the Seventeenth and Eighteenth Centuries* (Cambridge, 1986), p. 7.

4   Clark, 'On Hitting the Buffers', p. 199.

effective ways of reintegrating the history of England into that of continental Europe.'[5]

The revisionist thesis of an *ancien régime* indubitably engages with several of the most fundamental of all historiographical concerns involved in the study of eighteenth-century England. On their refusal to accept anachronistic assumptions of several generations of scholars, the revisionists should be congratulated. However, some elements in their model of eighteenth-century society had been anticipated by earlier writers. Many historians – not least Namier – had argued that eighteenth-century England retained many traditional features, not least the social and political predominance of the landed interest in general and of the aristocracy in particular. In 1985, just before the birth of revisionism, I wrote a lengthy review article for *The Historical Journal* which included John Cannon's *Aristocratic Century*, Ian Christie's *Stress and Stability in Late Eighteenth-Century Britain* and John Gunn's *Beyond Liberty and Property*. These books stressed the hierarchical basis of Hanoverian society, the aristocratic nature of its leadership, the conservatism of its pattern of thought and its adhesion to existing forms of behaviour, within a framework of traditional institutions and values. None of them would have gone as far as Jonathan Clark in describing England as *ancien régime* society but they would have agreed that traditional institutions and patterns of thought maintained their grip on eighteenth-century England.

Others would not have done. Social and economic historians were predictably unhappy with the *ancien régime* model because it appeared to ignore many of the modernizing elements upon which their careers depended: industry, capitalism, commerce and new patterns of consumption.[6] Revisionists, however, replied that economic development and rapid social change can occur within traditional societies, dominated by the monarchy, the church and the aristocracy, as is the case today in Japan and other Asian countries. 'To picture an ancien regime in the ways adumbrated in *English Society* is to remind ourselves of the substantial compatibility of the hegemony of the traditional elite and of the orthodox religion with broadly-diffused commercial activity and incipient industrial growth.'[7] In this manner, the idea of England as an *ancien régime* society becomes marvellously flexible. It incorporates the old and the new, industry and land, science and religion.

---

5   *Ibid.*
6   See, for example, Peter Earle, *The Making of the English Middle Class. Business, Society and Family Life in London, 1660–1730* (1989); *The Consumption of Culture*, ed. J. Brewer and A. Bermingham (1985); *Early Modern Conceptions of Property*, ed. J. Brewer and S. Staves (1995); C. Shammas, *The Pre-Industrial Consumer in England and America* (1993); *Consumption and the World of Goods*, ed. J. Brewer and R. Porter (1994); B. Lemire, *Fashion's Favourite. The Cotton Trade and the Consumer in Britain, 1660–1800* (1991); Peter Borsay, *The English Urban Renaissance. Culture and Society in the Provincial Town, 1660–1800* (Oxford, 1989).
7   Clark, 'On Hitting the Buffers', p. 203.

What precisely is to be understood by the term *'ancien régime'*? Oddly, Jonathan Clark refuses 'to construct models of what ancien regimes "essentially" or "typically" were'. Indeed, he is anxious merely to use the term for polemical purposes. 'The purpose of using the term was to negate former reifications in terms of bourgois modernity.'[8] In fact, it is just as questionable to import the term *'ancien régime'* to describe eighteenth-century England as it is to apply a term like 'industrial revolution' or 'bourgeois society', none of which were used by contemporaries. Indeed, the term *'ancien régime'* was not used in France until 1788 and so until then the English could not possibly have used it in order to describe themselves. The great French historian, Pierre Goubert, its most noted exponent, uses it to describe the old regime in France which was destroyed at the time of the French Revolution. His definition of the *'ancien régime'* is of cardinal significance. 'In reality, the ancien regime stands out only by contrast with what came after it. It becomes a distinctive entity only by its legal death, which defines and names it.' More directly, and more importantly, Goubert pronounces:

> The confusion which is the hallmark of the ancien regime derives from its nature. It is a conglomeration of mostly centuries-old, sometimes thousand year-old elements, none of which was ever discarded. Its profound conservatism often protected the obsolete, creating museum-pieces that were simultaneously respected, distorted, forgotten, revived and fossilised ... The ancien regime is like an immense turbid river carrying dead hulks of trees, rank weeds torn from its banks, and living organisms of all ages and sizes.[9]

If the reader is in some doubt about the applicability of such a term to eighteenth-century England, Goubert goes far towards dispelling it. In considering the factors which 'gradually tore the ancien regime apart' he specifically includes several of the cardinal, defining characteristics of English society during the eighteenth century such as 'accelerated transportation', 'the foundations of a reliable banking system', 'the decline of religious belief' and 'industrialization'.[10]

In noting the key features of an *ancien régime*, moreover, Goubert lists a number of properties which were of rapidly *declining* relevance to Hanoverian England.

> Economically, it is characterized by slow communications, the predominance of agriculture, the low status of iron-working in industry, itself of minor importance, and an almost non-existent banking system ... Politically, it remained the regime of juridical, linguistic and administrative diversity ... Mentally, it is distinguished by a blend of supernaturalism and christian fervour, widespread illiteracy, a very blinkered provincial and local way of life, and a uniformly weak, and sometimes non-existent,

8   J. C. D. Clark, 'Reconceptualising Eighteenth-Century England', *British Journal for Eighteenth Century Studies*, xv (1992), 135–6.
9   P. Goubert, *The Ancien Regime. French Society, 1600–1750* (1973).
10 *Ibid.*, pp. 18–19.

concept of state, nation and fatherland, except for the worship of the monarch and the physical presence of danger.[11]

Obviously, Goubert would have been amazed to find that the term *'ancien régime'* was being stretched to describe a society which exhibited *qualities which were its very antithesis*.

Of course, there were broad similarities between England and France. Like most European societies between the seventh and the twentieth centuries, eighteenth-century England was governed by a monarchy, a church and an aristocracy. Her society was hierarchical, her people inhabited scattered rural communities and her ruling class was a small and privileged aristocracy. Her manufacturing industries were generally small scale but directed towards internal and external trade in general, and, in particular, towards a rapidly expanding consumer market. Consequently, it would be most unwise to erect artificial contrasts between an economically dynamic England and an economically backward France. There is massive evidence, for example, that the French middling orders expanded both in numbers and in wealth during the century, as did those of England. At the same time, the French industrial sector prospered and diversified.

Yet serious differences between the economic structures of England and France remained.[12] London dominated the English economy in a way that far surpassed the economic influence of Paris. In 1750, for example, 11 per cent of the English population lived in London; only 2.5 per cent of the population of France lived in Paris.[13] England was an unusually urbanized country and an exceptionally high proportion of her inhabitants worked in manufacturing industry. Her neighbour, arguably, was much more backward. France was still subject to structural crises of food production, as the decade of the 1780s illustrated. In England, on the contrary, famine was a thing of the past. Indeed, the productivity of French agriculture was only one half that of the English. The surplus population of rural England flocked to the towns, where it could be used, in part at least, as a pool of cheap labour in the new, as well as the old, manufacturing industries. After the Act of Union in 1707, indeed, Britain comprised the largest free trade area in Europe, while the French economy was still inhibited by internal tolls. By the middle of the eighteenth century, England had become an importer of raw materials and an exporter of manufactured goods (principally textiles) on a scale that was unique in Europe.[14]

The financial structures of the two countries remained distinct. While France still laboured under the outdated system of tax farming and the inefficient tax collection

---

11 *Ibid.*, p. 20.
12 J. de Vries, *European Urbanization, 1500–1800* (1984); R. Price, *The Economic Modernization of France, 1730–1800* (1975). See also the interesting discussion in J. Innes, 'Jonathan Clark, Social History and England's "Ancien Regime"', *Past and Present*, 115 (1987), esp. pp. 191–7.
13 M. J. Daunton, *Progress and Poverty. An Economic and Social History of Britain, 1700–1850* (1995) pp. 137–8.
14 R. Davis, *The Industrial Revolution and British Overseas Trade* (1979).

which were to prove her undoing in the 1780s, England had developed an effective system of managing her national debt. Perhaps because England developed her central bureaucracy much later than France did, it was not overburdened with the sale of office, the existence of exemptions and privileges and the thoroughgoing corruption that was to defeat the French reformers of the 1780s.[15] As a consequence, the government was relatively free to innovate and to establish efficient systems of state borrowing. Indeed, the English system of financing the government deficit over a lengthy period of time helped to spread repayments fairly evenly between times of war and times of peace. The routines of parliamentary review which were established after the Glorious Revolution actually reinforced the power of the English state by strengthening the processes of consent which underpinned its financing.

Similarly, the political structures of England resembled those of many European states, such as France, but it is the differences which need also to be noticed. Effective royal powers and prerogatives survived the Glorious Revolution and the monarchy remained the hub from which executive action emanated. 'The rebellion of 1688 was not a bid for a weak monarchy, but for a Protestant monarchy. Consequently, the legislative expressions of that attempt which followed had much to do with religion, but little to do with placing limitations on the monarch's prerogative in other spheres.'[16] The English parliament remained a subsidiary partner of the monarch; its meetings were summoned – and dissolved – by the crown and it lacked the right to engage in a continuous review of government action. On the other hand, it was the crown-in-parliament which was all-powerful. The elimination of the powers of the highland chiefs after the '45 could not have happened in France, where the government lacked the power to override local separatism to this formidable extent.[17] Furthermore, the English fiscal-military state, characterized by a steadily growing bureaucracy, was as powerful as any in Europe. The control which the government enjoyed over trade and commerce was, moreover, if anything *more* powerful than that of any government in Europe. In general, the old whiggish assumption that the British were treading the path to constitutional government and liberal politics while her European neighbours were stumbling blindly on the road to 'absolutism', can no longer be taken seriously. Britain was like many other European states in her 'composite' structure, her union of crowns and the existence of different nations under the same crown.

As in the economic sphere, however, there were important political differences between England and France. There was, quite simply, nothing in the French state to compare with the English parliament. After 1707 there were no local estates or assemblies and, with the exception of the corporate towns, few privileged governing

---

15 T. Ertman, 'The Sinews of Power and European State-Building Theory', in *An Imperial State at War. Britain from 1689 to 1815*, ed. L. Stone (1994), pp. 33–51.
16 Clark, *Revolution and Rebellion*, p. 89.
17 Nicholas Henshall, *The Myth of Absolutism* (1992), ch. 5.

bodies. The function of parliament in the routines of politics was guaranteed through its indispensable role in public finance. Most of all, however, and never to be underestimated, were the contrasting religious purposes of the English and French political systems. In France, the established state religion was Roman catholicism. England, on the other hand, was a protestant state and it had been the purpose of the Glorious Revolution to perpetuate that state of affairs. In the same way, the function of her armed services was to defend her from the catholic Bourbon states.

Comparisons and contrasts between England and France could be endlessly pursued; those between England and the rest of Europe could be infinitely examined and variously concluded. Although England shared much with her continental neighbours it is most unwise to argue either for or against her compatibility with European models of political and social development. There was no *European* standard. France differed from Spain, from the Scandinavian countries, from Holland, from Prussia, from Poland and from Russia. To assume that France served as an 'absolutist' model for continental states is erroneous. The massive variations in the power enjoyed by monarchs and the number of large and important states in which monarchs were self-evidently *not* absolute – Britain, Sweden, Poland, Holland – and the irrelevance of such labels to so many parts of central and eastern Europe – all weaken the force of the *ancien régime* argument. European regimes in the eighteenth century may have been élitist, they may have been christian and they may have been monarchical but it is the differences between them which need emphasizing because it is the differences which explain differing patterns of national development. Even Professor Clark has noted that 'in respect of their ideological structure, there were at least three equally viable forms of the ancien regime: Roman Catholic, non-Calvinist Protestant, Russian Orthodox'.[18]

The differences exhibited by England were absolutely vital to her development. She was an island state, perched on the north western periphery of Europe, a naval rather than a military power. Her system of common law retained its distinctiveness and its native versions of protestantism their character. The established anglican and presbyterian churches were unique to Britain and her possessions. Her great victories in the French revolutionary and Napoleonic wars ensured that her territories were neither overrun nor dominated by France, thus enabling her to achieve economic preeminence in Europe, to establish a global maritime supremacy and to construct a largely non-white empire. To notice these developments is not to fall into a triumphalist and 'exceptionalist' historiography. If there was no European standard, it can hardly be 'exceptionalist' to identify the characteristic features of English history during the eighteenth century. Interestingly, moreover, it is surely significant that many of these characteristic features were not shared by France but were in fact tearing France apart. International economic competition was weakening the

18 Clark, *Revolution and Rebellion*, p. 79.

resources of the French state and, in particular, its system of internal taxation. Furthermore, imperial warfare was dangerously stretching the fabric of the *ancien régime* in France by the middle decades of the century.

It is quite unsurprising, then, that eighteenth-century Britons were strongly aware of their own individuality and their own identity. This is not so much to claim, along with Professor Colley, that a British national identity made its appearance during the eighteenth century. Such a development may well have been under way during the eighteenth century and, indeed, long before it.[19] It is, rather, to observe that they conceived of themselves less within *ancien régime* perspectives than within their direct opposite. The cluster of organizing concepts which meant so much to ordinary Englishmen cannot be contained within what is normally understood as an *ancien régime* model of social and political life: the freeborn Englishman, the Anglo-Saxon constitution, the freedom of the press, the virtues of a protestant nation, the Glorious Revolution. Englishmen congratulated themselves upon their dynamic and flexible society, their freedom, their extensive degree of religious toleration and – what is often under-estimated – their commercial inventiveness. They certainly *felt* themselves to be distinct, different from their neighbours. It does not seem to be sensible to discard these ideas, to which contemporaries returned again and again. Indeed, they would have been astonished to learn that Britain and France were both *ancien régime* societies since they spent so much time at war with each other. Contemporary observers were much more inclined to compare Britain with Sweden or Holland than with France. They may have been blinded through prejudice to the similarities between French and English social and political systems which historians may now identify. But they certainly did not consider England to have been a society of the *ancien régime*.

One of the reasons for this was the political arrangements of the period. It is too simplistic to affirm that England was a monarchical state. On the one hand, eighteenth-century England derived enormous strength and stability from its monarchy but it derived no little strength, too, from its ability to discipline and limit the powers of the monarchy and thus to acknowledge the powers and reputation of parliament. Contemporaries return again and again to this aspect of their politics. The Glorious Revolution had, of course, been concerned to establish a protestant monarchy but it had also been careful to establish a monarchy whose powers were circumscribed. Consequently, the Hanoverian regime derived strength and legitimacy from the status of parliament and its accountability to the public, from the confidence of the propertied public, from the emphatic repudiation of its (jacobite) alternative, from the calculated use of patronage, and, perhaps most important of all, from the new patriotism of the decades of the Revolutionary and Napoleonic wars.

19 Linda Colley, *Britons. Forging the Nation, 1707–1837* (New Haven, 1992).

The aristocracy played an invaluable, and sometimes heroic, part in the armed services during that period and it is beyond dispute that the regime derived enormous strength and stability from its aristocratic traditions of service and sacrifice. Yet a balanced view of the regime and its legitimacy demands a recognition of the prominent role played by those whom Professor Langford has accurately termed 'A polite and commercial people', those tens of thousands of people of the middling sort who were fashioning vital consumer, commercial and industrial developments. It was not just that their numbers were increasing. The regime positively welcomed their involvement in national life and actively sought their participation, especially in local administration. For one thing, the deficit financing of eighteenth-century governments depended upon the long-term investments of the middling orders. In other words, the middling orders were actively prepared to finance the 'fiscal-military state' and to enjoy the occupational and political benefits which flowed from it. Moreover, they were anxious to act as officers in the armed services, to staff the rising professional occupations and to occupy legal and administrative posts throughout society. They were particularly prominent throughout the economy and played indispensable roles in the rapidly expanding commercial sectors, both domestic and foreign. Indeed, the very revenues of the state depended upon the taxes of the middling orders, the customs dues of commerce, the trade of the empire and the wealth of the city of London. This global and commercial perspective to Hanoverian history requires emphasis. The rapid expansion and the sheer size and scope of the empire are often underplayed. Most historians concentrate unduly upon the North American empire when there is a growing imperial presence in India, Canada and Australia and, after 1815, many other parts of the world. England was an imperial state and becoming an imperial nation in the eighteenth century. To ignore and to neglect that dimension in favour of a little Englander conception of an unchanging *ancien régime* interpretation is regrettable. Consequently, it was not only the *ancien régime* engines of church, monarchy and aristocracy which preserved and strengthened the Hanoverian regime but the rising forces of commerce and empire.

Yet Jonathan Clark finds 'no room ... for bourgeois modernity' in Hanoverian England.[20] 'Until the evolution of class', he writes, in a brief passage that deserves careful study, 'hierarchical subordination was scarcely dissolved.'[21] Scarcely dissolved? Not even a little? By the middle of the eighteenth century the aristocracy was having to accommodate the middling orders, its regime coming to depend upon their service and their money. Because of this the aristocracy was making concession after concession to the values of the middling orders, to commerce and to trade. Indeed, the aristocracy was itself becoming less like an *ancien régime élite*. Its interests were becoming increasingly urban and its attitudes increasingly capitalistic.

---

20 Clark, *English Society*, p. 118. See also p. 94.
21 *Ibid.*, p. 86.

At least one principal reason for the revisionists' repudiation of modernity is presumably to be found in the concept of *ancien régime* England as a 'confessional state', that is to say, a state with a single confession of faith, a faith established by the law, to which the whole population should conform by regular attendance at church. This notion, with its assumption that social life should be imbued with the orthodox religion of the state, has profound implications for the life of the population more generally, for their employment, for their education, for the management of their hospitals and for the treatment of the very poorest among them. In this scheme of things, anglicanism was much more than a political theology. It was nothing less than an all-pervasive social cement which was the foundation of a deep-seated ideological consensus. The ideology of the confessional state maintained the force of a patriarchal and familial conception of society which legitimized the orders of society, their chains of command, inculcating humility and obedience into the minds and hearts of social inferiors.

Compelling and attractive though this 'self-image' of the Hanoverian regime may be, it trembles on the verge of a powerful ecclesiastical nostalgia. The idea of a confessional state may have meant much to the religious intelligentsia of the anglican church and, to some extent, to the paid officials of the Hanoverian regime but it meant considerably less to the mass of the people. This judgment does not refer merely to the patterns and rhythms of popular culture, which, while operating within a largely ecclesiastical calendar, assumed a somewhat secular, and even, pagan, quality that seems to have few points of contact with the official doctrines of anglicanism. It refers, more seriously, to the massive gulf between the clergy and the people. During the years of the American war, according to Professor Bradley, 'the dominant attitude of the clergy ... was not confidence, but deep distrust of the people and a fear of moral, political and social disorder'.[22] As we have seen, Englishmen professed a conception of themselves far removed from the picture of a docile and deferential parochial congregation.

There was good reason why they should resist such an identification of themselves. Their spiritual needs were not being met. Recent estimates reach the astonishing conclusion that in 1780 only 38 per cent of parishes had resident incumbents and that, correspondingly, 36 per cent of anglican clergy were pluralists.[23] Indeed, in most places less than 10 per cent of churches maintained a monthly communion.[24] It is hard to avoid Dr Gilbert's conclusion that between 1740 and 1800 'Anglicanism rapidly lost much of that constituency to which, in theory, it had exclusive access'.[25] Furthermore, it was institutionally impossible to undertake reform

---

22   J. E. Bradley, 'The Anglican Pulpit, Social Order and the Resurgence of Toryism during the American Revolution', *Albion*, XXI (1989), 377.

23   Peter Virgin, *The Church in an Age of Negligence. Ecclesiastical Structure and Problems of Church Reform 1700–1840* (Cambridge, 1989), pp. 191–6.

24   A. Gilbert, *Religion and Society in Industrial England* (1976), pp. 27–9.

25   *Ibid.*, p. 47.

of the church. A powerful laity defended its vested interests, especially at the local level, by resisting pressures for necessary reform. Even the bishops, in their dependence upon successive governments, promoted an ecclesiastical servility which was reflected lower down the social scale not only in a casual acceptance of secular control of the church but too often in a lamentable inattention to duty on the part of the anglican clergy. Human imperfection does not entirely dispose of the idea of a confessional state but there are surely limits to what can and cannot be reconciled with it. By the later decades of the eighteenth century, the church was losing its influence over the people to such an extent that such ideological consensus as might have existed in Hanoverian England could only be found in non-anglican sources. Two of these may briefly be mentioned. As Roy Porter has suggested, 'the ideology of the common law was one to which the great majority of the British people seem to have subscribed'.[26] Furthermore, at certain times, at least, ideological consensus was formed out of patriotic pressures, orchestrated by the press, pamphlet and celebration. Consequently, it is not necessary to mobilize the ideology of the confessional state in order to understand the ideological consensus which existed in Hanoverian England.

If this is so, then why should the idea of a confessional state have exerted such a powerful hold on some contemporaries and some historians. Perhaps the answer lies in the fact that the maintenance of the privileges of a confessional state depends vitally upon its own self-belief. A confessional state can neither admit its own weaknesses nor reach accommodations with its enemies. It is a magnificent exercise in self-projection, a beguiling corporate image.

It could not last for ever. With the repeal of the Test and Corporation Acts in 1828 and the passage of catholic emancipation in 1829 the religious props of the so-called *ancien régime* came crashing down. Nevertheless, there was, according to Jonathan Clark, no gradual slide into unbelief. Indeed, until the 1820s, England remained almost as much of a monarchical confessional state as it had been under the Stuarts. There had, of course, always been challenges to the confessional state, whether from civil war sectaries, restoration Roman catholics and quakers, post-revolution non-jurors, American dissenters and Irish catholics. As Clark notes: 'there was nothing unique about the challenges faced by the regime in the 1820s except their spectacular success'. What accounts for this spectacular success was 'a final and sudden betrayal from within' as much as the numerical erosion of anglicanism.[27] The bishops failed to fight in the last ditch for their church in 1828 and 1829 and, not surprisingly, they failed to oppose the Reform Bill of 1832 with sufficient vigour.[28] With the abandonment of the confessional state 'the cultural hegemony of the

---

26 Roy Porter, 'English Society in the Eighteenth Century Revisited', in *British Politics and Society from Walpole to Pitt*, ed. J. Black (1990), p. 35.

27 Clark, *English Society*, p. 409.

28 *Ibid.*, pp. 349–424, especially pp. 372–5.

aristocracy and gentry disintegrated with great rapidity'.[29] The days of the *ancien régime* were dramatically numbered.

However, to speak in terms of the collapse of the *ancien régime* might be somewhat premature. Almost every single historian who has investigated the matter has reported upon the substantial element of continuity between the regime which preceded repeal, emancipation and reform and that which succeeded it. The reason for this is plain. The regime which preceded it, far from being an old fashioned *ancien régime*, was marked by powerful, dynamic qualities which were entirely appropriate for a rapidly industrializing and urbanizing society. The point is an important one. It was not the monarchy, the church and the aristocracy which provided the dynamic for English society in the early nineteenth century. As we have seen, the development of the fiscal-military state enabled a strong central government, supported by powerful armed forces, to fight, and to win, the wars against the French revolution and Napoleon. At the same time, Britain was establishing commercial supremacy in Europe and acquiring a global empire. These developments rested less upon the institutional continuity of monarchy, church and aristocracy than upon the internal taxes levied by the British state and by the external revenues which it received. It was not, therefore, the *ancien régime* which was the key to British successes in this period but the emergence of wealthy, acquisitive and socially conformist elements within the population. The so-called *ancien régime* was not overthrown by an internal conspiracy of silence. When the nation grew tired of the fiscal-military state, the taxation and the expensive bureaucratic sacrifices it demanded, then the reform of the *ancien régime* was at hand.

In many ways, however, the *ancien régime* contained the seeds of its own liquidation. It had always been less the established and prescriptive qualities of the regime which had commanded assent and compelled legitimacy than its dynamic and conditional features. The hegemony of landed superiors unquestionably existed but it rested less upon compulsion and fear than upon subtle and complex webs of patronage, sustained by generalized sentiments of reciprocal deference. What this meant in practice was that landed superiors would normatively only seek to enforce their supremacy within a framework of mutual recognition and mutual dependence. I have argued this out in some detail with respect to their electoral supremacy.[30] That supremacy, with its qualities of influence, nomination and personal pressures, can be dismissed as corruption or intimidation or even as aristocratic domination. On the other hand, landed 'control' of the electoral system, so complete and 'hegemonic' when viewed from a distance, looks very different when examined more closely. First, the exercise of power within the electoral system was in the hands of local men and their ability to establish relations with the voters, their families and their associates.

29 *Ibid.*, p. 411.
30 Frank O'Gorman, *Voters, Patrons and Parties. The Unreformed Electorate of Hanoverian England, 1734–1832* (Oxford, 1989).

Second, the values which governed the electoral system were not handed down by the aristocracy but were the product of decades of negotiation between the needs of the community and the values of neighbouring (and sometimes not so neighbourly) landowners. Third, the issues upon which contested elections were fought were not always chosen by the patrons themselves but often owed more to local pressures and tended to reflect community sentiments. Fourth, elections were not merely occasions for the election of members of parliament. They were opportunities for patrons to defend their record of service to the local constituency, in particular, and local communities more widely. In such ways, the social and political leadership of the landed classes was conditional upon the fulfilment of local needs.

Similarly, as Professor Baugh has argued,[31] aristocratic control of the navy appears to be complete when viewed from a distance. Closer inspection, however, reveals that naval patronage operated within the service according to its own precedents and traditions, conforming to its own values and in response to its own needs and requirements. Aristocratic 'control' had to take account of these values, needs and requirements, to recognize and to honour them. They could not be swept aside through an arbitrary exercise of aristocratic power.

In this way, the seeds of the ultimate transformation of the Hanoverian ruling order was less any 'sudden betrayal' by its guardians, still less any of the admittedly powerful external forces with which it had to contend, even though the aristocracy made concession after concession to the values of commerce and trade. The secret of its dynamism and, ultimately, its transformation, lay in the internal, reciprocal features of the regime itself. Discussion, dissent, discord and disagreement were by no means incompatible with a stable political order. Indeed, they were integral to it. In the end, it was the limited and conditional nature of aristocratic supremacy which enabled new groups and new forces to play such a prominent part in Hanoverian society. It is, therefore, precisely this conditionality of aristocratic leadership which permitted, indeed, necessitated, flexibility, concession and negotiation. In this way, the *ancien régime* could not be indefinitely preserved. It was always dynamic, always changing, always developing. Its ultimate transformation was both inescapable and unavoidable.

The key to understanding England in the eighteenth century, then, does not lie in adopting the ideology of an *ancien régime*. It is, perhaps, inherently unlikely that the complex and staggering achievements of Britain between 1660 and 1832 are to be explained simply by the fact that Britain had a monarchy, a church and an aristocracy. However, it is not enough merely to attempt a negative refutation of that interpretation or model. It is important also to advance an alternative model. I have argued in this paper that although eighteenth-century England derived enormous strength from her monarchy, her church and her aristocracy, she derived no little strength, too, from

---

31 Daniel A. Baugh, *British Naval Administration in the Age of Walpole* (Princeton, N.J., 1965).

her commerce and the rapid spread of consumer goods, from the growth of the new
bureaucratic and financial structures of the fiscal-military state and, not least, from
the incorporation of the middling orders. As Jonathan Clark concedes 'the residual
values of an ancien regime co-exist with and subtly modify apparently quite
contradictory values'.[32] It is not just that the eighteenth-century aristocracy had
discovered the principles of the free market. As Dr Porter recognizes, the old regime
'was remarkably adroit in devising new material means of perpetuating itself, through
stimulating and harnessing socio-economic change'.[33] Indeed it was, but my thesis
goes very much further. I have argued that the internal, reciprocal features of the old
order render it a dynamic and flexible regime. I have also advanced the view that the
conditional nature of aristocratic hegemony permitted vital social accommodations.
The Hanoverian *élite* was able both to maintain its own social pre-eminence and to
advance its own economic interests while acknowledging the claims of the middling
orders to participation in occupational and administrative spheres. However, the
middling orders remained, for the most part, strikingly uninterested in pursuing or
advancing any political objectives. Even when they began to do so in the early
nineteenth century, it was with a mixture of emulation for the culture and life-styles
of the aristocracy and a considered and well-cultivated distaste for the lower orders.
Here were yet further grounds for the much-vaunted, yet poorly understood,
avoidance of serious social dislocation between 1800 and 1832 as the regime was
slowly and silently undermining itself and steadily giving birth to a regime conspicuously like itself.

32 Clark, *Revolution and Rebellion*, pp. 168–9.
33 Roy Porter, 'English Society in the Eighteenth Century Revisited', p. 34.

3

British Whig Ministers
and the Irish Question 1714–1725[*]

D. W. HAYTON

Such limited discussion as there has been among historians of the development of British policy towards Ireland in the early eighteenth century[1] has tended to focus upon the extraordinary events surrounding the coinage of 'Wood's Halfpence' in 1722–5: the bitter opposition of Irish 'patriots'; the rage of a (predominantly protestant) public opinion inspired by Swift's *Drapier's Letters*; the parliamentary difficulties encountered by administration; and the ministerial *démarche* signalled by the appointment of Lord Carteret as lord lieutenant in 1724. Despite differences of interpretation there is general agreement that the Wood's Halfpence affair provoked British ministers into a reappraisal of their Irish policy: the traditional view held that the failure of Dublin Castle to secure acceptance of the Halfpence brought about the adoption of the so-called 'undertaker system', whereby the viceroy, instead of seeking to manage the Irish parliament himself, contracted out the responsibility to Irish politicians;[2] more recent reinterpretations have suggested that parliamentary management was already devolved to local managers, and that the events of 1722–5, far from precipitating the inauguration of an 'undertaker system', actually led ministers (and Walpole in particular) to reconsider the viability of this approach, and to try and build up a self-consciously 'English interest' in the Dublin administration, through the appointment of Englishmen to the judicial bench, to the episcopate and

*   For permission to consult and to quote from documents in their possession I am grateful to Lord Bolton; the earl of Midleton; Lady Ravensdale; Lord Rossmore; the earl of Shannon; Lord Walpole; the British Library Board; the Governing Body of Christ Church, Oxford; the county archivists, Hertfordshire, Leicestershire and Surrey Record Offices; the director, Public Record Office of Northern Ireland; and the Board of Trinity College, Dublin.

1   J. L. McCracken, 'The Undertakers in Ireland and their Relations with the Lords Lieutenant, 1724–1771', Queen's University of Belfast M.A., 1941; Francis Godwin James, *Ireland in the Empire 1688–1770* (Cambridge, Mass., 1973); Joseph Griffin, 'Parliamentary Politics in Ireland during the Reign of George I', National University of Ireland (University College, Dublin) M.A., 1977; D. W. Hayton, 'The Beginnings of the "Undertaker System"', in *Penal Era and Golden Age. Essays in Irish History, 1690–1800*, ed. Thomas Bartlett and D. W. Hayton (Belfast, 1979), pp. 32–54; *idem*, 'Walpole and Ireland', in *Britain in the Age of Walpole*, ed. Jeremy Black (1984), pp. 95–119; Robert E. Burns, *Irish Parliamentary Politics in the Eighteenth Century* (2 vols., Washington, D.C., 1989–90); Patrick McNally, 'Patronage and Politics in Ireland 1714–1727', Queen's University of Belfast Ph.D., 1993.

2   McCracken, 'Undertakers', chs. 2–3.

to the Irish privy council.[3] It is the contention of this essay, however, that by focusing on Wood's Halfpence we are in danger of missing important clues to the evolution of ministerial thinking on Ireland in this period. If we take a longer perspective, we can see that an earlier crisis over Irish political management had occurred in the Irish parliamentary session of 1719, after which English ministers seriously considered and then rejected a radically different, integrationist approach to Irish government, in favour of muddling through, until a second set of political difficulties, over the Halfpence, prompted changes that were more in the nature of pragmatic readjustments than fundamental reforms.

I

It would be true to say that in discharging their responsibilities for the government of Ireland, British ministers in the first half of the eighteenth century consistently opted for pragmatism over principle. This was understandable, since their somewhat limited objectives rarely necessitated a bold or imaginative stroke of policy. The essential requirements of the crown and its servants from the government of Ireland had scarcely changed since Tudor times, despite the intervening rebellions, conquests, plantations and immigration, all of which had so greatly expanded the British presence there. These requirements were: the maintenance of order; the security of Ireland (and by extension the British mainland) from foreign invasion or the destabilising effects of foreign-inspired conspiracy; and the preservation of political stability, so that the Irish 'political nation' remained free of any factional conflicts which might reverberate dangerously at Westminster. Determining everything was the financial imperative. The Irish treasury had to collect sufficient revenue to support the civil administration and military power without subvention from Whitehall, and without putting at risk national defences (by weakening the army), social order (by pressing intolerably upon ordinary people), or political stability (by over-taxing the propertied *élite*). In the eighteenth century taxation meant parliamentary subsidy. The 'hereditary revenue' of the Irish crown (derived from customs, tonnage and poundage, import and inland excise, hearth tax, crown and composition rents, quit rents, prizage, aulnage duties, ale, wine and spirits licences, and other casual revenues) was not enough by itself to pay for the large army which the post-Revolution monarchy wished to station on Irish soil, and members of King William's Irish parliaments, unlike their predecessors at the Restoration, had not been prepared to grant their 'deliverer' any further powers of taxation in perpetuity but had held a tight grip on the power of the purse, granting fixed-term subsidies. By the reign of George I the Irish treasury was running a deficit, and the Irish parliament had settled into a practice of giving 'additional duties' for only two years at a time. Regular sessions of parliament strengthened the necessity for the maintenance of political

---

3   Hayton, 'Beginnings of the "Undertaker System"'; *idem*, 'Walpole and Ireland'.

stability within Ireland. Viceroys and lords justices were now responsible not only for military and civil administration but also for parliamentary management. In each sphere of responsibility what they and their cabinet colleagues wanted, more than anything else, was a quiet life.

The exceptions to this rule were the party politicians of the reign of Queen Anne. The appearance in the Irish parliament of recognizable whig and tory parties, on the English model, presented a viceroy with opportunities or problems, depending on his point of view. A committed partisan, like the tory duke of Ormond (1703–7, 1710–13) or the whig earl of Wharton (1708–10), would naturally wish to advance the interests of fellow tories or whigs in Ireland, altering the composition of the Dublin administration to give power to his natural supporters, and purging politically undesirable elements from central and local government. A self-consciously 'moderate', or neutral lord lieutenant, like the earl of Pembroke (1707–8) or the duke of Shrewsbury (1713–14), would try to construct a 'mixed ministry' and steer a course between the 'hotter' elements in both factions.[4] But party politics involved more than the dispensing of offices and influence. Each side held certain ideological commitments, or, more accurately, prejudices, which impacted upon government in the way that ministers enforced or modified the ecclesiastical settlement. Irish whigs took a strong line in defence of the 'protestant interest' in general, against what they saw as the international intrigues of the pope, the French king and the jacobite Pretender; tories argued more narrowly in defence of the established church, against the political ambitions of the increasingly populous and powerful Scottish presbyterian community in Ulster. Thus the whigs urged ever more severe penal legislation against Irish catholics; tories demanded action to reinvigorate the Church of Ireland (for example, by the recall of convocation) and to staunch the spread of presbyterianism.[5] The conflict came to focus on the issue of dissenters' access to political power, restricted by the imposition in 1704 of a sacramental test on all crown and municipal office-holders. Even though a clear majority of Irish M.P.s firmly supported the continuance of the test, British whig ministers were determined to obtain repeal, in order to promote that unity among protestants which alone, in their view, would deter the designs of the jacobites. In 1707 Pembroke raised the issue, at the behest of the whig junto, only to be rebuffed by the Irish house of commons, while his successor as viceroy, Wharton, having entered upon the government of Ireland with a determination to carry repeal, was equally unsuccessful in his attempts to persuade Irish M.P.s of the error of their ways.[6]

4   D. W. Hayton, 'Ireland and the English Ministers, 1706–16', University of Oxford D.Phil. 1975, pp. 159–60, 168–9, 177–82; D. W. Hayton, 'The Crisis in Ireland and the Disintegration of Queen Anne's Last Ministry', *Irish Historical Studies*, XXII (1980–1), 201–7.

5   Hayton, 'Ireland and the English Ministers', ch. 5; S. J. Connolly, *Religion, Law and Power. The Making of Protestant Ireland 1660–1760* (Oxford, 1992), pp. 74–84.

6   D. W. Hayton, 'Divisions in the Whig Junto in 1709: Some Irish Evidence', *Bulletin of the Institute of Historical Research*, LV (1982), 209–12.

The rapid break-up of the tory party in the Irish parliament following the Hanoverian succession dramatically transformed the political landscape in Ireland, and returned British ministerial policy to its previous reactive, or managerial, mode. Of course, the mass of Irish tories did not suddenly abandon their beliefs; indeed, it was possible to identify a 'tory' interest in many localities, and even in the Irish house of commons, as late as 1730.[7] But they became far less numerous and important, and parliamentary politics in Ireland ceased to be dominated by a conflict of parties. The Irish electoral system, so much less 'open' than its English counterpart, could not sustain a 'popular' opposition, and tories suffered grievous losses at the polls in 1715. Committed 'Hanoverian' tories, of whom there were a substantial number in Ireland, and careerist politicians like the former attorney- and solicitor-general, Sir Richard Levinge and Francis Bernard, crossed over.[8] A predominantly whig court party now faced a mixed parliamentary opposition, which coalesced around issues of general concern – 'corruption', economic distress, absenteeism, British parliamentary 'interference' in Irish affairs – and characterized itself as 'the country party', or, increasingly as time went by, the 'patriots'.[9] In consequence, viceroys no longer landed in Ireland with a pre-arranged, partisan agenda, determined to reconstruct the Dublin administration on party lines or to pursue a distinctive programme of legislation. The fact that in England, by contrast, party divisions and issues had retained much of their importance, and that in an English context the viceroys themselves would have professed a whig allegiance and a whig ideology, seems to have made relatively little difference to their conduct of government in Ireland. Presbyterian agents who expected whig ministers after 1714 to continue to press strongly for the repeal of the test, were disappointed. Fair words were forthcoming, but no decisive action. A limited scheme of relief in the 1715-16 parliamentary session was soon abandoned; and presbyterian representations in 1717 were ignored.[10] When Lords Stanhope and Sunderland picked up the issue again in 1719 it was, as we shall see, with English political interests uppermost in their minds. In short, the whig government of Ireland under the early Hanoverians was essentially conservative, aiming at efficient administration and successful management rather than reform.

7   Hayton, 'Beginnings of the "Undertaker System"', p. 46; Public Record Office of Northern Ireland (hereafter P.R.O.N.I.), Shannon MSS, D2702/A/1/2/39: Arthur Hill to Henry Boyle, 15 Apr. 1729; B.L., Add. MS 21123, f. 32.

8   Edith M. Johnston, *Great Britain and Ireland 1760–1800* (Edinburgh, 1963), pp. 120–78; Patrick McNally, 'The Hanoverian Accession and the Tory Party in Ireland', *Parliamentary History*, XIV (1995), 276–7, 280–1.

9   Hayton, 'Beginnings of the "Undertaker System"', pp. 46–8; Connolly, *Religion, Law and Power*, pp. 85–97

10 *Records of the General Synod of Ulster, from 1691 to 1820* (3 vols., Belfast, 1890–8), I, 365; *The Correspondence of Robert Wodrow*, ed. T. McCrie (3 vols., Edinburgh, 1842–3), II, 48; James Seaton Reid, *History of the Presbyterian Church in Ireland*, ed. W. S. Killen (3 vols., Belfast, 1867), III, 66–79; J. C. Beckett, *Protestant Dissent in Ireland, 1687–1780* (1948), pp. 71–4.

Naturally, this was easier said than done. In particular, ministers found stable parliamentary management an elusive commodity in the first decade of Hanoverian rule, and without readily compliant parliaments the chronic defects in the Irish public revenue were hard to repair. The basic objectives of government, public order and national security, were not in themselves problematic. Military defeat, exile and expropriation, followed by legislative restrictions on surviving landed and professional families, had intimidated the catholic interest; the jacobites were frankly uninterested in Ireland as a possible theatre of rebellion; and in any case large detachments of British soldiers were garrisoned in Ireland, a 'standing army' hidden from the objections of Westminster back-benchers.[11] But troops, and the supporting bureaucracy, cost money. Irish government expenditure had swollen horribly since the Revolution. In 1692 the combined civil and military establishments totalled some £309,000, while by 1715 the figure had risen to over £408,000, an increase of around 33 per cent. Most of this new expense was military in origin. In 1704, during wartime, there had been 21 regiments on the Irish establishment; in 1715, during peace, there were 28; in 1717 as many as 30.[12] Moreover, the ways and means taken by successive Irish parliaments to cope with increased government spending proved consistently inadequate. Arrears accumulated after the jacobite war until in 1707 they reached £130,000, and, even though some efforts were made to cut the deficit, helped by the slowing down of the war effort on the part of the tory ministry prior to the Treaty of Utrecht, the failure of the short-lived Irish parliament of 1713–14 to vote any 'additional duties' beyond Christmas 1713, and the dumping of extra regiments on the Irish establishment in peacetime, combined to produce a further deterioration. In 1715 the Irish treasury initiated a 'national debt', running at first at a little over £16,000. This quickly multiplied. The temporary disappearance of 'additional duties' in 1713 had a disastrous long-term effect. Merchants took advantage to stock up with tobacco and other imported excisable goods. As a result, when the duties were re-imposed by the 1715–16 parliament their yield failed to reach expectations. By 1717 arrears on payments had jumped to nearly £250,000, while the 'national debt' was now almost £80,000.[13] It was far from clear how this money could be raised. Irish M.P.s resisted increases in taxation no less vigorously than the representatives of every other propertied class in eighteenth-century Europe. They may even have been less tractable than British M.P.s, for they did not succumb to a land tax, and in 1710 a substantial number flatly opposed granting any additional subsidy.[14] In 1717 there was talk at last of a land tax, or a poll tax, the outgoing viceroy Lord Townshend

---

11 Connolly, *Religion, Law and Power*, pp. 233–49.
12 Hayton, 'Ireland and the English Ministers', pp. 49, 90, 92; P.R.O., S.P. 63/362. On this subject, see now C. I. V. McGrath, 'The Irish Revenue System: Government and Administration 1689–1702', University of London Ph.D., 1997.
13 Hayton, 'Ireland and the English Ministers', pp. 90–3.
14 Surrey R.O. (Guildford Muniment Room), Midleton MSS, 1248/2, ff. 380–1.

having failed in his 'utmost endeavours' at retrenchment.[15] Such was the popular reaction, however, that the government's parliamentary managers eventually settled instead for the continuing escalation of arrears and debt.

It is against this background of fiscal pressure that the development of government policy has to be understood. Of course, in comparison with Britain the levels of expenditure and debt were minuscule. The Nine Years' War, which ended in 1697, left the English government some £16,700,000 in debt; by 1720 this amount had become an astronomical £50,000,000.[16] But such comparisons blur the issue. Ireland was economically backward, with little industrial development and primitive banking facilities; a predominantly agricultural economy with at best uneven growth, still suffering periodic crises of production. There was a chronic shortage of coin; rents were slow; trade erratic and fragile. The depth of bitterness engendered by the controversial proposal for a Bank of Ireland in 1721, and by Wood's Halfpence a year later, showed the potential for popular unrest, and the need for administration to proceed in fiscal matters with caution and on the basis of a parliamentary consensus. There was no real alternative: the possibility of baling out the Irish treasury from British funds was simply not considered; nor does it seem that ministers ever seriously contemplated taxing Ireland from Westminster. Besides the likely outcry in Ireland, this would have meant subjecting Irish policy to the scrutiny of the British house of commons (as had happened once before, in 1693),[17] thus offering extra opportunities for the British parliamentary opposition to make trouble.

II

Soothing the Irish parliament, therefore, was the central purpose of English policy after 1714. At the outset, the omens seemed favourable. The crisis over the succession had shown the strength of pro-Hanoverian sentiment, and in particular the events of the turbulent parliamentary session of 1713 seemed to indicate a natural superiority for the whig interest over the tory among the protestant propertied élite. Despite the strenuous efforts of Lord Chancellor Phipps and other high tories in the Irish government, the 1713 election returned only a narrow tory majority in the commons, which was then overturned by the abstention and cross-voting of a squadron of moderate or 'Hanoverian' tories. After the whig leader Alan Brodrick had been elected to the Chair inquiries were set on foot into the alleged 'oppressions' perpetrated by Phipps and his colleagues in the Irish privy council, until eventually the lord lieutenant, Shrewsbury, was obliged to adjourn and then prorogue the session without the hoped-for vote of supply. Tories had maintained a majority in the Lords,

15 P.R.O., S.P. 63/375/59, 162–3.
16 John Brewer, *The Sinews of Power. War, Money and the English State, 1688–1783* (1989), p. 114.
17 James I. McGuire, 'The Irish Parliament of 1692', in *Penal Era and Golden Age*, ed. Bartlett and Hayton, pp. 25–6; Henry Horwitz, *Parliament, Policy and Politics in the Reign of William III* (Manchester, 1977), p. 111.

but that was of less value to government, since it was in the Commons that supply bills originated.[18] What appeared to be the naturally whiggish bent of Irish protestant opinion was duly confirmed by the results of the 1715 election, and before the new parliament met the ministry also took care to doctor the composition of the upper House: a raft of new peerage creations, drawn from the front rank of the Commons opposition of 1713, supported by partisan appointments to vacant bishoprics (this time a mixture of Irish and English nominees), and the advancement of Brodrick to the lord chancellorship.[19]

In fact, things worked out rather differently. Neither house of the new parliament proved as amenable as ministers hoped. The changing nature of parliamentary conflict, from whig against tory, to 'court' against 'country', meant that instead of being able to capitalize on the party loyalty of a whig majority in each house, successive viceroys found themselves seeking to explain and defend what were perceived as Anglocentric policy decisions to a hostile coalition of self-appointed 'patriots'. The government's difficulties became so acute in 1720 as to induce a fundamental re-evaluation of the system of political management, in which serious thought was given to abandoning the Irish parliament altogether, though without a clear idea of how money was to be raised in its absence. And although this particular crisis was overcome, the Walpole/Townshend ministry stumbled into further difficulties in 1722–4 over Wood's Halfpence, which necessitated a humiliating climb-down on the issue of the Halfpence itself, and an eventual change of direction in management that was less drastic than the proposals of 1720 and effective enough in its own way, but which involved some compromising of ministerial and viceregal authority.

There were two structural weaknesses in parliamentary management after 1714: difficulties in the Commons arose principally from the prolonged confusion between rival 'managers' or 'undertakers', and the indecision of viceroys and ministers in choosing between them; while management in the Lords was bedevilled by the emergence of a 'patriot' interest, seemingly immune to the influence of patronage.

It was in the nature of the Irish political system in the early eighteenth century that viceroys would require assistance from influential local politicians in order to secure the passage of important business and suppress embarrassing criticism. With the exception of the duke of Ormond under Queen Anne, the viceroys themselves were Englishmen (or in the case of Lord Galway, a Frenchman). In general they had little prior acquaintance with the kingdom, although some attempts were made to

---

J. G. Simms, 'The Irish Parliament of 1713', in *Historical Studies IV*, ed. G. A. Hayes-McCoy (1963), 82–92; Hayton, 'Crisis in Ireland', pp. 202–7; B.L., Add. MS 61640, ff. 29–30: list of the Irish house of lords, prepared for Lord Sunderland, [1714/15].

McNally, 'Hanoverian Accession and the Tory Party', pp. 274–5; *idem*, '"Irish and English Interests": National Conflict within the Church of Ireland Episcopate in the Reign of George I', *Irish Historical Studies*, XXIX (1994–5), 296–7; B.L., Add. MS 61640, ff. 27–8, 31–2.

remedy this defect by reappointing previous chief governors: Galway, who served as lord justice with the duke of Grafton between 1715 and 1717, had held the same post before, in 1697–1700, with the duke of Bolton, lord lieutenant from 1717 to 1720, as one of his colleagues; Grafton was subsequently reappointed as lord lieutenant himself in 1720. More to the point, perhaps, was the fact that these men were chosen less for their abilities than for their wealth, or their rank in the peerage. Bolton and Grafton were distinctly second-rate, the former henpecked and easily led, perpetually casting about for advice; the latter referred to contemptuously by the duke of Newcastle as 'the child'.[20] Able men were occasionally given the viceroyalty, but usually as an insult or a penance. Neither Lord Sunderland (1714–15) nor Lord Townshend (1717) ever had the slightest intention of travelling to Ireland, and resigned rather than do so. Lord Carteret (1724–30) did take up his post, but he was a rare exception, sent to Dublin Castle by Walpole and Townshend as a kind of internal exile.

As a stranger to Ireland, and to the configurations of Irish politics, a viceroy required informed advice. This would be unlikely to come from the chief secretary, almost always a junior political appointee, for whom the office was a first step on the ladder of preferment. (Only Galway's chief secretary, Martin Bladen, made himself a force to be reckoned with on the Dublin scene.) Nor could the secretariat at Dublin Castle fill the gap: there were a few permanent civil servants (the under-secretary, deputy vice-treasurer, accountant-general) but they were regarded as possessing insufficient political weight to give reliable counsel. So the viceroy would turn to men of experience in Irish politics. Grafton, for example, trusted in a kitchen cabinet made up of his chief secretary, Speaker William Conolly, and Lord Chief Justice Whitshed, supplemented on occasion by various drinking cronies, 'Lord Fitzwilliam, Ben. Parry, Lord Shannon (when well), and now and then Lord Tullamore, and now and then Lord Shelburne'.[21] These advisers would often double as parliamentary managers. The viceroy could not undertake the day-to-day business of managing parliament himself, since he was not a member of either house, and his chief secretary would have neither sufficient knowledge nor connexions to be able to manage on his behalf. In the historiography of eighteenth-century Ireland these parliamentary managers have come to be known as 'undertakers', a pejorative term rarely employed by contemporaries until the political crises of mid-century, when the managers became the subject both of popular resentment and ministerial opprobrium. The concept has a spurious precision: 'undertakers' can be defined as those who '"undertook" to provide the government with a majority in the Commons in return for a voice in policy-making and a substantial share of the official patronage for themselves and

20 Burns, *Irish Parliamentary Politics*, I, 69; B.L., Add. MS 32686, f. 372.
21 Sir Richard G. A. Levinge, *Jottings of the Levinge Family* (Dublin, 1877), pp. 65–6.

their dependants'.[22] In reality the degree of influence the 'undertaker' enjoyed, his functions and duties, and his relationship with the viceroy (and chief secretary) could alter considerably according to personality and circumstances. But the essential point common to all who held or aspired to this position was that they were men whose influence in parliament was independent of office, who could command votes by virtue of kinship, friendship, clientage, electoral patronage, the power of oratory, even character, and who put their influence at the service (rather than at the disposal) of government.

For this kind of delegated management to work two things were required: a manager or 'undertaker' of sufficient influence to be able to carry out what he had promised; and a firm understanding between viceroy and undertaker(s), publicly acknowledged and publicly demonstrated. Any sign of disharmony or distrust, and management ran the risk of collapse. During the heyday of 'party' politics, viceroys and their parliamentary managers worked for the most part in harmony. Only the 'moderate' administrations of Lords Pembroke and Shrewsbury departed from the principle: Pembroke's 'moderating scheme' in 1707 benefited from an unusual and fortuitous combination of circumstances, which brought the parties to vie with each other in their loyalty to the crown and willingness to vote supply; Shrewsbury's abject failure was the more predictable outcome, when the line of government favour was not established clearly, and government forces appeared to be divided.

III

The problem facing ministers after 1714 was that, despite the unprecedented purge of office-holders which took place after the death of Queen Anne, and the widespread dispersal of patronage to the different family- and regionally-based interest groups which made up the whig party in Ireland, resentments and rivalries soon came to the surface of the new political establishment. Within a few months there were rumblings from a handful of malcontents who felt themselves inadequately rewarded for their efforts, 'a small party that for some time gave themselves airs', as Alan Brodrick put it.[23] But it was not just a matter of 'outs' against 'ins'. More important was the fact that the unity of the court whigs themselves was broken, as two competing power-blocs emerged within the Irish administration, each seeking a privileged access to power. Brodrick was the key figure. At first his acceptance of a peerage and the lord chancellorship had seemed to bring him to the very top of the greasy pole. Then the drawbacks of the office became apparent: the patronage directly at his disposal as lord chancellor, pricking sheriffs, issuing new commissions of the peace and militia,

22 Hayton, 'Beginnings of the "Undertaker System" ', p. 32: a definition that has regrettably become too frequently cited and too little questioned. Patrick McNally, *Patriots and Undertakers. Parliamentary Politics in Early Hanoverian Ireland* (Dublin, 1997), ch. 6, provides a subtler and more qualified interpretation.

23 B.L., Add. MS 61636, ff. 121–2: Alan Brodrick to [Sunderland], 29 Dec. 1714.

was in reality no great asset, since in many counties there were few enough protestants, let alone few enough whigs, to make it practicable to distinguish between them; and to make matters worse, Brodrick's new eminence meant that he was no longer involved personally in the business of the house of commons, where a manager could make himself most useful to government, in arranging for generous grants of supply.

The necessity in 1714–15 of filling the judicial bench with reliable whigs, and of reinforcing the court party in the Lords, had taken almost all the party leaders out of the lower House, with one important exception: William Conolly, the *nouveaux riche* Ulsterman who had been chief commissioner of the revenue under Wharton and who was earmarked to take over that post under the new administration. Conolly was the obvious choice for the Chair, which automatically put him at the head of the court party in the Commons. (In Ireland the Speakership was a much more overtly political office than at Westminster.)[24] Moreover, the chief commissionership of the revenue afforded much greater opportunities for exercising patronage than Brodrick enjoyed as lord chancellor. The expansion of the revenue service was one of the most striking features of Irish bureaucratic growth in the decades after the Revolution; and the commissioners' administrative independence of the Castle, being directly responsible instead to the English treasury, left them considerable freedom of manoeuvre. In practice the commissioners themselves determined appointments up to the most senior level, and the chief commissioner, although technically only *primus inter pares*, could exercise a decisive influence.[25] Conolly made the most of his position, and within a few years some observers claimed that he had made the revenue his own personal political preserve, and the engine of what was to become a powerful political machine.[26]

Ironically, Brodrick himself had recommended Conolly to Lord Sunderland for the chief commissionership, expressing the hope that this office might not be seen as incompatible with the Commons' Chair.[27] He was soon to recognize the error of his ways. By Christmas 1715 Brodrick was writing to his brother in England (in a characteristically allusive style):

> Let me assure you I am credibly informed [that] while I am spending my lungs and impairing my health in endeavouring nothing may go wrong in the House where I sit, some people (and I think the triumvirate is your friend, the Speaker, and one who fancies he could well fill the seat in which the King has placed me) are endeavouring

24 A. P. W. Malcomson, 'John Foster and the Speakership of the Irish House of Commons', *Proceedings of the Royal Irish Academy*, LXXII (1972), 271–7.
25 Hayton, 'Ireland and the English Ministers', pp. 51–3; McNally, 'Patronage and Politics', ch. 3.
26 McNally, 'Patronage and Politics', pp. 107–9. Bishop Evans of Meath complained bitterly that Conolly 'puts into places his own dependants etc. so that among them an E[nglish]man can't get bread': Christ Church, Oxford, Wake Papers, Arch.W.Epist. 12 (unfoliated): Evans to [Archbishop Wake], 20 May [1718].
27 B.L., Add. MS 61636, f. 114: Brodrick to [Sunderland], Oct. 1714.

to possess the [lords] justices as if I had an intention to distress or break their government: and I am told one of the justices was so frank to say it must not be wondered at, if they endeavoured to break him who aimed at breaking them ...[28]

In Brodrick's view Conolly was the aggressor, aided and abetted by Chief Secretary Bladen, whom other commentators agreed was 'entirely with' the Speaker, while 'bearing a most implacable hatred to the chancellor'. Brodrick detected an ambition in his rival to demonstrate a superior interest in the Commons, and a greater willingness to serve the crown, by offering to 'increase the supply' and also to secure a substantial measure of relief for protestant dissenters.[29] Conflict between the two factions did indeed break out in the Irish house of commons over these two issues. Brodrick's eldest son St John, at the head of the chancellor's friends, kinsmen and followers, obstructed both schemes, once clashing publicly with Bladen in debate.[30] The strategy was cleverly calculated. The Brodrick 'squadron' did not oppose administration openly and consistently, as did the permanently malcontent whigs of the 'country party' (under the leadership of Colonel John Allen).[31] Rather, they chose the right moment to add their weight to opposition in a popular cause. Moreover, Brodrick *senior* did not involve himself personally, and could distance himself from his son's behaviour. It was a strategy that worked well enough to be employed repeatedly in succeeding sessions.

The replacement of Galway and Grafton, first by the absentee Lord Townshend, and subsequently by the duke of Bolton, offered the possibility of reconciling the two factions sufficiently for them to be able to work together in parliament, however much they distrusted and disliked each other. Not only was the partisan Bladen replaced by a more even-handed chief secretary, the eventual appointment of Bolton was regarded as having pushed the pendulum of court favour back towards Brodrick, who was connected to the new viceroy by marriage. Conolly expected the worst, but was pleasantly surprised by the outcome. Brodrick, elevated in the peerage as Viscount Midleton, may indeed have been able to establish himself as the viceregal confidant, but Bolton had sense enough not to antagonize the Speaker at the same time. 'His grace is very civil to me', wrote Conolly, 'and as I am not nor do I desire or expect to be in the first rank of his favour I cannot say that I am in the last ... the only favour I begged of his grace was that he would take no representation of me but from myself and my actions.'[32] The parliamentary session of 1717 thus passed off without the two factions coming to blows. There was talk of a trial of strength over the chair of the committee of accounts, before Conolly's candidate withdrew; and talk of opposition, or at the very least obstructionism, by some of the Speaker's followers

28 Surrey R.O., Midleton MSS 1248/3, ff. 283–4.
29 *Ibid.*, ff. 280, 289, 293; B.L., Add. MS 47028, ff. 156–7.
30 Burns, *Irish Parliamentary Politics*, I, 57–66; B.L., Add. 47028, ff. 109–11.
31 Burns, *Irish Parliamentary Politics*, I, 65; B.L., Add. MS 47028, ff. 154–5.
32 Trinity College, Dublin, MS 2534, p. 297; P.R.O., S.P. 63/375/99, 162–3.

in debates on supply, which also came to nothing (much to Midleton's chagrin, if we are to believe Conolly's own comments).[33]

The uneasy peace could not last. Midleton wanted a decisive public statement in his favour and expected it to be made when the ministry announced the appointment of the commission of lords justices, who would govern the country once the viceroy had returned to England. After he and Bolton had spent 'several hours' closeted together one Sunday evening at Dublin Castle it was assumed that he had prevailed, and that Conolly would be omitted.[34] But the Speaker had been intriguing with his English friends, especially Bladen and another former chief secretary, Charles Delafaye, who had the ear of Lord Sunderland, with the result that Bolton received instructions from Whitehall to reappoint the previous lords justices: Midleton, Conolly and Archbishop King of Dublin.[35] The chancellor was furious. Political rivalry and snobbery combined to render his rival's appointment intolerable. Midleton could not understand why the English ministers should 'support the interest of C., who even after this session of Parliament, and the very different parts he and I have taken ... can still be kept on a level with me'; and he abhorred the fact that the Speaker had been 'made my equal, and an office of the greatest honour and trust in the kingdom to be executed in a great measure by one of his birth and education'.[36]

Midleton blamed Sunderland for this insult, and seems to have determined upon revenge. The course he took in pursuit of this vendetta is at first difficult to follow, for although he joined his brother in the British house of commons early in the following year, and seems to have attended regularly, no reports of his speeches have survived. It may be that he paid some attention to the schismatic whig faction headed by Townshend and Walpole, with whom the Brodricks were subsequently linked, but the family correspondence fails on this point. What we do know is that by the spring of 1718 rumours were circulating in Dublin that Midleton was about to resign, and that later in the year experienced political observers in England were predicting his imminent dismissal.[37] He broke openly with the ministry in the spring of 1719, refusing to support the cherished Peerage Bill, 'though told by my Lord S[underland] and the Duke of B[olton] what the consequences of my doing so would be, almost in express terms'. He claimed to disapprove of the measure in principle, as a number of loyal whigs did, and in the face of personal representations from Sunderland himself, expressed himself determined to vote 'with my judgment' unless given leave to return to Ireland before the bill came to be debated. In the end Sunderland had to give way, and allowed him to depart, with a bad grace. A carefully prepared account

33 P.R.O., S.P. 63/375/152, 188, 204–5.

34 Ibid., 214.

35 Ibid., 216, 220, 222. Conolly was also in direct communication with Sunderland. B.L., Evelyn MSS, SJE 17 (temporary call number): William Evelyn to Sir John Evelyn, 2 Nov. 1717. I owe this reference to Clyve Jones.

36 Surrey R.O., Midleton MSS, 1248/4, ff. 90–1.

37 B.L., Add. MS 47028, f. 229. See also H.M.C., Portland MSS, v, 571.

of the episode survives in Midleton's papers, expounding the chancellor's principled resistance to ministerial pressure.[38] Intended to be shown to his friends and allies, it may also have been written with an eye to the opinion of posterity. Some historians have accepted its evidence at face value,[39] but the animosity that already existed between Midleton and Sunderland would permit a little cynicism: this was, after all, a critical moment for the ministry, and Midleton would have seen attractions in a well-timed desertion, either to exact his revenge or to serve as a reminder of his importance. The effect seems to have been to confirm Sunderland and cabinet colleagues in their determination to have a new lord chancellor of Ireland, though they held back from delivering the decisive blow.[40] The next Irish parliamentary session was imminent, and it was by no means clear that Conolly would be able to deliver a Commons majority on his own, especially with the Brodricks in open opposition.

Prospects were even more uncertain because of the deteriorating situation in the Irish house of lords. Here was the second chronic problem of management, how to restrain or suppress the enthusiasm of a determined and vociferous 'patriot' lobby in the upper House? Despite 'packing' the House with newly created whig peers and newly preferred whig bishops, the ministry had not immediately acquired a solid majority. Forecasts, suggesting a three-to-two preponderance for government over opposition, had proved hopelessly wide of the mark. In the most significant division of the first session of the Hanoverian parliament, in 1716, on a tory motion to admit the catholic convert peer Lord Mountgarrett, the court got its way by a mere 26 votes to 21.[41] The tories had continued to hold together well, under the formidable dual leadership of Lord Anglesey and Primate Lindsay, and on the issue of relief for protestant dissenters, when they were joined by whig bishops and some whig peers, had carried the day. After the Commons passed heads of a bill offering a measure of toleration and an temporary indemnity for militia and army officers who failed to take the sacramental test, the Lords, to show absolute opposition to any tampering with the test, had produced a draft of their own identical in every respect except for the indemnity clause, in a show of political strength which persuaded the British privy council to drop the entire measure.[42]

In retrospect, this episode was ominous, as far as ministers were concerned, for it showed their vulnerability in the Lords, and in particular how important it was to retain the loyalty of the whig bishops. On religious questions their recalcitrance could

---

38 William Coxe, *Memoirs of the Life and Administration of Sir Robert Walpole* (3 vols., 1798), II, 170–5.

39 See, for example, Connolly, *Religion, Law and Power*, pp. 90–1 (and the preliminary criticisms offered to his interpretation in McNally, 'Patronage and Politics', p. 245).

40 Bolton Hall, Wensley, N. Yorks., Bolton MSS, D/54: James Craggs to Bolton, 14 Apr. 1719.

41 B.L., Add. MS 61640, ff. 31–2; Surrey R.O., Midleton MSS, 1248/3, f. 283.

42 Seaton Reid, *History of the Presbyterian Church*, III, 66–79; Beckett, *Protestant Dissent in Ireland*, pp. 71–4; B.L., Add. MS 61640, ff. 95–6.

be frustrating, although it was unlikely to bring down the ministry. Unfortunately these same bishops could also be aroused by other issues. They were especially susceptible to appeals to 'patriotism', and sensitive to any slight offered to Irish interests, the more so, perhaps, when ministers reverted to earlier practice and brought in outsiders to the more lucrative Irish sees. The nomination in 1715 of the Welshman John Evans to Meath, and two years later of the Englishman William Nicolson to Derry, two patronage plums, were regarded as particularly insulting. Protests were inspired and orchestrated by Archbishop King, previously the leader of the whig faction within the Church of Ireland during the party struggles of Anne's reign. King's friends and protégés (most notably Archbishop Synge of Tuam, and Bishops Ashe of Clogher and Stearne of Dromore) formed the nucleus of an emerging 'Irish party' within the episcopate, which spearheaded 'patriot' protests among the Lords as a whole over a wide range of grievances, constitutional, political and economic.[43]

One issue in particular galvanized the 'patriot' opposition and drew widespread support, not just from opportunist tories and eccentric individualists, but even from some whigs with coronation peerages: the protection of the rights and privileges of the Irish house of lords, and by extension the Irish parliament in general, against what appeared to be the encroachments of Westminster. The cause was a dispute over jurisdiction. Was the Irish parliament the final court of appeal for legal cases originating in Ireland, or could Irish litigants appeal decisions to the British house of lords? This was a long-running controversy. In 1698 the chancery case of the *Bishop of Derry* v. *the Irish Society of London* (the company which had planted County Londonderry), was appealed first to the Irish house of lords, by the bishop, and then to Westminster, by the Society, where the English Lords declared themselves to be the proper judges in appeals from chancery in Ireland and the Irish Lords to be *coram non judice*.[44] At first denied the opportunity to respond directly, by the prorogation of their own parliament, the Irish Lords were quick to seize their chance when a similar case arose in 1703, *Edward Ward et al.* v. *the Earl of Meath*. This time they reaffirmed their original judgment in favour of Lord Meath, against an English decision for Ward, and went so far as to pass a series of resolutions vindicating their own right of jurisdiction. A persuasive viceregal intervention was required to compose differences between the litigants, and prevent the inter-parliamentary conflict from escalating.[45] But the issue had been postponed rather than resolved, and,

---

43 James, *Ireland in the Empire*, pp. 94–9; McNally, ' "Irish and English Interests" ', pp. 296–304.

44 James, *Ireland in the Empire*, pp. 99–100; Isolde Victory, 'The Making of the Declaratory Act of 1720', in *Parliament, Politics and People. Essays in Eighteenth-Century Irish History*, ed. Gerard O'Brien (Blackrock, Co. Dublin, 1989), pp. 10–12.

45 James, *Ireland in the Empire*, pp. 100–1; Victory, 'Making of the Declaratory Act', pp. 12–13; H.M.C. *House of Lords MSS*, new ser., III, 31, 297–9; *Calendar of State Papers, Domestic, 1703–4*, pp. 226–7, 491–3.

almost inevitably came to a head in a third *cause célèbre*, that of *Annesley* v. *Sherlock*.

Hester Sherlock's suit against Maurice Annesley, over Annesley's trusteeship of the Sherlock family estates, differed from the preceding cases only in so far as it had begun in the Irish court of exchequer. After an unfavourable judgment Mrs Sherlock appealed to the Irish house of lords, which in 1716 reversed the original decree. Annesley in turn appealed to the British house of lords, and duly received an order in his favour, whereupon Mrs Sherlock petitioned the Irish Lords in September 1717 for restitution of her property in accordance with their earlier decision. A point of no return had been reached. Despite Bolton's strenuous efforts, and powerful contributions from Midleton, arguing repeatedly for compromise, the issue was debated in terms of the relationship between the two parliaments, and eventually an overwhelming majority of lords insisted upon the right of their House to be the '*dernier* resort' in all appeals in cases originating in Ireland.[46] The political temperature climbed sharply. As one English resident observed:

> We are apt to think that our feuds and divisions in England run very high ... but alas, when compared with Ireland they are like little skirmishes and brangles. To preserve any temper or moderation is an intolerable crime ... The prodigious partiality and injustice that is daily practised doth perfectly astonish me, and put it beyond all doubt that there is no continuing upon this blessed spot of earth but upon such certain terms and conditions as cannot but be hateful and detestable ...[47]

What was striking was that divisions within the Lords followed 'national' lines. In the first vote, on 9 September, deferring a decision, as many as half of the 12 on the court side were Englishmen (Lords Strangford and Wharton, and the bishops of Kildare, Killala, Kilmore, and Meath).[48] A fortnight later, when the House agreed, this time without a division, to support its 'honour, jurisdiction, and privileges', and grant Mrs Sherlock possession, only the English lords and the chancellor dissented.[49] This exposed the bishops in particular to uncomfortable recriminations, and, not surprisingly, their letters home emphasized what they regarded as the unreasonable and bigoted national prejudice of the 'patriots', an impression which can only have increased the ministry's alarm, and the determination of the house of lords at Westminster to pursue its claim, which resulted in 1718 in further resolutions to restore Annesley.[50]

---

46 Victory, 'Making of the Declaratory Act', pp. 14–16.
47 National Library of Wales, Ottley MS 1715: Thomas Weedon to Bishop Ottley, 19 Sept. 1717. I owe this reference to Stephen Taylor.
48 Hertfordshire R.O., Panshanger MSS, D/EP F56, f. 24; Christ Church, Arch.W.Epist., 12: Bishop Godwin to [Wake], 10 Sept. 1717.
49 Christ Church, Arch.W.Epist., 12: Bishop Evans to [Wake], 23 Sept. 1717.
50 Victory, 'Making of the Declaratory Act', p. 16.

IV

The twin problems of parliamentary management, how to accommodate, or resolve, the rivalry between the Brodrick and Conolly factions in the Commons, and how to subdue the patriotic enthusiasm of a majority of the Lords, both came to a head in Bolton's second parliamentary session, in 1719. It is indicative of the absence of any strategic planning on the part of British ministers that nothing was done to tackle either of these deep-seated difficulties in advance. Everything was left to the viceroy himself. Sunderland and his colleagues would have liked to get rid of Midleton, but passed over responsibility for the decision to the man on the spot.[51] Nor were any suggestions made as to how Bolton might handle the ramifications of the *Annesley* v. *Sherlock* case, and the viceroy was reduced to seeking the advice of his old friend Lord Cowper, who had resigned as lord chancellor of Great Britain the year before and who was now in opposition. (In vain Cowper warned Bolton to obtain explicit instructions from Whitehall before committing himself to any course of action, in order to avoid being made a scapegoat.)[52] Ironically, Sunderland's only positive recommendation was on an issue which would have been better avoided: legislative relief for protestant dissenters.

Here he contrived to throw yet another spanner into the works, by raising again the issue of the sacramental test, and insisting that Bolton attempt a repeal. Indeed, the viceroy was presented with a draft bill for the purpose.[53] As religious toleration (for protestants) was a whig principle, and the fostering of unity among protestants a vital element in the traditional whig strategy for maintaining the Hanoverian succession, one might regard this resurrection of the repeal scheme as evidence of a proactive, reforming approach to Irish government. In reality, it had far more to do with the political situation on the mainland. Sunderland had not previously shown much interest in improving the condition of Irish dissenters as an end in itself, but was concerned to convince their English counterparts of his goodwill, and possibly had an eye to the opinion of Scottish presbyterian interests. Changing the religious settlement, and the bounds of the confessional state, was also part of a wider political strategy, to unify the rank and file of the whig party, and in particular to attract the support of certain radical, or 'country', whigs, who were known to be critical of the powers of the established church.[54] The removal of the test in Ireland would build on the ministerial success of the previous winter, in repealing the English Occasional Conformity and Schism Acts, and would do so relatively cheaply in political terms, since it would not put at risk parliamentary management at Westminster.

---

51 Bolton MSS, D/54: Craggs to Bolton, 14 Apr. 1719.
52 Hertfordshire R.O., Panshanger MSS, D/EP F56, ff. 33, 35.
53 P.R.O., S.P. 63/377/234–5; Bolton MSS, D/64b: 'A paragraph in my [Bolton] letter to Mr Craggs about the bill in easie [sic] to the Dissenters'.
54 See G. M. Townend, 'Religious Radicalism and Conservatism in the Whig Party under George I: The Repeal of the Occasional Conformity and Schism Acts', *Parliamentary History*, VII (1988), 24–44.

Sunderland had not, of course, taken into consideration the political situation in Ireland. Previous experience had shown that a strong majority in both Houses, whigs as well as tories, and court whigs as well as malcontent whigs, would oppose repeal, and would even balk at a generous toleration act. In the Lords the bishops who were at the forefront of 'patriotic' agitation over the question of the appellate jurisdiction would be further alienated by this attack on the church; in the Commons the scheme would offer unnecessary opportunities for the disaffected Brodrick faction to make mischief. Bolton had already warned against it before he left England. He repeated these warnings after his arrival in Dublin in June 1719, having consulted Midleton and Conolly. Both men were cautious. In private Midleton had always been ambivalent on the question, though he had made various professions of service to the dissenters themselves. Conolly was more genuine in his concern for their cause: as Bolton reported, the Speaker 'strongly espouses the dissenters' interest', and was the man 'in whom they entirely rely'. But even Conolly was against proceeding directly to repeal, and advised the viceroy instead to leave matters to the discretion of the members of the house of commons.[55]

At this point the two rivals were adopting contrasting political strategies. Conolly pinned his hopes on his English connexions, to whom he would show himself helpful and constructive, on such issues as supply and the test, though without putting at risk his standing in the Commons. Midleton, by contrast, relied on backstairs influence with the viceroy, whom he tried to assist in the escalating difficulties over *Annesley* v. *Sherlock*, but at the same time seems to have been prepared to obstruct ministerial ambitions, especially over the welfare of dissenters. There is some uncertainty here, because once again it was not Midleton himself who dabbled with opposition, but his son St John. As before, the chancellor tried to distance himself, a claim that Bolton endorsed.[56] The evidence of Midleton's private correspondence would bear out this charitable interpretation, were it not for the possibility that the chancellor may have expected his letters to be opened by the postmaster-general, Conolly's crony Isaac Manley, and thus consciously have avoided self-incrimination.[57] Certainly the ministers did not believe his protestations, and the chief parliamentary spokesman for Irish dissenters, Colonel Clotworthy Upton, reported the outcome of the Commons debates with a sardonic emphasis: 'my lord chancellor at last seemed pretty warm for us, but I fear too late; he was so unfortunate as not to be able to prevail on his son, brother, or any one of his friends, or those he formerly has had influence on'.[58]

55 P.R.O., S.P. 63/377/234–5. Midleton's ambivalence, which comes out most clearly in a letter to his brother Thomas of 13 Jan. 1708–9 (Surrey R.O., Midleton MSS, 1248/2, ff. 350–1) is noted in Connolly, *Religion, Law and Power*, pp. 164, 168.
56 Connolly, *Religion, Law and Power*, p. 165.
57 For Manley's affiliation to the Speaker's interest, see Surrey R.O., Midleton MSS, 1248/3, f. 365; and for Swift's belief that the postmaster interfered with the mails, *The Correspondence of Jonathan Swift*, ed. Harold Williams (5 vols., Oxford, 1963–5), II, 435.
58 Bolton MSS, D/73: Clotworthy Upton to [?John Barrington], 30 July 1719.

The end result was a serious disappointment for Sunderland's hopes. Bolton took the path of discretion and, instead of proposing a full-scale repeal, settled for a modest relief bill, which would have exempted from the provisions of the test justices of the peace and holders of other specified civil and military offices. But the Irish parliament insisted on further dilution. After much 'caballing' between the Brodrick faction and the tories, the Commons pre-empted the viceroy's bill, by introducing an even more limited measure, a toleration bill which did no more than repeal the unenforceable provisions of the Acts of Uniformity penalising recusancy. Efforts to widen the scope of the bill were defeated by huge majorities, which served to underline the strength of opinion and induced the ministry to drop its proposals, in return for the addition of a short-term act of indemnity, in favour of those who had taken militia commissions during the Anglo-Spanish crisis. For many dissenters this minimal relief was almost worse than no relief at all, and the general synod of Ulster asked sympathisers in England to do what they could to pressurize the ministry for more radical change.[59]

At the same time, the dispute over the appellate jurisdiction of the Irish house of lords exploded. Although Bolton's behind-the-scenes diplomacy brought about a financial settlement satisfactory to both parties in the original lawsuit, the quarrel between the two parliaments could not be patched up. At the storm centre was the figure of the sheriff of County Kildare, who had executed the judgment of the Irish house of lords in 1717 but had refused to acknowledge the countermanding orders of the British house of lords a year later, and had been fined for this disobedience by the barons of the Irish exchequer. On his behalf the Irish Lords now pursued the matter. It did not help that two of the exchequer barons, Jeffrey Gilbert and John Pocklington, were Englishmen who proclaimed a forthright, Anglocentric view of the constitutional issues at stake, even during interrogation by a committee of the Irish house of lords. In a dramatic move, all three barons were ordered into custody as 'betrayers of his majesty's prerogative and the undoubted ancient rights and privileges of this House and the rights and liberties of the subjects of this kingdom'.[60]

V

Matters had come to such a pass that some direct English intervention was necessary. As Lord Cowper had predicted, Sunderland and his colleagues blamed Bolton for the debacle over the appellate jurisdiction.[61] They had also had their fill of Midleton:

59 P.R.O., S.P. 63/377/167; Seaton Reid, *History of the Presbyterian Church*, III, 92–109; Beckett, *Protestant Dissent in Ireland*, pp. 75–81; Connolly, *Religion, Law and Power*, p. 165; *General Synod Records*, I, 508–10; P.R.O.N.I., Rossmore MSS, T 2929/2/48: John Henderson to Sir Alexander Cairnes, 31 Oct. 1719.
60 Victory, 'Making of the Declaratory Act', pp. 16–22.
61 Leicestershire R.O., Finch MSS, D97, box 4951, bundle 26: Edward Southwell to [Lord Nottingham], 17 Nov. 1719. Again, I owe this reference to Clyve Jones.

although he was retained as a lord justice in the immediate aftermath of the Irish parliamentary session of 1719, the ministry had determined on his removal from the lord chancellorship, and in February 1720 the seals were offered to an English lawyer, John Willes.[62] Indeed, there seems to have been a general feeling in ministerial circles that a more effective English presence was now required in Dublin. It had long been an *idée fixe* among English politicians that Irish protestants would 'aim at independency' if they could, and, by implication at least, the arguments of the Irish Lords about jurisdiction hinted at an assumption of legislative autonomy.[63] This anxiety was fuelled by the alarmism of the English-born bishops and judges in Ireland, whose letters exaggerated the intensity of 'patriotic' enthusiasm inside and outside the Irish parliament, and induced a knee-jerk reaction. 'There seems ... a resolution to employ more Englishmen in the high offices of trust there', wrote one observer, 'since they grow headstrong in that country, and forget their mother.'[64]

The one bright spot was the grant of an ample parliamentary subsidy in 1719. The Irish house of commons had made little or no difficulties about supply or ways and means, despite some early mutterings of discontent with further increases in the Irish army and in the pension list. Provision had been made for payment of the civil and military establishment over the full two years, and, for the first time, parliament had voted additional taxes towards the discharge of the national debt.[65] The significance of this success was not lost on the ministry, although overshadowed by the failure to repeal the test and the further embroiling of the two parliaments over jurisdiction. In a private letter to Bolton half-way through the session, Secretary Craggs commented: 'when you have two years beforehand, it is good elbow room'.[66]

At the very least, this generous supply afforded a long breathing-space. It also tempted some ministers to contemplate a more radical departure in their approach to the government of Ireland: the possibility that, for the future, the Irish parliament might have to be over-ridden or by-passed. Such drastic action would certainly have reflected Lord Sunderland's impetuosity and audacity, and would have been of a piece with the Peerage Bill, and his attacks on the privileges of the established church. To curtail the power and independence of the Irish parliament might have implied a betrayal of 'Revolution principles', and a break with the traditional whig emphasis on

---

62 B.L., Add. MS 61640, f. 194.

63 In their representation of their case the Irish house of lords explicitly denied aiming at legislative independence: *Journals of the House of Lords of the Kingdom of Ireland* (8 vols., Dublin, 1779–1800), II, 655–60 (published separately as *The Humble Representation Made to the Kings' Majesty by the Lords Spiritual and Temporal, in Parliament Assembled* (Dublin, 1719)). Nevertheless, their insistence that matters 'wholly' or 'only relating to this kingdom' should be 'finally determined' by an Irish parliament (*Lords Journals of Ireland*, II, 655, 659), had wide-ranging constitutional implications.

64 Leicestershire R.O., Finch MSS, D97, box 4951, bundle 26: Southwell to [Nottingham], 17 Nov. 1719.

65 P.R.O., S.P. 63/377/59, 91103, 121–2.

66 Bolton MSS, D/72: Craggs to Bolton, 25 July 1719.

the validity of legislative assemblies in colonial or dependent territories, but this was no obstacle. Whig administrations after 1714 had consistently displayed a ruthless intolerance of minor representative institutions which in any way obstructed or embarrassed government: elections were held to the convocations of Canterbury and of the Church of Ireland, but neither assembly was allowed to meet; and a similar fate befell the convocation of the stannaries in Cornwall, the so-called 'parliament of tinners'.[67] In practice whiggery was becoming associated with oligarchy, and the occlusion of parliamentary liberties, as successive whig administrations defended a standing army, rendered general elections less frequent, and opposed place and pension bills. The repression of Irish parliamentary ambitions would have been perfectly compatible with acquiescence in this general expansion of executive power.

We cannot say for certain what were the intentions of the ministry; and it may well be that Sunderland and his colleagues had not really thought through any change in policy, but all indications suggest a casting around for some alternative, non-parliamentary, form of political management. The first move was the introduction into the British house of lords in January 1720 of a bill, drafted by the English judges, 'for the better securing the dependency of Ireland upon the crown of Great Britain'. Passed into law the following April (as 6 Geo. I, c. 5), the Declaratory Act had two provisions: a clause declaring the right of the British house of lords to hear appellate causes from Ireland; and a second, affirming that statutes passed at Westminster were binding in Ireland. Clearly the first clause was intended as a final and indisputable pronouncement on the issue of jurisdiction. The purpose of the second clause is, however, unclear.[68] It may be interpreted as a simple tying-up of loose ends, settling a point on which the two parliaments had traditionally differed, and which was implicit in the narrowly focused parliamentary and pamphlet debates over appeals. Alternatively, it may have been included for tactical reasons, as some Irish pundits opined: a (successful) attempt to deflect potential opposition in the British house of commons, from the many M.P.s who resented any increase in the authority of the upper House, by raising an issue (the legislative pretensions of the Irish parliament) on which all but a handful of Westminster back-benchers would agree. Neither explanation would be plausible, however, if it had been intended that the Irish parliament should meet again in the short term. Given the uncertainties of parliamentary management in Ireland, gratuitous offence to Irish public opinion was obviously to be avoided. In bringing up the Declaratory Bill, Sunderland was signalling his intention to subsist, at least for a time, without another Irish parliamentary session.

67　J. C. D. Clark, *Revolution and Rebellion. State and Society in England in the Seventeenth and Eighteenth Centuries* (Cambridge, 1986), pp. 129–30; Clyve Jones, '"Venice Preserv'd; or A Plot Discovered": The Political and Social Context of the Peerage Bill of 1719', in *A Pillar of the Constitution. The House of Lords in British Politics, 1640–1784*, ed. Clyve Jones (1989), p. 105.
68　The possible motives behind the addition of the second clause are discussed at greater length in D. W. Hayton, 'The Stanhope/Sunderland Ministry and the Repudiation of Irish Parliamentary Independence', *English Historical Review* CXIII (1998), 610–36.

The second clause offered one means of constitutional circumvention: to legislate for Ireland at Westminster. If Sunderland had thought of taxing the Irish in this way it would have been a remarkable presumption, unprecedented and fraught with political dangers in the domestic sphere. But there were other possibilities, and the involvement of some radical or 'country' whigs in the passage of the bill, notably the committee chairman Grey Neville (a presbyterian himself and a spokesman for the dissenting interest in England) suggests that Sunderland may have hoped to buy support by promising to use the power enshrined in the second clause to repeal the Irish test. Ulster presbyterians had themselves proposed just such a stratagem, and Bolton went some way towards endorsing it in recommending that action be taken at Westminster to relieve Irish dissenters of some of their disabilities.

Whatever had been in Sunderland's mind during the passage of the bill was, however, obscured in April 1720 by the political revolution at court. The reconciliation between the king and the prince of Wales, and between the ministry and its whig opponents, led by Townshend and Walpole, changed the face of English politics. Sunderland no longer had a free hand at policy-making. Walpole in particular seems to have acted as a dead weight on the progress of the ministry's Irish strategy. The appointment of his and Townshend's ally, the duke of Grafton, as lord lieutenant in June, with Walpole's brother Horatio as chief secretary, was a sign of his influence. On the whole, Walpole took a view of parliamentary prospects in Ireland that was simultaneously more sanguine than Sunderland's and more cautious. On the one hand, he seems to have believed that the Irish parliament could be managed successfully despite the passage of the Declaratory Act and other English provocations (possibly encouraged in this optimism by his own connexions with Midleton, and Grafton's influence with Conolly); on the other, he argued against any dramatic and injudicious experiment.

After a summer of indecision Sunderland brought matters to a head. Chief Baron Gilbert was now his choice to replace Midleton as lord chancellor (in a calculated snub to Irish 'patriots'), and Sunderland persuaded the king to allow government officials to explore ways in which the necessity of recalling the Irish parliament the following year might be avoided. Craggs was officially informed that

> His majesty, having considered the present discontents and dispositions in Ireland to become independent of the crown of Great Britain, and that it may be for his service to have the administration and government there put upon the ancient foot, that the country may be eased of the additional duties, His Majesty not be under the necessity of calling a parliament every two years, and by that means the late differences between the two nations be prevented from coming to extremities, is desirous that some measures should be taken to make his hereditary revenue defray the charges of his government in that kingdom.[69]

---

69 Wolterton Hall, Norfolk, Walpole MSS: Sunderland and Stanhope to Craggs, n.d. (draft). These papers are now in the British Library.

Various proposals were then discussed, by a small *ad hoc* committee, to bring the expenditure on the Irish establishment within the compass of the crown's hereditary revenue. The committee met at Grafton's house in Westminster, and significantly did not include Walpole or Townshend. Sunderland was the prime mover.[70] Two broad strategies were considered: on the one hand, to maximize the yield of the hereditary revenue by 'a frugal management' or even by tax-farming, supplemented perhaps by income generated by chartering a national bank; on the other, to reduce expenditure, by transferring regiments to the West Indies.[71]

It soon became clear that the reduction of the military establishment was the only practicable expedient, and in September 1720 the king signed orders to this effect. At the same time, Grafton was informed of important changes in the Irish judiciary, beginning with the replacement of Midleton by Chief Baron Gilbert.[72] But it was too late. The lord lieutenant objected to the political risk involved, and was strongly supported by Walpole, who produced a clinching argument: the proposed retrenchment of expenditure could not take effect for several months, which meant that the Irish parliament would have to be recalled after all.[73] Delay had thus removed the possibility of the decisive action that Sunderland had wanted.

Given that another parliamentary session was inevitable, it made sense to postpone the reshuffle of the Irish judiciary. In their correspondence with Sunderland both Grafton and Walpole took this line. The viceroy's resolve was stiffened by the receipt of a letter of protest from Conolly, pointing out the 'dread consequences' of the appointment of Gilbert 'to his majesty's affairs and the ease of your graces' administration'. The general revulsion, Conolly feared, would make parliament unmanageable.[74] Walpole took a slightly different tack. He agreed that Gilbert's would be an unwise appointment, but appeared more concerned at the effect on the outgoing lord chancellor. The aggrieved Midleton might put himself at the head of the 'patriot' interest, 'of which your lordship knows what may be the consequence in parliamentary proceedings'.[75] Sunderland duly gave way on this second point, and in late December Midleton received a report from England that the decision to replace him with Chief Baron Gilbert had been rescinded.[76]

In all probability neither Conolly nor Walpole were entirely disinterested in their advice. Conolly had his own candidates in mind for promotion to the bench, and was

70 *Ibid.*: 'Minutes about Ireland, 20/21 June 1720'.
71 P.R.O., S.P. 63/379/61–72; Wolterton Hall, Walpole MSS: 'Memorial relating to schemes proposed for making such savings upon the military part of the establishment of Ireland, as may bring the charges of the government there within the produce of the hereditary revenue ... '
72 Wolterton Hall, Walpole MSS: Sunderland to Robert Walpole, 21 Sept. 1720; P.R.O., S.P. 67/7/81.
73 Wolterton Hall, Walpole MSS: Grafton to Craggs, 17 Oct. 1720 (draft); Robert Walpole to Sunderland, 11 Oct. 1720.
74 P.R.O.N.I., Conolly MSS, T2825/A/15: Conolly to Grafton, 18 Oct. 1720; P.R.O., S.P. 63/379/87.
75 Wolterton Hall, Walpole MSS: Robert Walpole to Sunderland, 11 Oct. 1720.
76 Surrey R.O., Midleton MSS, 1248/4, f. 377.

unhappy that Sunderland's scheme left them on the sidelines,[77] while Walpole may well have been acting out of concern for preserving in office his former ally, Midleton, and may have viewed the political consequences in the light of his own jockeying for position within the ministry. Behind both sets of arguments, however, lay an important reality. It was still far from clear which of the 'two great men' in Ireland was the stronger in parliamentary terms. The Speaker had been able to carry votes of supply in 1717 and again in 1719, but the outcome of the debates over the relief of dissenters had shown the dangerous potential in a combination of the Brodricks, 'patriots' and Tories. If the Irish parliament had to meet again it might be better to do nothing, to trust that the two rivals, each of whom had connexions at court, would compete in demonstrating their loyalty (as they had done in 1717) rather than in making mischief, and that the resentment of the house of lords, and of Irish public opinion generally, against the Declaratory Act, would burn itself out without inflicting any permanent damage.

VI

As things turned out, this was exactly what happened in the next parliamentary session, though as much the result of good fortune as design. Certainly Grafton prepared the ground carefully. First he invited Midleton's brother to call on him in London, and took pains to create a favourable impression. Then he arranged, 'in a handsome and obliging manner', for the chancellor's purse-bearer to have an army commission. Finally he wrote to Midleton himself. Expecting dismissal, Midleton was flattered to be asked instead for his co-operation.[78] When Grafton arrived in Dublin, the chancellor was seen to have 'favour and credit', of which he boasted 'to everyone'.[79] As a result, the parliamentary session began well. The 'patriots'' bluff seemed to be called, and the Declaratory Act was not mentioned in either House. Supply was voted without difficulty. Unfortunately, Grafton was not clever enough to be able to steer a course for very long between the rivals, and Midleton was in any case nervous of his own position and easily startled. It soon became clear that the real power behind the viceregal throne was the Speaker, 'a certain little fellow', as Midleton commented bitterly, 'who among our great men is believed to carry everything before him by his own interest'.[80] Factional conflict inevitably broke out again, although it did not create intolerable embarrassment for government. The central issue was the proposed national bank, which the ministry had agreed to support, in hopes of an infusion of cash from the projectors. A 'patriotic' opposition quickly formed, alarmed by the economic and political implications of the scheme,

77 P.R.O.N.I., Conolly MSS, T 2825/A/11–13: Conolly to Grafton, 2, 5 July 1720, memo on judicial promotions, [c. 5 July 1720].
78 Surrey R.O., Midleton MSS, 1248/4, ff. 401; 1248/5, ff. 35, 39, 43.
79 *Jottings of the Levinge Family*, p. 65.
80 Surrey R.O., Midleton MSS, 1248/5, f. 123.

into which Midleton joined. Conolly too, sensing the public mood, dropped his earlier commitment to the bank, and Grafton, left alone, could do no more than limit the damage as the proposal fell through. But this time there were no embarrassing criticisms of government, no expressions of anti-English sentiment.[81] The loss of an expected windfall was a small price for government to pay for an unexpectedly comfortable session.

Nevertheless, the fact that at the next time of asking, two years later, Irish political management once again fell apart, reveals the underlying frailty of the ministry's position. Grafton's initial success had been adventitious, and was unlikely to be repeated. In 1721–2 the two chronic problems of parliamentary management had been masked rather than solved. Minor skirmishes in the Commons had shown the continuing capacity of the Brodricks to cause trouble, while in the Lords the 'patriots' were only temporarily cowed. Archbishop King and his allies seem almost to have shocked themselves by the lengths they had gone in 1719. The passage of the Declaratory Act effectively called their bluff. No longer could they hide behind claims that they were only concerned with the narrow question of jurisdiction, since the constitutional debate had been taken to a higher plane, to the issue of legislative autonomy, and as yet few Irish protestants were willing to press their claims that far. But if the 'patriots' could find a more appropriate subject for their passions, they might still command a majority in the upper House. The defeat of the bank project, against which Midleton had mobilised 'patriot' peers and bishops, had demonstrated this amply enough.

It was in the agitation over Wood's Halfpence that these problems reappeared, in a sharper form. The details of this notorious episode in Anglo-Irish relations do not concern us here, so much as the causes of the government's difficulties, and the measures taken to put matters right. By the time Grafton returned to Dublin Castle in 1723, Midleton was thoroughly alienated, and not only from the viceroy himself but also from Walpole and Townshend, who now dominated the administration following the deaths of Stanhope and Sunderland. He had even begun an intrigue with their principal ministerial rival, Carteret.[82] So when popular resentment at the imposition of the Halfpence reached unprecedented proportions, Midleton grasped the opportunity to press home the political embarrassment, beyond the viceroy himself and as far as Whitehall and the court. The involvement in the affair of George I's mistress, the duchess of Kendal, who had been the original recipient of the patent for the coinage and who had sold her stake to Wood for £10,000, made the issue extremely sensitive in English as well as Irish terms. In the Irish house of commons

---

81 Burns, *Irish Parliamentary Politics*, I, 113–33; Michael Ryder, 'The Bank of Ireland, 1721: Land, Credit, and Dependency', *Historical Journal*, XXV (1982), 557–82. Cf. Isolde Victory, 'Colonial Nationalism in Ireland, 1692–1725: From Common Law to Natural Right', Trinity College, Dublin, Ph.D., 1984, pp. 162–3, 182–7.

82 Surrey R.O., Midleton MSS, 1224 8/5, ff. 174, 285; P.R.O., S.P. 63/382/17; B.L., Add. MS 32686, ff. 337, 357, 369.

there was now open warfare between the two 'parties': 'the contest ... was between [the Speaker] and Mr [St John] Brodrick, which one should guide the House'.[83] Grafton openly sided with Conolly. In the Lords the viceroy watched passively as his own 'constant companion' Lord Fitzwilliam led an attempt to censure the chancellor for neglect of duty; and privately he begged Walpole and Secretary Newcastle to dismiss Midleton.[84] But not even the revelation that St John Brodrick had threatened in the Irish Commons to move for the impeachment of Walpole himself proved sufficiently persuasive.[85] Walpole was still uncertain as to Conolly's capacity to 'undertake' alone, the more so because of the strength of feeling over the Halfpence, which the Speaker seemed impotent to restrain. Indeed, Conolly's reticence on the issue, which extended to an official resistance on the part of the revenue commissioners to enforce the acceptance of the new coin, enraged Walpole as much as Midleton's intrigues and outright opposition to the patent.[86] Walpole began to doubt whether any Irish political manager could be trusted to stand firm.

Walpole's eventual solution was a master-stroke of policy. Unlike Sunderland's response to the crisis of 1719 it involved no fundamental reconsideration of the system of government; it was, instead, the kind of high-political manoeuvre characteristic of eighteenth-century government, a ministerial reshuffle which removed the hapless Grafton from the viceroyalty, and inserted in his place the conspirator, Carteret. Responsibility for settling the disturbed state of Irish politics was left to the new lord lieutenant. Whatever happened, Walpole stood to gain: either Carteret resolved the impasse over the Halfpence, decided between Conolly and Midleton, and restored a workable scheme of management; or he floundered and sank in the mire in which his predecessor had struggled, and thus destroyed his own reputation with the king.[87]

Carteret's viceroyalty can be seen in retrospect as a remarkable success.[88] He stands out from the previous run of weak and incompetent lords lieutenant as a man prepared to take responsibility, and to tackle problems rather than postpone them. Moreover, he could claim to have quietened the furore against the Halfpence and to have stabilized parliamentary management. But he did so by surrendering the political initiative rather than by imposing his own will. On his advice the Halfpence were

---

83 Surrey R.O., Midleton MSS, 1248/5, f. 323; Hayton, 'Walpole and Ireland', pp. 103–5; Burns, *Irish Parliamentary Politics*, I, 138–43; D. W. Hayton 'Two Ballads on the County Westmeath By-Election of 1723', *Eighteenth-Century Ireland*, IV (1989), 7–30.

84 Surrey R.O., Midleton MSS, 1248/5, ff. 362–5; P.R.O., S.P. 63/382/96.

85 Coxe, *Walpole*, II, 280.

86 Albert Goodwin, 'Wood's Halfpence', repr. in *Essays in Eighteenth-Century History*, ed. Rosalind Mitchison (1966), pp. 122–3; P.R.O., S.P. 63/381/141; Coxe, *Walpole*, II, 285–6.

87 Hayton, 'Walpole and Ireland', p. 107.

88 This is the received view, presented for example in Burns, *Irish Parliamentary Politics*, I, 161–74, and ch. 4; and Hayton, 'Walpole and Ireland', pp. 107–12. For an important reassessment, see Patrick McNally, 'Wood's Halfpence, Carteret, and the Government of Ireland, 1723–6', *Irish Historical Studies*, XXX (1997), 354–76.

eventually withdrawn and the patent rescinded, though Walpole was reluctant to
concede and only did so under protest. Deprived of this major grievance, 'patriot'
anger quickly began to subside. The settlement of factional rivalry in the Commons
was a more difficult matter. At first Carteret sought to avoid a decision, followed the
line of non-partisanship which had occasionally worked, having brought Pembroke
success in 1707, Bolton a short-lived honeymoon in 1717, and Grafton some
temporary relief at the beginning of the 1721–2 session, but which more often than
not had ended in failure. Carteret's experiment, acting as his own 'chief minister'
during the 1724–5 session, and hoping to secure the goodwill and support of all sides,
foundered on the mutual hostility of Speaker and lord chancellor.[89] Midleton in
particular was quick to interpret the viceroy's studied neutrality as a rejection of
himself, and eventually resigned.[90] Even then Carteret did not hand over the
leadership of the court party to Conolly, but his belief in the capacity of a lord
lieutenant to act as his own 'undertaker' proved sadly misplaced, and before the next
session began he was obliged to come to an accommodation with the Speaker.

VII

Carteret's settlement with Conolly ended a lengthy period of confusion. Since 1715
the British and Irish governments had failed to speak clearly and with one voice as
to which among the competing groups of Irish whig politicians enjoyed the favour
and approval of the crown and its chief ministers. A glance at the aftermath of
Conolly's triumph might suggest that this alone restored stability to Irish political
management. The following parliamentary sessions were quieter and less troublesome: supply was voted without unduly warm debates on controversial or embarrassing subjects. But there were other contributory factors to the establishment of
political stability in Ireland, not least the deaths in rapid succession of St John
Brodrick and Lord Midleton, which robbed the opposition of leadership and
coherence. As far as the house of lords was concerned, the passing of the generations
and the long-term effects of the systematic dispensation of ecclesiastical patronage
resulted in a slow attenuation of the tory interest, among both temporal and spiritual
lords, and the gradual construction of a more powerful and compliant court party.
(The muted reaction to the Declaratory Act had in any case established the limit of
protestant constitutional ambitions, and without a popular grievance the 'patriot'
opposition was not hard to bridle.) Circumstances thus conspired to promote the
successes of what had been for the most part a series of pragmatic and piecemeal
changes.

89 I base this observation on the conclusions of Griffin, 'Parliamentary Politics', pp. 165–74; and
     McNally, 'Wood's Halfpence, Lord Carteret, and the Government of Ireland'. I am especially grateful
     to Dr McNally for permitting me to consult this paper in advance of publication.
90 Surrey R.O., Midleton MSS, 1248/6, ff. 165–6, 213.

There had been, however, one exception to the Walpolean ministry's conservative approach to Irish policy. Walpole and Townshend had taken the opportunity of a vacancy in the Church of Ireland primacy in 1724 to advance one of their own clerical dependants, Hugh Boulter, whom they clearly expected to act as their own 'eyes and ears' in the Castle administration, to represent 'English' interests with determination at the Irish privy council and to take over the leadership of the court party in the house of lords. The following year, on Midleton's resignation, they appointed an English lawyer, Richard West, as lord chancellor. Together, Boulter and West (and West's successor Thomas Wyndham) constituted the germ of an 'English party' in government, intended to check any centrifugal tendencies on the part of Irish political managers or 'undertakers'. They were to offer an alternative source of advice and recommendation, especially in the area of patronage, in case the viceroy 'went native', as Grafton was suspected of having done, and became too dependent on Irish advisers.[91] This was reminiscent of the instant reaction of Sunderland to the disasters of 1719, and represented a standard English response to political assertiveness by Irish protestants, reinforced, no doubt, by Walpole's belief that Conolly had let down government over the Halfpence, which bred a general distrust of 'undertakers'' ultimate loyalties. It was not a particularly happy innovation, however, as disputes over patronage brought Conolly and Boulter into conflict, and the involvement of the viceroy in these quarrels reintroduced the spectre of divided counsel which had haunted government between 1715 and 1725.[92]

British whig ministers in this period had no considered or consistent policy towards Ireland. They retained a theoretical commitment to the strengthening of the protestant interest by means of the conciliation of dissenters, but paid no more than lip-service to this principle unless they themselves stood to gain from it in the sphere of British domestic politics. Otherwise, changes in policy took the form of crisis-management, focused on securing political stability, suppressing parliamentary factionalism and notions of 'independency', and obtaining an adequate supply of 'additional' taxation. Viewed objectively and with hindsight, the problems that arose in the decade after 1714 seem neither very serious nor difficult to solve. That Irish protestants hankered after 'independency' was a myth; the complaints of parliamentary 'patriots' could be faced down by a determined government. In the house of lords a combination of tact and the careful deployment of ecclesiastical patronage would in time have produced a settled majority; in the Commons what was required was a clear expression of viceregal support for one political manager, or set of managers. Unfortunately, British cabinets reacted to failures rather than planning for success. Only once, after the setbacks of the 1719 parliament, did a chief minister,

91 Hayton, Walpole and Ireland', pp. 108–9; Burns, *Irish Parliamentary Politics*, I, 197–200; Christ Church, Arch.W.Epist., 14 (unfol.): Bishop Evans to Wake, 29 Jan. 1723–4; P.R.O., S.P. 63/381/141.
92 Griffin, 'Parliamentary Politics', pp. 168–9.

Lord Sunderland, seek to get to the root of the trouble. But his radical proposals were half-baked, and it was probably just as well for government that they were never implemented. Ironically, when George I's whig ministers did find an answer to their Irish question it was as a consequence of a high-political manoeuvre, contrived with a view to achieving a short-term advantage at court, and representing as much a recognition of the limitations of British government influence in Ireland as an exploitation of its potential strength.

4

Aboriginal Peoples and the British Press
1720–1763

DAVID MILOBAR

The continuing process of re-inventing a common identity with reference to changing circumstance is one of the most important aspects in the development of a national culture. Eighteenth-century British society was given coherence by a powerful web of historical myths based on protestantism, rule of law, the constitution, and the security of liberty and property. But these historical myths were not static. They were reconfigured constantly with reference to a changing world. The rise of the monied interest, the middle class and the military-fiscal state all challenged traditional beliefs about the relationship between the individual and the state. Improved communications brought regular news from around the world while the rise of the reading public allowed a larger segment of society to participate in public discourse. This study explores the relationship between the redefinition of empire, intellectual speculation about its non-European peoples and the rise of the popular press in eighteenth-century Britain.[1] Popular perceptions of North American Indians were shaped by metropolitan beliefs in the inherent moral, religious and constitutional superiority of the British empire. Missionaries, intellectuals and colonists readily accepted the proposition that Indian civilization was 'inferior' to European civilization; they sought to categorize aboriginal peoples according to well-defined criteria. These criteria judged the myriad of aboriginal groups according to their importance to Britain's economic/strategic interests, their commitment to Christianity, sedentary community structure and the adoption of European material culture. The British press built on philosophical speculation and colonial reports to make the American Indian an object of great interest to the reading public. The popular press refashioned the image of the Indian from an irrelevant irritant in the way of settlement to either a malevolent ally of the French or a noble, stalwart ward of the British crown; in the case of the latter the Indian became part of the 'noble experiment' that was the British empire.

Recent scholarship has reinvigorated debate about the influence of empire on eighteenth-century Britain's sense of national identity. John Brewer has shown the degree to which the military-fiscal state protected British commercial and strategic

---

1 For the purposes of this essay the popular press is defined as all forms of printed material available to the general public including newspapers, magazines, books and pamphlets.

interests that became a cornerstone in the establishment of a post-1707 sense of self.[2]
Ian Steele has explored the evolution of Atlantic communications and their role in the
establishment of a distinct trans-Atlantic perspective within colonial societies.[3] J. P.
Greene has revealed the political and constitutional dynamics of the rivalry between
metropolitan and periphery visions of imperial governance.[4] More recent interpretations build on this simple centre-periphery dichotomy to include the development of
distinctly provincial views on British definitions of self and empire.[5] Robertson argues
that the peoples of the Celtic fringe shared with their English counterparts a
commitment to the British empire but they did not embrace the concept of a London
centred British state with much enthusiasm.[6] The common element in all these works
is that by the first half of the eighteenth century most British *élites* were thoroughly
engaged in the process of establishing some sort of common identity through the
process of empire building.

The intellectual foundation of the discourse of common identity was constructed
on the antithetical concepts of land and commerce and republic and empire. J. G. A.
Pocock is representative of the significant body of scholarship stressing the evolution
of a republican and anti-imperial tradition within the British Atlantic.[7] Recent studies,
however, have highlighted the presence of a pro-imperial and authoritarian strain of
thought amongst social and political *élites*. H. T. Dickinson makes the point that
supporters of the traditional whig establishment not only maintained their status by
controlling the levers of power but by developing a conservative ideological
framework capable of justifying a more authoritarian king in parliament and winning
significant support within the political nation.[8] What Dickinson observes about the
political nation is also true for Britain's relationship with the empire as a whole.
Marshall argues convincingly that by the 1770s the ruling classes had accepted the
assertion that a culturally and racially polyglot authoritarian empire was of no threat
to the liberty of British subjects at home or abroad.[9]

2 John Brewer, *The Sinews of Power. War, Money and the English State, 1688–1783* (1989), pp.
   135–62.
3 Ian K. Steele, *The English Atlantic, 1675–1740. An Exploration of Communication and Community*
   (New York, 1986), pp. 273–8.
4 Jack P. Greene, *Peripheries and Center. Constitutional Development in the Extended Polities of the
   British Empire and the United States, 1607–1788* (Athens, Ga., 1986).
5 Ned C. Landsman, 'The Provinces and Empire: Scotland, the American Colonies and the
   Development of a British Provincial Identity', in *An Imperial State at War. Britain from 1689 to
   1815*, ed. Lawrence Stone (1994), p. 260.
6 John Robertson, 'Union, State and Empire: The Britain of 1707 in its European Setting', in *ibid.*, pp.
   224–7.
7 J. G. A. Pocock, *The Machiavellian Moment. Florentine Political Thought and the Atlantic
   Republican Tradition* (Princeton, 1975), pp. 423–52.
8 H. T. Dickinson, *Liberty and Property. Political Ideology in Eighteenth-Century Britain* (1977),
   pp. 121–63, 270–318.
9 P. J. Marshall, 'Empire and Authority in Later Eighteenth Century Britain', *Journal of Imperial and
   Commonwealth History*, XV (1987), 105–22.

While intellectual historians can infer the impact of empire on the sense of Britishness amongst the political *élite*, works focusing on the cultural impact of empire reveal its role in shaping a common identity amongst the general populace. Williams and Marshall have revealed a growing interest in the exotic peoples and places that were the British empire.[10] Kathleen Wilson has shown how the process of empire building, commercialism and civic virtue became embedded in British popular culture and sense of self. This enthusiasm for empire, Wilson argues, permeated Hanoverian culture and 'frequently transcended socio-economic and political allegiances'.[11]

A survey of scholarly literature would seem to indicate that aboriginal peoples of North America played little role in the integration of empire into the British sense of identity. The majority of works focus on the impact of British culture on aboriginal peoples, not the significance of the Indian to a British imperial identity. Recent scholarship, however, has began to examine just this issue. Glyndwr Williams argues that the popular image of the 'noble savage' was eventually crushed under the weight of the European conquest. But the debate about the place of aboriginal peoples in the hierarchy of world civilizations occupied a significant place in enlightenment analysis of the role of empire in British society. To many thinkers of this period the American Indian lived in a state of nature and thus provided insight into the first stage in human development.[12] Eric Hinderaker examines the relationship between the concept of the American Indian and the concept of empire through the prism of the London visit of four Iroquois 'kings' in 1711. He argues that the 'four kings' played a significant role the 'imaginative construction of empire' at a 'time when the English state and body politic were changing rapidly'.[13] The implication of Williams's and Hinderaker's studies is that the image of the Indian can be related to the convergence of that image with imperial and domestic changes that profoundly influenced the way the British public saw its world. The evolution of the image of the Indian and its significance to the development of popular perceptions of empire can only be understood with reference to the broader forces animating British history in the first half of the eighteenth century.

The mid-eighteenth century was in fact a period of profound political, economic and social change. The continuing process of state formation and heightened interest in continental affairs had increasingly involved England in European conflicts. Since the mid-seventeenth century England had steadily expanded its naval and land forces which were the cornerstone of any meaningful involvement in European diplomacy.

---

10 P. J. Marshall and Glyndwr Williams, *The Great Map of Mankind. British Perceptions of the World in the Age of Enlightenment* (1982), p. 3.
11 Kathleen Wilson, 'Empire of Virtue: The Imperial Project and Hanoverian Culture *c.*1720–1785', in *Imperial State*, ed. Stone, pp. 130–1.
12 Marshall and Williams, *Great Map of Mankind*, p. 222.
13 Eric Hinderaker, 'The "Four Kings" and the Imaginative Construction of the First British Empire', *William and Mary Quarterly*, LII (1996), 526.

Brewer points out a vigorous foreign policy required the state to devise a fiscal system capable of sustaining a large military force.[14] In fact this was part of a financial revolution extending from the late seventeenth to the first quarter of the eighteenth century. The creation of institutions such as the Bank of England and a stable system of national credit led to the establishment of a distinct socio-economic group, then known as the 'monied interest'. The creation of a new form of property and social group which controlled it encouraged many theorists to debate the relationship of that group to society, the state and the constitution.[15]

The rise of the fiscal-military state was not the only consequence of England's new-found interest in European affairs. Growing naval strength and sophisticated financial networks facilitated a rapid expansion of Britain's commercial strength. In many ways the union of England and Scotland was the first step in developing a structure capable of conducting vigorous trade throughout the globe. Furthermore, the acceleration of European trade was surpassed by even faster expansion of trade with Britain's colonies.[16] Underpinning this growth was an efficient communications network that allowed goods and information to be sent throughout the British Isles, to Europe and the imperial periphery. Steele has chronicled the steady reduction in trans-Atlantic communication time to the point where in 1739 London could inform Pennsylvania of the outbreak of war in 49 days.[17]

The development of an efficient postal system and packet boats raised public expectations of speed and reliability to the point where it was possible to obtain all manner of news from colonial America.[18] Newspapers hungry for news from the colonies give indications of how high public expectations were raised. By the 1740s many newspapers, even some provincial publications in seaports, had permanent foreign and imperial correspondents to ensure British readers received information as quickly as possible. For example in 1747 *F. Farley's Bristol Journal* announced it had 'engaged' Boston and Philadelphia correspondents to supply its readers with 'the most early Intelligences' from that part of the world.[19] Intelligence received from the colonies was printed quickly to inform readers and to try and beat competitors who had no scruples about reprinting the information as their own. A case in point was the fall of the French fortress on Cape Breton in June, which was being reported in the edition of the *Westminster Journal* of 3 August 1745. The edition of the *Gazetteer and London Daily Advertiser* of 5 January 1756 carried an extract of a letter dated 24 November with the news that on 6 November a soldier belonging to

14 Brewer, *Sinews of Power*, pp. xiii-xxii.
15 P. G. M. Dickson, *The Financial Revolution in England. A Study in the Development of Public Credit, 1688–1756* (1970).
16 E. B. Schumpeter, *English Overseas Trade Statistics, 1697–1808* (Oxford, 1960), p. 17.
17 Steele, *The English Atlantic*, p. 209.
18 *Ibid.*, pp. 113–212.
19 *F. Farley's Bristol Journal*, 14 Nov. 1747.

Fort Edward 'was killed and scalped by a party of Indians'.[20] That the speed the news in these case studies travelled was considered by the reading public to be unexceptionable points to the degree which they demanded and received news from abroad.

The rise of commerce, communication and the military-fiscal state created new wealth and opportunities throughout Britain. It also had a profound impact on Georgian social organization. By the mid-eighteenth century about half of Britain's population fell into the category of the middling sort as defined by Massie and King. Comprised of groups such as the lesser gentry, professions, merchants, shopkeepers and craftsmen the middling ranks included some of the most dynamic elements of eighteenth-century society. Weatherill notes that significant portions of this middle rank 'had distinctly consumerist tastes and a need to assert their position in society through the ownership of goods'.[21] The growing ranks of this middling sort began to be seen in urbanization and the establishment of a consumer society on a scale not hitherto achieved. The relative abundance of material possessions, therefore, represented a new code of behaviour and way of looking at the world as much as it represented conspicuous consumption.[22]

The impact of a middling consumer society could be seen in everything from the cloths they wore to the way they passed their leisure time. In consuming new products from around the globe British society was developing a world view in which the foreign and the exotic found itself into the life of even the lowest subject. Colonial commodities provided some of the most visual examples of the influence of consumerism at all levels of British society.[23] Coffee, tea, sugar, tobacco and spices were only a small part of a market in goods that brought the world into even humble British households.[24]

In keeping with a general rise in living standards Britons also experienced improvements in their intellectual life. Langford has noted that one of the principal cultural developments of the period was the rise of the reading public. The increase in literacy marched in step with the expansion of the middling order. The demand for published material was in part spurred on by marketing that made literature attractive to a wider social spectrum.[25] But it was equally a reflexion of polite society's desire to acquire knowledge of a wider world.

20 *Gazetteer and London Daily Advertiser*, 5 Jan. 1756.
21 Lorna Weatherill, 'The Meaning of Consumer Behaviour in Late Seventeenth- and Early Eighteenth-Century England', in *Consumption and the World of Goods*, ed. John Brewer and Roy Porter (1993), p. 210.
22 Neil McKendrick, 'The Birth of a Consumer Society: The Commercialization of Eighteenth-Century England', in Neil McKendrick, John Brewer, and J. H. Plumb, *The Birth of a Consumer Society. The Commercialization of Eighteenth-Century England* (1982), pp. 9–33.
23 Brewer, *Sinews of Power*, p. 185.
24 Carole Shammas, 'Changes in English and Anglo-American Consumption from 1500 to 1800', in *Consumption and the World of Goods*, ed. Brewer and Porter, pp. 199–201.
25 Paul Langford, *A Polite and Commercial People. England, 1727–1783* (Oxford, 1992), pp. 90–9.

The spread of popular reading from London to the provinces lead to the establishment of a vibrant provincial publishing industry. The revolution in the commercialization of popular reading was anchored on the printing room floor. Often printers or booksellers published newspapers, magazines, books and pamphlets on the same premises. Lack of copyright control and the need to fill their newspapers and magazines encouraged printers to borrow heavily from one another. Since the bulk of foreign and imperial news came through London metropolitan newspapers exercised a disproportionate influence on the types of stories and their interpretation to the national reading public.[26]

The potential impact of the metropolis on provincial interpretation of world events can be divined from the growing number of newspaper readers throughout the British Isles. By the 1750s the circulation of the average London paper numbered in the thousands while its provincial counterpart had a circulation of from 1,000 to 2,000 subscribers.[27] During this period approximately 20,000 London papers per week found their way from London to the provinces.[28] Harris estimates that London newspaper consumption came close to half a million copies per week. Furthermore the availability of newspapers in taverns and coffee houses meant that circulation figures only indicate a portion of the readership.[29] Contemporaries such as Joseph Addison thought 20 readers for each paper sold 'a modest computation'.[30] Add to these numbers circulation figures for magazines and other printed material and one may gain an appreciation of the power of the printed word for disseminating information to the reading public.[31] No longer was reading the prerogative of a closed circle of gentlefolk; by the first half of the eighteenth century the consumers of newspapers and magazines were drawn from all ranks of society.[32]

It is in this context that popular reading material provides the historian with insights into popular perceptions of the British identity and of the imperial 'other' that helped define it. The need for material as much as the public demand for the exotic encouraged publishers to include a significant number of stories from abroad. John Feather argues that history and geography titles were the fourth most popular category out of ten in the eighteenth century; he estimates that during that period almost 30,000 titles were published covering historical and geographical topics from

26 G. A. Cranfield, *The Development of the Provincial Newspaper, 1700–1760* (Oxford, 1962), ch. 4.
27 *Ibid.*, p. 176.
28 *Ibid.*, p. 180.
29 Michael Harris, *London Newspapers in the Age of Walpole. A Study of the Origins of the Modern English Press* (Cranbury, N.J., 1987), pp. 190–2.
30 Cited in Cranfield, *Development*, p. 177.
31 James R. Sutherland, 'The Circulation of Newspapers and Literary Periodicals, 1700–1730', *The Library*, 4th ser., xv (1935), 110–24.
32 Charles A. Knight, 'Bibliography and the Shape of the Literary Periodical in the Eighteenth Century', *The Library*, 6th ser., viii (1986), 242.

around the globe.[33] Out of this total culled from publishing lists contained in the *Monthly Review* 2,469 titles examined the history of North America and 371 works were devoted to geographical information on that part of the world.[34] These publishing records show that the public's desire to be educated and entertained with tales of non-European peoples only grew as the century progressed.[35]

In part the enthusiasm for knowledge of foreign nations and exotic colonies was a reflexion of the commercial spirit of the age; increased trade with foreign nations and empire made information on foreign climes of immense value to the mercantile classes.[36] Whether a large trader, a worker in a cottage industry or a small investor trans-Atlantic commerce involved a wide stratum of British society. Roger North observed with amazement that 'all men that are dealers, even in the shop trades, launch into adventures by sea... A poor shopkeeper that sells candles will have a bale of stockings or a piece of stuff for Nevis or Virginia.'[37]

But the growing interest in the 'other' also related to Britons' sense of identity. Commentators linked commerce, empire and the constitution as the foundation of a cultural fortress protecting the rights, freedom and property of all the king's subjects. As the duke of Newcastle proclaimed, 'by trade we do, and must, if at all subsist; without which we have no wealth; and without wealth we have no power, as without power we can have no liberty'.[38] These sentiments were echoed in a pamphlet written by Fayrer Hall. Hall argued that 'British strength and protection is ships and ships protect British liberty from foreign powers.' The colonies, he noted, provided material and economic activity that stimulated British shipping.[39] The notion that Britain must retain and develop itself as a pre-eminent trading nation and imperial power to protect its subjects' liberties from the malevolent designs of France encouraged the public to define itself with reference to a commercial and global perspective.

Public prints of all types exposed the population to the central tenets of a discourse that connected the progress of empire, commerce and Britishness; this discourse was also an expression of those enlightenment values that highlighted order and harmony. In a world where exploration and imperial expansion revealed ever growing numbers of plants, animals and humans Carl von Linne's *Systema Naturae*

---

33 John Feather, 'British Publishing in the Eighteenth Century: A Preliminary Subject Analysis', *The Library*, 6th ser., VIII (1986), 37.

34 *Ibid.*, p. 44.

35 Feather's research indicates that out of the almost 30,000 history and geography titles 18,390 were concerned with non-European parts of the globe. *Ibid.*

36 John Brewer, 'Commercialization and Politics', in McKendrick *et al.*, *Birth of a Consumer Society*, pp. 215–16.

37 Cited in Brewer, *Sinews of Power*, p. 186.

38 Cited in R. T. Cornish, 'A Vision of Empire: The Development of British Opinion Regarding the American Colonial Empire', University of London Ph.D., 1987, p. 89.

39 Fayrer Hall, *The Importance of British Plantations in America to this Kingdom* (1731), p. 59.

provided a system capable of ordering knowledge of the natural world.[40] In some sense newspapers and other popular prints were informal expressions of Linne's system of classification. Wilson notes 'the format and content of newspapers mirrored the contemporary conceptualizations of power and market relations, at home and abroad, and expressed the interests and priorities of those who read them'. Wilson's observation is equally applicable to popular printed material as representing an attempt to order knowledge of human society in a way the public would understand.

The production of histories and geographies represented one of the most diligent attempts to order knowledge pertaining to foreign and imperial peoples for the consumption of the reading public. One of the most influential representatives of this genre was John Oldmixon's *The British Empire in America*. First published in 1708, this work was re-edited and republished well into the eighteenth century. Oldmixon sought to produce an ordered study of the resources, climate, soil and development of each American colony to show his readers that 'our American Plantations are an Advantage, and a great one to this Kingdom'. Geographical grammars also sought to educate readers on the role of empire in spurring British trade and improving overseas civilizations.

Patrick Gordon's *Geography Anatomiz'd*, which ran to at least 17 editions, set out to catalogue the civilizations of the world.[41] Taking inspiration from Linne's system the American section described each colony under the subsections name, air temperature, soil, commodities, rarities, archbishoprics, universities, manners, language, government, arms and religion. Besides providing his readers with knowledge necessary to prosecute overseas commerce Gordon reflected the Georgian tradition connecting imperialism, consumerism and commerce with the development of politeness, morals and civic virtue within British society. In Gordon's dedicatory introduction to the archbishop of Canterbury he pointed out that the empire had facets concerned with issues beyond material gain; he praised the archbishop's efforts to encourage the Society for the Propagation of the Gospel that 'our implacable Adversaries [the French] can no longer upbraid us with supine Neglect of our Heathen American Neighbours, in their Spiritual Concerns'. The rivalry with the French was as much about demonstrating superior civic and moral virtue as it was about strategic and commercial dominance.

Other genres of published material sought to order knowledge and promote pride in empire to the public at large. The *Gentleman's Magazine*, *London Magazine* and *Scot's Magazine* were but the most prominent examples of a growing number of general periodicals that increasingly culled imperial news from newspapers and pamphlets as regular topics of discussion. In times of conflict this coverage was enhanced with lavish maps, illustrations and articles extolling the value of imperial

---

40 Cited in Robert F. Berkhofer, *The Whiteman's Indian* (New York, 1978), p. 40.
41 Patrick Gordon, *Geography Anatomiz'd: Or, The Geographical Grammar* (17th edn., 1741).

possessions to the metropolis. For example during a time of conflict in the 1740s the *Gentleman's Magazine* included a detailed map of New France with inserts detailing Quebec and Louisbourg, a chart of the coast of New England, Nova Scotia and Canada and remarks by N. Bellin, engineer to the marine office, criticizing French interpretations of British colonial boundaries. The editor dedicated the whole production 'to the British Merchants Trading to North America'.[42]

The most pervasive medium to connect the notions of empire and the imperial 'other' with Britishness was the newspaper. Relatively inexpensive and accessible to all levels of the reading public newspapers highlighted the role of empire in the everyday life of all levels of society. In the age of a consumer revolution advertisements for colonial products and shipping news made average citizens aware of Britain's place as a global commercial power. The appearance of sections entitled 'Plantation News' highlighted the importance of empire at home at the same time as it underlined its separation from domestic and European life. The main theme of news from the American colonies was the noble struggle of British settlers to carve a new life out of the wilderness. The obvious message to British readers was the inevitable triumph of the British settler over the French and their Indian allies; this, the public believed, was proof of the superior character of British peoples. In this way the colonies became barometers of the state of British civic virtue in general. One correspondent pointed out to the readers of the *Gentleman's Magazine* that the American colonies' 'Prosperity depends on the Freedom and good Constitution of their Government ... and such of them as have the freest and best Charter-Governments ... [are] the most populous, and consequently beneficial to us'.[43] The need to be vigilant in the protection of protestantism and the balanced constitution in the face of the French threat was made clear in numerous articles examining the importance of the American colonies; 'the introduction of [catholicism]', wrote one contributor, 'cannot but be fatal to our present constitution, since its natural influence is to affect all the civil rights of mankind'.[44] The steady material progress of the colonies and the apparent 'stagnation' of the French empire was therefore evidence that the British empire expanded because it was an empire of virtue.

At first glance it would appear that aboriginal peoples made little contribution to the debate about empire beyond providing entertaining stories of life on the frontier. The reading public was excited by lurid stories of violent crime of all types. Whether it was the exploits of a highwayman or a grizzly murder the eighteenth-century reader demanded and received the sensational.[45] Publishers of all genres of material found that the aboriginal as a subject could appeal to the public's love of the lurid and its lively interest in news from the empire. Public prints accused North America's first

---

42 *Gentleman's Magazine*, XVI (Feb. 1746), 75.
43 *Ibid.*, XI (Aug. 1741), 429.
44 *Ibid.*, XV (Oct. 1745), 581.
45 Cranfield, *Provincial Newspaper*, p. 71.

inhabitants of 'leading a Bestial Life' devoted to wars carried on with 'extreme cruelty'.[46] Publishers removed aboriginal society from its broader context that gave it complexity and meaning for the sake of 'confirming' their primitiveness or thrilling the reader with a sensational tale.

In an age of intense European and imperial warfare it is not surprising that aboriginal martial traditions were an area of particular interest to the public. Contemporary writers assumed Europe was the measure of all aspects of civilized behaviour, even in military tactics and rules of engagement. The public received regular reports that contrasted the seemingly cruel, sudden guerrilla campaigns of the frontier with open field, set piece battles that were the norm in Europe. Newspaper, magazine and pamphlet literature implied that aboriginal attacks on British settlers were the work of primitive cultures incapable of rising to the 'superior' level of European civilization. Readers were treated to the gory thrill of detailed descriptions of aboriginal attacks, scalping and their treatment of women and children. Typical of this type of story was an account carried in the *London Evening Post* describing a vicious and 'cowardly' attack on a settler named John Smith. The paper reported that Smith was the victim of an unprovoked attack by 'three or four Indians, who killed and scalped him, and took his Axe and split his Skull, leaving the Axe in his Head'. They then went to his house and killed his wife, 'scalped her, and split her Head with a Hatchet'.[47]

Besides connecting the image of the Indian with cruelty and savagery popular reading material associated aboriginal peoples with French schemes. Descriptions of French-Indian relations stressed a controlling role by the French in determining their actions. The language and imagery used to describe this 'unholy alliance' was very much in the style used to describe the martyrdom of French protestants by the French catholic crown. The *Gentleman's Magazine* printed a poem by Samuel Davies incorporating traditional anti-catholic and anti-French vocabulary to elicit a public response against the Indian held in thrall to his French masters.

> Long had a mungrel French and Indian brood
> Our peaceful frontiers drench'd with British blood.
> There horror rang'd, and her dire ensigns bore,
> Raw scalps her trophies, stiff with clotted gore;
> The heart and bowels smoking on the ground,
> Still warm with life, and mangled corpses round.[48]

The message of this poem was clear to the average eighteenth-century reader; in the wilds of North America the French catholic influence enticed their aboriginal allies to engage in violent attacks against hard working and virtuous British settlers. The

46 David Humphreys, *A Historical Account of the Incorporated Society for the Propagation of the Gospel in Foreign Parts* (1730), p. 278.
47 *London Evening-Post*, 1–3 Sept. 1757.
48 *Gentleman's Magazine*, XXVII (Feb. 1757), 83.

description of the massacre of some British settlers in Nova Scotia was ascribed 'to their good neighbours the French, whose priests have the conscience to tell the Indians, that our savior was born in France, and crucified in Britain; that the British are all heretics, and it is doing God good service to kill them'.[49] Traditional fears of catholicism and French cruelty were highlighted with stories of French treachery, even to the point where French officials ordered Indians allied to the British to be tortured upon capture.[50] This information was received by a public with a long national memory of French-catholic persecution and cruelty in a never ending struggle to bring an end to Europe's prominent bastion of liberty and protestantism.

Reports from the frontier provided the British reading public with object lessons on the virtues of British, French and aboriginal society. Popular prints defined British values in the language of English civic-humanism. A 'true Briton' was protestant, patriotic, hard working and frugal. He possessed the 'manly' characteristics of civic virtue and courage, as exemplified by Roman citizens at the height of its power.[51] Benjamin Franklin discussed these characteristics and how even in the colonial setting 'true born' Britons continued to possess them.

> Great Numbers of our own People are of the BRITISH RACE ... Our Neighbours of New-England afford the World a convincing Proof, that BRITONS, tho' a Hundred Years transplanted, and to the remotest Part of the Earth, may yet retain, even to the third or fourth Descent, that Zeal for the 'Publick Good', that 'military Prowess', and that 'undaunted Spirit', have we likewise of 'those brave People', whose Fathers in the last Age made so glorious a stand for our Religion and Liberties.[52]

Similarly the fall of Cape Breton inspired a host of favourable comparisons between the virtuous New England 'sons of the soil' and 'the ancient Romans leaving the plow for the field of battle, and retiring after their conquests to the plow again'.[53] The French people were a people whose ruling class was corrupted by luxury, cruel and deceitful. This perceived decay in *élite* social and political culture was visibly manifest in 'effeminacy' of manners and style. On the American frontier French influence was a major factor corrupting the 'noble savage' to the 'ignoble savage'.

The concepts of luxury, effeminacy and their threat to traditional British virtue was a common theme in eighteenth-century writing. The public showed a concern that in fact French society was first corrupting the British ruling class and then the nation as a whole.[54] Public prints did not pronounce aboriginal males to be 'effeminate' but they did utilize the vocabulary of gender in their analysis of their societies.

---

49 *Edinburgh Magazine and Literary Miscellany*, XV (Sept. 1753), 465.
50 *Gentleman's Magazine*, XXVI (May 1756), 227–9.
51 J. G. A. Pocock, *Virtue, Commerce and History* (Cambridge, 1985), pp. 246–53.
52 This pamphlet was an enormous success in the colonies and was reprinted in Britain. Benjamin Franklin, *The Plain Truth. Or Serious Considerations On the Present State of the City of Philadelphia and Province of Pennsylvania* (Philadelphia, 1747), p. 202.
53 *The Craftsman*, 3 Aug. 1745.
54 Kathleen Wilson, *The Sense of the People. Politics, Culture and Imperialism in England, 1715–1785* (Cambridge, 1995), pp. 185–205.

Nussbaum points out that 'the Other can never be fully "known" except in reference to the self'.[55] In the case of Britain, monogamy, the subordination of women with a focus on maternal concerns of the home provided many eighteenth-century thinkers with a definition that complemented their ideas about the role of the male in a civilized society. The American Indian, therefore, was to be judged according to British ideals of gender roles and characteristics. John Gregory's *Manuel of Modern Geography* presented the reading public with a negative but fairly common assessment of aboriginal peoples. His study of New York Indians judged the males to be lazy and devoted to games while the women were left 'to plow and sow'.[56] Another writer studying the aboriginal peoples of Nova Scotia implied that it was 'abnormal' relations between the sexes that provided a partial explanation for the 'natural' cruelty of Abeneki men. The author informed his audience that Indians of that area were great warriors who would 'try their Courage in a pitched Battle with their Wives' and if successful in the contest they would take it as an 'ill Omen' and not wish to go into battle. The reason for this belief, the reading public was told, was that a drubbing at the hands of one's wife would make the husband 'desperate' so as 'not daring to return home without the Laurel, for fear of a second Drubbing from his wife'.[57]

Polygamy, sexuality, morphology and dress were included in most discussions of aboriginal societies. The British ideal of monogamy and christian marriage was contrasted with aboriginal practices. Oldmixon expressed disapproval of aboriginal sexual mores and the seeming informality of relations between husband and wife. He informed his readers that if an Iroquois man 'dislikes his Wife, he turns her off for the least Offence; to cuckold her Husband is so little a one that no notice is taken of it... Their Maids do not keep that Name ... they lie with whom they please before Marriage.'[58] Another writer argued that the husbands of Abeneki women 'are quite Savages to their wives' and accepted polygamous relationships. Even when it proved that they did not generally engage in such marriages the author ascribed this 'not so much to their Chastity as to their Laziness'.[59] Newspaper and magazine correspondents provided detailed accounts of Indian attacks and almost never failed to mention that the 'young women' were either 'ravished' and scalped or 'carried away'.[60]

Writers described aboriginal morphology and dress so as to emphasize the primitive to the reading public. A typical description of aboriginal peoples included

55 Felicity A. Nussbaum, 'Polygamy, Pamela, and the Prerogative of Empire', in *The Consumption of Culture 1600–1800*, ed. Ann Bermingham and John Brewer (1995), p. 219.
56 John Gregory, *A Manuel of Modern Geography* (1740), p. 20.
57 Anon., *A Geographical History of Nova Scotia* (1749), p. 45.
58 John Oldmixon, *British Empire in America*, (2 vols., 1708), I, 279.
59 Anon., *A Geographical History of North America* (1749), pp. 42–3.
60 For some examples see: *Gentleman's Magazine*, XXVI (Jan. 1756), 6; John Wilson, *A Genuine Narrative of the TRANSACTIONS IN NOVA SCOTIA Since the Settlement, June 1749, till August the 5th, 1751* (1751), pp. 15–20.

mention of the strength of the males and the minimum amount of clothing they wore. Thomas Salmon informed his readers that the Indians of North Carolina 'are a manly well-shaped Race, the Men tall, women little' and the men wore only 'a piece of Cloth drawn through their Legs'.[61] Another correspondent noted with disapproval that before Europeans arrived Indian males wore only a loin cloth at most. He went on to inform his readers that American Indians were 'tall, straight in their limbs, and their bodies strong beyond the portion of most nations'. But this positive assessment of their strength served to highlight their primitive state as the Indian possessed 'a species of strength rather fitted for hunting than labour. It is the strength of a beast of prey.'[62]

Not all popular discourse was built solely on an interpretation of aboriginal culture as primitive and lacking any characteristics worthy of consideration by European thinkers. As the century progressed the reading public was exposed to a more subtle discussion of aboriginal society. The vocabulary of this analysis removed the Indian from their cultural context by incorporating words and terms whose meanings were understood readily by the reading public but provided little understanding of life in the context of aboriginal belief systems. The *Grub-Street Journal* reprinted stories from a number of London papers discussing the visit of a number of Indian 'kings', 'queens' and 'princes'.[63] Cadwallader Colden referred to each of the Five Nations as an 'absolute Republick', 'Common-Wealth' and Iroquois territory as an 'empire'.[64] In part the use of European terms to describe aboriginal society was connected to imperial claims with relation to other European powers. The growing importance of imperial possessions made it in the government's interest to enhance public perceptions of aboriginal groups allied to the British crown. The notion that Iroquois territory encompassed a vast 'empire' was the basis for laying claim to major portions of areas controlled by the French. If the Five Nations possessed an empire and they in turn were wards of the British crown then any territory under their control fell within the British empire. At the very least referring to leaders of aboriginal groups allied to the British as 'emperors', 'kings', 'queens' and 'princes' enhanced their stature in the popular mind and built pride in empire.

The use of aboriginal peoples in popular prints also pulled them into a broader discussion about empire and the lessons to be drawn from ancient history. Throughout the eighteenth century Britons engaged in a lively debate whether a society should be founded on the values of landed property or the modern ideal of a commercial society. The ideal of an agrarian society versus a modern commercial society naturally drew the concept of empire into the debate. Neither side in this debate was particularly concerned with Britain's sovereignty of a vast American empire; they

61 Thomas Salmon, *A New Geographical and Historical Grammar* (1749), p. 537.
62 *Lloyd's Evening Post, and British Chronicle*, II (6–9 Jan. 1758), 28.
63 *Grub-Street Journal*, 18 July 1734.
64 Cadwallader Colden, *The History of the Five Nations of Canada* (1747).

were settled largely by British subjects who occupied what many Europeans regarded as unclaimed territory traversed occasionally by nomadic, primitive tribes.

The introduction of the concept of 'barbarism' to this debate provided thinkers with the basis for a four stage theory of history; hunting, herding, farming and commerce represented phases of human progress that many thinkers used to create a taxonomy of the world's peoples and their development over time. This fascination with human development and the relationship between commerce and empire mirrored a public interest in using the experience of ancient Rome to gauge Britain's progress as an imperial power. Gibbon's *History of the Rise and Fall of the Roman Empire* marked a high point in the use of history to provide insight into the challenge of empire to civic virtue at home. Pocock points out that Gibbon's analysis of barbarian tribes was built upon the notion that they lacked agriculture. Agriculture was seen by Gibbon and his contemporaries to inculcate 'a sense of property which could moderate the sense of self'.[65] Therefore the Germanic barbarians studied by Gibbon lived within a society where a tribesman's passions were violent, alternating between 'lethargy' and 'melancholy' and a 'lively sense of his existence'.[66] Many eighteenth-century thinkers believed it was the control of these passions that was a precondition for a modern, commercial, civilized property owning society such as Britain.[67]

The popular press expressed sentiments similar to those later voiced by Gibbon when analyzing the connexion between the British empire and aboriginal peoples. Writers of the period often made explicit connexions between the Roman/barbarian experience and the contemporary British-aboriginal relationship. A correspondent to the *London Journal* told his readers that the establishment of Georgia was an act worthy of the best characteristics of early Rome. He informed the reading public that the British in America could be compared to the ancients because 'the Romans esteemed sending forth Colonies among the noblest of their Works'.[68] Colden compared the Iroquois to the 'greatest Roman Heroes' when it came to 'Love of their Country' or protection of liberty.[69]

In an atmosphere of growing imperial rivalry the public was introduced to a more subtle taxonomy for describing aboriginal groups. Writers tended to give more favourable assessments to groups allied to the British than to the French. The *London Magazine* printed a letter from James Oglethorpe painting a positive image of the pro-British Creek chief 'Tomo-chi-chi'. The letter appealed to public pride in empire with the chief's alleged recognition of British power and a superior sense of

65 Pocock, *Virtue, Commerce and History*, p. 16.
66 *Ibid.*
67 *Ibid.*, pp. 116–18.
68 *London Journal*, No. 684, 5 Aug. 1732.
69 Colden, *History of the Five Indian Nations*, p. v.

humanity. The chief was recorded as explaining the symbolic meaning of the gift of a buffalo skin with the head and feathers of an eagle on it:

> the Eagle signified Speed, and the Buffalo Strength. That the English were swift as a Bird, and as strong as a Beast; since, like the first, they flew from the utmost Parts of the Earth over the vast Seas; and like the second nothing could withstand them. That the Feathers of the Eagle were soft, and signified Love; the Buffalo's Skin warm, and signified protection; therefore he hoped that we would love and protect their little Families.[70]

This type of story served to reinforce the popular conviction that Britain possessed a global empire with a duty to protect its 'wards' while rising to the challenge of its destiny.

British writers constantly returned to the idea that Britain was a nation blessed by providence. Thomas Prince, a Boston pastor, published a sermon celebrating the British victory at Cape Breton and crediting it to God's hand. He also expressed the hope that God would continue to bless British arms 'till He extends His Empire from the Eastern to the Western Sea'.[71] Similarly Thomas Prentice compared the Cape Breton campaign to that of Israel against the king of Canaan. To this end he closely examined biblical text and compared it to events at Louisbourg to show that the hand of 'providence' directed the entire undertaking.[72]

The clergy picked up on the idea that divine providence was at work in British America to promote their activities amongst the various aboriginal groups. The Society for the Propagation of the Gospel in Foreign Parts produced numerous pamphlets describing their activities and highlighting the need to 'civilize' and christianize aboriginal populations. Their analysis echoed that of contemporary historians studying the relationship between 'barbarians' and the Roman empire. Just as the barbarians could not establish 'civil society' until they became sedentary agriculturalists so aboriginal peoples could not truly be converted to christianity until they had adopted a similar lifestyle. In developing a refined taxonomy distinguishing between the different aboriginal societies' semi-sedentary, agricultural and pro-British tribes were described by church interests as the best candidates for missionary activity. Writing for the S. P. G. Humphreys explained that the problems of converting the Mohawk stemmed from 'the roving life' they led. He concluded it was not possible 'to teach them the Christian Religion, before they were in some Degree civilized'.[73] John Bartram gave a much more positive assessment of the Iroqouis but he based it upon the view that agriculture and sedentary habitations were the prerequisite of civil society. He argued that the pro-British confederacy had hope for conversion to protestantism because they practised agriculture and lived in permanent

---

70 *London Magazine*, (Aug. 1733), 400.
71 Thomas Prince, *Mr Prince's Sermon on the taking of Cape Breton* (Boston, 1745), p. 17.
72 Thomas Prentice, *A Sermon Preached at Charlestown* (1745), p. 34.
73 Humphreys, *Historical Account*, p. 304.

villages. The controversialist even compared Onodago, the village acting as the centre
of the Iroquois confederacy, to Baden, political centre for the 13 cantons of
Switzerland.[74]

Within the propagandizing of the S. P. G. one may detect the impact of Rome on
interpretations of the importance of aboriginal civilization to the concept of empire.
John Shebbeare's conviction that the Roman empire collapsed because it strayed from
the path of virtue reflected a widely held concern about the challenge of reconciling
empire with civic virtue.[75] The *Monthly Review* reprinted a short tract denying that
the Iroquois deserved the appellation 'barbarian' and called upon Britons to grasp the
mantle of providence by copying 'those illustrious heros of antiquity ... by
propagating knowledge and useful arts among [the Iroquois] ... [and to] civilize our
pagan friends and neighbours, whose original soil we possess'.[76] Writers were careful
to stress that Britain acquired its American territories by settlement of unoccupied
land and treaty or purchase. Conquest, they argued, was only undertaken when a
particular group threatened British colonists.[77] The purpose of empire was not merely
commercial in nature. As a group of dissenting ministers explained: it was 'Diffusing
freedom and science, political order and Christian Knowledge through those
extensive regions which are now sunk in superstitious barbarism ... imparting even
to the most uncultivated of our species, the happiness of Britons'. Britain, therefore,
possessed its American colonies by virtue of moral duty to its first inhabitants as well
as national self-interest.

The desire to study exotic peoples and apply the lessons learned to British society
was manifest in a growing interest in the North American Indian. Seventeenth-century
philosophers had discussed the evolution of British society with reference to
developmental stages. The Bible provided the anchor for a belief in European
superiority while enlightenment thinkers sought to order knowledge of aboriginal
peoples into a comprehensible package. The concept of the garden of Eden and
natural man were at the heart of enlightenment discussions of civilization. Aboriginal
people were portrayed as living models of the development of civilization over time.
The notion of the noble/ignoble savage provided living examples of man living in a
'state of nature'.

But in many ways the ideas about aboriginal peoples were not new. For hundreds
of years they had served Europeans as living models of 'natural man'. They had
become the central figures in the Edenic myth and the romanticized belief in the very
origins of human development. But what gave power to the debate about the place

---

74 John Bartram, *Observations on the Inhabitants, Climate, Soil Productions, Animals, and Other
    Matters Worthy of Notice* (1751), p. 34.
75 John Shebbeare, *A Letter to the People of ENGLAND, on the Present Situation and Conduct of
    National Affairs. Letter I* (1755), p. 8.
76 *Monthly Review*, VIII (Jan. 1753), 291.
77 Oldmixon, *British Empire in America*, I, 74.

of aboriginal peoples in the 'great map of mankind' was the convergence of the debate about empire, commerce and civic virtue within an expanding arena of public discourse. The consumer revolution had created a reading public whose demand for the lurid and the sensational was balanced by their desire to know the 'other' and their place as a people in a global taxonomy. The notion of the 'other' and a global taxonomy was part of a growing pride in empire and a desire to redefine the concept of Britishness. Aboriginal people became North America's 'representatives' of an increasingly heterogeneous empire.

It was only natural that a nation which had once been part of the Roman empire sought inspiration in the historical examples it could provide. Aboriginal peoples were thus granted the unsolicited role of 'barbarians' in the contemporary play of history. Visual images of the eighteenth century only highlight this point. The Manchester Theatre's performance of a tableau depicting the death of Wolfe included 'an "Indian Prince" kneeling at [the feet of Britannia] resigning up "America"'. Similarly Benjamin West's famous depiction of the death of Wolfe included the figure of 'a noble savage' in the foreground contemplating the heroic death of a 'whiteman'. General Townshend a 'hero of Quebec' had statues of four Indian warriors holding his tomb in imitation of the Roman tradition of having defeated warriors carry the victorious leader through the streets of Rome. Joseph Wright of Derby's 'The Indian Widow' contained the highly romanticized figure of an aboriginal woman in a classical pose 'watching the arms of her dead husband'. The pro-American political satire the 'Deplorable State of America' featured Britannia attempting to give the Stamp Act to 'America' represented by an aboriginal figure.[78] These are but a few of the examples of the culmination of a process by which aboriginal people were established as a powerful icon linking ancient Roman empire with the contemporary empire of Great Britain in a discourse carried out within the arena of the reading public.

78 Kathleen Wilson, 'Imperialism and the Politics of Identity', in *Consumption of Culture*, ed. Bermingham and Brewer, p. 251; Linda Colley, *Britons. Forging the Nation 1707–1837* (New Haven, 1992), p. 179; Hugh Honour, *The European Vision of America* (Cleveland, 1975), pp. 184, 227.

5

Queen Caroline and the Church of England[*]

STEPHEN TAYLOR

The past two decades have witnessed the publication of a number of works which have re-fashioned our understanding of the Hanoverian period, and 'revisionism' has become one of the catchwords of historical debate. One of the most strident and self-consciously revisionist historians has been J. C. D. Clark, who has advanced an interpretation of eighteenth-century England as an *'ancien régime'* society which had 'three essential characteristics: it was Anglican, it was aristocratic, and it was monarchical'.[1] Clark's views have stimulated a great deal of comment and criticism,[2] but in the debate surprisingly little attention has been given to the monarchical element of this trinity. Clark himself has developed his views in this area – borrowing a concept developed to analyse continental European, and especially French, society in the early modern period, he has described eighteenth-century England as a 'court society'.[3] In addition, Robert Bucholz has published an important monograph on the court during the reign of Queen Anne, although his portrayal of that period as crucial to the decline of the court as the centre of political, social, intellectual and cultural life runs counter to the main tendency of Clark's argument.[4] Apart from these works, the importance of the court in eighteenth-century England has been neglected. The only modern scholarly work on the Hanoverian court is John Beattie's study of the reign of George I published in 1967, while those who wish to learn about the political influence of the monarchy have to turn to older works, such as those by Kemp and

---

* I would like to thank Hannah Barker, Elaine Chalus, David Hayton, Clyve Jones and John Walsh for the comments on an earlier version of this essay. The Georgian Additional manuscripts at Windsor Castle were used by the gracious permission of Her Majesty The Queen, and the Pearce Papers by permission of the Dean and Chapter of Westminster.

1 J. C. D. Clark, *English Society 1688–1832. Ideology, Social Structure and Political Practice during the Ancien Regime* (Cambridge, 1985), p. 7.

2 See especially Joanna Innes, 'Jonathan Clark, Social History and England's "Ancien Regime"', *Past and Present*, 115 (1987), 165–200.

3 *The Memoirs and Speeches of James, 2nd Earl Waldegrave, 1742–1763*, ed. J. C. D. Clark (Cambridge, 1988), pp. 1–21. Nicholas Henshall advances a similar argument in *The Myth of Absolutism. Change and Continuity in Early Modern European Monarchy* (1992).

4 R. O. Bucholz, *The Augustan Court. Queen Anne and the Decline of Court Culture* (Stanford, Ca., 1993).

Pares.[5] Good modern biographies of George I and George III do exist, though their existence highlights the neglect of George II, despite the fact that both J. B. Owen and Jeremy Black have suggested that traditional assumptions about that king's lack of political influence are mistaken.[6]

The last 30 years have also witnessed a huge growth of interest in women's history and there has been an enormous outpouring of work in this field. Given this, the lack of interest in George II's wife, Caroline of Ansbach, is all the more surprising. The queen has received almost no attention from historians since the publication of two biographies almost 60 years ago.[7] This neglect reflects a more general neglect of the political role of aristocratic and royal women, as historians have focused on women lower down the social scale and on the domestic sphere rather than the public. As Elaine Chalus has observed, 'political historians have presumed that [women] could not have been political actors and that [their] participation was limited, anomalous and ultimately secondary to men's'. Meanwhile, 'women's historians' have assumed that 'women and politics were mutually distinct categories prior to the suffrage movement', an assumption reinforced by the powerful 'separate spheres model'.[8] It is only recently that some historians have begun to demonstrate how women could exercise considerable influence, and even power, in the political world.[9] In the case of royal women this is most obviously true of queens regnant, a recognized special case in any study of women's political role. Inclination and illness

5 John M. Beattie, *The English Court in the Reign of George I* (Cambridge, 1967); Betty Kemp, *King and Commons 1660–1832* (1959); Richard Pares, *King George III and the Politicians* (Oxford, 1954); *idem, Limited Monarchy in Great Britain in the Eighteenth Century* (1957). In addition, for the reign of George III, see John Cannon, *The Fox-North Coalition. Crisis of the Constitution, 1782–4* (Cambridge, 1969); Ian Christie, 'George III and the Historians – 30 Years On', *History*, LXXI (1986), 205–21.

6 Ragnhild Hatton, *George I. Elector and King* (1978); John Brooke, *King George III* (1972); John B. Owen, 'George II Reconsidered', in *Statesmen, Scholars and Merchants. Essays in Eighteenth-Century History Presented to Dame Lucy Sutherland*, ed. Anne Whiteman, J. S. Bromley and P. G. M. Dickson (Oxford, 1973), pp. 113–34; Jeremy Black, 'George II Reconsidered: A Consideration of George's Influence in the Conduct of Foreign Policy in the First Years of his Reign', *Mitteilungen des Österreichischen Staatsarchivs*, XXX (1982), 35–56.

7 R. L. Arkell, *Caroline of Ansbach. George the Second's Queen* (1939); Peter Quennell, *Caroline of England. An Augustan Portrait* (1939). Very recently, however, John Van Der Kiste has published a popular biography of George II and Caroline. *George II and Queen Caroline* (Stroud, 1997).

8 Elaine Chalus, ' "That Epidemical Madness": Women and Electoral Politics in the Late Eighteenth Century', in *Gender in Eighteenth-Century England. Roles, Representations and Responsibilities*, ed. Hannah Barker and Elaine Chalus (1997), p. 152.

9 In addition to the articles by Chalus cited above and in this volume, see P. J. Jupp, 'The Roles of Royal and Aristocratic Women in British Politics, c.1782–1832', in *Chattel, Servant or Citizen. Women's Status in Church, State and Society*, ed. Mary O'Dowd and Sabine Wichert (Belfast, 1995), pp. 103–13; Amanda Foreman, 'A Politician's Politician: Georgiana, Duchess of Devonshire and the Whig Party', in *Gender in Eighteenth-Century England*, ed. Barker and Chalus, pp. 179–204; *idem, Georgiana, Duchess of Devonshire* (1998); Frances Harris, *A Passion for Government. The Life of Sarah, Duchess of Marlborough* (Oxford, 1991); Elaine Chalus, 'Women in English Political Life, 1754–90', University of Oxford D.Phil., 1997.

may have combined to ensure that the political impact of Queen Anne was limited, a fact which undoubtedly contributed to the real and perceived decline in monarchical power in the early eighteenth century. None the less, significant power and influence continued to reside with the monarch throughout the century. As long as this was the case, the court continued to provide a forum in which political manoeuvring took place, policy was discussed and appointments were influenced and often made. Moreover, since the court was a social arena, not a bureaucratic institution, power was not necessarily an attribute of office, but rather was determined by less tangible criteria, such as personal contacts, especially with the monarch, and possession of information. Because women were as much a part of court life as men, they too could acquire political influence in this world. In this context, popular attention has tended to focus on the role of royal mistresses, and there is no doubt that they could be influential, as a recent study of Charles II's favourite mistress, the duchess of Portsmouth, has revealed.[10] But no one was better placed to acquire and exercise power at court than a queen consort, if she possessed the inclination, commitment and knowledge.

Contemporary commentators agree that Caroline of Ansbach was precisely such a queen consort.[11] This essay, therefore, aims to fill a gap in the historiography by delineating the political influence of Queen Caroline. Or, to be more accurate, it will contribute to filling that gap by focusing on one area of royal activity, the distribution of ecclesiastical patronage. This subject has been touched on before, notably by Norman Sykes. Writing in 1926 Sykes sought to correct the then established orthodoxy, as articulated by Mark Pattison, that between 1727 and 1737 'the ecclesiastical patronage of the crown ... was secretly dispensed by Queen Caroline. For a brief period, liberality and cultivation of mind were passports to promotion in the Church.'[12] Sykes argued 'not only that the influence of the Queen was much less effective than is commonly supposed, but also that her attempt to favour Latitudinarian clergy was largely unsuccessful'.[13] However, as this essay will show, Sykes diminished Caroline's influence too much, and, in so doing, deprecated the still important role of the monarch in ecclesiastical affairs.

---

10 Nancy Klein Maguire, 'The Duchess of Portsmouth: English Royal Consort and French Politician, 1670–85', in *The Stuart Court and Europe. Essays in Politics and Political Culture*, ed. R. Malcolm Smuts (Cambridge, 1996), pp. 247–73.

11 See the accounts of Caroline in John, Lord Hervey, *Some Materials Towards Memoirs of the Reign of King George II*, ed. Romney Sedgwick (3 vols., 1931) and Hertfordshire R.O., Panshanger MSS, D/EP.F205: diary of Mary, Lady Cowper. Lady Cowper's diary was published as *Diary of Mary, Countess Cowper, Lady of the Bedchamber to the Princess of Wales 1714–1720*, ed. Spencer Cowper (2nd edn., 1865). However, the published edition is incomplete, and all references in this essay will be to the manuscript.

12 Mark Pattison, *Essays*, ed. Henry Nettleship (2 vols., Oxford, 1889), I, 109.

13 Norman Sykes, 'Queen Caroline and the Church', *History*, XI (1927), 333–9.

I

There is no doubt about Caroline's interest in religion or her committed protestant-ism. Born in 1683 the daughter of John Frederick, margrave of Brandenburg-Ansbach, she was educated as a lutheran. In 1703–4, however, she was approached as a possible bride for the Archduke Charles, the Austrian Habsburg candidate as king of Spain and future Emperor Charles VI. Initially, she indicated that she was prepared to convert to catholicism, an essential prerequisite to the marriage. But she clearly found her conversations with Father Orban, the Jesuit sent to show her the errors of lutheranism, traumatic, and after much soul-searching she finally decided that she could not accept conversion.[14] The impression was allowed to spread that she had turned down a formal offer of marriage, and Habsburg supporters in Germany could not 'bear the thought of having the King of Spain refused after it was publicly known the Emperor and he had desired the match'.[15] This was an episode of which Caroline herself was very proud. When, shortly after her arrival in England, John Robinson, bishop of London and dean of the chapel royal, waited on the princess 'to satisfie her in any doubts or scruples she cd. have in regard to our Religion & to explain any thing to her, wch she did not fully comprehend', Caroline was 'a little nettled'. She sent the bishop away, remarking to her companions that 'he is very impertinent to suppose yt I who refusd to be Empress for ye sake of ye Protestant Religion dont understand it'.[16] Indeed, Caroline's rejection of the future emperor acquired for her something of the status of a protestant heroine. This image was widely cultivated in England. The dissenter John Evans, preaching on the occasion of the coronation in 1727, hoped that 'her brave refusal to accept the Imperial Alliance at the expence of a good conscience, may inspire this age of indifference with a zeal for true religion', while Alured Clarke, writing after her death, simply drew attention to 'her steady adherence to the Protestant cause'.[17]

Following the death of Queen Anne the lutheranism of the new dynasty was the subject of some controversy, provoking the cry of 'the church in danger', and George I's conduct during church services – 'he omitted to say a silent prayer on entering the Church, he did not kneel down with the congregation, nor did he hold the prayer book in his hand, to follow the service and say the prayers' – did little to allay the fears of high anglicans.[18] The princess of Wales, on the other hand, was noted for her

14 Arkell, *Caroline of Ansbach*, pp. 8–14.
15 Quoted in *ibid.*, p. 14.
16 Hertfordshire R.O., D/EP.F205, f. 12v.
17 John Evans, *The King and his Faithful Subjects Rejoycing in God; and the Mouths of Liars Stopped. A Sermon Preached at Hand-Alley, October the 15th 1727. Upon Occasion of their Majesties Coronation* (1727), p. 21; [Alured Clarke], *An Essay Towards the Character of her Late Majesty Caroline, Queen-Consort of Great Britain, &c.* (1738), p. 17.
18 *A History of the Lutheran Church; Or, The Religion of our Present Sovereign King George Agreeable to the Tenets of the Church of England. Being an Essay to Unite All Good Christians, in Opposition to the Principles of the Church of Rome* (1714); Thomas Brett, *A Review of the*

attendance at daily prayers, and her conduct in chapel was described as the 'devoutest in ye world'.[19] She cultivated a number of English clergy, and within months of her arrival in England it is possible to identify a circle of divines around Caroline at court. Prominent among these was Samuel Clarke, the latitudinarian rector of St James's, Westminster, whose *Scripture Doctrine of the Trinity* expounded a moderate form of arianism.[20] In November 1714 he presented Caroline with copies of his writings, and within days she was praising them as 'the finest things in the world'.[21] Clarke rapidly emerged as one of Caroline's favourites. There were rumours that, during one of Archbishop Wake's illnesses, she prevailed on the king to appoint him archbishop of Canterbury. Even if the truth of that story may be doubted, the fact that it was common gossip in London indicates the high esteem in which Caroline held Clarke, and, after his death, she placed a bust of him in the grotto she created at Richmond.[22] Other latitudinarians were also admitted into Caroline's inner circle. Benjamin Hoadly, the author of the sermon which provoked the famous Bangorian controversy and later the editor of Clarke's *Sermons*, was enjoying audiences of up to three hours alone with the princess in 1716, while in the 1730s the noted arian and advocate of 'primitive christianity', William Whiston, was received at court and described by the queen as 'a sincere, honest man'.[23]

Caroline's connexions with latitudinarian clergy were reinforced by her confidante and mistress of the robes, Charlotte Clayton, later Viscountess Sundon. Mrs Clayton shared Caroline's enthusiasm for religious debate, she corresponded with many divines, and she attempted to use her position to advance their interests. Samuel Clarke appears once more, a prominent figure in Mrs Clayton's correspondence – indeed, on occasion he even acted as an intermediary between her and the princess.[24] Her other friends included many of the most prominent latitudinarians within the Church in the first half of the eighteenth century – Benjamin Hoadly; Robert Clayton, the future bishop of Clogher and author of *The Essay on Spirit*; William Talbot, bishop of Durham, who was reputed to hold views on the Trinity similar to those of

---

Lutheran Principles; Shewing, How Far they Differ from the Church of England (1714); Wolfgang Michael, *England Under George I. The Beginnings of the Hanoverian Dynasty* (1936), pp. 88–9.

19 Michael, *Beginnings of the Hanoverian Dynasty*, p. 89; Hertfordshire R.O., D/EP.F205, f. 12v.

20 On Clarke, see Maurice Wiles, *Archetypal Heresy. Arianism through the Centuries* (Oxford, 1996), pp. 110–34; J. P. Ferguson, *Samuel Clarke. An Eighteenth-Century Heretic* (Kineton, 1976), pp. 83–97; and Thomas C. Pfizenmaier, *The Trinitarian Theology of Dr Samuel Clarke – 1675–1729. Context, Source, and Controversy* (Leiden, 1997).

21 Hertfordshire R.O., D/EP.F205, f. 4.

22 *Bishop Burnet's History of His Own Time*, ed. M. J. Routh (2nd edn., 6 vols., Oxford, 1833), v, 323 note n; H.M.C., *Egmont Diary*, I, 99; Ferguson, *Samuel Clarke*, p. 223.

23 Beinecke Rare Book and Manuscript Library, Yale University, Osborn Shelves f.c.110.2, f. 22: Hoadly to Mrs Clayton, 23 Aug. 1716; H.M.C., *Egmont Diary*, I, 288; II, 188. For Whiston's beliefs, see James E. Force, *William Whiston: Honest Newtonian* (Cambridge, 1985), especially ch. 4; and Wiles, *Archetypal Heresy*, pp. 93–110.

24 Royal Archives, Windsor Castle, Geo. Add. MS 28, no. 54: Caroline to Mrs Clayton, n.d.

Samuel Clarke and to favour clergymen who tended towards arianism; and Alured Clarke.[25]

These networks meant that Caroline acquired the reputation, especially among tories and high churchmen, of being a patron of latitudinarianism and even heterodoxy. William Cole described her as 'the great protectress and encourager of Arianism in this kingdom', and others who shared this view included Sir John Hynde Cotton, the tory M.P. for Cambridge, and Richard Bundy, a royal chaplain.[26] This was precisely the view of Caroline, as the patroness of men of 'liberality and cultivation of mind', which won her the approval of Pattison in the mid-nineteenth century.[27] As will be seen, there is undoubtedly some truth in this portrayal. However, it is far from the whole story. As Archbishop Potter noted, on the basis of his own conversations with the queen: 'however she might screen or favour persons inclined to Arianism, she yet was never fixed in that way of thinking as far as he could discern'.[28]

Mrs Clayton's clerical circle was almost exclusively latitudinarian in character; Caroline's, on the other hand, was always much broader. In the years immediately after the Hanoverian succession one of her closest acquaintances among the clergy was William Wake, the bishop of Lincoln who was translated to Canterbury at the end of 1715. Wake was a whig, but he was firmly opposed to the latitudinarianism of Hoadly and others. The views they expressed in the Bangorian controversy horrified him; they represented a 'libertinism ... the most dangerous of anything to our established church'.[29] But he was also a frequent visitor to the princess of Wales, and, by his own account, he appears to have acted as her spiritual adviser.[30] Indeed, such was his attachment to Caroline that, following the quarrel between George I and his son in 1717, Wake was prepared to sacrifice his political influence by siding with the Waleses.[31] Even more striking is the presence at court of men like George Smalridge, bishop of Bristol and one of the most prominent tory clergy, whom

---

25 Mrs Anthony Thomson, *Memoirs of Viscountess Sundon, Mistress of the Robes to Queen Caroline* (2 vols., 1847), *passim*; Beinecke Library, Osborn Shelves f.c.110.2; Lewis Walpole Library, Farmington, Connecticut, Clarke-Sundon correspondence. For Talbot's views, see William Talbot, *Twelve Sermons Preached on Several Subjects and Occasions* (1725); H.M.C., *Egmont Diary*, II, 136.

26 *Burnet's History of His Own Time*, ed. Routh, v, 323 note n; H.M.C., *Egmont Diary*, I, 262; *The Diaries of Thomas Wilson, D.D. 1731–7 and 1750*, ed. C. L. S. Linnell (1964), p. 216.

27 Quoted above, p. 84.

28 John Chapman, 'Memorandums of Things which I have heard in private from Archbishop Potter's own Mouth, as certain Truths', *Christian Remembrancer*, III (1821), 336.

29 Norman Sykes, *William Wake, Archbishop of Canterbury, 1657–1737* (2 vols., Cambridge, 1957), II, 165: Wake to King, 23 May 1717.

30 Lambeth Palace Library, MS 1770, ff. 161, 162, 164, 167, 169, and *passim*: diary of Archbishop Wake, 11 Aug., 9 Sept., 31 Oct. 1715, 1, 26 Jan. 1716; Hertfordshire R.O., D/EP.F62, ff. 58–9: Wake to Cowper, 25 Dec. 1717.

31 G. V. Bennett, 'An Unpublished Diary of Archbishop William Wake', *Studies in Church History*, III (1968), 258–66.

Caroline described after his death as 'one of the greatest honour to the Bench'. Smalridge's influence was probably limited and brief and, in any event, he died in 1719, but he had enough access to the princess to cause concern to Wake and other whigs.[32] The role of a leading high churchman like Smalridge prefigures the favour shown by Caroline to Robert Freind, the headmaster of Westminster School and former friend of Francis Atterbury, and to Thomas Sherlock. At the time of George II's accession in 1727, Sherlock, who was widely seen as one of the leaders of the tory clergy, had 'oftner access [to Caroline] in private than anyone of the clergy', and he was known to be one of the most influential clergymen in her circle. His favour with the queen subsequently secured for him the promise of the bishopric of London on the assumption that Edmund Gibson would be translated to Canterbury on the death of Wake.[33]

Attracting such an eclectic group of clergymen, the court under Caroline naturally became a centre for theological discussion. Pierre le Courayer, the French priest who wrote a treatise defending anglican orders, was welcomed there. Caroline herself worked to obtain subscriptions for his translation of Sarpi's *History of the Council of Trent*, and, after its publication, she had a long conversation with the earl of Egmont about it, which then developed into a discussion of the reputations of Augustine, Erasmus, Luther, Calvin and Melancthon.[34] Other theological works were also discussed. These included not only the writings of Samuel Clarke, but more minor books, such as Passerini's *Philosophical Discourse upon Death*, which Caroline condemned for destroying 'all distinctions between good and evil, truth and falshood', and ephemeral pamphlets like *The Country Parson's Plea against the Quakers-Tythe Bill*.[35] But possibly the work which made the greatest impression on her was Joseph Butler's *Analogy of Religion*, which she 'spoke much in praise of' and recommended enthusiastically to others. 'She said it was very intelligible. That she had read it and understood it easily. That it was a scheme a Midway between Woolston and Dr. Clark. That he was a little too severe. Expected too much perfection in the world.'[36]

32 H.M.C., *Egmont Diary*, II, 233; Hertfordshire R.O., D/EP.F205, f. 4v; D/EP.F62, ff. 60–1: Wake to Cowper, 27 Dec. 1717.
33 B.L., Add. MS 32703, f. 323: Freind to Newcastle, 23 Sept. 1744; Cambridge U.L., Cholmondeley (Houghton) correspondence, no. 1508: Morice to Atterbury, 2 Jan. 1728; St Andrews U.L., Gibson Papers, MS 5203: Bishop Gibson to Walpole, [Dec.1727/Jan. 1728]; H.M.C., *Egmont Diary*, III, 328; Hervey, *Memoirs*, I, 89; II, 545; Lewis Walpole Library, Weston Papers, III: Sherlock to Edward Weston, 8 Oct. 1743.
34 Thomson, *Memoirs of Viscountess Sundon*, I, 415–16; H.M.C., *Egmont Diary*, I, 92; II, 77, 160, 217, 240.
35 Hertfordshire R.O., D/EP.F205, ff. 4–5; H.M.C., *Egmont Diary*, I, 299–300; II, 254.
36 *Diaries of Thomas Wilson*, ed. Linnell, p. 155; *The Yale Edition of Horace Walpole's Correspondence*, ed. W. S. Lewis (48 vols., New Haven, 1937–83), XX, 167: Walpole to Horace Mann, 2 Aug. 1750.

Some were sceptical about both the extent of Caroline's knowledge and the depth of her understanding. Even her husband 'often used to make a jest of his Queen's intermeddling so much in theological disputes'.[37] There may well be some justification for this. Her response to Bishop Robinson, for example, would suggest that she did not fully appreciate the differences between anglicanism and continental forms of protestantism.[38] Certainly it is difficult to ascertain what Caroline believed. As has been seen, Archbishop Potter was convinced that she never embraced arianism, though others interpreted her words and actions differently. It is clear that she was hostile to calvinism, describing predestination as a 'monstrous doctrine'. This attitude is hardly surprising given her lutheran upbringing, except that she also 'had no great respect for Luther, who was too violent'.[39] Apart from hints such as these, Caroline has left little evidence of her own religious opinions, and the eclecticism of her clerical circle provides us with little further insight. Consequently, it is tempting to agree with Horace Walpole that her beliefs were a mishmash: she 'had no aversion to a medley of religions, which she always compounded into a scheme of heresy of her own'.[40]

Equally, however, this scepticism may be unjustified. Her brusque rejection of Robinson's offer to instruct her in the finer points of anglicanism can be explained in other ways. Caroline almost certainly had a personal aversion to the bishop – he had been one of the British plenipotentiaries at the Utrecht conference, which was widely regarded in Hanover as a betrayal of the electorate. Against the views of her detractors must be set the testimony of others, like Leibnitz and the earl of Egmont, who were clearly impressed by Caroline's intellect.[41] Some of the doubts about her understanding may have been caused by her imperfect grasp of English and her lack of a formal education, which doubtless contributed, on occasion, to some imprecision in her expression of theological concepts. Some people, possibly even including George II, may well have felt that divinity was not an appropriate subject for female discussion. Moreover, if, indeed, her views were a mishmash, and even included some which orthodox clergy may have regarded with suspicion, they were probably not untypical of those of many laymen and women from the upper classes. When she was told that Bishop Smalridge 'was in Dr. Clarke's notions, but had not courage to own it. The Queen replied if the Bishop thought those notions necessary to salvation he did wrong not to own them and even preach them, but if otherwise, he was to be commended for not disturbing the world with them.'[42] She also believed that the 39

---

37 Chapman, 'Memorandums', p. 336.
38 See above p. 85.
39 H.M.C., *Egmont Diary*, II, 260.
40 Horace Walpole, *Memoirs of King George II*, ed. John Brooke (3 vols., New Haven, 1985), I, 45–6.
41 *State Papers and Correspondence Illustrative of the Social and Political State of Europe from the Revolution to the Accession of the House of Hanover*, ed. John M. Kemble (1857), pp. 528–45; H.M.C., *Egmont Diary*, II, 259–60.
42 H.M.C., *Egmont Diary*, I, 233.

articles were 'drawn up with a latitude of opinion left'.[43] Views such as these would suggest that Caroline shared the irenic, undogmatic protestantism which was so common among the laity in mid-eighteenth-century England.

II

It is clear, therefore, that Caroline was a committed protestant (even if her beliefs may have been somewhat idiosyncratic), that she was interested in religious debate, and that, from the time of her arrival in England in 1714, she acted as the focus for an eclectic circle of clergymen. But to say that she had an interest in religion is, of course, very different from demonstrating that she exercised any influence over ecclesiastical policy or church patronage. It is not, however, the intention of this essay to claim that the queen influenced the religious legislation of the Walpole administration. She supported both the government's attempts to repeal the sacramental test in Ireland, and its opposition to similar moves in England.[44] Interestingly, she was initially sympathetic to the Quaker Tithe Bill, which was introduced with Walpole's support in 1736. Later she was convinced that 'it touched the clergy's property' and, like some prominent members of the ministry in the Lords, was pleased to see the bill defeated.[45] But, if her views often reflected those of the ministry, there is no evidence that she made any contribution to the formulation of its policy. There is no doubt that the power of the monarch to determine the legislative objectives of the government had declined markedly since 1688. However, church patronage was a different matter, and the remainder of this essay will explore the often considerable influence which Caroline exerted over the distribution of crown patronage after she became queen in 1727 and assess the impact of her interventions on the religious policy of the whig ministry.

Before doing so it is important to establish the extent of the crown's ecclesiastical patronage. In theory it was quite extensive, as the crown was patron of 9.6 per cent of all church livings in England and Wales.[46] But much of this was vested in people other than the king. The lord chancellor nominated to all livings worth £20 or under in the king's books without reference to the king himself, and further livings were in the hands of the chancellor of the duchy of Lancaster. In fact, only 86 parochial livings were in the gift of the king. But this statistic is misleading, because the king also appointed almost all the most prominent higher clergy, the governors of the Church – all 27 bishops, 25 deans, the canons of Westminster, Windsor and Christ

43 *Ibid.*, II, 260.
44 Thomson, *Memoirs of Viscountess Sundon*, II, 20: Bishop Clayton to Mrs Clayton, n.d.; H.M.C., *Egmont Diary*, II, 254.
45 H.M.C., *Egmont Diary*, II, 254; *Diaries of Wilson*, ed. Linnell, p. 188.
46 D. R. Hirschberg, 'The Government and Church Patronage in England, 1660–1760', *Journal of British Studies*, XX (1980–1), 112–13.

Church, nine of the 12 canons of Canterbury, and the four residentiaries of St Paul's.[47]

As recently as the reign of Queen Anne, it is clear that the monarch herself exercised considerable personal influence in the disposal of patronage. Her ministers placed great weight on securing key preferments for their candidates, but Anne was quite capable of acting without consulting them. She did this most famously in 1707, when she helped to provoke a political crisis by promising the sees of Exeter and Chester to Offspring Blackall and William Dawes, two friends of Archbishop Sharp, her 'spiritual adviser, friend and confessor'.[48] After 1714 George I took less interest in the Church than his predecessor, and, unlike Mary or Anne, he did not seek advice from any of the leading bishops. It became an established convention that church livings in the gift of the king were granted on the recommendation of the king's ministers, and, in particular, of the prime minister and the senior secretary of state. Successive ministries, however, relied heavily on the advice of bishops, and through most of George I's reign it is possible to identify one bishop who filled the unofficial post of 'Church minister'.[49] From the early 1720s this person was Edmund Gibson, bishop of Lincoln and, from 1723, of London. In the latter half of George I's reign all the evidence suggests that the management of church patronage was controlled by three people – Townshend, Walpole and Gibson. In the final analysis, however, the appointments were the king's; ministers only made recommendations. It was George I's inaction which allowed his ministers to monopolize appointments. Later monarchs still retained the right to intervene personally in the disposal of ecclesiastical patronage, and they continued to exercise that right well into the nineteenth century. Consequently, the court remained an arena of some importance in the distribution of ecclesiastical patronage; recommendations could be made there to the king through channels independent of his leading ministers.[50]

III

On the accession of George II in 1727, there was, therefore, plenty of scope for Caroline to make her clerical preferences known and, through the king, to influence

47 These figures have been calculated from John Ecton, *Thesaurus Rerum Ecclesiasticarum. Being an Account of the Valuations of all the Ecclesiastical Benefices in the Several Dioceses in England and Wales* (2nd edn., 1754). The figure of 27 bishoprics includes that of Sodor and Man. The 25 deaneries included those of Windsor, Westminster and Ripon. The deaneries of St Asaph, Bangor and Llandaff were not in the gift of the crown and there was no dean of St David's. A slightly fuller analysis can be found in Stephen Taylor, '"The Fac Totum in Ecclesiastic Affairs"? The Duke of Newcastle and the Crown's Ecclesiastical Patronage', *Albion*, XXIV (1992), 409–33.

48 G. V. Bennett, 'Robert Harley, the Godolphin Ministry, and the Bishoprics' Crisis of 1707', *English Historical Review*, LXXXII (1967), 726–46; Norman Sykes, 'Queen Anne and the Episcopate', *English Historical Review*, L (1935), 433–64.

49 St Andrews U.L., MS 5203: Gibson to Walpole, [Dec. 1727/Jan. 1728].

50 On the role of both the king and the court in the latter part of George II's reign, see Taylor, 'Newcastle and Ecclesiastical Patronage', pp. 419–28.

appointments to church livings. But it would be wrong to suggest that Caroline's influence was merely exerted behind the scenes through her husband. On the contrary, her power was quite remarkable for a queen consort. It was not only the case that, as one might expect, she acted during the king's absences in Hanover and assumed responsibility for appointments in her own household and that of the prince of Wales.[51] But, in addition, George II seems to have been prepared to hand over church patronage to his wife, just as William III had entrusted it to Queen Mary.[52] (Both, by contrast, retained firm, personal control over military promotions.) In the ten years between 1727 and the queen's death, the king was very rarely mentioned in discussions of church patronage. Instead, repeatedly, in correspondence and memoirs, it was Caroline who appeared as the crucial figure. She received recommendations, gave promises, made appointments, and even imposed vetoes on candidates for preferment.[53] From the very beginning of the reign, no one was in any doubt where power lay. When Gibson was asked to submit a list of whig clergy deserving of preferment, he knew that it was 'no less ye Queen's motion because it comes immediately from ye King'.[54] What is more, her role quickly came to be publicly known, William Morice reporting in January 1728 that 'the Queen seems chiefly to manage that Branch' of affairs.[55] At the very least, another partner was added to the triumvirate of Townshend, Walpole and Gibson. If anything, Caroline's influence increased in the last months of her life, following Gibson's 'resignation' as 'Church minister' in the aftermath of the controversy over the Quaker Tithe Bill in 1736. Gibson himself told Thomas Wilson, a clergyman who waited on him in his search for crown patronage, that, though Bishop Potter 'was now consulted with' about these matters, 'the Queen would take the disposal of Church Preferments into her own hands'.[56]

51 Lewis Walpole Library, Weston Papers, II: Gibson to Townshend, 8 July 1729; Thomson, *Memoirs of Viscountess Sundon*, I, 406: Hugh Lewis to Mrs Clayton, 20 Nov. 1729.

52 Like Caroline, Mary had close contacts with a circle of English divines. But, in many ways, Caroline's influence over ecclesiastical patronage is more surprising. Unlike Caroline Mary was English and had been educated as an anglican, thus providing a reassuring contrast with her Dutch calvinist husband. For Mary's control of church patronage and some important reservations about its extent, see W. A. Speck, 'William – and Mary?', in *The Revolution of 1688-1689. Changing Perspectives*, ed. Lois G. Schwoerer (Cambridge, 1992), pp. 137–8 and n. 23.

53 See, e.g., *Diaries of Thomas Wilson*, ed. Linnell, p. 125; Thomson, *Memoirs of Viscountess Sundon*, I, 379–81: duchess of Somerset to Mrs Clayton, 17 Sept. [1728]; Walpole, *Memoirs*, I, 45–6; Lambeth Palace Library, MS 1741, ff. 96–7: Waterland to Gibson, 15 Sept. 1734. On this occasion Gibson clearly assured Waterland that the queen had not put 'an absolute negative' upon his promotion. But an anecdote of Archbishop Potter would suggest that Waterland's suspicions may have been correct, although 'at length, she was quite reconciled to him'. Lambeth Palace Library, MS 1741, ff. 98–9: Waterland to Gibson, 16 Sept. 1734; Chapman, 'Memorandums', pp. 336–7.

54 St Andrews U.L., MS 5202: Gibson to [Walpole?], n.d.

55 William Coxe, *Memoirs of the Life and Administration of Sir Robert Walpole, Earl of Orford* (3 vols., 1798), II, 240: Morice to Atterbury, 2 Jan. 1728.

56 *Diaries of Thomas Wilson*, ed. Linnell, p. 169. See also pp. 177, 181, 186, 204.

How much influence, then, did Caroline have over the disposal of church patronage? Pattison's account, quoted at the beginning of this essay, is an exaggeration. But there is no doubt that Caroline did exercise a degree of influence which was probably greater than that of any other Hanoverian monarch. Some indication of her interest in church affairs and her ability to advance the careers of her favourite clergymen is provided in the early years of the Hanoverian succession. During Archbishop Tenison's last illness towards the end of 1715, Wake was publicly talked of as one of the candidates to succeed him at Canterbury. He was, however, little known to the king, and the dominant 'Junto' of ministers preferred either Talbot or Trimnell as his successor. Even so, three days after Tenison's death Wake was nominated as the new archbishop, and it was generally agreed that the princess of Wales had been instrumental in securing his promotion.[57] A year later Caroline worked with Wake and Earl Cowper to secure the bishopric of Exeter for Lancelot Blackburne.[58] Inevitably, however, the split in the royal family in November 1717 brought Caroline's influence to an end.

Caroline thus only really came into her own after the accession of George II in June 1727. It was widely assumed that the whig regime in church and state would be dismantled, but that did not happen. Just as Walpole and Townshend managed to defeat the challenge from Spencer Compton, so Gibson survived as 'Church minister'. However, whereas Caroline's support was crucial to the survival of Walpole, it was the queen who posed the greatest threat to the continuation of the old regime in the Church. Gibson was in no doubt that 'we and our Conduct' were 'condemn'd' at court, explaining such 'misrepresentation' as the work 'of one [Wake], who thinks we have kept him out of Power for some years; and of two others [Hare and Sherlock], who think we have all that while kept them off the Bench'.[59] Wake did indeed regain some influence in the first weeks of the new reign. In the summer of 1727 Gibson wrote to Newcastle noting that the queen was 'very unwilling' to give 'jealousies to ye Archbp'.[60] But this situation did not last long. His recommendations were ignored, including that of White Kennett for the bishopric of Bath and Wells, and soon he retired once more to Lambeth where he told 'every body he has no interest at court'.[61] One reason for Wake's disappointment was Caroline's marked preference for Thomas Sherlock, dean of Chichester, as her ecclesiastical adviser. For some months Gibson expected that he would be replaced by Sherlock,

57 Bodl., MS Add. A. 269, pp. 40, 43, 49, 52: Edmund Gibson to Bishop Nicolson, 6, 20 Oct., 10, 20 Dec. 1715; Christ Church, Oxford, Arch.W.Epist. xv, f. 39: Wake to Smalridge, 24 Dec. 1715; *ibid.*, ff. 41–2: Smalridge to Wake, 29 Dec. 1715.

58 Hertfordshire R.O., D/EP.F59, ff. 10–11: Countess Cowper to Earl Cowper, [Dec.? 1716]; Christ Church, Arch.W.Epist. vii, ff. 448–9: Wake to George I, 23 Jan. 1717.

59 St Andrews U.L., MS 5203: Gibson to Walpole, [Dec. 1727/Jan. 1728].

60 *Ibid.*, MS 5200: Gibson to Newcastle, [1727].

61 Coxe, *Walpole*, ii, 240: Morice to Atterbury, 2 Jan. 1728; B.L., Lansdowne MS 1016, ff. 23–4: Wake to Kennett, 19 Sept. 1727.

possibly acting in conjunction with Francis Hare, despite the fact that he still retained the confidence of Walpole and Townshend. At one point, Edward Chandler, bishop of Lichfield, was mooted as a possible compromise candidate for the position of 'Church minister', being someone in whom both the queen and the ministry could have reasonable confidence.[62] Ultimately, Sherlock's challenge to the old regime also failed, and the ministry succeeded in retaining the services of Gibson. Between 1727 and 1736 Gibson had little to do with Caroline personally and was never really trusted at court. Nevertheless, he continued to be an influential voice within the ministry and at least three of the twelve bishops created in this period – Tanner, Sydall and Claggett – owed their appointments primarily to him.[63]

These comments reveal clearly the limits to Caroline's power. The dominant voice in the formulation of religious policy, and thus in the distribution of church patronage, was the ministry's. Caroline failed to replace their 'Church minister' with one more to her taste. But this does not mean that, as one commentator suggested, after the early months of the reign 'sir R. W. ... gained his point in relation to church preferments, and ... Her majesty ... consults and does nothing without sir R.'s leave on that head'.[64] One way of gaining a clearer impression of the extent of Caroline's influence is to look at the appointments to bishoprics in the ten years between 1727 and her death in 1737. During that period 13 bishops were created, 12 of them before Gibson's resignation in 1736. In support of his claim that Caroline's influence was very limited, Norman Sykes argued that only three of those 12 owed their position to the queen.[65] One might suggest that, in the context of the decline in the power of the monarchy in the eighteenth century, this was not an insignificant number. It would, for example, be impossible to make a similar claim for George II in the years after Caroline's death. However, if these 13 appointments are examined afresh, there is a strong case for attributing even more influence to the queen.

There is no doubt that Caroline was primarily responsible for the creation of the three bishops attributed to her by Sykes: Sherlock, Hare and Butts. Sherlock's appointment to the bishopric of Bangor will be discussed later.[66] Francis Hare had been a member of Caroline's circle through the mid-1720s and his elevation to the episcopate was demanded by her immediately after her accession on the death of Bishop Hooper of Bath and Wells in September 1727. The ministry, encouraged by Gibson, objected to him succeeding Hooper, on the grounds that it would cause

62 St Andrews U.L., MS 5200: Gibson to Walpole, [1727]; MS 5201: same to same, [1727]; MS 5203: same to same, [Dec. 1727/Jan.1728].
63 All three appear on the list of whig clergy suitable to be made bishops which Gibson prepared at the queen's request in 1727 or 1728. *Ibid.*, MS 5202: Gibson to Walpole, n.d. Sydall was made bishop of St David's in 1731, while Tanner and Claggett were appointed to St Asaph and St David's respectively in 1732.
64 Coxe, *Walpole*, II, 242: Morice to Atterbury, 8 May 1728.
65 Sykes, 'Caroline and the Church', pp. 338–9.
66 See below p. 98.

divisions on the bench if a presbyter was appointed to one of the wealthier sees over the heads of the younger bishops. As a result, Bishop Wynne was translated to Bath and Wells, creating a vacancy for Hare at St Asaph.[67] Robert Butts had been a preacher at Bury St Edmunds, where his assistance in parliamentary elections obtained for him the favour of Lord Hervey. Hervey's influence with the queen secured for Butts first the deanery of Norwich in 1731, and then promotion to the bishopric two years later. This represented a decisive victory for Caroline, since Butts was made a bishop in the face of strenuous opposition from Gibson.[68]

To these three should be added John Harris, who was made bishop of Llandaff in 1729. Harris had close connexions with Caroline having served as dean of the chapel to George II while prince of Wales and then, from 1727, as clerk of the closet to the queen herself. In addition, there is strong evidence that Caroline at least assisted in the creation of two more bishops. Horace Walpole recalled that Thomas Secker was advanced by the queen first 'to the living of St James ... and afterwards to the bishoprics of Bristol and Oxford'.[69] Some caution needs to be expressed about Walpole's account, as Secker himself recalled that Gibson played a part in his appointment to St James's in 1733. But, as Secker was a *protégé* of Bishop Talbot and owed his royal chaplaincy to the support of Bishop Sherlock, both of them rivals of Gibson, it seems likely that his career benefited from some support from both Gibson and Caroline.[70] A similar conclusion is also plausible in the case of Isaac Maddox, who was consecrated as bishop of St Asaph in 1736. Maddox is commonly thought to have owed his preferment to Gibson, on the grounds that Gibson had supported him through university. But he also had a close attachment to Caroline, having succeeded Harris as her clerk of the closet.[71]

There is very little evidence for the other four bishops promoted during this period – Charles Cecil, George Fleming, Martin Benson and Thomas Gooch. Fleming's connexions on the bench – between 1736 and 1739 he deposited his proxy with Gibson or Smalbroke, who wrote a memoir of Gibson – would suggest that he owed his promotion to Gibson. However, there are reasons to suggest that the queen may have had a hand in the appointments of both Benson and Gooch. The latter was Sherlock's brother-in-law, and it is at least plausible that Caroline may have supported the efforts of one of her favourite clergymen to secure preferment for such a close relation. Benson's nomination to the see of Gloucester at the end of 1734 marked the recognition by the court that it could not secure the appointment of Thomas Rundle. Secker noted that Gibson, 'fearing that some Person would be put

67 St Andrews U.L., MS 5194: Gibson to Townshend, [18 Aug. 1724]; MS 5203: Gibson to Walpole, [Dec. 1727/Jan. 1728]; MS 5201: Gibson to Walpole, [1727].

68 H.M.C., *Egmont Diary*, II, 40–1; Hervey, *Memoirs*, II, 532–3.

69 Walpole, *Memoirs*, I, 45–6.

70 *The Autobiography of Thomas Secker, Archbishop of Canterbury*, ed. John S. Macauley and R. W. Greaves (Lawrence, Kansas, 1988), pp. 8–9, 13, 15.

71 *D.N.B.*; Thomson, *Memoirs of Viscountess Sundon*, I, 406.

in, whom he disliked', finally 'insisted ... that Dr Benson should take it'.[72] But there is no evidence to suggest that Gibson saw Benson as *his* candidate. On the contrary, in 1724 Gibson had opposed his appointment as regius professor of history at Oxford because he suspected him of a tendency to toryism. In fact, Benson, like Secker, had been a *protégé* of Bishop Talbot, and it is likely that his nomination to Gloucester was, at least in part, an attempt by the queen to compensate Lord Chancellor Talbot for her failure to fulfil her promise to appoint Rundle.[73]

There is, therefore, good evidence that Caroline was the most important influence behind four of the 13 episcopal creations between 1727 and 1737, that she played a major part in two others, and that she probably had some influence over two more. Moreover, three of these bishops – Hare, Sherlock and Secker – won rapid promotion, to the sees of Chichester, Salisbury and Oxford respectively. Translations were also given to Chandler and Potter. Both of these had remained loyal to Wake after he had lost all political influence in the late 1710s and, like Wake, both had been members of Caroline's circle while she was princess of Wales. Potter's favour with the new king and queen was made clear when they chose him to preach their coronation sermon in 1727.[74] Chandler was translated to Durham in 1730, while, much to Gibson's disgust, Potter was known to have the promise of the archbishopric of York.[75] Blackburne's longevity defeated this plan, but, following the affair of the Quaker Tithe Bill, the court publicly fixed on Potter as Wake's successor, 'a *reversionary Archbishop*', as Gibson described him.[76] In his *Memoirs*, Lord Hervey claimed the credit for persuading the queen to appoint Potter. However true his account may be, there is no doubt that Caroline was just as influential in securing Potter's elevation to the primacy in 1737 as she had been in promoting his predecessor in 1715. As Francis Hare, another candidate for the archbishopric noted, 'What has hitherto appeared in this matter, has arisen entirely from the Q[ueen].'[77]

The final testimony to Caroline's influence is that it extended after her death. In his memoirs, Zachary Pearce recorded that he was made dean of Winchester in 1739 in fulfilment of a promise made by Walpole to the queen shortly before her death that he should have the first deanery to become vacant. In the mid-1730s Pearce had become one of Caroline's favourites and was 'frequently honoured with her conversation at her Drawing-room'. His account of the queen's role in his promotion is the more plausible because he was a close friend of William Pulteney, the leader of

---

72 *Autobiography of Secker*, ed. Macauley and Greaves, p. 15.

73 P.R.O., S.P. 35/50/1: Gibson to ?, 2 June 1724; H.M.C., *Egmont Diary*, II, 23, 137.

74 These three bishops all entrusted their proxies to each other through the 1720s. H.L.R.O., proxy books. See also Coxe, *Walpole*, II, 351: Newcastle to Townshend, 1 Nov. 1725.

75 St Andrews U.L., MS 5285: Gibson to Walpole, 18 Dec. 1733. Gibson's disgust arose primarily from his objection to making promises of livings before they were vacant.

76 St Andrews U.L., MS 5315: Gibson to Hare, [10 Aug. 1736]; *Diaries of Thomas Wilson*, ed. Linnell, pp. 169, 190.

77 Hervey, *Memoirs*, II, 546–8; St Andrews U.L., MS 5316: Hare to Gibson, 12 Aug. 1736.

the whig opposition in the Commons, and thus someone who was hardly likely to benefit from Walpole's patronage.[78] However, few clergymen owed more to Caroline than Joseph Butler. Having made his reputation as preacher of the rolls, by the early 1730s he was 'buried' in comfortable obscurity in the Durham living of Stanhope. But in 1736 Caroline brought him back to London as her clerk of the closet, and from this time he was 'in high favour at Court'. The queen was unable to provide for him before her death in 1737, but she recommended him 'particularly and by name' on her deathbed. The following year he was created bishop of Bristol, retaining both the rectory of Stanhope and a prebend of Rochester *in commendam*.[79]

IV

It is clear from this discussion of episcopal appointments between 1727 and 1737 that Caroline exercised considerable influence over ecclesiastical preferments. Indeed, by comparison with any other Hanoverian monarch her power was quite remarkable. None the less, most of these appointments were relatively uncontentious. In so far as almost all of the recipients of crown patronage in this period were whigs, Caroline's influence was not inconsistent with the main thrust of whig ecclesiastical policy as developed and pursued by Townshend, Walpole and Gibson since the early 1720s. The ministry sought to create a whig church loyal to the Hanoverian monarchy and committed to the revolution settlement in church and state. To this end it confined crown patronage to whigs and low churchmen, while simultaneously trying to reassure the tory and high-church clergy that the Church was safe in whig hands. As Gibson expressed it, 'My great point, was to bring ye body of ye Clergy and ye two Universities, at least to be easy under a Whig Administration.'[80] In some ways, however, Caroline's interventions in patronage represented a threat to this policy. This became apparent immediately after George II's accession, when she made it clear that she wished to bring onto the bench Francis Hare, Thomas Sherlock and Samuel Clarke.[81] Hare has already been discussed. The real objection to him was promoting him immediately to one of the wealthier sees, and his appointment to St Asaph was relatively uncontentious. His whig credentials were impeccable – he had

---

78 'The Life of Dr Zachary Pearce', in *The Lives of Dr Edward Pocock ... by Mr Twells; of Dr Zachary Pearce ... and of Dr Thomas Newton ... by Themselves; and of the Rev. Philip Skelton, by Mr Bundy* (2 vols., 1816), I, 386–92. The quotation has been corrected following the manuscript among Pearce's papers. Westminster Abbey Muniment Room and Library, Pearce Papers, WAM 64856A.

79 *Autobiography of Secker*, ed. Macauley and Greaves, pp. 13, 15; H.M.C., *Egmont Diary*, II, 476; Hervey, *Memoirs*, III, 908.

80 St Andrews U.L., MS 5219: 'My Case in Relation to the *Ministry* and the *Whigs*', n.d. But see also, Norman Sykes, *Edmund Gibson, Bishop of London, 1669–1748. A Study in Politics and Religion in the Eighteenth Century* (1926), chs. 4–5.

81 St Andrews U.L., MS 5201: Gibson to Walpole, [1727].

been Walpole's tutor at university and was an old friend of Townshend.[82] Sherlock
and Clarke, however, were much more controversial candidates, and Caroline's
support for them threatened to undermine whig ecclesiastical policy in two ways.

On the one hand, Sherlock was reputed to be a tory. His promotion would thus
have breached the policy of confining crown patronage to whigs. Even more
seriously, he was known to be one of the queen's closest advisers and it was
suspected that Caroline wanted him to replace Gibson as 'Church minister'. Gibson
warned the ministry of the dangers of 'this new Experiment of Whig in the State and
Tory in ye Ch[ur]ch'.[83] He believed that he would be 'much mistaken, if he [Sher-
lock] be not found at ye head of ye Tory-Clergy in a twelve' month after he is made
Bp'. As far as Gibson was concerned, it mattered little whether or not Sherlock was
the 'favourite': if he was 'they will come to him; if not, he will go to them'.[84] The
ministry did succeed in preventing him from becoming bishop of Norwich, perhaps
fearing for whig influence in the city, but the queen was insistent and early in 1728
Sherlock was nominated to the bishopric of Bangor. The concerns about his toryism,
however, proved to be largely unfounded. He caused a stir in 1729 when he
attempted to fill the list of chaplains to the prince of Wales with tories, and he
continued to remain a patron of tory clergy for many years. But from the time he took
his seat in the Lords, his political conduct was irreproachably whig, and he rapidly
emerged as one of the administration's most prominent advocates on the episcopal
bench, attracting the attacks of opposition politicians for his pro-ministerial speeches
on issues like the Pension Bill of 1731.[85]

In the case of Samuel Clarke, on the other hand, it was theological liberalism
which posed a threat to ministerial policy. Clarke was the most prominent arian, or
semi-arian, in England. His *Scripture Doctrine of the Trinity*, 'a sort of textbook of
modern Arianism', had been complained of in the convocation of 1714, and he had
only saved himself from prosecution by an apparent recantation and a promise never
to preach again on the subject of the Trinity. His elevation to the episcopate,
therefore, would have been greeted with horror by the clergy. Gibson hardly needed
to remind Walpole 'how universally and with what resent such a step would be

82 Hervey, *Memoirs*, II, 547; B.L., Add. MS 32686, ff. 251–2: Newcastle to Bishop Bowers, 6 June
    1723.
83 St Andrews U.L., MS 5200: Gibson to Newcastle, [summer 1727]; MS 5201: Gibson to Walpole,
    [1727].
84 *Ibid.*, MS 5203: Gibson to Walpole, [Dec. 1727/Jan. 1728].
85 Coxe, *Walpole*, II, 240: Morice to Atterbury, 2 Jan. 1728; St Andrews U.L., MS 5203: Gibson to
    Walpole, [late 1727/early 1728]; B.L., Add. MS 32717, f. 38: Pelham to Newcastle, 7 Oct. 1748;
    H.M.C., *Egmont Diary*, III, 328; Cobbett, *Parl. Hist.*, VIII, 847–52; T. F. J. Kendrick, 'The Church-
    Whig Alliance, the Anti-Clericalists and the Government of Sir Robert Walpole, 1727–37',
    University of Toronto Ph.D., 1961, pp. 154–61.

condemn'd by the whole body of ye Clergy, Whig as well as Tory'.[86] Indeed, his promotion could have fatally undermined efforts to convince the clergy that the Church was safe in whig hands. Clarke may have been the queen's favourite clergyman, but the ministry was never going to consent to making him a bishop. On this occasion Caroline was persuaded to drop her proposal, and there is no evidence that it became known publicly. Even so, for the next ten years her patronage of latitudinarian and heterodox clergy continued to create problems for the ministry and to disrupt its religious policy, as the Rundle affair made only too evident.

At the end of 1733 the bishopric of Gloucester fell vacant by the death of Elias Sydall. The new lord chancellor, Lord Talbot, sought to secure the see for his chaplain, Thomas Rundle. On the surface, Rundle appeared an eminently suitable candidate for preferment – not only was he Talbot's chaplain, but he had previously served as chaplain to Bishop Talbot, from whom he had received valuable preferments in the diocese of Durham. Gibson, however, vigorously opposed him. He told Walpole that rumours of Rundle's preferment had 'given very great offence to the Clergy; and I may truly add, that the uneasiness is general, among the Whig as well as Tory part of them'.[87] The fundamental objection to Rundle was his arianism, a charge he made no effort to deny. But, in addition, at the end of December 1733 a London clergyman came forward with reports of conversations some years earlier which made Rundle appear as a freethinker.[88] As a result, the bishopric remained vacant for 12 months, while controversy raged in the press. Talbot and Gibson were portrayed as the leading protagonists, the former standing up for the rights of the laity against the priestly ambitions of the latter.[89] Finally, Gibson emerged victorious. Martin Benson was nominated to the see of Gloucester, while Rundle was compensated with the rich Irish bishopric of Derry in the following February.

The queen's role was barely mentioned in the controversy, but she could be regarded as its cause. She had promised Talbot that Rundle would be promoted to the bishopric, and it appears that she gave this undertaking before Gibson was consulted and possibly without even discussing the matter with Walpole. This engagement was crucial. Caroline may have come to regret it; early in March 1734

---

86 C. J. Abbey and J. H. Overton, *The English Church in the Eighteenth Century* (2 vols., 1878), I, 494; St Andrews U.L., MS 5201: Gibson to Walpole, [1727]; Ferguson, *Samuel Clarke*, pp. 83–97. I have found no evidence to support Coxe's claim that Walpole tried to persuade Clarke to accept a bishopric and the story must be treated with caution. Coxe, *Walpole*, I, 275–6.

87 St Andrews U.L., MS 5285a: Gibson to Walpole, [Dec. 1733].

88 *Ibid.*, MS 5288: Richard Venn to Gibson, 27 Dec. 1733; MS 5286: Gibson to Walpole, [27 Dec. 1733]; H.M.C., *Egmont Diary*, II, 23; Jonathan Swift, 'On Dr Rundle, Bishop of Derry' (1735), in *The Poems of Jonathan Swift*, ed. Harold Williams (3 vols., Oxford, 1937), III, 819–21.

89 Some account of this literature is provided by Stephen Bland, 'The Affair of Dr Rundle. An Examination of Ecclesiastical Patronage under Walpole', University of Cambridge B.A., 1985. See also, Christine Gerrard, *The Patriot Opposition to Walpole. Politics, Poetry, and National Myth, 1725–1742* (Oxford, 1994), pp. 27–31.

the earl of Egmont reported that she was 'puzzled ... what part to take'.[90] But through the year Talbot continued to insist that the promise was fulfilled; he made no secret of the fact that he preferred 'they should send for the great Seal' rather than fill up the bishopric with another person.[91] From the ministry's point of view, Caroline's support of Rundle was far more damaging than her advocacy of Clarke. Not merely was Walpole faced with the unenviable choice between alienating the new lord chancellor or his 'Church minister' – Gibson had made it clear that, if Rundle did become bishop of Gloucester, he would resign.[92] Far more seriously, Rundle's promotion threatened to undermine the ministry's ecclesiastical policy. Such an appointment would have been perceived as the abandonment of its declaration that heterodoxy was a bar to preferment in the Church.[93] If Walpole had any doubt about this, it was removed by the fierce opposition of both Hare and Sherlock to Rundle. Indeed, Gibson very much doubted that it would be possible to find enough bishops to consecrate him.[94] Moreover, the reverberations continued to be felt long after Benson had been nominated to Gloucester. Gibson's position became far more difficult. On the one hand, he was subjected to ever more virulent attacks from whig anticlericals.[95] On the other hand, he became even more sensitive than before to 'the charge of sacrificing the interests of Religion and the Established Church' to his own political ambition.[96] Viewed from this perspective, Francis Hare's comment, in the aftermath of the crisis over the Quaker Tithe Bill, that the 'unhappy affair of Rundle has been ... ye true cause of all ye unhappy misunderstandings that have since followed', appears perceptive.[97]

V

Three points are worth emphasizing by way of conclusion. First, from the time of her arrival in England, Caroline showed great interest in the Church and religious affairs. She gathered around herself a circle of clergymen which was never limited to one party in the Church but embraced a wide spectrum, ranging from tory high churchmen like Thomas Sherlock to advanced latitudinarians like Samuel Clarke. Moreover, she sought to use her position, first as princess of Wales and later as queen, to advance her favourites to positions of power and influence within the Church. In this she was remarkably successful. Two successive archbishops of

90   H.M.C., *Egmont Diary*, II, 49, 23.
91   H.M.C., *Egmont Diary*, II, 136; Lewis Walpole Library, Clarke-Sundon Correspondence: Alured Clarke to Lady Sundon, 15 Dec. 1734.
92   St Andrews U.L., MS 5285a: Gibson to Walpole, [Dec. 1733].
93   H.M.C., *Egmont Diary*, I, 262.
94   *Ibid.*, II, 23; St Andrews U.L., MS 5287: Gibson to Walpole, [1734].
95   See, e.g., the satirical print 'The Parallel: Or, Laud and C-d-x Compared', reproduced in Paul Langford, *Walpole and the Robinocracy* (Cambridge, 1986), p. 123.
96   St Andrews U.L., MS 5285a: Gibson to Walpole, [Dec. 1733].
97   *Ibid.*, MS 5311: Hare to Gibson, 2 Aug. 1736.

Canterbury owed their promotions in large measure to her intervention, while at least four, and possibly as many as eight of the 13 bishops consecrated between 1727 and 1737 can be credited to her influence. Her influence should not, of course, be exaggerated. She could not secure the preferment of clergymen, like Clarke and Rundle, whose liberalism placed them well outside the broad theological consensus which characterized the episcopal bench during the whig supremacy. Nor is there any evidence that Caroline had any influence over the making of the ministry's religious policy. Even so, the cases of Sherlock, Clarke and Rundle make it clear that her interventions in the distribution of crown preferments could have serious repercussions for that policy.

Second, Caroline's ability to influence, perhaps even on occasions to determine, who received crown patronage suggests that commonly accepted interpretations of the limited power of the monarchy in the eighteenth century require some revision. It has long been recognized that the Church was one of the areas in which Hanoverian monarchs could wield 'a significant, and often decisive, influence'.[98] Even so, Caroline, who was, it should be remembered, only a queen consort, was more successful in securing the promotion of her candidates to bishoprics than her father-in-law, her husband after her death, or her grandson. Her success provides some indication of what could be achieved in this field by an informed, politically astute and determined ruler.

Third, this study also suggests that the role of royal and aristocratic women in eighteenth-century politics might merit more attention than it has received hitherto. There is no doubt that such women were exceptional, but, as this examination of Caroline and church patronage reveals, they could play a significant role in politics, especially perhaps in those arenas where power was still exercised in more informal and personal ways. The court, though in decline, was just such an arena, providing access to the king which was not controlled by his ministers. None the less, it should be recognized that Caroline was more exceptional and her power greater than most comparable women – her ability to exert such influence over ecclesiastical preferments stemmed from the fact that her husband was prepared to hand over to her most of his power in this area.

[98] Owen, 'George II Reconsidered', p. 121.

6

The House of Lords and the Fall of Walpole*

CLYVE JONES

Walpole's resignation as prime minister in February 1742 was triggered by the ministry's defeat in the house of commons on 28 January by one vote over the disputed election at Chippenham.[1] In the 20 years of his administration, Walpole had lost other divisions in the Commons, so why did this particular defeat lead to his departure from office? The answer *may* be found in several underlying causes, which one historian has dated as far back as 1733, when Walpole suffered the defeat of his excise proposals.[2] If Walpole's power began to weaken in 1733, the process has been seen by some historians to accelerate at various points: in 1736, the clash with the Church over the Quakers Tithe Bill;[3] in 1737, the disillusionment of the Scots over parliament's treatment of the Porteous riots, the quarrel in the royal family and the going over to the opposition of Frederick, prince of Wales, which strengthened the loose alliance of the tory party with dissident 'patriot' whigs, and the death of Queen Caroline, Walpole's staunchest supporter at Court;[4] the noticeable decline of Walpole's health from 1738;[5] in 1739, the outbreak of war with Spain, which

---

* This essay has benefited from the comments of David Hayton and Stephen Taylor. The Stuart papers were used by the gracious permission of Her Majesty The Queen, the Harrowby MSS by permission of the earl of Harrowby, the Devonshire MSS by permission of the duke of Devonshire and the Trustees of the Chatsworth Settlement, and the Wentworth Woodhouse MSS by permission of the Olive, Countess Fitzwilliam's Wentworth Settlement Trustees.

1 Walpole took the decision to resign on 31 Jan. 1742. There were a further seven defeats in the Commons before he resigned on 11 Feb. J. B. Owen, *The Rise of the Pelhams* (1957), pp. 33–5, 87. See also H.M.C., *Egmont Diary*, III, 247.

2 Reed Browning, *The Duke of Newcastle* (New Haven, 1975), p. 111. For the excise affair see Paul Langford, *The Excise Crisis. Society and Politics in the Age of Walpole* (Oxford, 1975).

3 Walpole's 'ecclesiastical settlement had collapsed in 1736': Browning, *Newcastle*, p. 111 . For the crisis see Stephen Taylor, 'Sir Robert Walpole, the Church of England, and the Quakers Tithe Bill of 1736', *Historical Journal*, XXVIII (1985), 51–77, though the author does not see 1736 as a stepping-stone to Walpole's fall.

4 The Rev. Henry Etough recorded the opinion that the death of Caroline did not seriously weaken Walpole's hold over the king: B.L., Add. MS 9200, ff. 60–1: Etough's history of the reigns of George I and George II to 1745. However, Geoffrey Holmes, 'Sir Robert Walpole', in *idem, Politics, Religion and Society in England, 1679–1742* (1986), pp. 165–6, considered 1737 to be the turning point in Walpole's fortunes.

5 E. A. Spriggs, 'The Illness and Death of Robert Walpole', *Medical History*, XXVI (1982), 421–8. See also *The Letters of Philip Dormer Stanhope, 4th Earl of Chesterfield*, ed. Bonamy Dobrée (6 vols., 1932), II, 401: to Stair, 3 Dec. 1739; H.M.C., *Egmont Diary*, III, 228. To the end, Walpole's health was a cause for comment and concern. Chatsworth MSS (the duke of Devonshire, Chatsworth,

Walpole opposed, exacerbated by resulting disagreement amongst his cabinet colleagues on the conduct of the war,[6] and the public outcry, after some initial successes, against the disastrous progress of the war in 1740;[7] and in 1741, the poor performance of the ministerial whig party at the general election which reduced the ministry's majority in the Commons from 42 in the previous parliament to 18.[8] Though I do not wish to suggest a steady uninterrupted decline in Walpole's fortunes from the mid-1730s, all these factors weakened the underlying structure of the ministry and Walpole's position in it. Thus when war with Spain came, a crisis of unprecedented magnitude, the ministry was in a worse position to deal with it than it might otherwise have been.

It is not the contention of this essay that Walpole's loss of control of the Lords precipitated his resignation, though I hope to show that the upper House was a factor of some importance in the collapse of his administration. One peer, at least, was quite clear in his belief that the Lords did not have the power to bring down a government: 'I could, I confess', wrote the earl of Haddington in 1734, 'never be brought to believe that we are able to put down a minister whose all was at stake and who was not only in great favour but had command of money.'[9] That the Lords did not force Walpole's resignation is clear. None the less, there were signs in the 1741–2 session that the ministry was loosing its grip on the upper chamber,[10] as was witnessed by the serious decline of the ministerial majorities in divisions: from 51 at the end of the 1740–1 session, on a vote on the Austrian Succession, to a low of 12 on 28 January 1742, on a vote on the garrison at Minorca.[11] Though it is arguable that the ministry's position in the Lords may well have been only one reason in Walpole's decision to go, there can be little doubt that events in the upper House do cast light on the problem

Derbyshire), 245.11: Edward Walpole to Devonshire, 9 Jan. 1742.
6 Romney Sedgwick, 'The Inner Cabinet from 1739 to 1741', *English Historical Review*, XXIV (1919), 290–302.
7 Robert Harris, *A Patriot Press. National Politics and the London Press in the 1740s* (Oxford, 1993), pp. 95–115.
8 Owen, *Rise of the Pelhams*, pp. 5–7. *The Life and Correspondence of Philip Yorke, Earl of Hardwicke*, ed. Philip C. Yorke (3 vols., Cambridge, 1913), I, 205, gives 14; while Edward Southwell, M.P. for Bristol, thought 17, though Lord Egmont doubted it was so great. H.M.C., *Egmont Diary*, III, 242 (17 Jan. 1742). Cf. Linda Colley, *In Defiance of Oligarchy. The Tory Party, 1714–60* (Cambridge, 1982), pp. 229–30, which gives 26. All commentators agree that the war of the Austrian Succession was the most important long-term factor in the fall of Walpole. Browning (*Newcastle*, p. 111) dates Walpole's loss of the control of the policy of his administration from 1739.
9 H.M.C., *Polwarth MSS*, v, 85: Haddington to Marchmont, 28 Mar. 1734.
10 See Clyve Jones, 'The House of Lords and the Growth of Parliamentary Stability, 1701–1742', in *Britain in the First Age of Party, 1680–1750. Essays Presented to Geoffrey Holmes*, ed. Clyve Jones (1987), p. 91.
11 Low majorities had been reached in 1739 (seven on 19 Feb. on the South Sea Company Directors) and 1740 (eight on 27 Mar. on the state of the nation), but these had been in poorly-attended Houses. The ministry had quickly recovered by pulling in supporters for crucial votes and by 1741 the low majorities were a thing of the past. However, the low majorities in early 1742 were in well-attended Houses and, as we shall see, the government was unable to retrieve the situation.

of confidence in the ministry and Walpole's management in the final crisis of his administration. The collapse of ministerial support in the Lords parallels that in the Commons. It is the purpose of this essay to trace the reasons for these shrinking majorities in the Lords, and to assess the importance of the upper house in the Walpolean parliamentary system.

I

The war with Spain proved to be significantly different from any of the previous crisis faced by Walpole. It created a source of tension and conflict in the ministry, in parliament, and in the country at large, which could not be removed by Walpole's own actions. That the collapse of confidence in the ministry's handling of the war did not affect Walpole's position more quickly than it did was due partly to the disunity of the opposition. In 1740, the earl of Chesterfield, a senior figure in one faction and considered by some as the central figure of the opposition, lamented that '[t]he Opposition is, in truth, become no Opposition at all ... [for] [t]he views of the individuals are too different for them to draw together ... [and] [i]n this distracted state of the opposition, you will not be surprised that nothing is done, and the Court triumphs'. The earl's only comfort was in the next election, from which he was in 'hopes of having a better Parliament'.[12] That election, however, was not due for another year, and, despite the fact that the misconduct of the war not only began to alienate public opinion but also to strain relations within the ministry, the opposition, split into two factions, seemed powerless throughout the session of 1740–1. At the beginning of that session one faction wanted to give 'no opposition to the Address, nor to the supplies that should be asked, but afterwards to express our dislike of last year's conduct [of the war]'; the other wanted 'to oppose the Address directly the first day in both Houses; to say we had complimented long enough, and that it was now time to represent and remonstrate'.[13] This latter, more aggressive policy was eventually adopted by the opposition, but its culmination – motions in the Lords and Commons in February 1741 to address the king to remove Walpole – failed in each case by substantial majorities.[14] These defeats were the result of a walk-out in the Commons by many opposition members and of support for Walpole in the Commons and Lords by some of the opposition who disagreed with the tactics employed by their own side.[15] The continuing fissiparous nature of the whig opposition in the

12 *Letters of Chesterfield*, ed. Dobrée, II, 404–5: to Stair, [May, 1740]. William Pitt certainly thought that Chesterfield was central to the success of the opposition. P.R.O., (Chatham papers) 30/8/6, ff. 28–33: three draft letters to Chesterfield, [July–Aug. 1741].
13 *Letters of Chesterfield*, ed. Dobrée, II, 433–4: to G. Lyttelton, 5 Nov. 1740.
14 The majority in the Lords on 13 Feb. 1741 was 49: opposition 47 present, plus 12 proxies; ministry 89 present, plus 19 proxies.
15 E.g., in the Lords 'We had Lord Oxford zealously with us in both Questions, and the Duke of Leeds, and Benson and Secker 2 [whig] Bishops [of Gloucester and Oxford] who are generally against us'. National Library of Scotland, MS 16584 (Fletcher of Saltoun MSS), ff. 51–2: Ilay to [Milton], 14

Lords was further illustrated on 9 April 1741 when, upon an address over a subsidy to the queen of Hungary, Chesterfield claimed that he and the duke of Argyll forced a division largely to reveal the weakness of the Carteret whig faction in the opposition.[16] The result was a thumping majority for the ministry of 51 (76 to 25), many opposition peers failing to support Argyll and Chesterfield.

As a consequence Chesterfield, bearing in mind the continuing split and the lack of preparation of the opposition, looked forward to the 1741–2 session of parliament with foreboding.[17] However, by the time he returned to England from France in early November 1741 his outlook had begun to change: '[t]he minority is a considerable and a willing one; and if we can frustrate the designs of some few, who want to divide and weaken it, some good, I think, may be done'.[18] Indeed, some on the ministerial side viewed the coming session with trepidation, the premier's son forecasting 'greater violence the moment the Parliament meets', and later, after it had met, that 'this winter is to be all ups and downs'; while the earl of Ilay prophesied that it would be 'a very warm session'.[19] The cause of this change in attitude was undoubtedly the opposition's success in the spring general election.

II

A clue to the importance of the Lords in the fall of Walpole may lie in the prime minister's comment, at his resignation, to the duke of Devonshire: 'To give your grace a short view of this revolution, I must inform you that the panick was so great among what I should call my own friends, that *they all* declared my retiring was become absolutely necessary with honour and security &c.'[20] An influential number of these friends would have been some of Walpole's cabinet colleagues who, with one exception besides Walpole, were all members of the Lords. Such men may have been

---

[Feb. 1741].

16 *Letters of Chesterfield*, ed. Dobrée, II, 448–9: to Marchmont, 24 Apr. 1741. The split amongst the opposition whigs continued into the 1741/42 session with Chesterfield, Argyll and others not being supported by Carteret. See, e.g., Nat. Lib. Scotland, MS 16585, f. 284: [John Maule, M.P. and Ilay's secretary] to [Milton], 5 Dec. 1741.

17 This was despite at least one meeting held in hopes of 'healing the breach the motion made last Session, and animating our friends to attend and act with spirit and unanimity in the next'. *Letters of Chesterfield*, ed. Dobrée, II, 450, 476–7: to Marchmont, 24 Apr. 1741; to Lyttelton, 19 Oct. 1741 n.s. This meeting of opposition 'friends' took place in Oxford on 18 Aug. 1741 and included Lords Lichfield and Gower, and the M.P.s Lord Quarendon and Sir James Dashwood. P.R.O., 30/8/33/69–70: Gower to William Pitt, 17 Aug. 1741.

18 *Letter of Chesterfield*, ed. Dobrée, II, 480: to Marchmont, 12 Nov. 1741.

19 *The Yale Edition of Horace Walpole's Correspondence*, ed. W. S. Lewis (48 vols., New Haven, 1937–83), XVII, 171, 250: Walpole to Horace Mann, 19 Oct., 24 Dec. 1741; Nat. Lib. Scotland, MS 16584, f. 82: Ilay to [Milton], 24 Sept. [1741]. Horace Walpole, in his letter of 19 Oct., indicated that his father was depressed by the coming session.

20 William Coxe, *Memoirs of the Life and Administration of Sir Robert Walpole, Earl of Orford* (3 vols., 1798), III, 592. The italics are in the original. The earl of Wilmington confirmed to Egmont that Walpole went 'unwillingly, but his friends prevailed on him' to go. H.M.C., *Egmont Diary*, III, 248.

panicked by the collapse of the ministry's majority in the Commons, but proceedings in the upper chamber are also likely to have had an effect on them as they struggled to keep the ministry afloat in increasingly stormy seas.

One problem was that the ministry was rent with faction almost as much as the opposition. We must not make the mistake of thinking that Walpole totally dominated his own administration, a picture painted by opposition propagandists. In many ways he was only *primus inter pares*, even though policy and management were guided by him until almost the very end. The ministry was not monolithic, being made up of a coalition of interests, including several significant political figures whose views had to be taken into consideration.[21] In 1740 the earl of Egmont, 'one of the shrewdest of political observers in Walpole's time',[22] noted '[t]hat there are three parties in the Court': first, the prime minister's own 'posse', which included the dukes of Devonshire (lord lieutenant of Ireland) and Grafton (lord chamberlain of the household); secondly, a connexion headed by the duke of Newcastle (secretary of state for the south) and Lord Hardwicke (lord chancellor), the only other political heavy-weights in the cabinet, who both favoured a more trenchant foreign policy than Walpole; the third was headed by the earl of Wilmington (lord president) and the duke of Dorset (lord steward). Perhaps significantly, Lord Harrington (the secretary of state for the north, and nominal 'leader' of the house of lord) stood outside these factions, for he was 'so indolent [that] he joins himself to none'.[23] The presence in the cabinet of Wilmington and Harrington well illustrates one of the limits of Walpole's power. The former's alienation from the prime minister had increased when he failed to succeed Walpole as premier in 1727 on the accession of George II, as was almost universally expected. Wilmington, however, remained (as did Harrington) a favourite of the king and thus Walpole was unable to remove him from the cabinet.

The division within the cabinet which probably led to the most tension, however, was that between Newcastle and Lord Hervey. Newcastle, a ponderous, though on occasions an effective performer in debate, disliked the wittier and more eloquent Hervey, a dislike which turned to intense jealousy when Hervey was promoted to the post of lord privy seal against Newcastle's wishes. In the autumn of 1739 Newcastle considered 'withdrawing from the administration' if Hervey gained the office.[24] Newcastle regarded himself as the real leader of the ministry in the Lords, and had

21 Stephen Taylor, 'Robert Walpole, First Earl of Orford', in *A Biographical Dictionary of British Prime Ministers*, ed. Robert Eccleshall and Graham Walker (1998). This point, especially in relation to Walpole's control of the house of lords, was noted by A. S. Turberville, *The House of Lords in the XVIIIth Century* (Oxford, 1927), pp. 232–3.

22 Owen, *Rise of the Pelhams*, p. 12.

23 H.M.C., *Egmont Diary*, III, 141.

24 *Life of Hardwicke*, ed. Yorke, I, 232: Newcastle to Hardwicke, 14 Oct. 1739. Hervey's 'unprincipled and profligate *Clich*', in the words of the Rev. Etough, consisted of the M.P.s Stephen and Henry Fox, Thomas Winnington and Charles Hanbury Williams, who formed 'a separate Phalanx' and 'gave Sir Robert a great deal of trouble, but after his retreat from Office, they thought it advisable to be the most violent and outrageous Walpolians'. B.L., Add. MS 9200, f. 211 (original emphasis).

probably done so since the resignation of Townshend in 1730. He considered Hardwicke the only other member of the cabinet with a claim to such a leadership – both men being employed 'in preparing business for the House of Lords'[25] – though, as lord chancellor, Hardwicke posed no political threat. In late 1739, however, the duke did regard Hervey's proposed elevation as a threat to himself and Hardwicke, fearing that Hervey 'would go one step further and set him[self] quite at the head of the House of Lords'. If this came to pass, Hervey and 'all his *little click*' would be able 'to be an immediate check, both in Council and in Parliament, upon those who may ever have presumed ... to have differ'd from them'.[26] Hervey's promotion finally took place in April 1740, and Newcastle's relations with Walpole deteriorated so badly that, by mid-January 1742, he and the prime minister were obliged by the king to make up, at least 'in appearance'.[27] It is likely that this was no more than a public reconciliation and that privately the relationship was unchanged. Among other things, Newcastle's fears could only have been strengthened by the elevation to the peerage of Hervey's close friend Stephen Fox, as Lord Ilchester, in May 1741. Fox, Henry Bromley (raised to the peerage two days earlier as Lord Montfort) and John Howe (raised as Lord Chedworth the day after Fox) had the reputation of being useful speakers in the Commons.[28] Their elevation almost certainly was an attempt by Walpole to boost the performance of the ministry in the Lords (as had been those of Hardwicke, Hervey and Talbot in 1733). Indeed, Henry Fox described his brother's elevation to the Lords as taking place 'at a very seasonable Juncture'.[29]

Well before 1742 the secretary of state for the north had become regarded as the nominal leader of the Lords.[30] Until his resignation in 1730 Townshend, as secretary of state for the north, appears to have occupied that position. He was succeeded as secretary (and possibly as leader of the Lords) by Harrington, with Newcastle remaining as secretary for the south, a position he had occupied since 1724. Certainly the annual pre-sessional meetings of pro-ministerial lords (the organization of which has been taken as indicating who was leader of the House) were held in Harrington's office.[31] Harrington, because he had the king's favour, was a powerful figure within

25 *Life of Hardwicke*, ed. Yorke, I, 276: Newcastle to Hardwicke, 10 Jan. 1742.

26 *Ibid.*, p. 230: same to same, 14 Oct. 1739. There is some evidence that Walpole initially may not have supported Hervey's promotion, but was prevailed upon by the king. If true, this throws an interesting light on Walpole's supposed dominance of the ministry, particularly as the same report gives two other instances of the king thwarting Walpole's wishes. Perhaps significantly, Walpole was reported as 'in a bad state of health' at the time. H.M.C., *Egmont Diary*, III, 140.

27 H.M.C., *Egmont Diary*, III, 238, 243, 244 (quotation: 18 Jan. 1742). Egmont's information came from Newcastle's brother-in-law, Sir John Shelley, M.P.

28 Romney Sedgwick, *The House of Commons, 1715–1754* (2 vols., 1970), I, 492; II, 49, 155.

29 B.L., Add. MS 51417, ff. 76–7: H. Fox to Ilchester, 17 Dec. 1741.

30 Jones, 'Lords and the Growth of Political Stability', pp. 97–8; Clyve Jones 'The Origins of the Leadership of the House of Lords Revisited', *Historical Research* (forthcoming).

31 J. C. Sainty, 'The Origins of the Leadership of the House of Lords', *Bulletin of the Institute of Historical Research*, XLVII (1974), 53–73.

the ministry, able on at least one occasion to change the plans of the cabinet unilaterally.[32] From the surviving evidence, however, he seems to have had a lower profile within the house of lords than many of his cabinet colleagues. Indeed, Newcastle once wrote, with perhaps pardonable hyperbole, that Harrington 'scarce ever speakes his opinion in Council and never says one word in Parliament'. The duke also claimed that Wilmington took 'no share in the debates'.[33]

As well as this possible uncertainty within the ministry about the 'leadership' of the house in the late 1730s and early 1740s, the poor performance of key ministers in the Lords may also have weakened the ministry there.[34] Thus the imposition of a 'loose cannon' in the form of Lord Hervey may have further damaged the perception, by both supporters and opponents, of the ministerial team in the Lords at a crucial time for Walpole's administration. Newcastle himself confessed during the 1741–2 Christmas recess that 'nothing is yet thought of, or at least, determined for us to do in the House of Lords, on the State of the Nation' due to be debated in mid-January. He wrote pessimistically to Hardwicke that 'I believe (as things are going) your Lordship and I, shall not be employed very often, for the future, in preparing business for the House of Lords; or advising measures of administration'.[35] Hervey himself was to be absent for more than half of the sittings of the house in December 1741 and January and February 1742. Though reported as ill during this period, it is possible that his absences were due to his uneasy negotiations with the opposition. As Horace Walpole put it, Hervey 'lives shut up with my Lord Chesterfield and Mr Pultney [a leader of the opposition whigs in the Commons], a triumvirate who hate one another more than any one they could proscribe had they the power'.[36] Hervey's absence (or possible abstention) on 19 January from the crucial division on the state of the nation

---

32 *Life of Hardwicke*, ed. Yorke, I, 228: Newcastle to Hardwicke, 28 Sept. 1739. Walpole eventually was able to restore the original cabinet plan.

33 *Ibid.*, pp. 228, 230. For Wilmington see also H.M.C., *Egmont Diary*, III, 250; Horace Walpole, *Memoirs of King George II*, ed. John Brooke (3 vols., New Haven, 1985), I, 30; John, Lord Hervey, *Some Materials Towards Memoirs of the Reign of George II*, ed. Romney Sedgwick (3 vols., 1931), I, 174. Though there is evidence of Harrington and Wilmington speaking in debates, and sometimes crucially (see, e.g., Nat. Lib. Scotland, MS 16585, ff. 238–9, 284: [J. Maule] to [Milton], 16 Jan. 1741, 5 Dec. 1741; Harrowby MSS [the earl of Harrowby, Sandon Hall, Staffordshire], Vol. 1195A: Dudley Ryder's Political and Parliamentary Notes, 4 Dec. 1741), the majority of reports of debates show that the intervention of Harrington and Wilmington was rare and that the bulk of the defence of the ministry in the late 1730s and early 1740s was carried by Cholmondeley, Hardwicke and Newcastle. By Jan. 1742, however, one report claimed that 'Lord Harrington is become a great Speaker'. Hertfordshire R.O. (Panshanger papers), D/EP.F20: John Savage to [Cowper], 30 Jan. 1741[–2].

34 E.g., Newcastle on 22 Dec. 1741 and Hervey on 28 Jan. 1742. See Hertfordshire R.O., D/EP.F20: Savage to [Cowper], 24 Dec. 1741, 30 Jan. 1741[–2].

35 *The Correspondence of the Dukes of Richmond and Newcastle, 1724–50*, ed. T. J. McCann (Sussex Record Society, LXXIII, 1984), p. 81: 9 Jan. 1742; *Life of Hardwicke*, ed. Yorke, I, 276: Newcastle to Hardwicke, 10 Jan. 1741[–2].

36 *Walpole's Correspondence*, ed. Lewis, XVII, 275–6: Walpole to Mann, 7 Jan. 1742. For Hervey and the opposition see also *Letters of Chesterfield*, ed. Dobrée, II, 476: to Lyttelton, 9 Oct. 1741 n.s.

(see Appendices 1 and 2), could be interpreted as symptomatic of a deep malaise within the ministry. His behaviour would certainly have reinforced the message to the opposition in the Lords of division, weakness and confusion at the heart of government; and what was most damaging was that Hervey was known to be close to the king.

In an earlier essay, I outlined the case for there having been a collective leadership of the Lords by the mid-1730s, comprising Harrington (against whom the lack of evidence demands there be a question mark), the earl of Cholmondeley (Walpole's son-in-law), Newcastle, Hardwicke, Ilay (in charge of Scottish affairs, but who, in the early part of the 1741–2 session, while attending, was too ill to be involved in debates) and the prime minster himself.[37] More evidence has since emerged to show that Walpole was indeed closely involved in the running of the house,[38] but none has yet been found for his involvement in the 1741–2 session. We must be careful not to place too much emphasis on this lack of evidence, but if Walpole was not much involved in the management of the Lords between December 1741 and February 1742, all his time and energy being taken up with attempts to manage the Commons, it may be a further pointer to the breakdown of ministerial control in the upper chamber. This could only lead to the opposition exploiting such a situation, and Walpole's supporters, faced by the serious difficulties of the ministry, possibly questioning the administration's viability.

III

Besides a handful of defections from the ministry to the opposition, there were two major factors for Walpole's loss of control over the house of commons in January and February 1742: first, his reduced majority resulting from the general election in the spring of 1741 (which further declined as contested election cases went against him), and secondly, the fact that towards the end many erstwhile supporters absented themselves, enabling the opposition to overwhelm his declining majority.[39] As Walpole's son observed on Christmas Eve of the M.P.s absent from Westminister, '[t]he time is a touchstone for wavering consciences'. The three week Christmas

---

37 Jones, 'Lords and the Growth of Parliamentary Stability', pp. 98–101. For Ilay's illness in Dec. 1741, see Nat. Lib. Scotland, MS 16586, ff. 163–4: Somervile to [Milton], 22 Dec. 1741.

38 See, e.g., (1) tactical interventions in debates – Royal Archives, Windsor Castle, Stuart papers 206/106: T. Carte to D. O'Brien, 4 May 1738; H.M.C., *Carlisle MSS*, p. 117; (2) the organization of proxies – Sheffield City Lib., Wentworth Woodhouse Muniments, M3/7, 58: R. Sutton [?] to [Malton], 8 Feb. 1736; Walpole to [Malton], 6 Nov. 1739; (3) appearance 'incognito' to exert moral pressure – *Life of Hardwicke*, ed. Yorke, I, 194; (4) canvassing for the election of the Scottish representative peers – P.R.O., S.P. 36/2/145: Richmond to [Townshend], 13 Aug. 1727; (5) canvassing the support of absent and doubtful lords – B.L., Add. MS 33002, f. 404; 33034, ff. 1–3, 21–4; 35876, ff. 86–7; 47000, ff. 111–12.

39 Owen, *Rise of the Pelhams*, pp. 20–6, 34; see also Coxe, *Walpole*, III, 588: Walpole to Devonshire, 23 Jan. 1742.

recess would prove crucial, he thought, for '[a]ll depends upon the practises of both sides in securing or getting new votes during the recess', and indeed much 'trafficking deeply for votes during the holidays' went on.[40] Was what was true for the Commons also true for the Lords?

In June 1741, George Bubb Dodington, M.P. for Bridgwater and a leading oppositionist, buoyed up by the results of the general election of the previous month, was convinced that 'the state of our country depends upon the behaviour of the parliament', but confined his optimism to the house of commons for it was 'one of the crimes of this administration, which has almost irretrievably disabled one of the hands given for our defence [i.e. the house of lords]'. Presumably, though he did not say so, Dodington was referring to the corrupting patronage of offices and pensions and, possibly, the elevation of unsuitable men to the peerage. Lord Chesterfield, three months later, was in agreement with Dodington: '[a]s to our most flagitious house, I believe you agree there is nothing to be done in it; and for such a minority to struggle with such a majority, would be like the late king of Sweden's attacking the Ottoman army at Bender, at the head of his cook and his butler'.[41] This pessimism of the opposition seemed amply justified, when on 4 December 1741, the second day of the session, on the division on the address, the ministry's majority was 45 (88 to 43). Reporting this victory, Horace Walpole wrote that it came 'with some converts'.[42] Thus at the beginning of the session, it seems some lords were moving *to* the administration *from* the opposition. However, the next division, only five days later on the 9th, over a motion by the tory Bathurst for a day to consider the state of the nation, the majority was only 14, though in a much smaller house of 74 (44 against 30).[43] On 22 December there were two further votes, concerning the foreign policy of the government, in which the administration majorities recovered somewhat to 27 (59 to 32) and 30 (60 to 30).[44] However, three days before these two divisions, Lord Ilay (a politician of long experience, having sat in the Lords since 1707) thought he perceived a growing equality of parties in the house, reminiscent of the days of King

---

40 *Walpole's Correspondence*, ed. Lewis, XVII, 251, 253, 271–2: Walpole to Mann, 24 Dec. 1741, 7 Jan. 1742.

41 Coxe, *Walpole*, III, 566, 581: Dodington to Argyll, 18 June 1741; Chesterfield to Dodington, 8 Sept. 1741 [n.s.?]. The reference to the late king of Sweden is to Charles XII who was killed in 1718.

42 Unfortunately, while giving the majority as 41, Walpole gives no details of how many 'converts' or who they were. *Walpole's Correspondence*, ed. Lewis, XVII, 231: Walpole to Mann, 10 Dec. 1741.

43 No further lords had taken the oaths by 9 Dec., so the same forces were theoretically available as on the 4th – 93 to 46, plus two doubtfuls (calculated from attendance figures in *L.J.* and the record of support in Appendix 1). Thus 47 per cent of the ministry's potential supporters voted on 9 Dec. as against 65 per cent of the opposition's. For Bathurst moving the motion, see Hertfordshire R.O., D/EP.F250: Savage to [Cowper], 11 Dec. 1741.

44 By 22 Dec. one further ministerial lord had taken the oaths (giving a total of 94), but a further five opposition lords had (a total of 51): in the first of two votes on 22 Dec. 62 per cent of the ministry's supporters voted as against 63 per cent of the oppositions; on the second vote the figures were 64 and 59 per cent respectively. Thus between 9 and 22 December the ministry's performance was improving, while the opposition's was declining.

William III and Queen Anne.[45] Indeed, the three divisions which took place between the end of the Christmas recess on 14 January and the fall of Walpole did seem to indicate such a shift as Ilay perceived. The ministry's majorities, two on the state of the nation and one on an aspect of foreign policy, were 24 (19 January 1742), 16 (26 January) and 12 (28 January). The important difference between these declining majorities and the low one of 14 on 9 December 1741 was that they all took place in well attended sittings – 130, 128 and 126 lords respectively voted in person, which suggests that the opposition's ability to sustain voting numbers was greater than the ministry's.

As we have seen, the opening of a parliamentary session in the Lords was normally preceded by a meeting of ministerial supporters, at the house or the office of the northern secretary of state. Here the government's tactics would be outlined, the speech from the throne read, and agreement reached on who should move and second the address. Such a meeting did take place on 3 December 1741.[46] The 141 lords who took the oaths on the first two days of the session was an unusually large number, so we can perhaps assume that a good number attended this pre-sessional meeting.[47] However, an attendance figure of 141 was never quite reached at any of the sittings of the House. A significant number of lords registered proxies shortly after the opening of parliament and either did not sit again[48] or attended infrequent-

45 Nat. Lib. Scotland, MS 16584, ff. 105–6: Ilay to [Milton], 19 Dec. 1741. Uncertainty amongst leading ministerial peers is evident from Ilay's earlier forecasts in Oct. of a majority of 20, and in early Dec., after parliament's first sitting, of 40. *Ibid.*, ff. 86, 103: Ilay [to Milton], [–] Oct. 1741, 3 Dec. [1741].

46 Because the parliament was newly elected in 1741, the first day of the session in the Lords (1 Dec.) was occupied with the taking of the oaths. The first day of business was on the second day (4 Dec.), thus what would normally have been the 'pre-sessional' meeting took place on 3 Dec. Huntington Library, San Marino, California, ST 57 (Stowe papers), vol. 55, p. 309: [Chandos] to Harrington, 3 Dec. 1741.

47 Four peers (Bathurst, Carlisle, Grafton and Mansel) are recorded as sitting on 1 Dec. though recorded as taking the oaths only on 4 Dec., while one (Bruce) is recorded as taking the oaths on the 1st but not sitting. Sandwich is recorded as sitting on 1 Dec. and later, but is never recorded as taking the oaths. (This error also applies to the bishop of Hereford who first attended on 16 Dec. and continues to attend regularly but is not recorded as taking the oaths. *L.J.*, XXVI, 15.) The Commons also saw a large number of M.P.s sworn in on the first day – 513, which, according to William Hay, was 'a greater Number than ever had been known'. *Tory and Whig. The Parliamentary Papers of Edward Harley, 3rd Earl of Oxford, and William Hay, M.P. for Seaford, 1716–1753*, ed. Stephen Taylor and Clyve Jones (Parliamentary History Record Series, I, Woodbridge, 1998), p. 167.

48 Blackburne, archbishop of York, and Huntingdon and Crawford registered proxies on 2 Dec. and never sat again (though the proxy book indicates that Crawford vacated his proxy by his presence, it gives no date, and the *Journals* show he did not attend again this session); while Gibson, bishop of London, registered his proxy on 3 Dec. and never sat again. Poulett and Stamford registered proxies on 8 and 14 Dec. and never sat again (H.L.R.O., proxy books, XVII).

ly.[49] The largest number appearing on any one day before Walpole's fall was 137 on 19 January.[50]

High attendance figures usually betoken both a high level of interest among members and good organization by the ministry and opposition. The larger than normal attendance throughout most of December 1741 and January 1742 was no exception.[51] Attendance at the beginning of the session of 1741–2 was higher than at the beginning of any of the sessions in the years immediately preceding.[52] This may have been partly because the 1741–2 session was the first session of a new parliament, and the larger attendance figures may have been accounted for by the need for the members of the Lords to take the oaths before they could sit. Also, and perhaps more importantly for some, the oaths had to be taken before any peer or bishop could register a proxy, something the ministry or opposition would hope for from its supporters who could or would not attend. However, leaving that factor aside, the large attendance figures of 89 for the last sitting day before the Christmas recess, and of 79 and 137 on the first and second sittings days in January 1742 after the holiday, point to the beginning of this session as being a period of crisis in the Lords.[53]

The sense that members of the Lords were taking a higher level of interest in proceedings at the beginning of the 1741–2 session than was normal so early in a parliament is also shown by the proxy records.[54] It was normal for a number of proxies to be registered before the house met, but this was not possible prior to the 1741–2 session, as proxies could not be entered until a lord had taken the oaths in person in the chamber, it being the first session of a new parliament. The 38 proxies entered between the opening of parliament and the Christmas recess, however, was

---

49 E.g., Bishop Butts of Ely, who was a protégé of Hervey and to whom he owed his preferment, registered his proxy on 17 Dec., having only sat on 1 and 4 Dec., and vacated it by attending on 1 Feb. (the proxy book mistakenly gives the date as 18 Feb.). Thereafter he attended irregularly on a further ten days, only registering proxies between 13 and 20 May and from 31 May until the end of the session on 15 July. H.L.R.O., proxy books, XVII; *L.J.*, XXVI, 3, 5, 49, 55, 69, 74, 83, 87, 89, 90, 96, 115, 129, 160. Salisbury took the oaths on 19 Jan. 1742, failed to support the ministry in the vote, and left his proxy on the 20th and never sat again.

50 *L.J.*, XXVI, 33.

51 There was also a high attendance level in the Commons. On 21 Jan. 1742, 508 were present at a division which, according to William Hay, was '[a] fuller House than anyone remembers', an assessment with which Edward Harley agreed. *Tory and Whig*, ed. Taylor and Jones, pp. 54, 175.

52 Although 115 lords are recorded as taking the oaths on 1 Dec. 1741, 119 are recorded as attending. *L.J.*, XXVI, 3–5. On the second full day of business 132 attended. The figures for 1740–1 were 106 and 77; for 1739–40, 110 and 52; for 1739, 106 and 74; for 1738, 102 and 78; for 1737, 85 and 51; and for 1736, 94 and 44.

53 In 1740–1 the figures were 48 (pre-Christmas sitting), and 72 and 87 (first two in January), while in 1739–40 they were 53, and 32 and 50. The sources for the figures in notes 52 and 53 are *L.J.*, XXIV, 436, 438, 445, 568, 573–4; XXV, 3, 8, 11, 158, 161–2, 277, 281, 426, 429–30, 444–6, 535, 541–2, 558–9; XXVI, 3–4, 5–6, 22–3, 33.

54 The following information about proxies comes from H.L.R.O., proxy books, X (1735) – XVII (1741/2).

a low figure compared with the two immediately preceding sessions: 69 in 1740–1 and 53 in 1739–40. This figure of 38 proxies entered does point to a higher level of political activity and interest in December 1741 than in the equivalent period in previous years, for fewer lords seem to have been tempted to stay away. It was normal to regard the pre-Christmas sittings both as a dead period and as an inconvenience, as peers usually had to return to their families and country estates for the festivities within a few weeks of arriving in London. That a higher level of attendance than normal was maintained into the new year of 1742 is also indicated by the fact that 17 of the 38 proxies entered in December were vacated between 14 January (the first sitting after the Christmas recess) and the 19th when the first post-Christmas division took place.

An analysis of the political stance of those who left their proxies shows that 15 of those 17 who vacated their proxies between 14 and 19 January were ministerial supporters. Thus it might be assumed that ministers were pulling out all the stops to gain maximum attendance for their side (and there is evidence of a tactical meeting of ministerial lords at Harrington's on 18 January).[55] However, because only two opposition peers vacated their proxies, does this mean the opposition's organization was poor? Certainly in the eighteenth century the opposition's political organization tended to lag behind that of the ministry, one reason being that the opposition did not have the financial resources open to government. Also, historically the tories (who in 1741 formed the bulk of the opposition) were less well organized than the whigs.[56] On both the ministerial and the opposition sides a high attendance was the key to victory, and an organization capable of getting members to Westminster, and *keeping them there*, was crucial to success.[57] The leaders of the opposition, particularly Chesterfield and Dodington, were alive to these problems. Earlier Dodington had urged that '[t]he most eminent amongst us should call us together, countenance us, and enliven our meetings', but even he knew that old habits die hard and did not expect Argyll, the recipient of his letter, 'considering where you are [Scotland], [and] the fatigues you have gone through', to be 'among those who I think ought to meet with all convenient speed'. Dodington suggested that the most prominent available lords of the opposition – Oxford, Thanet, Cobham, Gower and Bathurst – get together (Chesterfield at that time being still abroad, 'and poor lord Carlisle's family employs him too disagreeably'). Dodington was prepared to 'make a visit to lord Bathurst or Bruce', carrying Argyll's instructions. This was written on 18 June, in the flush of excitement after the opposition's gains in the general election. By 3 July,

---

55 Hertfordshire R.O., D/EP.F250: Savage to [Cowper], 18 Jan. 1741[/2].

56 See Geoffrey Holmes, *British Politics in the Age of Anne* (1967, rev. edn. 1987); Colley, *In Defiance of Oligarchy*.

57 Dodington also urged opposition attendance. Coxe, *Walpole*, II, 569: to Argyll, 18 June 1741. In the event, the opposition's attacks turned out to be very effective. See, e.g., Carteret on 22 Dec. 1741 and Argyle on 28 Jan. 1742. Hertfordshire R.O., D/EP.F250: Savage to [Cowper], 24 Dec. 1741, 30 Jan. 1741[/2].

having gone up to London and 'found no body of consequence but Mr. Pultney and Lord Carteret', Dodington had less confidence: Pulteney was unwilling to act, saying that he 'was weary of being at the head of a party' and 'thought a fortnight before the session would be time enough'.[58] Dodington concluded that he himself would 'never meddle with affairs either in or out of the house' without Argyll's commands; that he would return to Dorset 'from which I shall not stir, ... till the day before the session'.[59] Argyll, on the other hand, *was* prepared to do his bit, intending to leave Scotland in early September and travel to Oxfordshire to see Cobham and Bathurst.[60] Chesterfield, though agreeing with Dodington on the necessity of having 'meetings to concert measures some time before the meeting of parliament', also saw 'insurmountable difficulties' in the form of '[f]ox hunting, gardening, planting, or indiference, having always kept our people in the country, till the very day before the meeting of parliament', a habit which he had been endeavouring unsuccessfully to overcome for the past seven years.[61] In October 1741, only six weeks before parliament met, Chesterfield was complaining that 'though I have often pressed it, I could never get them [the opposition leaders] to meet in town till two or three days before the parliament'. None the less, upon his return to England in early November, he began urging supporters to hurry to London, perhaps sensing that victory might be within the opposition's grasp: '[t]he minority is a considerable and a willing one; and if we can frustrate the designs of some few, who want to divide and weaken it, some good, I think, may be done'.[62]

Indeed, there was whipping by the opposition, particularly as it became clear that the ministry's position was weakening. At least two meetings of opposition politicians took place in December, and one in early January, where tactics were discussed.[63] As a result the opposition maintained a better attendance record than the administration. However, by 19 January 1742 (the crucial debate on the state of the nation which first showed a rapid decline in the government's majority in the Lords) only 55 opposition lords had taken the oaths,[64] whilst the ministry by the same reckoning had 98

58 Pulteney apparently changed his mind. Between July and October 1741 he toured England and Wales holding meetings with local tories and opposition whigs. Colley, *In Defiance of Oligarchy*, pp. 230–1.

59 Coxe, *Walpole*, III, 572, 575–6, 578: Dodington to Argyll, 18 June, postscript 3 July 1741.

60 *Ibid.*, p. 578: Argyll to Dodington, 15 August 1741.

61 *Ibid.*, pp. 580–1: Chesterfield to Dodington, Spa, 8 Sept. 1741.

62 *Letters of Chesterfield*, ed. Dobrée, II, 477, 480: to Lyttelton, 19 Oct. n.s., to Marchmont, 12 Nov. 1741.

63 Coxe, *Walpole*, III, 582; *Walpole's Correspondence*, ed. Lewis, XVII, 243; Royal Archives, Stuart papers 239/58: A. Cockburn to J. Edgar, 11 Jan. 1741/2. See also Archibald S. Foord, *His Majesty's Opposition, 1714–1830* (Oxford, 1964), p. 209.

64 Thirty-seven had taken the oaths on 1 Dec. 1741, nine on the 4th, two on the 22nd, one on 14 Jan. 1742, and five on the 19th. To these should be added Sandwich who was sitting but appears not to have taken the oaths (see above, note 47). *L.J.*, XXVI, 4–6, 8, 15, 32–3. 'Theoretical supporters' means that on their past record up to the start of the 1741–2 parliament (see Appendix 1) they should have voted with the opposition.

supporters.[65] This should have given the government a majority of 43 rather than the 24 it had on 19 January; and the majority was to sink further to 16 and 12 on 26 and 28 January.

IV

In the Lords, as in the Commons, absenteeism by ministerial supporters was more significant than desertions to the opposition. If those lords who on their past record (from Appendix 1) could be considered potential government supporters are compared with those voting on 19 January 1742 (the last division list we have for Walpole's regime), we find 37 who did not vote (see Appendix 2). Of these, 13 had not taken the oaths,[66] but five had valid reasons for not doing so: Ancaster and Bishop Weston of Exeter had recently died; Devonshire was in Ireland as lord lieutenant; Hopetoun was ill in Scotland and died soon after; while Hyndford was abroad as envoy to Prussia. Of the remaining eight who had not taken the oaths, two took them later: Lauderdale on 20 January and Bishop Peploe of Chester on 18 February. Ill health and infirmity may account for some of the remaining six. However, far more significant to the ministry's fortunes in the upper House were the 24 lords (see Appendix 2) who had taken the oaths but did not vote on 19 January (15 of whom had left proxies).[67] Perhaps most significant of all were the seven officeholders who did not vote,[68] of whom Lord Privy Seal Hervey stands out.[69]

If the opposition is analysed in the same way, 19 potential supporters did not vote, of whom 10 had taken the oaths.[70] In turn, of these 10, five (Brooke, Burlington, Macclesfield, Rockingham and the prince of Wales) appear to have abstained (see Appendix 3).

---

65 Seventy-seven had taken the oaths on 1 Dec., 16 on the 4th, and four on 19 Jan. To these should be added the bishop of Hereford who sat from 16 Dec. but who appears not to have taken the oaths. *L.J.*, XXVI, 4–6, 8, 15, 32–3. Two peers who were considered doubtful had also taken the oaths on 1 and 4 Dec.

66 Ancaster, Clarendon, Dartmouth, Devonshire, Hopetoun, Hyndford, Lauderdale, Leicester, Say and Sele, Trevor, and Bishops Peploe of Chester, Weston of Exeter and Wynne of Bath and Wells. See Appendix 2.

67 Six of this 15 had left proxies after the call of the house on 16 Dec. 1741 to attend after the Christmas recess, and one of these, Percy, had left his with Brooke, an opposition peer who, in the event, did not vote. See Appendices 2 and 3; H.L.R.O., proxy books, XVII.

68 Seven in section 2 and Hervey in section 3 of Appendix 2. Five of the eight had left proxies (one, Holderness, since the call of the House).

69 He was present on the day but is not recorded as voting, thus he either abstained or left the chamber before the vote. On the list for the division on 19 Jan. 1742 whoever was marking a presence list (possibly Newcastle) with two series of running numbers (one for the pros and one for the cons) as the lords voted started to write the number 4 against 'Ld Privy Seal [Hervey]', abandoned it and marked 'Ld Steward [Dorset]' with a 4. B.L., Add. MS 33034, f. 71.

70 As things turned out only one other lord (Lauderdale, a new Scottish representative peer who was regarded as probably doubtful) took the oath (on 20 Jan.) before Walpole resigned.

Thus, of the 98 ministerial supporters who could have voted on 19 January, Walpole had at the time of the vote lost 24 per cent of his strength; the opposition with 55 potential voters had lost 18 per cent.Clearly the support of the administration was declining at a faster rate by 19 January than the opposition's, and continued to do so in the two later divisions on 26 and 28 January when the majority dropped to 16 and 12 respectively (though we have no division lists to enable us to analyse this decline exactly). This loss of supporters must have greatly disturbed the leaders of the ministry in the Lords.[71]

Besides the absentees there were also deserters from ministry to opposition. The division list for 19 January shows none at this stage, with the possible exception of Bishop Egerton (see below). However, other sources reveal at least two (Dudley and Lymington), who voted against the ministry on 28 January when the majority slumped to 12.[72] There may also have been other desertions which were not recorded. But even if there were no more, the ministerial leaders in the Lords may have wondered how many more there might be. A few deserters similar to Dudley, Bishop Egerton and Lymington might have been tolerated by the ministry without the loss of its majority in the Lords. However, on 9 February Lord Egmont reported a conversation with Lord Lovel, whom he described as 'a creature of Sir Robert's', in which Lovel

> owned the Lords were falling off, particularly the Duke of Dorset and Duke of St. Albans. He added, that it was suspected the Earl of Islay, although he pretends much zeal for the Court, played false in causing such a strange pack of Scotch Lords to be elected this Parliament, and so many Commoners who have deserted Sir Robert, ... that the Duke of Dorset is a creature of Lord Wilmington and always hated him [Walpole].[73]

Clearly this analysis partly refers to the jostling for position immediately prior to Walpole's resignation, but it also applies to the period before. Dorset and St Albans were officeholders; Dorset was in the cabinet and close to Wilmington, who was a favourite of the king and, in the event, Walpole's successor. The loss of Dorset, on

---

71 A comparison of the 131 lords attending on 4 Dec. 1741, when the ministerial majority in a division was 45, with the 128 attending (though only 126 voted) on 28 Jan. 1742, when the majority was 12, confirms that a higher absentee rate by supporters of the ministry than the opposition and a better attendance rate by the opposition than the ministry, rather than abstentions and defections, were the two most important factor in the decline of the ministerial majority in the Lords. Between 4 Dec. and 28 Jan. the ministry's vote declined by 19 from 88 to 69 while the opposition's increased by 14 from 43 to 57. On 28 Jan. there were 20 lords attending who had not done so on 4 Dec., and of these four were ministerial supporters while 16 were supporters of the opposition or were considered doubtful by the ministry. The other side of the coin is that there were 23 lords present on 4 Dec. who were absent on 28 Jan., of whom 17 supported the ministry and six the opposition or were doubtful. *L.J.*, XXVI, 5–6, 46.

72 Coxe, *Walpole*, III, 591: Hartington to Devonshire, 30 Jan. 1741–2 (gives Lymington); Hertfordshire R.O., D/EP.F250: Savage to [Cowper], 30 Jan. 1741[–2] (gives Lymington and Dudley).

73 H.M.C., *Egmont Diary*, III, 249. Hervey confirms Dorset's hatred of Walpole. *Memoirs of George II*, ed. Sedgwick, I, 174

top of the large number of absentees, might have been a potentially crippling blow to the administration in the Lords.

Lovel's comments on Ilay and the Scottish members of the Lords is of interest. Ever since the first general election in 1708 following the Anglo-Scottish Union, ministries had exercised careful control over which representative peers were returned. Even though occasionally, as in 1713, a ministry could not always determine all those who appeared on the official list, only once in 1722 had a peer (Aberdeen) been elected who was not on such a list, and there is evidence that Aberdeen had a measure of favour from some ministers.[74] Once elected the representative peers were usually kept in order by places and pensions, but sometimes (often over Scottish issues) they broke ranks and voted against the ministry or withdrew support by absenting themselves. They were also apt to be late arriving for a session, distance, travelling conditions, and poverty being the excuses. Buccleuch and Bute, two of the replacements elected in 1734 for the four representative peers dropped by the ministry for opposition to the 1733 excise scheme and the 1734 dispute over the election of Scottish peers, were themselves in constant opposition by the late 1730s. They in their turn were dropped from the king's list in 1741 and failed to be re-elected, along with Atholl who was also dismissed (though he continued to sit in the Lords by his English title of Lord Strange inherited in 1737). Cathcart, first elected in 1734, had died in December 1740 and had not been replaced. These four 'vacancies' were filled at the 1741 election by Home, Lauderdale, Moray and Somerville – presumably the 'strange pack' referred to by Lovel, the other 12 representative peers remaining the same. Of the 16 elected in 1741 only a few, apart from Ilay, represented the higher social ranks of the Scottish peerage, and none, apart from Ilay, Dunmore and Hopetoun had more than ten years experience in the Lords.[75]

Ilay, who was in charge of Scottish affairs under Walpole and had at one time been labelled 'the Scots W[al]p[o]le',[76] was in something of an equivocal position in 1741–2. Apparently a loyal supporter of Walpole since the 1720s, he was the supreme political survivor, with the requisite qualities of ruthlessness, deviousness, and ultimate loyalty to himself, family and clan. He had been placed in a somewhat invidious situation in 1739 when his elder brother, the duke of Argyll (an effective debater in the Lords), finally deserted the ministry for the opposition where he became a leading and influential figure. The 1741 general election saw limited gains in the Commons in Scotland for the opposition as a result of Argyll's defection.[77] This

---

74   See 'The Letters of Lord Balmerino to Harry Maule, 1710–13, 1721–22', ed. Clyve Jones, in
       Miscellany XII (Scottish History Society, 5th ser., VII, 1996 for 1994), pp. 116–20.

75   See, J. C. Sainty, *A List of Representative Peers for Scotland, 1707 to 1963, and for Ireland, 1800
       to 1961* (H.L.R.O. Memorandum No. 39, 1968). On the social side, Somerville, though the twelfth
       peer of that title, could not compare with the replaced Buccleuch, who had extensive estates, a
       dukedom, and was the great grandson of Charles II.

76   Scottish R.O. (Mar and Kellie papers), GD 124/15/1431: [Cleland] to [Grange], 21 Mar. 1734.

77   Owen, *Rise of the Pelhams*, pp. 7–8.

could only have weakened Ilay's position both in Scotland and within the ministry. Lovel's comment may also have reflected a more general unease and dissatisfaction in the administration with Ilay, though apparently it was not shared by Walpole.[78] However, Ilay's sense of self-preservation may have led him to question his position and loyalty to the ministry, as Hervey and Dorset may have been doing. The loss of only some of the votes of the Scottish peers in the Lords could have been critical to the ministry. In the event the vote on 19 January shows that 11 of the 16 representative peers voted for the ministry; all five who did not vote were absent (only two of whom, Crawford and Portmore, had left proxies).[79] Three of the four new peers elected in 1741 voted for the ministry, while Lauderdale had not yet taken the oaths.

Besides gains in the number of M.P.s in Scotland at the 1741 election, advances also had been made in Cornwall by the opposition, where the electoral influence of the prince of Wales had been used against the government. He had 21 followers, including 19 placemen, in the Commons,[80] but only two placemen in the Lords.[81] His influence, however, undoubtedly spread wider than the number of his direct supporters. As heir to the throne, the prince might succeed at any time. In the uncertainty of a major political crisis, such as that of 1741–2, his position undoubtedly carried weight and influence. After he had rejected Walpole's last-minute attempt in January 1742 to win over his support and that of his followers in the Commons his stand must have been crystal clear, especially to any waverers. Indeed it was reported in mid-January that 'the Prince's refusal to return to Court unless Sir Robert Walpole be dismist, ... has fixt several members of the opposition, who were wavering on suspicion that the Prince might be prevailed on to accept conditions from his Majesty'.[82]

Though the prince is not recorded as voting against the ministry – he abstained on 19 January (see Appendices 1 and 3) – he was clearly regarded as an opponent (see Appendix 1), and his record of attendance (when compared with that of the previous session of 1740–1) is instructive. In 1740–1 Frederick attended 13 sittings out of 73. Five of these 13 attendances were associated with formal occasions, when

78 See the evidence of the Rev. Henry Etough, who was close to Walpole, quoted in *ibid.*, p. 8. See also B.L., Add. MS 9200, f. 211v.

79 Hopetoun was dying in Scotland, Hyndford was on an embassy in Prussia, and Lauderdale only took the oaths on 20 January. However, Hopetoun had been regarded in a mid-January forecast as a doubtful supporter of the ministry, while Lauderdale had so been forecast, but had then been crossed off the list. See Appendix 1.

80 Owen *Rise of the Pelhams*, pp. 8, 79.

81 Scarbrough was treasurer to the prince's household, and North was a gentleman of the bedchamber. John Chamberlayne, *Magnae Britanniae Notitia* (1741), pp. 257–8. By the end of 1742 the earls of Halifax and Darnley (Lord Clifton in the English peerage) had both become gentlemen of the bedchamber. *Ibid.* (1743), pp. 225–6. Cf. A. N. Newman, 'The Political Patronage of Frederick Lewis, Prince of Wales', *Historical Journal*, I (1958), 73, where he states that at this time there were three peers in Frederick's household.

82 H.M.C., *Egmont Diary*, III, 240: 14 Jan. 1742. For Walpole's approach to the prince, see Owen, *Rise of the Pelhams*, p. 79.

he accompanied the king who passed bills, delivered a speech or pronounced prorogation. Of the rest, some were certainly political appearances, coinciding with major opposition protests and the attack on Walpole on 13 February 1741. In 1741-2 he attended 12 times out of 88 sittings; but apart from three attendances at formal occasions with his father, all the other attendance were before Walpole's resignation. He took the oaths on 22 December 1741 and attended on the first day after the Christmas recess (14 January) and thereafter on seven out of the 12 sittings before the fall of the great minister, including three of the four occasions on which a division took place.[83] There can be little doubt that his presence was designed to encourage waverers to support the opposition or, at least, not to support the ministry.

Finally a word needs to be said about the bishops, that bloc of 26 votes, which traditionally in the eighteenth century has been seen as subservient to the ministry. By 1742, 19 of the 26 bishops owed their initial appointment to Walpole, and six of the remaining seven had been promoted by him to richer sees. From 1723 to 1736 these episcopal troops had been well disciplined by Edmund Gibson, bishop of London. The first major revolt by the bench occurred in 1736 over the Quakers Tithes Bill, when all 15 bishops present voted against the ministry. This bill also led to the rupture of relations between Gibson and Walpole. Though the bishop remained loyal to the ministry, he never again attended the Lords during the life of the ministry, other than to take the oaths, giving his proxy to a colleague of known ministerial loyalty. Gibson's unique position as ecclesiastical supremo was never filled, and, while clerical patronage passed to Walpole and Newcastle, parliamentary management of the bench largely lapsed. Towards the end of the ministry a group of four or five bishops were to be found on occasions in opposition to the administration. On 19 January 1742 only 14 bishops voted for the ministry, while four – Benson, Egerton, Reynolds and Smalbroke – voted against. Of these, Benson, Reynolds and Smalbroke had a history of opposition, but Egerton appears to have voted for the first time against Walpole (see Appendix 1).[84] This small but significant weakening of the bishops' support, yet another straw in the wind, was detected early in 1742 by Newcastle.[85]

83 *L.J.*, XXV, 535–664; XXVI, 3–160.
84 The remaining eight bishops were absent from the vote, of whom four – Blackburne, Butts, Gibson and Hoadly – left proxies. See Appendix 2. Of the four remaining absentees, Weston had recently died, Hough and Wynne were probably too ill or fragile to attend, while Peploe did not attend until 18 Feb. See also Stephen Taylor, 'The Bishops at Westminster in the Mid-Eighteenth Century', in *A Pillar of the Constitution. The House of Lords in British Politics, 1640–1784*, ed. Clyve Jones (1989), pp. 143–4.
85 See his assessment of six bishops as doubtful. Column 4, Appendix 1. The political impact of nearly a quarter of the parliamentary active episcopal bench in January 1742 voting against the ministry over secular matters, a rare occurrence since the days of Queen Anne, should not be underestimated.

V

Absenteeism (plus a few abstentions), rather than a mass desertion to the opposition, was the reason for the rapid decline in the ministry's majorities in the Lords early in 1742. This paralleled what was happening in the Commons. Indeed the lower House, through the family connexions and political interests of the peerage, may possibly have been influenced by the upper House. Further, in the Lords a significant number of absentees (and one possible abstainer who was a member of the cabinet) were officeholders, and these lords who voted with their feet must have had an effect on the house as a whole and on the calculations of the ministerial leadership as to the survival of Walpole. The 'domino effect' may have come into play in the collapse of confidence in the prime minister: once one or two lords showed their hand others followed, and, if he had not resigned, the trickle might have turned into a flood. Thus perception (a factor historians have become increasing aware of as important in historical change) rather than reality may have played a part; perception that the end of the regime might be nigh. This, combined with battle fatigue after 20 years of supporting the prime minister, might well have been enough to bring Walpole down. As the Revered Etough, who was close to Walpole, put it,

> [t]he number of those who exerted themselves in his cause was more considerable, than what had before appeared, on a like trying occasion [presumably the attempt to gain Walpole's dismissal in 1741], but the same uniformity, vigor, and constancy, especially where numbers on each side are nearly equal, is not so natural to those, who are on the defensive, as to those who are stimulated by fierce and eager appetites.[86]

It is clear, however, that there were several underlying reasons which could have weakened the resolve of ministerial supporters in the upper House.

Sir John Shelley, M.P. and brother-in-law of Newcastle, reported to Egmont in early January 1742 that 'a rebellion or civil war' might break out if 'the Parliament is obstinate to have Sir Robert Walpole out, [and] the King is not less determined not to part with him'. Egmont affirmed that the nation did not want Walpole, and that the sense of the nation could not be judged by court members in parliament, 'who are engaged by places, pensions and expectations to support Sir Robert'. Egmont thought rebellion rather than civil war more likely, 'because a few hot headed men are able to raise one ... in hatred to the Minister'.[87] Were Shelley and Egmont expressing a more widespread fear of civil disturbance? The centenary of the English civil war had fallen in 1741 and the fear of a return to '41 was part of the long political memory shared by many politicians of the early eighteenth century.[88] More significant, given his closeness to the self-confessed leader of the Lords, is that Shelley may have been expressing Newcastle's fears as well as those of other ministerial peers.

---

86 B.L., Add. MS 9200, f. 145.
87 H.M.C., *Egmont Diary*, III, 236–7: 9 Jan. 1742. Shelley repeated his fears on 14 Jan.: *ibid.*, p. 240.
88 Langford, *Excise Crisis*, pp. 17–18; *Tory and Whig*, ed. Taylor and Jones, p. 213.

Besides these forebodings among the political *élite*, Egmont's diary also gives the historian further reasons as to why some peers might have turned against Walpole's regime. In a conversation with Lovel on 9 February, Egmont said 'it could not fail but the Lords would fall off, because he that paid their pensions must have them'.[89] In other words, some peers holding patronage from the ministry, detecting a change in the wind, may have decided to trim their sails in relation to a possible new source of patronage should the prime minister fall. The absenteeism of some officeholders gives some credence to this idea.[90]

A second reason may have been a general desire to see the end of parties. William Hay, a ministerial M.P., in March 1742 wrote in his journal 'that all Party distinctions were to be at an end'.[91] Lovel, in conversation with Egmont, said, of a major player in the opposition, that 'the Duke of Arguile's plan is to extinguish party names, and lay the foundation of government so large or broad, that all who have opposed the Court may find their account in it, and a lasting peace at home be fixt for 20 years to come'. The end of party was a cry that went back to at least the beginning of the century, and had been given wide circulation in the 1720s and 1730s by the opposition writings of Lord Bolingbroke. However, if Lovel, a firm follower of Walpole, thought that Argyll's 'plan was good if it could be executed', such a utopian ideal might well have appealed to the less committed peers, who might have then absented themselves to help bring it about. Lovel, on the other hand, went on to argue that it probably would not work for 'they who were not provided for in it, would in a little time endeavour to form a new party, but the mischief was that very few Courtiers had reputation enough to head it, Sir Robert having filled the House with insignificant tools'.[92]

This mention of Walpole's 'insignificant tools' brings us to a third, more long-standing reason for Walpole's fall, which was expressed to Egmont by three peers from different factions of the whig party: Wilmington, lord president, cabinet minister, and long-standing rival of Walpole, on 4 February 1742 'complained that Sir Robert had been very faulty in preferring low insignificant persons instead of men of fortune or character'. Five days later, Lovel, joint-paymaster general and strong supporter of the prime minister, 'said, Sir Robert Walpole's great fault was preferring

89 H.M.C., *Egmont Diary*, III, 249.
90 For the defection or deliberate absenteeism of some army and placemen M.P.s, who were to prove the crucial element in the loss of Walpole's majority, because the ministry seemed about to lose control of patronage, see Colley, *In Defiance of Oligarchy*, p. 233.
91 *Tory and Whig*, ed. Taylor and Jones, p. 177.
92 H.M.C., *Egmont Dairy*, III, 249–50. See Colley, *In Defiance of Oligarchy*, p. 231, for a similar feeling about the 'losing all Party Distinctions' amongst some M.P.s. Two days before his appointment as first lord of the treasury, Wilmington was reported by Egmont to believe that 'the true interests of England was to have no chief minister ... [and] He also is for making the basis of the Government so broad, that many interests may be taken in'. H.M.C., *Egmont*, III, 550. These sentiments were shared by Chesterfield who, in his paper, *Common Sense*, supported a 'broad-bottom' alliance. Marie Peters, *The Elder Pitt* (1998), p. 24.

mean scoundrels, by choice, to men of family and honour and fortune, who would stand by him in his present adversity, whereas he now finds the others desert him'. Significantly, revealing the social sensitivity of the peerage, he went on to blame Walpole for 'procuring his bastard daughter to take the place as an Earl's daughter, and his thoughts of a pension of 4,000*l.* on the Excise'. (This refers to Walpole's illegitimate daughter, Maria Skerrett born in 1725, who was granted the precedence of an earl's daughter when on 6 February Walpole had been created earl of Orford. According to Egmont this, and the offer of a pension, caused outrage in the City and parliament, while William Hay, M.P., noted that Miss Skerrett's new precedence 'disgusted the Nobility, and brought more Odium on him [Walpole] than perhaps any Act of Power'.) On 13 February, Carteret, a leading dissident whig working with the opposition, also stated that 'it was Sir Robert Walpole's fault to prefer mean, contemptible persons to others of family and fortune more deserving, merely because the later would not be equally subservient to his measures'.[93] It was further reported about the opposition 'without doors ... that its plain all the old true familys are for the Country Interest, And so long as they have them they do Not value any New up start or hyreling: this is their language to their followers'.[94]

The feeling that under Walpole men of inferior quality and status had been promoted to office, granted patronage, and even raised to the peerage may well have been widespread among the social and political *élite*. George Lyttelton, M.P., had written to his friend William Pitt in May 1741 that, having had enough of electioneering, he felt 'that my Ambition wou'd be better satisfied in being only a Member of the House of Lords', and that he was 'at least as well Qualified for [it] as any of the three last created', meaning Stephen Fox (Ilchester), Henry Bromley (Montfort), and John Howe (Chedworth).[95] There is more than a hint here that there was a perception that men of inferior wealth and status had been elevated to the peerage. The resentment

93 H.M.C., *Egmont Diary*, III, 248–51; *Tory and Whig*, ed. Taylor and Jones, p. 176. Of the 14 peers created between 1723 and 1741 (see Appendix 4) who were still alive to vote on 19 Jan. 1742, all supported the ministry, with the exceptions of Malton, who was absent, Hervey, who abstained, and Ker. Four of the 18 created in those years had died, and of their successors in the title, King was absent, Raymond voted pro and Graham and Talbot con. An analysis of all those who voted on 19 Jan. (excluding Scottish representative peers, Scots with British tiles and the bishops) bears out the claim that the older established families in the peerage supported the opposition. The mean age of the title of a ministerial supporter was 53 years, while that for the opposition was 82 years. However, perception (propaganda?) may have been more influential on voting and absentee patterns than reality.

94 Royal Archives, Stuart papers 238/139: A. Cockburn to J. Edgar, 7 Dec. 1741.

95 P.R.O., 30/8/48/243–4: Lyttelton to Pitt, 23 May [1741]. George II expressed disquiet in 1756 at 'having raise so young a peer as Lord Ilchester [to an earldom] above so many ancient barons'. Walpole, *Memoirs of George II*, ed. Brooke, II, 179.

of newcomers amongst the older peerage families, though often concealed, was ever present,[96] and this resurfaced in the political crisis of 1741–2.

The 13th Lord Willoughby de Broke had been a loyal supporter of Walpole since the 1720s, but in 1734 quarrelled with the prime minister, and was reported as having renounced his pension over the latter's patronage given to Willoughby's younger brother whom the peer accused of depriving him of his estate. Willoughby wrote to Walpole that the prime minister had insulted him 'in the House of Peers where my ancestors have sat many years', assured him that 'His Majesty knows too well How much Interest and credit he Gains by the Support of His Peers superior to His Commons', concluding that 'I can get more by my Peerage than any Pension you Gave.' Willoughby then voted with the opposition. However, relations seem to have been patched-up as Willoughby returned to supporting the government shortly after. In a series of letters of 1741 to Newcastle, Willoughby revealed he had a pension of £600 a year from Walpole, and went on to ask Newcastle to apply to the prime minister for £50, he having been robbed by a highwayman on his way to Edinburgh. Walpole complied and within two months Willoughby had the money.[97] None the less, though he did attend the beginning of the session (up to 9 December) and was considered a supporter in the mid-January 1742 forecast, Willoughby was absent on the 19th (see Appendices 1 and 2), and he had not left a proxy. Willoughby's former anger with and opposition to Walpole may well have been only the visible tip of a much bigger iceberg: the disintegration of some of the peerage's support for the prime minister because he disregarded what the peers saw as their justifiable claims on the government, and promoted men whom they regarded as social inferiors.[98] It would be ironic indeed if one of the reasons for the fall of Walpole was the very same as had marked a major stage in his rise to political power. In 1719 he destroyed the Peerage Bill (which had been supported by the vast majority of the peers because they

96 It is instructive that shortly after Walpole's reconciliation with the ministry and his return to power in 1720 Lord Orrery wrote that 'the ministry upon this new Bargain with their old friends have been forc'd to put some into Peers, they had Such for their purpose enough before, and therefore perhaps the reproch of making continual additions to the Peers and especially of prefairing men of very in different characters, as most of their favourites are may do 'em more prejudice than this encrease of strength may do 'em good'. Royal Archives, Stuart papers 47/106: to the Pretender, 18 June 1720, o.s.

97 B.L., Add. MS 32696, f. 509: Willoughby to [Newcastle], 12 May [1741]; 32697, ff. 78, 138, 291: same to [same], 26 May, 1 June, 8 July [1741]; Cambridge U.L., Cholmondeley (Houghton) papers, Correspondence 3214: Willoughby to [Walpole], four undated letters. For the dating of these last four letters to 1734, see Hervey's letter printed in *Lord Hervey and His Friends, 1726–38*, ed. the earl of Ilchester (1950), pp. 190–1: to H. Fox, 31 Jan. 1734. The brother referred to was John Verney (d. 5 Aug. 1741), M.P. for Downton and master of the rolls. Elected as a tory, he had by 1727 moved to support Walpole having been made a Welsh judge in 1726. Sedgwick, *House of Commons*, II, 495–6. Willoughby's journey to Edinburgh may have been concerned with the peerage election and his claim to be earl of Carrick.

98 For a social analysis of the new peers created during Walpole's premiership, see Appendix 4. Is it fanciful to hear again an echo of 1641 when the majority of the aristocratic opposition to Charles I came from the 'ancient nobility' of the pre-Stuart creations?

feared that the peerage was being diluted as a social *élite* by unsuitable newcomers)[99] by opposing the creation of a closed-off caste at the head of society and politics. In 1742 certain peers may have unwittingly taken their revenge. Furthermore, Walpole's dismissal of the duke of Bolton and Lord Cobham from their regiments in 1733 for opposition to the ministry, which was regarded as an attack on property, provided another reason for resentment by the peerage. In the words of the duke of Montagu, this '[t]urning people of quality and fortune out of the army' engendered enmities which one historian considers 'were not to be cooled until the days of the Pelham regime'.[100]

VI

This essay has shown that while it may have been the loss of his majority in the Commons that was the main cause of Walpole's fall from office, the Lords (along with other factors) played a part in his resignation, and the drastic decline in the ministry's majority in the upper House was another symptom of a widespread desire to see an end of the 'great minister'. As in the Commons, it was the substantial absenteeism in the Lords (in some cases by very senior erstwhile supporters) that proved the writing on the wall.

A comparison of the 1741–2 crisis with that of 1733–4 over the collapse of the excise scheme and its aftermath is instructive. Despite the fact that the upper chamber never got to debate the excise because Walpole had withdrawn it before its possible defeat the Commons, the prime minister's brother reported that 'another reason for giving up the Bill was the falling away of friends in the House of Lords'.[101] The aftermath of the 1733 crisis, in which order in the upper House was only restored by the timely dismissal of the senior rebellious court peers from office and, in some cases, their regiments, showed clearly the kind of trouble the administration was heading for in January 1742.[102] Loss of control in the Lords in 1733 was an indication of a much more significant loss of control by the ministry, that of the court. Despite retaining the confidence of the king, a chief minister in the eighteenth century could not survive the loss of the support of parliament and the court. In 1733–4 Walpole was able to retrieve the situation and regain control of the Lords and the court, having first safeguarded his rear in the Commons. In 1742 Walpole could not sustain

---

99 For worries by the peerage over its dilution in 1719, see Clyve Jones, '"Venice Preserv'd; or A Plot Discovered": The Political and Social Context of the Peerage Bill of 1719', in *A Pillar of the Constitution*, ed. Jones, pp. 79–112.

100 Langford, *Excise Crisis*, p. 148. Bolton, after a period in opposition, returned to supporting the ministry in the late 1730s, while Cobham remained steadfastly in opposition. Montagu had sold himself to Walpole for the price of Bolton's office of governor of the Isle of Wight and remained a supporter.

101 H.M.C., *Egmont Diary*, I, 359.

102 For a full study, see Clyve Jones, 'The House of Lords and the Excise Crisis, 1733–34: The Storm and the Aftermath', (forthcoming).

HOUSE OF LORDS AND THE FALL OF WALPOLE   125

his administration in the face of a possible rebellious house of lords and court having lost the support of the Commons. The king alone could not save him.

The crisis of 1742 is also important in demonstrating that, despite the house of commons being the main seat of parliamentary power, the upper House was not insignificant.[103] As a historian of the excise crisis has written, '[u]nder Walpole the House of Lords was not the safe preserve of government that it was later to become'.[104] Many major political figures practised their craft in its chamber, and many from the Commons were only too eager to pass through its portals.[105] The political *élite* understood the Lords' important position in the constitution.

103 I have previously described the Lords at this time as the 'dominant partner in the constitution'. J. V. Becket and Clyve Jones, 'The Peerage and the House of Lords in the Seventeenth and Eighteenth Centuries', in *A Pillar of the Constitution*, ed. Jones, p. 18. This was an overstatement on my part, and I have been taken to task for it by John Cannon in 'The Nobility Ascendant: The Hanoverian Settlement, 1714–1832', in *The House of Lords. A Thousand Years of British Tradition* (1994), p. 106. However, I still maintain that the Lords retained a great deal of authority and influence and could, at times, threaten the survival of a ministry. Moreover, the loss of the Lords could presage a loss of the court, and no eighteenth-century minister could remain in office if he lost control of both. J. H. Plumb, *Sir Robert Walpole* (2 vols., 1972), II, 275, 277.

104 Langford, *Excise Crisis*, p. 85.

105 Lyttelton (see above, p. 122) was not alone in desiring a peerage. Dodington moved into opposition to Walpole in 1740 largely because the prime minister would not recommend him for a peerage before others who had more pressing claims. Another obstacle was that the king 'was in nothing so hard to be persuaded as to make peers'. Dudley Ryder's diary, 9 Aug. 1740, quoted in Sedgwick, *House of Commons*, I, 501–2.

Appendix 1
Forecast and Division Lists, 1740–1742

	1	2	3	4	5	6
Abergavenny	p	p	p	p	p	
Abingdon	c	c	c	c	c	
Albermarle	p	p	p	p	p	
Ancaster	a/pp	p	p	–	–	d. 13 Jan. 1742
Anglesey	a/pp	p	pp	p	p	
Arundell of Trerice	a	d	a	–	–	
Aylesford	c	c	c	c	c	
Barnard	a/cp	c	cp	c/ad	–	
Bathurst	c	c	c	c	c	
Beaufort	c	c	c	c	c	
Bedford	c	c	c	c	c	
Berkeley	a/pp	p	p	p	–	
Berkeley of Stratton	–	–	–	–	c	succ. 24 Mar. 1741
Berkshire	c	c	c	c	c	
Bolton	p	p	p	p	p	
Boyle of Marston (Orrery)	a/cp	c	c	cp	–	s. English title
Bridgwater	c	c	c	c	c	
Bristol	d	cq	c	c	c	
Brooke	–	d	a/n	c	a	
Bruce (Ailesbury)	c	c	c	c	–	succ. as Ailesbury 16 Dec. 1741
Burlington	a	c	a	c	a	
Butler of Weston (Arran)	d	c	a	c	–	s. English title
Cadogan	a	p	p	p	–	
Cardigan	d	d	a	p	–	
Carlisle	c	c	c	c	c	
Carteret	c	c	c	c	c	
Chandos	p	p	p	p	–	
Chedworth	–	–	–	p	p	cr. 12 May 1741
Chesterfield	c	c	c	c	c	
Cholmondeley	p	p	p	p	p	
Clarendon	p	p?	–	pd?	–	
Cleveland	a	d	–	–	–	
Clifton (Darnley)	c	c?	a/n	c	c	s. English title
Clinton	a/cp	c	c	c	c	
Cobham	c	c	c	c	c	
Conway	p	p	p	p	a	
Cornwallis	p	p	p	p	p	
Coventry	c	c?	a/n	c	c	
Cowper	p	p	p	–	–	
Craven	c	c	c	c	c	
Dartmouth	p	p	p	pd	–	
De La Warr	p	p	p	p	p	

	1	2	3	4	5	6
Denbigh	c	c	c	c	c	
Derby	a/cp	c	cp	c	c	
Devonshire	p	p	–	–	–	
Dorset	p	p	p	p	p	
Ducie	p	p	p	p	p	
Dudley	a/pp	p	p	pd?	p	
Effingham	p	p	p	p	p	
Essex	p	p	p	p	p	
Exeter	c	c	c	c	c	
Falmouth	c	c	c	c	c	
Fauconberg	p	p	p	p	p	
Fitzwalter	p	p	p	p	p	
Foley	c	c?	a/n	c	c	
Gainsborough	a/pp?	c	cp	c	–	
Godolphin	p	p	pp	p	–	
Gower	c	c	c	c	c	
Grafton	p	p	p	p	p	
Graham	c	c	a	c	c	
Grantham	p	p	p/n	p	–	
Greenwich (Argyll)	c	c	c	c	c	s. British title
Griffin	a	c	a	cd?	–	
Halifax	c	c	c	c	c	
Harborough	p	p	p	pd	p	
Harcourt	p	p	p	p	p	
Hardwicke	p	p	p	p	p	
Harrington	p	p	p	p	p	
Hatton	a	–	–	–	–	
Haversham	c	c	c	c	c	
Hay (Kinnoull)	p	p	p	p	p	s. British title
Hereford	c	c	–	–	c	
Hervey	p	p	p	p	a	
Hobart	p	p	p	p	p	
Holdernesse	p	p	p	p	–	
Hunsdon	a/pp	p	p	p	–	
Huntingdon	a/cp	c	cp	c	–	
Ilchester	–	–	–	p	p	cr. 11 May 1741
Jersey	p	p	p	p	p	
Ker (Roxburghe)	c	cq	c	c	c	succ. as Roxburghe 27 Feb. 1741; s. British title
King	p	p	p	pd?	–	
Kingston	a	p	p	p	–	
Leeds	d	c?	p	cd	c	
Leicester	a/pp	p	pp	pd	–	
Leigh	a	c	c	c	c	
Lichfield	c	c	c	c	c	
Lincoln	–	–	–	p	p	
Lonsdale	a	d	–	cd?	p	
Lovel	p	p	p	p	p	
Lymington	p	p	p	p	p	voted c 28 Jan.

	1	2	3	4	5	6
Macclesfield	a	c	c	c	a	
Malton	p	p	p	p	–	
Manchester	p	p	p	p	p	
Mansell	c	cq	cq?/c	c	c	
Marlborough	p	p	p	p	p	
Masham	c	c	c	c	c	
Maynard	c	c?	a	cd?	–	
Middleton	c	c	cp	c	–	not sworn until 18 Feb. 1742
Monson	p	p	p	p	p	
Montagu	p	p	p	p	p	
Montfort	–	–	–	p	p	cr. 9 May 1741
Mountjoy	c	c	c	c	c	
Newcastle	–	p	p	p	p	
North and Guilford	c	c	c	c	c	
Northampton	c	c	c	c	c	
Onslow	a/pp	p	p	pd	p	
Oxford, 2e	c	c?	p	–	–	d. 16 June 1741
Oxford, 3e	–	–	–	c	c	
Pembroke	p	p	p	p	p	
Percy (Hertford)	a/pp	p	p?	pd	–	ca. (Somerset)
Peterbrough	p	p	p	p	p	
Pomfret	a/pp	p	pp	p	p	
Portland	p	p	p	p	p	
Poulett	a/pp	p	pp	p	–	
Poulett of Hinton	p	p	p	p	p	ca. (Poulett)
Radnor, 3e	a/pp	p	–	–	–	d. 1 Feb. 1741
Radnor, 4e	–	–	p	p	p	
Raymond	p	p	p	p	p	
Richmond	p	p	p	p	p	
Rochford	p	p	p	p	p	
Rockingham	c	c	c	c	a	
Romney	c	cq	cq?	c	c	
Rutland	d	pd	p	pd	–	
St Albans	p	p	p	p	–	
St John	a	c	cp	–	–	d. 8 Apr. 1742 aged 90
St John of Bletso	a	c	c	c	c	
Salisbury	a/pp	p	pp	pd?	a	
Sandwich	c	c	c	c	. c	
Say and Sele	a/pp	p	pp	pd	–	
Scarbrough	a	c?	cp	c	–	
Shaftsbury	c	c	c	c	c	
Somerset	a/cp	c	cp	–	–	
Stamford	a/cp	c	c	c	–	
Stanhope	c	cq?	cq?	c	c	
Stawell	a	d	–	cd?	–	d. 23 Jan. 1742
Suffolk	c	c?	p	c	c	

	1	2	3	4	5	6
Tadcaster (Thomond)	a/cp	c	cp	–	–	d. 20 Apr. 1741; s. British title
Talbot	c	c	c	c	c	
Tankerville	a/pp	p	p	pd?	p	
Thanet	a/cp	c	c	c	c	
Torrington	p	p	p	p	p	
Townshend	c	c	cp	c	–	
Trevor	a/pp	p	pp	pd	–	
Uxbridge	a	d	–	–	–	
Waldegrave, 1e	a/pp	p	p	–	–	d. 11 Apr. 1741
Waldegrave, 2e	–	–	–	p	p	
Wales, prince of	c	–	n	c?	a	
Walpole	p	p	p	p	p	
Ward	a	c	c	c	c	
Warrington	a/cp	c?	a	c?	–	
Warwick	p	p	p	p	p	
Westmorland	c	c	c	c	c	
Weymouth	p	p	p	p	p	
Willoughby de Broke	d	p	a/p	p	–	
Willoughby of Parham	p	p	p	p	p	
Wilmington	p	p	a/p?	p	p	
Winchilsea	c	c?	c	c	c	

Scottish Representative Peers

	1	2	3	4	5	6
Atholl (Strange)	p	p	p	p	p	dis. 27 Apr. 1741; s. English title L. Strange from 14 Mar. 1737
Breadalbane	a	p	pp	p	p	
Buccleuch	c	c	c	–	–	dis. 27 Apr. 1741
Bute	a/cp	c	cp	–	–	dis. 27 Apr. 1741
Cathcart	a	–	–	–	–	d. 20 Dec. 1740
Crawford	a/pp	p	pp	p	–	
Dunmore	p	p	p	p	p	
Findlater	p	p	p	p	p	
Home	–	–	–	p	p	el. 13 June 1741
Hopetoun	a/pp	p	pp	pd	–	d. 26 Feb. 1742
Hyndford	p	p	p	–	–	
Ilay	p	p	p	p	p	
Lauderdale	–	–	–	pd?	–	el. 13 June 1741; not sworn until 20 Jan. 1742
Lothian	p	p	pp	p	p	
Loudoun	p	p	p	p	p	
Moray	–	–	–	p	p	el. 13 June 1741
Morton	p	p	p	p	p	
Portmore	p	p	p	p	–	
Somerville	–	–	–	p	p	el. 13 June 1741
Sutherland	p	p	p	p	p	

	1	2	3	4	5	6
Bishops						
Benson (Gloucester)	p	p	p	pd?/c	c	
Blackburne (York)	a/pp	p	pp	p	–	
Butler (Bristol)	p	p	p	p	p	
Butts (Ely)	a/pp	p	pp	p	–	
Chandler (Durham)	p	p	p	p	p	
Claggett (St Davids)	p	p	p	p	p	
Clavering (Peterborough)	p	p	pp	pd?	p	
Egerton (Hereford)	p	p	p	pd?/c	c	
Fleming (Carlisle)	a/pp	p	p	p	p	
Gibson (London)	a/pp	p	pp	p	–	
Gilbert (Llandaff)	p	p	p	p	p	cons. 28 Dec. 1740
Gooch (Norwich)	p	p	p	p	p	
Herring (Bangor)	p	p	p	p	p	
Hoadly (Winchester)	p	p	p	p	–	
Hough (Worcester)	a	–	–	–	–	d. 8 May 1743
Maddox (St Asaph)	p	p	p	p	p	
Mawson (Chichester)	p	p	p	p	p	
Peploe (Chester)	a/pp	p	p	pd	–	
Potter (Canterbury)	p	p	p	p	p	
Reynolds (Lincoln)	c	c	c	c	c	
Secker (Oxford)	p	p	p	pd?	p	
Sherlock (Salisbury)	p	p	p	p	p	
Smalbroke (Lichfield and Coventry)	d	c	c	c	c	
Weston (Exeter)	a/pp	p	p	–	–	d. 8 Jan. 1742
Wilcocks (Rochester)	p	p	p	p	p	
Wynne (Bath and Wells)	a/pp	p	pp	pd?	–	d. 15 July 1743

Sources for Appendix 1

(1) *Late Dec. 1740 to mid Jan. 1741.* Pre-sessional forecast. B.L., Add. MS 33002, ff. 407–8.

    p = for
    pp = listed as proxy for
    c = against
    cp = listed as proxy against
    d = doubtful
    a = absent

(2) *28 Jan. 1741.* Forecast of support and opposition to the ministry (subsequently annotated as a division list for the vote on 13 Feb. 1741). B.L., Add. MS 33034, ff. 1–3.

    p = for
    c = against
    d = doubtful
    q = marked 'Q' [query?] on list
    ? = crossed off list

(3) *13 Feb. 1741.* Those voting for and against the motion for an address to the king to remove Walpole. B.L., Add. MS 33034, ff. 21–4; 35876, ff. 86–7; 47000, ff. 111–12 (lists those neuter);

A True and Exact List of the Lords Spiritual and Temporal ... who voted for and against the Address to remove a certain Great Man (1741), marked also with those who were neuter.

    p = against (i.e., supporting the ministry)

    pp = proxy vote against

    c = for

    cp = proxy vote for

    a = absent

    n = neuter (abstained?)

    q? = query? (crossed off on list, B.L., Add. MS 33034)

Note: the proxy voting is calculated from comparing the lists with the lists of registered proxies in the H.L.R.O., proxy books, XVII.

(4) *Mid-Jan. 1742*. Forecast of support and opposition (? on a possible impeachment of Walpole). B.L., Add. MS 33002, ff. 400–1.

    p = for

    c = against

    d = doubtful (marked 'D')

    ? = crossed of list

(5) *19 Jan. 1742*. Those voting for and against the motion to appoint a date for a committee of the whole house on the state of the nation. B.L., Add. MS 33034, f. 71.

    p = against (i.e., supporting the ministry)

    c = for

    a = abstained? (recorded as present in the *L.J.* but not voting)

There are several technical problems concerning this list. The presence list printed in *L.J.* is based on that complied by the clerk assistant to the House and recorded in the H.L.R.O., manuscript minutes. There are occasional discrepancies between these two sources, as changes were made between the minutes and the manuscript journal which is the basis of the printed version. The list in *L.J.* for 19 Jan. 1742, however, has 17 more lords in it than the list in the manuscript minutes. There is also one lord (the bishop of St Davids) recorded in the minutes but not in *L.J.* He and 15 of the extra 17 lords listed in the *L.J.* are recorded as voting in the duke of Newcastle's list (Add. MS. 33034), which is headed 'Lords present January 19th 1741[/2]'. This list also gives the prince of Wales and the earl of Burlington (who are not recorded in the minutes but are in the *L.J.*) as present, but not voting (abstaining?), as well as recording Lords Brooke, Conway, Hervey, Macclesfield, Rockingham and Salisbury (who all appear both in the minutes and the *L.J.*) as present but not voting. The Newcastle list also has the earl of Lichfield as present and voting, though he is not recorded in either the minutes or the *L.J.* Finally, the total recorded as voting on Newcastle's list are 78 for the ministry and 53 for the opposition, while the official figures of the clerk in the minutes are 77 and 53. These discrepancies are irreconcilable. For the purposes of compiling column 5 Newcastle's list has been taken at face value. Any inaccuracies are likely to be insignificant for the analysis based on this list.

(6) ca. = called to Lords in father's barony (courtesy title by which known) (father's title)

    cons. = consecrated bishop

    cr. = created a peer

    d. = died

    dis. = dismissed from ministry's list of peers at general election and not re-elected

    el. = elected

    s. = sat in Lords by virtue of British or English title (Irish or Scottish title by which known)

    succ. = succeeded to title

Appendix 2
The ministerial lords who did not vote on 19 January 1742

1. Those who had not taken the oaths:
   Ancaster, died Dec. 1741; successor took oaths 18 Feb. 1742
   Clarendon
   Dartmouth
   Devonshire, in Ireland
   Leicester
   Say and Sele
   Trevor
   Scottish representative peers
   Hopetoun, died in Scotland Jan. 1742
   Hyndford, on an embassy in Prussia
   Lauderdale, took oaths 20 Jan. 1742
   Bishops
   Peploe of Chester, took oaths 18 Feb. 1742
   Weston of Exeter, died 8 Jan. 1742
   Wynne of Bath and Wells

2. Those who had taken the oaths but did not attend (o = officeholder; p = had left a proxy vote; x = had left proxy after the call of the house):

Berkeley		
Cadogan		p x
Cardigan		
Cowper	o	p
Godolphin	o	p
Grantham		p x
Holderness	o	p x
Hunsdon		p x
Kingston	o	p
Malton		p x
Percy	o	p
Poulett of Hinton		
Rutland		
St Albans	o	
Willoughby de Broke		

   Scottish representative peers

Crawford	p
Portmore	p

   Bishops

Blackburne of York	p
Butts of Ely	p x
Gibson of London	p
Hoadly of Winchester	p

3. Those who abstained (were recorded as present but not as voting; o = officeholder):
   Conway
   Hervey   o
   Salisbury

Appendix 3
The opposition lords who did not vote on 19 January 1742

1. Those who had not taken the oaths:

   Gainsborough
   Griffin
   Maynard
   Middleton, took oaths on 18 Feb. 1742
   St John, very elderly and died shortly afterwards
   Somerset, elderly and infirm
   Stawell, died shortly afterwards
   Townshend
   Warrington

2. Those who had taken the oaths but did not attend (p = had left a proxy vote; x = had left proxy after the call of the house):

Boyle of Marston	p x	
Bruce (Ailesbury)	p x	(held the proxy of Stamford)
Huntingdon	p	
Scarbrough		
Stamford	p	

3. Those who abstained (were recorded as present but not as voting):

Brooke	(held the proxy of Percy)[1]
Burlington	
Macclesfield	
Rockingham	
Wales, prince of	

[1] Brooke has been counted as an opposition supporter in this analysis though his only firm listing as such was in the mid-Jan. 1742 ministerial forecast; otherwise he appears as doubtful or neuter. Percy has been counted as a supporter of the ministry; his record is clearer than Brooke's, but the mid-Jan. forecast lists him as doubtful supporter. See Appendix 1. It was very unusual at this time for a proxy to be given to a lord of the opposite political stance; perhaps Percy giving his proxy to Brooke shows that he was by this time moving into opposition.

Appendix 4

The social and political background of those raised to the peerage
1722–1741

Date and title	1	2	3	4	5	6	7	8	9	10	11	12	13	14
1722														
Graham	x^a													
Ker	x^b													
1723														
Walpole									x	x^c				
1725														
King					x	x					x^d	x	x	x
1728														
Wilmington	x^e					x			x					
Hobart		x^f		x	x	x	x		x					
Monson			x	x	x	x	x							
Malton		x^g	x		x	x	x							
Lovel			x		x	x	x	x^h		x				
1730														
Harrington						x			x^i					
1731														
Raymond					x	x			x			x	x	
1733														
Hervey	x^j					x			x					
Hardwicke					x	x			x		x^k	x	x	x
Talbot						x^l			x			x		
1734														
Poulett of Hinton	x^m								x					
1741														
Montfort						x	x^n	x^o			x^p			
Ilchester						x	x	x^q	x		x^r			
Chedworth		x^s				x				x				
Totals:														
18	5	3	3	2	7	14	6	3	10	3	4	4	3	3

Sources: G. E. Cokayne, *The Complete Peerage*, ed. V. Gibbs (new edn., 13 vols., 1910–40); R. Sedgwick, *The House of Commons, 1715–1754* (2 vols., 1970); A. S. Turberville, *The House of Lords in the XVIIIth Century* (Oxford, 1927), pp. 505–8. They are arranged by date order of their patents. Royal princes created peers have not been included.

Columns:

(1) Son of a peer
(2) Other relation of a peer
(3) Married to the daughter of a peer
(4) Baronet at time of creation

(5)   Knight at time of creation
(6)   M.P. before creation
(7)   Possessor of an electoral interest
(8)   Wealthy
(9)   Officeholder at time of creation
(10) Relation or close friend of Walpole
(11) Of low social origin
(12) A lawyer
(13) Became a judge
(14) Became lord chancellor

Notes:

a   Eldest son of 1st duke of Montrose; a minor, he took his seat in 1727 (d. 1731); succ. by his brother, also a minor, who took his seat in 1733
b   Eldest son of 1st duke of Roxburghe; a minor, he took his seat in 1730.
c   Son of Sir Robert Walpole, raised to the peerage in consideration of his father's political work.
d   Son of a grocer.
e   Second son of the 3rd earl of Northampton.
f   Nephew of the 2nd earl of Stamford.
g   Grandson of the 2nd Lord Rockingham.
h   Average income from estates in 1728–33 was £8,875. R. C. A. Parker, *Coke of Norfolk. A Financial and Agricultural Study, 1707–1842* (Oxford, 1975), pp. 22–3. Cf. Sedgwick, who states that he 'succeeded to estates worth over £10,000 a year, which, in spite of heavy losses in the South Sea bubble, had increased by 1741 to £15,000 … [in 1730 he said] "I have an estate sufficient for an earl or a viscount at least"'. Sedgwick, *House of Commons*, I, 565.
i   Soldier and diplomat.
j   Eldest son of the 1st earl of Bristol; raised to the peerage in father's barony.
k   Son of a solicitor; married the niece of Lord Somers.
l   Son of the bishop of Durham.
m   Eldest son of the 1st Earl Poulett; raised to the peerage in father's barony.
n   Reputed to have spent £100,000 by the time of his death in supporting the government interest in Cambridgeshire. Sedgwick, *House of Commons*, I, 493.
o   He and Fox are reported to have paid £30,000 between them for their peerages. H.M.C., *Egmont Diary*, III, 259–60.
p   Grandson of a pedlar, who became a wealthy West Indian sugar planter.
q   In 1716 he inherited estates which brought in £6,500 a year 'over and above all encumbrances'. Christopher Clay, *Public Finance and Private Wealth. The Career of Sir Stephen Fox, 1627–1716* (Oxford, 1978), pp. 328–9. In 1736 he had married an heiress.
r   Son of a footman, who became paymaster of the forces.
s   Cousin of the 2nd Viscount Howe [Irish peerage]; married the niece of the 1st Viscount Weymouth.

During the eighteenth century the creation of peerages was severely limited, particularly in the reign of George II. As the table above shows there were only 18 new members added to the house of lords during Walpole's ministry. John Cannon in his book *Aristocratic Century. The Peerage of Eighteenth-Century England* (Cambridge, 1984) has shown (pp. 11–26) that, though peers with low social backgrounds were not unknown, they were usually as a result of a turn of fate which caused a peer to succeed to the title unexpectedly. Further he shows that the cry that the peerage was being diluted by the creation of unsuitable candidate was fairly constant down the ages and should not be taken at face value. He goes on to demonstrate that very few peers indeed were created who did not have a connexion with an existing peerage family. However, his concept of 'connexion' is very wide indeed including such far flung relatives as great-great-nephews of peers. Though, as he argues persuasively, such connexions were often used for advancement, a far narrower definition would seem more appropriate for the present analysis.

The first three columns of the above table show fairly close family ties to the peerage, and 61 per cent of the 18 had such a connexion.[1] A further two had inherited baronetcies by the time of their creation, and seven had been knighted (including the two baronets). Only four can be considered to have originated from a low social family (King, Hardwicke, Montfort and Ilchester). Significantly the first two of these were eminent lawyers who became judges and lord chancellors, and it had always been necessary to draft legal talent into the Lords (the highest court in the kingdom) as the sons of the peerage rarely went into the law. One of the other Walpolean creations became lord chancellor (Talbot, the son of a bishop) and another a senior judge (Raymond, the son of a senior judge). The last two creations from lowly families, Montfort and Ilchester were, along with Lovel, men of considerable wealth who had no problem, at least to begin with, in keeping up the style associated with their title.

The favoured route to a title at this time was, as was usual in the eighteenth century, a career in politics, and with those listed above it seems to have been the most important: 14 of the 18 had been M.P.s before their elevation, and for some their performance in the Commons had been a strong factor in their selection for the upper chamber. Of these 14 six had extensive electoral interest which had been put at the disposal of the government, and 10 were officeholders at the time of their elevation (in one case, Harrington, his performance in diplomacy seems to have been the only reason for his title). Only three had a family tie with, or were close friends of, Walpole.

Cannon noted few examples of the purchase of peerages in the eighteenth century (p. 8), but there were rumours that Montfort and Ilchester had bought their peerages via the king's mistress, the countess of Yarmouth. Whether true or not, the fact that their was such a rumour may not have done much for the reputation of the two peers, especially as both were from low family backgrounds.

The 18 men raised to the Lords seem to conform somewhat to the pattern of creations found by Cannon in the rest of the century, except that the stricter interpretation of a connexion with the peerage used here produces a non-aristocratic origin of 39 per cent of total creations as opposed to his 13.6 per cent over similar period (p. 26). Perhaps the fact that over a third of the new peers had no close connexion with the peerage, that few had sufficient wealth (outside their perquisites of office) to maintain their new status, and that some of those very few who did have the wealth were from low social backgrounds and possibly acquired their titles by dubious methods, did indeed cause some outrage amongst the established peerage. The three creations of 1741 may have merely underlined what some peers regarded as a regrettable trend. The rank of an earl's daughter given to Walpole's illegitimate offspring on his elevation to the earldom of Orford in 1742 could only have reinforced perceptions of this trend.

1 Two (Graham and Ker) of the 11 who had a close connexion with the peerage were sons of Scottish peers. In 1711 the house of lords had passed a resolution preventing Scottish peers who were granted a British title sitting by right of their British title. This resolution had social and xenophobic as well as political origins (the Lords feared being swamped by new British peers from what the English generally regarded as a second-rate foreign peerage, whose members were usually much poorer than English peers). However, Graham and Ker, being commoners at the time of their creation, were not covered by the 1711 resolution (as, indeed, neither was Lord Dupplin, son of the earl of Kinnoul, created Baron Hay in 1711, and whose creation raised little comment at the time, nor in 1719 when he succeeded as Lord Kinnoul and continued to sit in the Lords by virtue of his British peerage). However, the survival of the fear of 1711 of an influx of Scottish peers is attested to by the dispute that arose in 1727 over Lord Graham's patent, and this fear may well have formed part of the unease peers felt in 1742.

7

Surrendering Rites:
Prisoners on Colonial North American Frontiers[*]

Ian K. Steele

Amerindians and Europeans, whose own feuds had developed complex, ritualized limits, initially faced each other as complete aliens. Taking captives, as curiosities, hostages, informants, interpreters, sacrifices, or slaves, was one of the first interactions between these unrelated peoples.[1] Assumptions about the taking and treatment of prisoners differed markedly, collided explosively and evolved only slowly. New complications surfaced in the eighteenth century, when Europe's professional military effectively extended new 'honours of war' conventions to America. These new rules generated renewed confusion, conflict and compromise involving Amerindians, European colonists and imperial soldiers. What follows is an invitation to explore this subject more intensively and comparatively. Much that otherwise seems chaotic and arbitrary can be better understood by appreciating each of these three perspectives, and noticing their persistence, interaction and adaptation.

[*] My thanks are due to commentators on earlier versions of this paper presented at East Carolina University, Greenville, N.C., 10 Nov. 1995; the Americanists Seminar at York University, Toronto, Ont., 19 Nov. 1995; and the Eighteenth Century Interdisciplinary Seminar, University of Western Ontario, London, Ont., 26 Jan. 1996.

[1] Recent studies of captives include: J. M. Bumsted, 'Carried to Canada: Perceptions of the French in British Colonial Captivity Narratives, 1690–1760', *American Review of Canadian Studies*, XIII (1983), 79–96; Colin G. Calloway, 'An Uncertain Destiny: Indian Captivities on the Upper Connecticut River', *Journal of American Studies*, XVII (1983), 189–210; John Demos, *The Unredeemed Captive. A Family Story from Early America* (New York, 1994); Norman J. Heard, *White into Red. A Study of the Assimilation of White Persons Captured by Indians* (Metuchen, N.J., 1973); Frances Row Kestler, *The Indian Captivity Narrative. A Woman's View* (New York, 1990); James Lynch, 'The Iroquois Confederacy and the Adoption and Administration of Non-Iroquoian Individuals and Groups Prior to 1756', *Man in the Northeast*, No. 30 (1985), 83–99; June Namias, *White Captives. Gender and Ethnicity on the American Frontier* (Chapel Hill, N.C., 1992); Daniel K. Richter, 'War and Culture: The Iroquois Experience', *William and Mary Quarterly*, 3rd ser., XL (1983), 528–59; Peter Stern, 'The White Indians of the Borderlands', *Journal of the Southwest*, XXXIII (1991), 262–81; Richard Van Der Beets, *The Indian Captivity Narrative. An American Genre* (Washington, 1984); Alden T. Vaughan and Daniel K. Richter, 'Crossing the Cultural Divide: Indians and New Englanders, 1605–1763', *Proceedings of the American Antiquarian Society*, XC (1980), 23–99.

I

North American Amerindian societies varied greatly in 1500, but none regarded captured warriors as behaving honourably unless they escaped quickly or died defiantly. Captivity was, by definition, failure as a warrior. Captive warriors were often presumed dead by their own people, did not expect to be exchanged, and might be forced to undergo purification ceremonies if they did return.[2] Defenders of an Amerindian stronghold did not expect to discuss terms upon which they would surrender. When Amerindians controlled a victory over each other or over Europeans, surrender was usually unconditional.[3] A comprehensive exchange of prisoners was not a part of Amerindian peacemaking, though the return of a few recently-captured prisoners might be both a token of intent to negotiate and a vehicle for discussion. Surviving records of negotiated terms of surrender during intertribal war are invariably European, and suggest European influences.

Amerindians regarded all members of enemy societies as legitimate prisoners, though captive women and children were more likely to be incorporated successfully. Military success added to the population of victorious communities, and weakened the defeated. Captives who became wives could also become diplomatic or social connexions between societies, though they could also act as spies and dissidents. The numerous Huron captives living among the Five Nations of the Iroquois in the 1650s, for instance, proved to be particularly effective preservers and transmitters of christianized Huron values.

A warrior's quest for personal martial reputation usually meshed well with communitarian assumptions about property and its redistribution. During military actions, a prisoner remained the personal responsibility of the captor. There were no facilities to hold prisoners, so the taking of prisoners, rather than scalps, usually brought a raid to an end.[4] In some societies a prisoner, like a scalp, was a personal trophy, and clearly the captor's property. Since status was linked to the ability to gather and distribute resources, successful warriors could maintain or enhance their status through the trade in captives. War chiefs who organized raids were sometimes awarded additional captives. Grieving clan matrons, whose suffering provoked 'mourning war' raids by the Five Nations and 'crying blood' expeditions by the

2 Lawrence H. Keeley, *War before Civilization* (New York, 1996), pp. 85–8. In a 1725 incident, a returned Cherokee underwent a four-day purification ritual. Theda Perdue, *Slavery and the Evolution of Cherokee Society, 1540–1866* (Knoxville, 1979), p. 6.

3 For the unusual battle of Long Sault (1660) see J. A. Dickinson, 'Annaotaha et Dollard vus de l'autre côté de la palissade', *Revue d'Histoire de l'Amerique Française*, XXXV (1981), 163–78. Colonial examples of such unconditional surrender include Lachine (1689), Schenectady (1690), Deerfield (1704), Saratoga (1746), Fort Bull (1756), and German Flats (1757).

4 Montcalm's intense negotiation with his allies from the *pays d'en haut* after their successful battle of Sabbath Day Point in July of 1757 illustrates several aspects of this convention that were seen as extremely inconvenient by French regulars. Ian K. Steele, *Betrayals. Fort William Henry and the 'Massacre'* (revised edn., New York, 1993), pp. 88–91.

Catawba, could, like certain Shawnee matrons, be arbiters of the lives of prisoners.[5] As a result, those sachems and paramount chiefs who negotiated with outsiders on behalf of Amerindian communities had no authority to promise the return of prisoners who were not their own, and sachems were likely to control fewer prisoners personally than did war chiefs.

The varied fates of prisoners taken by Amerindians have often appeared entirely arbitrary to European survivors and historians. Prisoners might be killed along the trail by individual acts of brutality or, more often, to avoid a counterattack made more likely by howling children or slow-moving captives. A small proportion of adult male prisoners were subjected to ritual torture unto death, and there were also a few authenticated reports of cannibalism. Apparently gender mattered more than race to Amerindian captors. There are early reported cases of black male prisoners being tortured to death, though many Amerindians eventually came to regard blacks as saleable plunder. Women captives were seldom tortured to death.[6] Prisoners might be fully adopted into families, or held as slaves outside the protection of specific clan membership. Repentant murderers within the Mohican or Shawnee communities, for example, could offer a slave captive as part of a ransom to save their own lives.[7] Unadopted prisoners could also be given as diplomatic gifts or sold to other Amerindian communities. The Apache, for example, routinely sold war captives to Pueblo communities for corn, textiles and pottery. The Comanche, from earliest accounts, were known as traders of Apache captives.[8]

If the usefulness of prisoners could influence their fate, there is value in comparing prisoners taken by hunting as opposed to farming societies. Hunting, fishing and gathering societies that did not grow grain, like the Ottawa, Abenaki and Calusa, could not absorb many prisoners. Any rapid population increase would entail a war for larger hunting grounds, except in the wake of epidemics. These hunter-warrior societies were economically and culturally more male-dominated than were farming societies, even before the European fur trade reinforced this tendency. Unless prisoners were excellent hunters, or could be sold promptly and profitably,

5   Daniel K. Richter, 'War and Culture: The Iroquois Experience', *William and Mary Quarterly*, 3rd ser., XL (1983), 528–59; James H. Merrell, *The Indians' New World. Catawbas and their Neighbors from European Contact through the Era of Removal* (Chapel Hill, N.C., 1989), pp. 121–2.
6   Cornelius Jaenen, *Friend and Foe* (New York, 1976), p. 139; Kenneth Wiggins Porter, *The Negro on the American Frontier* (New York, 1971), pp. 23–6; Steele, *Betrayals*, pp. 8, 116, 123, 127, 140, 156. For 'Morning Star' female sacrifices, see James R. Murie, *Ceremonies of the Pawnee* (Lincoln, Neb., 1989), pp. 114–36.
7   *The First Report of the American Society for Promoting the Civilization and General Improvement of the Indian Tribes in the United States* (New Haven, 1824), p. 45; Dwight L. Smith, 'Shawnee Captivity Ethnohistory', *Ethnohistory*, II (1955), 36–7.
8   Elizabeth A. H. John, *Storm Brewed in Other Men's Worlds. The Confrontation of Indians, Spanish and French in the Southwest, 1540–1795* (College Station, Texas, 1975), p. 6; Thomas W. Kavanagh, *Comanche Political History. An Ethnohistorical Perspective, 1706–1875* (Lincoln, Neb., 1996), pp. 66, 83.

they were liabilities. The reputed martial ferocity of hunting societies may be linked, at least indirectly, to the lack of any incentive to take a prisoner rather than their scalp.

Amerindian farming societies, or those that combined hunting with reliable farming, could often make more effective use of prisoners. If farmland was available, adult workers could raise more than twice as much corn, beans and squash as was needed to sustain themselves. Societies that lived on grown or purchased corn had an additional use for servile labour; the grinding of hard Indian corn was, in most seasons, a daily chore that consumed about one hour for every adult person to be fed.[9] Since women grew and ground the corn in most Amerindian communities, female prisoners could more easily earn their keep. Societies like the Cherokee, who used both male and female slaves in their fields, could be somewhat less discriminating about the gender of their captives.[10]

Farming societies routinely sustained population densities at least seven times those of hunting societies, but were susceptible to higher losses during epidemics. Rapid adoption of numerous prisoners, especially women and children, helped rebuild Amerindian societies shattered by disease. The well-known Five Nations adoptions of numerous Iroquoian-speaking Huron (1649), Petun (1650), Neutral (1651), Erie (1657) and Susquehannock (1680) illustrate this strategy. However, the limits of cultural absorption were exceeded when the Mohawk became outnumbered by adoptees in their own villages in the 1650s. The disruption of the Mohawk, including re-christianized Huron adoptees, led to the northward migration that peopled Caughnawaga (Kahnawake), contributed to the growth of Lac des Deux Montagnes (Oka), and added Mohawk to the Huron village of Lorette.[11]

By the mid-eighteenth century, only one portion of the Amerindian-European frontier in North America could be said to involve Amerindian farmer-hunters who raided without a major European market for their captives. These were the comparatively new and mixed upper Ohio villages of Delaware, Shawnee and Mingo.[12] When they participated in the defeat of the all-male garrison at Fort Necessity in 1754, they took no prisoners at all. In this confusing pre-war clash, Canadian and American colonial participants were allowed to negotiate a surrender they considered generous, European, and guaranteed by the taking of two Virginian officers as 'hostages' of the Canadians. In the attack on Braddock's column the

9   Lois Green Carr, Russell R. Menard and Lorena S. Walsh, *Robert Cole's World. Agriculture and Society in Early Maryland* (Chapel Hill, N.C., 1991), pp. 71, 96, 102, 302 n.51.
10 Perdue, *Slavery*, p. 15; Rudi Halliburton, *Red Over Black. Black Slavery among the Cherokee Indians* (Westport, Conn., 1977).
11 Daniel K. Richter, *The Ordeal of the Longhouse* (Chapel Hill, N.C., 1992), pp. 70–4, 108–9, 112–32.
12 Richard White, *The Middle Ground. Indians, Empires, and Republics in the Great Lakes Region, 1650–1815* (Cambridge, 1991); Michael N. McConnell, *A Country Between. The Upper Ohio Valley and Its People, 1724–1774* (Lincoln, Neb., 1992).

following year, the few prisoners taken included 12 men who were tortured to death and eight adults who were sold to the Canadian military; the van of a European army was not a rewarding place to capture valuable prisoners.[13] In the next decade, however, an estimated 2,700 captives were taken in scores of Amerindian raids conducted on the frontiers of Pennsylvania, Maryland and Virginia.[14] Although adult male captives outnumbered adult female captives two to one, men killed in raids outnumbered women 19 to one. Women and children, who could help feed and populate an embattled society without threatening it, were a priority.

Amerindian views of prisoners of war not only depended upon specific customs, and on differences between hunters and farmers, but also changed through interaction with Europeans. Canadians brokered a substantial and successful prisoner exchange between the Ottawa and Five Nations in 1701.[15] Eleven years later, however, the French treacherously negotiated with the Fox at Detroit, then watched while as many as 1,000 Fox were slaughtered by the Ottawa, Huron and Potawatomi.[16] Onondaga orator Teganissorens emphasized continuing differences when he upbraided Governor Robert Hunter of New York in 1711: 'We are not like you Christians for when you have taken Prisoners of one another you send them home, by such means you can never rout one another.' An Ottawa chief echoed the same view 46 years later.[17]

Amerindian acceptance of the occasional exchange of numerous prisoners amongst themselves was a minor change compared with the impact of the white market for captives as slaves or servants. For Abenaki hunters, especially those living at Canadian missions, this new trade in prisoners revived and sustained the resources and reputations of hunters in a region increasingly depleted of game. Captives could be part of traditional tribal victory celebrations, and could then be adopted or sold. The adopted were sometimes rented, were less likely to be sold and brought higher prices if they were.[18] Those who were sold in New France were being 'ransomed' by

13 *Documents Relative to the Colonial History of the State of New York*, ed. Edmund B. O'Callaghan and Berthold Fernow (15 vols., Albany, N.Y., 1856–87) [hereafter *N.Y.C.D.*], VII, 282; Samuel G. Drake, *Indian Captivities* (Buffalo, 1854), p. 184; Huntington Library, San Marino, California, Merlin Stonehouse Transcripts, IV: deposition of Mrs Miller of the 44th, 13 Dec. 1757; *Pennsylvania Gazette*, 6 Sept. 1759, No. 1602.

14 Tentative and preliminary results of the author's study of newspaper accounts, captivity narratives and archival sources. Cf. Matthew C. Ward, 'Fighting the "Old Women": Indian Strategy on the Virginia and Pennsylvania Frontier, 1754–1758', *Virginia Magazine of History and Biography*, CIII (1995), 297–320.

15 Bruce Trigger, *The Children of Aataentsic* (2 vols., Montreal, 1976), II, 649, describes a likely parole and exchange of Tokhrahenehiaron for Guillaume Couture in 1645. Richard Haan, 'The Problem of Iroquois Neutrality: Suggestions for Revision', *Ethnohistory*, XXVIII (1980), 320.

16 R. David Edmunds and Joseph L. Peyser, *The Fox Wars* (Norman, Okla., 1993), pp. 61–75; White, *Middle Ground*, pp. 149–59.

17 N.Y.C.D., V, 274; Steele, *Betrayals*, p. 131.

18 Account by Enos Bishop in *New York Mercury*, 11 Aug. 1755; Titus King, *Narrative of Titus King of Northampton, Mass. A Prisoner of the Indians in Canada, 1755–1758* (Hartford, Conn., 1939), p. 15.

the Canadian purchaser, often to replace the farm labour of busy Canadian militia in wartime. After 'working off' the price of their ransom, or being ransomed again by the Canadian government or their own relatives or communities, these prisoners might still continued to be held during Anglo-French wars, awaiting a 'prisoner of war' exchange. When New England and New France were not at war, and the demand for labour in New France was lower, the Abenaki raided in accordance with their own diplomatic timetables. When the Massachusetts governor objected to Canadian tolerance for these Abenaki raids in peacetime, Governor Michel-Ange Duquesne de Menneville replied that the Abenaki were slave-raiding, which English colonists surely understood, and the captives were 'slaves fairly sold' once bought by Canadians. Duquesne, whose own kindnesses to prisoners/hostages was criticized by his successor as overly generous, claimed that he would certainly have returned the captives if they had been prisoners of war.[19]

The sale of captives was much more prevalent in the southern British mainland colonies and in French Louisiana, though all colonies in eastern North America had some access to slave markets. South Carolina led the British colonies in the export of Amerindian slaves; of more than 5,500 Amerindians taken before 1752, about 85 per cent were exported.[20] The Westo, Savannah and Tuscarora took turns being slavers for the South Carolinians, before being taken as slaves themselves. When Creek raiders, accompanied and supplied by their South Carolinian trading partners, completely destroyed the Apalachee missions of Florida in 1703, Amerindian slaves briefly constituted 26 per cent of the colony's bound labour. Stronger Amerindian confederations, French arming of the Choctaw, and fears that came in the wake of the Tuscarora and Yamasee wars greatly reduced the trade in Amerindian slaves in the Carolinas after 1718.[21]

The expanded trade in Amerindian slaves had affected the conduct of Amerindian warfare. Dead or wounded victims were of less value that healthy prisoners; a scalp was now a trophy with a measurable price. Slaughter of the defeated could be limited, as at the Battle of Flint River (1702) where 600 of 800 Apalachee combatants were

19 Quoted in Emma Lewis Coleman, *New England Captives* (2 vols., Portland, Me., 1925–6), II, 267. On the captivity of Robert Stobo and Jacob van Braam, see Robert C. Alberts, *The Extraordinary Adventures of Major Stobo* (New York, 1965).
20 William Robert Snell, 'Indian Slavery in Colonial South Carolina, 1671–1795', University of Alabama, Ph.D. 1972; Almon Wheeler Lauber, *Indian Slavery in Colonial Times within the Present Limits of the United States* (New York, 1913); Stanford Winston, 'Indian Slavery in the Carolina Region', *Journal of Negro History*, XIX (1934), 433–6; Jerome Handler, 'The Amerindian Slave Population of Barbados in the Seventeenth and Early Eighteenth Centuries', *Caribbean Studies*, VIII (1969), 38–64; Richard S. Dunn, *Sugar and Slaves. The Rise of the Planter Class in the English West Indies* (Chapel Hill, 1972), pp. 74, 227–8, 269–70.
21 Russell R. Menard, 'The Africanization of the Lowcountry Labor Force, 1670–1730', in *Race and Family in the Colonial South* (Jackson, Miss., 1987), pp. 81–108. The Choctaw may have lost as many as 2,000 men to this trade between 1690 and 1710. Richard White, *The Roots of Dependency. Subsistence, Environment, and Social Change among the Choctaws, Pawnees, and Navahos* (Lincoln, Neb., 1983), pp. 35–6.

spared and sold into slavery. At the burning and storming of the Tuscarora stronghold of Neoheroka (1713) nearly 400 of the 584 defenders were sold as slaves. Amerindians from the *pays d'en haut*, who had come for the 1757 Fort William Henry campaign, were taught by the Abenaki about the profits of the captive trade, tempering the willingness of some to kill and eat a prisoner. However, the slave trade also greatly expanded Amerindian warfare. As in West Africa, Europeans selling guns for slaves promoted a desperate race to become slavers in order to avoid becoming slaves. Predawn raids captured entire villages for a trade that could include male and female, adult and child.[22] Although widely held Amerindian assumptions about the capture, adoption and exchange of prisoners persisted throughout the colonial period and beyond, development of major colonial trades in Amerindian and white captives was revolutionary.

Three frontier zones of Amerindian captivity can be distinguished in colonial North America, depending on the availability of a trade in captives with Europeans. Northern hunters became linked to the substantial, but variable, trade in white and Amerindian captives to New France. Eighteenth-century Ohio Valley Amerindians raided for captives who were almost all absorbed into their own communities. A number of Amerindian societies of the southern frontiers were completely destroyed by the apparently limitless colonial demand for slave labour. Amerindians preserved central characteristics of their own conventions concerning captives, and adapted to colonial opportunities without accepting colonial perspectives.

II

Migrants to North America from Reformation Europe carried two ancient and complementary traditions about prisoners of war. Plato had proposed rules for war between Greeks. Captured Greek prisoners should not be robbed or sold into slavery, though he suggested that 'barbarians be treated as Greeks had been treating Greeks'. Cicero urged Romans to be magnanimous to the conquered, sparing those who had not been bloodthirsty. (Was the American colonial and revolutionary mantra about 'blood-thirsty savages' evoking this time-honoured distinction?) Cicero also advocated the protection of prisoners and the parole of officers. Like Plato, he considered war with 'barbarians' as outside these conventions and justifying barbarous methods.[23]

---

22 See W. A. Richards, 'The Import of Firearms into West Africa in the Eighteenth Century', *Journal of African History*, XXI (1980), 43–59; Jan S. Hogendorn, 'Slave Acquisition and Delivery in Precolonial Hausaland', in *West African Culture Dynamics*, ed. B. K. Swartz and Raymond A. Dumett (The Hague, 1980), pp. 477–84; J. E. Inikori, 'The Import of Firearms into West Africa, 1750–1807: A Quantitative Analysis', in his *Forced Migration. The Impact of the Export Slave Trade on African Societies* (1982), pp. 126–53.

23 Plato, *The Republic*, V. 15–16; Cicero, *De Officiis*, XII. 23; Josiah Ober, 'Classical Greek Times', in *The Laws of War. Constraints on Warfare in the Western World*, ed. Michael Howard, George R. Andreopoulos and Mark R. Shulman (New Haven, 1994), pp. 12–26.

Medieval christians had attempted to distinguish several kinds of war. *Guerre mortelle*, or *bellum romanum*, was merciless war, usual against Islam, common between feuding individuals, but rare between recognized christian leaders. Indicated by flying a red banner, *guerre mortelle* meant no quarter, no prisoners and no ransom. Open, public war between christian sovereigns was more likely to be *bellum hostile*, which presumed unrestrained plundering and extortion but included the hope that non-combatants of either gender would be spared. Knights and squires who surrendered could hope to be ransomed for about one year's revenue from their estates, and to be paroled to assemble that money. Common soldiers could not give or receive such mercies, and were spared only if they could be profitably sold. Siege warfare commenced with the attacker calling for a surrender that, if refused, meant the inhabitants could expect no mercy. Garrison commanders sometimes held written contracts from their lords specifying the length of siege they were to endure, and surrenders were sometimes made conditional on failure of reinforcements to arrive by a specified time.[24]

The Reformation disrupted such limited civilities of western European war, as heretics were readily considered just as alien as infidels and barbarians. Fighting under the red flag became more common in these ideological wars. Old Testament tribalisms, that could call for the execution of entire defeated communities,[25] gained acceptance over New Testament calls for individual rather than communal responsibility for evil, and for mercy that included freeing captives. Biblical ambiguities about slavery were also applied; slaves were prisoners of war, so prisoners of war could be slaves.

Although slavery was considered a 'natural evil' to be borne as God's will, this perception did not always prompt resigned submission. When Barbary and Algerian 'pirates' captured the seaborne as revenge for the expulsion of Moors from Spain, a large redemption industry developed, including religious orders created specifically to ransom captives. Captured soldiers on either side in the long Dutch war for independence could, from the 1590s, expect their army to ransom them promptly, in part to discourage enlistment with their captors. By the early seventeenth century, Franco-Spanish reciprocity concerning prisoner exchange included the enlisted.[26]

Although Europe's migrants, colonists, and military officers brought these confused and evolving notions to North American conflicts, European prisoners

24 M. H. Keen, *The Laws of War in the Late Middle Ages* (Toronto, 1965), pp. 156–85; Robert C. Stacey, 'The Age of Chivalry', in *The Laws of War*, ed. Howard, Andreopoulos and Shulman, pp. 27–39.
25 Geoffrey Parker, 'Early Modern Europe', in *The Laws of War*, ed. Howard, Andreopoulos and Shulman, pp. 40–58; Numbers xxxi. 17–18; Deuteronomy XIII. 12–18; but see Deut. XXIV. 16 where 'a man shall be put to death only for his own sin'.
26 Ellen G. Friedman, *Spanish Captives in North Africa in the Early Modern Age* (Madison, Wisc., 1983); Geoffrey Parker, *The Army of Flanders and the Spanish Road, 1567–1659* (Cambridge, 1972), pp. 169–70.

captured there were usually exchanged. There were notable exceptions, however. The hatred between Spanish Catholics and French Huguenots surfaced in the slaughter of soldiers who had been granted quarter at Fort Caroline, Florida, in 1565 and 1567. As late as 1664, after Europe's diplomatic world had formally expanded to include the Americas, Dutch defenders of New Amstel on the Delaware River were still judged by their English conquerors to have forfeited their lives by refusing to surrender. After the fort was overrun, the 27 survivors were not put to the sword, but were sold into servitude in Virginia.[27]

Transactions for exchange of prisoners between colonial governments became routine, but could be complicated. When New York officials sought to recover Dutch settlers adopted by Canadian mission Amerindians, the Canadian governor reported that the adoptees were not for sale, but their Amerindian families would consider an exchange for Amerindian slaves.[28] There were relatively few Canadian prisoners in the British colonies, and they were prized by merchants to justify 'flag of truce' trips that masked lucrative illegal trade with Montreal, Louisbourg or Martinique. However, most British colonial governments had no strategic incentive to exchange prisoners with New France during war; the British colonial manpower advantage made it useful to retain French prisoners, especially if the captives were skilled frontier fighters.[29] English prisoners held in New France served their governments better, occasionally by smuggling out military intelligence, but more reliably by consuming scarce Canadian victuals to the point that military operations had to be delayed. Louisbourg, which imported virtually all of its food, was particularly vulnerable to shortages caused by successes like the Canso expedition of 1744, which brought 137 prisoners to the fortress. French and Canadian privateers repeatedly endangered Louisbourg themselves by dropping off captured prisoners, then taking captured ships and provisions elsewhere for sale. Bermuda was the only British colony in which the return of prisoners could be justified by a shortage of provisions.

European colonials did not usually take white women and children prisoner, but readily 'ransomed' them from Amerindian allies. If Canada and the British colonies were not then at war, these captives either 'worked off' their debt or were ransomed by relatives, parishes, or colonial governments. With the return of Anglo-French hostilities, English captives of either sex who had been sold to Canadians were treated as indentured and, once they had served their time, were then regarded as prisoners of war.[30]

27 C. A. Weslager, *The English on the Delaware, 1610–1682* (New Brunswick, N.J., 1967), pp. 176–96.
28 Ansel Judd Northrup, *Slavery in New York* (Albany, 1900), p. 307; J. C. Hamilton, 'The Panis: An Historical Outline of Canadian Indian Slavery in the Eighteenth Century', *Proceedings of the Royal Canadian Institute*, new ser., I (1898).
29 *The Dictionary of Canadian Biography* [hereafter *D.C.B.*] (13 vols., Toronto, 1966–94), IV, 633–6.
30 For example, Sarah Gerish of Dover, Massachusetts was exchanged for a Canadian soldier while the ill-fated Phips expedition was besieging Quebec in 1690. Drake, *Indian Captivities*, p. 70.

Race was a more fundamental category than gender in colonial views of prisoners. Non-white prisoners of either sex were an accepted part of plunder for seventeenth-century European soldiers and colonists in North America. Occasionally, Amerindian prisoners were held as hostages to provoke negotiation, as in Boston in 1687, Montreal in 1747, or Fort Prince George in 1759. Mohawk prisoners might even be sent to man Louis XIV's Mediterranean galleys, a royal whimsy that caused enough Iroquois outrage to prompt the return of the survivors.[31] Most Amerindian and African prisoners were sold into slavery, from the first Spanish raids on the Calusa and Timucua of Florida and on the Caddoans of the southern Great Plains. French traders bought so many Pawnee slaves that they used their name for all Amerindian slaves, though Apache and Caddoans were also enslaved in large numbers.[32] English fishermen were selling New England Amerindians, like Squanto, even before the Pilgrims landed, and Virginians were selling Amerindian captives in the West Indies from the 1630s, a half century before slavery became a significant feature of their tobacco industry.[33] South Carolinians bought and sold Amerindians from the founding of that colony. As late as 1760, North Carolina recruitment terms for the Cherokee War included personal ownership of captives as a major incentive.[34] Colonial militia, English colonial volunteer regiments, and Canadian *troupes de la marine* all sought Amerindian captives as plunder, occasionally to the detriment of their military objectives.[35] The 1716 peace negotiations between the defeated Fox and their Amerindian and Canadian opponents revealed a logical extension of this preoccupation. The Fox were required to make war 'in distant regions to get slaves, to replace all the dead who had been slain during the course of the war'.[36]

Despite their ready treatment of Amerindians as outside the bounds of civilized military conventions, European colonials made several adaptations concerning prisoners. Initially, prominent or promising Amerindians were taken back to Europe for display and advertisement, and to become informants and interpreters on subsequent voyages. The Spanish took Francisco Chicora and Paquiquineo (Don Luis de Velasco). The French took Donnacona's sons. The English took a considerable number, including Skidwarres (Abenaki) and Epenow (Wampanoag). The European

31 Jaenan, *Friend and Foe*, p. 136; Paul W. Bamford, 'Slaves for the Galleys of France, 1665 to 1700', in *Merchants and Scholars*, ed. J. Parker (Minneapolis, Min., 1965), pp. 173–91.
32 George E. Hyde, *The Pawnee Indians* (2nd edn., Norman, Okla., 1974), pp. 24, 46, 57, 70, 91, 94; Daniel H. Usner, jr., *Indians, Settlers, and Slaves in a Frontier Exchange Economy. The Lower Mississippi Valley Before 1783* (Chapel Hill, N.C., 1992), pp. 7, 46–51, 56–9.
33 Helen C. Rountree, *Pocahontas's People. The Powhatan Indians of Virginia Through Four Centuries* (Norman, Okla., 1990), pp. 85–6; James H. Merrell, *The Indians' New World. Catawbas and their Neighbors from European Contact Through the Era of Removal* (Chapel Hill, N.C., 1989), pp. 36–7.
34 Perdue, *Slavery*, p. 25.
35 Unsuccessful sieges of San Augustín in 1702 and 1728 were particularly blatant examples.
36 *The French Regime in Wisconsin, 1634–1760*, ed. Reuben G. Thwaites (3 vols., Madison, Wisc., 1902–8), I, 343. The Fox did not fulfil this condition.

assumption, that exposure to their civilization would turn these captive Amerindians into willing agents of European expansion, almost always proved erroneous.[37]

Before the development of a regular trade in Amerindian prisoners, Europeans occasionally used fire and sword on Amerindian defenders, indiscriminately killing all who tried to escape their burning towns or villages. Soto did this at Mabila in 1541, claiming he was provoked by treachery. Captain John Underhill, a Netherlands-trained soldier and instructor of the early Massachusetts militia, planned the slaughter of the Pequot at Mystic Fort in 1637, and did the same to a Siwanoy village in Kieft's war seven years later.[38] It is noteworthy that these atrocities occurred where and when there was no regular trade in Amerindian prisoners. The context was different by 1675, when a New England army attacked a Narragansett stockade in the Great Swamp Fight. The attackers were anxious to capture both needed supplies and valuable prisoners, but set fire to both when the battle failed to go as planned.[39]

A trade in Amerindian slaves might be expected to replace exterminating attacks with more profitable captures, but slavery did not moderate slaughter along all frontiers. New Englanders kept some Amerindian slaves, but did not develop a major Amerindian slave trade to the English West Indies. The Barbados Assembly, shocked by news of King Philip's war, apparently prohibited the import of New England Amerindian captives, and decided 'to send away and transport those already brought to this island from New England and the adjacent colonies, being thought a people of too subtle, bloody and dangerous inclination to be and remain here'.[40]

A more widespread adaptation was the scalp bounty, which was variable in itself and in relation to the bounty/ransom which colonial governments paid for Amerindian prisoners. In the 1690s, for instance, the Canadian government offered twice as much for male captives as for females, with a scalp bounty at the lower price. Given the risks and costs of holding prisoners, some premium was required of governments seeking information. In the same period Massachusetts escalated its scalp bounty until there was no premium at all for keeping Amerindian prisoners alive.[41] This perversion of Amerindian custom created a land-based privateering industry, as in the Massachusetts-Abenaki war of the 1720s. Investor syndicates sent private armies to take scalps. If the bounties offered for scalps versus prisoners was a barometer of a

37 On Squanto's exceptional reaction see Neal Salibury, 'Squanto, Last of the Patuxets', in *Struggle and Survival in Colonial America*, ed. David Sweet and Gary Nash (Berkeley, 1981), pp. 228–46.

38 Cf. Increase Mather, *A Relation on the Troubles in New England* (Boston, 1677), pp. 50–4.

39 Ian K. Steele, *Warpaths. Invasions of North America* (New York, 1994), p. 102.

40 The act was of short duration, and was not renewed, but something similar was passed again in 1688. Handler, 'Amerindian Slave Population', pp. 57–60.

41 Canadian prices were 20 and 10 ecu respectively. Thomas-Marie Charland, *Histoire des Abénakis d'Odanak* (Montreal, 1964), p. 49. *The Glorious Revolution in Massachusetts. Selected Documents, 1689–1692*, ed. Robert E. Moody and Richard C. Simmons (Boston, 1988), p. 282; Richard I. Melvoin, *New England Outpost* (New York, 1989), pp. 201, 228, 229.

colony's fear, Connecticut in the 1740s was in terror. That government was paying £400 for a male Amerindian scalp, which was £25 more than they paid for a prisoner.[42]

European colonists regarded themselves as fundamentally different from Amerindians, whom they considered outside the prisoner conventions that they afforded most fellow Europeans. Usually the only colonists taken prisoner by other colonists were adult males, and most of these captives worked to sustain themselves in captivity until they were exchanged.[43] Most Amerindians of either gender and any age were considered booty, and were enslaved, if not scalped, by bounty hunters. Canadians may have shared these British colonial views, but had numerous Amerindian allies whose presence often confused their own and even their enemies' distinctions.

A revised set of martial conventions spread through western Europe after the middle of the seventeenth century, led by the French. Aristocratic officers in the service of the crown ritualized, professionalized and 'ennobled' military life as taught in the new officer training schools.[44] This development interacted with the evolution of international law, pioneered by sixteenth-century scholars like Franciscus de Vitoria and Francisco Suarez, then elaborated and secularized into 'the law of nations' by writers such as Alberico Gentili and Hugo Grotius.[45] The new etiquette of siege and surrender was symptomatic, helping defending commanders pick the appropriate time to surrender in order to avoid either execution by their own courts-martial or slaughter by their conquerors. After a stout defence that lasted until the wall was breached at ground level, defenders of a fortress were to withstand one assault on that breach, then raise the white flag. A brief parlay could be held to ensure that this event or its equivalent had occurred. The coveted 'honours of war' then allowed the defenders to keep their arms, standards and personal effects and, after agreeing not to fight for a specified period, they could proceed to the nearest post held by their own side without becoming prisoners at all.

After 1648, all ranks were routinely to be taken prisoner in western European warfare, were not to be treated as criminals, and were to be exchanged by cartel or

---

42 See J. L. Sibley and C. K. Shipton, *Harvard Graduates* (8 vols., Cambridge, Mass., 1873–1951), VI, 407–8 and VII, 176–7 re investments; John K. Mahon, *History of the Militia and the National Guard* (New York, 1983), p. 22.

43 The government-funded 'prisoners house' in Quebec City was one exception, and British colonial governments occasionally paid locals for the maintenance of soldier-prisoners.

44 Norbert Elias, 'The Courtization of Warriors', in his *The Civilizing Process* (2 vols., New York, 1978), II, 258–70; cf. Armstrong Starkey, 'War and Culture, a Case Study: The Enlightenment and the Conduct of the British Army in America, 1755–1781', *War and Society*, VIII (1990), 1–28. The increasing separation of women from armies accompanied early modern developments, perhaps as part of 'the divorce between gainful labor and family life which is a feature of the modern economic order'. John U. Nef, *War and Human Progress* (New York, 1968), pp. 210–11.

45 James Turner Johnson, *Ideology, Reason, and the Limitations of War. Religious and Secular Concepts, 1200–1740* (Princeton, 1975).

as specified in peace treaties. The holding of substantial numbers of prisoners on both sides generally encouraged better treatment, or at least allowed threats of reprisals in the event of gross mistreatment. Prisoners could also be security against counterattack, for all cultures agreed that prisoners would be killed if their guards were attacked. Prisoners' own governments were to compensate captors for the pay and upkeep of prisoners and were to provide supplements like the French royal bounty that improved the diet for French subjects held by the British. Armies and navies actively recruited among prisoners of war, and occasionally allowed other governments to do so as well.[46]

Military officers who were taken prisoner were to be paroled in order to find a prisoner of comparable status held by their own government, and they routinely returned to captivity if this search proved unsuccessful. The stigma of captivity was moderate; the pay of officers continued while they were prisoners though they were not eligible for promotion. Cartels and exchanges of all prisoners became common, according to a recognized hierarchical scale of values. A field marshal, for instance, could be exchanged for 3,000 rank-and-file.[47]

Amid their new civilities, European soldiers still distinguished sharply between those afforded 'the law of nations' and those excluded. Emmerich de Vattel, Swiss jurist whose influential *Droit des gens* was published in 1758, claimed 'When we are at war with a savage nation, who observe no rules, and never give quarter, we may punish them in the persons of any of their people whom we take.'[48] There were three other arguments that were used to justify indiscriminate war against Amerindians. Firstly, kin-ordered societies were not treated as nations at all in eighteenth-century international law. Secondly, irregular troops, like the Austrian pandours, French chasseurs, and partisans, were all regarded as fighting less nobly, and were routinely shot upon capture.[49] Thirdly, rebellious subjects were often considered as criminals who were outside military conventions.[50] Those grandiose British claims to extensive Amerindian lands in the Treaties of Utrecht (1713) and Paris (1763) were not harmless puffery, for they allowed the Amerindians to be regarded as rebels in the 1720s and in 'Pontiac's Rebellion' of 1763–5. Whether regarded as barbarians, as kin-ordered communities, as irregular warriors or as rebels, Amerindians were easily

---

46 After Naseby, the French and Spanish were allowed to recruit among royalist prisoners. Geoffrey Parker, *The Military Revolution* (Cambridge, 1988), pp. 50–1.

47 Christopher Duffy, *The Military Experience of the Age of Reason* (1987), pp. 265–7.

48 Emmarich de Vattel, *Laws of Nations* (Philadelphia, 1861), p. 348.

49 Duffy, *Military Experience*, p. 277.

50 The main parties in the English Civil War usually accorded the new conventions to their opponents. Barbara Donagan, 'Codes and Conduct in the English Civil War', *Past and Present*, 118 (1988), 65–95. After the Jacobite risings of 1715 and 1745, most of the captured 3,471 men, women and children who survived incarceration were transported to the colonies without trial. Those with commissions in French regular regiments, however, were exchanged. Bruce Lenman, *The Jacobite Risings in Britain, 1689–1746* (1980), pp. 271–5.

excluded from the peculiar new conventions of eighteenth-century European warfare, provided those Amerindians fought alone.

These 'enlightened' conventions of European warfare arrived gradually in North America along with military governors, naval officers, fulsome colonial newspaper accounts of European warfare, training manuals and terms of European peace treaties. When European courts made global peace, and ordered the return of all prisoners, there were persistent difficulties in recovering captives from Amerindians. After the peace of 1697, a New York mission to Canada and a Canadian mission to Iroquoia both found that most of those adopted by Amerindians were so resistant to returning that a semblance of exchange could be achieved only by forcing those under 12 years of age to return.[51] The Peace of Utrecht called for a general exchange of prisoners, but English converts to catholicism were left at liberty to remain in Canada. The Peace of Aix-la-Chapelle had a similar clause, causing private efforts to redeem captives to become a complex five-year diplomatic wrangle about the return of some colonial captives and the redemption of others. These negotiations also sought the release of 26 Abenaki held near Boston during most of the war, and of three prominent Mohawk held prisoner in Canada.[52] Holding these Amerindian prisoners was itself unusual, apparently intended to provoke separate negotiations with the Amerindian allies of one's European opponents.

III

Mixtures of the three military cultures occurred in North America throughout the century after 1660, but became much more frequent in the two decades after 1744: one decade involving few European regulars, and the next one featuring many. The four formal sieges and surrenders that concerned Massachusetts governor William Shirley during the war of the Austrian Succession can illustrate the first of these periods of renewed confusion and adaptation. Shirley was an English lawyer with no military experience who had lived in Boston for a decade before becoming governor in 1741.[53] The sieges of Canso (1744), Louisbourg (1745), Fort Massachusetts (1746) and Grand Pré (1747) involved a variety of forces, conventions and outcomes. At Canso, a Canadian-led force defeated the remnants of four decrepit and locally recruited British companies commanded by Nova Scotia-born Captain John Bradstreet. Not only the garrison but also their families were taken prisoners of war.

---

51 *Calendar of State Papers, Colonial Series, America and the West Indies, 1700*, pp. 443–4; *N.Y.C.D.*, IV, 340–1, 343–5, 347–51, 435–6; W. J. Eccles, *Canada under Louis XIV, 1663–1701* (Toronto, 1964), pp. 205–6.

52 See *N.Y.C.D.*, VI, 484–7, 494–5, 500, 512–13, 520, 539–40, 542, 720–1; X, 185–6, 192, 209–11, 214–15.

53 John A. Schutz, *William Shirley: King's Governor of Massachusetts* (Chapel Hill, N.C., 1960); William Pencak, *War, Politics, and the Revolution in Provincial Massachusetts* (Boston, 1981), pp. 115–47.

The 50 women and children were soon sent from Louisbourg to Boston as the first act of what would be a complete release of prisoners by a governor who could not feed them. The victors had been promised booty, as was common in intercolonial war, but the valuable captured fish was apparently treated as the prisoners' personal effects and therefore exempt from plundering. The captives immediately sold the fish to the Canadian officers at extremely low prices.[54] In another garbling of the newer European conventions, the captives initially agreed to a clause making them prisoners of war for one year. Louisbourg's governor Jean-Baptiste-Louis le Prévost Du-quesnel, a career French naval officer,[55] had these prisoners sign a more conventional parole of honour, agreeing not to fight for a year after their release and promising the return of Canadians held prisoner in Boston.[56] In a surrender that had not involved Amerindians, Canadians and British Americans had observed some approximation of recent European conventions.

Aided by the released prisoners, Governor Shirley organized the 1745 New England assault on Louisbourg. Louis du Pont Duchambon, commander of the Canadian colonial regulars, proposed surrender terms after nearly seven weeks under siege. As finally negotiated with New England merchant-prince William Pepperrell and Commodore Peter Warren of the royal navy, all 900 civilians would be sent to France along with the defeated garrison. Duchambon's peculiar request for two covered wagons was granted, on condition they 'be inspected only by one officer of ours, that no warlike stores may be contained therein'. Anyone whom the governor did not want the victors to see, including at least four Canso turncoats, could 'go off masked'. French sick and wounded would be tended 'in the same manner with our own', reflecting the precise sentiments attributed to Louis XV at the battle of Fontenoy that same year.[57] These terms were conditional upon the return of all New England prisoners, and the taking of an oath by the inhabitants of Louisbourg that they would not take up arms against the British for a year. It was only at the final stage in these negotiations that Duchambon asked for the ritual aspects of the 'honours of war'. The conquered were allowed to leave the fortress with their muskets and with regimental colours flying, but these were to be surrendered to the British until arrival in France.[58] Although threatened with retaliation for minor

---

54 *Louisbourg in 1745. An Anonymous Lettre D'un Habitant De Louisbourg*, ed. G. M. Wrong (New York, 1897), p. 34. National Archives of Canada, C¹¹B, 26: 'Statement made by Messrs. Garrerot, Sabatier and Bigot concerning the booty taken at Canso, June 20, 1744'.

55 *D.C.B.*, III, 392–3.

56 William G. Godfrey, *Pursuit of Profit and Preferment in Colonial North America. John Bradstreet's Quest* (Waterloo, Ont., 1982), p. 22; *Boston News Letter*, 27 Sept., 6 Dec. 1744.

57 Starkey, 'War and Culture', p. 1.

58 'Journal of Roger Wolcott at the Siege of Louisbourg, 1745', *Collections of the Connecticut Historical Society*, I (1860), 144–7; *Correspondence of William Shirley*, ed. Charles Henry Lincoln (2 vols., New York, 1912), I, 239–41; G. A. Rawlyk, *Yankees at Louisbourg* (Orono, Me., 1967), pp. 144–52; J. S. McLennan, *Louisbourg from its Foundation to its Fall* (4th edn., Halifax, 1979), pp. 162–5, 178–80.

Amerindian raids in which scalps had been taken,[59] and cursed by New England troops who were deprived of promised plunder,[60] Europe's newer conventions had prevailed.

Although only 120 miles west of Boston, newly-stockaded Fort Massachusetts was in another world in 1746. François-Pierre de Rigaud de Vaudreuil, Montreal-born son of a former governor of Canada, led the attack. He was accompanied by 20 *troupes de la marine*, 400 Canadian militiamen and some 300 Amerindians, predominantly Iroquois and Abenaki from the mission settlements around Montreal.[61] After a day and a half of musket exchanges had produced numerous casualties on both sides, there was a two-hour truce to allow Sergeant John Hawks and the remaining 21 Massachusetts militiamen, three women and five children to consider their situation. Revealing terms were agreed upon:

> I. That we should be all prisoners of the French; the general promising that the savages should have nothing to do with any of us.
>
> II. That the children should all live with their parents during the time of their captivity.
>
> III. That we should all have the privilege of being exchanged the first opportunity that presented.
>
> Besides these particulars, the general promised that all the prisoners should have all christian care and charity exercised toward them; that those who were weak and unable to travel should be carried in their journey; that we should all be allowed to keep our clothing; and that we might leave a few lines to inform our friends what was become of us. [62]

These terms reflected a lifetime of experience and apprehension on this frontier. They indicated a preoccupation with avoiding Amerindian captivity, an assumption that wives and children were captives, and a fear that the wounded would be killed if they could not keep up with this war party. There was no point in specifying that the 'captives' or 'prisoners' were technically prisoners of war, though prompt exchange was sought. 'Honours of war' were not even mentioned; these were not yet part of the military culture on this frontier.

Despite the agreement, 16 of the captured were promptly turned over to the Amerindians, no doubt to fulfil recruiting promises. By this action, Rigaud treated his allies justly, but confirmed suspicions that the terms of a capitulation were not

---

59 Massachusetts Historical Society, Louisbourg Papers, IV, nos. 7, 8, 14; Pepperrell Papers, I, f. 178. See also Wrong, *Louisbourg in 1745*, pp. 53, 55; 'Walcott Journal', pp. 133–4.

60 L. E. DeForest, *Louisbourg Journals 1745* (New York, 1932), pp. 91, 92; Shirley, *Correspondence*, I, 260; *Journal of the Taking of Cape-Breton, Put in Metre, by L. G. One of the Soldiers in the Expedition* (Boston, 1745); Douglas E. Leach, 'Brothers in Arms? – Anglo-American Friction at Louisbourg, 1745–1746', *Proceedings of the Massachusetts Historical Society*, LXXXIX (1977), 36–54.

61 *D.C.B.*, IV, 660–2; Jay Cassel, 'The Troupes de la Marine in Canada, 1683–1760', University of Toronto, Ph.D. 1988, Appendix D.

62 Rev. John Norton, *Narrative of the Capture and Burning of Fort Massachusetts* (Albany, 1870), pp. 15–16.

inviolate.[63] Nothing is known about the method of allocating these prisoners among specific participating warriors; after such a formal capitulation no one could claim to be the captor of a specific prisoner. Amerindian care of these prisoners was later commended, including their carrying the wounded and ill.[64] Ten of the Amerindians' prisoners were immediately ransomed by Canada's government, and rejoined those being sent to the 'prisoner's house' in Quebec. Whatever additional arrangements were made with their Amerindian masters, the other six rejoined the larger group within six weeks.[65] The mission Amerindians had been able to bring captives home for a village triumph, be paid a ransom, and then send their prisoners along to conform roughly with Europe's view of what constituted fair treatment for prisoners of war. The other 14 prisoners were apparently taken to Canada as prisoners of individual Canadian officers.[66] This view, that these prisoners were initially private possessions rather than prisoners of the king of France, reflected both Amerindian and earlier European practices.

Soon after arrival in Canada all these prisoners were ransomed by the government and sent to the 'prisoner's house' in Quebec, where their treatment was determined by that veteran naval officer who had been governor general of New France for two decades, the marquis de Beauharnois.[67] These prisoners were not hired out as farm labourers; the government of Canada maintained them until they could be exchanged the following year, by which time 16 of the 30 were dead of fevers and scurvy.[68] The four surviving prisoner journals convey the terrible misfortunes of this situation, but with surprisingly little rancour against their captors.[69] The Rev. Benjamin Doolittle, who attempted a judicious New England account of this frontier war soon thereafter, argued 'the French treated our Men civilly and tenderly: So also did the Indians those with them according to their Manner'.[70] There had been none of the feared

63 A decade later, when Montcalm refused to do likewise at Oswego and at Fort William Henry, mission Indians killed and captured prisoners. Steele, *Betrayals*, pp. 79, 109–28.
64 Norton, *Narrative*, p. 21, reported that Rigaud had promised rewards for Indians helping the feeble.
65 *Ibid.*, pp. 19–51; William Pote, *The Journal of Captain William Pote ... May 1745 to August 1747*, ed. V. Paltsits (New York, 1896), p. 133.
66 Norton became the personal prisoner of Lieutenant Jacques-Pierre Daneau de Muy of the colonial regulars. Sergeant Hawks was taken by St Luc de la Corne. Norton, *Narrative*, pp. 17–18; Arthur Latham Perry, *Origins of Williamstown* (2nd edn., New York, 1896), pp. 145–7, 187; *D.C.B.*, III, 161–3. Cf. Emma Lewis Coleman, *New England Captives Carried to Canada between 1677 and 1760 during the French and Indian Wars* (2 vols., Portland, Me., 1925–6), II, 205.
67 *D.C.B.*, III, 41–51; Dale Miquelon, *New France 1701–1744. 'A Supplement to Europe'* (Toronto, 1987), pp. 95–123.
68 Perry, *Williamstown*, p. 187; Norton, *Narrative*, *passim*; Coleman, *New England Captives*, II, 203–10.
69 Norton, *Narrative*; Nehemiah How, *Narrative of the Captivity of Nehemiah How* (Boston, 1748); Pote, *Journal of Captain William Pote*, ed. Paltsits; Anon, 'From my Private Notes in Rhode Island, Anno 1748', in *Colonial Captivities, Marches, and Journeys*, ed. I. M. Calder (New York, 1935), pp. 3–136.
70 Benjamin Doolittle, *A Short Narrative of Mischief Done by the French and Indian Enemy on the Western Frontiers of the Province of Massachusetts Bay* (Boston, 1750), p. 9.

Amerindian cruelty, hard labour, or forced conversion to catholicism that had marked the popular literature about earlier captivities. Elements of Amerindian, colonial, and new imperial conventions had been meshed effectively.

For Governor Shirley, the last formal capitulation of this war occurred along the Nova Scotia frontier at Grand Pré in February of 1747, and again showed a blending of martial conventions. Captain Nicholas-Antoine Coulon de Villiers led a winter raid by some 235 Canadians and 42 Malecite, Micmac, and Abenaki. Their target was some 470 Massachusetts volunteers who had been sent by Governor Shirley to occupy the Acadian village of Grand Pré. Most of that scattered garrison survived the initial attack and retreated to a stone house, defending it well enough to be offered terms. Neither the militiamen nor the Amerindians would undertake a direct assault on a well-defended position. Captain Benjamin Goldthwait, a Bostonian who had served at the siege of Louisbourg, negotiated for the New Englanders.[71] He was unsuccessful in seeking the return of all prisoners and plunder already captured. He also sought the honours of war, specified as: being allowed a vessel to take them to Annapolis, keeping their muskets, powder and ball, and carrying six days' provisions in their haversacks. The Canadians and Amerindians allowed the defeated to *march* to Annapolis, equipped as suggested, provided they would not fight in that theatre for six months. The sick and wounded, except for paroled Captain Howe, were to be cared for by the Canadians, and returned when well. Captain Howe's parole included his exchange for a Captain 'Lagrois' and all other French prisoners at Boston.[72] The Canadians and Amerindians had acquired enough traditional plunder and captives to honour these terms and head home.

Arrival of European regulars in large numbers after 1755 would bring victory for the new martial values, but only after confusion that can only be hinted at here. After the battle of Lake George, William Johnston treated captive General Jean-Armand, baron de Dieskau, with every fashionable civility, while sending other French captives as presents to help his Mohawk friends mourn their dead. Montcalm's capture of Oswego in 1756 meant that 1,800 prisoners of war arrived in a Canada that did not have enough grain to feed them. Next year, after his victory at Fort William Henry, Montcalm avoided taking prisoners by paroling the 2300-man garrison, which promised to stay out of the war for 18 months. The subsequent attack on the parolees, dubbed a 'massacre', demonstrated Amerindian ability to frustrate European

---

71   *D.C.B.*, III, 259–60.

72   Daniel-Hyacinthe-Marie Liénard de Beaujeu, 'Journal de la Campagne de Détachement de Canada à l'Acadie et aux Mines en 1746–47', in *Collection de documents inédits sur le Canada et l'Amerique* (3 vols., Quebec, 1888), II, 59–75; *D.C.B.*, III, 149–51, 400–2; Francis Parkman, *A Half-Century of Conflict* (2 vols., Boston, 1905), II, 182–200. Stephen Coffen, a soldier in the garrison, was taken prisoner by Indians, but only lived with them for three weeks before being put to work with Canadian fishermen at Gaspé. *N.Y.C.D.*, VI, 835–7. It is noteworthy that Coleman, *New England Captives*, does not include these captives. A Sieur de Lagroix was captured off Labrador, 24 July 1745 and returned from Boston 28 May 1747. Archives Nationales, Paris, Colonies, C^{11}A 87, pp. 43–4. Dr Jay Cassell kindly provided this information.

conventions that would have cost them the scalps, prisoners and booty they had been promised. Consequently, British regulars refused to grant the honours of war to infuriated French regulars at Louisbourg, Quebec and Montreal; the garrison at Fort Niagara was allowed only the ritual honour of leaving the fort 'with their arms and baggage, drums beating, and match lighted at both ends, and a small piece of cannon' before going to New York as prisoners of war. The 30 Amerindian defenders of Fort Niagara, who had earlier talked with a Six Nations legation, were simply released.[73]

A striking confusion of conventions occurred in the Cherokee War (1759–61). British regulars took hostages and burned the deserted Cherokee towns as though earlier, or colonial, conventions still prevailed, but unwisely sought the 'honours of war' when starved into surrendering Fort Loudoun to the Cherokee in August of 1760. The Cherokee agreed, and the freed garrison began a 200-mile retreat to the nearest British fort. After two days on the trail they were attacked; all but one officer was killed and the survivors were retaken as prisoners.

However, British regulars had already begun a major adaptation to war with Amerindians. Early in 1760 Colonel Archibald Montgomery made the return of all prisoners into a precondition for peace talks with the Cherokee. This tactic is not known to have been an established part of European, colonial or Amerindian military conventions. The Cherokee promptly returned 113 prisoners, perhaps those controlled by the negotiators and their close dependents, but would not surrender more without some ransom or exchange of people or gifts.[74] Later that same year, Ohio Amerindian communities anxious to make peace faced the same British demand, which was a major threat to their new composite communities. The British regulars insisted that all prisoners be returned without ransom or exchange, including those adopted and even those wishing to remain in Amerindian communities. Compliance was predictably slow and limited, and British negotiators were too anxious to conclude expensive military operations to pursue the matter further.[75]

Return of all captives had been a colonial war objective that became a clever imperial tactic which tested Amerindian interest in peace more reliably than did the promises of negotiating chiefs. For Amerindians, however, compliance was difficult. Surrendering prisoners without reciprocity or payment implied that participation in the war had been a great crime rather than an honourable vocation. Chiefs without traditional authority to force the surrender of captives were lured or bullied into promises that were beyond their power to keep. Chiefs could, and did, surrender their

---

73 Terms are reprinted in Brian L. Dunnigan, *Siege – 1759. The Campaign against Niagara* (Youngstown, N.Y., 1986), pp. 100–1; Pierre Pouchot, *Memoirs on the Late War in North America Between France and England* (Youngstown, N.Y., 1994), pp. 246–8, nn. 746, 747.

74 David H. Corkran, *The Cherokee Frontier. Conflict and Survival, 1740–1962* (Norman, Okla., 1962), pp. 142–272.

75 *The Papers of Sir William Johnson*, ed. James Sullivan (14 vols., Albany, 1921–65), III, 550; X, 198–206, 317–18; Richard White, *The Middle Ground. Indians, Empires, and Republics in the Great Lakes Region, 1650–1815* (Cambridge and New York, 1991), pp. 261–3.

own prisoners, but could not effectively order the return of others. Compliance would devastate upper Ohio Valley communities that had absorbed so many prisoners for a decade. No wonder this innovation was resisted and ignored whenever possible. The British regular officers had devised a policy that was wise only if the resulting peace was perpetual; such a policy could make the taking of scalps much more honourable than the taking of prisoners.

As they began negotiations to end the explosive Amerindian War of 1763–5, the British regulars again demanded that all prisoners be returned as a preliminary to peace talks.[76] Colonel Henry Bouquet had the recently-won military reputation, the Amerindian hostages, and the British bayonets to force compliance from Ohio tribes. He insisted on the return of all prisoners 'English men, Frenchmen, women & children whether adopted in your tribes, marry'd or Living amongst you under any denomination or pretense whatever'. Children of captives were to be returned as well.[77] Ecstatic and pathetic scenes of 'redemption' at Muskingam River, Fort Pitt and Carlisle, Pennsylvania, in 1764 and 1765 destroyed more families than were reunited.[78] Amid some happy reunions there were disrupted interracial marriages, returning spouses who discovered they had been superseded, and youths who would soon run back to their Amerindian homes. White and métis children had to be tied hand and foot, and could not understand a word their parents spoke, if their parents could be identified at all. In their zeal to redeem all the captives, and extract abject Amerindian submission, the British army had converted prisoners of war into prisoners of peace.

IV

Over more than two centuries, Amerindian views of captives had been asserted, adapted, blended, confused and suppressed, but never entirely extinguished. Colonists had made clear racial distinctions in applying Reformation Europe's views of treatment of prisoners, granting quarter and exchange to fellow-Europeans while routinely regarding Amerindian prisoners as fit only for slavery or death. Even when substantial numbers of colonists were held among the Amerindians, colonists seldom took Amerindian captives for exchange, and there was little Amerindian interest in such exchanges.[79] This complete lack of reciprocity, which Amerindian negotiators frequently denounced by the 1750s, fit very well with the assumptions of the European regulars who arrived after 1755. While they largely completed colonial conversion to the 'honours of war', and apparently did not participate in a slave

76 Steele, *Warpaths*, p. 243.
77 Huntington Lib., HM 569; *Pennsylvania Gazette*, 15 Nov. 1764, No. 1873.
78 William Smith, *An Historical Account of the Expedition Against the Ohio Indians, in the Year 1764, Under the Command of Henry Bouquet Esq.* (Philadelphia, 1766); *Pennsylvania Gazette*, 9 Sept. 1762, No. 1759.
79 One intriguing exception is claimed in Mather's *A Relation on the Troubles*, pp. 50, 53.

trade, the regular officers routinely excluded Amerindians from their conventions. While refusal to return prisoners was in keeping with Amerindian custom, insistence upon a unilateral return of 'every drop of European blood' was a wrenching innovation accepted only under duress. With the Anglo-French struggle suspended, Europeans were insisting upon a racial definition of identity that Amerindians were, most reluctantly, being forced to accept.

8

Tea, Tribute and the East India Company
*c.*1750–*c.*1775

H. V. BOWEN

In 1788, a former director of the East India Company, Thomas Bates Rous, wrote of the tea trade, 'It is difficult to convey to the imagination of those who are unused to consider the subject, the mighty size of the object.' He then went on to suggest that 'on mentioning the article, it appears almost ludicrous, but when considered, as it is now unhappily become the food of the whole people of Great Britain, it must soon draw the serious attention of every well-wisher to his country'.[1] In his last years, Philip Lawson devoted a considerable amount of serious attention to the growth of the eighteenth-century tea trade, convinced that it allowed important and meaningful connexions to be made between different areas of historical study. His work on the 'empire of tea'[2] examined the social and cultural impact of the trade and he acknowledged the part that it played in shaping the British imperial experience. Tea drinking and its accompanying rituals represented a 'transatlantic addiction' which, he argued, helped to define the social and cultural contours of the Anglo-American world.[3] As far as the East India Company was concerned, he wrote that 'the eighteenth century was undoubtedly the age of tea',[4] and he gave due emphasis to the way in which the growth of the trade helped to redefine the economic terms of reference within which Britain's Indian empire was placed. Observing that the tea trade had become a 'cash cow to be tendered with great care',[5] he linked different forms of overseas expansion. Military and political success in Bengal had brought the Company control of large revenues which were used to stimulate the China tea trade as part of an attempt to facilitate the transfer of 'tribute' or revenue surpluses from India to Britain. Territorial expansion thus helped to dictate patterns of commercial

[1] Thomas Bates Rous, *An Explanation of the Mistaken Principle on Which the Commutation Act was Founded; And the Nature of the Mischiefs that Must Follow from a Perseverance in It* (1788), p. 4. Rous (M.P. for Worcester 1773–4 and 1774–84) had followed in his father's footsteps and served as a director of the Company during the 1770s.

[2] Philip Lawson, 'Tea, Vice and the English State, 1660–1784', in *idem, A Taste for Empire and Glory. Studies in British Overseas Expansion* (Aldershot, 1997), item XIV, p. 2.

[3] Philip Lawson, 'Sources, Schools and Separation: The Many Faces of Parliament's Role in Anglo-American History to 1783', in *Parliament and the Atlantic Empire*, ed. Philip Lawson (Edinburgh, 1995), pp. 20–1.

[4] Philip Lawson, *The East India Company. A History* (1993), p. 100.

[5] *Ibid.*, p. 100.

expansion, with the growth of the tea trade after 1760 being driven by both consumer demand in Britain and the urgent need to service an extended and much-changed Indian empire.

In recent years, other historians have also explored the importance of the tea trade in helping to underpin and sustain British imperial activity. A great deal of detailed information and analysis is now available on how the eighteenth-century trade operated and was regulated. The effects of smuggling have been examined, and much is now known about how the commodity was marketed, distributed and consumed.[6] More generally, within a context provided by an attempt to establish links between the process of domestic industrialization and the development of the British overseas presence, J. R. Ward has shown how the growth of the China tea trade helped to strengthen and expand the British Indian empire during the later part of the eighteenth century.[7] In particular, he argues that, because an expansion of the 'country' or inter-Asian trade with Canton helped European agency houses in India to generate substantial profits after 1780, the tea business helped to underwrite British imperialism by providing some of the vital resources that were made available to the East India Company in the form of loan finance. Indeed, as borrowing from Indian capitalists diminished, a small number of agency houses became the 'main source of loans', and this more than anything else allowed the Company to maintain large armies which could be deployed in wars of conquest. Developments within an industrializing metropolitan economy are thus held by Ward to have played a key role in allowing this to happen because any expansion of the China trade depended ultimately upon increased domestic consumption of the tea that was shipped into Britain in an ever-growing amount after 1750. Hence Ward not only analyses how tea imports were paid for in China through the export of manufactured goods from Britain, but he also stresses the importance of the strength of the consumer demand that was evident within an industrializing and urbanizing economy.

On the whole, this interpretation is a convincing one, yet, although it embraces the entire century before 1850, and focuses in particular on the years 1790 to 1820, Ward's article, like the work of others, treads rather lightly over the period between 1750 and 1775 when the East India Company's tea trade underwent a considerable expansion. Indeed, rather surprisingly, the third quarter of the eighteenth century

---

6 See, most notably, K. N. Chaudhuri, *The Trading World of Asia and the English East India Company, 1660–1760* (Cambridge, 1978); W. A. Cole, 'Trends in Eighteenth-Century Smuggling', *Economic History Review*, 2nd ser., X (1957–8), 395–410; idem, 'The Arithmetic of Eighteenth-Century Smuggling: A Rejoinder', *ibid.*, XXVIII (1975), 44–9; Hoh-Cheung and Lorna H. Mui, 'Smuggling and the British Tea Trade Before 1784', *American Historical Review*, LXXIV (1968–9) 44–73; idem, '"Trends in Eighteenth-Century Smuggling" Reconsidered', *Economic History Review*, 2nd ser., XXVIII (1975), 28–49; idem, *The Management of Monopoly. A Study of the East India Company's Conduct of its Tea Trade 1784–1833* (Vancouver, 1984); idem, *Shops and Shopkeeping in Eighteenth-Century England* (1989).

7 J. R. Ward, 'The Industrial Revolution and British Imperialism, 1750–1850', *Economic History Review*, 2nd ser., XLVII (1994), 55–65.

represents a somewhat neglected period in the history of the Company's tea trade. Where the trade has received attention from historians, this has often been in a context provided by analysis of smuggling or the series of events that led to the Boston Tea Party in 1773.[8] Little attention has been paid to the commercial and imperial preconditions of the 1760s and 1770s which dictated the sudden expansion of the tea trade, helping to push the Company to the very brink of bankruptcy and plunging the British empire into the deep political crisis which resulted in the eventual loss of the American colonies.

Here, those preconditions are examined, and attention is devoted to some of the primary reasons which help to explain why it proved so difficult, in the face of prevailing commercial expectations, for the Company to exploit the growth of the tea trade during the 1760s and 1770s. In theory, the trade promised much to the Company and the British government, but in the short term it proved to be a conspicuous failure. The foundations upon which the trade rested during this period were ill-adapted to the new demands made upon it by the Company's directors and politicians. It was only after radical action was taken and import duties were cut back from 119 to 12½ per cent following the passage of Pitt's Commutation Act in 1784 that conditions were properly established for successful and sustainable long-term growth. Until that time, the Company was unable to exploit its most prized commercial asset in the way that had been anticipated, with the result that the newly won material benefits of the Indian empire remained unrealized. Indeed, it can be argued that, far from underwriting British imperialism during the 1760s and 1770s, the tea trade did exactly the opposite and began instead to undermine it.

During the first half of the eighteenth century the East India Company's tea trade underwent considerable growth.[9] From humble origins in the seventeenth century the trade had expanded, despite marked annual fluctuations, to the point where the Company was importing around 3,500,000 pounds of tea a year into Britain from China during the 1750s. This figure, which marked a fivefold increase on the figures for the 1720s, represented such a rate of expansion that by mid-century the trade, supported by the spread of the tea-drinking habit, had become a key part of the Company's commercial operations. Tea accounted for around 25 per cent of the value of all goods imported into Britain by the Company, and sale receipts from tea were such that the commodity had risen to a position of 'prized profit-making status'. These developments were not without their problems, however, and several features of the tea trade regularly troubled the directors of the Company. Most notably, there was evidence of a significant imbalance between supply and demand which meant that

8   B. W. Labaree, *The Boston Tea Party* (New York, 1964); P. D. G. Thomas, *The Townshend Duties Crisis. The Second Phase of the American Revolution 1767–1773* (Oxford, 1987); *idem, Tea Party to Independence. The Third Phase of the American Revolution 1773–1776* (Oxford, 1991). For smuggling see above, note 6.
9   The following paragraph is based upon Chaudhuri, *Trading World of Asia*, pp. 385–406.

the Company several times during the 1710s and 1730s accumulated a 'glut' of tea in its London warehouses and chose not to purchase additional supplies in Canton. A combination of over-trading, foreign competition (in the face of high import duties levied on Company tea), and smuggling all played their part in causing this problem. These factors underlined the important point that although the Company enjoyed a legal monopoly on British trade with China, it did not act as sole supplier of tea to the domestic market. Without such a position, the Company was always likely to run into difficulties with over-supply problems, and this lay at the heart of the Company's problems during the 1760s and 1770s.

There was no uninterrupted growth of the Company's tea trade, even though the selective use of consignment figures might suggest otherwise.[10] Close examination of the statistics reveals that this was far from being the case during the 30 years or so before 1784. The level of annual imports did indeed move in an upward trend, although marked year-to-year fluctuations were caused by warfare and the hazards presented by the long journey from the east. As far as annual sales for domestic consumption were concerned, however, growth remained steady if rather sluggish, with the annual amount of 'home sales' by the Company increasing from 3,089,049 pounds in 1753/4 to 4,460,721 pounds a decade later.[11] These figures represented between 85 and 95 per cent of total Company tea sales, but with annual import levels running at over 6,500,000 pounds by 1764 levels of supply began to outstrip sales by a considerable margin. The outcome manifested itself in a tea 'mountain' that was beginning to rise in the Company's London warehouses. By 1765, the Company's accrued surplus of tea stood at 3,150,446 pounds, a figure which suggests that for all the rapid expansion of sales earlier in the eighteenth century, the problem of oversupply had now become a major cause for concern. In view of this, it can be argued that the mid-1760s was hardly the most appropriate time for the Company to embark upon the sudden further expansion of its tea trade. This, however, was exactly what happened.

The problems associated with over trading and competition that were already evident by 1765 were greatly exacerbated by the consequences of the East India Company's political and military success in Bengal. During the mid- to late-1760s, the balance between the supply of, and demand for, Company tea was tilted dramatically and dangerously in favour of the former. Historians have long recognized the importance of this, and they have fully explored the political consequences which manifested themselves in the events leading to the American revolution. Little attention has been paid, however, to the reasons for this over-supply situation occurring in the first place. In part, this reflects the fact that a great deal of general analysis of the growth of the tea trade has been informed by discussion of demand rather than the equally important supply factors.

10 Ward, 'The Industrial Revolution and British Imperialism', p. 51.
11 The figures in this paragraph are taken from Labaree, *Boston Tea Party*, p. 334.

Most historians, including Philip Lawson, have tended to stress the importance of domestic demand in their analyses and explanations of the growth of the eighteenth-century tea trade. Placing tea within terms of reference defined by the 'consumer revolution', they have identified important dynamics of growth in areas related to advertizing, fashion, income and marketing as they chart the spread of the tea-drinking habit from the social *élite* to the population at large between the 1720s and the 1780s.[12] Yet to ignore the supply side of the equation is to overlook important factors beyond the straightforward commercial response to widespread craving for the leaf. The marked increase in East India Company tea imports from China that was clearly evident after the mid-1760s can be attributed to reasons beyond those narrowly associated with increased levels of demand for the product in Britain and elsewhere. Instead, the great increase in investment in tea by the Company, which often only occasions comment from historians when they refer rather vaguely to the elasticity of supply, can be seen to have been stimulated in large part by other rather unorthodox and only partly commercial factors. As the Company sought to come to terms with Lord Clive's acquisition of a large territorial empire in Bengal, the tea trade with China was widely seen as an established commercial link between east and west which could be easily adapted to the purpose of transferring newly acquired financial resources from India to Britain via Canton.

When, in the Treaty of Allahabad of 1765, the Mughal Emperor Shah Alam II granted the East India Company the position of *dīwan* or revenue collector in the provinces of Bengal, Bihar and Orissa,[13] he not only bestowed a considerable territorial and financial prize upon the British, but he prompted those guiding the Company's affairs to reassess their economic *raison d'être*. Having long pursued purely commercial objectives, the Company now had to come to terms with revenue collection in the territories under its control, and this raised a whole series of practical problems as well as the larger question of what type of organization the Company had now become. Clearly the Company no longer represented a stereotypical joint-stock organization, for its responsibilities drew it into local administrative and political affairs in such a way that it began to take on the form of a governing agency acting in a quasi-official capacity on behalf of the British crown. Contemporaries marvelled at this largely unforeseen transformation, often noting that the 'trader is now become sovereign', but they often failed to identify the full extent of the problems that this would cause the Company. In particular, few anticipated how difficult it would be to

---

12 See, for example, Ward, 'The Industrial Revolution and British Imperialism', pp. 52–5, and Woodruff D. Smith, 'Complications of the Commonplace: Tea, Sugar and Imperialism', *Journal of Interdisciplinary History*, XXIII (1992), 275–8.

13 The background to, and consequences of, this important event are examined in H. V. Bowen, *Revenue and Reform. The Indian Problem in British Politics, 1757–1773* (Cambridge, 1991), pp. 5–15. More broadly, see P. J. Marshall, *Bengal: The British Bridgehead. Eastern India 1740–1828* (Cambridge, 1987).

establish a reliable mechanism for effecting the transfer of surplus revenues or 'tribute' from Bengal to London.

Carried along on a surging tide of optimism sustained by those with speculative interests in India stock, and eventually overcoming any misgivings that they might have held about the reported size of the Bengal revenues, the directors of the Company considered how best they might 'bring our great acquisitions to centre in England'.[14] No simple transfer of bullion or specie was possible, or even considered, because it was understood that such a strategy was not only hazardous but would serve quickly to ruin the Bengal economy by reducing the amount of coinage in circulation.[15] Instead, the directors concentrated their attention on increasing their annual investment in Asian goods, using the revenue surplus to prime the Company's commercial pump in Bengal. It became generally accepted within Company circles that 'No part of the revenues can be realised in England, except through the cost of the investments or cargoes sent home from India or China.'[16] Recognizing the need to concentrate on products for which there was a long history of demand in Europe, the directors singled out silk, fine cloth and tea for special attention. No effort was to be spared to increase the volume and quality of goods procured in Bengal, but the Company's employees in India were also exhorted to direct bullion as well as goods towards Canton so that the supercargoes there could purchase larger quantities of tea. Dispatches to the east emphasized that the tea trade had now become a 'national concern' because it offered one of the few channels through which revenue income could flow to Britain.[17] As a result, there were sharp increases in the value of the goods shipped to Britain in the year of the Company's acquisition of the *diwani*. The 'prime cost' of the cargoes sent home from Bengal rose from £276,772 in 1764–5 to £437,511 in 1765–6 (May to May), and the purchase value of those sent from Canton rose from £393,122 to £544,948.[18] The overall effect of this upon the Company was, as the Abbé Raynal later wrote, that 'They are no longer a *commercial society*, they are a *territorial power* who make the most of their revenues by the assistance of a traffic that formerly was their sole existence.'[19]

14 This phrase was used by Company chairman, George Dudley, in a letter he wrote to Lord Clive in May 1766 (National Library of Wales, Aberystwyth, Clive MSS, 52, p. 179).

15 See, e.g., the comments made by the chancellor of the exchequer, Lord North, in 1769, quoted in P. J. Marshall, *Problems of Empire. Britain and India, 1757–1813* (1968), p. 83.

16 Nathaniel Smith, *Remarks on the East India Company's Balances in England from Their Trade and Revenues* (1781), p. 1. Smith (M.P. for Pontefract 1783 and Rochester 1784–90 and 1792–4) was a director of the Company for much of the period between 1774 and 1794.

17 See, e.g., *Fort William – India House Correspondence and Other Contemporary Papers Relating Thereto (Public Series)*, V: 1767–9, ed. N. K. Sinha (New Delhi, 1949), p. 136: the directors to the Bengal Council, 11 Nov. 1768.

18 *Reports from Committees of the House of Commons, 1715–1801* [hereafter *R.C.H.C.*] (15 vols., 1803), IV, 60–9.

19 Quoted in George Tierney, *The Real Situation of the East India Company Considered, With Respect to Their Rights and Privileges, Under the Operation of the Late Acts of Parliament* (2nd edn., 1787), p. 9.

In the immediate aftermath of the acquisition of the *diwani,* few observers of East Indian affairs acknowledged the extent to which the restructuring of the Company's trade represented an abandonment of the tried and trusted practices and principles which had hitherto allowed those in London to make well-informed and logical decisions about their commercial activities. Not only was trade being subordinated to greater economic considerations – the transfer of revenue – but it was being driven to a considerable degree by a resource system over which the directors had little direct control. In earlier years, Company trade had been funded by ploughed-back profits and working capital raised through short-term loans and bonds issued in Britain. Now, financial input was being derived from a new and unfamiliar source, the revenues, and this made it almost impossible for the Company to calculate and predict levels of profitability on its trade. Although this later greatly exercised the minds of those charged with monitoring the Company's affairs, it did not loom large as a serious problem during the mid- to late-1760s. In part, this was because, at first, it appeared that a successful overall strategy was being pursued. As far as tea was concerned, the directors secured their primary objective and the annual amount of the commodity imported into Britain by the Company began to rise, albeit rather unevenly. Just under 7,000,000 pounds had been imported in both 1764 and 1765; thereafter, with the exception of 1768 and 1769, annual figures of over 8,500,000 pounds were recorded and a pre-1775 peak of almost 13,000,000 pounds was reached in 1772.[20]

If the initial stimulus for the expansion of the Company's tea trade after 1765 can be attributed to the factors outlined briefly above, much of course depended upon a level of demand which would allow the release of supplies on to the market in a profitable manner, offering eventual satisfaction to stockholders and the ministers who now claimed a share of the Bengal revenues for the state.[21] But although most within the Company deemed an increase in investment in tea to be quite appropriate and proper, very little thought appears to have been given to how the domestic market could be expanded in line with the increased volume of imports. At first sight, this might appear rather surprising in view of the successful competitive challenge that had long been offered to the Company by those who smuggled large quantities of duty-free tea into Britain. A considerable amount of the tea being consumed around the country was finding its way into tea pots without ever passing through the hands of the Company, and this was damaging to the interests of both Company and state. Yet when the structure of the domestic tea trade, and the heavy hand of established commercial practice, are considered, it becomes readily apparent that, in

---

20 Labaree, *Boston Tea Party,* p. 334. Labaree's figures are based on a return in B.L., Add. MS, 8133B, ff. 326–7.

21 The ministry's claims upon the Bengal revenues are examined in detail in H. V. Bowen, 'A Question of Sovereignty? The Bengal Land Revenue Issue, 1765–7', *Journal of Imperial and Commonwealth History,* XVI (1987–8), 155–76.

spite of its legal monopoly of supply, the Company was ill-positioned to affect the distribution and consumption of tea in Britain.

Of considerable importance was the fact that information about the overall state of the domestic tea market was extremely sketchy during this period, and contemporaries were deeply uncertain about how much of the product was, or could be, sold for home consumption each year. This arose, in large part, from difficulties in assessing the amount of tea that was illegally 'run' from returning East Indiamen,[22] or, more importantly, smuggled into the country from mainland Europe. The amount of tea seized by hard-pressed customs officers gave no indication of the scale of the problem because it was widely believed that most smuggled tea chests slipped through the net. Between 1769 and 1773 an average of 135,428 pounds of illegal tea was seized each year by officers based in London and the outports,[23] but perhaps as much as 50 times that amount was finding its way safely ashore. This is the conclusion arrived at by historians who, struggling with far from perfect data, suggest that approximately 7,000,000 pounds of tea was being smuggled into Britain each year during the 1770s.[24] Contemporaries, who did not have access to a range of different sources of information, could only hazard rough guesses, although one well-informed student of the trade arrived at much the same figure.[25] In general, no-one could assess with any degree of confidence how much tea was being sold in total, either illegally or legally, at any given moment. This was later acknowledged by a director of the Company, Francis Baring, who remarked that before 1784, 'the quantity of tea consumed in these kingdoms was known to very few persons'.[26] One of those who did try to assess overall levels of consumption was the deputy accountant-general of the East India Company, William Richardson, who put the figure at 18,000,000 pounds for Britain and Ireland during the early 1780s.[27] Prior to that time, however, there is little evidence that any form of market research was ever undertaken by the Company, and thus it was impossible for the directors accurately to assess the potential maximum volume of domestic sales of their tea. This, of

---

22 The Company's deputy accountant, William Richardson, believed that 1,000 – 3,000 chests of Hyson tea were 'frequently smuggled' ashore from returning China ships. He calculated that each loss of a 1,000 chests of Hyson cost the Company around £7,500 in profit. B.L., India Office Records, L/AG/18/2/1, p. 11.

23 *First Report From the Committee on Illicit Practices Used in Defrauding the Revenue* (1783), in *R.C.H.C.*, XI, 240–1. By 1778–82 recorded seizures had increased slightly to 148,192 lbs. a year.

24 Different estimates and methods of calculation are to be found in the works cited in note 6 above. The most recent estimate, based upon decades of work on this complex subject, is provided by the Muis who put the figure at *c*.7–8 million lbs. a year for the 1770s. *Shops and Shopkeeping*, p. 250.

25 William Richardson's estimates are to be found in B.L., I.O.R., L/AG/18/2/1, p. 11. For other figures produced by Richardson see Mui and Mui, 'Trends', p. 29.

26 Francis Baring, *The Principle of the Commutation Act Established by Facts* (1786), p. 33. Baring was a director for much of the time between 1779 and 1810, the year of his death.

27 Mui and Mui, 'Trends', p. 29. The Muis observe that this estimate 'proved remarkably accurate' and was borne out by domestic consumption of Company tea after the introduction of the Commutation Act.

course, presented them with an insurmountable problem as they endeavoured to reduce warehouse stockpiles and regulate future levels of supply. By the mid-1780s, when the effects of Pitt's Commutation Act were being felt and a heavy blow was being dealt to smugglers, expert opinion was in a much more secure statistical position to suggest that 'the East India Company cannot sell more than 12,000,000 pounds annually'.[28] Before that time, no such assertions could be made with any confidence and the Company's domestic commercial targets remained hazy to say the least.

Uncertainties about the size of the market were compounded by the fact that the Company did not itself have direct contact, or a commercial relationship, with consumers of tea. As was the case in all spheres of its activities, the Company did not become involved directly in production or distributive processes in Britain. Instead, it made use of specialists and limited circles of intermediaries to establish contact with different sections of the wider economy. This applied, for example, to shipbuilding and bullion procurement as well as to the supply of tea to the domestic market. In the case of tea, the Company co-operated with a small group of London dealers who purchased consignments of tea at half-yearly March and September sales. This was to all intents and purposes a closed shop arrangement designed to ensure that the market in legal tea remained quite stable and predictable, a state of affairs that was reinforced by the Company sticking rigidly to long-established procedures and relationships. Acting in concert with the dealers, the Company never did anything unexpected that might introduce an element of uncertainty into the proceedings.[29] There were obvious benefits in such an arrangement, but it also worked to the Company's disadvantage. It meant, for example, that the Company was always one step removed from the world of marketing and retail sales. Beyond lobbying government for the reduction of duties on tea, it could do little, except through careful quality control and wholesale price adjustment, to affect the general state of the domestic market. Moreover, the Company's cause was not helped by the fact that little, if any, assistance in this important matter was ever forthcoming from the London dealers. The dealers had long focused their commercial attentions upon the wealthier sections of society, concentrating on quality rather than price, and they were simply not able or inclined to assist in any attempt to create a mass market for Company tea. As a result, the legal tea trade lacked the increasingly sophisticated and systematic sales techniques and methods that were being developed in other branches of domestic retail sales at this time.[30] Moreover, as far as the sale and distribution of tea was concerned, adhering to a practice of public auctions regulated by statute meant that the Company was never fully able to exploit its privileged position as sole legal importer of the product into Britain. Reaching consumers through the network

---

28 Baring, *The Principles of the Commutation Act*, p. 33.
29 Chaudhuri, *Trading World of Asia*, pp. 132–4, 364.
30 Mui and Mui, *Shops and Shopkeeping*, pp. 250–4.

of intermediaries who made the market, the Company had no choice but to accept the sums for lots offered by dealers who knew that their own customers had alternative sources of (illegal) supply upon which they could draw. Thus, although the relationship between the Company and the dealers was seldom characterized by tension or a serious clash of interests, there were times when concerted action by dealers could result in a significant lowering of bid-up prices at tea auctions.[31] Some contemporaries took a dim view of this and argued that the way in which the sales were regulated served only to harm the Company's interests. One pamphleteer, clearly a friend to the Company, argued in 1776 that 'They are obliged to sell all their goods publicly to the highest bidder and often, by the combination of brokers, for less than the prime cost and contingent expenses.'[32]

In spite of being hampered in these different ways, the Company never considered the possibility that it might reach beyond the dealers and engage in marketing and retail sales on its own account. Although, as K. N. Chaudhuri has observed about an earlier period, it is remarkable that, like its Dutch rival, the Company made 'little effort to reach the consuming markets directly',[33] it must be remembered that this was an institution driven along lines of development determined by routine, precedent and a very strong inbuilt suspicion of change. Reform was never willingly embraced by those who drew collective strength from systems and working practices that often remained unaltered for 100 years or more. The Company's long-standing reluctance to refine or modify its procedures and core relationships was later succinctly expressed by a director writing about shipping arrangements. Sir Joseph Cotton declared in 1798 that 'innovations in an established system are at all times dangerous',[34] and the strength of this maxim was such that no director or official ever sought to disturb business arrangements in Britain. Thus, even though modern commercial logic might suggest that the interests of the Company would have been much better served if it had taken a more active role in sales and marketing, such a development would have required a quantum leap of the imagination in the minds of those who were in charge of corporate strategy and policy making.

Although the domestic tea trade was characterized by structural and organizational imperfections, any weaknesses were always highlighted by the Company's inability to counter the threat offered by tea smugglers and illicit dealers. Such was the extent of tea smuggling that, by the 1770s, illegal operators were commanding a much larger share of the domestic market than licensed traders. Indeed, it has been estimated that between 1773 and 1783 the amount of tea being smuggled into Britain

31 *Ibid.*, p. 250; *idem*, 'Smuggling', p. 52.
32 Anon., *An Essay on the Rights of the East India Company to the Perpetuity of Their Trade, Possessions, and Revenues in India* (1776), p. 46.
33 Chaudhuri, *Trading World of Asia*, p. 132.
34 Joseph Cotton, *A View of the Shipping System of the East India Company* (1798), p. 15. Cotton was a director of the Company for much of the period between 1795 and 1823.

each year was twice that passing through legal channels.[35] Smugglers offering cheap duty-free tea were able to establish great influence in parts of the country where they secured direct points of access to regional markets, unlike the retailers of legal tea who relied on the product being channelled through London and the formal sales and distribution systems. This played its part in helping to ensure that London dealers, even if they had been so inclined, would have found it very difficult to establish a 'national' market for their tea.[36] But although smuggling had long been a major source of irritation to the Company and those involved in the legal trade, the London dealers had for the most part managed to co-exist alongside smugglers in separate markets until the mid-1760s. Legal traders had generally been content as long as demand for their commodity was increasing, even if that demand was nowhere near its potential maximum strength. Competition from smugglers was only deemed to be threatening when the size of the market for legal tea was significantly reduced, and this does not appear to have been the case between 1745 and 1764 when sales of Company tea suggest a 'profitable and brisk trade'.[37] At the end of the Seven Years' War, however, the general recovery of European trade with China led to a great increase in the volume of cheap smuggled tea being shipped into Britain. This development was facilitated by the development of a new system of smuggling after 1763 which saw well-resourced large-scale operators using a greatly enhanced carrying capacity, and efficient credit and distribution networks, to displace their smaller unsophisticated competitors in local markets. Restructuring on such a scale enabled illicit traders to establish a much stronger position which, in turn, restricted Company access, via the dealers, to the usual retail outlets. The market position of legal tea, which had been untroubled for 20 years or so, was thus threatened at precisely the moment the Company was seeking to increase levels of investment in the product. In such circumstances, unless prompt action was taken, supply would greatly outweigh demand and the Company's plans to put the revenues in train would lay in ruins.

Unable to do much by itself to increase domestic consumption of tea, and facing a stern challenge from the smuggling community, the Company took the only course of action open to it and, backed by the tea dealers, appealed for assistance from government. In particular, it sought the removal of taxes and duties on tea in an attempt to reduce the retail price in the country at large. This represented an entirely appropriate strategy in view of the heavy customs and excise burdens, amounting to over 100 per cent *ad valorem*, that had been applied to tea over the years. By 1766, Company teas carried a 23.93 per cent import customs duty, as well as an excise duty

35 Mui and Mui, 'Shops and Shopkeeping', p. 250.
36 For full details on the organization and methods of those involved in smuggling see Mui and Mui, 'Smuggling and the British Tea Trade'. Unless otherwise stated, the following paragraph is based on this source.
37 *Ibid.*, p. 52.

levied at a rate of 25 per cent of the Company's auction purchase price and an 'inland duty' of one shilling a pound on tea destined for home consumption.[38] Reducing rates of duty was not without precedent. Such a policy had secured the desired effect, later described as a 'happy success',[39] during the late-1740s when the domestic consumption of legal tea increased in response to the downward adjustment of excise rates introduced in 1745 to counter greater levels of smuggling activity.[40] Since that time, the government's search for revenue had seen the rate of customs duty on tea rise, in two stages, from 13.93 per cent to 23.93 per cent, and this had served to offset some of the advantages gained by the reforms of 1745. It was against this background that representations were made to government, and in the spring of 1766 rumours suggested that the Company would soon be offered a 'bounty on the importation of low priced teas; which it is thought, will be an effectual means to suppress the smuggling this commodity into the Kingdom from France, Holland, etc'.[41] Nothing happened on this occasion, but when representatives of the Company met with ministers at the end of the year and they found the government receptive to the idea of adjusting rates of duty in order to boost domestic and export sales of tea. Hence formal proposals submitted early in 1767 requested the removal of the inland duty and a rebate or 'drawback' of at least 20 per cent of the customs duty that was paid on tea re-exported from Britain. After lengthy negotiations, which took place against the background of the first parliamentary inquiry into East Indian affairs, the Company was granted its wishes for a five-year period. The inland duty was removed from all black teas and cheap green (Singlo) tea, and a full drawback of customs duty was granted on all teas exported to North America and Ireland. A complicated formula was agreed by which the Company undertook to compensate the government for any revenue lost under the scheme, and the whole arrangement was then formalized under the terms of the Indemnity Act (7 Geo. III, c. 56).[42]

Company approval of this outcome was soon qualified, however, by the unwelcome news that some of its commercial advantages were likely to be offset by the effects of government policy towards the American colonies. This was because, as part of Charles Townshend's plans to raise revenues from the colonies, an import duty of three pence a pound was to be levied upon all tea shipped into North America. Some within the Company complained bitterly that the chancellor was giving to them with one hand while taking away with the other, but the Company's tea destined for the colonies was still far cheaper after the introduction of the

38 Full details of the customs and excise rates of duty applied to tea during the eighteenth century are to be found in Mui and Mui, 'Trends', p. 29.
39 Thomas Bates Rous, *Observations on the Commutation Project* (1786), p. 22.
40 Mui and Mui, 'Smuggling', p. 51.
41 *Lloyd's Evening Post*, 28–30 Apr. 1766.
42 Bowen, *Revenue and Reform*, p. 109.

Townshend duty than it had been before 1767.[43] With tea destined for the colonies already being free from the inland duty that had long been applied in Britain,[44] merchants in the America trade found that the new drawback on customs duty rendered the price of re-exported tea much more competitive, despite the effects of the Townshend duty. This was borne out by a sharp increase in tea exports to America in 1767–8, although shipment levels later fell sharply as colonists began to boycott the trade in response to the government's levying of duties on glass, paper and painting materials, as well as tea.[45]

As far as the situation in Britain was concerned, the removal of the inland duty had a significant short-term effect upon the Company's position in the domestic tea market. Sales of Company tea for home consumption almost doubled, from 3,731,903 pounds in 1766–7 to 6,586,829 pounds in 1767–8,[46] with the average price of the popular Bohea tea sold at the auctions falling from 30.6d. per pound in 1766 to 24.6d. per pound by 1769.[47] Contemporary critics later condemned the 'absurdity' of this experiment, pointing out that because the structure of the domestic trade remained unaltered, 'it was soon found that speculators stood between the [Company] sales and the consumer'.[48] Unscrupulous dealers seeking a quick return purchased cheaper duty-free tea and, without passing any of this benefit on to the consumer, were able to increase their short-term profit margins by retaining retail prices at somewhere near their previous levels. The effect of this upon the market and the domestic consumer was such that the *status quo ante* was quickly restored and 'the smuggler held the same advantage as before'.[49] Speculative pressures forced the price of tea to rise again,[50] and 'home' sales of Company tea levelled off and then began to fall. The Company sold 6,687,386 pounds in 1768–9 and 6,870,691 pounds in 1769–70, but the amount fell to 5,683,570 pounds in 1770–1.[51] This could not

43 Thomas, *Townshend Duties*, pp. 27–9. Townshend hoped that the 3d. a pound levy on tea imported into North America would raise £20,000 a year with taxes on the other commodities, plus a cancelled rebate on exports of china, also raising £20,000. *Ibid.*, p. 30.

44 Inland duty had been paid on re-exported teas between 1745 and 1748. Mui and Mui, 'Trends', p. 35.

45 Colonial resistance to the duties, and the boycott of imported tea, is discussed in Thomas, *Townshend Duties*, pp. 76–93, 142–59, and Labaree, *Boston Tea Party*, pp. 15–57.

46 B.L., Add. MS 38397, ff. 224–5. The first figure covers the period 30 June 1766 to 5 July 1767; the second covers the period 5 July 1767 to 5 July 1768. The new duty and indemnity arrangements came into effect on 5 July 1767. The same figures are used Labaree (*Boston Tea Party*, p. 334.) but are applied instead to the calendar years 1766 and 1767.

47 Mui and Mui, 'Smuggling', p. 54. The price of Bohea had already fallen from 39.5d. per pound in 1765 as a result of coordinated action by the dealers.

48 Rous, *Observations*, pp. 22–3.

49 *Ibid.*, p. 23. Rous reported that one unidentified dealer, who had once been a director of the East India Company, cleared a profit of £20,000, declaring that as a 'merchant he had a right to do, if the government gave him the opportunity' (p. 24).

50 Mui and Mui, 'Smuggling', pp. 54–5.

51 B.L., Add. MS 38397, ff. 224–5. Labaree's figures show that domestic sales then rose to 7,511,907 lbs. in 1772, before falling again to 4,134,125 in 1773. Labaree, *Boston Tea Party*, p. 334.

have happened at a worse time for the Company. Not only did sales of tea for export also begin to slip from the heights reached in 1769, but the levels of annual importation from China, driven upwards by the investment of revenue surpluses, reached new peaks in 1770 and 1772.[52]

By 1772, the amount of tea lying unsold in the Company's warehouses stood at over 17,500,000 pounds. At prevailing sale prices, this tea mountain, a depreciating asset, was worth over £2 million, a figure which represented approximately 63 per cent of the total value of all the Company's unsold goods.[53] The Company could ill-afford this at a time when it was coming under acute financial pressure from several other directions, and matters were made worse by the effects of the terms and conditions of the Indemnity Act. The act had caused annual wrangling between the Company and the treasury over how much should be paid to the government *in lieu* of lost revenue.[54] The level of agreed compensation was quite substantial, and between 1768 and 1772 the Company paid the government almost £300,000.[55] Moreover, when the Indemnity Act expired at the end of its five-year term in July 1772, the Company incurred further losses, totalling over £500,000, by agreeing to indemnify those tea buyers who, having purchased tea since 1767, had continued to store it in the Company's warehouses and were now obliged to pay the restored inland duty of one shilling per pound.[56] Well-informed contemporaries were not too wide of the mark when they estimated that the Indemnity Act had cost the Company a million pounds.[57] There could be no doubt whatsoever that the Company had been the 'losers' under the arrangement of 1767, as the veteran East India politician Lawrence Sulivan remarked in the house of commons.[58] Others taking a wide view

---

52 Labaree, *Boston Tea Party*, p. 334.

53 H. V. Bowen, 'British Politics and the East India Company, 1766–1773', University of Wales (Aberystwyth) Ph.D., 1986, pp. 504–5.

54 For these disputes and details of amending legislation see *ibid.*, pp. 507–9.

55 *R.C.H.C.*, IV, 40–59.

56 T. Shearer, 'Crisis and Change in the Development of the East India Company's affairs, 1760–1773', University of Oxford D.Phil., 1976, p. 108. The decision to compensate the tea buyers was taken by the court of directors on 1 July 1772. B.L., I.O.R, B/88, p. 96. The value of the tea stored in the Company's warehouses that had been purchased by dealers stood at £5,395, 880 in 1772. *R.C.H.C.*, IV, 58.

57 Sir George Colebrooke, *Retrospection: or Reminiscences Addressed to my son Henry Thomas Colebrooke Esq.* (2 vols., 1898–9), II, 18. Colebrooke was chairman of the Company in 1772–3. See also the evidence of Company deputy secretary Richard Holt given to the house of lords (*Public Advertiser*, 25 Dec. 1772).

58 Sulivan made this comment on 11 Feb. 1772 when seconding Lord North's motion to introduce a bill to explain and amend the Indemnity Act. *Proceedings and Debates of the British Parliaments Respecting North America 1754–1783*, ed. R. C. Simmons and P. D. G. Thomas (6 vols., New York, 1982–6), III, 408.

of the matter were convinced that the indemnity scheme was a major factor contributing to the financial crisis that was fast overtaking the Company.[59]

The Company's general finances were now in a state of complete disarray, and the directors were obliged first to default on customs payments and then to seek assistance from the government.[60] It became clear that the acquisition of the *diwani* had failed to yield the financial results that had been widely anticipated, not least because the size of the Bengal revenue surplus had been greatly exaggerated in the first place. Against a background of crisis, recrimination and ministerial intervention in the Company's affairs, critics condemned both the general restructuring of the Asian trade and the methods that had been used to encourage the domestic consumption of tea. With regard to the revised framework for overseas operations, one pamphleteer had already anticipated that 'alterations of the mode of trade' would only bring discord and confusion to the Company's affairs, both at home and abroad.[61] Concern was now also voiced about the way in which the Company had abandoned tried and trusted commercial principles as it endeavoured to ensure that the China trade 'afforded a channel for remitting our revenues to England'.[62] Such views were later echoed by a select committee of the house of commons which declared in 1782 that the 'principle and oeconomy of the Company's trade' had been 'compleately corrupted by turning it into a vehicle for Tribute'.[63] With perceptions of the Company altering in this way, commentators began to look again at the benefits arising from the acquisition of the *diwani*. By the mid-1770s, the unqualified endorsement that had once been offered to Lord Clive's military and political actions was being replaced by gloomy retrospective assessments which suggested that the Company had gained very little from its expansionist activity in Bengal. One commentator argued that experiences to date were such that 'this extraordinary success, instead of producing only advantage, has hitherto been the bane of the Company'.[64] In view of this unhappy state of affairs, some questioned whether the Company should continue its pursuit of wealth derived from possession of a territorial empire, and they argued that the commercial arrangements that had been in place before 1765 had offered ample scope for extensive, and sustainable, profit-making

---

59 Anon., *The Present State of the English East India Company's Affairs, Comprehending the Accounts Delivered in to the Treasury Which were Laid Before the Committee of Secrecy* (1772), pp. iv–v. Two committees of the house of commons, a select committee and a secret committee, were appointed to examine the Company's affairs in 1772.

60 For the Company's financial crisis and the political response see Bowen, *Revenue and Reform*, pp. 119–86, and L. S. Sutherland, *The East India Company in Eighteenth-Century Politics* (Oxford, 1952), pp. 213–68.

61 Anon., *A Letter to L[aurence] S[ulivan]* (1769), p. 7.

62 Anon., *A Second Letter to the Committee of Twenty-Five Proprietors of India Stock* (1773), p. 20. This pamphlet contains a lengthy detailed attack upon the Company's handling of the tea trade since 1766.

63 *R.C.H.C.*, VI, 60.

64 *An Essay on the Rights of the East India Company to the Perpetuity of Their Trade*, pp. 24–5.

activity. Such an attitude informed the opinion of one pamphleteer who wrote: 'I know nothing we want but a maritime trade; this was the original plan we acted on, and to support the trade properly would bring all the wealth to this nation that would be desired or expected.'[65] As time went on, a tiny minority even began to suggest that the Company, and the nation, might almost be better off without any Indian territorial possessions at all.[66]

Critics who focused more narrowly on the tea trade drew attention to mismanagement and a lack of sound commercial judgment among those in the highest Company circles. One pamphleteer and Company politician declared that ill-informed directors had extended their consideration of the problem no further than seeking the removal of duties in an attempt to boost sales. He conceded that the 'trial at the joint risque of the Exchequer and the Company' had an effect in the short term because it temporarily weakened the position of smugglers, but he argued with some justification that this should have represented only one element within a broader based, and more detailed, policy.[67] 'The execution of so complex a scheme, as this was now become', he wrote, 'required a constant, vigilant attention, a minute and accurate knowledge.' Instead, he argued, the directors had not considered the type of tea they imported or whether supply was now well suited to the level of demand. With attempts to reduce the number of ships sent to China each year being thwarted in the court of directors,[68] the consequences were now all-too evident in the form of overstocked Company warehouses. Blame for this unsatisfactory state of affairs could only be attached to those 'who pretended to understand the *whole* system of the commerce, and who *ought* to have known what *effect* the possession of revenues might produce in England'.

Those who criticized the theory and practice of Company attempts to stimulate the tea trade could point, with some justification, to a commercial performance that was, in view of earlier optimism, producing surprisingly poor results by the early 1770s. The profit margins on tea sold by the Company remained good,[69] but not enough of the product was being disposed of at home and abroad. As a result, tea

65 *Letter to L[aurence] S[ulivan]*, p. 9.
66 See, for example, B.L., I.O.R., Home Miscellaneous Series, 211, p. 261: George Dempster to Lord [?], 8 Nov. 1781. Dempster (M.P. for Perth Burghs 1761–8 and 1769–90, director of the Company 1769, 1772–3) foresaw that the impending loss of the 13 colonies would not prevent Britain having a 'very beneficial trade' with North America, and he suggested that the same might apply to India.
67 All the quotations in this paragraph are taken from *A Second Letter to the Committee of Twenty-Five Proprietors*, pp. 22–9.
68 The author claimed that Thomas Rous senior had argued for this in 1770. *Ibid.*, p. 29.
69 William Richardson's rough calculations, based on the subtraction of prime cost, customs and freight charges from the sales price with discount deducted, suggested that during the 1770 the rate of profit on its China cargoes stood at between 14.4 and 26.1 per cent. This was much better than the rate of return on goods imported from Bengal, Bombay, and Madras. Indeed, Richardson calculated that Bengal goods were being sold at an increasing level of loss after 1775. B.L., I.O.R., L/AG/18/2/1, pp. 18–23.

was far from assuming any position of dominance among the commodities imported from India and China. On the contrary, analysis of Company accounts reveals that after 1765 the position of tea and the China trade worsened quite considerably in relation to other commodities and trades.

In spite of the vigorous attempts to increase levels of investment in tea which resulted in a much greater volume of the product being shipped to Britain during the late-1760s, the position of China cargoes in the overall profile of the Company's import trade worsened quite considerably following the acquisition of the *diwani*. In 1764–5, the 'prime cost' of goods from China accounted for 43.6 per cent of the value of all Company imports into Britain.[70] Thereafter, there was a reduction in the proportionate value of goods imported from China and, after a brief recovery in 1769–70, they accounted for only 28.8 per cent of the total by 1770–1. While the relative value of cargoes from Madras and Bombay also fell over time, much more success was had with goods despatched from Bengal. In 1764–5, the value of Bengal cargoes had represented 30.7 per cent of Company imports, but this increased to exactly 50 per cent in 1767–8 and 55.5 per cent in 1770–1. The invoice value of imported Bengal goods rose more or less evenly, doubling from £437,511 to £865,878 between 1766 and 1772, and this rate of increase applied to all the major categories of commodity: piece goods, silk, saltpetre and drugs.[71] In 1771, as the problems of the tea trade began fully to manifest themselves, the prime cost of the Bengal cargoes stood at almost double the value of the goods shipped from Canton.

The Company's success in increasing the value of goods imported from Bengal was matched by its ability to dispose of such products when they arrived in Britain, even though the rate of return was poor and annual losses could be sustained from time to time.[72] As a result, the sale of Indian goods was reflected in important changes that occurred to the broad pattern of the Company's income distribution. During the late 1750s and early 1760s, cash received by the Company from tea sales in London had usually represented between 30 and 38 per cent of all income.[73] This figure leapt to 48.3 per cent in 1767–8, when the Company earned over £2,000,000 from its tea sales for the first time, but thereafter it fell away significantly as domestic

70 Unless otherwise stated, the calculations in this paragraph are based upon trade figures in *R.C.H.C.*, IV, 60–9.

71 *Ibid.*, VI, 112.

72 William Richardson's calculations suggested that losses on Bengal cargoes were incurred in 1772 and 1775–9. When losses were not incurred, he calculated that the rate of profit on Bengal cargoes stood at between 1.6 and 3.6 per cent. See note 69 above.

73 In the absence of the Company's tea ledgers, which were destroyed during the nineteenth century, information relating to commodity income has been taken from the cash journals. B.L., I.O.R., L/AG/1/5/17–23. Among numerous other types of entries, these journals, which were placed at the heart of the Company's day-to-day accounting and control procedures, record monthly cash income carried over from the tea, calico, and drug and chinaware ledgers. As far as tea is concerned, figures relate to the sums received for tea sold and a small number of deposits paid by dealers in anticipation of future purchases.

and export demand weakened. By the early 1770s, the Company was receiving less than 30 per cent of its income from tea, and in some years, such as 1772–3 (£839,580) and 1778–9 (£804,963), the proportion stood at less than 20 per cent of the total. Of course, during this period the Company began to receive a large amount of income in the form of emergency loan finance (especially from the government and the Bank of England) as it attempted to stave off bankruptcy, and this had a some effect upon the relative position of cash received from tea sales. Having said that, however, the proportionate share of income derived from other types of commodity was subjected to exactly the same pressures from loan finance, but the outcome was rather different. In particular, the amount of cash received from the sales of goods recorded in the 'calico leger' rose steadily over time, roughly doubling between the mid-1750s and the mid-1770s, and this was reflected in an increased proportion of Company income being derived from this source. Like the proportion derived from tea sales, the percentage figure fluctuated from year to year, but it did not fall away during the 1770s. Indeed, after 1772–3, the proportion of Company income represented by sales recorded in the calico leger usually stood at over 35 per cent of the total, and in cash terms this translated to more than £1,500,000 a year. It was only after the introduction of the Commutation Act that a decisive shift occurred in favour of tea. Only then, after a vigorous government-assisted attempt to capture the domestic market, did the tea trade assume a dominant position within the Company's commercial activities.[74]

The East India Company's inability to put its revenues 'in train' during the period immediately following the acquisition of the *diwani* had a considerable effect upon the long-term development of the British empire in India. Along with growing concern about British conduct in Bengal, the financial crisis that undermined the Company during the early 1770s acted as a spur to government intervention in East Indian affairs. In a formal sense, this led to state-Company relations being recast by Lord North's Regulating Act of 1773. At the same time, it was widely recognized that the restructuring of the Company's commercial affairs that had taken place after 1765 had not served its intended purpose. In particular, it had become all-too evident that the Company simply did not possess the capacity to sustain a greatly expanded tea trade because the structure of British markets, and the Company's position therein, did not allow for the easy diffusion of the product through the country at large. The Company, hitherto reasonably efficient and profitable, revealed itself to be incapable of adapting to new conditions in India, and arguments in favour of a 'free' East India trade began to gather strength once more. The long-standing difficulties associated with the China trade now lay at the very heart of the Company's problems, and the large stockpiles of unsold tea served as a stark reminder of how uncomfortable and largely unsuccessful the transition from trader to sovereign had been for the

74 This is evident in the 'cash received' figures for the years after 1784. Full details will be made available in a forthcoming study of the Company's finances between 1756 and 1813.

Company. The directors had sought to exploit the wrong product at the wrong time, and the consequences of their misjudgment, together with a poorly executed general strategy, ultimately inflicted considerable damage upon the British empire in both east and west.

9

'George, Be a King!': The Relationship between Princess Augusta and George III

JOHN L. BULLION

When textbooks in history focused on kings, queens and presidents more than they do today, writers sought the origins of the American revolution in the characters of the most prominent participants. The role of principal villain was George III's, and authors seeking to explain why he took that part often referred to what he learned as a youth from his mother, Augusta, the dowager princess of Wales. 'George', Augusta commanded the boy, 'be a King!' Her son took this injunction to heart, and resolved to assert his personal authority over his subjects. Ultimately this resolution fated him to be the last king of most of Britain's North American possessions.[1]

However familiar the story of the princess's command was to generations of schoolchildren in Britain and America, scholars of eighteenth-century Britain have long regarded it as apocryphal. To support this judgment, they have pointed to its provenance. None of the great memoirists *cum* gossips of the 1750s and 1760s mentioned such a vignette. Nor is there any reference to it in contemporary letters, diaries, pamphlets or caricatures. The story first appeared in 1820, in the autobiography of John Nicholls. Nicholls had been a student at Exeter and Oxford during the 1750s, and had no contact whatsoever with the court at Leicester House, the princess's residence. Thus historians have seen fit to dismiss it as a piece of unsubstantiated gossip, passed off as fact, and of no great historical import. So sceptical of the truth of Nicholls's tale was the great historian Sir Lewis Namier that he was wont to joke that Augusta was probably criticizing her son's table manners. The Namier version went this way: ' "George! sit up straight! take your elbows off the table! don't gobble your food! do you want to look like your uncle Cumberland? George, be a King!" '[2] Whether or not other scholars agreed with Sir Lewis's

---

1 For a description of this story, see John Brooke, *King George III* (1972), pp. 86, 390. I can remember reading this story in an elementary school textbook during the 1950s.

2 *Ibid.*, p. 390. For biographical details about John Nicholls, see Sir Lewis Namier and John Brooke, *The House of Commons 1754–1790* (3 vols., 1964), III, 202. J. C. D. Clark has also cautioned historians about the possibility that Nicholls may have nursed a grudge against Augusta and her son. His father, Dr Frank Nicholls, had been one of George II's physicians. When George III succeeded his grandfather, Dr Nicholls lost his position to a Scotsman who, according to Samuel Johnson, was 'very low in his profession'. *The Memoirs and Speeches of James, 2nd Earl Waldegrave, 1742–1763*, ed. J. C. D. Clark (Cambridge, 1988), p. 129 n.

explanation, they clearly shared his doubts about the significance of Nicholls's account. Augusta's impact on her son has been left largely unexplored, except for some perfunctory condemnations of her for isolating the prince of Wales from society and politics. Far more attention has been paid to the critical part George's 'dearest friend', the earl of Bute, played in shaping his character during the 1750s and determining his political fate in the 1760s.[3]

This oversight needs correcting. Certainly Bute did have a significant effect on his young protégé, but it is equally certain he had the opportunity to accomplish what he did solely because Augusta chose him to tutor the prince in secret. Precisely how she explained her decision to George is unknown. A surviving letter from the earl to his royal pupil does reveal, however, that she stressed to her son that Bute was her trusted friend.[4] That recommendation may have had an important effect at the beginning of the intimate friendship the prince and his mentor formed. The man who served as George's governor during that period, Earl Waldegrave, was positive that it was 'by the good offices of the Mother' that Bute 'became the avow'd favorite of the Young Prince'.[5] Embittered by her friend's usurpation of his responsibility, Waldegrave later claimed that 'long before [George's] coming of age, none who approached him preserved the least influence, except the mother and those who she confided in'.[6] To test the truth of these charges, looking at the relationship between mother and son is necessary.

Waldegrave's recollections point to another reason to assess Augusta's role in the life of George III. The earl was positive that the dowager princess had a definitive impact on the young prince as his character developed. When Waldegrave began his service as governor, he 'found his Royal Highness uncommonly full of Princely Prejudices, contracted in the Nursery, and improved by the society of Bed Chamber Women and Pages of the Back Stairs'; this situation he blamed on Augusta.[7] Other contemporaries were equally convinced. Indeed, they believed that the princess's sinister control over her son continued after the advent of Bute, and was even heightened by the earl's winning of George's heart and mind. Vivid proof of the popular convictions about Augusta's role may be found in the satirical caricatures that appeared in London windows after George III's accession to the throne.

3   See the treatment of Augusta and Bute in Brooke, *George III*, pp. 29–72; Stanley Ayling, *George the Third* (New York, 1972), pp. 33–60; Sir Lewis Namier, *England in the Age of the American Revolution* (2nd edn., 1961), pp. 83–93; idem, 'King George III', in *Crossroads of Power. Essays on Eighteenth-Century England* (1962), pp. 124–40; and John L. Bullion, 'The Prince's Mentor: A New Perspective on the Friendship between George III and Lord Bute during the 1750s', *Albion*, XXI (1989), 34–55.

4   *Letters from George III to Lord Bute, 1756–1766*, ed. Romney Sedgwick (1939), pp. liii–liv: earl of Bute to the prince of Wales [summer 1755].

5   Earl Waldegrave, 'Memoirs of 1754–1757', in *Memoirs and Speeches of Waldegrave*, ed. Clark, p. 176.

6   *Ibid.*, p. 229.

7   *Ibid.*, p. 176. See also Waldegrave, 'An Allegory of Leicester House', in *ibid.*, p. 229.

Constantly, she and her reputed lover were portrayed as duping, or blindfolding, or lulling into a politically and personally damaging slumber, or even poisoning – *à la* Claudius and Gertrude in *Hamlet* – the young king. These images not only effectively undercut the royal authority, they served as well to communicate and confirm widespread fears about the power George's mother had to narrow his vision of reality and to lead him astray. Given the widespread broadcasting of such 'verses and indecent prints', it is not surprising that on 16 November 1760, immediately after his accession, George III heard 'in the avenues to the Play house the mob crying out No Scotch Government, No Petticoat Government'.[8]

Historians should not, of course, accept Waldegrave's opinion and popular caricatures as incontestable proof of Augusta's power over her son. Nevertheless, that so many were so certain that she enjoyed great influence over him and used it to control his thoughts and acts makes an investigation of the accuracy of their perceptions worthwhile. That requires a careful analysis of the relationship itself, and of the extent and significance of his mother's role in George III's life. The proper place to begin that analysis is with Augusta herself.

I

Before her husband Frederick died in 1751, few people at court paid much attention to Augusta. When they did, it generally was due to some *gaffe* of his. Two examples must suffice.

Although the sexual liaisons of George II were openly conducted and widely known, the king did not treat his wife publicly as the prince did his. During their marriage, the court was sure Frederick had two mistresses, Lady Archibald Hamilton and Lady Middlesex. Each was a frequent source of embarrassment to Augusta. Immediately after their marriage in 1736, the prince persuaded his wife to name Lady Archibald Hamilton one of the ladies of the bedchamber, after Queen Caroline had refused to do so, saying 'it was impossible for her to put Lady Archibald about the princess without incurring the contempt of the whole world'.[9] The court's reaction to Augusta's yielding to her husband's wishes was not contempt, however. Rather, it was one of sympathy for her, and appreciation for her willingness to obey and endure. 'Poor creature', Caroline once remarked, 'if she were to spit in my face, I should only pity her for being under a fool's direction, and wipe it off.' The queen was 'always remarkably and industriously civil' to Augusta, and thought 'there was

8   Examples of these prints, and a stimulating analysis of their content and significance, may be found in Vincent Carretta, *George III and the Satirists from Hogarth to Byron* (Athens, Ga., 1990), 68–71. The quotations are from 'Leicester House Politics, 1750–1760, From the Papers of John, Second Earl of Egmont', ed. Aubrey N. Newman, *Camden Miscellany XXIII* (Camden 4th ser., VII, 1967), p. 227: diary of the earl of Egmont, 16 Nov. 1760.

9   *Lord Hervey's Memoirs, Edited From a Copy of the Original Manuscript in the Royal Archives at Windsor Castle*, ed. Romney Sedgwick (1952), p. 176.

no sort of harm in her, that she never meant to offend, was very modest and very respectful'. To be sure, Caroline considered Augusta to be neither witty nor intelligent. Still, she invariably reproached herself whenever exasperation led her to lament 'the silent stupidity' of her daughter-in-law and forget her virtues.[10]

In a like manner, Frederick's behaviour with his other mistress elicited from observers pity for her situation and respect for her behaviour. While Lady Middlesex was enduring a difficult pregnancy in 1750, Horace Walpole reported that the prince attended her as constantly as did the midwife. One morning 'the Princess came [to Lady Middlesex's house] to call him to go to Kew; he made her wait in her coach above half an hour at the door'.[11] Episodes such as these led even Walpole, who came to detest Augusta and pilloried her in his memoirs as a passionate and domineering woman, to praise 'the quiet inoffensive good sense of the Princess (who had never said a foolish thing, or done a disobliging one since her arrival [in England], though in very difficult situations)'.[12]

Caroline's comments, and those of Walpole, reveal the perspective they and others at court had on Augusta. To them, her virtues were apparent. She obeyed her husband and followed his directions, just as the social mores of the eighteenth-century court demanded. She accepted the twin realities that men could commit adultery with virtual impunity from society's censure, and that men with royal blood could conduct their affairs in public, without any protest. The fact that she did not respond to Frederick's actions, which went beyond the acceptable boundaries of even royal behaviour by exposing her to public humiliation, improved others' opinion of her.[13] It is important to note, though, that this did not mean these observers had great respect for the princess's abilities. Implicit in their remarks is the judgment that Augusta's preservation of dignity and adherence to society's standards was more passive than active, the reaction of a person of limited wits, spirit and experience rather than the calculated determination of an intelligent, politically and socially aware woman. In this reading of her character, they were mistaken. When the earl of Shelburne summed up his impressions of Augusta, he observed, 'it seems to have been her fate through life to have been neglected and undervalued'.[14] Whatever the truth of these remarks for her later years, they certainly described her fate while she was Frederick's wife.

Shelburne himself did not feel the princess's virtues had been underestimated. Instead, he believed the court had not accurately gauged her natural aptitudes for

---

10 *Ibid.*, pp. 186–7.
11 *The Yale Edition of Horace Walpole's Correspondence*, ed. W. S. Lewis *et al.* (48 vols., New Haven, 1937–83), xx, 122: Horace Walpole to Sir Horace Mann, 25 Feb. 1750.
12 Horace Walpole, *Memoirs of King George II*, ed. John Brooke (3 vols., New Haven, 1985), I, 53.
13 For comments about contemporary attitudes toward adultery, see Lawrence Stone, *The Family, Sex, and Marriage in England, 1500–1800* (1977), pp. 501–7.
14 Lord Fitzmaurice, *Life of William, Earl of Shelburne, Afterwards First Marquess of Lansdowne, with Extracts from his Papers, and Correspondence* (2 vols., 1912), I, 46.

'dissimulation and intrigue', which 'the perpetual mortifications she submitted to pressed and obliged her to exert'.[15] These cutting words were deliberately chosen by a man who intensely disliked the princess. What they amount to is this: Augusta successfully concealed from interested observers at court her real strengths as a person and as a princess. A central part of her character, her devoutness, went largely unremarked. Yet when she first came to Britain, she insisted that her beliefs would not allow her to take communion in the Church of England, and went instead to a Lutheran chapel. The argument of the prince, that when this became known it would be very unpopular, had no impact on her. According to Frederick, 'she only wept and talked of her conscience'. Ultimately a political point overrode her scruples. The Act of Succession required heirs to the crown to take communion only from the Church of England on pain of losing the throne if they did not comply. When Augusta learned that this could possibly be applied to her, and if so would result in her being sent back to Germany, she 'dried her tears, lulled her conscience, and went no more to the Lutheran Church'. She began regularly attending anglican services at the chapel at Kensington, and 'received the sacrament like the rest of the royal family'.[16] Undoubtedly, this decision was inspired in the first instance by political expediency. Still, there is reason to believe that once made, the change in communions was not continued cynically. Augusta's critical attitude during the 1750s toward the immorality of young aristocrats, and the freedom with which an intimate adviser of hers could criticize latitudinarian clergy, indicate that she had genuinely transferred her religious commitment to a strict anglicanism.[17]

Augusta's ability to adapt her commitment to ideals to the reality of the particular circumstances of her life in Britain is evident in other areas as well. Most notably, she succeeded in winning the affection and trust of a difficult and capricious husband. Despite Frederick's apparent infatuation at different times with other women, she learned how to attract and hold his attention. The proof of this is not merely the birth of nine children in 14 years of marriage. It may be found as well in 'The Charms of Sylvia', a poem written by Frederick in praise of his wife. In it, he celebrated the princess's 'lovely range of teeth so white', her 'gentle smile ... with which no smile could e'er compare', 'that chin so round, that neck so fine', 'those breasts that swell

---

15 *Ibid.*, p. 49.
16 *Hervey's Memoirs*, ed. Sedgiwck, pp. 182–3. Augusta's presence at the chapel at Kensington was conspicuous, because, according to Hervey, Frederick insisted that she arrive late. Perhaps he did so to draw attention to her observance of anglican rites.
17 Augusta frequently complained about the immorality of young people at court, both to people she was personally close to, such as George Bubb Dodington, and those she was less well acquainted with, such as Earl Waldegrave. For example, see Dodington's diary entry for 27 May 1755, in *The Political Journal of George Bubb Dodington*, ed. John Carswell and Lewis Arnold Dralle (Oxford, 1965), p. 300; and Waldegrave, 'An Allegory of Leicester House', in *Memoirs and Speeches of Waldegrave*, ed. Clark, p. 229. For the scathing comment by James Cresset that the latitudinarian bishop of Norwich was a 'bastard and atheist', see *Walpole's Correspondence*, ed. Lewis, XX, 344: Walpole to Mann, 11 Dec. 1752.

to meet my love', and 'that easy sloping waist, that form divine'. The verses themselves are awkward and hackneyed, and afforded much amusement to London's *cognoscenti*, but Frederick was sufficiently pleased with them and his wife to publish them. Significantly, he emphasized in the poem that Augusta's physical attractions 'below' and 'above' – as he gracelessly referred to them – were not what bound him most closely to her.

> No – tis that gentleness of mind, that love
> So kindly answering my desire,
> That grace with which you look and speak and move,
> That thus has set my soul on fire.[18]

One example of how the princess's 'gentleness of mind' comforted and strength-ened Frederick has survived. During his fatal illness in 1751, Augusta, who believed he was getting 'much better [and] only wanted to recover his strength', confided to the earl of Egmont, his closest political adviser, that the prince 'was always frightened for himself when he was the least out of order but that she laughed him out of it and never would humor him in these fancys'. After these wifely ministrations he had as always – in this case, incorrectly – concluded 'he should not die this bout but for the future would take more care of himself'.[19] Long familiarity with her husband's fears and foibles enabled her to manipulate his moods away from despair and toward optimism.

Frederick's affection for his wife was matched by his trust in her discretion. Those politicians who plotted with the prince to oppose the king's government sooner or later realized that the princess was privy to his political secrets. It is doubtful that she played an active role in formulating his plans, for her husband's proudest boast was that he, unlike his father, would never fall under the domination of his wife.[20] But Augusta was present on one occasion when Frederick and Egmont sifted through the political loyalties of some M.P.s, and the fact that the earl expressed no surprise in his diary that she remained in the room indicates that he did not find this unusual. Once the two men were ready to begin discussing their strategies for establishing themselves firmly in power immediately after George II's death, however, 'the Princess at [Frederick's] intimation then withdrew'. Probably the prince wanted to

---

18 Frederick, 'The Charms of Sylvia', in Walpole, *Memoirs*, ed. Brooke, III, 145. A parody of the poem circulated in London that included these lines: 'No – tis that all-consenting tongue/ That never puts me in the wrong.' See also Walpole's comment on Frederick as poet in *ibid.*, I, 54.

19 'Leicester House Politics', ed. Newman, p. 197.

20 Princess Caroline, who detested her brother, once scornfully rejected Lord Hervey's hypothesis that, if Frederick became king, within a month Queen Caroline 'would have more weight with him than anybody in England' with these words: 'Jesus! ... My good Lord, you must know him very little if you believe that; for in the first place he hates Mama; in the next, he has so good an opinion of himself that he thinks he wants no advice, and of all advice no woman's; for the saying, no woman ought to be let to meddle with business or ever did any good where they did meddle, is perhaps the only thing in which I have not heard him ever contradict himself.' *Hervey's Memoirs*, ed. Sedgwick, pp. 218–19. See also Brooke, *George III*, pp. 29–30.

underline his freedom from feminine control. It is also conceivable he did not want
Augusta to know that he was taking the dangerous step of loaning Egmont a copy
of his scheme for a few days.[21] Certainly she was familiar with the plan's existence
and its details. When Frederick died unexpectedly on 20 March 1751, he was not
even cold before she sent for Egmont. Mastering her shock and horror at her
husband's death, she warned the earl that 'she did not know but the King might seize
the Prince's papers – that they were at Carlton House – and that we might be ruined
by these papers'. She gave Egmont the keys to three trunks there, commanded him
to hurry to Carlton House, remove incriminating evidence, and bring it back to her.
She even supplied him with a pillow case to hide the papers in. After the earl
accomplished his mission, she supervised the destruction of the plans. Only then did
Augusta turn to considering what to do about Frederick's body and when to inform
his father.[22] It was an impressive and disciplined performance, one that revealed not
only her knowledge of her husband's schemes, but a political acumen and decisive-
ness that would have surprised many.

When Augusta remarked 'we might be ruined by these papers', she was not
including Egmont in her thoughts. The earl served a useful purpose by smuggling the
dangerous material out of Carlton House, but the princess was already determined
to sever her ties with him. What concerned her was the possibility that George II
would seize upon any plausible excuse to take her children away from her control. In
particular, she feared that the new heir to the throne, her son George, would be
removed to the king's household. In the time immediately after Frederick's death, the
purpose behind Augusta's manoeuvres was to avoid giving George II any justification
for that measure. Thus she destroyed Frederick's plans, stopped seeing Egmont, and
sought a reconciliation with the king.[23]

The princess succeeded in her design, and convinced George II to agree to her
becoming regent should he die before his grandson came of age. On 30 March, the
two met for 15 minutes, then sent for the children. According to Egmont's informant,
'the King embraced Prince George, said he loved him, bid him be honest and brave,
and mind his mother who was the best of women'. Then he 'embraced the Princess,
desired nobody might come between him and her, and that he would do everything
for her'. This 'abundance of speeches and a kind behaviour to her and the children'
ended by 'captivat[ing] Prince George who said he should not be frighted any more

21 'Leicester House Politics', ed. Newman, pp. 196–7. Others also assumed Augusta was conversant
    with Frederick's political negotiations. After his death in 1751, some tories appealed to the princess
    to confirm to George II that they had rejected his overtures in 1747 to join him and his friends in an
    open opposition to the ministry. During the next year, Dodington asked the same favour of her,
    reminding Augusta as he did so that they had both hoped Frederick would follow 'a plan of temper
    and moderation' in 1749. *Dodington Journal*, ed. Carswell and Dralle, pp. 135, 165: 2 Oct. 1751
    and 16 July 1752.
22 'Leicester House Politics', ed. Newman, pp. 198–9.
23 Augusta's manoeuvres may be followed in detail in *ibid.*, pp. 199–213.

with his grandpapa'.[24] Augusta's performance at what was the supreme political and personal crisis of her life to that point, plus the reaction of her son, meant that George and the other children would continue to be with her. She would have the opportunity to mould the character of the next king of Britain. Perhaps because she was so keenly aware that she might have lost it had she not disarmed the suspicions of George II, she intended to make the most of this opportunity.

II

The historical record is nearly silent about what sort of parent Augusta had been for George and her other children before Frederick's death. Almost all contemporary comment centred on the prince, and focused in particular on his obvious preference for his second son, Edward.[25] His 'great Passion' for this boy was openly avowed. It also inspired Frederick to use Edward to execute his favourite political plan of separating Great Britain from Hanover. When he became king, he informed Egmont in 1750, he would make his second son the elector of Hanover. George would not dare object, he went on. Frederick intended to force him to acquiesce by first offering him an annual allowance of £100,000, and then withholding it until he agreed to this settlement.[26]

The prince planned to manipulate his heir in other ways as well. Aware that George might want to command the army, he intended to make him lord high admiral instead. The reasoning behind this decision was no compliment to George. Frederick believed 'if he was to be bred among Troops [it] might turn his head dangerously to a love of regular Troops with all the fopperies of the Trade which naturally captivate young men'. Being lord high admiral would 'turn his attention and vanity to the fleet'. One should not be deceived by the prince's reference to the natural tendency of young men. That was not what worried Frederick. He believed Edward could avoid the temptations army service provided, for he meant to give his second son command of a regiment of guards. What concerned the prince was a weakness he perceived in George's character, a weakness that would make him unable to avoid the showy follies and idle affectations of importance that Frederick identified with officers in the regular army. Only if George was placed in a better environment would his attention and pride be turned toward proper objects; left to himself, he could not do it.[27]

Why the prince reached this conclusion is not clear. As Horace Walpole archly observed, 'it ran a little in the blood of the family to hate the eldest son', but this does not seem to have been the case with Frederick. Even Walpole conceded he was a

---

24 *Ibid.*, p. 207.
25 For example, see Walpole, *Memoirs*, ed. Brooke, I, 51; and Brooke, *George III*, p. 41.
26 'Leicester House Politics', ed. Newman, pp. 175, 193.
27 *Ibid.*, p. 175. For a contemporary understanding of what 'foppery' meant, see Samuel Johnson's *Dictionary of the English Language*.

much better parent than George II.[28] His preference rested on a different foundation, one made up at least in part of Edward's physical and psychological resemblance to him. In appearance, Edward looked much more like Frederick than George did. The second son's mercurial moods and his often indiscreet glibness also perfectly matched his father's temperament.[29] George was much the quieter child, with a less facile mind and tongue. His social mannerisms were marked by, as the sympathetic Lady Louisa Stuart observed, an 'awkward hesitation'. While Edward was praised, when George 'ever faltered out an opinion, it was passed by unnoticed [and] sometimes knocked down at once with "Do hold your tongue, George: don't talk like a fool."'[30] In his father's mind, he was the son who would require careful guidance and supervision, or he would learn the wrong lessons.[31] This did not mean that Frederick was unremittingly harsh or cruel to George. The few surviving letters from him to his eldest son reveal a father capable of mixing judicious encouragement and mild criticism.[32] Nevertheless, the prince was determined to monitor and control George's life closely, and could not help comparing this necessity with what he presumed to be Edward's intelligence, spirit and independence.

At least outwardly, Augusta concurred with her husband's assessment of their two oldest sons. Lady Louisa Stuart recalled that she openly preferred Edward, often ignored George, and at times corrected him sharply.[33] Other observers' memories were much the same.[34] Of course, after Frederick's death the situation changed dramatically. George would obviously become king far sooner than anyone could have anticipated. Paying less attention to him than to the favourite son was no longer

---

28 Walpole, *Memoirs*, ed. Brooke, I, 51.

29 Henry Fox remarked on the physical and psychological resemblance between Frederick and Edward by noting the son was the 'express image of his worthless father'. Henry Fox, 'Memoirs on the Events Attending the Death of George II, and the Accession of George III', in *The Life and Letters of Lady Sarah Lennox, 1745–1826*, ed. the countess of Ilchester and Lord Stavordale (1902), p. 12. Walpole also called attention to the similarities between the two in a letter to Mann, 24 May 1767. *Walpole's Correspondence*, ed. Lewis, XXII, 521. For some remarks on Edward's notorious indiscreetness, see Horace Walpole, *Memoirs of the Reign of King George III*, ed. G. F. Russell Barker (4 vols., 1894), I, 110; and *Walpole's Correspondence*, ed. Lewis, VII, 365–6: 'Account of the duke of York's Journey to Paris and Comprègne, and his death at Monaco' [1767].

30 Quoted in Brooke, *George III*, p. 41.

31 For examples of Frederick's political advice to his children, see his remarks on Sir Robert Walpole, in *Walpole's Correspondence*, ed. Lewis, XVIII, 219: Walpole to Mann, 25 Apr. 1743; on George II, in 'Leicester House Politics', ed. Newman, p. 207; and on his brother, the duke of Cumberland, in Fox, 'Memoirs', in *Lady Sarah Lennox*, ed. Ilchester and Stavordale, pp. 33–4.

32 These letters are described in Brooke, *George III*, p. 23.

33 *Ibid.*, p. 41.

34 For example, see Shelburne's comment that the treatment of George by his mother and father 'went the length of the most decided contempt of him, if not aversion, [by] setting up his brother [Edward's] understanding and parts in opposition to his, and undervaluing everything he said or did'. Fitzmaurice, *Life of Shelburne*, I, 53–4. The surviving letters from Frederick to George strongly suggest that this account is too harsh.

possible; his preparation for the throne could not be delayed. The princess accordingly began to focus her attention and efforts on George.

During the first months after Frederick's death, Augusta learned very little about 'the real disposition' of George. At the end of that time, she complained to one of her husband's old political allies that he knew her son almost as well as she did. He was, she thought, 'very honest'. Still, 'she wish'd he were a little more forward, and less childish, at his age.' He also was not learning his schoolwork as rapidly as she had hoped. This slowness as a student concerned her rather less, though, than his immaturity. Augusta believed his instructors bore the lion's share of the responsibility for his lack of progress in education. But his childishness meant the boy remained dangerously impressionable. His character was still malleable, and therefore the possibility of his being impressed by the wrong people was still very real. For the present, Augusta was 'very glad' that George did not take 'very particularly to anybody about him but his brother Edward'. 'The young people of quality', she believed, 'were so ill educated, and so very vicious, that they frighten'd her.' She hoped that his instructors would soon succeed in improving the boy's studies and his maturity. For now, she could summarize what was good in George's character more briefly: 'he was a very honest boy, and ... his chief passion seem'd to be Edward'.[35]

George's learning did not improve during the next three years. Even after Bute became his 'dearest friend' and tutor, he continued to be afflicted by a debilitating indolence in intellectual pursuits. (One of Bute's greatest accomplishments was convincing his pupil that he could resist this weakness.)[36] Nor did George's childishness wane. His mother complained about it and feared its possible consequences for years. When an effort was made to remove some of the prince's instructors on the grounds of jacobitism, Augusta's sensitivity to George's vulnerability to manipulation caused her to see it as a plot to remove him from her. The aim of her enemies, she believed, was 'to get the Prince to their side, and then, by their behaviour, to throw her off from her temper, and so make their complaint to the King stronger and make her disoblige him [by] defending the accus'd'. They were confident 'if they could have forc'd her into any indiscreet warmth', that they would carry 'the Prince into those other hands, at last, by taking him from the people now about him and by degrees, consequently, from her'. Augusta was sure she defeated this only by keeping George II 'in very good humour with her and the children'.[37] Later she justified her suspicions and actions by recalling that Lord Harcourt, the prince's governor, 'always spoke to the children of their father, and his actions, in so disrespectfull a manner, as to send them to her almost ready to cry, and did all he could, to alienate them from

35 *Dodington Journal*, ed. Carswell and Dralle, pp. 178–9: 15 Oct. 1752.

36 See Bullion, 'The Prince's Mentor', pp. 43–6.

37 *Dodington Journal*, ed. Carswell and Dralle, pp. 192–3: 28 Dec. 1752. Lucid accounts of this struggle may be found in Brooke, *George III*, pp. 35–9; and in Clark's introduction to *The Memoirs and Speeches of Waldegrave*, pp. 54–63.

her'. After Harcourt's removal, the boys themselves became aware of his attempts. 'George ... mentioned to her once, that he was afraid he had not behav'd to her so well as he ought sometimes, and wonder'd he could be so misled.' Augusta soothed her son by assuring him that he had never acted improperly toward her, but only 'now and then' treated her 'not with quite so much complaisance, as a young gentleman should use to a lady'.[38] But she did not wonder at his being misled so easily. This narrow escape strengthened her conviction that she must maintain her pre-eminent influence on the life of her immature son. It would be up to her to imprint certain virtues on his heart and mind, virtues that would enable him to live up to her ideas of what a king should be.

III

As had been Frederick's habit, Augusta often defined what a king should be by what she believed George II was not. A monarch should not be dominated by his ministers, unlike George II, whom 'she reckon'd ... no more than one of the trees we walk'd by (or something more inconsiderable, which she named)'.[39] A king should maintain his dignity and authority, and not childishly claim to be able to accomplish deeds he could not. The man presently on the throne 'would sputter and make a bustle, but when [the ministers] told him that it must be done from the necessity of his service, he must do it, just as little Harry [her son Henry, who was eight] must when she came down' to discipline him.[40] A king should observe his obligations to his family, without cavilling or being tightfisted. George II was notoriously miserly, and ever ready to divert funds that should have gone to his grandchildren to his own purse.[41] A ruler of Great Britain should not favour the interests of Hanover when they conflicted with those of Britain. Augusta 'wish'd Hanover in the sea, as the cause of all our misfortunes'; 'in the manner it had been treated [by George II], it had been the foundation of all just complaints, and bad measures'.[42] Finally, a king should not be governed by the women his love and lust attracted him to. 'Princes when once in women's hands', she believed, 'make miserable figures'.[43] She was determined that her son would be the reverse of his grandfather, and not simply because she 'could have nothing so much at heart as to see him do well, and make the nation happy'.[44] Her determination was also fuelled by a dislike for the king so intense that a friend

---

38 *Dodington Journal*, ed. Carswell and Dralle, p. 207: 3 Mar. 1753.
39 *Ibid.*, p. 199: 25 Jan. 1753.
40 *Ibid.*, p. 203: 8 Feb. 1753.
41 *Ibid.*, pp. 176–7: 15 Oct. 1752. See also entry for 29 May 1754, *ibid.*, pp. 271–2.
42 *Ibid.*, p. 316: 6 Aug. 1755.
43 One can see what Augusta taught George about the consequences of the king's attraction to women in a letter from the prince to Bute in 1759 in *Letters from George III to Bute*, ed. Sedgwick, p. 37. The princess was hardly the only person who believed a succession of women had essentially ruled George II. See Hervey, *Memoirs*, ed. Sedgwick, p. 194.
44 *Dodington Journal*, ed. Carswell and Dralle, p. 180: 15 Oct. 1752.

could only remember her speaking favourably of him once, and by the bitter awareness that she had to behave prudently, stay in his good graces, and never reveal her dislike and contempt as long as he lived.[45]

Augusta had three basic strategies for moulding her son into the right sort of man and monarch. One was the time-honoured parental stratagem of seizing on appropriate chances to reinforce good and criticize bad behaviour. We have seen how she reminded George that a gentleman should always be complaisant toward ladies, when he was remorseful about his behaviour toward her. Similarly, whenever George and Edward 'behav'd wrong, or idly (as children will do) to any that belong'd to the Prince, and are now about her, she always ask'd them how they think their father would have lik'd to see them behave so to anybody that belong'd to him, and that he valued'. 'They ought', she reminded the boys, 'to have more kindness for them, because they had lost their friend and protector, which was [the children's] also.' This effort to induce feelings of loyalty and obligation to one's friends, she found, 'made a great impression upon them'.[46] Augusta also made certain that her sons showed the proper respect to the rank of those who were trying to serve them. Although she regarded the bishop of Norwich as an enemy, she assured him that she had constantly supported him as the prince's preceptor, and 'always inculcated to the children to show him great respect'. 'Not for love of you, my Lord', she bluntly told the bishop, 'but because it is fitting and necessary; for if they are suffer'd to want respect that is due to one degree, they will go on to want it to another, till at last it would come up to me, and I should have taught them to disregard me.'[47] This took a considerable act of will on her part. Both Augusta and the boys thought the bishop was an incompetent instructor, and the princess probably shared her secretary's opinion that his latitudinarianism made him virtually an atheist.[48] Nevertheless, paying the respect owed a man of his station was an important enough principle that it could not be overlooked, even in this case. Not that Augusta blinked at criticism at the right times when it was called for. She regularly assessed the moral fitness of those about her, and those in politics and at court. It must be assumed that she passed both these judgments and her readiness to judge along to George. As Waldegrave later

---

45 *Ibid.*, p. 215: 29 Mar. 1753. There are indications that George II sensed Augusta's real feelings, yet felt himself thwarted by her prudence from taking action. Horace Walpole heard that the king told Henry Pelham soon after Frederick's death that 'You none of you know this woman, and you none of you will know her until I am dead.' Quoted in *The Memoirs and Speeches of Waldegrave*, ed. Clark, p. 54.

46 *Dodington Journal*, ed. Carswell and Dralle, p. 179: 15 Oct. 1752. See also entry for 17 Nov. 1753: *ibid.*, p. 241.

47 *Ibid.*, p. 191: 28 Dec. 1752.

48 For their reaction to the bishop of Norwich as an instructor, see *ibid.*, p. 203: 8 Feb. 1753. George and Edward had been complaining about the bishop for some months prior to this. See Clark's introduction to *The Memoirs and Speeches of Waldegrave*, p. 54. For Cresset's remarks about the bishop's religious views, see n. 17 above.

remarked, even as a young man he paid 'rather too much attention to the sins of his neighbour'.[49]

Augusta's second stratagem was also traditional, one customarily resorted to by devout parents. Although direct evidence on this is lacking, it seems likely that the woman who had insisted on taking communion in the Lutheran chapel until she was convinced this was politically unwise encouraged her children to observe the rites of the anglican church faithfully and wholeheartedly. Her efforts were most successful with her eldest son. Well before he ascended the throne, George had concluded that God's will applied to kings as well as to lesser mortals, and had to be accepted and obeyed.[50] He had a sense of the active role of providence in the lives of men and nations that was far keener than most of his contemporaries in Britain, and resembled more closely the providentialism of his subjects in New England.[51] These convictions were genuinely held. As Waldegrave remarked, George's 'Religion is free from all Hypocrisy'. The earl did qualify this observation by noting it 'is not of the most charitable sort'.[52] One should recall, though, that this was the critique of a worldly man not particularly concerned about the presence of sin in himself or others.[53] What Waldegrave's comment unintentionally points out about George is his knowledge of christianity's moral rules and his conviction that he and others should live by these precepts.

But could her son manage to live by these rules? This question haunted Augusta. He was childish and impressionable, and the weak will and heedlessness of children did not bode well for resisting the temptations and snares of the world. The princess had no reason to be confident in his capacity for resistance, even with her aid and the

49 Waldegrave, 'Memoirs', in *The Memoirs and Speeches of Waldegrave*, ed. Clark, p. 148.
50 See *Correspondence of George III with Bute*, ed. Sedgwick, p. 31: the prince to Bute, [7 Sept. 1759]. In his reply, Bute recalled that the prince's religious feelings were not new, for he was 'accustomed from [his] childhood to look up to Heaven' so he could 'in the day of affliction put full confidence in Him who gives and resumes at pleasure'. The cause of George's unhappiness was the death of his sister Elizabeth. A few years later, when he drafted a 'sketch of the Education I mean to give my Sons', George III noted, 'Religion should be instilled from the most tender Youth as that teaches that the All Wise Creator is not a respecter of persons and that in his Eyes all Men are judged by their conduct not their birth.' For this reason he believed the end of their education should be 'the making them Christians, & Usefull Members of Society'. Royal Archives, Windsor Castle, Add. Georgian MS 32/1732–3: 'The Plan of Education for a Prince'. I would like to thank Her Majesty The Queen for her gracious permission to quote from papers in the Royal Archives.
51 It is striking to compare the prince's providentialism with that of the Massachusetts soldiers so well described by Fred Anderson in *A People's Army. Massachusetts Soldiers and Society in the Seven Years' War* (Chapel Hill, N.C., 1984), pp. 196–7, 209–10, 216–18. For examples of George's providentialism during the Seven Years' War, see Bute Papers (the marquess of Bute, Mountstuart, Isle of Bute), Correspondence with George III, nos. 73, 25: the prince to Bute [early Aug. 1759], [19 Oct. 1759]; and in *Letters from George III to Bute*, ed. Sedgwick, p. 32: the prince to Bute [19 Oct. 1759].
52 Waldegrave, 'Memoirs', in *The Memoirs and Speeches of Waldegrave*, ed. Clark, p. 148.
53 For an excellent description of Waldegrave's social milieu and his worldliness, see Clark's introduction in *ibid.*, pp. 41–8.

church's counsel. Indeed, she had reasons other than her son's temperament to be apprehensive. Augusta had managed to get her way on important points with both her husband and her father-in-law, but she had no illusions about the limits of her powers. The diary of her confidante George Bubb Dodington offers ample evidence of her frustrations over her inability to change George II and the necessity of prudently avoiding antagonizing the king.[54] If the world ever gained a foothold within her son, and offered him a rationale for gratifying impulses, the influence she had might not be sufficient to overcome it. When Dodington claimed that 'all good men plac'd their chief hopes in the Prince's continuing chiefly in her hands and direction, and in her preserving this influence over him which was justly due to her from her prudence as well as from nature', he articulated her heartfelt convictions.[55]

To accomplish this, Augusta adopted her third stratagem. She was certain it was essential to isolate her son as much as possible from worldly contaminations. 'The young people of quality', as we have seen, 'were so ill educated, and so very vicious, that they frighten'd her.' Thus she was glad in 1752 that George clung to the company of his family, and encouraged this tendency in her eldest son.[56] When Edward complained in 1753 about this 'subjection ... and of his brother's want of spirit', she was alarmed. At this time, Dodington argued that the prince should have more company, but the princess 'seem'd averse to the young people, from the excessive bad education they had, and the bad examples they gave'.[57] This close supervision of their social life continued to chafe Edward, while George bore it docilely. In 1755, Augusta conceded that he needed the company of men, because 'women could not inform him' about his duties in government and opportunities in politics. 'But if it was in her power absolutely', she rhetorically asked Dodington, 'where could she address him? What company could she wish him to? What friendships desire he should contract? Such was the universal profligacy, and the character and conduct of the young people of distinction' that she did not know where to turn. Then Augusta revealed her deepest concern. 'She would be in more pain for her daughters', she told her friend, 'than for her son, if they were private persons, [because] the behaviour of the women was so indecent, so low, so much against their interest, by making them so cheap.'[58] The princess had realized that the wedge which could split George apart from her, and destroy what potential he had for being a good monarch, was unbridled sexual appetite. All her careful instruction in morals and manners, she believed, would be swept aside if he ever yielded to lust.

Augusta did not spell out to Dodington why she believed this, but her reasoning may be easily inferred. In part, she assumed that her son, like other men, had

54 *Dodington Journal*, ed. Carswell and Dralle, pp. 177–8, 193–4, 197–200: 15 Oct., 28 Dec. 1752, 25 Jan. 1753.
55 *Ibid.*, p. 194: 28 Dec. 1752.
56 *Ibid.*, p. 178: 15 Oct. 1752.
57 *Ibid.*, p. 244: 18 Dec. 1753.
58 *Ibid.*, p. 300: 27 May 1755.

powerful sexual hungers to satisfy. She was certain, as she told her friend, that he would have 'many' children.[59] In part, too, she had the example of what lust had done to George II. To the princess, the king's unrestrained pursuit of sexual pleasure had helped make him a cipher. Finally, it is possible that Augusta blamed Frederick's erratic behaviour on his penchant for adultery, and resented the way his amours had exposed her to public humiliation. She was determined to prevent the still immature George from repeating the mistakes of his grandfather and father. To do this, she tried to isolate him from feminine temptation for as long as she could, until, she hoped, he accepted the necessity of avoiding the dangers of lust. Her efforts were successful. Augusta did not manage to keep George completely separated from women she regarded as immoral. Indeed, George Lewis Scott, the prince's subpreceptor from 1750 to 1756, noticed that his pupil 'has the greatest temptation to gallant with the ladies, who lay themselves out in the most shameful manner to draw him'. But she did persuade him that 'Princes when once in their hands make miserable figures, the annals of France and the present situation of government in the Kingdom I most love are convincing proof of' that. She taught him to believe that such women were attracted not to him but to his power, and sought an ascendancy over him to turn that power to their own purposes. He learned that lesson well enough to remark to Scott that 'if he were not what he is, they would not mind him'. Finally, she convinced him that he had to resist the passions of 'boiling youth', in the expectation that in time a proper 'marriage will put a stop to this combat in my breast'. Fortified by these precepts, the prince had, as Scott noted, 'no tendency to vice, and ... as yet very virtuous principles'; the ladies' efforts were 'to no purpose'.[60] Another, and more important, proof of the princess's success came in August 1755. Rumours were circulating that George II was thinking of arranging a match between his grandson and a princess of Brunswick. To Augusta, such a marriage was premature and, because of the personality of the proposed bride, unwise. She was

---

59 *Ibid.*, p. 317: 6 Aug. 1755.

60 Augusta's precepts are revealed in *Letters from George III to Bute*, ed. Sedgwick, p. 37: the prince to Bute [1759]. In it, George told Bute that he had 'long resisted the charms of those devine creatures', which indicates that the moral he stated in the letter dated from before his friendship with Bute. His mother's observation about people flattering him because of his position rather than his personal qualities clearly impressed the young prince. He remembered it for years. Indeed, when he planned the education of his sons, he commented that 'the most severe trials a Prince has to combat are those occasioned by his rank; the most efficacious means of destroying this dangerous charm would be the making him acquainted with his own weakness, his own ignorance, and the keeping him perhaps distant from Courts'. The king even mused that it might be wise 'to hide his rank from him till he shall possess virtue enough to be frightened at the being acquainted with it'. He conceded, however, that 'custom, that most powerful of Tyrants, will never permit this to be adopted'. Royal Archives, Add. Georgian MS 32/1732: George III, 'The Plan of Education for a Prince'. The comments in this paragraph by George Lewis Scott are quoted in Ayling, *George the Third*, p. 36. Waldegrave, a much less sympathetic judge of the prince than Scott, confirmed his resistance to temptation. The earl pointed out that George had 'great command of his Passions', and noticeably avoided the pursuit of pleasure. Waldegrave, 'Memoirs', in *The Memoirs and Speeches of Waldegrave*, ed. Clark, pp. 148–9.

delighted when she found that George understood her objections, and, far from yielding to lust, 'was much averse to [the marriage] himself'.[61]

Underlining what the princess had achieved is important. She had taught her son, by frequent precept and with the assistance of isolating him as much as she could from contact with 'indecent' and 'cheap' women, that chastity before marriage and fidelity afterwards were virtues. This was an unusual lesson, to say the least. Augusta lived in an age when male fornication and adultery were at worst venial sins, and often expected behaviour. Chastity and fidelity were strictly feminine virtues. Under this double standard, royal males differed from their aristocratic and commoner counterparts only in the fact that they conducted their sexual adventures more publicly.[62] Augusta succeeded in training her eldest son so well that even when he was most afflicted with 'boiling youth', he shrank from any lustful, immoral designs on women.[63]

Edward did not absorb these lessons. To his mother's disgust, he celebrated coming of age by courting a married woman, sleeping with whores and professing latitudinarian religious doctrines that permitted him to do both without feeling guilty.[64] The difference between the two brothers was aptly summarized by another son, Prince Frederick. In 1759, the nine-year old Frederick and George saw a famous courtesan pass by. 'The child named her – the Prince, to try him, asked, who that was? – "Why, a Miss" – "A Miss", said the P[rince] of W[ales], why, are not all girls Misses?"' Frederick replied that she was a certain kind of miss, one who sold oranges. George teasingly asked, '"Is there any harm in selling oranges?"' The boy rose to this bait by answering, '"Oh! but they are not such oranges as you buy – I believe they are of a sort that my brother Edward Buys."'[65]

As time passed, it became clear Frederick was a consumer of the fruit Edward bought. Among Augusta's sons, George alone adopted the virtues that she taught

---

61 *Dodington Journal*, ed. Carswell and Dralle, p. 317: 6 Aug. 1755.

62 See Stone, *Family, Sex, and Marriage*, pp. 503–7.

63 See *Letters from George III to Bute*, ed. Sedgwick, pp. 36–39: two letters from the prince to Bute [1759]. In describing his infatuation with Lady Sarah Lennox, George protested 'before God I never have had any improper thought with regard to her, ... having often flatter'd myself with hopes that one day or other you would consent to my raising her to a Throne'.

64 For Edward's pursuit of Lady Essex, and the princess's presumed reaction to it, see *Walpole's Correspondence*, ed. Lewis, xxi, 53–4: Walpole to Mann, 29 Jan. 1757. Two weeks later, on 13 Feb. 1757, Walpole wrote to Mann: 'Prince Edward's pleasures continue to furnish conversation: he has been rather forbid by the Signora Madre to make himself so common; and has been rather encouraged by his grandfather to disregard the prohibition.' *Ibid.*, p. 57. For Edward's relationship with the earl of Eglintoun, who encouraged his protégé in both pleasurable activities and latitudinarianism, see Fox, 'Memoir', in *Lady Sarah Lennox*, ed. Ilchester and Stavordale, pp. 16–17; and *James Boswell. The Earlier Years, 1740–1769*, ed. Frederick A. Pottle (New York, 1966), pp. 47–52. Boswell, in his 'Sketch of the Early Life of James Boswell, Written by Himself, for Jean Jacques Rousseau, 5 December 1764', explicitly linked latitudinarianism and sexual licence in this way: 'My Lord [Eglintoun] made me a deist. I gave myself up to pleasure without limit. I was in a delirium of joy.' *Ibid.*, p. 4. Eglintoun was Edward's mentor as well.

65 *Walpole's Correspondence*, ed. Lewis, ix, 237: Walpole to George Montagu, 16 May 1759.

them all.[66] He became an anomaly not only at court and in politics, but within his family as well: a man who believed being virtuous meant being chaste and faithful, and practised those womanly virtues. This pleased his mother greatly. In August 1755, she proudly informed Dodington that the prince of Wales 'was not a wild, dissipated boy, but good natur'd, and cheerful, but with a serious cast in the whole'. She also told her friend that 'those about [the prince] knew him no more than if they had never seen him; that he was not quick, but with those he was acquainted with, applicable and intelligent'.[67] These were the words of a mother satisfied with her son's moral progress and confident he would realize his potential as a king. Although Dodington neither knew nor guessed this, these were also the sentiments of a woman who knew that the final step in the moulding and maturation of George's character was taking place. Unknown to the politicians at court, the princess's friend Lord Bute had begun to tutor the prince. Moreover, Bute was proving to be a remarkably successful instructor.[68]

This success was crucial to Augusta's plans for her son. As early as May 1754, she had 'wish'd [the prince] saw more company'. By this, she meant that 'he had acquaintance older than himself'. More specifically, she wanted him to know men who could guide him in the ways of politics without compromising her efforts to make him virtuous. Even that early she may have had Bute in mind. But she 'durst not recommend', she told Dodington, 'for fear of offense: while he had governors &c., was under immediate inspection, all that they did not direct, would be imputed to her'. Unwilling to give George II any excuse for taking his grandson from her, she refrained. 'In a year or two', she hoped, the prince 'must be thought to have a will of his own, and then he would, she hop'd, act accordingly'.[69]

The reason for her concern is clear. Augusta had learned from Frederick's detailed plans for his first days on the throne that 'it was of infinite consequence how a young reign set out'. The fact that George was leading an isolated life had thus far yielded very good results, but, if it continued much longer, it might have very bad ones. The princess did not believe that 'women could ... inform him' about the realities of power, and she 'was highly sensible how necessary it was that the Prince should keep company with men'.[70] This was the case in part because she thought men had political skills and knowledge not available to women. Moreover, Augusta worried that unscrupulous men might convince George that his reliance on his mother

---

66 Indeed, Frederick may have been precocious. When nine, he unbuttoned his trousers and offered to show Lady Charlotte Edwin how eunuchs were made. *Ibid.* For his later escapades, and those of his other brothers, see Brooke, *George III*, pp. 270–82.

67 *Dodington Journal*, ed. Carswell and Dralle, p. 318: 6 Aug. 1755.

68 Bute began his work with George in June–July 1755. See *Letters from George III to Bute*, ed. Sedgwick, p. 2: the prince to Bute [1 July 1756].

69 *Dodington Journal*, ed. Carswell and Dralle, p. 271: 29 May 1754.

70 *Ibid.*, p. 300: 27 May 1755. For Frederick's detailed plans for the first days of his reign, and Augusta's knowledge of them, see 'Leicester House Politics', ed. Newman, pp. 104–20, 198.

was unmanly, and thus sever their relationship. Bute expressed her fear vividly in a letter to the prince, when he warned him against those who 'sooner or later' would whisper in his ear that 'Lord Bute ... only means to bring you under your mother's government, sure you are too much of a man to bear that.'[71] Driven by her sense she had to do something soon, not merely to forestall such tactics, but because of George II's advancing age and the deepening crisis with France, she decided during the early summer of 1755 to ask Bute to take over the education of the prince. To prevent discovery, the two adopted the subterfuge that the earl was visiting her.[72] Bute and George established with surprising quickness a rapport that went well beyond the usual teacher-pupil relationship. Delighted that a male friend who shared her ideas about morality and her commitment to making George a patriot king was now her son's 'dearest friend', Augusta urged Bute to continue to pursue his 'worthy efforts' and 'imprint his grate sentiments' on the prince.[73] Her choice of 'imprint' to describe this process is significant. She expected Bute would duplicate in his political education of George her own successful effort to fix within his heart and mind her religious and moral beliefs and practices. This duplication would not merely complete the fashioning of his character as a virtuous man and monarch. It would also guarantee that the ways of the world would not overturn the lessons of his mother.

IV

Augusta's success with her son was soon obvious, at first to those who saw him most frequently at court, and then to the wider world that gossiped and speculated about events at Leicester House. His devotion to religion and his insistence on maintaining morality were apparent to Waldegrave, who viewed them coolly, and to Bute, who was overjoyed by his protégé's willingness to submit to the laws and the will of God.[74] His commitment to chastity excited even more comment. No doubt this was because it had no precedent among his male ancestors in the house of Hanover and

71 The quotation is from *Correspondence of George III with Bute*, ed. Sedgwick, p. liii: Bute to the prince [1755]. Bute went on to note that if the prince were 'well acquainted with this nation, with the people you are to govern, with the individuals you are one day to employ, with the business of the Kingdom, you would have no occasion for the Princesses advice nor would she offer it'. Until that time, however, he warned George to 'look on him as your most determined enemy who attempts to breed suspicions in your breast against her'.

72 This deception led observers at court to conclude that Augusta and Bute were having an affair. The gossip about them played a crucial role in preventing politicians from guessing that the earl was in fact tutoring the prince. This episode and its importance are discussed by John L. Bullion, 'The Origins and Significance of Gossip about Princess Augusta and Lord Bute, 1755–1756', *Studies in Eighteenth-Century Culture*, XXI (1991), 245–65.

73 *Letters from George III to Bute*, ed. Sedgwick, p. 4: Augusta to Bute [1755].

74 Waldegrave, 'Memoirs', in *Memoirs and Speeches of Waldegrave*, ed. Clark, p. 148; *Letters from George III to Bute*, ed. Sedgwick, p. 31: Bute to the prince [7 Sept. 1759].

was so different from the reactions of Edward, who could not wait to embrace both latitudinarian religion and all available women.[75]

The fact that George's 'chastity had ... remained to all appearance inviolate, notwithstanding his age and sanguine complexion', did not surprise the cynical Horace Walpole. He explained the princess's success by confidently asserting that she had 'fettered' George's mind. Indeed, Walpole believed that 'could she have chained up his body' as well, 'it is probable she would have preferred his remaining single' in order to maintain her control over him.[76] Such an interpretation is unjust to Augusta. She expected her son would marry, and wanted him to preserve the line of descent. She also knew that his most intimate male advisers would come to have, and rightly so, more influence on his political behaviour than she ever would. As for fettering his mind, she clearly had less impact on Edward and her other sons than she did on George. Other explanations for her decisive role in shaping his character must be sought.

Foremost among these must be George's receptiveness to her moral training. Augusta was right when she realized that the young prince was pliable, was susceptible to having patterns of thought and behaviour imprinted on him. She was also correct to observe that he was 'good natur'd', not merely in the sense that he was complaisant, but in the fact that he wanted to be virtuous. What his mother accomplished was convincing him that he could be good, that virtue was within his power if he committed himself to christianity and to following its rules of morality. Bute then built upon this foundation, by persuading his pupil that a monarch could be moral politically as well as personally, and could be a patriot king if he learned and observed certain procedures and policies.[77] Both his mother and his 'dearest friend' appealed to the deep-seated desire within George to be a good man and monarch. Far more than his other brothers, he was in this crucial respect his mother's son.

V

Gauging the historical significance of Augusta's influence on George requires asking two separate questions. The first is the more difficult to answer. How did George's perceptions of himself as an honest and moral man, a faithful husband and a conscientious father, affect his political judgments? Such a question must be answered in the immediate context of his decisions, and the answers will on occasion not be obvious. To return to Augusta's putative role in the coming of the American revolution: if as some scholars have argued, that revolution may be understood in important ways as a revolt against patriarchalism, how would a king determined to

75 Even before Edward came of age, Scott observed that he was 'of a more amorous complexion' than his older brother. Quoted in Ayling, *George the Third*, p. 36.
76 Quotations from an excerpt from Walpole's original draft of his 'Memoirs of George III', published in *Walpole's Correspondence*, ed. Lewis, XXI, 517 n. 15: Walpole to Mann, 23 July 1761.
77 Bullion, 'The Prince's Mentor', pp. 44–7.

be a good father to his family and his people react to an assault on his paternal as well as his political authority? George III's correspondence after the beginning of armed conflict in 1775 reveals his absolute commitment to reducing the mother country's rebellious children to obedience. P. D. G. Thomas has suggested that this deeply felt determination was the result of his personal character, 'a resolution not to give way, that is very marked throughout his political life, combined with an inability to see an opponent's point of view; perhaps also a sense of lese-majesty towards himself as sovereign'.[78] Asking whether the king's sense of himself as a virtuous man with moral imperatives he had to follow helped form these character traits and contributed to his determination might illumine his own character and his role in the American revolution further. Certainly such subjects deserve careful and sensitive examination.

The other question involves assessing the significance of his people's perceptions of George III as a moral, religious monarch who was particularly and conspicuously virtuous in the domestic sphere of his family. Here Linda Colley has provided us with some intriguing food for thought. As Colley has pointed out, George's public reputation improved dramatically after the end of the American War of Independence. Central to that improvement, according to her, was the king's 'undoubted domestic probity and obstinate patriotism'. In a time of national flux and humiliation, these qualities 'seemed to many to represent a reassuring stability ... [and] honest uncomplicated worth in contrast with those meretricious, complex and/or immoral politicians who had failed'. As years passed, George III's morality and stability seemed even brighter and more meritorious in contrast to his heir's sexual and political escapades. In this case, the king may have been the beneficiary of 'a general rise in female politicization' in the early nineteenth century.[79] That should not be surprising. Many of the virtues George's people had come to prize – his unfeigned commitment to christianity, his fidelity to his wife, his morality in general and his dedication to domestic responsibility in particular – were, as we have seen, feminine.

That George III had these virtues was the result of his mother's efforts and example. She served him well. George reigned during a time when European monarchs were toppled from their thrones by popular revolutionary fervour and war. In contrast to them, he enjoyed the support and affection of his people, and became the national symbol of resistance to French ideas and armies. That affection was deeply rooted in the morality the princess imprinted within him. John Brooke closed his comments on Augusta by asserting that 'during the reign of her son she was of no consequence in politics'.[80] This is true only in the most literal sense, in terms of direct

---

[78] For the interpretation of the American Revolution as a revolt against paternalism, see Jay Fliegelman, *Prodigals and Pilgrims. The American Revolution against Patriarchal Authority, 1750–1800* (Cambridge, 1980); for Thomas's remarks, see P. D. G. Thomas, 'George III and the American Revolution', *History*, LXX (1985), 30–1.

[79] Linda Colley, 'The Apotheosis of George III: Loyalty, Royalty and the British Nation, 1760–1820', *Past and Present*, 102 (1984), 104–5, 124–5.

[80] Brooke, *George III*, p. 266.

intervention in political events. Insofar as broad influences on George III were concerned, it was she, after all, who instilled in him what it meant to be a king. Indeed, she did more than that. Years after her death, her lessons of domestic virtue and genuine piety helped him remain one.

10

Israel Mauduit: Pamphleteering and Foreign Policy in the Age of the Elder Pitt

Karl Schweizer

The eighteenth century witnessed dramatic expansion in the English press. Enjoying unprecedented growth, vitality and appeal, periodical, newspaper and pamphlet publications became an important part of the country's socio-political fabric, at once reflecting, shaping and co-ordinating public opinion on diverse matters of local and national concern.[1] While scholarship of late has shown growing consensus regarding the impressive upsurge of press activity during the Hanoverian era, less agreement exists about the actual impact of this 'culture of print': its role as a mode of political communication, its function in the factional conflicts of the period, and, above all, its significance in the area of foreign policy, one of the major topics of public and ministerial debate at this time.[2] Thus, several recent studies have questioned whether, given the problems associated with circulation figures, readership, literacy, press control and other issues (aggravated by gaps in the surviving materials) press influence can ever be precisely established; other works *per contra*, while recognizing these problems nevertheless see a double link between press activity – the printed dissemination of ideas and information – and policy formulation.[3] Whatever its bearing on specific diplomatic manoeuvres, the English press, so runs the argument,

[1] For excellent introductions to both the seventeenth- and eighteenth-century press see: *Newspaper History: From the Seventeenth Century to the Present Day*, ed. G. Boyce, J. Curran and P. Wingate (1978); *The Press in English Society from the Seventeenth to the Nineteenth Centuries*, ed. M. Harris and A. Lee (1986); *The Culture of Print. Power and the Use of Print in Early Modern Europe*, ed. R. Chartier (Cambridge, 1989); M. Harris, *London Newspapers in the Age of Walpole. A Study in the Origins of the Modern English Press* (1987); J. Black, *The English Press in the Eighteenth Century* (1987); R. R. Rea, *The English Press in Politics, 1760–1774* (Lincoln, Neb., 1963); E. Eisenstein, *The Printing Press as an Agent of Change* (Cambridge, 1973).
[2] J. Black, 'Foreign Policy and the British State, 1742–1793', in *idem, British Politics and Society from Walpole to Pitt, 1742–1783* (1990), ch. 6; *idem, British Foreign Policy in the Age of Walpole* (Edinburgh, 1985), preface; *Politics and the Press in Hanoverian Britain*, ed. K. W. Schweizer and J. Black (Lewiston, N.Y., 1989), introduction.
[3] J. Black, *A System of Ambition? British Foreign Policy, 1660–1793* (1993), ch. 7; M. Harris, 'Periodicals and the Book Trade', in *Development of the British Book Trade, 1700–1899*, ed. R. Myers and M. Harris (1981), pp. 37–62; V. Berridge, 'Content Analysis and Historical Research on Newspapers', in *The Press in English Society from the Seventeenth to Nineteenth Centuries*, ed. M. Harris and A. Lee (Rutherford, N.J., 1986), pp. 201–8; J. P. Thomas, 'The British Empire and the Press in English Society, 1763–64', University of Oxford D.Phil., 1982.

helped to create a climate of opinion that was important in two respects – in influencing foreign perceptions of British strength and, perhaps more intangibly, in affecting the views held by the British political nation, thereby creating an atmosphere or milieu likely to inhibit or promote certain policy options. As such, the press, in its various forms, was critical in providing a bridge between 'public opinion' (however defined)[4] and the high political sphere.[5] Pamphlets especially were considered an effective means of analysing diplomatic issues and influencing public opinion: compact and accessible, catering to a diverse audience well informed and actively interested in court, parliament and beyond. 'Quicker and easier to produce than books, as well as being less expensive, they provided an opportunity for developing views at greater length than that offered by newspapers.'[6] Indeed, every issue of importance, and many of none, engaged writers to such a degree that one could establish the scale of pamphleteering as one of the indexes by which the importance of an issue can be measured.

A problem central to all the above works, whatever their conclusions, is that they tend to discuss the subject over protracted time spans, an approach which fails to capture the true nature of eighteenth-century press activity: at no time continuous or consistent, but fluid and variable, ever susceptible to amorphous pressures or conditioning influences. Drawing attention to this problem in his recent book on the English press, Jeremy Black has suggested, by way of solution, that to understand the political role of individual publications or of the press in general, it will henceforth be necessary to consider specific political circumstances and conjunctions: the precise context that gives press productions their meaning. 'It is probable that a stress on specificity is going to be one of the key developments in eighteenth century historiography.'[7]

The aim of the following chapter is to contribute to this process through a detailed case study of the famous pamphlet *Considerations on the Present German War* by the writer Israel Mauduit – a pamphlet important not only as a significant contribution to political journalism, but one whose publication history and remarkable

---

4   For a working definition of 'public opinion' as used in this paper see M. Peters, 'Historians and the Eighteenth-Century English Press', *New Zealand Journal of History and Politics*, XV (1987), 48 n. 37. She writes, 'public opinion is understood to be something more than the mere aggregate of private opinion or the opinion of interest groups. Certainly more than the opinion of "topic people". Its development is obviously closely connected with the growth of political consciousness and means of public communication and also with the development of the role of government from the mere holding of power towards the conscious exercise of power for the supposed benefit of some or all of those governed. Such a definition can best provide a basis for consideration of substantive issues, such as the ways in which, in a particular historical context, public opinion was perceived by contemporaries and can be seen by historians to exist, manifest itself and be influential.'

5   Black, *English Press*, p. 114; Schweizer and Black, *Politics and the Press*, p. xi.

6   J. Black, 'Dr Johnson: Eighteenth-Century Pamphleteering and the Tory View on Foreign Policy', *Factotum*, XXXII (1990), 15. Cf. Craig Harline, *Pamphlets, Printing and Political Culture in the Early Dutch Republic* (1987).

7   Black, *English Press*, p. 114.

appeal also illuminate some striking aspects of the interconnexion between press activity and policy formulation in a wartime setting. By contributing to a sustained debate of national significance – the controversy over continental intervention – it focused both metropolitan and provincial sensibilities, elicited responses and counter responses and so constituted a critical mechanism by which public opinion could be articulated and developed, thus producing an impact both locally and nationally. As such, Mauduit's work highlights the complex relationship between political decisions and the role played by ideas in determining certain choices of action and legitimating those chosen.

Born in 1708, Israel Mauduit began his career as dissenting minister and woolen trader in the City of London, subsequently becoming an agent for Massachusetts in England in addition to preaching in protestant chapels, advising British ministers on the intricacies of colonial affairs and writing political pamphlets.[8] While never more than a minor figure in English political life, Mauduit had influence among those in power: as seasoned lobbyist, contact man and consultant, with a flair for writing which he avidly employed in the service of successive administrations, prior to and during the difficult years of the American revolution. At his death in 1787, the Gentleman's Magazine gave him nearly a full column in its obituaries while The European Magazine and London Review featured a two installment memoir including an engraved portrait.[9]

Although involved in the earlier press controversy involving the loss of Minorca,[10] Mauduit first rose to prominence as the author of a pamphlet entitled Considerations on the Present German War, published in 1760, a work which immediately established his reputation as a leading polemicist. Indeed, as J. Corbett once observed, with the exception of Swift's Conduct of the Allies, no such pamphlet had ever produced so deep an effect on England and no student of the period can afford to ignore it either on political or strategic grounds.[11]

Selling over 5,000 copies in five editions, within the space of a few months,[12] the Considerations was inspired by, and contributed to, the debate then raging concerning Britain's proper strategy in her conflict with France at a time of diminishing resources and discontent especially with the German part of the war: the defensive operations which Britain and her continental allies, Prussia, Brunswick and Hanover,

8   R. J. Taylor, 'Israel Mauduit', New England Quarterly, XXIV (1951), 208–30.
9   The Gentleman's Magazine, LVII (June 1787), 549; The European Magazine, XI (June 1787), 383–4; The London Review, XII (July 1787), 6–8.
10 A Letter to the Right Hon. Lord B—g being an Enquiry into the Merits of his Defense of Minorca (1756).
11 J. Corbett, England in the Seven Years War (2 vols., 1907), II, 144.
12 The total print-run was 5,750 copies, considerably greater than that of the most influential pamphlets of the decade. Cf. the total printing of 3,250 for Burke's Thoughts on the Cause of the Present Discontents. J. Brewer, Party Ideology and Popular Politics at the Accession of George III (Cambridge, 1976), p. 146; B.L., Add. MS 48800, ff. 129–32; 48803, ff. 51, 61–3.

had been conducting since 1757.[13] Beginning as a limited enterprise – small scale military contributions to a continental army financed by subsidies to German confederates – the war in Europe had by 1760 accelerated into a major, seemingly unlimited commitment of troops and funds, the cost of which was ever mounting and increasingly resented.[14] As one political observer wrote in December 1760: 'In general ... many people of this country are cooled in their ardour and even disaffected with regard to the war in Germany.'[15]

One consequence of this was a revival of the strategic controversy dating from Elizabethan days over the inter-relationship between sea power and land war, between naval and military priorities and over the best policy to follow in the light of national interests and resources.[16] Involved here were two opposing arguments or schools of thought: continental and maritime. The former advocated continued British involvement in Germany as a vital prerequisite to imperial success; the latter argued for exclusive concentration on colonial maritime war – the need for either European intervention or a standing army was denied.[17]

Unless France, the continentalists maintained, was compelled to keep some of her resources diverted from sea to land, to remain enmeshed in British financed European campaigns, Britain would not be able to maintain the superiority in maritime power necessary for further victories overseas. Naval objectives themselves, therefore, dictated some commitment to, and involvement in, the German theatre of war.[18] In the words of one eminent proponent of interventionism, 'France will outdo us at sea when they have nothing to lose by land ... I have always maintained that our marine should protect our alliances upon the continent; and they, by diverting the expense of France, enable us to maintain our superiority at sea.'[19]

Equally, there was the problem of Hanover, the king's electoral domain, an area chronically vulnerable to attack whenever Britain and France were at war. Dynastic ties, combined with strategic factors, meant that Britain was obliged to make

13 The origins and evolution of Britain's continental commitment can be followed in R. Savory, *His Britannic Majesty's Army in Germany during the Seven Years War* (Oxford 1966), and K. W. Schweizer, *Frederick the Great, William Pitt and Lord Bute. Anglo-Prussian Relations, 1756–1763* (New York, 1991), pp. 1–3.

14 Schweizer, *Frederick the Great*, pp. 99–100; C. Eldon, *England's Subsidy Policy Towards the Continent during the Seven Years War* (Philadelphia, 1938), pp. 132–4; B.L., Add. MS 32916, ff. 88–9, 329; 6839, ff. 208–9, 210–11.

15 B.L., Add. MS 6839, f. 203 v.

16 On this controversy see, R. Pares, 'American versus Continental Warfare, 1739–1763', *English Historical Review*, LI (1936), 429–65.

17 K. W. Schweizer, 'An Unpublished Parliamentary Speech by the Elder Pitt, 9 December 1761', *Historical Research*, LXIV (1991), 94.

18 D. A. Baugh, 'Great Britain's Blue-Water Policy 1689–1815', *International History Review*, X (1988), 33–58; P. H. Kennedy, *The Rise and Fall of British Naval Mastery* (1976), p. 4.

19 B.L., Add. MS 35410, f. 140: Newcastle to Hardwicke, 25 Aug. 1749.

provisions for Hanover's defence, and thus for continental war, by subsidies to allies, through an expeditionary force, or both.[20]

To these interventionist arguments, the 'maritime' or 'blue water' school offered the reply that foreign subsidies, alliances and troops were both a waste of money and a diversion of effort, a costly departure from Britain's primary objective: expansion and protection of overseas trade, the central point to which all other activities were subsidiary.[21]

Initially, while in opposition, the elder Pitt had been a leading figure among the maritime strategists, outspokenly hostile to entanglements in Europe which he deplored as hampering Britain's quest for naval/commercial supremacy.[22] But whereas Pitt, after taking office, had modified his ideas, generally coming to insist on the totality of war, continental as well as American, longtime colonial advocates (including George III and Bute) remained unconvinced, their hostility to Britain's German commitments intensifying in direct proportion to the prolongation and ever rising cost of the struggle abroad.[23]

Among the numerous proponents of 'blue water' strategy none ultimately was as forceful or persuasive as Israel Mauduit, whose famous pamphlet was written specifically to challenge Pitt's war policy and advance the isolationist cause. Britain's naval/colonial dominance, argued Mauduit, was virtually achieved, yet expenditures continued to soar, in large measure because of the German war from which no financial or territorial returns could be expected. Thus, rather than constituting a diversion, as the continentalists claimed, Germany was rapidly becoming the main theatre of operation, the scene of costly but indecisive campaigns where Britain, faced with French military superiority, could never hope to prevail. Since 1759, the year of Hawke's victory at Quiberon Bay, 'the German war, far from being a diversion of the French force from invading us, has been nothing but a diversion of English treasure to exhaust us'.[24] France's failure to send adequate reinforcements overseas was owing

20 R. Hatton, *The Anglo-Hanoverian Connexion, 1714–60* (1983); Uriel Dann, *Hanover and Great Britain* (Leicester, 1991), p. 1; H. Wellenreuther, 'Die Bedeutung des Siebenjährigen Krieges für englisch-hannoveranische Beziehungen', in *England und Hannover*, ed. Adolf M. Birke and K. Kluxen (Munich, 1986), pp. 145–75.
21 Pares, 'American versus Continental Warfare', *passim*; I. Mauduit, *Occasional Thoughts on the Present German War* (1761), pp. 8–10; Bute MSS (the marquess of Bute, Mountstuart, Isle of Bute), 2/93: Dodington to Bute, 10 July 1762.
22 Eldon, *England's Subsidy Policy*, pp. 69–71; P. C. Yorke, *The Life and Correspondence of Philip Yorke, Earl of Hardwicke*, (3 vols., Cambridge, 1913), I, 198–9, 230–1, 236–8; P.R.O., Chatham Papers, 30/8/89, ff. 148–61: an account of the Anglo-Prussian correspondence after the Convention of Westminster.
23 B.L., Add. MS 32918, f. 390; *The Devonshire Diary. William Cavendish, Fourth Duke of Devonshire, Memoranda on State Affairs, 1759–1762*, ed. Peter D. Brown and Karl W. Schweizer (Camden 4th ser., XXVII, 1982), pp. 74–6; K. W. Schweizer and John Bullion, 'The Vote of Credit Controversy, 1762', *British Journal for Eighteenth-Century Studies*, XX (1992), 176–88; J. Brooke, *King George III* (1972), pp. 58–60.
24 Israel Mauduit, *Considerations on the Present German War* (1761), p. 14.

not to the German war but to Britain's command of the sea and her blockading efforts. European alliances (subsidies) and armies, therefore, were all a waste of money, an expensive distraction from Britain's imperial interests: 'should this same war of diversion go on much longer, we shall find that instead of fighting in Germany for America, we shall have really lost America in Germany'.[25]

Britain's foremost enemy, stressed Mauduit, was France, and the only effective way of fighting France in Europe was not by subsidizing minor German states but through a recreation of a grand alliance, the policy of William III. Germany, Holland and England must be the basis of every confederacy which can be of avail against the land power of France.[26] In assisting, as Britain was presently doing, Prussia's struggle with Austria, she was merely prolonging and exacerbating a German civil war – a conflict which ought to be settled so both adversaries could redirect their forces against France. Every resolve which has a tendency to uniting the powers of Europe among themselves and against France, must therefore be for the general good of Europe, and the particular interest of England: and every measure which tends to set the states of Germany, Holland and England, either at war with each other, or among themselves, must be a measure calculated for the good of France.[27] With relentless cogency, Mauduit stressed the military absurdity of meeting France on her own ground, all for the integrity of an insignificant state (Hanover) in which Britain really had no interest: indeed, the only reason Hanover was attacked in the first place was because France knew the British would defend it.[28] Instead of spending millions of pounds for the protection of Hanover, Britain ought to withdraw, so urged Mauduit, and let the electorate be defended by the Empire, or, that failing, procure compensation for it when settling with France.[29]

Mauduit's strictures also extended to England's alliance with Prussia: its lack of a common, unifying purpose,[30] Frederick the Great's subsidy – dubbed tribute – for which Britain received nothing in return, and Prussia's growing weakness, a liability that might cost Britain dearly in the future. 'The time may come', warned Mauduit,

> when the nation, being exhausted by the German war and perhaps intimidated by that
> very Prince it is now upholding, may be forced to give up its own conquests to buy him
> a peace. Then every member of the administration will disown this excessive regard
> to Germany and each individual will say that for his part he was always against it.[31]

Although showing a generalized concern for peace, Mauduit advocated accelerated hostilities as the best means of inducing France to negotiate – but hostilities directed at French possessions overseas not continental operations. Taking everything France

25 *Ibid.*, p. 16.
26 *Ibid.*, pp. 20–7.
27 *Ibid.*, pp. 13–15, 31–3.
28 *Ibid.*, p. 38.
29 *Ibid.*, pp. 51–2.
30 *Ibid.*, pp. 43–6.
31 *Ibid.*, p. 51.

has left 'will drive them to peace or pay us the annual expense of our Naval war'.[32] By remaining entangled as was presently the case in the costly German war, Britain sacrificed the benefits of her insular position, as well as risking her maritime supremacy, all to sustain a ruler (Frederick II), 'who never can have it in his power and who is yet to give us the proof of his ever having had the will to do us any service'.[33] Mauduit concluded by urging his countrymen ('whose riches and naval power were at their height') not to neglect 'their own war, to go upon a distant land war, in support of a little remote state, scarce heard of before', and made important only by its British connexion.[34] The moment had come, in their words, to sever all ties with continental allies and recall British forces from Europe without delay.

On the whole, Mauduit's narrative was strongly partisan in bias, his arguments frequently contrived or simplistic – continental operations, for instance, are treated as a separate war rather than defensive parts of the whole. The pamphlet, in short, ignored the need to harmonize the use of naval and military power for the sake of a unified, co-ordinated strategy. It was also politically opportunistic; colonial war was traditionally popular and especially known to be so with the future king, George III, and his closest advisers whose favour Mauduit hoped to gain. Hence his advocacy of commercial/maritime interests and constant neglect of historical examples that in any way challenged or contradicted his supporting arguments. Accordingly the pamphlet's appeal derived more from effective writing than faultless argumentation, though obviously it also registered the prevailing shift of public opinion against an aspect of the war that no longer seemed relevant. In the words of Symmer, writing to Andrew Mitchell, Britain's envoy to Prussia: 'There is nothing new in the arguments the author employs but they are handled in a manner not unlikely to raise a flame among the vulgar and abet the prejudices of many.'[35]

While numerous replies appeared immediately attempting to offset the public impact Mauduit's polemic had made, none quite succeeded either in substance or style. At worst they either flatly contradicted him or argued absurdly; at best, they were merely point-by-point refutations, larded with substantial quotations from the *Considerations* and lacking in overall coherence.[36] If anything, the ensuing press debate, continuing well into 1761–2, set opinion even more against the German war, Hanover, the Prussian alliance and in favour of peace. 'The pamphlets in circulation', as one contemporary observed, 'have so influenced the minds of the people that the great number are more violent than ever against a war on the continent.'[37] Mauduit

32 *Ibid.*, p. 92.
33 *Ibid.*, p. 68.
34 *Ibid.*, p. 140.
35 B.L., Add. MS 6839, f. 202v.
36 M. Peters, *Pitt and Popularity. The Patriot Minister and London Opinion during the Seven Years War* (Oxford, 1980), p. 184.
37 B.L., Add. MS 6839, f. 242v.

himself, in part through further anti-German tracts written subsequently,[38] appears to have increased his influence on public opinion generally as the war progressed, both in London and nationally. Thus Horace Walpole's observed that Mauduit's critique 'had more operation in working a change in the minds of men than perhaps ever fell to the lot of a pamphlet'.[39] Smollett gave the pamphlet similar praise at court and Lord Egmont observed that its arguments gained credence 'in a very surprising manner',[40] while the *Critical Review*, in a survey of opposition papers in 1763, remarked 'that Mr Pitt, during his administration, can scarcely be said to have experienced an attack from the press, till the *Considerations on the German War* appeared'.[41]

The impact of the pamphlet, judging by public interest, can be further gauged from the vigorous ways in which it was publicized, the notices it received in other publications – reviews, newspapers, magazines – and the fact that it broadened its exposure by being read and discussed in coffee houses, taverns and inns,[42] made available in circulating libraries and pamphlet clubs, and, like many important pamphlets of the period, privately distributed on an impressive scale. Nor was the pamphlet effective in London only: interesting is the emergence of an increasingly coherent anti-German sentiment radiating from the metropolis to the provinces, a process fostered at least in part by the steady dissemination of Mauduit's message in the country press.[43] There, as in the capital, influential pamphlets – the *Considerations* included – were stocked in private subscription libraries, such as those that existed in Birmingham, Bristol, Coventry and Newcastle, discussed in pamphlet clubs, and reviewed or excerpted in provincial papers and magazines.

Although it is difficult to determine precisely the segments of society influenced most by Mauduit's arguments (or even the degree to which public opinion generally, remained divided over the issue of the German war), there is direct evidence indicating that the pamphlet made significant inroads in parliament, impressing especially the country M.P.s, who for some time had felt the burden of rising taxes without understanding the principles behind the governments military/diplomatic schemes; those who had maintained all along that British energies should have been

---

38 *Further Considerations on the Present German War* (1761); *Occasional Thoughts on the Present German War.*

39 Horace Walpole, *Memoirs of the Reign of George III* (4 vols., 1894), I, 33.

40 A. Newman, 'Leicester House Politics, 1750–1760, from the Papers of John, Second Earl of Egmont', *Camden Miscellany XXIII* (Camden 4th ser., VII, 1969), p. 227.

41 *Critical Review*, XVI (Oct. 1763), 280.

42 Such as, for instance, the Cocoa Tree Coffee House, a widely popular tory stronghold. Cf. Warwickshire R.O., Newdigate MSS, Diary, 1760–1770; Brewer, *Party Ideology and Popular Politics*, pp. 148–9.

43 A. Gee, 'English Provincial Newspapers and the Politics of the Seven Years War', University of Canterbury M.A., 1985, pp. 26–9; *Newcastle Journal*, 5, 13 Dec. 1760; *Norwich Mercury*, 6 Dec. 1760.

devoted exclusively to the war in America with its harvest in colonial prizes.[44]
Therefore, in discrediting Pitt's continental strategy and the expenditures this
entailed, Mauduit's pamphlet not only appealed to a wide range of gentry opinion in
the Commons, it also became a fertile source of anti-ministerial comment used so
often in opposition harangues that Pitt scornfully observed on one occasion, 'A
certain little book, that was found somewhere or other has made a great many orators
in the House.'[45]

Since the support given by the landed interests in parliament helped define
opposition strength, Pitt could not remain indifferent to these forces – the pressures
they exerted or the threat their alienation presented to his political standing. This
explains why in early 1761 he advised postponement of the controversial Prussian
subsidy, the previous session having revealed growing hostility to the agreement with
speeches adapted directly from Mauduit's pamphlet.[46] It was Newcastle who secured
renewal of the subsidy treaty for another year.[47] Still, the German war declined in
appeal and criticism intensified in parliament where, on 13 November 1761, during
the debate on the king's speech, 'continental connexions', the Prussian alliance and
Pitt himself came under bitter attack.[48] More strained yet was the atmosphere on 9
December during the deliberations on the German estimates, where £21 million had
to be voted for continental reinforcements and supplies. The estimates were passed,
but again not without another heated debate. Although Charles Townshend, secretary
of war, made a strong case for the German conflict – 'Mr. Pitt's divine plan', as he
put it[49] – he found himself bitterly opposed by Richard Rigby, leading opposition
spokesman, who not only delivered what amounted to a full scale attack on Pitt's
ministerial record, but, echoing Mauduit, urged the immediate recall of British forces
serving abroad and the speedy resumption of peace negotiations with France. Here
he was supported by John Delaval who, speaking next, likewise criticized Pitt's war
policy and, drawing extensively on the *Considerations*, predicted inevitable bankruptcy if continental operations continued for another year.[50] Both Rigby and Delaval,
in their strictures against Britain's commitments in Europe, claimed to be speaking
for the landed classes, those 'opposed to a war in every instance prejudicial to the
interests of this nation', and reportedly the sympathy of the House was clearly with

44 Peters, *Pitt and Popularity*, pp. 182–3; B.L., Add. MS 6839, ff. 208–9: Symmer to Mitchell, 30 Jan.
    1761; Bute MSS: Jenkinson to Bute, 9, 17 Dec. 1761; Geheimes Staatsarchiv Preussischer Kultur-
    besitz Abteilung, Merseburg, Rep. 33, E, ff. 100–4: Knyphausen to Frederick II, 17 Nov. 1761.
45 Basil Williams, *The Life of William Pitt, Earl of Chatham* (2 vols., 1915), I, 68.
46 *Correspondence of John, Fourth Duke of Bedford*, ed. Lord John Russell (3 vols.,1846), II, 426;
    Schweizer, *Frederick the Great, William Pitt and Lord Bute*, pp. 106–8.
47 Reed Browning, *The Duke of Newcastle* (New Haven, 1975), p. 277; cf. B.L., Add. MS 32918, ff.
    45–6.
48 Bute MSS: Jenkinson to Bute, 9, 17 Dec. 1761; B.L., Add. MS 32931, ff. 45–9.
49 B.L., Add. MS 32932, ff. 78–81.
50 *Ibid.*, ff. 80–1.

them.[51] This bitter debate, by revealing serious divisions over national policy, could not but be embarrassing to Pitt. More generally, the ever deepening national aversion to Britain's continental involvement, articulated so ably by Mauduit, put Pitt very much on the defensive *vis-à-vis* Prussia and the German war, resulting in diversionary tactics designed to help him avoid responsibility for controversial measures and possibly contributing to his final resignation in the autumn of 1761.[52]

Mauduit's influence again emerges conspicuously during the parliamentary session of 1762, when several peers, in supporting the duke of Bedford's motion for an immediate recall of the British forces serving abroad, utilized arguments quoted almost verbatim from the *Considerations* in support of their case.[53] In fact, Bedford's own speech preceding his motion similarly relied on the pamphlet for inspiration and we know that, among those in power, certainly George Grenville and Lord Bute (if not George III himself) were familiar with Mauduit's work and on their own admission were influenced by his arguments. 'One thing is certain', wrote one contemporary observer, 'that many in high places are so far from disapproving of it [the *Considerations*] or opposing its influence that if one may judge by the part their friends take, they favour it not a little.'[54] This is further confirmed by Mauduit himself. Seeking a place in December 1762, writing to Bute, he assessed his contribution this way:

> I have had the honour of first pointing out to the public a deception, which had generally prevailed over the kingdom ... a deception which, under the double guard of eloquence and popular prejudice, had so firmly fixed itself, that no man in either house dared to attack it. No man will now deny my having broke the enchantment. The Duke of Bedford was so gracious as to assure me that I had first opened his eyes. And your Lordship, upon the present happy change was so very condescending, as to say that I now saw the fruits of my work and that I was the beginner of it ... twice had honorable mention been made of me in the House of Lords ... twenty times I heard myself speaking through other men's mouths in the House of Commons.[55]

Mauduit's influence is indeed visible in Bute's overall approach to foreign affairs, an approach that was, as has recently been shown, decidedly non-interventionist: opposed to large scale involvement in Europe, hostile to Hanover and averse to extensive alliance commitments.[56] As such, the *Considerations* is an important guide to

---

51 *Ibid.*, ff. 123–5; 35365, ff. 403–4.

52 As suggested by the opposition press throughout the autumn of 1761. See, *London Chronicle* (1761), 10–13; *The Right Honourable Annuitant Vindicated* (1761), pp. 16–25; *A Letter from a Right Honourable Person and the Answer to it Translated into Verse* (1761), pp. 6–24.

53 P.R.O., 30/8/70/5, ff. 26–35: Sir James Caldwell to Lord Newton, 1761.

54 B.L., Add. MS 6839, f. 210 v: Symmer to Mitchell, 30 Jan. 1761.

55 K. W. Schweizer, 'A Note on Israel Mauduit's "Considerations on the Present German War"', *Notes and Queries*, CCXXV (1980), 45–6.

56 K. W. Schweizer, 'The Draft of a Pamphlet by John Stuart 3rd Earl of Bute', *Notes and Queries*, CCXXXII (1987), 343–5; *idem*, 'Lord Bute and British Strategy in the Seven Years War: Further Evidence', *Notes and Queries*, CCXXXVI (1991), 189–91; *idem*, 'Lord Bute and the Prussian Subsidy: An Unnoticed Document', *Notes and Queries*, CCXXXIV (1989), 58–61.

certain of the fundamental assumptions behind official policy in 1760 to 1763, and hence a key to its better understanding. In focusing discontent on interventionism – the central tenet of post-1688 government strategies – Mauduit exemplifies uniquely a perspective that has been generally marginalized, one that could be described as tory. British attitudes in the second half of the century in particular are commonly seen in terms of a rising swell of nationalist feeling, a proto-imperialism derived from the 'patriotic' opposition to Walpole that was reflected in such works as *Rule Britannia* and that maintained that Britain should extend her sway, that her destiny was one of maritime mastery and colonial acquisitions, a destiny that made conflict with the Bourbon powers necessary and inevitable.[57] Mauduit represents a different viewpoint – not only the more cautious, if not sceptical, perception that on principle Britain must be wary of excessive continental obligations and the expenditures these entailed, but the conviction also, as shared by ministers like Bute, that an unchecked expan-sionist policy could only lead to Britain's ultimate ruin. This belief, in large measure, was based on the conviction that Britain's fiscal and political situation precluded limitless reliance on national credit and confidence – on that funding capacity upon which government and an active foreign policy depended. Unlike politicians solidly committed to a system in Europe, Bute took a more prudential line on the issue of continental connexions and expenditures. The same considerations were also to play a role in the post-war world, the generation of ministers, who sought to tax cider or redefine the financial nature of Anglo-American relations, being similarly reluctant to underwrite ventures which had little apparent relevance to British diplomatic trad-itions or current priorities. This prudential tendency matched the parameters of public debate in parliament and the press, and one should view that debate, substantially shaped by the *Considerations*, as permeating the political discourse that policy makers formulated to guide and explain their actions. Eighteenth-century foreign policy was not fashioned in a closed, bureaucratic setting, but by prominent figures who were primarily politicians and therefore influenced by other ministers, the wishes of the crown and domestic pressures, including powerful expositions in the press. Consequently, Mauduit's pamphlet (like other leading pamphlets of the period) performed multiple functions in the political sphere, its rhetoric attracting high level support and providing the interpretation – the line of critical inquiry and comment – around which opposition activity as well as the wider discussion of government policy could be organized. At the same time, by addressing issues that linked activity at high political levels with the deep rooted concerns of the nation at large, Mauduit directly contributed to the political education of his extensive readership, enabling those outside court, cabinet and parliament to become more informed about the dynamics of government policy. As such he played a part, albeit small, in widening the political nation and thus changing the context in which political decisions were made, a development of far greater consequence than he ever

57 Black, 'Dr Johnson', p. 16.

intended. By the same token, the case of Mauduit's pamphlet suggests that press influence in eighteenth-century Britain must be seen as centred on issues, occasions and particular political conjunctures rather than any general relationship between the press and society, government or public opinion. Here, as in other recent studies,[58] it is ultimately only through highly specific 'content analysis' that the direct impact of press activity on political actions can be established.

---

58 Charles Clark, *The Public Prints. The Newspaper in Anglo-American Culture, 1665–1740* (New York, 1994); Thomas, 'British Empire and the Press'; J. Black, 'Press and Politics in the Age of Walpole', *Durham University Journal*, LXXXVII (1984), 87–93.

11

'*My Minerva* at my Elbow': The Political Roles of Women in Eighteenth-Century England[*]

ELAINE CHALUS

In 1979, Karl von den Steinen, in a ground-breaking essay on the discovery of women in English political life, was terse in summing up historians' approach to women and politics in the eighteenth century: 'one must now choose between politics without women or women without politics'.[1] Unfortunately, to a large extent, this comment still stands today. Barring periodic recourse to the larger-than-life figures of the duchesses of Marlborough and Devonshire at opposing ends of the century,[2] and mandatory references to the notoriety of the 1784 Westminster election, most historians would still be hard put to name more than a scattering of politically active eighteenth-century women and at a dead loss to explain what roles women played in political life as a whole.[3]

This lacuna exists due to the differing concerns and assumptions of political and women's history. Gender has usually been assumed to have acted as an insuperable barrier to women's involvement prior to the suffrage agitation of the nineteenth century: unreconstructed notions of women's place in eighteenth-century society,

[*] I would particularly like to thank Paul Langford, Mark Pottle, Hannah Barker and Roey Sweet for their comments on earlier versions of this essay, and the participants at seminars at the Universities of Oxford, Sussex, and Reading, where it was presented. I would also like to acknowledge the Social Sciences and Humanities Research Council of Canada, the Committee for Graduate Studies, University of Oxford, and Wolfson College, Oxford, for supporting the research. Permission to consult the Wentworth Woodhouse Muniments is by courtesy of Olive, Countess Fitzwilliam's Wentworth Settlement Trustees and the Director.

[1] Karl von den Steinen, 'The Discovery of Women in Eighteenth-Century English Political Life', in *The Women of England From Anglo-Saxon Times to the Present*, ed. Barbara Kanner (Hamden, Conn., 1979), p. 247. See also, *idem*, 'The Fabric of an Interest: The First Duke of Dorset and Kentish and Sussex Politics, 1705–1765', University of California (Los Angeles) Ph.D., 1969.

[2] Frances Harris's balanced and comprehensive biography of Sarah, duchess of Marlborough, is outstanding as an examination of the most political of all early eighteenth-century political woman. Amanda Foreman's forthcoming biography of Georgiana, duchess of Devonshire, provides a fascinating insight into the life of the best-remembered of all eighteenth-century political women and dispels once and for all the belief that the 1784 Westminster Election marked the end of her political involvement. Frances Harris, *A Passion for Government. The Life of Sarah Duchess of Marlborough* (Oxford, 1991); Amanda Foreman, *Georgiana, Duchess of Devonshire* (1998). I would like to thank Amanda for allowing me to consult her work prior to publication.

[3] The most significant exception to this is the far too brief treatment of women and politics in Linda Colley's examination of 'womanpower' in *Britons. Forging the Nation, 1707–1837* (1992).

combined with the customary political constraints which prevented women from voting, holding places, or seats in parliament, have fostered a belief that their involvement was limited, anomalous and ultimately secondary to men's. At best, women were assumed to have been political actors at one remove, operating 'indirectly' or 'behind the scenes' through their manipulation of men and situations. Their activities, and the social and personal aspects of politics in which they were involved, have traditionally been viewed with distaste by political historians who saw them as symptomatic of the lack of accountability and 'old corruption' of the unreformed political system.[4] For women's historians, not only has the equation of politics with enfranchisement and the nineteenth-century woman's movement tended to overshadow and devalue women's pre-feminist, pre-suffrage, political involvement,[5] but assumptions that women were increasingly relegated to a private, separate, domestic sphere during the century have also tended to discourage research.

An examination of over 250 personal, general and political correspondences by male and female members of the political *élite* for the second half of the eighteenth century challenges both of these notions.[6] While the nature of the sources means that

---

4   The trivialization of women's political involvement has a long history. J. Grego, writing of eighteenth-century female canvassers in 1886, attributed their success to 'the seductive wiles of female charms and persuasions', a view which differs little from Frank O'Gorman's portrayal, a century later, of women's canvassing as 'the public flaunting of fairly innocent sexual and sartorial behavior' – cynically male-directed sexual exploitation for political ends. J. Grego, *History of Parliamentary Elections and Electioneering in the Old Days* (1886), p. 292; Frank O'Gorman, *Voters, Patrons and Parties: The Unreformed Electorate of Hanoverian England, 1734–1832* (Oxford, 1991), p. 93.

5   This is especially noticeable in the anthologies by Bridget Hill and Vivien Jones, *Eighteenth-Century Women: An Anthology*, ed. Bridget Hill (1987); *Women in the Eighteenth Century: Constructions of Femininity*, ed. Vivien Jones (1990). It has also generated continuing interest in exceptional women such as Mary Astell, Catherine Macaulay and Mary Wollstonecraft, who demanded change that current scholars identify with feminism. For Astell, see Bridget Hill, *The First English Feminist. Reflections on Marriage and Other Writings by Mary Astell* (1986); J. K. Kinnaird, 'Mary Astell and the Conservative Contribution to English Feminism', *Journal of British Studies*, XIX (1979), 53–75; Ruth Perry, *The Celebrated Mary Astell. An Early English Feminist* (1986). For Macaulay, see especially Bridget Hill, *That Republican Virago. The Life and Times of Catharine Macaulay, Historian* (Oxford, 1992). Wollstonecraft's life and works have become a specialized field of study in their own right: see, for instance, Gary Kelly, *Revolutionary Feminism. The Mind and Career of Mary Wollstonecraft* (Basingstoke, 1991); Jennifer Lorch, *Mary Wollstonecraft. The Making of a Radical Feminist* (Oxford, 1990); Claire Tomalin, *The Life and Death of Mary Wollstonecraft* (rev. edn., 1992). The search for origins has also manifested itself in large debates with political implications, such as the long-standing debate over the relative merits of economic factors and patriarchy in explaining the historical experience of women and work. See, for example, Judith M. Bennett, 'History That Stands Still: Women's Work in the European Past', *Feminist Studies*, XIV (1988), 269–83, and 'Women's History: A Study in Continuity and Change', *Women's History Review*, II (1993), 173–84; Bridget Hill, 'Women's History: A Study in Change, Continuity or Standing Still?', *Women's History Review*, II (1993), 5–22.

6   For women's electoral involvement, see Elaine Chalus, '"That Epidemical Madness": Women and Electoral Politics in the Late Eighteenth Century', in *Gender in Eighteenth-Century England. Roles, Representations and Responsibilities*, ed. Hannah Barker and Elaine Chalus (1997), pp. 151–78, and *idem*, 'Women in English Political Life, 1754–1790', University of Oxford D.Phil., 1997.

conclusions must be drawn from the weight of evidence rather than quantification, they reveal a largely familial political culture, where the boundaries between the social and political arenas were blurred and where some degree of female political involvement was frequently assumed, expected, or even demanded. More importantly, they suggest that women's political participation – primarily familial, albeit sometimes personal or factional – can be roughly divided into four roles: those of confidante, adviser, agent and partner.[7]

These roles form a pyramid, with that of confidante encompassing the largest group of women at the bottom, up to a small group of highly political women at the very top. The division between adviser and agent is perhaps the most significant, as it marks the shift from indirect to direct participation (a shift that was often, but not always, also one from private to public). The women at the top – those who acted as agents, and even more importantly, as partners – generally possessed the most political knowledge, social adroitness and self-confidence of all political women. Their involvement tended to be more independent, direct and public; furthermore, their relationships with political men reflected the greatest trust and intimacy. Taken as a whole, these four roles are not mutually exclusive or even sharply divided; instead, they take shape through a process of accretion, with each subsequent role building on those roles beneath it. Women could, and occasionally did, fulfil only one role, but they were more likely to combine several roles, or to shift back and forth among them depending upon situations or circumstances.

Confidante

The role of confidante was the most widespread, but also the most private and passive of women's political roles. There is evidence to suggest that the majority of women who were closely connected to leading politicians acted as confidantes; moreover, it is clear that the bulk of political men found confidantes in either their female friends or in the female members of their families, at least at various points in their lives. Most women in the political *élite* may have been brought into contact with the political world in this way. Few women, however, appear to have acted solely as confidantes. Not only does the tendency to proffer advice in return seem to have been nearly insuperable, but also the reality of women's participation in social politics would have made it difficult to maintain such a passive role, or even to remain consistently politically aloof. Thus, 'confidante' shades into 'agent'. Despite this, it is worth retaining the separation between the two, for the one-sidedness of some

---

[7] Pat Jalland has suggested that Victorian and Edwardian political wives had three very general political roles: mistresses of households and political hostesses, confidantes, and election campaign workers. While useful, this breakdown does not take enough account of the full range of women's political involvement. Pat Jalland, *Women, Marriage and Politics, 1860–1914* (Oxford, 1986), ch. 7.

sources makes it impossible to ascertain whether all women who acted as confidantes were also agents.

As confidantes, women's connexion to the political world and their participation in it was dependent upon men, and primarily directed by male concerns. The apparent asymmetry could, however, mask women's ability to encourage and elicit confidences. This seems to have been especially true in the case of couples not long married. In July 1767, the duchess of Portland encouraged her husband to keep her informed about political developments: 'I shall not be a little impatient to know how these affairs are settled, for tho' I am not a great Politician yet I have not a desire of remaining quite Ignorant.'[8] Nearly 20 years later another young wife, Lavinia, Lady Spencer, elaborated upon the same theme:

> I long for the account you will send me (or have sent) of the debate in the House of C:
> last Tuesday – I never was a politician before but I confess I feel myself at present a
> little agitiated & anxious about public affairs – At so important a juncture if one did
> not – all pretentions to any more feeling than there is in a block of Marble must be laid
> aside –[9]

Success as a confidante seems to have depended upon two factors: a modicum of interest (real or simulated) on the part of the women; and varying but potentially significant amounts of trust from their male counterparts. Women who were confidantes were essentially listeners; they provided the men in their lives with shoulders to cry on, or ears to bend. They acted as outlets for the men's needs. This was especially true in the literary catharsis of correspondence, which made confidences doubly safe through the intimacy of the relationship and the distancing (both real and psychological) of the medium. Men who had female confidantes expected them to be interested, sympathetic and understanding. The sources indicate that they were.

In 1766, during her first lengthy separation from the duke, the duchess of Portland's correspondence with him was made up largely of love letters and political confidences. Portland, who was in London, was facing the most difficult decision of his young political career. Despite being encouraged by his friends and male relations not to resign with the rest of the first Rockingham administration, he was agonizing over his decision. He depended upon the duchess, whose pregnancy had kept her in the country, to provide him with a sympathetic hearing and give him a safe outlet for the frustrations and fears that he could not express in London:

> I have ten thousand things to say to you … I never was so perplexed about any part I
> was to take; I never as yet acted contrary to my own inclinations without being
> convinced, & now dread that I am upon the brink of that precipice & that I shall be
> exposed to reproach & censure: which I shall almost be inclined to think I deserve.
> They all tell me, nay even Lord John, that I ought not to quit. So that in short I am

8 Nottingham U.L., Portland papers, PwG 37: duchess of Portland to 3rd duke, 11 July 1767.
9 B.L., MS Coll. Althorp, G. 289: Lavinia, Lady Spencer to George, Lord Spencer, 29 Nov. 1781.

quietly patiently tamely to see my friends abused & insulted, am to appear as if I
separated myself from them, & for what reason, why, upon account of some few
enthusiastick ravenous followers of a man of whom I never had or can have any
opinion, & upon a pretence of preserving the Whig Cause. Thus much I could not help
troubling you with.[10]

Political confidences were part of continuing relationships based on mutual trust
and respect. Sons who had been raised by political mothers – especially those whose
mothers had been widowed while the young men were still minors – often took their
mother's role as confidante for granted. In December 1783, when the Fox/North
coalition was forced to resign, George, Lord Spencer was quick to pass this
information on to his mother. He reported the rumours he had heard about an
upcoming dissolution of parliament and expanded at length on his ideas for the
elections. This type of political sharing was a regular and valued part of their
relationship: 'I thought you would like to hear my ideas on most of these subjects &
for the rest I am really so accustomed to talk to you unreservedly upon them, that it
is quite grown into a natural habit to me.'[11]

Sisters and daughters also acted as confidantes, especially if their brothers were
unmarried or their fathers widowed. Men who were caught up in the middle of
political developments, as J. H. Addington was in 1782, tended to not to even
question their sisters' political interest:

I assure you I had fix'd upon to-day as a day of special Indulgence to you for almost
this Week past, that I might give you an Account of the Event of our Election. – 'Nevill
for ever' – is in every Mouth; they will soon teach the babbling Gossip of the Air to
cry out 'Nevill.' You can have no Idea of the universal Exultation which his Success
has occasion'd. [12]

For some men, this presumption may have been derived from a mistaken belief that
anything that interested them had to be fascinating to the women in their lives, but in
the majority of cases, their expectations appear to have been valid, and the interest
was reciprocated. Fathers who confided in their unmarried daughters may have also
had an additional purpose in mind. Lord Granville (Carteret) regularly sent his 15
year old daughter Sophia his opinions on the political developments of the day as part
of her education. Whether he was consciously grooming her for marriage into a
political family is debatable, but she subsequently married Lord Shelburne and her
involvement in political life as an adult implies that her early lessons were well
learned.[13]

---

10 Nottingham U.L., Portland papers, PwF 10527: 3rd duke of Portland to the duchess, 29 July 1766.
11 B.L., MS Coll. Althorp, F. 14: George, Lord Spencer to Dowager Countess Spencer, Brookes's, [19 Dec. 1783].
12 Gloucester R.O., Bragge Bathurst papers, D421 C8: J. H. Addington to Charlotte Addington, Feb. 1782.
13 Bodl., MS Lyell, Empt. 35: letters to Lady Sophia Carteret. See, for instance, his letters to her in 1759–60.

In general then, women acted as confidantes for a mixture of personal, political and social reasons. For some women, participation had less to do with an interest in politics than it had to do with a personal and emotional investment in the men themselves (although initial lack of interest, especially early in a marriage, seems to have often been short-lived). Involvement could also stem from a strong sense of duty, which might suggest that women internalized at least a certain amount of contemporary prescriptive literature's emphasis on adopting and sharing men's – especially husbands' – interests.

In addition, for members of the political *élite* the social and political arenas were closely intertwined, and being a confidante could pay dividends. Politics was, after all, the soap opera of the day, replete with stars and scandal. Confidantes not only took part in political life vicariously, but were also able to put the knowledge that they gained to social ends. It could be a weapon in the carefully orchestrated battles of social one-upmanship that occurred among eighteenth-century women and, in the larger political arena, it could also give status by suggesting the proximity of the possessor to the 'fountain head' of power, thus intimating potential political influence. Inside information was useful during elections or periods of political tension or crisis, when current political developments formed a significant part of everyday conversation, never mind at those times when politics took on epidemic proportions, dominating society and dividing even social events along political lines.

Adviser

Advisers extended the range of involvement manifested by confidantes. Correspondence suggests that most of the women who acted as confidantes also acted as advisers. All advisers performed similar tasks. Primarily, they provided political men with a discreet combination of support, criticism, direction and strategy, either through correspondence or in person. They also acted as sources of political information, by gathering news from the public arena, screening it, and then relaying it. A similar combination of public and private informed their actions as intermediaries among various family connexions or political groups. The primary difference in terms of advisers' political involvement was one of degree, both in terms of politicization and the extent to which they attempted to influence or direct political decisions. The most detailed and specific advice usually came from intelligent, assertive women who tended to form an *élite* within the political *élite*. Contemporaries recognized that advisers could possess significant – if, in hindsight, unquantifiable – political influence. In spite of this, even the most active advisers' involvement still took place through men, and their influence was dependent upon their abilities to persuade or manipulate.

While much of what advisers did entailed reacting to men's confidences and providing them with feedback, they were more autonomous than confidantes, supplying men who were absent from their localities, the capital, or the country with 'news'. Among the political *élite*, 'news' was generally first political, then social. Women who were at the centre of political action, by being in London during the parliamentary season or in the country during periods of intense local politics, were in the best position to act as advisers. Even politically uninterested women like Hester, Lady Newdigate became involved. When Lady Newdigate was in London during the early 1780s and her country gentleman-cum-M.P. husband, Sir Roger, was in the country, her letters to him regularly included electoral as well as parliamentary information.[14] She advised him of political developments as she heard of them, not because she was personally interested, but because it was expected of her. Women who were more interested in the political developments made far more exciting correspondents. Lady Temple was in London during the excitement caused by the massacre of the Pelhamite innocents, and her comments reflect the way that political news and gossip were interwoven at the time:

> there have been this day several coming in & turning out 3 have kiss'd hands & the places are all to be fill'd in a moment it is believed & given out that even to a hund. cousin of those that have not behaved well are to march out of the most trifling places, it well if your two window peepers won't be call'd upon.
>
> Mr. Ellis is secretary at War. Mr. Rigby treasurer of Ireland Lord Charles Spencer is out ranger of Windor forest with something else that comes to 12 hundred pd. pr. Annum my Lord & Lady Vere mighty uppish some sarcasms thrown at my head & Mr. Brand came in for a snub pretty often because he did not entirely agree with them my Lord Vere thinks it perfectly right that they shou'd take away the smallest place & make a thorough cleaning for it was always done in all ministrys Lord George & Mr. Brand deny'd it & said it was impolitick & foolish to go so far as those trifling places it wou'd raise them a flame for nothing, Lord Vere said the Duke of Newcastle did it, they both answer'd it was no such thing.[15]

Whether advisers were based in London or in the country, their prerequisites were the same: they had to be sensitive to their correspondents' political interests, able to gauge the depth of political feeling in the locality, and aware of the latest political or parliamentary developments. Sometimes, women's participation emerged in response to men's spoken or unspoken demands; at other times, it formed part of a continuing, transactional process which operated at differing levels of mutual understanding and interest.

The extent to which advisers annotated the news they sent varied greatly. As levels of women's politicization and interest rose, so did their personal involvement. Advisers who were highly aware and keenly interested frequently provided their correspondents with significantly more analysis and direction than information. When Lady Betty Waldegrave sent her brother Lord Gower news of the duke of Newcastle's negotiations with William Pitt and Henry Fox in 1756, she summed up the situation, then went on to discuss Newcastle's probable reaction:

14 Warwickshire R.O., Newdigate papers, CR136B.2705–2858.
15 B.L., Add. MS 57806, ff. 119–20: Lady Temple to Lord Temple, 17 Dec. [1762].

then what is to be done next? rather than give up, wch. is the advice of his sincerest friends: his Grace will attempt to govern without either; & in spight of all their oratory will flatter himself with numbers, there are people & not fools neither; they think he may succeed in this, if he has resolution enough to stand it. I do not think this new scheme can last, above one Sessions; perhaps that, it may.[16]

Highly politicized advisers tended both to give their own opinions and try to influence men's decisions. This was particularly noticeable among women who united political families (generally as a result of being brought up in one and then marrying into another), or political groups. Once again, Lady Betty Waldegrave provides a good example. As an intermediary between two prominent political leaders, her brother Gower and her brother-in-law the duke of Bedford, she helped to maintain their political connexions by relaying political information between them. At one point during the aforementioned negotiations, she wrote to tell Gower that he should expect to receive a summons to town from Bedford. Her frustration with his political indolence overcame her, though, and she ended by giving him a piece of her mind:

I shall not enter into any particulars, with regard to politicks: but only say in general that I believe never were such times, nor such rogues; as now, you will be surprised & from your own good heart, will I dare say, be a Dydemus. But for Godsake come up & hear & judge for yr-self, for I will not say one word more upon these subjects.[17]

Lady Betty's annoyance was symptomatic of the fundamental limitations placed on women by their position as intermediary. It presented them with the unenviable task of facilitating understandings and negotiating compromises, but chiefly by means of persuasion or manipulation. Final decision-making power remained firmly under male control.

Where Lady Betty used a variety of tactics to try and motivate her brother, Emily, Lady Kildare depended predominantly upon manipulation when advising her husband. Her ability to manoeuvre her way around pompous and mule-headed Lord Kildare was remarkable. By judiciously demanding the benefit of Kildare's 'superior' judgment in insignificant matters, she freed herself to speak her mind on political affairs. By the age of 23 (in 1755), Lady Kildare had already settled on the method of combining political analysis with advice and astute flattery that was to become her hallmark. Her comments about Irish political affairs are revealing:

I am glad to hear you say *our affairs look well.* I hope you mean by that the heads of our party are likely to be reasonable, which is all you can judge of as yet, and what I own I had my doubts about. Don't let them work you up to expect too many concessions from these people. Nobody cou'd be more inclined to peaceable measures than you were, and I hope you will continue so; tho' rather than be dirty or do any thing that had the appearance of being bought off I wou'd renounce all expectations and

16 P.R.O., 30/29/1/17/965: Lady Betty Waldegrave to Lord Gower [1756].
17 P.R.O., 30/29/1/17/967: Lady Betty Waldegrave to Lord Gower [1756].

oppose as violently as ever. My dear Jemmy has always used me to talk to him upon
this subject and tell my mind freely, so I hope he don't think I have said too much.[18]

She was careful to couch what she said in such a way as to cushion Kildare's ego, but
her advice was definite – and she clearly expected her views to be taken seriously.

As the sister of the duke of Richmond and the sister-in-law of Henry Fox, Lady
Kildare's family background provided her with a set of connexions and an understanding of politics that spanned the social and political worlds in both Ireland and
England. She had two ambitions and she used her role as adviser to advance them:
her long-term goal was to obtain a dukedom for Kildare (he was created duke of
Leinster in 1766);[19] her short-term goal was to acquire for him some lucrative place
and the possibilities of 'future emoluments' to help support their rapidly expanding
family and allow them to proceed with their 'schemes for improvements'.[20] When
Kildare became disillusioned with politics in 1759 and considered resigning a post
worth £1,500 per annum, thus threatening their future prospects, her advice dropped
its subordinate posturing:

> Indeed, my dear Lord K., I am more of that opinion than ever; because I hear all your
> enemies here triumph so much in it, and are so much delighted at the thoughts of you
> giving up so good a thing as this in a huff. If 'tis done when you receive this you will
> hate me for telling you this, but I will run the risk of that in the hopes that if you are
> inclined to keep the employment it may strengthen you in any such intention.[21]

Political mothers also acted as advisers. Familiar as they were with giving
personal and moral guidance, the step to political guidance was relatively small,
especially for widows who had been involved in maintaining the family political
interest while their sons were minors. Political mothers seem to have been particularly
concerned to provide sons on the grand tour or at university with the political
information and direction necessary to make wise political judgments on their
majorities. Elizabeth, Lady Pembroke maintained just such a steady correspondence
with her son Lord Herbert while he was away on the continent. Not only did she
discuss current political developments with him, such as the court martial of Admiral
Keppel and the ministry's handling of the American war, but she also gave him subtle
political guidance, either through her analysis of political situations, or by expressing

18 *Correspondence of Emily, Duchess of Leinster (1731–1814)*, ed. Brian Fitzgerald (3 vols., Dublin,
    1949–57), I, 14: Lady Kildare to Lord Kildare, 12 May [1755]. As a woman who played all of the
    political roles with consummate skill, it is worth noting that Lady Kildare's political involvement took
    place in spite of almost constant pregnancies. Married at age 15, she bore no less than 17 children
    in 26 years; nevertheless, maternity seems to have been less appealing to her than politics, for her
    ever-expanding family played a decidedly secondary role in her correspondence. For Lady Kildare
    and her sisters, see Stella Tillyard, *Aristocrats. Caroline, Emily, Louisa and Sarah Lennox,
    1740–1832* (1994).
19 *Correspondence of Duchess of Leinster*, ed. Fitzgerald, I, 40: Lady Kildare to Lord Kildare, 2 June
    [1757].
20 *Ibid.*, I, 92, 161–4: Lady Kildare to Lord Kildare, 22 May [1759], 23 [Dec. 1762].
21 *Ibid.*, I, 92: Lady Kildare to Lord Kildare, 22 May [1759].

her own political opinions and commenting on the political actions of others. For instance, as a strong believer in morally guided political independence, she felt that politicians were correct in occasionally opposing the administration but drew the line at a determined opposition. When her husband moved into open opposition in 1780 after the loss of his lord lieutenancy, her advice was only slightly veiled :

> I hope & believe he will go on very properly in his Political line, he seems to see that this is his first appearance in that way, & that it is of consequence; I wish him to oppose what he dissaproves with coolness, firmness, & *avoid all* pitifull, frothy abuse, by which means he will raise the dignity of his character, & make himself of more consequence. I assure you, you was much mistaken in thinking me Ministerial, I am quite the contrary, but my head is not yet enough turn'd by *Party* not to see reason now & then, that's all.[22]

Later the same year, she dropped the veil entirely when she drew on her own knowledge of court politics to give Herbert explicit directions about how to forward his application for a position in the prince of Wales's household:

> to be sure you must not attend the Address, whatever may happen afterwards, as the Queen at least is so good & the K. too as to be really I believe taking *your affair* into consideration, & trying to twist it about so as not to seem to partial in the eyes of others; I do not think we are likely to succeed, but they are at least civil in not taking the heart to say no at once, as was certainly natural in our situation.[23]

As a widow, Agneta Yorke did her best to protect the political interest of her step-son Philip (later 3rd earl of Hardwicke) while he was a minor. She took pains over his political education and was determined that he should understand the importance of social politics. After having given an election dinner in his name (in the lead-up to the 1780 election), she was quick to make a political lesson out of the event:

> The feast which was given in your name at Hamels did a great deal more good than I expected, Mr Wolfe wrote me word that it had a great share in the success of the Day; above four hundred People partook of the Crums which fell from your Table eight Hogsheads of Ale were emptied, and I rejoice they were made so good a use of, for you will find the benifit of such a conduct when you are of age nothing obtains popularity sooner than a free and generous use of the goods of fortune, & as you come after an old gentleman who lived in that style of Hospitality People will see that his fortune is well bestowed.[24]

Agneta Yorke's problematic relationship with the rest of the Hardwicke family, and especially with the second earl, seems to have prompted her to be especially clear

---

22 *Henry, Elizabeth and George, 1734–80*, ed. Lord Herbert (1939), p. 416: Lady Pembroke to Lord Herbert, 23 Feb. [1780]. This volume, and the subsequent *Pembroke Papers (1780–1794)*, ed. Lord Herbert (1950), provide an interesting insight into a devoted political mother's actions. Lady Pembroke's deteriorating relationship with her husband undoubtedly encouraged her to take extra pains to provide her son with careful political guidance.

23 *Pembroke Papers*, ed. Herbert, p. 54: Lady Pembroke to Lord Herbert, 24 Oct. [1780].

24 B.L., Add. MS 35386, f. 60d: Agneta Yorke to Philip Yorke, 6 Mar. [1780?].

in her political advice. After a difference of political opinion with Hardwicke, who
was supporting the administration, she encouraged Philip to base his future political
conduct around honourable independence:

> for my part I should not have been sorry if all the addresses had met with the same fate.
> – notwithstanding Lord Hardwickes different opinion. Indeed Philip I did not think I
> should have lived to have seen such an alteration in the Political principles of your
> Family – It is true they have laid themselves under obligations to the crown & therefore
> I suppose think themselves bound to support the measures it adopts, whether right or
> wrong –. What a blessing is independancy! and who would forfeit it that has enough
> to live on comfortably. You my dear Yorke may enjoy that blessing, & I hope will
> never forfeit the freedom your large Fortune will give you.[25]

Like many other political mothers, once Philip had achieved his majority she
ostensibly retreated from involvement: 'my important Part is entirely over. – Yet tho
I am no longer the watchful Guardian, I shall ever be the anxious Friend.'[26] Not
surprisingly though, she continued to provide him with advice whenever she felt he
was in danger of making a political misstep. When Hardwicke informed her that
Philip was planning to go to Wimpole on his own in the election year of 1780, just
after having reached his majority, she drew on her own political experience and
pointed out the problems that this could pose:

> I cannot conceive what use your being there alone, & without an establishment, can be.
> I rather think it may do harm, for all the lower order of Freeholders will swarm about
> you, & if your Larder & Cellar are not open to Them, you may assure yourself it will
> be remembered in due time & place. The Gentlemen too, in the Neighbourhood, will
> expect to be entertained when they call upon you … But these things considered, I own
> it is *my opinion* that you had better not go till His Lordship is there.[27]

Political wives and mothers were not the only women who acted as advisers;
sisters often filled this role admirably. Sir Joseph Yorke's correspondence with his
sister Elizabeth, Lady Anson echoes with his thanks for her 'inimitable letters' that
'contain so clear an account of our Confusion, that I have as compleat an Idea of it
as if I was within the Circle myself'.[28] Stationed as he was at the Hague, Sir Joseph
depended upon 'my dear Emissary Westminster'[29] to provide him with parliamentary
news, details of the political schemes and intrigues of the moment, and analyses of the
state of the English political world. Although he was in continuous contact with male
politicians through his correspondence with his father and the duke of Newcastle, his
appreciation for the additional information and new insights provided by his sister was
genuine: 'I cannot sufficiently express how sensible I am of your friendship to me, &
how anxious you are to inform me, of everything that is going forward in these

25 *Ibid.*, f. 68d: Agneta Yorke to Philip Yorke, 5 Dec. [1780?].
26 *Ibid.*, ff. 256–7: Agneta Yorke to Philip Yorke, 5 Sept. 1779.
27 *Ibid.*, ff. 281d–2: Agneta Yorke to Philip Yorke, 28 Apr. [1780].
28 *Ibid.*, f. 101: Sir Joseph Yorke to Lady Anson, 30 Sept. 1755.
29 *Ibid.*, f. 185: Sir Joseph Yorke to Lady Anson, 13 July 1756.

troublesome times';[30] or, 'Your accounts are so exact & so curious, that you must forgive my repeating to you a thousand times over, how much I am flatter'd with your attention to me.'[31]

Lady Anson was a highly intelligent woman whose advisory role was only a part of her overall involvement in political life. Her participation extended through detailed political correspondences with her brothers to direct electoral involvement for both her husband and her father, and included specific political tasks, even writing and publishing a defence of the admiralty's actions over Minorca.[32] As the daughter of the lord chancellor and the wife of the most important naval administrator of the day, she was ideally placed to gather the most up-to-date political news and gossip, speak to the most powerful politicians, and forward those causes that she felt most worthy.

Lady Charlotte Wentworth was Lord Rockingham's sister, and another woman who was at the very heart of the political world. She was politically astute and both of the Rockinghams seem to have usually accepted her political advice. Occasionally, however, she and her brother differed over politics. In one such instance, Lady Rockingham at first attributed Rockingham's 'tart stile as if you [was] in a Tiff at something ... to the quantity & quality of the Oranges you had eat', but she later decided that Lady Charlotte must have put him into such 'a political puzzle' and resolved quite calmly that it was also up to her to 'put you out of it again'.[33] Lady Charlotte's worth as an adviser was far too high for Rockingham to be annoyed with her for long. Her advice on men and measures was well thought out, and she even went so far as to provide him with direction in preparing his speeches:

> *If* you should attend on Wednesday & mean to speak, I have a notion you wd: find a passage in Blackstone which you wd not dislike to introduce – it is in his 1st Vol: speaking of the excellency of the Constitution as settled at the Revolution – he says something to this purpose 'That notwithstanding all the precautions taken the Crown is every day gaining an accession of power; which is the more dangerous as it is less observed – ' The Stern Voice of *Prerogative* indeed is not longer heard but the milder power of Influence pervades the whole – I spoil it, but it is worth your looking at –[34]

30 *Ibid.*, f. 9: Sir Joseph Yorke to Lady Anson, 19 Mar. 1754.
31 *Ibid.*, f. 11: Sir Joseph Yorke to Lady Anson, 22 Mar. 1754.
32 For references to Lady Anson's electoral participation, see *ibid.*, f. 3d: Sir Joseph Yorke to Lady Anson, 8 Feb. 1754; ff. 6–6d: 5 Mar. 1754; ff. 57–58: 21 Mar. 1755; ff. 61–2: 1 Apr. 1755. For Sir Joseph's comments on her publication on the invasion of Minorca, see *ibid.*, f. 135: 17 Feb. 1756; for her collaboration with Lord Royston on this publication, see B.L., Add. MS 35376, ff. 132–3: Lady Anson to Lord Royston, [8 Aug.?] 1756. The piece was published in the *Public Advertiser*, Friday, 27 Aug. 1756.
33 Sheffield City Libraries, Wentworth Woodhouse Muniments (hereafter W.W.M.), R168–102: Lady Rockingham to Lord Rockingham, n.d.
34 This speech was given on 16 April 1777 during the second debate of the session on the address to the king on the payment of the civil list. See W.W.M., R169–129: Lady Charlotte Wentworth to Lord Rockingham, 14 Apr. 1777. I would like to thank Stephen Farrell for drawing my attention to this and allowing me to consult his unpublished paper, 'Lady Rockingham – Politician?'.

Advisers were well-known figures in the eighteenth-century political world. The stock character of the favourite, replete with all its connotations of undue influence, was an adviser whose power and lack of accountability inspired at best envy, at worst, fear. As contemporary comments about the duchess of Bedford's influence over her husband indicated, female as well as male advisers could be thought to possess overweening power. Not enough of her own correspondence survives to shed light on the extent of her influence, but numerous contemporary references suggest that she was believed to be one of the primary political forces behind the Bedford faction.[35] In 1762, when Bedford was involved in peace negotiations in France, she personally carried to him the political details that were too sensitive to put in writing.[36] By 1765, Lord Ilchester classed her and Richard Rigby as Bedford's most influential advisers: 'I hear it is with much difficulty that Rigby & the Duchess have prevaild with the Duke of Bedford not to resign his employment *now*.'[37] This view was shared by the ex-prime minister George Grenville, who always kept a close eye on the duchess when gauging his reception by the duke.[38] The most damning indictment of the duchess, however, and thus a most useful insight into her methods, as well as a strong assertion of her influence, comes from Lord Charlemont's memoirs:

> The duke, a man of excellent parts, though deficient in common sense, was in the highest degree passionate, but perfectly good-natured. By thwarting his temper, her wily grace was wont to provoke him, which was not difficult, to hasty, rude, and even savage expressions of anger, well knowing that his subsiding passion would give way to unbounded penitence; and in those moments of contrition her powers were without limits. Of this lady (the most artful and dangerous of women) I am almost afraid to speak.[39]

While the duchess of Bedford's overall political involvement was by no means confined to her activities as an adviser, for many women the role of adviser may have been the ideal means of accessing the political world. Being a valued political adviser meant being acknowledged and respected by political men. The role legitimated women's political awareness and interest, provided them with an acceptable avenue for expressing political opinions, and allowed them to affect political decisions with little risk to reputation. As advisers, they could have significant political influence, but since their participation remained indirect and was usually private, it was impossible for contemporaries to calculate the extent of their power or to hold them publicly accountable for political decisions.

35 John Brooke, *The Chatham Administration, 1766–1768* (1956), pp. 30–2.
36 *Correspondence of John, Fourth Duke of Bedford. Selected from the Originals at Woburn Abbey*, ed. Lord John Russell (3 vols., 1842), II, 131–2: Richard Rigby to duke of Bedford, 30 Sept. 1762.
37 B.L., Add. MS 51421, f. 98: Lord Ilchester to Lord Holland, [31 May] 1765.
38 B.L., Add. MS 42083: Grenville Papers, I. See, for instance, ff. 172d–3, 237.
39 H.M.C., *12th Report, Appendix, Part X*, p. 10.

Agent

The dividing line between advisers and agents can also be drawn between indirect and direct political participation, and between private and public involvement. When changing situations forced women to make decisions on their own, they moved beyond the role of adviser to act directly (often publicly) as agents, or beyond that, as partners. The role of agent incorporated those of confidante and adviser and extended them through increasingly public, direct and autonomous political involvement. As agents, women were the acknowledged delegates of their families, friends, or political connexions. They could hold positions of trust and responsibility. Their activities extended across the political spectrum: from the social politics of racemeets, assemblies and balls, through the non-institutional politics of patronage, to direct electoral involvement. For some women, especially the wives of leading politicians, being an agent also meant identifying with, and participating in, factional politics.

Agents operated under varying degrees of supervision; nevertheless, they took a direct part in the political world and worked with men as individuals or in groups. At their most involved, they were in leadership positions over men and made political decisions. Even Lady Chatham, that most uninspiring of all political wives, was forced to act as 'a borrowed hand' in taking over Chatham's correspondence, and as his personal representative and link to the political world, during his extended illness.[40] Other political wives also acted as secretaries for their husbands (with varying amounts of individual input), reading their mail and managing their correspondences if they were ill, busy or away from home, especially during elections. Lady Rockingham's services as a copyist were often much in demand, but it was her ability to whip in members and solicit votes that made her truly valuable.[41] She acted as Rockingham's personal representative, and by extension as the faction's representative, whenever she took over the Rockingham correspondence network. As an old friend, Sir George Savile was very familiar with this division of labour and accordingly addressed his correspondence to her during the lead-up to the 1774 general election:

> Lady Rockingham knows that I have long plac'd her near the head of my list of Politicians, & therefore altho' the letter beginning *Dear Sr George* & written in the Hand of the Lady is sign'd by the Gentleman, I yet shall write my answer to Wentworth. I gather indeed from the Servant as well as from Lady Rockingham's

40 B.L., Add. MS 43771, ff. 45–6: Lady Chatham to John Calcraft, 10 Apr. 1770. For a good example of the latter, see Lady Chatham's dealings with the duke of Grafton during the Chatham administration: Augustus Henry Fitzroy, *Autobiography and Political Correspondence of Augustus Henry Third Duke of Grafton*, ed. Sir William R. Anson (1898); Brooke, *Chatham Administration*.
41 Nottingham U.L., Portland papers, PwF 9161, 9162: Lady Rockingham to 3rd duke of Portland, 28 June 1767. The first of these notes is dated at three in the afternoon, the other past midnight (and thus is actually misdated); in the second note, she protests that she is 'tired to death with sitting all day watching the Nod of my Sovereign & writing Notes for him'.

Postscript that Ld Rockingham does not return to Wentworth between the
Northallerton Business & York Races.[42]

During elections, those political women who chose to become involved could act
as personal representatives of their families and get involved in the rough-and-tumble
world of eighteenth-century electioneering – as did the duchess of Devonshire, her
sister Lady Duncannon, and their opposition Lady Salisbury, when they canvassed St
Albans for their respective brothers during the 1784 election – or they could stay at
home and turn their homes into political control centres. Often, they did both.
Georgiana, Lady Spencer had a lifelong love–hate relationship with politics, yet her
ambivalence did not stop her from being one of the most active of agents, representing both her husband and her son at various points in time. When her husband learned
of the dissolution of parliament in September 1780, he immediately dispatched her
and Lord Althorp to different towns to manage the family's elections:

> he has no Opposition either at Northampton or St Albans, yet he packt off Ly Spencer,
> & Ld Althorpe at Nine o'clock that Night, *she* to St Albans with Mr Sloper who is to
> come in there in the room of Sir Richard Sutton, and she is to stay there till after the
> Election, which comes on next Friday, and Expresses are sent, or receiv'd two or three
> times a day.[43]

By the time of the 1784 election Lady Spencer was a widow and her movements
were temporarily curtailed by a bad knee, but she nevertheless managed the St Albans
election from her home. Never one to value other people's abilities highly, it was not
at all out of character for her to take charge of the election committee itself, in spite
of the demands that this made on her time and energy. After the election was over,
she explained the time commitment to her friend Mrs. Howe: 'I have for some time
got up invariably at 6. – & the two or three busiest day's of the Election my
Committee & I met at a little after five.'[44]

The demands placed upon agents did not necessarily require them to be more
politically aware than advisers, but rather to be more openly involved if the
opportunity arose. Although it is impossible to quantify the number of women who
acted as agents, the sources suggest that fewer women acted as agents than as
confidantes or advisers. They tended to be women who were closely connected to
men who were important in local or national politics – themselves a relatively small
proportion of the political nation. The wives of members of parliament and
occasionally their mothers, sisters and daughters were most likely to be agents. Their
political involvement, like that of their male counterparts, was not continuous, but
varied both with the time of the year and the state of political nation.

---

42   W.W.M., R1–1498: Sir George Savile to Lady Rockingham, 10 Aug. 1774. See also Nottingham
     U.L., Portland papers, PwF 10744: duchess of Portland to 3rd duke, 4 Oct. 1780.
43   P.R.O., 30/29/4/6/77, f. 1108: Rachel Lloyd to Lady Gower, 5 Sept, [1780].
44   B.L., MS Coll. Althorp, F. 53: Lady Spencer to Mrs Howe, 5 Apr. 1784. Lady Spencer's
     correspondence on her involvement in the 1784 St Albans election runs through F. 14, F. 53, F. 109,
     F. 114–115, F. 119–121, F. 123, F. 130–131, G. 276, G. 287, and G. 289.

Partner

The dividing line between agents and partners was often difficult to pinpoint, as the principal difference was one of degree. Partners were the most highly politicized, directly involved and independent of all political women. They acted in conjunction with men but often made political decisions independently. Their political judgment was trusted and their influence recognized, or even feared. Just as the most active male politicians formed a small select group at the top of the political world, the women who acted as partners were the apex of female political involvement. The majority of partners were the wives or mothers of politically active men, which is not surprising given the predominance of familial politics in the eighteenth century, but there were also some women whose claim to political involvement was based on the irrefutable eighteenth-century grounds of control over property, including political interests and patronage.

Partnership was highly individual. Partners combined intelligence, confidence and assertiveness with sensitivity to social and political nuance, and highly developed personal skills. They were accomplished operators, who used their comprehensive knowledge of people and politics to advantage. As the need arose, they acted as confidantes, advisers and agents. They shared not only the concerns but also many of the fatigues of male politicians. Of course, not all women, even those from highly political families, could meet – or wanted to meet – these criteria. For instance, as daughters of the second duke of Richmond, Lady Kildare and Lady Caroline Fox shared the same political heritage and upbringing; furthermore, both married politicians and went on to raise politically active sons. Yet Lady Caroline's peevishness and chronic insecurity hardened into a distaste for politics that never prompted her to become more than her husband's adviser. Lady Kildare, on the other hand, found politics a natural outlet for her vivacity and made good use of her ability to manipulate both people and situations. She became her husband's partner within a short time of their marriage.

Women who acted as partners were likely to be involved directly and publicly in political life. They filled a variety of positions: secretary, whip, manager, co-ordinator, negotiator, canvasser, broker and even patron. Some controlled family interests or took leading roles in political connexions. On the whole, though, they were more independent and more likely to make political decisions than other groups of women. To cite only one example, Urania, Lady Portsmouth was faced with the difficult decision of deciding whether her son should stand for parliament when he returned from the grand tour in time for the 1790 general election. The family political interest had been carefully maintained for him and, if all had gone well, this would have been a matter of course. Things, however, had not gone well, and Lady Portsmouth was forced to recognize that even time on the Continent had done nothing to cure his mental deficiencies. She consulted with male relatives, but, as she told Sir John Griffin Griffin, the decision, and the responsibility for it, rested with her:

every flattering hope of his supporting a public Station with Credit is almost entirely vanish'd. With this melancholly Knowledge can we consistently with our Duty towards him Place him in a Station which will contiually expose his Imbecillity to the World? On the other hand can we with justice deprive him untried of that which I cannot help considering as a part of his Birth-Right? Or how can we possibily justify ourselves for seting him aside without being Ourselves the Proclaimers of his Misfortunes? Here my Lord, is our Distress – here is the Difficulty which we have to encounter – a difficulty which presses the more hardly upon me – because *I* must determine, *I* must bear the blame or Praise of the Determination, and what adds not a little to my Affliction is, let me, determine or Act which way I will, I am almost certain to incur the Censure of the world, which must in a great Measure be ignorant of the Reasons or Motives of my Conduct.[45]

Partners were potentially the most powerful political women in the eighteenth century. Male and female contemporaries acknowledged them as political actors with influence or interest, and approached them as such. Political partners existed at all levels of the political *élite*, but a brief examination of one of the best known political partners in the second half of the eighteenth century will suffice. Lady Rockingham identified closely with her husband's political concerns and appears to have found politics intriguing, intellectually stimulating and fulfilling. Lord Rockingham quickly came to value her political acumen and her shrewd management of people. Very soon after their marriage she became a member of his most intimate political circles. While she was still consolidating her role as partner in the 1750s, she was eager to reassure him that she preferred politics to the social whirl,[46] but by the 1760s their partnership was well established and she had become an accomplished political actor. She worked in conjunction with Rockingham and also made decisions in her own right.

This combination of joint and independent action was perhaps best displayed in the Rockingham party's approach to William Pitt in 1765. Pitt was always difficult, but as the year went on, it became apparent that the Rockingham administration needed his support in order to survive. Lady Rockingham became the point of contact between the politicians. Both she and Pitt were at Bath for their health, which provided her with the excuse she needed to initiate the contact and with a less highly charged political atmosphere in which to operate. Her light touch and her subtle flattery allowed her to manoeuvre around Pitt's ego and to establish a comfortable rapport. Ostensibly, she approached him because she wanted to buy a pair of his horses; in actuality, she and Rockingham were discussing the best way to put out political feelers to Pitt. In the end, she bought the horses, managed the negotiations, and facilitated the transmission of political papers from Rockingham to Pitt without compromising anyone involved.[47]

45 Essex R.O., Audley End papers, D/DBy C9/53: Urania, Lady Portsmouth to Sir John Griffin Griffin, Lymington, 30 June 1789.
46 W.W.M., R168–21–1: Lady Rockingham to Lord Rockingham, n.d.
47 See W.W.M., R156 for letters between Lord and Lady Rockingham regarding her approach to Pitt.

Later that year when the duke of Cumberland died, she was still at Bath; however, her poor health did not stop her from providing Rockingham with detailed political advice. She was secure enough in her partnership by this time, personally and politically, to tell him at length, without excuses or apologies, what she felt he should do to capitalize on the temporary political instability:

Was I you I would take the first opportunity of speaking to the K—g upon the subject of this Melancholy Event, & I would speak boldly & openly for I think all Political success will greatly turn upon the Channel his Confidence now falls into, & therefore I would hasten as much as possible to draw his mind to *a right* decision & determination at this time – in short I would tell him this, that the juncture was now more critical than *ever*, that every real Friend to his M—y must deeply lament the Loss he sustains in his Uncle, whose abilities & judgmt: were of so superior a sort as to be irreparable, that the only attempt to any degree of equivalent must be the superadded assiduity of his Administration to endeavour to make his M—y & the publick suffer as little from the blow as the nature of such a sad Event can admit, & that his Ministers can only be enabled so to do by the concurrence of his Majesty's firm & unreserved Confidence; that therefore you humbly presumed to submit it to his consideration whether he was so far satisfied with the Conduct of his present Ministers as to think they merit the continuance of that full & *undevided* Confidence they Must expect to enjoy, in order to serve him well, if so you could answer for yourself that yr: endeavours to carry on his business should be indefatigable; that on the other hand, you should be ready with the greatest submission to resign the Trust to his better choice, if any other plan should be more to his inclination or interests, for the same motive would influence you on, every occasion, & does so at this present instant of beseeching his Majesty that his Confidence & his Ministers may ever be undevided of whomsoever his administration is composed; as no other method can secure permanent benefit nor any set of Ministers could either in conscience or prudence venture, to build without that head corner Stone the complete Confidence of their Sovereign.

Something to this effect, in yr: words, I mean, & would have said at first, to show him that the confidence he placed in the Duke must now it its full scope be transferr'd to *All* of you; & instantly, for I think now wd: be the time for *certain past Influences*, to try to revive in case they find themselves *too much down*, & this also wd: be the period most likely for it to succeed in some degree, for when the mind is again on flat for a repositary it is the more liable to sink back into old habits; You are all in a manner Strangers to the King, my Politicks are to fix him now, or give him up for ever—[48]

Given the depth of political knowledge and perspicacity that this, and other of her letters reflect, it is no wonder that Rockingham relied on her judgment, lamenting the loss of '*my Minerva* at my Elbow' when they were apart.[49] Moreover, her political contribution was well known to contemporaries, and, when Edmund Burke advised

48 W.W.M., R168–177–1–2: Lady Rockingham to Lord Rockingham [Nov. 1765].
49 W.W.M., R156–9: Lord Rockingham to Lady Rockingham, 31 Mar. 1767.

her to preserve her correspondence alongside her husband's, his tribute to her was more than empty flattery:

> Pray therefore let them be returned to keep company with the rest and to remain with the family as documents of the constant support and assistance you have uniformly given to your excellent Lord in the Course of that Conduct which will make this age a pattern of Virtue to the next, and to many more succeding, notwithstanding its having its full share of evil examples. Your Names indeed ought to go down together; for it is no mean part you have had in the great services which that great and good man has done to his Country.[50]

50 *The Correspondence of Edmund Burke*, ed. Thomas W. Copeland *et al.* (10 vols., Cambridge, 1958–78), v, 45–7: Burke to Lady Rockingham, Beaconsfield, 20 Nov. 1782.

12

Creation of Empire:
James Murray in Quebec

LINDA KERR

To understand fully the historical development of Canada it is vital to embrace imperial history. An ignorance of imperial history has led Canadian scholars to misunderstand and to misrepresent the actions of governor-in-chief, James Murray. As the first governor of the newly acquired territory of Quebec, Murray's actions and philosophy are critical to the way in which British policy in Canada developed.[1] Indeed influential Canadian historians have, in a backhanded way, placed the credit or blame for the creation of the present day conditions in Canada *vis-à-vis* Quebec (the preservation of French politics, language and culture) on Murray. In the present climate of separatism or renewed federalism (which has been the subject of much discussion of late) the actions of Murray have been misrepresented and this could only be the result of a total unfamiliarity with eighteenth-century imperial politics. But imperial politicians had to rely heavily upon their governors. Therefore it is also necessary to look at the theory and the practicalities of the running of an empire. Although understandable, it is narrowly xenophobic to pretend that Britain has never influenced the course of Canadian history and equally wrong to blame the ensuing political developments on the supposed 'narrow' vision of a man whom, until now, no one has cared to study in any depth. Imperial history is the linchpin in eighteenth-century history.

Philip Lawson understood this and devoted much time to Quebec and the empire. That this study has yet to be fully integrated into the university-level Canadian history curriculum is distressing, for an understanding of the politics of empire is the most necessary element in any examination of the implications of the change from French to British political control. There was no colonial office in 1763 and Quebec had to wait its turn behind pressing domestic issues and crises in other parts of the empire.

If Murray can be faulted at all it would have to be for his political naivety and his falling political star in London after 1764. Because of the state of imperial politics in the early 1760s it was all but impossible even for governors to get the attention of key London politicians and easy to use Murray as a scapegoat when impractical orders

---

[1] Linda Kerr, 'Quebec. The Making of an Imperial Mercantile Community, 1760–1768', University of Alberta Ph.D., 1992, pp. 37–108.

could no longer be implemented. Murray had an unusual background for a governor; he had seemingly impeccable political ties, but the taint of jacobitism dogged his career and cost him promotions time and again until finally it seemed that his patronage by Bute and Newcastle had overcome this with his posting to Quebec. Throughout his brief but crucial stay at Quebec his effectiveness was constantly challenged by the lack of vision at Whitehall for this new part of the empire. The interplay of the local official and London politicians with their hastily formed plans for empire makes for interesting reading. It was the practicalities of empire that soon triumphed over the theory of empire.

James Murray became governor-in-chief of Quebec in 1763. He had come to the colony as part of Wolfe's conquering force and remained as military governor of Quebec until the end of the war. Murray remained in Quebec as the governor-in-chief of the new colony because of political lobbying by his friends in London and the hasty retreat of the two other potential candidates, Brigadiers Monckton and Townshend. Murray held this post from 1763 until 1768. He proudly refused to curry the favour of anyone but Pitt and the king, but he wanted the job.[2] If he had understood that he would not have had both civil and military control of the province it is doubtful that he would have been so anxious to assume these responsibilities. He was first and foremost a military man. It was standard procedure that British troops overseas were always under military control and never under the civil command of a governor, and Murray must have been aware of this fact.[3] To observers in London, Murray seemed the perfect choice for the post of military governor of Quebec, but a less obvious choice to head the civil government. In fact his aristocratic background, his family's political ties (though some of these brought notoriety) and his long service in the British army made him the perfect candidate for such a colonial posting. In the eighteenth century it was often the case that political patronage rather than ability was responsible for success in the job market. While it is true that Murray obtained the post because of his good relationship with the ministry in London, it is clear from his correspondence that he was very interested in, and conscientious about, his posting.

A brief look at Murray's problems in Quebec from the beginning of civil government shows the mixed signals which he received from London and the practical barriers that stood in the way of the efficient running of even one small corner of the empire. The chaos and uncertainty in Quebec in the 1760s had less to do with Murray and his temperament than with the intransigence of successive British ministries who wanted to reach a reasonable settlement for the new colony but seemed incapable of completing this task.

---

2   Cromartie Correspondence (the earl of Cromartie, Castle Leod, Strathpeffer, Ross-shire), Bundle XXII: Murray to George, former earl of Cromartie, 17 July 1761.

3   A. A. Wetherell, 'General James Murray and British Canada. The Transitions from French to British Canada, 1758–1766', St John's University, N.Y. Ph.D., 1979, p. 293.

By the articles of the negotiated peace, Quebec became a British colony – part of the newly forming empire – but the home government took another year to send instructions and commissions to the new governor. By the royal proclamation of 1763 George III and his ministers treated Quebec the same as his other new acquisitions. In choosing a unitary settlement the crown overlooked the potential problem of assimilating a European people within the bounds of a British empire and ignored the economic needs of the colony. Murray came to understand Quebec in a way that the men who framed the royal proclamation did not. In an age of political patronage it was good fortune that Murray was chosen for the post, because, at the very least, he had been resident in the province since 1759 and was aware of its problems. Most political appointments to Quebec were sold to deputies in London and the patentees never caught sight of the shores of the St Lawrence.

Murray's letters reveal his belief that in order to keep Canada within the British empire, the British had to earn the respect of Canadians; this viewpoint took precedence over pandering to the merchants by allowing an assembly to operate in the colony. This position posed a dilemma. Murray could not give the British in the colony a general assembly because it would be unfair to the Canadians, yet by denying this right to the British settlers he was showing both groups how arbitrary British rule could be.

In the final analysis, the political settlement in Canada was not controlled by Murray but by his political masters in London, and the 1760s were a decade of political instability. The search for the meaning and purpose of empire was well underway, but the differences between a theoretical settlement in London and its actual effect on the empire was soon to become apparent. This dichotomy was especially true of the debates in the house of commons over the East India Company and the empire in the east. It should be kept in mind that these were the early days of the global British empire and broad based settlements were practical only when they showed some flexibility locally and when they were closely supervised.

The fate of Quebec was only one of many items on the ministerial agenda after the war ended. Until the recent work by Philip Lawson on the peace settlement, it was argued that there was some debate about whether the British government should seek to keep Canada or Guadaloupe.[4] Lawson's work has shown, through its examination of the decision-making process at the peace negotiations, that the French did not want New France back and that British negotiators were well aware of this. From as early as 1761 British ministers were conscious of the fact that they could be left with Canada.

The road towards peace had not been straightforward since the hardliners in cabinet – Pitt, Temple and Halifax – had wanted to continue the fight but the king

---

4   The account of British politics in the 1760s which follows in the next four pages is indebted to Philip
     Lawson, *The Imperial Challenge. Quebec and Britain in the Age of the American Revolution*
     (Montreal and Kingston, 1990), pp. 13–36, 104.

wished for peace. Pitt and Temple had to resign late in 1761 after the cabinet rejected
their war aims. The new ministry included Bute, Newcastle, Halifax and the earl of
Egremont with Grenville in the Commons. Murray had some ties with this group of
politicians, as we can see from his appointment as governor-in-chief, but even this
ministry, which had the ear of the king, would not be enough to produce a clear
policy for the newly acquired territory. First of all, the decade was one of political
upheaval, changes of ministry and more than one reorganization of colonial
responsibilities. It was not until the end of the decade that the position of colonial
secretary was created and even then it would be virtually powerless in its first year
of operation because of the jealously guarded jurisdictions of other departments.
There were many questions outstanding on the role of overseas possessions that still
remained to be thrashed out and policy decisions were a matter of juggling
information from a variety of sources and passing them on to the treasury and
customs board. Nothing was done quickly because there was no colonial office to
plan things – power was vested in ministers and there was no separation of domestic
and colonial issues. The possessions of Great Britain *were* Great Britain. Colonial
issues were not handled as foreign affairs; they had no special claim on the time of the
house of commons and no specific ministers in charge of them. Finding solutions to
problems was not helped at all by the power struggles between the treasury and the
secretary of state for control on matters of executive policy. The board of trade, the
customs board and the plantations committee of the privy council were all attempting
to gather some control over colonial affairs for themselves. It was generally agreed
by all three bodies that military rule had to be ended in Quebec and civil government
established, but there the agreement ended. By May 1763, Egremont had called for
a settlement but the combination of his death and worries caused by Pontiac's rising
forced the government into action before it was ready. The result was the royal
proclamation and its choice of representative government reflects how little the
ministry knew about Quebec. The stream of reports sent by Murray and others were
not even considered until after the proclamation had been publicly declared. A high
turnover in the decision-making personnel involved with the new acquisitions was a
recurring problem in policy making for Quebec.

   As soon as Murray was placed in charge of the colony there were a number of
issues that he had to deal with, but, before he could take any practical steps, he had
to wait for his instructions to arrive. The instructions and his commission did not
reach him until the autumn of 1764, although his letters are full of frenzied enquiries
about them.[5] The instructions themselves show that the British government really had
no idea that its latest acquisitions had moved the empire into a new era.[6] Murray's

---

5   Public Archives of Canada, Ottawa, MG 11 Q Series, Vol. 1: Murray to Egremont, 27 Sept. 1763;
     MG 11 Q Series, Vol. 2: Murray to the commissioners of trade and plantations, 24 Apr. 1764.
6   Lawson, *Imperial Challenge*, pp. 181–204.

commission gave him the power to call an assembly whenever circumstances allowed, one to be duly elected by the majority of freeholders. It is obvious from its references to cities, boroughs, ports and harbours that this was a standard format and was not one put together specifically for Quebec. Why had Murray's report and the reports of others, including merchants, on the state of Quebec failed to have any impact at Whitehall? This is a difficult question to answer but some general comments can be made. It took almost two years after the proclamation was published for ministers to address the question of the Quebec settlement. This was partly because they had been rushed into a settlement in 1763. There were too many departments handling colonial affairs and questions from the colonies arrived in the various departments in a jumbled heap. In the end it took the British government until 1774 to respond to the very special demands of Quebec.

The first problem that Murray faced was in the winter of 1759 when he had to find food and shelter for over 7,000 troops and an equal number of civilians.[7] This was no easy task in a town devastated by war where over 500 houses had burned, including almost all of the lower town.[8] The troops therefore had to camp on the plains where they were kept well away from the civilians. By all accounts it was a severe winter not helped by the chronic shortages of food, fuel and shelter and Murray's letters detail the scurvy and dysentery among his men which even imbibing spruce beer could not prevent.

From the very beginning there was a problem with funds in the colony. It was only in May 1760 that the colony received any cash, a lump sum of £20,000, and Murray complained that it was not much considering that the garrison had been without pay for nine months.[9] There was also confusion because there were so many different kinds of coins in circulation and tables of equivalencies had to be set up. The Halifax rate was in use in Quebec and the New York rate in Montreal until Murray reorganized both in 1764 to bring some form of standardization to the whole colony. The British also limited the use of leather money to a maximum value of one shilling.[10] Murray suggested to Egremont in his 1762 report that the lack of currency should be one of the home government's top priorities. He explained that because of the lack of specie the English merchants could not sell their goods, and that the best response would be for the government to send a lump sum over to allow commerce to continue unabated. Murray proposed that the tidy sum of £100,000 sterling would do, but indicated that even then his problems would not be over because the Canadians would probably not use the money in case it proved as unreliable as French paper had been in 1760. To build confidence in British currency he thought that some of it could be handed out as rebuilding loans, merchants could use it to pay duties and

7   Hilda Neatby, *Quebec. The Revolutionary Age, 1760–1791* (Toronto, 1966), p. 18.
8   Wetherell, 'General James Murray', p. 69.
9   Public Archives of Canada, MG 23 GII Series 1, Vol. 1: Murray to Amherst, 19 May 1760.
10 Fernand Ouellet, *Economic and Social History of Quebec 1760–1850* (Ottawa, 1980), p. 60.

the civil government could use it for public works.[11] In the meantime, British merchants accepted the French paper of the habitants at a 50 to 80 per cent discount.[12] It soon became clear that paper money was the object of speculation and that merchants were gambling on the French government paying back a substantial amount on the bills. Local merchant Samuel Jacobs told his storekeeper Charles Curtius to sell part of the store's goods for paper money: 'if you sell at 80 livres to a dollar that'd be selling at good profit, take it, paper money is 100% profit'.[13] News of these activities disturbed the government and in 1763, Murray was ordered to find out how many 'Canada bills' were in the colony and to note how each bill had been acquired. He was also instructed to keep track of any claims from the Canadians that they had been hoodwinked into selling at a low rate.[14] Murray was well aware that local merchants were indeed speculating in the bills and in a letter to Halifax named agents working for the London merchants, Rybot and Lynch. He noted that 'there is hardly an English merchant who has not taken of this specie and a considerable amount encouraged to it by the great prospect of gain if a part is even paid'.[15] Murray also wrote that he had assembled the Canadian merchants and told them that it was senseless to sell so low and that they should instead register their money. It has been estimated that the losses from this speculation were £300,000 to Canadians and £110,000 to British traders, but, because the latter were fewer in number and most of the bills had been held within the colony, the losses were more severe for the British.[16]

Lord Sandwich, the northern secretary, was in charge of the British side of the negotiations with the French over these 'Canada bills' between August 1763 and July 1765.[17] The French government was aware that a substantial number of the bills had been sold at a huge discount to British merchants. These sales did not endear them to the idea of a quick settlement. Successful London merchants – Watson, Crokatt, Lynch and Rybot, to name but a few – were involved in the Canada bills trade. It was not only British merchants in Quebec who managed to sell to the London merchants, but successful Canadian fur trade families, such as the Babys, also passed large amounts to Francis Rybot.[18] Throughout 1764 Murray continued to tally and send in the amounts of paper money registered, but at the end of the year he received a brief letter from Halifax which, in an unusually sharp tone, lamented that Murray's total

11   Public Archives of Canada, MG 11 Q Series, Vol.1: Murray to Egremont, 7 June 1762, enclosed with the report on the state of Quebec.
12   Isabel Craig, 'Economic Conditions in Canada 1763–83', University of Ottawa M.A., 1968, pp. 206–7.
13   Public Archives of Canada, Jacob's Estate Papers, Vol. 8, 1760–3: Jacobs to Curtius, June 1763.
14   *Ibid.*, MG 11 Q Series, Vol. 1: Halifax to Murray, 9 Dec. 1763.
15   *Ibid.*, Vol. 2: Murray to Halifax, 14 Feb. 1764.
16   Ouellet, *History of Quebec*, p. 68.
17   Lawson, *Imperial Challenge*, p. 57.
18   Dale Miquelon, 'The Baby Family and the Trade of Canada, 1750–1820', Carleton University M.A., 1966, p. 35.

was now two million livres over the previous one and that unfortunately it was too late to hand this over to the French government.[19] The Canada bills issue caused Murray to believe that the British merchants were taking advantage of Canadians. But in fact, French merchant houses were accepting these bills at a 65 per cent discount.[20]

Another general concern of the military administration was to maintain a contented population. One way to do this was to fix prices. In 1760 the sale of wheat and bread was regulated in the town of Quebec and there were heavy fines for any violations.[21] Clerks of the court became inspectors of bakeries and butcher shops; they stamped goods and these were then sold for amounts determined by a standard chart of prices.[22] Licences were also a necessity in the provisioning trade.[23] There was a very real chance of famine in the winter of 1759–60 and again the following year. The British merchants gathered £500 and handed it over for the purchase of provisions, while Murray and Amherst corresponded regularly about which colonial city could best provide supplies. The Quebec garrison also chipped in by handing over some of the soldiers' provisions each week to help fend off famine.[24]

A number of measures were taken to ensure that there was a minimum of contact at first between the army and civilian population. When the guard was mounted in the town the men were not dismissed until they were back at the garrison.[25] Any non-commissioned officer who owed money to the merchants for goods purchased on credit and who did not pay was to be reduced to the ranks.[26] To maintain good will between the occupiers and the occupied, it was ordered in November 1759 that any measures having to do with the general population were to be published in both languages so that there were no misunderstandings. The task of the governors, and especially of Murray, was to keep order in Quebec until the peace was signed. Despite problems with the currency and with food shortages Murray did a remarkably good job. He established a council of seven which included two well respected Canadians, a few merchants and his most trusted companions. Throughout the period all instructions for Murray came through Jeffrey Amherst with whom he was on the best of terms. He appears to have been devoted to Amherst and later took it very badly when Amherst returned to England and was replaced by Thomas Gage, former governor of Montreal.

19 Public Archives of Canada, MG 11 Q Series, Vol.2: Halifax to Murray, 8 Dec. 1764.
20 Elizabeth Arthur, 'The French-Canadian under British Rule, 1760–1800', McGill University Ph.D., 1949, p. 235.
21 Wetherell, 'General James Murray', pp. 93–4.
22 Ouellet, History of Quebec, p. 54.
23 Public Archives of Canada, MG 23 GII Series 1, Vol. 1: 15 Jan. 1760.
24 Wetherell, 'General James Murray', p. 87.
25 Public Archives of Canada, MG 23 GIII 23, Vol. 4, f. 5: John Nairne Papers, Orderly Books, 17 Aug. 1762.
26 Ibid., Orderly Books, 26 Nov. 1762.

Murray wrote to Pitt on 22 October 1760 with his observations on the colony. This was one of his first deliberations on the newly conquered territory and it provides us with his first impressions of Quebec and its people.[27] This letter has been generally ignored by historians in favour of the report of 1762; this lack of interest is unfortunate because his observations paint a vivid picture of the potential of the colony. In Murray's estimation there did not appear to be any trouble looming on the horizon, especially from the hard working habitants. He estimated the population at 80,000, most of them landholders, except for the small urban populations found in the three towns. Habitants were portrayed as self-sufficient farmers who could turn their hand to anything. He emphasized the potential the place held for the production of naval stores. This preoccupation with naval stores was typical – colonies were most often judged on two criteria: their ability to absorb and pay for British manufactured goods or their ability to give the navy a secure supply of naval stores including pitch, tar, hemp, flax and, most of all, masts. In fact Quebec had neither the immediate ability to absorb manufactured goods nor could it fulfil the second criterion. Murray extolled the virtues of the east coast fisheries which were the eastern equivalent of the fur trade. The fisheries had been very productive in the French regime and at first were targeted by those British merchants who had large amounts of cash at their disposal. Interested as he was in the east coast, Murray was also very interested in the fur trade.

Murray's letter to Pitt was optimistic, emphasizing how diligent the Canadians were, how rich the resources of the province were and how only mismanagement would cause the colony to be a financial drain on Great Britain. He expressed the hope that the example of his well regulated management of Quebec would somehow end a century of attachment to the French crown and bring the colonists into the orbit of British influence. In the meantime he opened the fur trade to all, promised to keep watch in case the Indians were mistreated and put an agent in charge of the king's posts to maintain some continuity of local trade practices. At the same time Murray wrote to Lord Colvill of the admiralty, explaining the importance of the posts and how they operated, and asked for a passport for his agent to move freely to and from the area.[28] This did not have the desired effect for later in the year Murray told Pitt that Colvill had allowed the produce of the posts to be claimed as a navy prize and sold.[29] Murray was also kept busy with the question of dutiable goods and with the difficulties of supplying the garrison, but his main task in the early years was to compile a comprehensive report on the colony.

27 Public Archives of Canada, MG 23 GII Series 1, Vol. 3: Murray to Pitt, 22 Oct. 1760.
28 *Ibid.*, Vol. 1: Murray to Colvill, 26 June 1760.
29 *Ibid.*: Murray to Pitt, 22 Oct. 1760.

Murray's report of 1762 is well enough known to historians but there are a few sections which are of special interest.[30] He gave a lucid account of the revenues and expenses of the government before 1759, including all duties that were customarily levied, and this information gave the British government a sound basis from which to impose duties after 1763. Overall the report confirmed that New France was a normal and well regulated colony which in either regime would require a similar type of infrastructure – public works, crown officials, courts, forts and garrisons. Murray then produced an economic plan for the colony which focused first on its potential to create income. He expected that a duty levied on spirits would bring enough to support the civil establishment. He would have liked to revive the duty on wine but he thought the habitants could ill afford it, and, more importantly, thought this would not endear them to British rule. He also wanted to maintain the tax on houses but because of the bombardment of Quebec this was not possible. There had been a duty of three per cent on dry goods before 1759 but he counselled that this should not be revived as it had been a temporary war measure. Murray introduced the idea later followed up by Carleton, that the civil officers be given small salaries rather than fees. As with the report to Pitt, he discussed in detail the productive capability of the land, but his estimation of the agricultural abilities of habitants had changed radically in two years. His attitude was typical of eighteenth-century European reflexions on farmers who did not practice new techniques and use the new agricultural tools available. The report did pin-point some of the potential growth areas in the economy to which the British merchants would apply themselves in the near future – hemp, flax and potash. He thought that potash in particular could be produced more cheaply in Quebec than in Britain, but there proved to be too many obstacles to overcome for potash to be a profitable venture in the early years. The trouble was that potash production was expensive and the habitants would not co-operate by bringing in their wood ashes. Again the report spoke of the importance of the fisheries, especially those in the gulf of St Lawrence. He was kept well informed about the benefits of the east coast fisheries by the seigneurs who had fishing concessions on the coast and who knew exactly how much could be made from exports, not only in fish, but train oil, sealskin and whalebone.

Overall, the report exuded enthusiasm for the great potential of the country. In Britain this exuberance spilled over into the pages of the British press which extolled the virtues of the colony and showed it worthy of the attention of British entrepreneurs.[31] Along with this report Murray also sent a letter to Egremont, the secretary of state, which stated in no uncertain terms some of the most basic difficulties he

---

30 Public Archives of Canada, MG 8 EI: report of the government of Quebec and dependencies thereof 1762, 5 June 1762.

31 Philip Lawson, '"The Irishman's Prize": Views of Canada from the British Press 1760–1774', *Historical Journal*, XXVIII (1985), 586–7.

faced in the colony, and it was here that he declared the Canadians not yet ready for the typical forms of British colonial government.[32]

The proclamation had come as a great relief to the new British population in Quebec. It meant the end of martial law and the promise of an assembly. The British merchants of Quebec, many of whom had now been there since 1760, felt confident that the future held good prospects. Some had been in regular contact with London merchants and this contact extended past their business transactions into the realm of politics. Their petitions of 1764 and 1765 to the ministry in London hint at the economic prospects of Quebec and the obstacles that lay ahead. But by the terms of the proclamation, the merchants had lost the east coast fisheries and Pontiac's rising had effectively closed the west to most traders. The only mercantile occupation left untouched after 1763 was participation in the transatlantic trade as consignees, retailers or wholesalers of imported goods. But the costs of participation in this trade were high. Civil government did not bring merchants the freedom which they had hoped for; they still had to abide by the rules laid down by the governor and his council. Civil government under Murray brought no relief because it was the loyalty of the Canadians, and not the profits of the British in Quebec, which interested his governing council. The British merchants were upset at the speed of change, but the business of governing had to go on and merchants were forced to vent their spleen in a petition to the board of trade in December 1763.[33]

Murray corresponded regularly with the British ministry, with Burton at Montreal, and with George Ross his agent, in his first unofficial year as governor-in-chief. First of all there were the settling in problems to deal with, such as the need for an admiralty court (which he could not have because he had not yet been made admiral, though this was later rectified in his instructions). Murray argued that, although he had asked the lords of trade for a customs house and a collector, his hands were virtually tied because, even if smugglers were caught, there was no court of justice. Murray had been warned by the new customs deputies that these vessels had to be passed to the nearest admiralty court and, if anything happened *en route*, he would be held personally responsible. On three occasions Murray mentioned this fact to the lords of the treasury but received no reply.[34] In a series of letters to the treasury in 1762 he pointed out that large volumes of brandy were entering Quebec illegally despite his efforts to stop this practice, and, as it was a source of revenue for the crown, he suggested an imposition of a 6*d.* per gallon duty on brandy and an increase of 6*d.* on spirits.[35]

---

32 Public Archives of Canada, MG 11 Q Series, Vol.1: Murray to Egremont, 5 June 1762.
33 William L. Clements Library, Ann Arbor, Michigan, Shelburne Manuscripts, 66, ff. 1–4.
34 Public Archives of Canada, MG 11 Q Series, Vol. 1: Murray to Egremont, 27 Sept. 1763.
35 *Ibid.*, Treasury I, Vol. 421: seizure of foreign brandies 1762, Murray to the secretary of the lords of the treasury, 9 Mar. 1762; MG 40 D9 TS II, Vol. 419: Murray to the secretary of the lords of the treasury, 4 Nov. 1762.

The issue of liquor duties plagued him during his tenure as governor-in-chief and continued to confound the courts long after he was gone. Murray thought that this might well be the one and only way that he could legally, and without an act of parliament, raise revenue. Murray continued to collect the old French duties on wines and spirits, and, in return for a five per cent commission, John Gray was appointed collector in November 1761.[36] The main bone of contention within the merchant community at Quebec was whether or not the government had the right to collect duties or taxes when there was no assembly, and whether or not British brandy came within the definition of brandy at all, since French brandy was made from wine and the British spirit was made from corn. There was general agreement that the British equivalent had no right to be called brandy at all and that it could not be taxed, as it had not existed in Quebec during the French regime. The merchants quickly realized that they had a good argument and wasted no time in taking advantage of their sound legal position. In fact, in his instructions, Murray had been directed to do nothing to affect the liberty of the king's subjects, including imposing duties and taxes, and the merchants attempted to use this directive to their advantage by saying that maintaining the old French duties was wrong. John Gray informed Murray in November 1764 that merchants in Quebec were about to prosecute him for the amounts that he had already collected.[37] Murray swore to get Gray the best legal representation possible after receiving word from England that the original decision to collect the duty was to be upheld.[38] In London the government had its law officers Norton and de Grey take Murray's action over duties in Quebec under consideration, and they declared it legal in August 1764.[39] It had been clear from correspondence between Murray and the British ministry, after his report of 1762 reached London, that duties were seen as the most favoured way to raise funds to support the civil establishment, and there was nothing in the letters from Britain which could have led Murray to believe that this was going to be a problem. The government eventually decided that only the amount necessary to cover government expenditure would be raised from the collection of duties. Murray was disappointed because he had hoped the revenues would bring in enough funds to allow for some reconstruction in the colony. At the same time, the British response speaks volumes about how optimistic the government in London was about the expected windfall from liquor duties, although the revenues from this sector had fallen from £13,000 during the French regime to £3,000 under Murray.[40] A full account of all duties paid amounting to £11,897 Halifax currency was made public in the *Quebec Gazette* on 18 July 1765. This list in the *Gazette* gives

36   Public Archives of Canada, CO 42 MG 11 No. 1, Part 2, Vol. 4, p. 136: 16 Nov. 1764.
37   *Ibid.*, CO 42.2, Part 1, p. 107: Gray to Murray, 16 Nov. 1764.
38   Ibid., MG 23 GII, Vol. 1(2), 1763–5: Murray to Gray, Nov. 1764.
39   Lawson, *Imperial Challenge*, p. 56.
40   John Mappin, 'The Political Thoughts of Francis Maseres', McGill University M.A., 1968, p. 22.

an idea of the diversity of spirits imported. Colonial merchants felt that they were the victims of double taxation since most imports were from American ports.

A constant theme in Murray's letters to the British ministers was the chronic lack of funds. He complained to the lords of the treasury in July 1765 'that it is impossible without money to carry on the King's service' and, to emphasize this point, said that not only had he spent all the duties collected but he had also drawn on the treasury for £300 to pay some local merchants for services rendered.[41] Murray also wrote to the lords of trade, complaining of the impossibility of carrying on government in Quebec without a shilling. When they failed to respond, he contacted Halifax to bemoan the task of governing with no funds.[42]

Murray showed his impatience with the creakings of the government machinery in a tetchy letter to the treasury in the autumn of 1765, in which he pointed out that, because of their lack of response and failure to make provisions for the province, he had been obliged to draw on them through his agent George Ross for £3,000.[43] He also wasted no words in his explanation of why the duties had not been sufficient: there was approximately £3000 outstanding in liquor duties because of the pending court case. The privy council stepped in and tried to resolve the matter of duties. The merchants were put at arms length from the governor by following Murray's lead and Grenville's plan of 1764 which had suggested giving a resident receiver-general and his collectors the power to collect the revenues previously collected by the French government.[44] This order was sent to Quebec at the end of 1765.

Francis Maseres, who replaced George Suckling as attorney-general in 1766, argued, in a report for the government which was suppressed, that any taxation of the inhabitants of Quebec should be done by an act of parliament so that its legality could not be questioned. Once in Quebec, Francis Maseres issued writs against the merchants who had yet to pay their duty. In the meantime, the merchants continued with their legal challenge. Their case was heard in October 1766 by the newly appointed chief justice who asked the jury to return a special verdict allowing him to refer the whole matter to London. The jury refused and returned a verdict of not guilty and repeated this two years later when Maseres tried once more to resolve the issue.[45] The issue of the liquor duties and the difficulties of raising revenues to allow the civil government to run properly provide an opportunity to examine the way in which the London and Quebec administrations operated. Murray began collecting duties in 1760 and regulating the contraband trade by carrying on the French practice

---

41 Public Archives of Canada, MG 23 GII Series 1, Vol. (1)2: Murray to the lords commissioners of the treasury, 20 July 1765.
42 *Ibid.*, MG 11 Q Series, Vol. 2: Murray to the lords of trade, 3 Mar. 1765; MG 11 Q Series, Vol. 2: Murray to Halifax, 24 June 1765.
43 *Ibid.*, MG 23 GII Series 1, Vol. (1)2: Murray to the lords of the treasury, 31 Aug. 1765.
44 Sheffield City Library, Wentworth Woodhouse Muniments, R62–12. These manuscripts were used by permission of the Olive, Countess Fitzwilliam's Wentworth Settlement Trustees.
45 Mappin, 'Francis Maseres', p. 30.

of using duties to raise the necessary revenues. It took the government in London five years to say, yes, this procedure is what we want and we will give you the power to continue. At times the ministers did say that this practice was indeed what they wanted and on occasion they hinted that they may give the necessary powers to the governor-in-chief to collect duties. But the constant turnover of ministers and the changing circumstances in Quebec meant that approval of the tactics and the power to implement them never coincided. Once military rule was ended, the last thing the merchants wanted was to be taxed.

Remarkably enough there is little in Murray's correspondence about the economic impact of the closure of the west in 1763, followed by the restrictions imposed on the Indian trade in the interior and the loss of the east coast fisheries on which he had been so keen in the 1762 report. The decision to reduce the boundaries of Quebec was taken at the peace talks in February 1763. The province of Quebec was to revert to its original borders. All lands outside these boundaries and not in the hands of Indians were to be reserved to them; there was to be no white settlement there. Licences were to be issued free of charge to traders who applied to the governor. Traders were no longer to range far and wide but were forced to trade at designated posts. These restrictions dealt a blow to fur traders and trade merchants in Montreal which was the hub of the fur trade, but the impact was also felt at Quebec which was the emporium for the whole colony.[46]

The decision to change the structure of the fur trade had its origins in the report which Thomas Gage, lieutenant-governor of Montreal, sent to the secretary of state in 1762.[47] Once again this issue showed not only the British government's tendency to take its time making policy decisions but also its unerring ability to miss the mark altogether. It had created a policy best suited to the Albany merchants and applied it to an area unsuited for such restrictions. Early in 1761, Jeffrey Amherst, commander-in-chief for North America, proclaimed that trade with the Indian nations was now open. He put into place, along with Sir William Johnson, a four point plan for the regulation of the Indian trade that included the practice of licencing, trading only at military posts, fixed prices for goods and enforcement of the regulations by commandants at the posts.[48] The board of trade, after taking into consideration both Amherst's proposal and Gage's report which criticized monopolies, the sale of permits and the problem of trading in Indian villages, came up with its own plan.[49] All the elements of Amherst's plan were to be implemented except that the trade was to be supervised by an Indian department rather than be controlled by the military. When trade did reopen in the spring of 1765 licences were issued by the colonial governors,

46 E. E. Rich, *The Fur Trade and the Northwest to 1857* (Toronto, 1967), p. 133.
47 Marjorie G. Jackson, 'The Beginnings of British Trade at Michilimackinac', *Minnesota History*, XI (1930), 232.
48 M. G. Lawson, *Fur – A Study in English Mercantilism, 1700–1775* (Toronto, 1943), p. 52.
49 Jackson, 'British Trade', p. 234.

trade was restricted to the forts, prices were fixed and there was to be no wintering. Recognition of what this meant for business can best be seen in the 1766 memorial of Benjamin Frobisher to the board of trade on the state of the Indian trade. Frobisher not only pointed out the difficulties for Quebec merchants in the fur trade but also the ill effect the new policy was having on the Indians. He concentrated on explaining the need for wintering and said that 'perhaps this will appear incredible, but it can only be to those, who are entirely unacquainted with the situation of the country, and the advantages it has by nature, for carrying on such a commerce'.[50] Such well thought out memorials belied Murray's often vitriolic attacks against merchants he claimed were uneducated and ignorant.

By 1766 the board of trade, headed by Shelburne, investigated the petitions it had been receiving on the perils of a fur trade which did not allow wintering or monopolies.[51] The system in place had proved so inflexible that the government found itself under increasing pressure to make some changes and in 1767 Sir William Johnson, superintendent of the northern department, yielded on the question of wintering. This signalled the beginning of the end for the board of trade plan which by 1768 was in tatters. The management of Indian lands was handed over to the local control of the 13 colonies and Quebec, but this policy was reversed in 1774.

Murray was far more interested in the potential of the east coast fisheries and their loss was a source of immense aggravation to him, not least because of the number of petitions he received for the restoration of the boundaries.[52] From the earliest settlement of New France its inhabitants had fished the lower St Lawrence up to the coast of Labrador. It was the eastern equivalent of the fur trade, producing a rich mix of fish, seals, oil and whalebone, all of which could find ready made European markets. Seal skins, for instance, were used to cover boxes and trunks and the oil was used in lamps.[53] The posts were held by seigneurs and French factors, and some were sold to British merchants after 1763. The fact that a number of grants had been made to British merchants in 1763 only added to the general alarm when it was discovered that the coast of the gulf of the St Lawrence was to be part of the jurisdiction of the governor of Newfoundland. It was not until the Quebec Act of 1774 that the borders in the east and west were restored.

The case of Daniel Bayne and William Brymer offers some insights into the effect of the boundary change in the east. On 26 April 1763, Brymer was granted the use of the seal post at Cape Charles for four years. Brymer had access to considerable money and goods through his position as the Quebec agent for the army provisioners

50 William L. Clements Lib., Shelburne Manuscripts, Vol. 50, p. 351: Memorial on the state of the Indian trade, 10 Nov. 1766.
51 Jackson, 'British Trade', p. 252.
52 Public Archives of Canada, MG 11 Q Series, Vol. 2: petition on the loss of the fisheries, 14 Feb. 1764.
53 Peter Kalm, *Travels into North America* (1772), entries for 25, 31 Aug. 1750.

in London. He was able to use this position to help establish himself in the business which involved a large outlay of capital for building materials, labour costs, provisioning and maintenance of vessels. The governor of Newfoundland, Thomas Graves, was replaced in 1765 by Captain Hugh Palliser who took a different view of what he saw as interloping on the part of Quebec merchants; he did have the proclamation on his side. The boundaries after all had been reduced and the east coast was to become part of the British Atlantic possessions for the use of British fishermen. The boundary changes were not enforced until the arrival of Palliser. All land in Labrador was made crown property on 8 April 1765 and private property was no longer recognized. Bayne and Brymer had their post destroyed and its equipment seized, taken to Newfoundland and auctioned off. They were also warned that they were not welcome and their vessels would be seized if they attempted to work the area again.[54]

The partnership spent the next five years petitioning the king and suing Palliser for £5,000. The case moved from the board of trade to the privy council to the court of king's bench to the lords commissioners of trade and plantations and back to the privy council. In the end, however it was left to Lord Hillsborough to decide the issue. He found that, while there was nothing wrong with the original grant, neither was there anything illegal in Palliser's actions. Bayne and Brymer had won, but because Palliser had been acting within his powers the government paid his damages. The tribulations of Bayne and Brymer sent the message to others that, however lucrative this business had been in the past, there was no percentage in investing in it now until the borders were reconstructed. The British government had originally listened to submissions from fishermen at Bristol and other outports before enforcing the boundary decisions and again ignored the petitions from merchants and officials in the colony. Murray had handed out land grants in good faith and, after merchants had invested valuable time and money, they had been cast adrift with their losses. Murray was neither powerful enough to take on the British ministers nor able to square off against Palliser. This case offers another insight into the muddle that was colonial policy at this local level.

In the midst of the acrimony between the merchants and the governor on the issues of duties and economic policy, the Stamp Act came into force on 1 October 1765. The Stamp Act affected an incredible range of mercantile activity from licences for public houses to newspaper advertisements, legal documents and, more importantly for Quebec, ships' clearances. In Quebec, the only newspaper, the *Quebec Gazette* shut down completely while the act was in effect. The new duty had raised the price at the news-stand from a half dollar to two dollars.[55] That Quebec merchants were not in favour of the imposition of any such tax can be seen in a letter

54 G. O. Rothney, 'The Case of Bayne and Brymer', *Canadian Historical Review*, XV (1934), 270.
55 W. B. Kerr, 'The Stamp Act in Quebec', *English Historical Review*, XLVII (1932), 648.

published in the *Quebec Gazette* of 28 July 1766, which stated that they were further hampered because they could not even protest against the act because they had no assembly and therefore no political voice. It was a good opportunity to express their displeasure with the governor. The merchants thought that Murray could give them an assembly but was being deliberately obstinate. Their perceptions were wrong, because, in reality, the board of trade had in 1765 dealt with the question as it related to the collection of revenues and in a report that was never made public, admitted that it did not foresee an assembly for Quebec in the near future.[56] The merchants had no quarrel with this act in principle, but they did oppose both the duty on dry goods and the liquor duties because they were part and parcel of the French regime. It is possible that given a choice between fighting over the three per cent duty, the liquor duty, and the stamp duty which was gathering on the horizon like a thundercloud, it was more politic to accept those measures passed by parliament. Yet, strangely enough, of the three duties it was the Stamp Act that fell by the wayside while the merchants expended their energies railing against the others. Contemporary experts consulted by the government on possible opposition to the Stamp Act in Canada responded that unless the crown had specifically exempted the colony, parliament could 'tax them as they want'.[57] The Stamp Act was repealed on 18 March 1766 after less than one month of debate in both houses.[58] Merchants in Quebec added this to the list they were compiling against the governor.

Murray's description of the merchants at Quebec as 'Licentious Fanatiks' has become the phrase most commonly associated with his troubles at Quebec.[59] Yet is this a fair analysis of Murray's views on the whole mercantile community after the conquest? At various times he had no fault to find with the merchants and was even in their debt. His relationship with them as a group cannot be considered without understanding all the other crises in the colony, including the basic problem of running the government with no funds, looking after the welfare of the army in its various garrisons and trying to maintain the goodwill of the Canadians. On the other hand, it is easy to overstate the importance of the petitions against Murray and take these statements of his arbitrary rule at face value. The British merchants in Quebec were not always aware of decisions taken in London nor did they fully understand the workings of that government. Murray was not likely to go to the merchants and tell them that he was having some trouble enforcing his orders. Merchants in Quebec were well aware of the seasonal nature of shipping and, therefore, of information, and chose deliberately to ignore the political reality that distance from London meant delays in sending and implementing instructions. The time lag in communicating

56 Lawson, *Imperial Challenge*, p. 70.
57 Sheffield City Lib., Wentworth Woodhouse Muniments, R65–5d 1765: Dr Fothergill's consideration on American affairs laid before Lord Dartmouth.
58 P. D. G. Thomas, *British Politics and the Stamp Act Crisis* (Oxford, 1975), pp. 233–43.
59 Public Archives of Canada, MG 11 Q Series, Vol. 2: Murray to the lords of trade, 29 Oct. 1764.

orders and requests did not just affect the colony in its relationship with London but also affected internal communication links.

Murray survived the merchants' fury in 1765, but, with the dismissal of the Grenville ministry in July 1765, his patrons were gone. It no longer mattered, as his sister had put it only months before, that 'you are the darling of your countrymen and in high favour with the present ministry'.[60] Murray was not unaware of the political turbulence in London, for he had been warned of as much in a letter that 'things are in confusion here, disunion and faction in the administration and opposition'.[61] Anyone connected to Lord Bute was in danger but Murray was not an immediate victim because his friend Cramahe was in London trying to counteract the petitions of the Quebec merchants. He sent Murray a list of hints on how best to serve his cause, including some very down to earth instructions such as writing to the first lord of the treasury and president of the board of trade by name, and he told him who to contact in case of any extraordinary matters. It was in this letter too that he warned Murray not to let his frustration show by hinting at resignation.[62]

The Cramahe letters show just how difficult it was to obtain an audience with the appropriate politicians in London. After one month Cramahe had still not been received by Lord Bute and had spent all his time sitting outside doors. Waiting became a normal occurrence and when finally received it was usually for only a brief meeting which ended in promises that the right people would read his reports. Even Grenville had not read the account of revenues that Cramahe carried with him and so there was not much to discuss when they met in February 1765.[63] It was not until August, after the change of ministry, that Cramahe was received by Lord Dartmouth. Compared to the Grenville ministry, the new administration worked quickly, but, even so, Cramahe was told by Mellish, secretary of the treasury, that the administration had so much business on hand that they could not review the question of the Quebec revenues for a while.[64] By this time Cramahe suspected that his friend Murray might be in trouble and wrote to tell him to 'act only as requires immediate decision and refer such as can admit of delay home for instruction but give your own thoughts along with it'. He also warned in August 1765: 'You cannot be too cautious.'[65] He was still in London when the ministry changed and realized that this meant starting the process all over again. His letters show Canada was not high on the new ministry's list of priorities, yet it would be this Rockingham administration which began to look seriously for a practical settlement for Quebec. Murray welcomed the words of advice from Cramahe because he failed to understand why he was left in

60 Scottish R.O., GD32/24/18: Mary Murray to James Murray, 19 Feb. 1765.
61 *Ibid.*, GD32/24/19: unknown correspondent to Murray, Mar. 1766.
62 Public Archives of Canada, MG 23 GII Series 1, Vol. 3: Cramahe to Murray, 12 Jan. 1765.
63 *Ibid.*: Cramahe to Murray, 9 Feb. 1765.
64 *Ibid.*: Cramahe to Murray, 10 Aug. 1765.
65 *Ibid.*

limbo, receiving few responses from the government on basic questions of common concern. As late as November 1765, Murray complained to his friend, the member of parliament, James Oswald, that he had not heard from the board of trade since August 1764 and it was now over one year later.[66] Murray was asked to return to London to give an account of the colony and acquitted himself admirably. After a short stay in London he decided against returning to Quebec. He was replaced, temporarily at first, by Guy Carleton whose position became permanent in 1768.

Murray presided over the transition from French to British rule and from military occupation to the establishment of civilian government. He left the colony with a stable economy despite the difficulties raised by the boundary changes of 1763. As governor-in-chief he wanted the colony to be able to pay for its own civil government and, with the backing of the government in London, he began a system of duties that dovetailed with the old French system. Murray received his salary only once while in the colony, but he had to use it to pay the salaries of his civil officers and, as a result, ended up in great financial embarrassment.

Like the British ministers he served, Murray's vision of Canada's future was based on the arrival of a wave of responsible settlers and diligent merchants, the willingness of French Canadians to embrace and understand the intricacies of British colonial government, and the economic viability of the colony. Murray, this much maligned Scot, was responsible for the well-being of Quebec. He not only tried to follow in the footsteps of other colonial governors, but he also had a vision of Quebec's place in the empire and conscientiously tried to ensure that its people would receive only the best from Britain. He also ensured that the colony would not go unforgotten in the quest of British ministers to define what being part of an empire really meant.

Murray's actions in Quebec have been misjudged and misunderstood by historians because of a flawed reading of the political and economic structure of both the colony and British politics in the 1760s. Political instability in Britain, the pressure to deal first with events in India and then America, and the uncertainty caused by the Catholic question are important in any discussion of post-conquest Quebec. But it is impossible to understand Quebec without understanding what Murray was trying to achieve; the creation of a well-run colony that could prove itself central to the future needs of Great Britain. He was part of a long tradition of the Scots *élite* who served the crown in imperial service. He had an extra incentive to make things run smoothly – he wanted to prove his loyalty and ensure his place at the top – and he did have reason to worry because his family's political influence did not extend to the Rockingham circle. Murray was undone by the lack of vision among the ruling *élite* and by its political instability.

---

[66] *Ibid.*: Murray to James Oswald, 11 Nov. 1765.

But he was also witness to a positive political change for Quebec, the fall of the Grenville ministry and the rise of the Rockinghams. This new administration took steps to regulate the Quebec situation and accomplished more in its brief time in power than anyone had in the previous five years. To assist in this task Murray was asked to return and give an account of the civil administration. He was never tarred by any hint of wrongdoing but decided not to return to the colony. With this decision, Quebec lost the man who had guided it through defeat and set it on the path to recovery. In the process, for reasons good or bad, he had made certain that the British ministry should take notice of Quebec and include it in their plans for the expanding empire.

13

Opium and Imperial Expansion:
The East India Company
in Eighteenth-Century Asia*

RICHARD CONNORS

While Britons had been trading with the peoples of the Indian subcontinent since the founding of the 'Company of Merchants of London, Trading into the East Indies' – the English East India Company – in 1600, it was not until the 1750s, with Clive's victories at Arcot, Chandernagore and Plassey, that India became significant enough within the 'British political consciousness' to inspire widespread artistic representations of interaction between east and west.[1] Samuel Foote's satirical and highly popular play *The Nabob* reminded those attending the theatre in 1772 that Indian wealth and ways of life could corrupt weak willed Britons, while Henry Vansittart's *Narrative of Transactions in Bengal, 1760–1764* (1766), Alexander Dow's *History of Hindustan* (1768), and Robert Orme's *History of the Military Transactions of the British Nation in Indostan* (1763–78) quenched some of the thirst for information about a mysterious Indian subcontinent and helped to propel India into the mental worlds of Hanoverian Britons.[2] This growing cultural interest in India and Asia was

---

* This is a revised version of a paper given at the 'International Conference on Opium in East Asian History', held at the Joint Centre for Asia Pacific Studies, University of Toronto, in May 1997. I am grateful to the participants for their comments and for the advice of Chris Bayly and Peter Marshall.

1 On this point see B. Allen, 'From Plassey to Seringpatam: India and British History Painting, *c.* 1760–1800', in *The Raj. India and the British 1600–1947*, ed. C. Bayly (1990), pp. 26–37. For a broader discussion of the intellectual and ideological influences of Anglo-Indian interaction upon Britain and India see B. Cohn, *Colonialism and its Forms of Knowledge* (Princeton, 1996); J. J. Clarke, *Oriental Enlightenment. The Encounter between Asian and Western Thought* (1997); E. Said, *Culture and Imperialism* (1993); P. J. Marshall and G. Williams, *The Great Map of Mankind. Perceptions of the New Worlds in the Age of Enlightenment* (Cambridge, Mass., 1982), pp. 67–184; T. R. Metcalf, *The New Cambridge History of India, III, 4: Ideologies of the Raj* (Cambridge, 1994); P. J. Marshall, 'Taming the Exotic: The British and India in the Seventeenth and Eighteenth Centuries', in *Exoticism in the Enlightenment*, ed. G. S. Rousseau and R. Porter (Manchester, 1990), pp. 46–65; and R. Connors, 'Colonial Knowledge and Cultural Imperialism', *Journal of Historical Sociology* (forthcoming).

2 Scholars are becoming increasingly interested in the construction of imperial knowledge. See C. A. Bayly, *Empire and Information. Intelligence Gathering and Social Communication in India, 1780–1870* (Cambridge, 1996); Cohn, *Colonialism and Its Forms of Knowledge*; S. Tammita-Delgoda, 'Disillusionment and Decline: A Picture of the Changing Face of British India', *Indo-British Review*, XXI, 36–41; B. Anderson, *Imagined Communities* (revised edn., 1991); R. Inden,

well illustrated in 1778 by the directors of the English East India Company when they commissioned the Italian artist Spiridion Roma to paint the ceiling of their rather stark headquarters on Leadenhall Street, London. Roma's rendering, entitled 'The East offering its Riches to Britannia', captured the *mentalité* of the Company merchants and was a mixture of imperious patriotism and the purely commercial.[3] Britannia, seated on a rock with a lion at her feet, protects the East India Company which is depicted as children. The genius of the Ganges pours forth at her feet. Under the supervision of Mercury, the Roman god of acquisitiveness and thievery (commerce), various Asian provinces present tribute to Britannia. In the centre an Indian woman offers strings of jewels and pearls. Another woman, presumably China, grasps a large porcelain urn and a chest of tea. Other figures approach with bundles of textiles, calicos and muslin. In the distance an East Indiaman riding at anchor prepares to set sail with these treasures, a potent reminder to the viewer that Britain was the beneficiary of this outpouring of Indian and Asian wealth and that Britannia and her subjects were part of an increasingly integrated global trade network focussed upon London.[4]

Curiously missing from Roma's painting were the chests of Indian opium which increasingly helped to finance and drive British imperial expansion in the Indian subcontinent and south-east Asia in the late eighteenth and early nineteenth centuries. For if there was one product that reflected the riches and mystique of the east it was opium. Like their Roman forebears,[5] eighteenth-century Britons appreciated opium for its medicinal qualities – Samuel Johnson took it to alleviate headaches, while Robert Clive relied upon it to counter chronic stomach pain.[6] However, in the

Imagining India (Oxford, 1990); N. Dirks, 'Castes of Mind', *Representations*, XXXVII (1992), 56–78; M. H. Edney, *Mapping an Empire. The Geographical Construction of India, 1765–1843* (Chicago, 1996).

3   B.L., F. 245, Spiridion Roma, 'The East Offering its Riches to Britannia'. On the relationship between art and imperial expansion see, P. Lawson, ' "Arts and Empire Equally Extend": Tradition, Prejudice and Assumption in Eighteenth-Century Press Coverage of Empire', *Journal of History and Politics*, VII (1989), 119–46; P. Godrej and P. Rohatgi, *Scenic Splendors. India Through the Printed Image* (1989); M. Archer and R. Lightbown, *India Observed. India as Viewed by British Artists 1760–1860* (1982); and J. MacKenzie, *Orientalism. History, Theory and the Arts* (Manchester, 1995).

4   On this voluminous subject see, K. N. Chaudhuri, *The Trading World of Asia and the English East India Company* (Cambridge, 1978); D. Hancock, *Citizens of the World. London Merchants and the Integration of the British Atlantic Community, 1735–1785* (Cambridge, 1995); H. Bowen, *Elites, Enterprise and the Making of the British Overseas Empire, 1688–1775* (1996); P. Curtin, *The Rise and Fall of the Plantation Complex* (Cambridge, 1990); A. L. Stinchcombe, *Sugar Island Slavery in the Age of Enlightenment. The Political Economy of the Caribbean World* (Princeton, 1995); *The Rise of Merchant Empires. Long-Distance Trade in the Early Modern World, 1350–1750*, ed. J. Tracy (Cambridge, 1990); and *The Political Economy of Merchant Empires. State Power and World Trade, 1350–1750*, ed. J. Tracy (Cambridge, 1991).

5   On this subject see J. Scarsborough, 'The Opium Poppy in Hellenistic and Roman Medicine', in *Drugs and Narcotics in History*, ed. R. Porter and M. Teich (Cambridge, 1995), pp. 4–23.

6   See, e.g., J. Ausiter, *An Essay on the Effects of Opium, Considered as a Poison. With the Most Rational Method of Cure, Deduced from Experience, etc.* (1763); G. Young, *A Treatise on Opium,*

Hanoverian mind opium was also, as Johnson characteristically reminded Boswell, a symbol of the orient which was to be adopted with great care.[7] These reservations aside, the growing involvement of the British in Indian opium production and the Asian opium trade mirrored their increasing imperial presence in the Indian Ocean and the orient. In the early eighteenth century the East India Company was primarily a commercial enterprise which bought and sold and imported and exported goods and commodities from its 'factories' in Bombay, Calcutta and Madras, and was incapable of exerting a great deal of influence on the dynamics of power and the internal politics of the subcontinent and the moribund Mughal empire.[8] In the aftermath of the events which culminated in the defeat of Nawab Sirajuddaula and his French allies at Plassey, the Company increasingly involved itself in, and was increasingly drawn into, the intricate and internecine world of politics in Bengal and Bihar.[9] By 1815, the Company had acquired, and continued to maintain, the most powerful armies in India and governed, formally or informally, Bengal, much of the upper Ganges basin and extensive areas of eastern and southern India.[10] Equally important, the Company was expanding its spheres of political and economic power and becoming a major player in Asia as late eighteenth-century conflicts in Arabia, Mauritius, the Moluccas and Java attest.[11] By the turn of the nineteenth century, representatives of the East India

Founded upon Practical Observations (1753); J. Jones, *The Mysteries of Opium Reveal'd* (2nd edn., 1701). For a broader discussion of this subject consult, A. H. Maehle, 'Pharmacological Experimentation with Opium in the Eighteenth Century', in *Drugs and Narcotics in History*, ed. Porter and Teich, pp. 52–76; and V. Berridge and G. Edwards, *Opium and the People. Opium Use in Nineteenth-Century England* (New Haven, 1987).

7   J. Boswell, *The Life of Samuel Johnson LL.D.* (2nd edn., 1793). On 23 March 1783 Boswell 'breakfasted with Dr, Johnson, who seemed much relieved, having taken opium the night before. He however protested against it, as a remedy that should be given with the utmost reluctance, and only in extreme necessity.'

8   J. F. Richards, *The New Cambridge History of India, I, 5: The Mughal Empire* (Cambridge, 1993); and S. Subrahmanyam, 'The Mughal State – Structure or Process? Reflections on Recent Western Historiography', *Indian Economic and Social History Review*, XXIX (1992), 291–321.

9   The 'Plassey revolution' has been the subject of considerable discussion since 1757. See, for example, S. Chaudhuri, 'Sirajuddaulah, the English Company and the Plassey Conspiracy – A Reappraisal', *Indian Historical Journal*, XIII (1986–7), 111–34; *The History of Bengal, 1757–1905*, ed. N. K. Sinha (Calcutta, 1967), pp. 7–8; and K. Chatterjee, *Merchants, Politics and Society in Early Modern India. Bihar: 1733–1820* (Leiden, 1996), pp. 101–27.

10   P. J. Marshall, *The New Cambridge History of India, II, 2: Bengal: The British Bridgehead, Eastern India 1740–1828* (Cambridge, 1987), pp. 93–136; K. de Schweinitz jr., *The Rise and Fall of British India. Imperialism as Inequality* (1983), pp. 86–117; G. J. Bryant, 'The Military Imperative in Early British Expansion in India, 1750–1785', *Indo-British Review*, XXI, 18–35; D. M. Peers, *Between Mars and Mammon. Colonial Armies and the Garrison State in Nineteenth-Century India* (1995); P. Marshall, 'Empire and Authority in the Late Eighteenth Century', *Journal of Imperial and Commonwealth History*, XV (1987), 105–17; E. Ingram, *Commitment to Empire. Prophecies of the Great Game in Asia, 1797–1800* (Oxford, 1981); idem, 'Timing and Explaining Aggression: Wellesley, Clive, and the Carnatic, 1795–1801', *Indo-British Review*, XXI, 104–15; idem, *In Defence of British India. Great Britain in the Middle East, 1775–1842* (1984).

11   C. Bayly, *Imperial Meridian. The British Empire and the World 1780–1830* (1989); idem, *The New Cambridge History of India, II, 1: Indian Society and the Making of the British Empire*

Company in Asia were no longer merely men of business, they were overlords of an empire which rivalled that of ancient Rome. Not only did contemporaries – such as Edward Gibbon, Richard Price, Josiah Tucker, William Robertson, Adam Smith and Edmund Burke – reflect upon the virtues and similarities of these empires,[12] but Britons also relied upon classical Greek and Roman architecture in all sorts of building projects (from the Arcadian classical buildings at Stowe and the development of Edinburgh's New Town to Wellesley's extravagant building programme for Calcutta) to reveal their new found imperial authority.[13] These processes of expansion are well known since a great deal of imperial historiography has focussed upon them and related subjects, and has taught us much about the rise and fall of the East India Company and the growth of the British empire.[14]

While scholars offer a variety of contending interpretations for the rise of the British *imperium*,[15] most would agree that the union of the powers of state and the wealth of the propertied, broadly conceived, helped propel Hanoverian Britain into the imperial club.[16] Indeed, it has been recently suggested by Thomas Brady jr. that

(Cambridge, 1988); D. Judd, *Empire. The British Imperial Experience, From 1765 to the Present* (1996), pp. 1–8; Linda Colley, *Britons. Forging the Nation 1707–1837* (New Haven, 1992).

12 Recent writings on the perspectives of these individuals and the ideology of empire include, Metcalf, *Ideologies of the Raj*; P. Miller, *Defining the Common Good. Empire, Religion and Philosophy in Eighteenth-Century Britain* (Cambridge, 1994); A. Pagden, *Lords of All the World. Ideologies of Empire in Spain, Britain and France, c.1500–c.1800* (New Haven, 1995); E. H. Gould, 'American Independence and Britain's Counter-Revolution', *Past and Present*, 154 (1997), 107–41; J. G. A. Pocock, 'Political Thought in the English-Speaking Atlantic, 1760–1790: (i) The Imperial Crisis', and *idem*, 'Political Thought in the English-Speaking Atlantic, 1760–1790: (ii) Empire, Revolution and the End of Early Modernity', in *The Varieties of British Political Thought, 1500–1800*, ed. J. G. A. Pocock, G. J. Schochet and L. G. Schwoerer (Cambridge, 1993); *Edward Gibbon and Empire*, ed. R. McKitterick and R. Quinault (Cambridge, 1997); *William Robertson and the Expansion of Empire*, ed. S. J. Brown (Cambridge, 1997); and F. G. Whelan, *Edmund Burke and India. Political Morality and Empire* (Pittsburg, 1996).

13 On this subject see Godrej and Rohatgi, *Scenic Splendours*; D. Watkin, *English Architecture. A Concise History* (1979), pp. 124–53; *The Cambridge Cultural History, Volume 5: Eighteenth-Century Britain*, ed. B. Ford (Cambridge, 1991); J. Summerson, *Architecture In Britain, 1530–1830* (5th edn., 1969); P. Borsay, *The English Urban Renaissance. Culture and Society in the Provincial Town, 1660–1760* (Oxford, 1989).

14 For a recent discussion of the historiography on this voluminous subject see P. Lawson, *The East India Company. A History* (1993).

15 The literature on this subject is immense. The following works briefly summarize the field: D. Cannadine, 'The Empire Strikes Back', *Past and Present*, 147 (1995), 180–94; P. Lawson, 'The Missing Link: The Imperial Dimension in Understanding Hanoverian Britain', *Historical Journal*, XXIX (1986), 747–51; A. Burton, 'Who Needs the Nation? Interrogating "British" History', *Journal of Historical Sociology*, X (1997), 227–48; P. Buckner, 'Whatever Happened to the British Empire?', *Journal of the Canadian Historical Association*, IV (1993), 3–32; V. Kiernan, *Imperialism and Its Contradictions* (1995); P. Wolfe, 'History and Imperialism: A Century of Theory, from Marx to Postcolonialism', *American Historical Review*, CII (1997), 388–420.

16 For discussions on the early modern British state see J. Brewer, *The Sinews of Power. War, Money and the English State, 1688–1783* (1989); P. Corrigan and D. Sayer, *The Great Arch. English State Formation as Cultural Revolution* (Oxford, 1985); Colley, *Britons*; *The Imperial State at War. Britain from 1688–1815*, ed. L. Stone (1994); M. Braddick, 'The Early Modern English State and

imperial expansion readily facilitated the development of centralized western European states by reminding us that 'nations [were] postecclesiastical Europe's solution to the problem of mobilizing populations for imperial and other purposes' and that 'the first nations were the first imperial peoples – England, Spain, Portugal, the Netherlands and France – and other peoples invented nations either to imitate the imperial states or to get free of them'.[17] At the centre of these complex processes of state-building and imperial expansion were the great chartered enterprises such as the East India, Royal Africa and Hudson's Bay Companies. Granted the rights of monopoly to conduct trade in certain parts of the globe, during the eighteenth century these merchant venturers slowly became representatives of not only British economic, but also British imperial interests abroad. Despite this transformation, the Companies continued to seek out profitable trading opportunities and marketable commodities. In the case of the English East India Company this was particularly true after their mid-eighteenth-century successes in Bengal.[18]

One commodity which attracted the interest of East India Company servants in Bengal and Bihar was Indian opium. Other products such as pepper, salt, cotton, saltpetre, silk, coffee and indigo proved profitable to the Company, but opium was the first to fall completely under the control of the Company in Bengal, Bihar and Orissa.[19] As the British began to increase their control over Bengal, they sought to monopolize the produce of the poppy fields of the region. Unlike other agricultural products or foodstuffs, little or no Indian opium was imported into Britain during the period.[20] The trade had traditionally been restricted to the Indian subcontinent and Asia and European traders, first the Dutch and then the British, were content to keep

the Question of Differentiation, from 1550–1700', *Comparative Studies in Society and History*, XXXVIII (1996), 92–111; M. Mann, *The Sources of Social Power* (2 vols., Cambridge, 1986–93), I, 451–516; S. Clark, *State and Status. The Rise of State and Aristocratic Power in Western Europe* (Montreal, 1995), pp. 80–119. On the subject of property in the eighteenth century see P. Langford, *Public Life and the Propertied Englishman* (Oxford, 1991); J. Innes, 'Politics, Property and the Middle Class', *Parliamentary History*, XI (1992), 286–92; *Early Modern Conceptions of Property*, ed. J. Brewer and S. Staves (1995). For specific discussions of the relationship between the state, property and empire see, N. F. Koehn, *The Power of Commerce. Economy and Governance in the First British Empire* (Ithaca, 1994); H. V. Bowen, *Revenue and Reform. The Indian Problem in British Politics, 1757–1773* (Cambridge, 1991); P. J. Cain and A. G. Hopkins, *British Imperialism. Innovation and Expansion 1688–1914* (1993); A. Porter, '"Gentlemanly Capitalism" and Empire: The British Experience since 1750?', *Journal of Imperial and Commonwealth History*, XVIII (1990), 265–95.

17 T. A. Brady jr., 'The Rise of Merchant Empires, 1400–1700: A European Counterpoint', in *The Political Economy of Merchant Empires*, ed. J. D. Tracy (Cambridge, 1991), p. 148.

18 This subject is discussed in detail in P. J. Marshall, *East India Fortunes. The British in Bengal in the Eighteenth Century* (Oxford, 1976); idem, 'Empire and Opportunity in Britain, 1763–75', *Transactions of the Royal Historical Society*, 6th ser., V (1995), 111–28; H. Furber, *Private Trade and Company Profits in the India Trade in the Eighteenth Century* (Aldershot, 1997); Lawson, *The East India Company*; Chaudhuri, *The Trading World of the Asia*; C. Bayly, *Rulers, Townsmen and Bazaars. North Indian Society in the Age of British Expansion* (Cambridge, 1982).

19 Chaudhuri, *The Trading World of Asia*, pp. 313–83.

20 H. Furber, *Rival Empires of Trade in the Orient 1600–1800* (Minneapolis, 1976), p. 257.

it that way. Furthermore, opium was not only a commodity which created private fortunes in Asia, but it also proved a primary means for transmitting home imperial revenues through trade with South-East Asia and China. Therefore, the destinies of the British in India and in the Far East were inextricably linked not merely to their increasing domination of the trade routes and commercial potency of early modern Asia – with which K. N. Chaudhuri and R. Mukherjee have made us familiar – but also with the monopolization of the opium trade in India and the domination of it in Asia.[21] The fortunes of the East India Company also reveal the somewhat obvious, but often neglected point, that in the case of British interests in Asia the flag followed trade.

The story of the British and the Asian opium trade in the nineteenth century has been the focus of considerable scrutiny by numerous scholars. While the question of how the English gained control of the Bengal and Bihar poppy fields in the eighteenth century has also been discussed by historians, recent research on the related issue of the tea trade reveals that the place of Indian opium in the imperial trade nexus requires recapitulation and re-evaluation. This paper explores the means by which the English East India Company and its employees monopolized the procurement and the sale of opium throughout Bengal, which was in the eighteenth century the principal producer of the drug in Asia. Secondly, it considers the relationship between Company fortunes in the Indian opium trade and, as Huw Bowen has shown, their misfortunes in the China tea trade in the later eighteenth century.[22] Finally, these economic developments provide the background against which one can consider the debate about the monopolization of opium precipitated within the Company and in Britain itself. During this intense discussion which took place within and without the Company boardrooms and parliament, a number of arguments were made to justify Company involvement in Indian politics and in the opium trade in particular.

With the defeat of Sirajuddaula (nawab of Bengal) and the conquest of Bengal and Bihar in 1757, the Company not only impressed itself upon North India and the Mughal empire, it also ensured that the opium trade, like most other trades in the area, would eventually pass into English hands. These aggrandizing tendencies were reinforced in October 1764 when the Company and its Indian allies defeated the forces of the Mughal Emperor Shah Alam II, Shujauddaula (the wazir of Awadh) and Mir Kasim (nawab of Bengal since 1760) at Buxar. In recognition of its power, the Mughal emperor offered the Company the office of *diwan* which made them revenue collectors and regional administrators of Bengal, Bihar and Orissa.[23] As a result of the

---

21 K. N. Chaudhuri, *Asia before Europe. Economy and Civilisation of the Indian Ocean from the Rise of Islam to 1750* (Cambridge, 1990); *idem, Trade and Civilisation in the Indian Ocean. An Economic History from the Rise of Islam to 1750* (Cambridge, 1985); *idem, The Trading World of Asia*; R. Mukherjee, *The Rise and Fall of the East India Company* (New York, 1974).

22 See H. V. Bowen, 'Tea, Tribute, and the East India Company *c*.1750–*c*.1775', above ch. 8.

23 For the influence of these events on Britain, see Bowen, *Revenue and Reform*, pp. 5–29; *idem*, 'A Question of Sovereignty? The Bengal Land Revenue Issue, 1765–67', *Journal of Imperial and*

elevation of the Company to the office of *diwan* of these three imperial provinces, Bihar poppy cultivation (which was confined to the central Gangetic tract of land about 300 miles in length and 200 miles in depth, bound on the north by the Himalayan mountain range and on the south by the Ramgarh uplands and forests) fell under the scrutiny, and later the control, of Company servants. Much of the Bihar opium was produced in the environs surrounding Patna and was transported by Indian merchants and middlemen to the factories at Patna, Chandernagar and Calcutta. Late seventeenth-century estimates of Bihar opium production put the figure at roughly 4,300 chests of the drug of approximately 140 lbs each (602,000 lbs). Of this output only about one per cent was used in Bihar, while about ten per cent was sent to other parts of Bengal. Exports to the north and west, to centres such as Agra and Allahabad, which were the principal distribution centres for the north Indian market, accounted for 39 per cent. The remaining 50 per cent was exported to other parts of the subcontinent and abroad to international markets such as Indonesia, through which – and by country traders – some Bihar opium reached consumers in China.[24]

While the Company had been marginally involved in the opium trade before 1757,[25] British success at Plassey presented individual servants of the East India Company with the opportunity quickly to displace the Dutch and Indian merchants who dealt in opium.[26] Furthermore, because of their political authority in the three provinces, the English were also able to encourage and coerce the producers and the suppliers of the drug into dealing directly and exclusively with them. This was initially accomplished by Company employees acting as private traders who claimed the privilege of monopoly of the drug for a given locality. Inevitably, this also meant that the Company servants obtained the opium at below market prices since they were the only individuals to whom producers could sell their product. In 1761 William McGwire, the chief of the English factory at Patna, extricated from Ram Narain (naib subahdar of Bihar) a *parwana* (a letter of authority and entitlement) stating that he

Commonwealth History, XVI (1988), 155–76; P. Lawson, 'Parliament and the First East India Inquiry, 1767', *Parliamentary History*, I (1982), 99–114; P. Lawson and B. Lenman, 'Robert Clive, the "Black Jagir", and British Politics', *Historical Journal*, XXVI (1983), 801–29. For a discussion of the broader implications of the granting of the *diwani* on India, see Chatterjee, *Merchants, Politics and Society in Early Modern India*, pp. 101–27; and R. Guha, *Dominance without Hegemony. History and Power in Colonial India* (Cambridge, Mass., 1997), pp. 1–5.

24 This information is drawn from O. Prakash, 'Opium Monopoly in India and Indonesia in the Eighteenth Century', *The Indian Economic and Social History Review*, XXIV, (1987), 64–5. On the subject of the Dutch trade in opium and the Indonesian archipelago see O. Prakash, *The Dutch East India Company and the Economy of Bengal, 1630–1720* (Princeton, 1985), pp. 54–60, 145–56.

25 See for example *Fort William – India House Correspondence and Other Contemporary Papers Relating Thereto (Public Series), Vol. I: 1748–1756*, ed. K. K. Datta (New Delhi, 1958), pp. 330–1, 801: 24 Feb. 1748/9 and 7 Dec. 1754 which discuss 'Dutch pretences to an exclusive trade in opium'.

26 B.L., India Office Library, L/Parl/2/15, Appendix 57 to the 'Ninth Report from the Select Committee appointed to take into consideration the State of the administration of justice in the provinces of Bengal, Bihar and Orissa', 25 June 1783.

possessed the exclusive privilege to contract with opium producers for the purchase of opium. We know of this train of events because McGwire tried to have this arrangement authorized by Calcutta and even offered a share of the profits to the governor, Henry Vansittart. Vansittart disapproved of the scheme and ordered McGwire to withdraw the *parwana*.[27] Moreover, it was clear that the directors of the Company in London had also heard of McGwire's actions because they informed Vansittart and his colleagues at Fort William, Calcutta, in March 1763 that

> we have received intimations of an extraordinary nature from the Dutch Company that Mr McGwire when Chief of Patna, made an attempt to obtain an exclusive grant for himself of the Ophium trade there, this is a matter of such consequence, that we direct it to be enquired into and if there appear good grounds to suspect he has made such an attempt, he must expect to meet with our resentment. As we think if such a step had been taken it is an insult upon our Authority, for any servant to presume to sollicit separate Grants or Privileges of Trade for his own Advantage and emolument.[28]

The directors clearly did not wish to see Company servants assuming the authority of the Company without their approval, particularly when it did nothing for the firm's finances. By undermining McGwire's monopoly, Vansittart perceived, as he informed Warren Hastings, that he had made 'all the world ... free to buy opium'.[29] Vansittart had actually disciplined William McGwire before the correspondence from the directors in London had arrived at Fort William.

Vansittart's actions owed something to the fact that from April 1762 he feared that Anglo-Indian relations in Bengal were deteriorating and that 'the unjust authority exercised all over the Country in the English name deserve[d] immediate attention'.[30] In the immediate circumstances more was at stake in Bengal than the private profits of unscrupulous Company servants in Patna. McGwire's misfortune at the hands of his Company masters did not dissuade his successor at Patna, William Ellis, from compelling local producers to provide him opium at preferential prices and from warning off Dutch, English or other private traders. Vansittart again found it necessary to discipline his subordinates over their intervention in the Patna opium trade. Writing to Hastings he commented, 'you remember how much I censured Mr McGwire last year for an attempt to monopolize it [opium], this year Mr Ellis has orders to provide fifty chests for the Company and that is all'.[31] To add insult to injury Ellis not only took potential opium profits from the Company coffers, but his activities in Patna had incensed Mir Kasim, nawab of Bengal (1760–3), and in part, contributed to the outbreak of hostilities between the Nawab and the Company in July

---

27 B.L., I.O.L., Bengal Public Consultations, Range I, vol. 36, ff. 274–81: 3 Oct. 1763.
28 *Fort William – India House Correspondence and Other Contemporary Papers Relating Thereto (Public Series), Vol. III: 1760–1763*, ed. R. R. Sethi (New Delhi, 1968), p. 197: 9 Mar. 1763.
29 B.L., Add. MS 29132, ff. 224–5: George Vansittart to Warren Hastings, 27 June 1762.
30 *Ibid.*, f. 169: H. Vansittart to W. Hastings, 2 May 1762. These concerns are also evident in Vansittart's writings on his time in India. See H. Vansittart, *A Narrative of the Transactions in Bengal 1760–1764*, ed. A. C. Banerjee and B. K. Ghosh (Calcutta, 1976).
31 B. L., Add. MS 29132, ff. 224–5: H. Vansittart to W. Hastings, 27 June 1762.

1763.[32] The general conduct of Company officials in the three imperial provinces not only antagonized the nawabs of Bengal and the Mughal emperor, but English interventions into the opium trade infuriated their European rivals, the French and Dutch East India Companies.[33] These Dutch and French protestations over the drug trade met with little sympathy from the English merchants who merely countered by offering to sell the Europeans a fixed and limited number of chests of opium. For example, the Dutch Company saw its share of Bengal opium drop from approximately 1,200 chests per year in the 1750s to 430 chests in 1765.[34]

In the same year, 1765, English Company factors at Patna agreed to hold collectively the monopoly on opium for it was 'one of the principal emoluments of the factory'.[35] At this stage, therefore, the monopoly was 'owned as a resource for persons in office; was managed chiefly by the civil servants of the Patna factory, and for their own benefit'.[36] Profits from the opium monopoly still did not find their way onto the Company ledgers. The factors themselves did not take an active part in the actual trade in opium, but sold it to prospective vendors who included Indian merchants, other private English traders and the Dutch Company. The gross profits earned by the Patna factors was somewhere between 200 and 400 per cent. Opium, which could be produced for about 200 rupees a chest, was selling at Calcutta in 1772 for 550 rupees, in 1773 for 650 rupees and in 1774 for 800 rupees.[37] Surprisingly this trade structure endured until the early 1770s, despite the fact that it was unacceptable to the East India Company and to Indian, European and English private traders alike.

This arrangement was torn asunder in 1773 when, upon the advice and guidance of Warren Hastings, the English Company assumed the monopoly on opium for itself.[38] In April 1772, Hastings was made governor-general with the aim of reorganizing the structure of administration in British India. To lend greater stability and continuity to the decision making process at India House, the directors in London were offered appointments of four years rather than annual elections to the position. The voting rights of stockholders were also restricted, but the most important

32 These events are discussed in Marshall, *Bengal. The British Bridgehead*, pp. 83–9.

33 Discussion of Dutch and French complaints about the English opium monopoly can be found in *Fort William – India House Correspondence, III*, pp. 197, 451, 473, 556–7: 9 Mar. 1763, 30 Oct. 1762, 14 Feb., 19 Dec. 1763; *Fort William – India House Correspondence and Other Contemporary Papers Relating Thereto (Public Series), Vol. XVI: 1752–1781: Secret and Select Committee*, ed. A. Prasad (New Delhi, 1985), pp. 138, 350, 370, 399: 16 May, 3 Aug., 20 Dec. 1775, 20 Mar. 1776.

34 These statistics are drawn from Prakash, 'Opium Monopoly in India and Indonesia', pp. 75–6.

35 Bodl., Papers of George Vansittart, Dep. b. 103, f. 7: Vansittart to Warren Hastings, 11 Dec. 1772. I would like to thank Professor P. J. Marshall for drawing this archival material to my attention.

36 B.L., I.O.L., L/Parl/2/15, p. 35 under heading 'Opium'.

37 Bodl., Dep. b. 93, p. 38: G. Vansittart to J. Price, 25 Oct. 1772; p. 132: G. Vansittart to J. Holland, 15 Apr. 1773; Dep. b. 94, p. 70: G. Vansittart to R. Palk, 12 Mar. 1774.

38 B.L., I.O.L., L/Parl/2/15. H. R. C. Wright, *East-Indian Economic Problems in the Age of Cornwallis and Raffles* (1961), pp. 106–89.

changes took place in India. The presidencies of Bombay and Madras were brought under the control of Calcutta which, in turn, gained a supreme council composed of government appointees who were overseen by Warren Hastings himself. This was no easy task for Hastings, not only because of the difficulties the British experienced with neighbouring and increasingly hostile nawabs, but also because of the factiousness of the council itself.[39] On the subject of the opium trade, Hastings clearly saw the need for some form of monopoly, though he also acknowledged the virtues of free trade. After evaluating the issue, Hastings submitted to the Bengal council three options for dealing with the production of poppy and the sale of opium. Firstly, he suggested that the Company could offer the concession to an individual or group of merchants. This amounted to contracting out the monopoly. A second option was for the Company to take over the whole process of producing, manufacturing and selling the drug. Thirdly, it was suggested that all restrictions could be lifted and a free trade in opium could prevail. Hastings then discussed the advantageous and disadvantageous aspects of each plan. Monopoly conditions inherent in options one and two could hinder the growth of the industry and prevent the product from selling at its true worth. However, Hastings inveighed more heavily against a free trade in the drug for he noted that 'it is not a necessary of life, but a pernicious article of luxury, which ought not to be permitted but for the purposes of foreign commerce only, and which the wisdom of government should carefully restrain from internal consumption'.[40] On 23 November 1773, the council resolved to relieve the Patna council of its opium monopoly, and thereafter the Company assumed the right of exclusive purchase of the drug in Bengal, Bihar and Orissa and then arranged for its sale to merchants through public auctions held in Calcutta. Indian intermediaries were not removed from the trade completely, for after 1773 they were appointed on a yearly basis as contractors to collect the opium and deliver the chests to the Company.[41] Public notices were posted inviting interested individuals to apply for the position; most often, however, it was filled by patronage appointees of the governor-general.[42] The initial contract in 1773 was granted to Meer Muneer, an aging Indian merchant who had acted as a contractor for the Patna factors, and Ram Chand Pandit, an young entrepreneur who came to dominate Patna's export market in the 1770s and

39 Lawson, *East India Company*, pp. 116–25.
40 B.L., I.O.L., L/Parl/2/15, Appendix 59A: Extract of the Proceedings of the President and Council at Fort William in Bengal, in their Revenue Department, 15 Oct. 1773.
41 On the importance of Indian agents in the opium trade see, J. F. Richards, 'The Indian Empire and the Peasant Production of Opium in the Nineteenth Century', *Modern Asian Studies*, XV (1981), 59–82; and S. Sanyal, 'Ram Chand Pandit's Report on Opium Cultivation in Eighteenth-Century Bihar', *Bengal Past and Present*, LXXXVII (1968), 181–9.
42 Fine examples of these notices can be found in B.L., I.O.L., L/Parl/2/15, Appendix 62: Extract, Bengal Revenue Collections, 23 May 1775.

1780s.[43] In 1775, the contract passed into the hands of Warren Hastings' friend, Richard Griffith, for the next two years, and thereafter it was regularly given, though not without debate and infighting, to patrons of the Bengal council. Griffiths's contract was followed by a three year appointment for John Mackenzie, a colleague of both Hastings and Philip Francis, a member of the supreme council. In 1781, it was decided to extend the contracts to four year terms and not surprisingly Stephen Sulivan (the son of Lawrence Sulivan who was then chairman of the court of directors in London who was closely tied to Hastings) was granted the monopoly. In fact, these appointments, especially that of Sulivan, were subjected to considerable scrutiny during the impeachment proceedings conducted against Hastings in the late 1780s. After Hastings' departure from Bengal in 1785, it was resolved to alter the system slightly, replacing the patronage system by offering the office to the highest bidder at a public auction.

These administrative adjustments were made to the monopoly in the hope that the Company would extract more wealth from the industry. However, the production process and trade in opium changed little in these decades. The contractors received a pre-arranged price for the chests of opium. It was common practice to advance half of the total payment since the contractor was expected to do the same for the *ryots* or peasant producers of the poppy. This owed something to the fact that poppy cultivation and opium extraction and production were labour intensive and unprofitable for the vast majority of the peasant cultivators.[44] To ensure a quality product all opium was collected and delivered to Calcutta in a crude state where it was then manufactured under the supervision of the Company.[45] The majority of the Company controlled opium was purchased by private merchants or 'country wallahs' (a name for those who traded between India and other places in the east) who were often Indian or British, but also Dutch, Portuguese, Armenian and Arabian. They then

43 *Ibid.*, L/Parl/2/15, Appendix 61: Extract, Bengal Revenue Consultations, Translation of a Contract under the Seals of Mahomed Muneer, and Ram Chunder Pundit; dated 16th Rumran in the Bengal Year 1180, or 2 Dec. 1773. On the careers of Muneer and Pandit see Chatterjee, *Merchants, Politics and Society in Early Modern India*, pp. 164–76, 220–36; and Sanyal, 'Ram Chand Pandit's Report'.
44 *The Cambridge Economic History of India Vol. 2: c.1757–1970*, ed. D. Kumar and M. Desai (Cambridge, 1983), pp. 146, 312–15; K. Banerjee, 'Grain Traders and the East India Company: Patna and its Hinterland in the Late Eighteenth and Early Nineteenth Centuries', *Indian Economic and Social History Review*, XXIII (1986), 403–29; Bayly, *Rulers, Townsmen and Bazaars*, p. 289. For broader implications of the opium trade on Indian society see, B. Chandra Barui, 'The Smuggling Trade of Opium in the Bengal Presidency, 1793–1817', *Bengal Past and Present*, XCIV (1975), 123–36; G. N. Chandra, 'Some Facts about Opium Monopoly in Bengal Presidency', *Bengal Past and Present*, LXXVI (1957), 123–36; K. P. Mishra, 'Growth of Opium Culture in Banares, 1775–1795: A Quantitative Study', *Bengal Past and Present*, XCI (1972), 17–24.
45 R. Prasad, *Some Aspects of British Revenue Policy in India, 1773–1833* (New Delhi, 1970), pp. 148–50; G. Watt, *A Dictionary of the Economic Products of India* (6 vols., 1892), VI, pt. I, 37–40; B. Chowdhury, *Growth of Commercial Agriculture in Bengal, 1757–1900* (Calcutta, 1964).

shipped the chests of opium for the 'country trade' to Malaya, the Dutch East Indies or China.[46]

The opium enterprise was undoubtedly profitable for the English East India Company, the contractors and other intermediaries participating in the business. From the perspective of the Company, an obvious advantage was in terms of an accretion to the revenues of Bengal. After 1775, the profits from opium were treated as excise or tax revenues rather than as receipts from the trade. Evidence available in the documentation of the Company suggests that between 1774 and 1784 there was an upward trend in the revenue from opium. From £14,250 in 1773–4, the revenue grew to £56,225 in 1775–6, to £68,912 in 1781–2 and to £78,300 in 1783–4.[47] As a proportion of total Bengal revenues, the revenues from opium are estimated to have accounted for 5.2 per cent in 1792, 7 per cent in 1812, 10 per cent in 1822 and as much as 20 per cent in 1842.[48] Opium was of even greater significance to Company merchants and traders as a commodity to utilize in offsetting the cost of China tea, a product for which Britons of the Atlantic archipelago seemed to have unquenchable thirst. It would seem that the eighteenth-century British addiction to tea matched that of opium users in Asia. The figures on tea imported into Hanoverian Britain are truly staggering, as Philip Lawson and Huw Bowen have shown, and help to put the Company's need to sell marketable commodities like opium into better perspective.[49] In the 1690s only a few hundred pounds of the best China teas were imported into Britain by the Company to help eliminate a glut in the sugar market. Thereafter the supply of, and the demand for tea, grew at a meteoric rate. In 1717, 200,000 lbs. came to London from Canton. By 1757 this figure had climbed to three million lbs. and 25 years later, in 1772, 12 million lbs. were imported. Moreover, because of stipulations in the Company charter, to maintain its monopoly it had to bring in the product every year and as a result, by the outbreak of the American Revolution, the

---

46 On this voluminous subject see D. K. Bassett, 'British "Country" Trade and Local Trade Networks in the Thai and Malay States, c.1680–1770', *Modern Asian Studies*, XXIII (1989), 625–43; J. R. Rush, 'Opium in Java: A Sinister Friend', *Journal of Asian Studies*, XLIV (1985), 549–60; A. C. Sahu, 'Genesis and Growth of Indo-Chinese Opium Monopoly under East India Company', *Journal of Indian History*, LVII (1979), 163–9; T. Chung, 'Foreign Mud on Good Earth: British Opium Enterprise vis-a-vis China', *China Report*, XVII (1981), 9–41; and R. K. Newman, 'Opium Smoking in Late Imperial China: A Reconsideration', *Modern Asian Studies*, XXIX (1995), 765–94; Prakash, 'Opium Monopoly', pp. 74–80; D. Washbrook, 'South Asia, the World System and World Capitalism', *Journal of Asian Studies*, XLIX (1990), 479–508.

47 B.L., I.O.L., Home Miscellaneous Series, MS 209, no. 3, p. 167.

48 T. Chung, 'The British-China-India Trade Triangle (1771–1840)', *The Indian Economic and Social History Review*, XI (1974), 422–3.

49 P. Lawson, 'Tea, Vice and the English State, 1660–1784', in *idem, A Taste for Empire and Glory. Studies in British Overseas Expansion* (Aldershot, 1997), item XIV, pp. 1–21; Bowen, *Revenue and Reform*, pp. 121–2; Chaudhuri, *The Trading World of Asia*, pp. 385–406; H. C. Mui and L. H. Mui, 'Smuggling and the British Tea Trade before 1784', *American Historical Review*, LXXIV (1968), 44–73; Furber, *Rival Empires of Trade*, pp. 125–46. The statistics which follow are drawn from Lawson and Bowen.

Company had stockpiled in warehouses on the banks of the Thames some 17 million lbs. of the addictive leaf.[50] Despite the loss of 2.5 million tea-drinking, freedom-loving American colonists in 1783, the Company continued to import massive amounts of China tea.[51] For Company merchants in the 1790s, the sale of Bengal opium directly to China was a natural step in balancing the Company ledgers. It was timely that the Company appropriated the opium monopoly in Bengal, Bihar and Orissa since their massive investments in Bohea tea were proving so problematic in the north Atlantic world. Between 1773 and 1784 Company profits from opium amounted to £534,009.[52] While this figure may not have offset the total purchase price of China tea by the Company, it went some way to improving a dismal financial situation. Nevertheless, Indian opium production was not the answer to the tea problem. One of the solutions to that problem was to be found by botanical imperialists such as Joseph Banks and those tending to the empire's fledgling botanical gardens, for they seized on the potential of producing tea on plantations in India.[53] In the nineteenth century, the Company did indeed begin producing tea in India and continued to sell opium for the Indonesian and Chinese markets, thereby reducing their dependence on the Canton tea connexion, while maintaining an outlet for Indian opium sales.

Notwithstanding these fortuitous developments for the British in India and Asia, the acquisition of the monopoly on Bengal opium production by the Company was not without controversy. Monopolies in the hands of Company servants had often been condemned by the court of directors and by parliament for fear that it lead to price fixing and in the case of poppy production to the oppression of *ryots* or agricultural labourers. In Bengal, Henry Vansittart feared that the monopolization of opium would sew seeds of hostility between the Company and the Indian *élites*, merchants and the peasant population. This was a serious consideration since Indian merchants and bankers played a crucial role in financing British ventures in the subcontinent and Asia. Antagonizing Bengali bankers and merchants merely to satisfy a few Company servants was a risk Vansittart was not willing to take in the early

---

50 Bowen, *Revenue and Reform*, p. 122.
51 H. C. Mui and L. H. Mui, *The Management of Monopoly. A Study of the East India Company's Conduct of its Tea Trade 1784–1833* (Vancouver, 1985); Chung, 'The Britain-China-India Trade Triangle', pp. 411–31.
52 B.L., I.O.L., Home Miscellaneous Series, MS 209, no. 3, p. 167.
53 On these matters see D. P. Miller and P. H. Reill, *Visions of Empire. Voyages, Botany and Representations of Nature* (Cambridge, 1996); J. Gascoigne, *Joseph Banks and the English Enlightenment. Useful Knowledge and Polite Culture* (Cambridge, 1994); D. Mackay, *In the Wake of Cook. Exploration, Science and Empire, 1780–1801* (1985); L. H. Brockway, *Science and Colonial Expansion. The Role of the British Royal Botanical Gardens* (New York, 1979); Z. Baber, *The Science of Empire. Scientific Knowledge, Civilization and Colonial Rule in Colonial India* (Albany, 1996), pp. 168–70; R. Drayton, 'Science and the European Empires', *Journal of Imperial and Commonwealth History*, XXIII (1995), 503–10; M. Vicziany, 'Imperialism, Botany and Statistics in Early Nineteenth-Century India: The Surveys of Francis Buchanan', *Modern Asian Studies*, XX (1986), 625–60.

1760s as his perspective on McGwire and Ellis clearly shows.[54] In Britain, broader and often more philosophical issues were at stake. Adam Smith condemned the effects of monopolies on trade arguing that they 'derange[d] the natural distribution of the stock [produce and goods] of [a] society'.[55] He elaborated upon this subject at some length in *The Wealth of Nations*, but also specifically discussed the East India Company and opium. Smith argued that while the Company had only recently assumed a principal role in the governance of Bengal, he feared that by the 'arts of oppression' they would ignore the interests of the indigenous population or those of their customers. He illustrated this by arguing that monopolies drove up the prices of commodities. More ominously, the Company also tampered with rice and food cultivation in India to increase the production of poppy. On 'occasion ... a rich field of rice or other grain has been ploughed up, in order to make room for the plantation of poppies; when the chief [factor] foresaw that extraordinary profit was likely to be made by opium'.[56] A free market in goods, unhindered by monopolistic practices would alleviate these concerns because the East India Company would be in no position to dictate the terms of the opium trade either to peasant producers or to purchasers of the drug. There were individuals within the Company who agreed with this Smithian perspective. Philip Francis objected to Warren Hastings' move to monopolize opium for the Company in 1773.[57] Instead he advocated free cultivation and sale of the poppy and a 30 per cent exportation tax on opium. Objections to the monopoly were again raised in 1775, when a new council general was appointed to look into the drug trade. Strong doubts about the propriety of the opium monopoly were voiced by Sir John Clavering, George Monson and Philip Francis. Their objections were taken seriously in London and the directors of the East India Company left the council 'at liberty to throw the trade open, under a Duty, if they thought it practicable'.[58] Clavering, who had most severely censured the monopoly, wavered for he 'supposed it impossible, with the Power and Influence which must attend British Subjects in all their transactions, that monopoly could be avoided, and he preferred an avowed monopoly which brought benefit to Government to a virtual engrossing, attended with Profit only to Individuals'.[59] Francis continued to staunchly

---

54 S. Chakrabarti, 'Intransigent *Shroffs* and the English East India Company's Currency Reforms in Bengal, 1757–1800', *Indian Economic and Social History Review*, XXXIV (1997), 69–94; K. Chatterjee, 'Collaboration and Conflict: Bankers and Early Colonial Rule in India, 1757–1813', *Indian Economic and Social History Review*, XXX (1993), 283–310; C. Bayly, 'The British Military-Fiscal State and Indigenous Resistance: India 1750–1820', in *The Imperial State at War*, ed. Stone, pp. 322–54; and for a general discussion of power relationships see J. C. Scott, *Domination and the Arts of Resistance. Hidden Transcripts* (New Haven, 1990).

55 A. Smith, *An Inquiry into the Nature and Causes of the Wealth of Nations* (Glasgow edn., 2 vols., Oxford, 1976), II 631–2.

56 *Ibid.*, p. 636.

57 On Philip Francis consult, T. H. Bowyer, 'India and the Personal Finances of Philip Francis', *English Historical Review*, CX (1995), 122–31; Marshall, *East India Fortunes*, pp. 184–6, 207–8.

58 B.L., I.O.L., L/Parl/2/15.

59 *Ibid.*

oppose the Company's policy of monopolization, be it of opium or any other commodities, and highly recommended their abolition in a plan which he subsequently sent to the court of directors in London. In the end, this power struggle within the council had little effect on the opium trade. The importance of the trade in the ledger books and for the economic vitality of the Company ensured the maintenance of the monopoly. Hastings' stance on the monopoly was reinforced by the fact that opium was practically the only commodity that could be exported directly to China from Bengal to provide the supercargoes with the funds necessary to purchase the vast amounts of tea needed to satisfy demand back in Britain.

General criticisms like those held by Francis were also levelled at the right of any monopoly held by the Company. There were those in Britain who feared the wealth which the Company acquired from the traffic in opium. As one commentator put it in a letter to the *Public Advertiser* on 20 December 1776, if luxury was the only benefit to be derived from oriental trade, 'it would be better that Britain allow France the honour of it'. If wealthy individuals like Clive and Hastings returning from the east were not prevented from 'contaminating by their vices the manners of the Mother Country what benefit will arise from all the riches of the East?' What lent substance to these concerns was the fact that these monopolies (on both opium and tea) were on commodities which were exotic in the truest sense of the word. These goods came from the 'orient' and produced vast amounts of money for those involved in their trade. By the late 1770s, this combination proved unfortunate for the Company because there were those in Britain who had become apprehensive of the influences that territorial aggrandizement in the Americas and Asia, and wealth creation in the east, were having upon British society.[60] These objections included moral concerns about the treatment of eastern peoples and their cultures. For example, in 1773, one commentator noted that 'in the east the laws of society, [and] the laws of nature have been enormously violated. Oppression in every shape has ground the faces of the poor defenceless natives; and tyranny in her bloodless form has stalked abroad.'[61] These concerns were also eloquently elaborated upon by Edmund Burke.[62] Concerns were also raised about the political and constitutional implications of imperial conquest upon Britain from the vast amounts of overseas wealth entering the country, particularly because many saw it as the spoils of nabobbery, ungentlemanly conduct and dubious monopolistic business practices in

60 See Lawson, *East India Company*, pp. 103–43; Bowen, *Revenue and Reform*; and *idem*, '"Dipped in the Traffic": East India Stockholders in the House of Commons, 1768–74', *Parliamentary History*, v (1986), 39–53.
61 *London Magazine*, (1773), p. 12, cited in P. Langford, *A Polite and Commercial People. England 1727–1783* (Oxford, 1989), p. 534.
62 See, e.g., his speech on Amas Ali Khan, 30 July 1784, in *Pre-Revolutionary Writings of Edmund Burke*, ed. I. Harris (Cambridge, 1993), pp. 277–97. See also *The Writings and Speeches of Edmund Burke. V: India: Madras and Bengal 1774–1785*, ed. P. Marshall (Oxford, 1981).

Asia. Moreover, the hostilities to these commodities revealed 'a deep rooted resistance to changes in the traditional way of conducting trade and exchange'.[63]

Similarly Edmund Burke attacked any monopolistic rights of the East India Company, not just those pertaining to opium, because open trade was more beneficial to all parties, but also on deeper philosophical grounds. Like the vast majority of his fellow countrymen Burke did not object to the trade in opium itself (since the discussion on opium had not yet become a moral or legal issue) but he argued that Company officials acted in arbitrary ways when they bought or sold the opium monopoly as patronage to favoured friends below the market price without advertising its availability to other potential purchasers. This was one of the central points made during the protracted discussion upon proceedings to impeach Warren Hastings in the house of commons.[64] Burke was thoroughly convinced that the Company had used its political authority in India systematically to undermine the sub-continent's economy in the blind pursuit of profit. In Burke's opinion, one of the finest examples of this careless and callous approach to its political and fiscal responsibilities, was the way in which contracts for the opium monopoly had been dispensed by supreme council while under Hastings' leadership. The case of Sulivan's opium contract was specifically drawn upon by Burke to illustrate this dubious and destructive behaviour.[65] Despite the acrimonious debates about Company policy in India which took place during the long impeachment trial of Hastings, and Burke's repeated requests that Englishmen should profit without oppressing Indians, it was agreed that Britons and the East India Company should stay on the subcontinent. One reason Burke was so unsuccessful in his attack on Hastings and monopolies was because the right to control the opium trade was seen by Hanoverian Britons as a form of private property. The principle of private property had significance not only in social and economic terms, but also, as John Locke reminded his late seventeenth- and eighteenth-century readers of *Two Treaties of Civil Government*, the defence of private property was the crucial responsibility of government. The preservation and protection of private property, even monopolies on Indian opium, were cornerstones of eighteenth- and nineteenth-century political and legal thought, as responses to the

63 Lawson, 'Tea, Vice and the English State', p. 14. On this topic see also, P. Lawson and J. Philips, '"Our Execrable Banditti": Perceptions of Nabobs in Mid-Eighteenth-Century Britain,' *Albion*, XVI (1984), 225–41; and J. Raven, *Judging New Wealth. Popular Publishing and Responses to Commerce in England 1750–1800* (Oxford, 1992), pp. 221–48.

64 On this subject see P. J. Marshall, *The Impeachment of Warren Hastings* (Oxford, 1965); Whelan, *Edmund Burke and India*, pp. 83–6; N. Sen, 'Warren Hastings and British Sovereign Authority in Bengal, 1774–80', *Journal of Imperial and Commonwealth History*, XXV (1997), 59–81.

65 Burke's observations on the opium trade can be found in his 'Ninth report of the Select Committee Appointed to take into Consideration the State of the Administration of Justice in the Provinces of Bengal, Bihar and Orissa', 25 June 1783, reprinted in Burke, *Writings and Speeches: Madras and Bengal*, pp. 270–86; and in *The Writings and Speeches of Edmund Burke. VI: India: The Launching of the Hastings Impeachment 1786–1788*, ed. P. Marshall (Oxford, 1991).

Boston Tea Party revealed in the 1770s, and as British actions later reminded the Chinese during the opium wars of the mid-nineteenth century.

In the face of these growing concerns about the nature of territorial expansion and trade policy, the East India Company offered a number of justifications for their conduct in the subcontinent and for their monopoly on opium. First, the policy was justified on the general and mercantilist grounds that monopolies were needed to protect British interests against incursions from foreign Companies, primarily the Dutch and French East Indian Companies. More specific reasons which were peculiar to the commodity itself were also suggested:

> to the nature of the trade; and to the state of the country; the security against adulteration; the preservation of the excessive home consumption of a pernicious drug; the stopping of excessive competition, which, by an over-proportioned supply, would at length destroy the market abroad; the inability of the cultivator to proceed in an expensive and precarious culture, without a large advance of capital; and ... the incapacity of private merchants to supply that capital on the feeble security of wretched farmers.[66]

These arguments were often drawn upon to justify the activities of the Company in a trade about which even its own directors in London had grave reservations. Throughout the 1760s, East India House ordered Company officials on the ground in Bengal to foster positive relations and continue to trade opium with the Dutch and French Companies.[67] Ironically, the directors endorsed the monopoly so as to ensure the growth of poppy and production of opium, but objected to becoming distributors. Such an attitude was evident when Hastings and Bengal merchants sent a cargo of opium to Malacca and China on the Company accounts. The ships, the *Betsy* and *Nonsuch*, were also armed by Company soldiers and loaded with approximately 3,000 chests of opium. The *Betsy* was captured by a French privateer before the majority of her cargo had been sold and the *Nonsuch* ran into problems when it actually reached Canton. The *Nonsuch* arrived to find that the price of the drug was low, and 'being a business altogether new to us' and 'prohibited' by the Chinese authorities, the supercargoes handled the matter with trepidation. The venture was a disaster and the Company lost £14,000.[68] The directors in London condemned the transaction and noted that 'under any circumstances it is beneath the Company to be engaged in such a clandestine trade, we therefore, hereby positively prohibit any more opium being sent to China on the Company's account'.[69] Thus, they forbade the shipping of opium

---

66 B.L., I.O.L., L/Parl/2/15, Appendix 59B.

67 See, e.g., correspondence between London and Fort William. *Fort William – India House Correspondence and Other Contemporary Papers Relating Thereto (Public Series), Vol. IV: 1764–66*, ed. C. S. Srinivasachari (New Delhi, 1962), p. 17, 44–5, 78: 22 Feb., 16 May 1764, 15 Feb. 1765.

68 M. Booth, *Opium. A History* (1996), pp. 111–12.

69 B.L., I.O.L., L/Parl/2/15, Appendix 87. This extract can also be found in *Fort William – India House Correspondence and Other Contemporary Papers Relating Thereto (Public Series), Vol. IX: 1782–1785*, ed. B. A. Salatore (New Delhi, 1959), p. 61: 12 July 1782.

to China, preferring instead to establish trading stations in Indonesia from which 'whatever opium might be in demand by the Chinese, the quantity would readily find its way thither without the Company being exposed to the disgrace of being engaged in an illicit commerce'.[70] There were plenty of private traders willing to make the trip from Bengal to China and Indonesia, even if the Company was not. While Hastings worried little about the effects of opium upon the Chinese and Asian populations, he looked upon Indian opium consumption in a different light. One reason for maintaining the monopoly was to prevent the use of the drug in India itself. As Hastings urged, opium 'was not a necessary of life', and one which should not be encouraged within the empire. Thus profits could be made from the sale of the drug, while at the same time the population of Bengal would be insulated from the effects of opium production and addiction.

It was also argued that the 'dispositions and the habits of the natives' necessitated a monopoly.[71] Vansittart's observations further elaborated on the subject by noting that 'had every merchant free liberty to make [the Indian suppliers and producers] advances, they would receive money in abundance, they would dissipate a part of it, [and] they would be unable to manufacture opium sufficient to complete their Engagements'.[72] In order to justify the monopoly, the Company went so far as to create an elaborate myth that a state monopoly of opium had existed under the Mughals. In a letter sent to Dutch merchants at Hugli, Governor-General John Macpherson of the Calcutta council noted that

> the opium of this country was always managed by the native government [Mughal empire] as a monopoly and we have the evidence before us of a person who held a considerable office at Buxbandar for above sixty years, and who is now alive that opium and saltpetre were purchased by the foreign companies as they could from the persons enjoying the exclusive privilege of this monopoly in the like manner as by private merchants.[73]

Scholarship on the Dutch and Mughal trade hardly suggest the existence of a state monopoly or arrangements between Patna merchants and suppliers of opium. The English were really seeking to avoid criticisms of unfair trading which were being levelled at them from other Europeans, the Dutch, who found the monopoly an inconvenience to their supply of opium. These concerns by foreign competitors fell on deaf ears, as did domestic criticisms of the opium trade, for ultimately the strongest justification for the practice lay in the value of the trade for the imperial economy. Successive Bengal governors and their councils convincingly argued that abolishing

70 Parliamentary Papers, 1787, cited in J. Rowntree, *The Imperial Drug Trade* (1905), pp. 17–18.
71 Algemmen Rijkearchief, Hooge Regeering Batavia 211 (unfoliated): John Macpherson and Council at Calcutta to Eilbracht and van Cittars, members of the Dutch Council at Hugli, 8 Sept. 1785, cited in Om Prakash, 'Opium', p. 66.
72 B.L., I.O.L., L/Parl/2/15, Appendix 57, Ninth Report: Extract, Bengal Revenue Collections, 23 Nov. 1773.
73 Macpherson to Eilbracht and van Cittars, 8 Sept. 1785, cited in Om Prakash, 'Opium,' p. 67.

the monopoly would glut the market, that profits would drop as a result of over-production and competition, and finally that the East India Company would have no control over the trade and would not be able to protect the peasant producer from exploitative middlemen and merchants.[74] Officials in Calcutta also informed the directors in London that, despite metropolitan reservations, the trade of Bengal and Bihar opium for Chinese tea was 'not a matter of choice but necessity',[75] because there was little else China wished to purchase. This fact was underlined in 1793 when China's Emperor Ch'ien Lung reminded Lord Macartney that 'we have never valued ingenious articles, nor do we have the slightest need for your country's manufactures'.[76] In such circumstances Company officials in India perceived that they had little choice but to continue to encourage the production of the drug in British India and the carriage by private traders of opium to waiting markets in China.

The East India Company presented these arguments for the monopolization of the opium trade in Bengal and Bihar to counter growing concerns in Britain about the virtues of such privileges. These justifications helped to ensure that the Company and its investors continued to profit from the drug trade. While opium may have proven the key to paradise for the Romantic poets of the early nineteenth century and to Thomas de Quincey in particular,[77] it offered unremitting hard labour and most often grinding poverty for the peasant producers of Bengal and Bihar's poppy fields. For the merchants of the Company it remained a readily marketable monopolized commodity which could be sold to sustain and increase their imperial presence in Asia. In the short term, the profits of the opium trade and the *imperium* it helped create were seen in the architectural and aesthetic edifices such as Roma's ceiling painting adorning East India House and in the burgeoning ledgers kept in Leadenhall Street, London. In the long term, opium assisted in recasting Britain's perceptions of the peoples of Asia, and in so doing precipitated and perpetuated an imperial state of mind that conceived of buildings like Wellesley's Government House in Calcutta and which figured so prominently in the daily life of successive generations of British imperialists and Indian colonial subjects on the shores of the Bay of Bengal for the next 150 years.

---

74 B.L., I.O.L., L/Parl/2/15, Appendix 57 and Appendix 59.
75 *Fort William – India House Correspondence, IX*, p. 378: 5 April 1783.
76 *An Embassy to China. Being the Journal Kept by Lord Macartney during his Embassy to the Emperor Ch'ien-lung, 1793–1794*, ed. J. L. Cranmer-Byng (1962), pp. 337–41.
77 Thomas De Quincey, *Confessions of an Opium Eater* (1865), pt. 2, in which he famously wrote, 'thou hast the keys of Paradise, oh just, subtle, and mighty opium!'

14

'Bill of Rights Morris':
A Welsh Wilkite Radical and Rogue
Robert Morris (1743–1793)[*]

PETER D. G. THOMAS

'The man was a pretended enthusiast, and offered himself to the Court as a martyr, and to the people for one of their representatives. The Ministers refused him the first honour, and the people the second.' Horace Walpole thus dismissed the attempt in 1770 of Robert Morris, a young supporter of John Wilkes, to emulate his mentor. His comment is characteristically unfair – doubly so; there was nothing feigned about the radicalism of Robert Morris, who remained an opponent of authority, an anti-establishment figure in modern parlance, throughout his life; and there is no evidence that Morris cherished any political ambitions for himself. Posterity has paid little heed to a man whose behaviour made him notorious at the time for both political and personal reasons.[1] Morris outdid Wilkes in his political zeal, for he was impetuous whereas Wilkes was calculating. And certain aspects of his private life seemed to contemporaries to be more reprehensible than anything Wilkes had done. To suggest that Robert Morris outdid Wilkes himself in some respects has a wider connotation than that of mere politics.

'[His] pride is to be thought one of the lower class of the people.' So noted the *Middlesex Journal* about Robert Morris on 19 March 1771. That was inverted snobbery with a vengeance, or a misleading attempt to claim appropriate political credentials. For Morris came of gentry stock, was educated at Charterhouse and Oxford, and had by then gained a substantial inheritance from a father who had been a prosperous industrialist.

---

* This paper has been prepared for publication by Mrs Margaret White, secretary of the Department of History at Aberystwyth, who herself has warm memories of Philip Lawson as a postgraduate student.

1 Horace Walpole, *Memoirs of the Reign of King George the Third*, ed. G. F. Russell Barker (4 vols., 1894), IV, 155. Morris does not appear in the *Biographical Dictionary of Modern British Radicals*, ed. J. O. Boylan and N. J. Gossmer (4 vols., 1978–88), and neither is he mentioned in S. Maccoby, *English Radicalism 1762–1785. The Origins* (1955). J. E. Ross edited his diary of 1772–4, with an introductory account of his life in *Radical Adventurer. The Diaries of Robert Morris, 1772–74* (Bath, 1971). There is a popular sketch by Wyn Jones, 'Robert Morris, the Swansea Friend of John Wilkes', *The Glamorgan Historian*, XI (1975), 126–36.

The Morris family arrived in the Swansea area of Glamorganshire in South Wales early in the eighteenth century, and during the 40 years before his death in 1768 Robert's father, another Robert, made a substantial fortune from the copper industry there. The senior Robert Morris married in 1725 a Margaret Jenkins from Machynlleth in Montgomeryshire, heiress to a small estate in that county. Six of their 12 children died young, and Robert, born on 4 August 1743, was to be his father's heir, though he had four older sisters. Robert was sent to Heath School in Yorkshire where, so he later recalled, he had an unhappy time, and then to Charterhouse: in his diary for 17 May 1774 he records meeting an old school-fellow from there named Green, with whom he 'held a good deal of old school chit-chat', even though with characteristic mischief he gave the wrong name for himself of Chapman.[2] In 1760, at the age of 16, he went on to Oriel College, Oxford, and, before he graduated there in 1764, had been admitted in January 1763 to Lincoln's Inn, where he was called to the bar on 6 May 1767.[3]

Robert Morris had hardly commenced his legal practice before he became involved in a case that attracted much notoriety, for he assisted in the successful defence of Lord Baltimore against a charge of rape in March 1768. A wealthy widower, Lord Baltimore was already infamous for his sexual promiscuity. His acquittal, obtained because the woman was too frightened to give evidence, did not convince public opinion of his innocence, and social ostracism caused him to live abroad thereafter.[4]

The next month Robert's father died, and when his will was proved in June the young lawyer became a man of some property, inheriting two small estates in Glamorgan, a house at Swansea, shares in his father's copper business and £500 in cash. Other property would revert to him on the death of his mother.[5] The law, however, remained his chosen profession, and his younger brother John managed the copper firm. For several years Robert retained chambers at Lincoln's Inn, and also practised on the South Wales circuit.

But as the storm of the Middlesex elections case began to break, the pull of politics proved too strong a temptation for a young man who evidently held very advanced views. John Wilkes was already a symbol of popular resistance to government because of the *North Briton* case of 1763–4, when he had been expelled from parliament, and eventually outlawed for refusing to face a legal trial for seditious libel on George III in that periodical. He had now returned from exile in France and won a seat for Middlesex at the general election of 1768. The ministry of the duke of Grafton, urged on by an indignant sovereign, was determined not to allow Wilkes

2   Ross, *Radical Adventurer*, pp. 175–6, 179. It seems improbable that he also attended Shrewsbury, a more customary school for Welsh boys, as is stated elsewhere. Jones, 'Robert Morris', p. 127.
3   Ross, *Radical Adventurer*, pp. 1–2.
4   For reports of and comments on the trial see the *Gentleman's Magazine*, XXXVIII (1768), pp. 180–8.
5   For a copy of his father's will see Ross, *Radical Adventurer*, pp. 5–6.

to sit in parliament. He was expelled on 3 February 1769 on a composite charge of libels, and on 17 February declared ineligible to sit after his return at a by-election the previous day.[6]

That was the background to the formation of the Bill of Rights Society. John Wilkes, currently in the king's bench prison for his libel offences, was due for release in April 1770; but by early in 1769 his financial debts were thought to amount to over £14,000. This burden carried the threat that Wilkes on his release would simply be transferred to the Fleet prison for debtors. While most of this debt had been incurred by personal extravagance, some had arisen from political expenses, and Wilkites therefore had good ground for coming to the aid of the champion of 'liberty'. Three days after Wilkes had been declared incapable of election, and thereby deprived of any prospect of parliamentary immunity from creditors, a meeting of his friends on 20 February 1769 subscribed over £3,000 and decided to establish a permanent organization to support him. On 25 February this was formally created as the Bill of Rights Society, and Robert Morris was elected secretary. There is no evidence as to how or why this choice was made, or of his previous connexions with any Wilkites; but already he probably knew two Welsh members of the society, Robert Jones of Fonmon Castle in Glamorgan, and fellow-lawyer Watkin Lewes. Young Morris brought zeal and energy to the post, and the society members, nearly all men of substance, were probably glad to find someone eager to do the administrative chores. Robert Morris was the public face of the Bill of Rights Society, for it was over his names that all its notices appeared. According to the later recollection of diarist William Hickey he was publicly denoted in the press as 'Bill of Rights Morris'. Much of his time must have been taken up with the society, for it met every Tuesday, alternatively in full session and in committees.[7] When Morris resigned 18 months later it was professedly because he was 'tired of my share of the burden'.[8]

The first notice issued by Morris appeared in the *London Chronicle* of 28 February 1769, and no doubt also in other newspapers. It gave the society's name as 'Supporters of the Bill of Rights', and declared that 'their sole aim is to maintain and defend the legal constitutional liberty of the subject. They mean to support Mr. Wilkes and his cause, as far as it is a public cause. For this purpose only they solicit the countenance and encouragement of the public.' The notice had been drafted by John Horne, the vicar of Brentford, and the key figure in the society until Wilkes emerged from prison. He was seeking, by this advertisement and otherwise, to give the society a wider objective than the mere payment of the debts of John Wilkes; but for the moment that problem had to be given priority. It came to resemble the task of killing the many-headed hydra of Greek mythology, whose heads grew again as

---

6   P. D. G. Thomas, *John Wilkes. A Friend to Liberty* (Oxford, 1996), pp. 70–99.
7   *The Memoirs of William Hickey*, ed. A. Spencer (4 vols., 1925), IV, 60; N. C. Davies, 'The Bill of Rights Society and the Origins of Radicalism in Britain', University of Wales M.A., 1986, pp. 93–9.
8   *London Evening Post*, 6 Sept. 1770.

they were cut off. For fresh debts appeared as fast as others were settled. When the flow of London subscriptions slackened, the society decided to launch a national appeal, and on 20 July a circular letter was issued in the name of Robert Morris. This purported to give 'friends of liberty at a distance' the opportunity to assist the cause, but the method adopted was insensitive. Numbered letters were sent with the circulars to targeted individuals, asking them to organize local subscriptions. The brash approach, which assumed, for example, that opposition M.P.s would publicly subscribe to pay Wilkes's debts, was probably counter-productive, if the reaction of William Dowdeswell, Commons' leader of the main opposition party of Lord Rockingham, was in any way typical. For he commented to his Rockinghamite colleague Edmund Burke on 10 August, 'I think of writing no answer. For if I do I must find fault with the forwardness of Mr. Morris.'[9] Political zealots tend to forget that not all sympathizers share their enthusiasm, but it is unclear how far Robert Morris was personally responsible for the failure of this fund-raising campaign. Horace Walpole's comment that it 'produced nothing' was all too near the mark.[10]

Despite this fiasco enough money was eventually raised for Wilkes to leave prison in April 1770. The most famous contribution, which arrived in February 1770, was £1,500 from the Assembly of South Carolina, and it fell to Robert Morris to compose an appropriate reply. At a meeting of the society John Horne savaged his draft as too flowery in style, and Morris withdrew it in favour of a composite one, drawn up by Horne but altered by other members. Much of the evidence for this incident comes from a letter of 1771 during the famous public dispute between Horne and Wilkes known as the 'Controversial Letters' episode. Wilkes then explained that Americans favoured 'a copious style' of writing and 'that in this style Mr. Morris excelled'. Horne had been 'peevish and ill-bred', whereas Morris had behaved in 'a good-natured manner'.[11]

Robert Morris would seem to have been something of a political idealist, genuinely fighting for radical causes, regardless of career disadvantages or what contemporaries thought of him. There is never any hint in his admittedly short political career that he himself might be a candidate even for any City office, let along a parliamentary seat. The rectitude of his principles made him uneasy about the compromises necessary in practical politics; and he criticized the temporary alliance in the City of London made during the summer of 1770 between the Wilkites and the Rockinghamite party, which resulted in the election of three Rockinghamites to City office, as the lord mayor and both sheriffs. In a letter of 6 August, published in the *London Evening Post* on 6 September, Morris denounced 'the great leaders of

---

9   *The Correspondence of Edmund Burke*, ed. Thomas W. Copeland *et al.* (10 vols., Cambridge, 1958–78), II, 54.
10 Walpole, *Memoirs of George the Third*, III, 240.
11 Quoted in Ross, *Radical Adventurer*, pp. 8–9.

Parliamentary opposition' for having failed to support Wilkes. 'I shall look upon them as interested men, more studious to do themselves good, than their country.'

It was in the same letter that Morris resigned as secretary of the Bill of Rights Society. Ostensibly he did so because he had expected the post to rotate among members and was finding it an onerous task, but he added a further explanation.

> The cause of Mr. Wilkes, as an injured and persecuted individual, has been the first and hitherto the only motive of my appearing in public. I have the satisfaction to say that I leave the cause in a better situation than I found it: though not the vanity to think, that much of our success (which indeed ought to have been greater) has been owing to my endeavours ... As for odium which may have fallen on my name from the conspicuous part I have appeared in, I shall esteem that my greatest reward, being satisfied it will only come from a quarter, whose enmity will be my greatest honour.

Morris did not abandon the radical cause, and during the next year was to offer deliberate provocation to the establishment institutions of court, parliament and the judiciary. His resignation may in part have been prompted by dismay at growing discord within the Bill of Rights Society, as John Horne led criticism of Wilkes for his assumption that the society existed only to fill his purse and enhance his reputation. In character the two men were as different as chalk from cheese. Horne was a serious-minded man, often of gloomy complexion and outlook, deeming the frivolous and self-interested Wilkes an unworthy champion of liberty. Robert Morris, on friendly terms with both men, was at first to side with Wilkes, whom he had probably never met before the formation of the Bill of Rights Society. He then made a habit of visiting him in prison, and of sending him delicacies to alleviate the tedium of his confinement.[12] And in October 1770, when Morris judged that Wilkes must have cleared the backlog of City business resulting from his election as an alderman when in prison, he invited him to visit South Wales. There Morris was playing his summer role of country gentleman. He wrote from Pontypool, where he was staying with Monmouthshire M.P. John Hanbury, and was 'now going with a large Glamorganshire party to the Races at Monmouth'. In a letter ending 'your sincere friend' Morris extolled the delights of the Welsh countryside, and still more of the women.

> It is the country and open air, that I imagine would suit your taste the best. If mountains, rivers, seas can charm, here you may have your fill; in short we have all sorts of prospects I think, and all sorts of animals to command, but women, for whom I shall say nothing. I don't know indeed, what conquests you may be able to make, for you are certainly a great favourite with the ladies.[13]

Although Morris offered to meet him at Bath or Bristol, Wilkes declined the invitation, and in his letter evidently raised a new political issue. The recent Spanish seizure of the British base in the Falkland Islands made war seem inevitable, and the

---

12 B.L., Add. MS 30871, f. 25.
13 *Ibid.*, ff. 40–1.

admiralty began to issue press warrants authorizing the seizure of men not specifically named for service in the navy. In his reply, from Swansea on 27 October, Morris made, or echoed, an obvious analogy: 'I entirely join with you in the affair of press-warrants. You shall have all my assistance in it. It rests upon no better footing than general warrants. All the usage in the world would not have made them legal, as the Judges declared; and I don't see, why the same might not be said of press-warrants.'[14] The condemnation of general warrants, used to arrest unnamed persons, had been one of the blows struck for liberty by Wilkes in the *North Briton* case. But this time the Wilkites, aware that the liberty of the subject had to be balanced in the scales of popular opinion against the vital needs of the navy, did not seek the legal condemnation of press-warrants. Instead they resorted to legal and practical obstruction in the City of London, until the controversy died early in 1771 when the international crisis was resolved without a war.

One controversy at a time was not enough for Robert Morris. He had meanwhile taken part, as witness not as learned counsel, in one of the trials arising out of the publication of a 'Letter to the King' by that noted anonymous political polemicist Junius in the *Public Advertiser* on 19 December 1769. This was almost universally deemed a libel, even by opposition M.P.s in parliament, and since the author was unidentifiable the North administration commenced prosecutions of the newspapers that printed it, and also of John Almon for selling at his bookshop the monthly *London Museum*, which had reprinted it. The last action was widely though to be spiteful revenge on a fearless journalist whose publications had long infuriated government, for he was the only person to be prosecuted merely for selling the offensive piece. He was tried and found guilty on 2 June 1770 in the court of king's bench, even though the evidence established that Almon had not personally been involved in any sales, and had promptly withdrawn the *London Museum* from his shop when he read it.[15] Not until 28 November did Almon come up for sentence, and that is when Robert Morris entered the fray. He submitted one of the six affidavits produced to alleviate the criminality. Morris deposed that he had called at Almon's shop 'a very few days after' the *London Museum* went on sale, and had been refused a copy by Almon himself. He later bought it elsewhere, gratuitously adding in parenthesis, 'verily believing in his conscience that the said pamphlet did not contain any libellous matter whatsoever'.[16]

Morris was the only one of those making depositions who was not involved in the publishing trade, and Almon's counsel made much of this. John Lee claimed that 'the affidavit of Mr. Morris, an independent gentleman, was the most incontrovertible proof of their being founded on fact that could possibly be produced, and that established, the whole was a strong alleviation of the defendant's criminality'.

14 *Ibid.*, ff. 42–3.
15 *A Complete Collection of State Trials*, ed. T. J. and T. B. Howell (34 vols., 1809–28), xx, 803–43.
16 There is a copy of Morris's affidavit in *London Evening Post*, 13 Dec. 1770.

Sergeant John Glynn, so the *London Museum* itself reported, 'mentioned, as a further proof of his client's innocence, that Mr. Morris was a friend of Mr. Almon's, and that Mr. Almon could not suppose that a gentleman of Mr. Morris's rank and character came to his shop with a design to inform against him, his refusing to sell him the Museum therefore was a plain proof'. But the denial by Morris that the Junius letter was a libel had provoked Judge Aston, who in his judgment declared that the court 'would not pay any regard to the affidavit of Morris, who could declare (though only in a parenthesis) that Junius's letter was not a libel'. The press report of the proceedings thereupon ended with this biting comment.

> The reasons given for throwing out of the consideration a material affidavit made by Mr. Morris, a witness totally disinterested, is really curious. He is a young barrister, and swears that he bought Junius's letter, not thinking it a libel. The judge thinks it is. ... Because, therefore, Mr. Morris is wrong in his legal notions, he is not to be credited as to matter of fact. It will not pass in Westminster Hall for fair inference, good logic, or pure justice.[17]

Junius himself, in a later note to a letter he published on 14 November condemning the judicial conduct of the trials arising out of his 'Letter to the King', singled out this incident: 'In the course of one of them Judge Aston had the unparallelled impudence to tell Mr. Morris (a gentleman of unquestionable honour and integrity, and who was then giving his evidence on oath) that *he should pay very little regard to any affidavit he should make.*'[18] Morris was not the man to let such an opportunity slip. He decided on a pamphlet, informing Wilkes on 1 December that he hoped 'to trim that Bully Aston whom I do not intend to spare'. He would submit his draft to Wilkes on 3 December, 'for your perusal ... that you may throw in where you see occasion a little of seasoning'.[19] It was published on 12 December, as *A Letter to Sir Richard Aston, Knight, one of the Judges of his Majesty's Court of King's Bench ... being a reply to his scandalous abuse, and a display of the modern doctrine of libels, by Robert Morris of Lincoln's Inn, Barrister at Law and Late Secretary to the Bill of Rights.* Priced at 1s. 6d., it achieved a second edition the next day, even though extracts had at once appeared in the newspapers. Having recapitulated what Judge Aston had said about him, Morris commented 'that the plain and obvious sense of these polite and elegant expressions, I take to be this. "Mr. Morris has, by this affidavit, shown himself to be a man of so abandoned a conscience, as not to deserve credit in a Court of Justice"'. Judges, he declared, 'ought surely to be the last to set an example of slander, or to incur that reproach ... of using the privilege of their

---

17 The report in *State Trials*, XX, 843–8, is stated to be from *Lloyd's Chronicle* of 20 Nov. 1770. There was no such newspaper, and probably *Lloyd's Evening Post* of that date is meant, but I have not found a copy. The same report, without the final comment, had appeared in the *Morning Chronicle* and the *General Evening Post* of 19 Nov. The *London Museum* report is printed in *State Trials*, XX, 848–50. Almon's punishment was mild; he was fined ten marks and bound over for two years.

18 *The Letters of Junius*, ed. J. Cannon (Oxford, 1978), p. 213. For the letter attacking the king, see *ibid.*, pp. 159–73.

19 B.L., Add. MS 30871, f. 48.

station, to cast abuse upon the characters of private men, who might attend to give their evidence'.[20]

Having had his fun at the expense of the bench, Morris was soon to turn his pen on parliament, provocatively to increase the impotent resentment there and at court against the great radical triumph of 'the Printers Case', which secured the freedom of the press to publish parliamentary debates. Ironically this success was achieved at the very time of the final break between Wilkites and Hornites. Matters came to a head on 9 April 1771 when Horne put a motion to dissolve the Bill of Rights Society. Robert Morris, aware that this would have fateful consequences whichever way the vote went, was one of five who vainly sought to postpone any decision. The motion was defeated only by two votes, 26 to 24, and the Horne faction promptly seceded to form a new Constitutional Society. Robert Morris was in the Wilkite majority, but was one of half-a-dozen who now sought to meet the damaging Horne criticism by insisting that the society should widen its objectives, by the threat that otherwise they also would secede. Wilkes himself put the appropriate motion at the next meeting of the society on 16 April.[21] The 'Printers' Case' may have hastened the break. Although John Horne was involved early on until Wilkes took over the initiative, some of his supporters, notably Alderman James Townsend, were deterred from active participation by disapproval of the parliamentary opposition, and at the society meeting of 9 April Robert Morris took Townsend to task on the matter.[22]

Hitherto the reporting of debates had been prevented by direct parliamentary punishment of defiant printers; but the public interest in politics generated by the Middlesex elections case resulted, for both commercial and political reasons, in the majority of London newspapers, a dozen or so, adopting this practice by early 1771. A fresh attempt was then made to stamp it out, supposedly instigated by the king himself and certainly soon taken up by the ministry of Lord North. Offending printers were as usual intimidated by being summoned to appear at the bar of the house of commons and ordered to cease their reporting forthwith. John Wilkes, Robert Morris and John Almon now concocted a scheme to thwart this prosecution of the printers. There was soon little secrecy about this plan, to set up one privilege against another, pitting against that of parliament the chartered rights of the City of London to an exclusive legal jurisdiction within its own boundary. John Wilkes, as an alderman, was *ex officio* a City magistrate, and the support of others was obtained, including that of the Wilkite lord mayor, Brass Crosby. Their accomplice was John Miller, printer of the *London Evening Post*, a Wilkite newspaper. The trap was sprung when on 12 March Miller was included in the next batch of printers to be summoned before the house of commons. Next day Morris sent this report to Wilkes.

---

20 *London Evening Post*, 11, 13 Dec. 1770.

21 *Ibid.*, 18 Apr. 1771. For the radical split, see Thomas, *John Wilkes*, pp. 121–4.

22 *London Evening Post*, 18 Apr. 1771. Morris mocked Townsend for refusing to act because 'no great man would support him in it'.

I have been all this day upon the wing about the business of the printers, and hitherto unable to call upon you, agreeable to my inclinations. I would not have this affair sleep for the universe. The ministry take care it shall not on their side; we must therefore be staunch on ours. You know what they proceeded to yesterday. Some of the six newly ordered to attend, I believe make their appearance tomorrow at the House... There will be business new for all of us, and each must have his share. Different games must be played.[23]

Of the six printers summoned on 12 March to attend the house two days later only Miller defied the Commons, and he was ordered to be taken into the custody of the house's sergeant at arms. Meanwhile a sub-plot unfolded, arising out of the earlier defiance of two other printers, John Wheble of the Hornite paper the *Middlesex Journal*, and Roger Thompson of the *Gazetteer*, which had resulted in a royal proclamation offering a reward for their capture. Robert Morris met both men on 12 March;[24] and two days later he deliberately provoked the house of commons by a piece of impudence. John Wheble sent a public letter to the Speaker, enclosing this opinion of his learned counsel, Robert Morris: 'I am clearly and decisively of opinion, that Mr. Wheble is not compellable by law to attend the House of Commons in pursuance of the written order.' The Speaker's warrant for his arrest was therefore invalid, since 'the Speaker of the House of Commons is no more a magistrate appointed to issue warrants of apprehension, then the House itself is a Court of Justice appointed to punish'. Next Morris pronounced that the king's proclamation of a reward was 'clearly illegal, Proclamations have no intrinsic force in this country'. He therefore gave it as his opinion 'that Mr. Wheble may well institute an action upon the case, against the counsellors, promoters, aiders, abettors and publishers thereof'. Altogether Morris advised Wheble to pay no attention to any of the documents: 'All are equally unjust and illegal. Mr. Wheble will be protected by Magna Carta and by numerous statutes which confirm our valuable code of liberties.'[25]

This was all rather tongue-in-cheek, and the legal opinions of Robert Morris were not tested as the administration lost interest in Wheble and Thompson when subsequent proceedings centred on John Miller. It was Wilkes, Lord Mayor Crosby and Hornite Alderman Oliver who enjoyed the high-profile role of City magistrates defying the house of commons, and there is little glimpse of Robert Morris. When on 15 March John Miller was arrested by a Commons' messenger and the case was heard by these three magistrates, Morris acted as counsel for Miller and made repeated interventions on legal points to add to this discomfiture of the Commons' officials. A public letter of 29 March, printed over the initials G. W. and often attributed to Junius, praised the legal arguments adduced by Morris on this and other occasions.

23 B.L., Add. MS 30871, ff. 69–70.
24 *Ibid.*
25 *London Evening Post*, 16 Mar. 1771. The opinion is printed in Ross, *Radical Adventurer*, p. 15.

I have forborne to take this business up on the same grounds as Mr. Morris has done, as it would only be a repetition of what he has very judiciously before transmitted to the public. It is sufficient for me to say that I think he has sufficiently demonstrated the illegality of the order of the House of Commons. I only meant to give additional strength to his observations.[26]

The role of Robert Morris was twice acknowledged by the City of London. The *Middlesex Journal* of 19 March announced that 'as a token of honour to Mr. Morris, for his intrepid conduct in the late affair of the Printers, we hear that gentleman has now received a general retainer for the City of London, in all actions and persecutions that may ensue'. And on 27 March Lord Mayor Crosby presented Morris to the freedom of the City as a symbolic gesture before he himself set out to face the house of commons and imprisonment in the Tower of London.[27] This honour was formally bestowed on Morris on 23 April by a *locum tenens* mayor in the absence of the still incarcerated Crosby.[28] The detention of Crosby and Oliver – the house of commons refused to tangle with Wilkes – provoked a determination in the City to support their cause by providing a safe haven for defiant printers, and the publication of debates soon resumed as before. The imprisoned magistrates were released at the end of the parliamentary session, and the North ministry wisely abandoned its attempt to prohibit parliamentary reporting.[29]

This success did not heal the breach among London's radicals. On the contrary, once the contest with parliament was over, Horne and Wilkes joined battle, notably in their famous press controversy. Robert Morris, despite his initial alignment with Wilkes, appears soon to have trimmed his sails. As early as 7 May he was the subject of an attack in the Wilkite *London Evening Post*.

A correspondent says, that the versatility of Robert Morris Esq. was never equalled but by the pliability of Lord Barrington,[30] and that he is at a loss to reconcile his present connections and conduct with his former declarations, and parts of his letter to the Supporters of the Bill of Rights.

There followed quotations of the laudatory remarks on Wilkes in the letter of resignation Morris had sent to the Bill of Rights Society on 6 August 1770. Another paragraph in the same paper suggested that Morris ought to apologize to Judge Aston for a false story, given him by John Horne, that he had profited from a large allocation of government lottery tickets, demand for which was so great that they could be re-sold at a premium on the open market. In the next issue on 9 May the *London Evening Post* published a reply from Morris; he conceded that Horne had

26 The letter is printed in Ross, *Radical Adventurer*, pp. 17–18. The attribution to Junius is not now accepted. *Letters of Junius*, ed. Cannon, p. 526.

27 *London Evening Post*, 30 Mar. 1771.

28 Ross, *Radical Adventurer*, p. 18.

29 For an account of the whole episode, see Thomas, *John Wilkes*, pp. 125–40.

30 Lord Barrington was notable, or notorious, for retaining continuous office under a succession of different ministers from 1746 to 1778.

been his source of information, but pointed out that Judge Aston had not denied the charge, made to his face at an Old Bailey dinner.

Morris was in fact attempting to distance himself from the quarrel between two men who were both his friends, but that proved to be impossible. He had earlier commented to Wilkes that Horne had never approved of him. Wilkes now used that as an excuse to publish a letter he had received from Horne in 1766, in which Horne described himself as 'a man who has always both felt for your sufferings, and spoken highly of your conduct in the public cause'. Horne complained about this publication of a private letter, so damaging in the context of the current quarrel. Wilkes said that he had done so in order to refute the statement by Morris, who in a public letter of 27 May to Wilkes denied that such a step had been necessary.

> I am unwilling to interfere in the dispute between you and Mr. Horne, who have both deserved well of the public, and are so fully qualified to fight your own battles: but ... I perceive a mistake in your last letter, where you mention my name, which it is in my power to correct. ... The sentiment you would have the world adopt is, that the first production of that letter was in consequence of what I said, and to corroborate your answer; therefore not a wanton or designed publication of a private and confidential letter.

Morris then complained that on the contrary Wilkes had shown the letter first to a dozen other gentlemen, 'at a meeting at the Devil's Tavern, called the Retribution Club', and only produced it for Morris when it was mentioned.[31] After commenting that apart from his quarrel with Wilkes the conduct of Horne had been 'in other respects equally honourable to himself and serviceable to you', Morris ended the letter with a declaration of neutrality.

> Having rendered this justice to Mr. Horne, I shall be equally ready to do the same justice to you, whenever I find him trespassing upon truth, either through wilfulness or mistake, in any matters, which come immediately within my knowledge. As to the parties who are now contesting, I have no reason to wish success on one side more than the other. ... It is the cause of liberty I wish to promote, and I care not by whose hand it triumphs. Of that cause alone I desire to be esteemed a partizan, and not of any individual.

Two days later Wilkes published this reply to Robert Morris.

> The fact is that you, Sir, had frequently said so to several of your friends, 'Mr. Horne told me he had always the same opinion of Mr. Wilkes', and once to myself before the meeting at the Devil Tavern. My answer had been to you, 'Not always the same. When I see you next, I will convince you of it'. I knew you were to dine at the meeting at the Devil Tavern. I brought the letter with me for your perusal. You came late. Several gentleman before your arrival mentioned your declaration about what Mr. Horne had

31 The only occasion Wilkes recorded in his diary of meeting Morris at the Retribution Club was on 1 Feb. 1771. W. P. Treloar, *Wilkes and the City* (1917), p. 266.

said. I then produced the letter, which was read before you came by the other
gentlemen, and by yourself afterwards.[32]

Wilkes must have known that Morris would be offended by this publication, and
the *Middlesex Journal* of 6 June forecast in humorous fashion that Morris would
soon break with him: 'Mr. Morris was never accused of steadiness till he attached
himself to Mr. Wilkes. His behaviour then was for a long time thought a great blotch
in his consistency. Of late it is imagined, Mr. Morris will get rid of this accusation of
his enemies.' Two days later the same newspaper reported that disgust and dismay
at the radical split would drive Morris to quit politics: 'Mr. Morris being much
chagrined at the quarrel between his friends Mr. Wilkes and Mr. Horne, it is thought
he will soon retire from all political squabbles into the country.'

That Robert Morris was drifting from the Wilkite to the Hornite faction can be
inferred from press reports. The *Middlesex Journal* of 13 June commented that if
Morris had attended the Bill of Rights Society two days earlier 'he would certainly
have been handled pretty roughly ... as a spy'. About this time Wilkes deliberately
published a reminder to Horne of how two years earlier he had scorned the letter
Morris had drafted as a reply to the South Carolina Assembly: 'Will you prevail on
your new friend Mr. Morris, to favour the public with his intended answer', so that
comparison could be made with Horne's own draft.[33] The Hornite *Middlesex Journal*
conceded on 15 June that 'Mr. Horne got the letter to be objected, and one of his
own substituted in its room'; but maintained that Mr Morris and Mr Horne were then
and always have been since 'very good friends'. And ten days later the same
newspaper added jocular confirmation of this. Morris had been robbed on the
Hammersmith road by the same men who had earlier robbed Horne there; 'from
whence 'tis conjectured they were supporters of the Bill of Rights'. Certainly if
Morris had still been active in that society he would have been among the 18
members named to draw up a political programme, a project close to his heart; but
he was not.[34] Yet his break with Wilkes was not complete or irrevocable. The diary
of Wilkes records that on 26 February 1772 he dined at the London Tavern 'with
Morris, Lewes, etc'.[35] And it was to John Wilkes that Robert Morris appealed for
help during the escapade that ended his legal career and political aspirations alike.

His downfall came over a woman, or rather a young girl. In his letter to Wilkes
on 27 October 1770 Morris had penned thoughts on women, the significance of
which is enhanced by hindsight.

There is no happiness without them; at least when our thoughts are turned their way.
We live by the hopes of such an acquisition, which, however, is rarely, if ever obtained.
There may be the widowed Bachelor, as well as the widowed husband, and widowed

32 Both letters were printed in the *Middlesex Journal* on 30 May 1771. Ross, *Radical Adventurer*, pp. 20–2, prints them and Horne's letter.
33 Ross, *Radical Adventurer*, pp. 8–9.
34 Davies, 'Bill of Rights Society', pp. 239–40.
35 Treloar, *Wilkes and the City*, p. 273.

wife. I am now in the former state, having no connection with females, and I sometimes think myself the happier for it.[36]

The event that changed the life of Robert Morris was the death of Lord Baltimore on 4 September 1771. His estate was bequeathed to his two illegitimate children. Henry Harford, 14 years of age, was to inherit Maryland, the American colony of which Lord Baltimore had been the proprietor. Frances Mary Harford, a mere 12 years old and known as Fanny, was to have £30,000. Morris must have earlier impressed Lord Baltimore by his role in the rape case of 1768, for he had been appointed one of the executors, and guardians of the children, being paid £1,500 and an annuity of £100. The boy was sent to Eton, and the girl placed by Morris at a school in Chelsea. He visited her frequently, and sometimes took her out to social occasions. On 15 May 1772 they were due to visit Robert's sister Jane and Susannah Vaughan, wife of Richard Vaughan of Golden Grove in Carmarthenshire, at the Vaughan house in London. Instead the couple made off to Dover, where they hired a boat to Calais. At Ypres on 21 May Robert and Fanny went through a marriage ceremony. The other guardians had meanwhile launched a hot pursuit, and Robert Morris was arrested at Lille on 24 May.[37] Next day he wrote to John Wilkes and John Glynn, professedly as a constituent of the M.P.s for Middlesex: 'As you have never been wanting to the care of public liberty, so I doubt not you will be attentive to that of an individual, however remote from his home; leaving the name and character of an Englishman everywhere to be respected, especially amongst our vanquished enemies.' This letter arrived on 1 June and was forwarded the next day by Wilkes and Glynn to Lord Rochford, who as southern secretary of state was the appropriate government minister.[38]

Morris was released, presumably through his own efforts, for Lord Rochford took no action.[39] The pursuit continued through the Netherlands and northwards to Hamburg, where the couple took refuge in a nearby tiny principality of Wandsbeck, which enjoyed its own separate jurisdiction and was connected to Denmark. Morris seldom dared to leave this refuge, and bought property to establish residence there, as a preliminary to a second marriage ceremony. In November 1772 he obtained permission for this from the king of Denmark, and went through another marriage with Fanny on 3 January 1773 at Ahrensburgh. But back in Britain the court of chancery had issued a writ on 9 July 1772 ordering Morris to appear before it with 'Frances Harford' on 5 August. When Morris, who burnt the writ, failed to appear that day the court ordered that he be debarred from acting as a trustee, restrained from matrimony, and committed to prison.[40]

---

36 B.L., Add. MS 30871, f. 43.
37 Ross, *Radical Adventurer*, pp. 23–7.
38 B.L., Add. MS 30871, ff. 130–1. Wilkes had been expelled as M.P. for Middlesex, but still claimed the seat, and so Morris acknowledged this in his letter.
39 *Ibid.*, f. 166.
40 Ross, *Radical Adventurer*, pp. 27–30.

During 1772 Morris wrote to Wilkes on 1 June, 21 July and 18 September, without obtaining any reply. But he did then receive this letter of 11 December: 'Mr. Wilkes has had the honour of writing four letters to Mr. Morris in France and at Hamburg, but as he has not heard of any of them being received, now makes a last effort, and if this paper reaches him, begs Mr. Morris to do Mr. Wilkes the justice of believing the real and warm sense he entertains of many past favours.'[41]

Morris sent a long reply on 22 December: 'By the step I have taken in relation to matrimony my private and public reputation I know has greatly suffered; which I did not at first foresee.' He was aware that he was accused of having betrayed a trust and taken advantage of a young girl, 'but if we loved each other all is justified'. The action of the court of chancery against him Morris compared to the great constitutional issues Wilkes had raised in the *North Briton* case:

> All comes very properly within the notion of a contempt; a term not less dangerous to the people of England, than general warrants and seizure of papers from which you have so gloriously relieved your countrymen, and in the room of which this has started up. I am satisfied that you will not be less active to relieve them from this new-fashioned instrument of tyranny, because it happens to be exerted in the case of another.[42]

That hope was as naive as his surprise at the reaction to his elopement. There is no record of any further correspondence or other contact between Wilkes and himself. His marital as well as political expectations both collapsed in 1773. Urged by Fanny to make a solo tour of Italy, Morris left her in Geneva on 1 November, penning this diary note two days later when encountering the Alps: 'I think I have seen worse mountains to cross in Wales.'[43] He visited Turin and Genoa, and returned through Toulon and Marseilles. On arrival in Geneva on 4 December he discovered that Fanny wished to end their marriage and had written to her family in London. Fourteen years old on 28 November, she now informed Morris that she had eloped only to escape from a disagreeable school and that any man would have served her purpose. Robert Morris thereupon took her to Paris, whence she left for London on 7 January 1774.[44]

Robert Morris himself returned to Britain on 28 April, landing at Harwich, where he found a letter from his brother John and took a coach to London. Next day he was re-united with John and sister Margaret. John, two years younger than Robert, had made a great success of the family copper business, so much so as to build Clasemont as a family mansion near Swansea in about 1772, and was about to be married to a daughter of Sir Philip Musgrave, a Cumberland squire. His career, culminating in a knighthood in 1806, affords a marked contrast to that of his volatile elder brother.

41 B.L., Add. MS 30871, ff. 135–6, 142, 144. There is no evidence of any previous letters by Wilkes, but the letter of 1 June had been forwarded to Lord Rochford.
42 *Ibid.*, ff. 166–7.
43 Ross, *Radical Adventurer*, p. 91.
44 *Ibid.*, pp. 89–112.

The two men alway remained on good terms, and John had assisted Robert with financial help on his European travels, receiving some property in exchange.[45] Robert was genuinely delighted at John's matrimonial coup: 'A most amiable young lady; fortune sufficient, and family most respectable and opulent. How happy for him! How happy would such a match have been for me! But how sincerely did I partake in his joy!'[46]

Robert Morris stayed on in London for some weeks, intending to prosecute his marital case in the court of chancery after his brother's marriage, not wishing to spoil that scene by public scandal. On 15 May he sent an emissary to the Harford household 'to demand the young woman as my wife in order to ground an action, if necessary to try one ... Mrs. Harford, putting on her best termagant voice hails him ... perhaps thinking it was me. ... "He claims a wife: he claims a gallows"'. It is doubtful whether barrister Morris believed that his behaviour had incurred the death penalty, although that was a possible interpretation of the law. But he was sufficiently alarmed by the news that the chancery writ for his arrest now carried a bonus payment of £100 to deem it expedient to quit London. He told John he would return to Hamburg to procure evidence for his matrimonial cause.[47]

He left for Newcastle on 16 May, but by a most circuitous route! He passed some ten days in the area around Manchester and Liverpool, fascinated by evidence of the embryonic industrial revolution, and noting how on 21 May he was reminded of his Welsh roots: 'I saw at Runcorn a pack of Aberystwith sailors; I enquired after my Aunt Lloyd; several of them had also been at Swansea and knew all my family connections there ... I daresay if £1,000 had been offered upon one's head, a fellow-countryman might have trusted his person with these fellows.'[48] On 30 May Morris sailed from Liverpool to Greenock, arriving in Glasgow on 2 June. Next day he discovered that 'as a preparatory to the celebration of the King's Birthday, boys go about, with a miserable Black figure held up, which they call Wilkes; and they accost everyone, "Won't ye give a Baubee to burn Wilkes?" I gave it to them, willingly; for the fun of saying I had done it.' It had evidently got beyond a joke on the following day, the birthday of George III, for Morris noted that he was 'perpetually plagued about the burning of Wilkes'.[49] Perhaps Morris was fortunate not to be identified as a former close associate of a man who was such a hate-figure in Scotland that he was accorded the Guy Fawkes treatment there. Morris went on to Edinburgh and thence to Cumberland, but had not reached Newcastle before his diary suddenly ended on

---

45 *Ibid.*, pp. 59, 116.
46 *Ibid.*, pp. 168–9.
47 *Ibid.*, pp. 172–4. For assistance on legal points I am indebted to my colleague Richard Ireland in the Law Department at Aberystwyth.
48 *Ibid.*, p. 181.
49 *Ibid.*, pp. 190–1.

5 July. It was unlikely that he ever went to Hamburg, for he was in Swansea by September.[50]

Throughout the next decade Morris fought to prevent annulment of his marriage. His diary makes it apparent that he was at first genuinely distressed at the loss of Fanny. He noted on 2 May 1774 that he had not made any 'attempt' on another woman since his elopement with her, and on 21 May poured out his heart: 'Could I take even temporary notice of another female I might find momentary relief. But the misfortune is, all the rest of womankind have lost their charms for me.'[51] The worldly-wise diarist William Hickey, far from portraying Morris as the villain of the Fanny escapade, depicted him as the dupe of a 'capricious damsel', who 'grew tired of her enamorata', tricked him into returning to Britain, and then concocted a pack of lies about the whole affair:

> Madam ... secretly made an application to the Lord Chancellor by petition for protection, stating that she being an uninformed, inexperienced girl of tender years, Mr. Morris ... by a thousand falsehoods and treacheries ... finally persuaded [her] to elope with him, directly conveyed her out of the kingdom, and had ever since kept her a close prisoner. She further stated that at the time she so went off with Mr. Morris she was not in her senses, and verily believed he had administered some drug to her to deprive her of her reason.

Although the greater part of these charges against Morris were void of all foundation in truth, the little hussy, having herself laid the plan for leaving her guardian's protection and certainly in her perfect senses, had voluntarily gone off with Morris, yet enough remained in the case to justify the interference of the Chancellor, who after a full investigation and discussion of the case, compelled Morris to give up the person of the young lady and restore her fortune.[52]

Not until 21 May 1784 did the court of king's bench pronounce both marriage ceremonies to Fanny to be void. Morris had strained the truth in his attempts to maintain their legality.[53] Hickey thought that his pertinacity was motivated not by attachment to Fanny but by the desire to lay hold on her fortune, since he had ruined his own inheritance by the lifestyle he had adopted even before his liaison with Fanny:

> Mr. Morris had originally a small patrimonial estate of a few hundreds a year, which he had nearly dissipated when he became known to Miss Harford, the being deprived of her property, added to the expense of contesting it, therefore reduced him to the greatest distress, and he was obliged to have recourse to a variety of schemes in order to obtain a subsistence. ... Notwithstanding it was notorious that Mr. Morris's little property was all gone, he appeared as much in public as ever, kept a carriage, servants with smart liveries, and dressed in the height of fashion, from which the world was not backward in forming very unfavourable opinions: some people carried this so far as

50   *Ibid.*, pp. 175–210.
51   *Ibid.*, pp. 170, 181.
52   *Hickey Memoirs*, ed. Spencer, IV, 60–1.
53   Compare the Morris diary in Ross, *Radical Adventurer*, pp. 51–115, with the legal proceedings described in *ibid.*, pp. 33–40.

to assert that he went upon the highway. It is more probable that he lived by cheating the unwary at the common gaming tables of the metropolis, many of which he was known to frequent, and he undoubtedly was a remarkably sharp, clever fellow.

Morris was thus suspected of being a highwayman, and made his way by cheating at gambling, loaded dice being his favourite method.[54] Even before he destroyed such character as he had left by this decade of dissipation in London it had been obvious that he could never have resumed his old way of life. Evidently debarred from pursuing a legal career, he was unable to resume his political one, seemingly being shunned on his return to Britain in 1774 by his former radical and journalist associates. After a fortnight in London he recorded in his diary for 12 May that of them all he had met only William Woodfall, proprietor of the *Morning Chronicle*, 'my constant and very good friend'.[55] There is no evidence that Morris ever again participated in the activities of London's radicals, but unsubstantiated stories suggest that he had not altogether lost interest in national politics and imply that he sympathized with the American cause in the War of Independence.[56]

In 1785 Morris turned over a new leaf, by a common method of doing so, matrimony. He returned to live in South Wales after his marriage on 28 June to Sarah Prichard, whose family owned Bach y Gwreiddyn, a small estate, perhaps only a farm, some five miles north-west of Swansea. It was near the Tredegar Fawr estate which Morris inherited the next year, among other possessions of his father which reverted to him on the death of his mother, who also bequeathed him her North Wales property. Now a landowner, Robert Morris settled down to the life of a small squire, making improvements to Tredegar Fawr, but his restless political soul soon led him to an active public life.[57] Actual local tyranny became his target as perceived national tyranny had been nearly 20 years before, the duke of Beaufort and his Swansea agent Gabriel Powell being identified as the enemy.

In 1787 Morris became involved in a campaign to obtain a Paving Act for Swansea, a measure opposed by Beaufort and talked out in committee by his ally Sir Herbert Mackworth, M.P. for Glamorgan Boroughs, after it had easily passed the second reading stage. In a pamphlet published on 17 September 1787 Morris warned against the alternative proposal, favoured by Beaufort and Mackworth, to levy

---

54 *Hickey Memoirs*, ed. Spencer, IV, 61–2.

55 Ross, *Radical Adventurer*, p. 172.

56 *Ibid.*, pp. 36–7, repeats a story that Morris was accused, and acquitted, of manslaughter after a duel in which the American loyalist Daniel Dulany was killed, Morris having been the second to Dulany's adversary. But Dulany died in Maryland in 1797. It is therefore doubtful how much credence can be given to another story from the same source. For what it is worth, it is that in 1782 Morris himself nearly became involved in a duel, being the reputed author of a pamphlet attacking General Benedict Arnold, who during the War of Independence had changed from the American to the British side. The pamphlet stated that Arnold had been transported from Britain to America for horse-stealing, whereas he had in fact been born in Connecticut. One of Arnold's officers challenged Morris, but the matter was reconciled.

57 Ross, *Radical Adventurer*, pp. 41–2.

charges on residents in proportion to their frontages, not the value of their properties. He questioned the legality of this procedure, and asserted that nothing short of an act of parliament would suffice.[58] Two other pamphlets on this subject have been attributed to Morris. One of 1787 by an 'Advocate of an Act of Parliament', addressed to 'The Inhabitants of Swansea', denounced this proposed scheme and warned that 'your town … will … dwindle to the wretched condition of an appendage to Morriston', the company town of his own brother's copper firm. The other, 'Caution', issued by Robert Morris on 26 June 1788, stated that the aim of this proposal was to prevent an act of parliament that might place management of the paving scheme in 'the hands of shopkeepers and other respectable house keepers'. Morris urged non-payment of the cost of the paving stones, supplied by Sir Herbert Mackworth for his own profit.[59]

The background issue in the dispute was the control over Swansea wielded by the duke of Beaufort; and the apparent failure of Morris and his friends to curb this power was more than balanced in any political scale by the overthrow of oligarchic power in the Glamorganshire parliamentary by-election of 1789, a success in which Morris played a leading role. Charles Edwin of Llanvihangel had been nominated county M.P. in 1780 by the coalition of magnates that had long dominated the Glamorgan political scene, the duke of Beaufort, Lord Mountstuart, Lord Vernon, Lord Plymouth and Thomas Mansel Talbot of Margam, who alone of them lived in the county. In 1789 Edwin, supposedly failing in health, sought to bequeath the seat to his son Thomas Wyndham, but his former sponsors would have none of it. To counter a canvass by Wyndham early that year, over two years before a general election was due, they put forward Lord Plymouth's brother Thomas Windsor. There ensued a vigorous campaign, and notable in the torrent of propaganda were the pamphlets of 'A Friend to the Independence of Glamorgan', usually identified as Robert Morris. He already had appropriate political connexions in the county. His old Bill of Rights Society friend Robert Jones of Fonmon Castle was an uncle of Thomas Wyndham; while in 1772 he had borrowed a coach to commence his elopement from Christopher Mansel Talbot,[60] brother of the Thomas Mansel Talbot who now broke ranks with his fellow magnates to sponsor Wyndham's candidature, and the Margam interest had long been the leading one in Glamorgan. The first broadside by Morris, on 13 May, declared the issue to be 'whether a few non-resident Lords shall name, or the freeholders elect, a member to represent the county of Glamorgan'.[61] Other pamphlets by Morris acclaimed Lady Dynevor for supporting Wyndham with the

58 National Library of Wales, Penrice and Margam MSS, no. 9125. This is a printed pamphlet, *An Address to the Owners and Occupiers of Property in the Town of Swansea, Relative to a Paving Act. By Robert Morris, Esq.* (Swansea, 1787).

59 These pamphlets are summarized in Llewelyn B. John. 'The Parliamentary Representation of Glamorgan, 1536–1832', University of Wales M.A., 1934, pp. 231–3.

60 Ross, *Radical Adventurer*, p. 25.

61 Nat. Lib. Wales, Tredegar MSS, no. 72/77.

Hensol estate influence, attacked Lord Mountstuart for putting pressure on voters, and criticized those who had succumbed to it. Windsor was scorned as a non-resident naval officer, whose duties would seldom permit him to attend parliament. If such a candidate was chosen, the oligarchs would have demonstrated that they could impose whomever they wished on Glamorgan.[62]

Windsor requested a public county meeting, but then failed to attend one called for 21 July, evidently sensing the trend of opinion. The meeting carried a series of eight resolutions in support of Wyndham. The sixth was moved by Robert Morris and denounced the non-appearance of Windsor as 'disrespectful to the county'.[63] His prominence in the campaign was signified by a popular election song 'The Champions of Liberty', for it included this line, 'And Morris that fame had long woo'd'.[64] Edwin took advantage of the wave of popular feeling by resigning his seat forthwith, and his son was not opposed by Windsor at the by-election on 4 September.

Such were now the pretensions of Robert Morris to respectability, and the strength of his new political connexions, that a rumour circulated that he would be named as a county magistrate when the next commission of the peace was announced. The very idea so scandalized the duke of Beaufort that in 1789 he informed Gabriel Powell that in such an eventuality he would personally visit Lord Chancellor Thurlow to have Morris struck off. And if Thurlow refused, he would see the king himself on the matter, doubtless to remind George III of the behaviour of Morris in his Wilkite heyday 20 years before. The duke was not alone in his dismay at such a prospect. The clerk of the peace for Glamorganshire, Thomas Edwards, on hearing the rumour in May 1790, commented that 'if he is admitted it will be a devil of a thing for the whole country'.[65]

It did not happen, for the life of Robert Morris took another downturn just when he seemed to have created a settled future for himself. His wife became ill in 1789 and was dead by the end of the year. Morris was so upset by this tragedy that he threw discretion to the winds, not for the first time in his life, and although the Swansea area was full of his relatives he applied in June 1790 for permission from the East India Company's court of directors to practice at the bar of the supreme court in Bengal. By December this had been granted, and Morris sailed for India in May 1791, having first made a will leaving his property to various members of his family, since his marriage had been childless.[66]

Morris arrived in Bengal without any letters of introduction to the four judges of the supreme court; and, according to the memoirs of William Hickey, which form the

62 *Ibid.*, nos. 53/58, 72/79; John, 'Parliamentary Representation of Glamorgan', pp. 115–18.
63 John, 'Parliamentary Representation of Glamorgan', pp. 119–20.
64 Nat. Lib. Wales, Tredegar MSS, no. 72/75.
65 *The Diaries of John Bird of Cardiff: Clerk to the First Marquess of Bute 1790–1803*, ed. Hilary M. Thomas (Cardiff, 1987), pp. 54–5.
66 Ross, *Radical Adventurer*, pp. 42–3.

sole source for what befell Morris in India, one of them, Sir William Dunkin, had, unluckily for Morris, known him during his years of London dissipation.

> Sir William Dunkin, in his days of gaiety, had more than once encountered him in situations highly disreputable; one in particular, where a young gentleman of rank and fortune who was playing with him at a common hazard table, detected him in cheating, and instantly accused him with having introduced loaded dice. Being directly seized by the company the dice he had in his hand were cut open and found to be loaded; two other pair of the same description were also taken from his pocket. Upon the discovery he was extremely roughly handled by the party and then kicked downstairs.

Dunkin therefore 'related to his legal brethren what he knew of Mr. Morris's former conduct, which, he added, in his opinion rendered him unworthy of a place at their Bar, or of being allowed to mix in the society of gentlemen'. The other judges agreed with Dunkin, but to avoid 'wounding the feelings of a man who perhaps had seen his errors and resolved upon a complete reformation' gave as the official reason for rejecting his application to practice at their bar the excuse that there already were enough barristers in their court. Morris pressed the issue, accusing the judges of partiality and injustice, whereupon the provoked Dunkin stated the real reason. 'I object to your being admitted an Advocate of the Court from the notoriety and infamy of your character, and from the vile, abandoned and disgraceful life you have led for many years past.'[67]

Morris, who had become something of a reformed character during his years back in Glamorgan, was greatly upset by this denunciation. He left the court without a word, and soon afterwards quitted Calcutta for the Bengal hinterland. 'Shortly after this Morris went up the country, making himself conspicuous by his violent conduct wherever he remained twelve hours', recalled Hickey. 'Among other whims he made it a practice to visit the gaols of every town he stopped at, enquiring into the particulars of each prisoner's case, and then assuring them that nine out of every ten were illegally confined and would be justified in using forcible means to obtain their liberty.' After describing how Morris had picked up a story that the former Governor-General Warren Hastings had been bribed to pardon a murderer, Hickey concluded his account of Robert Morris: 'Happily for society this dangerous and troublesome man was carried off by an attack of liver about eight months after he left Calcutta.'[68]

Robert Morris was buried in India on 29 November 1793.[69] A man of sharp mind and iconoclastic views, prepared to pronounce legal opinions in partisan fashion, he lacked both political judgment and stability of character. His notion in 1772 that Wilkes would make a popular cause out of the obscure and technical issue of 'contempt of court' was entirely unrealistic, with respect to both the subject and the man, and from that moment Wilkes had nothing more to do with him. His elopement

67 *Hickey Memoirs*, ed. Spencer, IV, 62–4.
68 *Ibid.*, pp. 64–5.
69 Ross, *Radical Adventurer*, p. 45.

of 1772 and his final idea of establishing a legal practice in India were acts of folly, impetuous steps which he undertook without assessing their practicability. Personality defects overshadowed his undoubted talents of intelligence and energy; for although he got on well with his family and intimate friends there was something about his character that caused him to be distrusted and disliked by too many people. He was too obviously a trouble-maker. Morris knew that full well himself, making in his diary for May 1774 this observation, which might serve as his epitaph: 'I do love bustle, variety and disturbance to my very soul.'[70]

70 *Ibid.*, p. 172.

15

Burke and Empire[*]

P. J. MARSHALL

In recent years eighteenth-century historians, with Philip Lawson very much to the fore, have begun to do justice to the intensity of Britain's engagement with empire, especially during the second half of the century. There are good reasons why this should be so. At no other time in Britain's history was imperial trade of greater significance to the national economy or was a larger proportion of Britain's armed forces deployed outside Europe in wartime. The extent of eighteenth-century intellectuals' preoccupation with empire is also becoming clear from some striking recent work, such as that of J. G. A. Pocock, Anthony Pagden, John Robertson and younger scholars, notably Peter Miller and David Armitage.[1] Empire is now firmly on the agenda of the eighteenth-century historian of ideas.

Edmund Burke plays surprisingly little part in current discussion of eighteenth-century theories of empire. There are a number of possible reasons for this. His work does not fit easily into either of what recent writing sees as the dominant contending models for empire: an 'incorporating', unitary empire under a single sovereignty or a 'confederal' empire with divided sovereignties. Burke clearly believed in an empire defined by a single sovereign, but there are so many qualifications on the apparent exercise of that sovereignty that Professor Pocock has recently argued that his theory of empire amounted to little more than one of 'informal empire'.[2] Moreover, as is inevitable for one fully engaged in the *mêlée* of day-to-day politics, any underlying principles that he may have held were inevitably obscured by his need to respond to events and to the immediate political pressures generated by a series of imperial crises ranging across the globe from North America to India.

[*] This paper is a revised version of one delivered at Trinity College, Dublin, at the Edmund Burke Bicentenary Symposium on 9 July 1997. I wish to express my gratitude to the organizers of the symposium for inviting me to speak at it and to the participants for their comments on my paper.

[1] J. G. A. Pocock, 'Political Thought in the English-Speaking Atlantic, 1760–1790, Part I, The Imperial Crisis', in *The Varieties of British Political Thought 1500–1800*, ed. J. G. A. Pocock (Cambridge, 1993); Anthony Pagden, *The Lords of All the World. Ideologies of Empire in Spain, Britain and France, c.1500–c.1800* (New Haven, 1995); John Robertson, *A Union for Empire. Political Thought and the British Union of 1707* (Cambridge, 1995); David Armitage, 'The British Empire and the Civic Tradition, 1656–1742', University of Cambridge Ph. D., 1992; Peter N. Miller, *Defining the Common Good. Empire, Religion and Philosophy in Eighteenth-Century Britain* (Cambridge, 1994).

[2] *Varieties of Political Thought*, p. 266.

This paper is an attempt to establish that a body of underlying principle can be found in Burke's responses to imperial problems over a long period. Although the emphasis undoubtedly changed, he seems to have maintained the essentials of his view of empire from the American crisis of the 1760s, at the outset of his political career, to the Hastings trial of the 1790s at the end of it. Burke therefore seems to deserve a place in the eighteenth-century debate about empire at least comparable to that currently accorded to the Scots, to French *philosophes*, such as Raynal or Diderot, to the founding fathers of the constitution of the United States, or even to British critics of empire like Josiah Tucker or Richard Price.

This paper is concerned primarily with ideas and only incidentally with any practical application that they may or may not have had. It tries to present Burke as an eighteenth-century intellectual wrestling with the problem of empire, as contemporaries conceived it. It will not therefore attempt to assess his contribution to the development of the later British empire nor will it hazard opinions as to whether he was or was not a wise imperial statesman in specific contexts. It will not try to answer such questions as whether Burke would, if he had been in a position to exercise decisive influence on imperial policy, have been able to avert the American revolution or the catastrophic happenings in Ireland in 1798 or whether he did or indeed could have ameliorated the effect of early British rule on India. Those questions are beguiling ones, but they are ultimately unanswerable, not least because they often have built into them unrealistic assumptions about the capacity of British imperial power to determine outcomes overseas. If one is really forced to try to answer them, my own view is that the answer has to be 'no' in every case, but this does not seem at all to detract from Burke's intellectual stature.

Burke's active political career began in the aftermath of the Seven Years War. This was a very important moment in the conceptualizing of ideas about a British empire. The usage of the term 'empire' has been subjected to close analysis in recent writing. Up to the sixteenth century, the term 'English empire', as in the Reformation statutes of Henry VIII's reign, had none of its later connotations of rule overseas. It simply meant the exercise of sovereignty within the realm of England. That meaning persisted into the eighteenth century, but from the reign of James VI and I the term 'British empire' came to be used for the integration of the kingdoms of England and Scotland, as it did again after 1801 for the union of Britain and Ireland. During the seventeenth century 'British empire' was a term sometimes extended to take in the seas around Britain. By the early eighteenth century many British people claimed an 'empire' over the world's seas in general, while the American plantations were added to conventional accounts of the British empire. But throughout the first half of the eighteenth century it seems to have been customary to talk about different empires in different parts of the world. For instance, there was a British empire of the seas or a British empire in America. Empire appears generally to have meant little more than an area where Britain exercised effective power. There seems to have been no real concept of a single British empire of rule over land and peoples throughout the world until the end of the Seven Years war. After that war, however, it became common-place to talk and write of a unitary British empire. In writing in 1773 of 'this vast empire on which the sun never sets and whose bounds nature has not yet ascertained', Sir George, later Lord, Macartney, was using what was becoming accepted contemporary usage.[3]

Burke was prominent among those who began to use the term British empire in what was to be its modern sense, as a single empire of rule throughout the world. As early as 1766, speaking specifically of North America, Burke is reported to have said: 'Without subordination, it would not be one Empire. Without freedom, it would not be the British Empire.'[4] In 1774 he told the electors of Bristol that he was now member not merely for a rich city, but for a 'great *Nation*, which however is itself but part of a great *Empire*, extended by our Virtue and our Fortune to the farthest limits of the East and of the West'.[5] He told an Irish catholic in 1779 that he wished to see 'every part of this Empire, and every denomination of men in it happy and contented and united on one common bottom of equality and justice'.[6] In opening the Hastings trial in 1788, Burke spoke of 'the Imperial justice which you owe to the people that call to you from all parts of a great disjointed empire'.[7]

What is particularly striking about Burke's sense of a British empire is the speed with which he incorporated India into it. In 1771, within six years of the grant of the Bengal *diwani*, he was explicitly referring to India as part of 'that vast, extensive heterogeneous Mass of Interests, which at this day forms the body of the British power' and arguing for its full integration: the East India Company's trade must be treated as British national trade, its revenues as British revenue and its army as a British army.[8] Whereas current scholarly writing on eighteenth-century theories of empire, for all its excellence, is, as Philip Lawson would surely be pointing out, disappointingly unwilling to engage with anything beyond the Atlantic, Burke's view of empire was truly world-wide. It embraced Ireland, North America, the West Indies and the Indian provinces of the East India Company.

In envisaging a world-wide British empire, Burke was thinking what was almost unthinkable for an eighteenth-century intellectual. The reality of Britain's world-wide expansion, greatly accelerated by the Seven Years War, was of course plain for all to see, but right-thinking opinion generally viewed the prospect with dread. World

3 *An Account of Ireland in 1773 by a Late Chief Secretary of that Kingdom* (1773). I owe this reference to Professor Thomas Bartlett.
4 *The Writings and Speeches of Edmund Burke*, ed. Paul Langford *et al.* (6 vols., Oxford, 1981–96), II, 50.
5 *Ibid.*, III, 70.
6 *The Correspondence of Edmund Burke*, ed. T. W. Copeland *et al.* (10 vols., Cambridge, 1970–80), IV, 121.
7 *Writings and Speeches*, VI, 277.
8 Sheffield City Library, Wentworth Woodhouse Muniments, Bk 9/23: draft for speech on East India Recruiting Bill, 12 Apr. 1771. These manuscripts were consulted by permission of the Olive, Countess Fitzwilliam's Wentworth Settlement Trustees.

empire was associated with Alexander, with imperial Rome, with the Spain of Philip II and with the France of Louis XIV. It was in no way an appropriate ambition for a free people. World empires of rule were by their nature unstable: they outgrew their strength and collapsed under the burden of their own weight. In the process they corrupted the virtue of a free people and undermined their institutions. The legacy of world empire would be luxury at home, standing armies and an eventual slide into despotism. The British should stick to an empire of the seas, based on trade and naval power, supplemented at the most by limited trading colonies of their own citizens enjoying the liberties of Englishmen overseas. The appropriate model of the past was Athens, whose colonies had been virtually independent partners of the mother country.[9]

Burke was well aware of the dangers of a territorial empire. In 1771 he acknowledged that 'It is frequently the Case that the Interest of our Empire clashes with the Interest of our Constitution.'[10] He believed that the war to reconquer America was having a deplorable effect on British society, militarizing and brutalizing it. If the war was to be won and America was to be subdued by military occupation, British liberties could not survive. He recognized every kind of danger from empire in India and expatiated on them at great length in his speeches at the impeachment: the power of the state would be greatly enhanced, the British would learn a taste for despotism, their political virtue and what he regarded as the simplicity of their manners would be corrupted; those who had learnt to be tyrants in India would become Jacobins at home.

Even so, Burke did not despair of empire, which, in any case, was an obligation imposed by divine providence on the British people and could not therefore be renounced. An overgrown territorial empire might prove to be the nemesis of Britain, but this need not be so. In a well conducted empire, British liberty and imperial power could be reconciled, as could the interests of the British people and those of the subject peoples of the empire.

For his model of a well conducted empire, Burke turned to a classical example and indeed to a Roman one: to the vision of empire enunciated by Cicero. A passage from *De Officiis* sums up Burke's ideal for eighteenth-century Britain:

> as long as the empire of the Roman People maintained itself by acts of service, not of oppression, wars were waged in the interests of our allies or to safeguard our supremacy; the end of our wars was marked by acts of clemency or by only a necessary degree of severity. The Senate was a haven of refuge for kings, tribes and nations; and the highest ambition of our magistrates and generals was to defend our provinces and

---

9 Pagden, *Lords of All the World*, p. 127.
10 Sheffield City Library, W. W. M., Bk 9/44: draft for speech on East India Recruiting Bill, 12 Apr. 1771.

allies with justice and honour. And so our government could be called more accurately
a protectorate of the world than a dominion.[11]

Three points in this passage seem to be particularly worth stressing for an
understanding of Burke's vision of empire. In the first place, the British empire, like
the empire of the Roman Republic, should be an empire of protection over a diverse
collection of allies and provinces, not a uniform empire of direct rule that sought to
impose uniformity on them. Secondly, Britain's imperial authority, like Cicero's view
of Rome's authority, should be exercised through doing justice, not through any
system of administration. Finally, the guarantee of justice was the vigilance of
parliament, the British senate.

'In the comprehensive dominion which the divine providence has put into our
hands', Burke told the sheriffs of Bristol in 1777, 'I was never wild enough to
conceive, that one method would serve for the whole; I could never conceive that the
natives of *Hindostan* and those of *Virginia* could be ordered in the same manner; or
that the *Cutchery* Court and the grand Jury of *Salem* could be regulated on a similar
plan.'[12] This is one of the clearest of his statements about the diversity of the empire
and the need to treat its different peoples in different ways.

In the vast corpus of his writing and speaking about India, Burke was generally
concerned not to exoticize or, in modern parlance, to 'orientalize' it. India was to be
made comprehensible to ignorant British audiences by stressing similarities between
it and their own world. Nevertheless, Burke believed that Indian society had
characteristics that made it unique. He described Hindus as possessing 'manners,
religion, customs and usages appropriate to themselves and no ways resembling those
of the rest of mankind ... [W]e, if we must govern such a Country, must govern them
upon their own principles and maxims and not upon ours.'[13] The British empire in
such conditions would take on a form totally different from that in any other part of
the world. Direct representation of Indians in their own government was totally out
of the question, although this did not mean that they would be governed despotically.
Burke wholly rejected conventional European stereotypes of 'oriental despotism'.
Government in India, like government anywhere else, was for him government
according to law. The law could not, however, be British law; it must be the law of
the Hindu and Muslim people over whom the British ruled. Indigenous systems of
property and land tenure must be cherished. The rulers in states under the Company's
protection must be preserved and, as far as was possible, authority within the
Company's provinces should remain in Indian hands.

The American colonies were at the opposite pole. In famous passages in his
'Speech on Conciliation' in 1775, Burke analysed the *'Temper and Character'* of the
Americans: their 'fierce spirit of Liberty', their English descent, their popular forms

11 Cicero, *De Officiis*, trans. Walter Miller (1913), p. 195.
12 *Writings and Speeches*, III, 316–17.
13 *Ibid.*, VI, 301–2.

of government, the strength of the 'dissidence of dissent; and the protestantism of the protestant religion', their litigiousness and their distance from Britain.[14] From all this he concluded that imperial authority must be administered with the lightest possible rein and a minimum of intervention. Above all, Britain must recognize the full competence of the colonial assemblies for all ordinary legislation and for taxation.

Burke saw Ireland's relations with Britain in imperial terms. He recognized both deep difference between Irish and English society as well as essential similarities. As Conor Cruise O'Brien has put it, from his childhood Burke had learnt 'to share directly in a considerable part of the experience of the Irish, Gaelic-speaking catholic people and to be at least somewhat affected by Irish catholic interpretations of history, and aspirations for the future'.[15] His opposition to the attempt to impose uniformity in religion and to exclude catholics from public life through the penal laws was total. He consistently urged catholics to make their voices heard and to be active in defending their interests.[16]

Yet for all his awareness of Ireland's particular history and culture, Burke also stressed the similarities between Ireland and England. Ireland had been made 'English, in civility and allegiance' over a long period by English laws and forms of legislature. 'It was not English arms, but the English constitution, that conquered Ireland.'[17] The Irish had gained a constitution 'favourable at once to authority and to freedom; such as the British Constitution boasts to be'. That constitution and the establishment of the Church of Ireland, for all its anomalies, must be preserved. Irish catholics should be absorbed into it and given its benefits. They must not be allowed to overthrow it. 'You cannot make the people Protestants – and they cannot shake off a Protestant Government.'[18]

For Ireland to be outside the empire would be a disaster for the Irish. Burke had serious reservations about the changed relationship with Britain brought about in 1782. 'That total independence of Ireland', in his view, added no 'security to its Liberty', but 'took it out of the common constitutional protection of the Empire'.[19] Britain's imperial authority was the ultimate protection for the catholic population against abuse of power by the Ascendancy. Within the empire, however, Ireland must maintain its autonomies. The Irish should resist undue intervention from England. He accused the North administration of trying to bring Ireland and England into 'a perfect state of Uniformity'.[20] He felt that the Irish in 1775 had a common interest in

---

14 *Ibid.*, III, 119–25.
15 *The Great Melody. A Thematic Biography and Commented Anthology of Edmund Burke* (1992), p. 23.
16 L. M. Cullen, 'Burke's Irish Views and Writings', in *Edmund Burke. His Life and Legacy*, ed. Ian Crowe (Dublin, 1997), pp. 62–75.
17 *Writings and Speeches*, III, 140.
18 *Ibid.*, IX, 651.
19 *Correspondence*, IX, 122.
20 *Ibid.*, II, 495.

the American cause in seeking to preserve the liberties 'of the dependencies of this Kingdom'.[21]

Burke seem to have been slow to recognize people of African origin in the British empire as being entitled to imperial protection and justice. He bitterly criticized Lord Dunmore's proclamation offering freedom for slaves in Virginia who joined the king's forces at the beginning of the war in America, seeing 'with shame the African slaves who had been sold to you on public faith, and under the sanction of Acts of Parliament, to be your servants and your guards, employed to cut the throats of their masters'.[22] In 1780, however, he drafted a 'code', based on the premises that trade 'in the persons of Men' and their 'detention ... in a State of Slavery' were contrary to 'the principles of true religion and morality, and to the Rules of sound policy'. The code consisted of measures 'to lessen the inconveniences and evils attendant on the said Traffic, and state of Servitude, until both shall be gradually done away'.[23] A gradual amelioration of the conditions of the slave trade and of slavery itself, leading to the eventual abolition of both, evidently remained the course that Burke most favoured. He sent his code to ministers in 1792. He was, however, prepared to give unequivocal support to Wilberforce's motion for immediate abolition of the trade in 1789. 'The Africans had that claim on our humanity that could not be resisted' and so what was no more than a 'system of robbery' must be abolished.[24]

Burke believed that Britain's responsibility for this diverse empire, varying from the near-democracies of North America to what he saw as the ancient hierarchical societies of India, was to provide protection from foreign enemies and from misgovernment and oppression and to ensure the due administration of justice. At one level, there was a great diversity of law: Islamic or Hindu legal systems seemed to be totally different to the common law exported from England to Ireland and the American colonies. The differences were, however, superficial. For Burke all human law was rooted in the natural law of God.

> There is but one law for all, namely, that law which governs all law, the law of our Creator, the law of humanity, justice, equity:– the law of nature and of nations. So far as any laws fortify this primeval law, and give it more precision, more energy, more effect by their declarations, such laws enter into the sanctuary and participate in the sacredness of its character.[25]

Thus it followed that

21 *Ibid.*, III, 245.
22 *Writings and Speeches*, III, 281.
23 *Ibid.*, p. 563.
24 *The Parliamentary History of England from the Norman Conquest in 1066 to the Year 1803*, ed. W. Cobbett (36 vols., 1806–20), XXVIII, 96, 98: speech on 21 May 1789. For further evidence of Burke's preference for a gradual abolition following reform, see William Windham's speech on 15 Mar. 1796, *ibid.*, XXXII, 894.
25 *Works of the Right Hon. Edmund Burke* (Bohn's British Classics, 8 vols., 1854–89), VII, 504.

the laws of morality are the same every where, and there is no action which would pass for an action of extortion, of peculation, of bribery and of oppression in England, that is not an act of extortion, of peculation, of bribery and of oppression in Europe, Asia, Africa, and all the world over.[26]

Rulers derived their power from God and it was their inescapable duty to do justice according to God's law as it was reflected in the diversity of human law and to prevent oppression.

Within the British empire these duties were entrusted to the British parliament. Like Cicero's vision of the senate, it was 'a haven of refuge for kings, tribes, and nations'. Administration played only a small part in Burke's vision of empire. Metropolitan authority should not interfere in detailed local matters. The role of secretaries of state or boards of trade was limited and Burke happily abolished them in 1782. Only parliament had the wisdom and the stature to exercise the general supervision that imperial statecraft required.

To perform its duties parliament had to have a supreme authority over all parts of the empire. In his 'Letter to the Sheriffs of Bristol', Burke wrote that 'if ever one man lived, more zealous than another, for the supremacy of parliament and the rights of this imperial Crown, it was myself'. He described the process by which 'What was first a single kingdom stretched into an empire; and an imperial superintendency of some kind or other became necessary. Parliament, from a mere representative of the people, and a guardian of popular privileges for its own immediate constituents, grew into a mighty sovereign.'[27] 'Without question this country must have the sole right of the Imperial legislation', he wrote of Ireland's relations with Britain.[28] Parliament's sovereignty extended to India, Burke believed, because the East India Company received its charter from parliament, which had a duty 'to interfere with effect, wherever power and authority originating from ourselves are perverted from their purposes and become instruments of wrong and violence'.[29]

The sovereignty of parliament meant that British statutes could override all enactments by local legislatures throughout the empire. Burke fully accepted this. He upheld the Declaratory Acts for Ireland and America, so long as he thought it practical statesmanship to do so. As is very well known, however, Burke insisted that this reserve legislative power would rarely be used and then only in ways that would usually be acceptable to the community that was being legislated for and which was thus unlikely to oppose it. Imperial legislation was not the means for the metropolitan power to impose its will on the peoples of the empire. The 'supreme power' was lodged in the British parliament 'not by force, or tyranny, or even by mere long

26 *Writings and Speeches*, VI, 346.
27 *Ibid.*, III, 313, 320.
28 *Ibid.*, IX, 488.
29 *Ibid.*, V, 385; see also VI, 281.

usage, but by the very nature of things, and the joint consent of the whole body'.[30]
Parliament's main function was not necessarily to legislate but to act as a forum to
which the peoples of the empire brought their concerns. The house of commons,
often through its committees, was the proper place to settle colonial disputes. Burke
took particular pride in the Free Port Bill of 1766 with which he had been much
concerned and which, he claimed, had 'perfectly reconciled' the interests of the West
Indies and North America.[31] The inquiries of the select committee on India from 1781
to 1783, of which he had been the moving spirit, had, he thought, laid the foundations
for Indian reform. Parliament's functions were also judicial. It was to call oppression
to account. For Burke the impeachment of Hastings became the embodiment of
parliament's role of inquiring into and redressing the grievances of the empire.

Burke's British empire was built on justice and existed for mutual advantage. Any
attempts made by Britain to gain benefits for herself at the expense of her dependencies would be entirely mistaken. Burke believed that within the Atlantic empire there
was a natural harmony of economic interests. The prosperity of each part of the
empire benefited all the rest. Restrictions on Irish trade merely damaged England.
'Ireland', he assured his Bristol correspondents, 'has never made a single step in its
progress towards prosperity, in which you have not had a share and perhaps the
greatest Share in the Benefit.'[32] Britain had prospered immensely from the success of
the American colonies. Mutual economic benefits were reinforced by a common
interest in defence against the same potential enemies and in sustaining shared
liberties on both sides of the Atlantic.

A properly conducted imperial relationship with India must also, Burke believed,
rest on mutual advantage. In return for protection, Burke considered that Britain had
a right to receive a justly assessed tribute from the revenues of India. Britain also had
a right to benefit from trade with India, but the trade must be on terms of freedom
and equality that were advantageous to both sides. This had been the case before the
grant of the *diwani* and it would be the case again if the commercial policies of the
East India Company were fundamentally reformed. The use of political power for
enforcing monopolies or fixing prices must be abandoned. They not only damaged the
Indian economy but undermined the profitability of the Company's own trade. As
with all other parts of the empire, policies that aimed at unilateral benefits for Britain
were self-defeating. 'All Attempts' which 'tend to the Distress of India, must, and in
a very short Time will, make themselves felt, even by those in whose Favour such
Attempts have been made.'[33]

Like most of his contemporaries, Burke believed that empire contributed very
materially to Britain's wealth and power. In a passage in his 'Speech on Conciliation'

30 *Ibid.*, IX, 488.
31 *Ibid.*, II, 55.
32 *Ibid.*, IX, 517.
33 *Ibid.*, V, 258.

Burke extolled the amazing extent of the American contribution 'to the growth of our national prosperity ... within the short period of the life of man'.[34] He believed that India too was responsible for the 'welfare of so great a part of the strength of Great Britain'.[35] In Burke's view it was entirely proper that Britain should benefit from empire, so long as she observed the golden rule that benefits must be equally reaped by all members of the empire. Yet for Burke, especially in his later years, empire was not primarily about wealth and power: it was the fulfilment of a divine dispensation, and the ultimate reward of empire was honour and renown.

'All dominion of man over man', Burke believed, 'is the Effect of the divine disposition.'[36] The origins of British rule might be discreditable – Burke admitted that empire in India was probably based on 'fraud or force' or 'a mixture of both'[37] – but it still fulfilled a divine purpose. In 1777 he had spoken of the 'comprehensive dominion which the divine providence has put into our hands' throughout the world.[38] In his Indian speeches this note became increasingly insistent. He saw conquest as 'a more immediate designation of the hand of God'.[39] In 1791 he asked the Lords whether their judgment would 'vindicate the dispensation of Providence that has committed so great an Empire to so remote a Country'.[40]

It was also in the Indian speeches that Burke gave the clearest expression to his conviction that in the government of their empire the British should be concerned with honour and reputation rather than with profit or power, which would be incidental benefits. For Britain to 'increase its commerce without increasing its honour and reputation' would be a 'bad bargain for the Country'.[41] He told the Lords that 'the credit and honour of the British nation' was at stake in the Hastings trial. He frequently spoke of other European nations watching and judging Britain by its record in India. 'Situated as this Kingdom is – an object, thank God, of envy to the rest of the world for its greatness and its power – its conduct, in that very elevated situation to which it has arisen will undoubtedly be scrutinized.'[42] Britain's rule over India should have 'done honor to Europe, to our Cause, to our religion, done honor to all the circumstances of which we boast'.[43] This had not been so, but he at least 'had laboured, though in vain, to rescue from ignominy and abhorrence the British name'.[44] In his very last words in public, at the close of the impeachment, he wished that the Lords might stand 'as unimpeached in honour as in power; ... as an ornament

---

34 *Ibid.*, III, 114.
35 *Correspondence*, IV, 310.
36 *Speeches and Writings*, VI, 470.
37 *Works*, VIII, 307.
38 See above p. 292.
39 *Writings and Speeches*, VI, 351.
40 B.L., Add. MS 24234, f. 359: impeachment minutes, 30 May 1791.
41 *Writings and Speeches*, VI, 282.
42 *Ibid.*, pp. 271, 277.
43 *Ibid.*, p. 315.
44 *Ibid.*, v, 476.

of virtue, as a security for virtue; ... the refuge of afflicted nations; may you stand a sacred temple, for the perpetual residence of an inviolable justice'.[45]

This paper has tried to reconstruct Burke's aspirations for the British empire. Whether they provided the basis for a practical programme of imperial statecraft is another question. If there is much that seems highly unrealistic about them, especially perhaps Burke's confidence that the British parliament could be the impartial disposer of imperial justice in the interests of all, what he proposed for America or Ireland is likely to have been a distinct improvement on the policies actually followed in the 1770s or the 1790s.

Whatever his influence on it in practical terms, the British empire did not and could not live up to Burke's hopes of what it ought to be. The 13 colonies left the empire. Rebellion broke out in Ireland, which remained within the empire at the price of union, an outcome of which Burke might perhaps have approved in the circumstances of 1801, in spite of his earlier insistence that Ireland maintain its autonomy. Even under Lord Cornwallis, of whom Burke spoke with respect, the British regime in India again became involved in wars and territorial expansion. Under Wellesley by the end of the century expansion was becoming uncontrolled. Victorian statesmen sometimes tried to appropriate Burke's name, but it is most unlikely that he would have approved of the later British empire. What he was offering was a vision of a world-wide empire based on universal justice. This is surely one to be set beside the aspirations of those enlightened critics of the European empires, Adam Smith, Price, Condorcet or Kant, who envisaged a universal brotherhood of independent peoples united by commerce.[46]

45 *Works*, VIII, 441.
46 Discussed in Pagden, *Lords of All the World*, ch. 7.

16

Toleration and its Limits
in the Late Hanoverian Empire:
The Cape Colony 1795–1828

R. E. Close

Philip Lawson's *The Imperial Challenge* was the first serious study of the constitu-tional implications of granting religious toleration to the French catholics of Canada, which was debated by parliament from 1763 until 1774.[1] According to Lawson, the Quebec Act was a precedent for religious toleration in Britain and would later provide the basis for toleration elsewhere in the empire. Religious toleration had long been unofficially recognized as East India Company policy in India.[2] Since its incorporation, the Company had remained somewhat neutral in its governance of the Hindu and Muslim population as a way of ensuring peaceful co-existence with the indigenous population and of ensuring better trading relationships. In his later work, *The East India Company*, Lawson noted this delicate balance between toleration and colonial government when finally the Company gave way to the evangelical pressure to retreat from toleration, and Lawson attributed the Company's rapid decline to its shift from sponsorship of orientalism to anglicism. With the rise of evangelicalism in Britain, the Company was increasingly expected to play an active role in promoting the salvation of the 'heathen' populations under its administration. The failure of the Company to restrict religious establishments in its territories in 1813, which Lawson claimed was fatal, contributed to the decline of its monopoly on trade and govern-ment in India.[3] The evangelization of the 'heathen' was an imperial dilemma not only for parliamentarians, but also for company officials, for missionary intervention in India shook the very foundations of the Company's administration. More importantly, it precipitated a growing vested interest in India by the British public that was commercial, religious and humanitarian.

The issue of toleration in the context of the Cape colony provides us with an interesting point of comparison with both Quebec and the East India Company. Similar to Quebec, the British promised the Cape Dutch a toleration of their civil and

---

1   Philip Lawson, *The Imperial Challenge. Quebec and Britain in the Age of the American Revolution* (Montreal and Kingston, 1989).

2   P. J. Marshall, *Problems of Empire. Britain and India 1757–1813* (1968), p. 72.

3   Philip Lawson, *The East India Company. A History* (1993), pp. 144–63.

religious institutions. The taking of the Cape in 1795 during the Napoleonic wars coincided with the evangelical revival when dissenters hoped to use the empire for their missions as well as to have greater religious freedom in new territories. The Cape of Good Hope became a popular destination for missionaries who were on route to India after the 1813 charter renewal, but it also was a convenient starting point for the conversion of Africa. As in India, the Cape administration had to grapple with the problem of an influx of civilians with different religious intentions. The first and most controversial group of newcomers was the London Missionary Society, whose members began to arrive in 1799.

In Quebec and India toleration of indigenous institutions was the eighteenth-century administration's way of creating sufficient goodwill to allow for a small military occupation force. The British administration at the Cape, by contrast, was increasingly able to impose its will over the colony once the colonial office realised the Cape's strategic importance as a naval base for defending the riches in the east.[4] As confidence in British military strength grew after the Napoleonic wars, colonial officials moved away from toleration of Dutch institutions toward anglicization.[5] At the Cape in particular, anglicization was a backlash against the growing number of dissenters in the colony who were disenfranchizing the anglican church from having any potential for growth among the civilian population. The London Missionary Society, comprised of congregationalists and presbyterians, was the main counter force to the colonial administration's religious policies. Because L.M.S. missionaries differed with the Dutch Reformed Church theologically, the society was unable to integrate into the existing community and became diametrically opposed to the administration's toleration of Dutch institutions. The society increased its influence over the colonial administration between 1790 and 1813 by appealing to the abolitionist public in Britain, targeting the administration's toleration of the system of slavery. The use of the public in the post-1813 period continued to be an important tactic for the L.M.S. as it struggled to impose its solution for the frontier problems between settlers and aboriginal communities such as the Khoikhoi and, later, the Xhosa.

This paper considers the two conflicting campaigns for toleration that took place at the Cape at the turn of the nineteenth century. The first of these movements demanded respect for Dutch institutions by a colonial government. Colonial officials of the nineteenth century approached change cautiously because of circumstances in the colony. The second was for religious freedom at the Cape for protestant dissenters. Missionaries tended to compound problems for colonial government by their insistence on immediate change, giving the Cape Dutch cause to fear for the survival of their culture. Of particular interest is the L.M.S. mobilization of the public

4   John S. Galbraith, *Reluctant Empire. British Policy on the South African Frontier 1834–1854* (Berkeley and Los Angeles, 1963), p. 22.
5   C. A. Bayly, *Imperial Meridian. The British Empire and the World 1780–1830* (1989) pp. 136–46.

in Britain on the question of slavery and later on the treatment of the aboriginal Khoikhoi, as it undermined the authority of the colonial government through the use of the missionary press.[6] The problem of slavery therefore made toleration of Dutch institutions increasingly difficult. Moreover, we shall see how both the missionaries and the colonial officials competed for control over the frontier between 1819 and 1828. Finally, the paper considers the consequences of this rivalry between the administration and popular politics as it eventually alienated the Cape Dutch from the British and, later, estranged the British settlers, the new arrivals to the frontier, from the mother country.[7]

Any assessment of the question of toleration in the South African context must first be situated within the context of the political circumstances of the conquest before an account is given of the origins of the slavery debate in the colony. The Cape found itself under British control twice during the Napoleonic wars. During the first occupation, from 1795 to 1803, the British had little intention of keeping the Cape, then a Dutch East India Company (V.O.C.) settlement. The British occupiers intended to leave the colony's institutions in tact in the event of a transfer back to V.O.C. authority at the end of the war. In 1803, the Dutch managed to reclaim the Cape for a short term. The British, who since the first occupation, came to see the strategic advantage of the Cape in the defence of their Indian territories reconquered the Cape in 1805. As with the first occupation, neither the British nor the Dutch colonists anticipated that British rule would be permanent. Under these circumstances, the British administration at the Cape channelled its energies into restoring order and peace in the colony as well as to ensuring that the military presence was not intrusive to the colonial Dutch way of life. Only until 1815 when the Congress of Vienna officially brought the Cape under British rule did either the colonial administration or the Dutch inhabitants have to reckon with the permanence of the arrangement.[8] The inhabitants for their part felt not unlike the French Canadians after the British conquest of Quebec, deserted by the mother country.[9]

---

6 Dissent and evangelicalism provided the values and the ideological impetus for slave emancipation. Evangelicals were also eager to become involved in the reforms of British institutions at home and abroad. See Edith F. Hurwitz, *Politics and the Public Conscience. Slave Emancipation and the Abolitionist Movement in Britain* (1973), pp. 17–18, 21–47.

7 As argued by Belinda Bozzoli in the South African context that a sense of community has always been strengthened by a 'hostile environment'. See Bozzoli, 'Class, Community and Ideology in the Evolution of South African Society', in *Class, Community and Conflict. South African Perspectives*, ed. B. Bozzoli (Johannesburg, 1987), pp. 1–43.

8 Stanley Trapido, *Van Riebeck Day and the New Jerusalem: Identity, Community and Violence in the Eighteenth- and Nineteenth-Century Cape* (Seminar on Societies of Southern Africa in the Nineteenth and Twentieth Centuries, 1993), p. 29.

9 Lionel Groulx, *Lendemains de conquête: cours d'histoire du Canada à l'Université de Montréal* (Montreal, 1920); Mason Wade, *The French Canadians 1760–1967* (2 vols., Toronto, 1968), I, 47–8.

The British were on the whole predisposed to granting the Dutch colonists the toleration of their institutions. Administrative change was retarded because of the complications of an economic structure that was dependent on the system of slavery.[10] As in Quebec, toleration as a policy attempted to freeze in time the institutions of the earlier regime by excluding the old inhabitants in the 'state building' process of the nineteenth century. The end result was that both the Dutch and the French Canadians were increasingly dispossessed by new emerging social hierarchies.[11] British missionaries were largely responsible for this exclusion because of their attack on the Dutch for their continued dependence on the system of slavery. The negative image of the Boer farmer as 'barbaric' and 'uncivilised', propagated by the missionaries, segregated the Afrikaner from the British and in many ways was responsible for the subsequent Afrikaner nationalism of the early 1830s.

At the outset of British rule, the British were confronted with varying degrees of hostility from the Dutch which made toleration expedient. In order to avert rebellion among the colonists, the military establishment sought the co-operation of the community. Crude classifications were observed between both English and Dutch of the anglomanen (anglophiles) and the jacobynen (jacobins). In Cape Town and Stellenbosche, former V.O.C. employees made the transfer over to George III rather easily. Opposition to British rule and a burgeoning independent sentiment lay in the hinterland in the region of Graaff-Reinet and Swellendam among the Boer farmers. The British found themselves exerting an enormous amount of energy trying to quell what they considered to be jacobin spirit among the Boers on the frontier even after the signing of the peace treaty in 1815.

What then exactly did the British come to tolerate at the Cape? And how did this toleration lead to a separate development of the two linguistic groups? For the most part, the British adhered to a toleration of Dutch institutions and laws during the first occupation. The Dutch Reformed Church was also fully recognized as the established religion of the Cape.[12] The D.R.C., which adhered to calvinism, resembled both the recognised established churches in Britain. There was no attempt to increase the influence of the Church of England because the church had sent out only a handful of military chaplains to attend to the needs of the British soldiers stationed there. It would only be with the increase of an British civilian population during the second occupation that the church would begin to increase its influence at the Cape.

The arrival in 1799 of the calvinist missionary Dr Johannes Van der Kemp, a Dutchman who came representing the British London Missionary Society, served to complicate rather than to simplify matters for both the British and the Dutch. A

---

10 Slave trade was abolished at the Cape in 1807 but slavery itself was not officially terminated until 1834.

11 These social hierarchies were the result of the infusion of British notions of private property and law. Bayly, *Imperial Meridian*, pp. 202–4.

12 G. M. Theal, *History of South Africa from 1795 to 1872* (6 vols., Cape Town, 1964), I, 26.

difference in theological views concerning slavery began the process of alienation of the Dutch community from the British establishment.[13] Not long after his arrival, Van der Kemp had been shocked to find that the D.R.C. was indifferent to slavery and more importantly to find that the D.R.C. could validate the system theologically, many of the church owning slaves themselves.[14] According to the D.R.C., slaves were not entitled to marriage, baptism or to enter the church. Conversion to christianity did not make the slave an equal to Europeans because he was born into the system as part of the divine plan.[15] Slaves according to this value system had no souls and therefore, according to Roman law in effect at the Cape, were not entitled to undertake legal obligations.[16] Confrontation between the two theological positions did not take long to surface once Van der Kemp started holding congregations of slaves in one of the D.R.C. churches. The Dutch community opposed this kind of missionary activity among their slave population and would later harbour the same hostility to the education of their Khoikhoi workers by the L.M.S. Van der Kemp, on the other hand, resolved that the spiritual welfare of these people, who outnumbered the Europeans, was not to be ignored.[17] Van der Kemp's mission to South Africa was to enlighten as many souls as was possible in his lifetime. The slaves and the Khoikhoi who were ignored by the other two denominations became his primary focus despite D.R.C. protest. These were the first signs of trouble for the British non-interventionist approach to administration at the Cape.

For the most part, Van der Kemp had the endorsement of the British governor, then Henry Dundas, who had offered Van der Kemp his assurance of protection. Dundas assumed that Van der Kemp's linguistic and cultural background would facilitate his integration into Cape society. Initially, Van der Kemp had been eager to co-ordinate his mission with pious members of the D.R.C. in forming the South African Missionary Society.[18] His theological views, however, which corresponded with his English sponsors on the issue of slavery, prevented him from seeking

---

13 The same response was common among planters of the West Indies who resisted education of their slaves. Conversion to christianity would entitle slaves to the same advantages under British laws as Europeans. In the case of the Cape Dutch, however, opposition to religious education for the slaves was based on religious convictions concerning the slaves' lack of moral being. Michael Craton, *Sinews of Empire. A Short History of British Slavery* (New York, 1974), p. 269; Mary Turner, *Slaves and Missionaries. The Disintegration of the Jamaican Slave Society, 1787–1834* (Urbana, 1982), pp. 1–37; Robert C. H. Shell, *Children of Bondage. A Social History of Slave Society at the Cape of Good Hope, 1652–1838* (Hanover, 1994), p. 342.

14 Ido H. Enklaar, *Life and Work of Dr J. TH. Van der Kemp, 1747–1811. Missionary Pioneer and Protagonist of Racial Equality in South Africa* (Cape Town, 1988), p. 81.

15 Jonathan Gerstner, *Thousand Generation Covenant. Dutch Reformed Church Theology and Group Identity in Colonial South Africa* (Leiden, 1991), pp. 167–70.

16 Dig.50.17.22, cited in Andre Malan Hugo, *The Cape Vernacular* (Cape Town, 1971), p. 9.

17 At the taking of the Cape, there were 22,000 European inhabitants to 18,000 slaves and 15,000 Khoikhoi, the aborigines of the region. Richard Elphick and Hermann Giliomee, *The Shaping of South African Society, 1652–1820* (1979), p. 30.

18 Enklaar, *Van der Kemp*, pp. 78–9.

acceptance by the Dutch community. His marriage to a Khoikhoi woman in 1800, which was sanctioned by the L.M.S. as long as it did not interfere with the interests of the mission in South Africa, also brought him criticism from the Dutch.[19] Instead, Van der Kemp immediately set out on the frontier where he could begin the prosletization of Africa out of the reach of the D.R.C. or the British administration. After doing a tour of the eastern cape region where he met with a few Xhosa chiefs, he reached the town of Graaff-Reinet in 1801–2. The town was ripe with anti-British sentiment after Dundas had crushed the Boer rebellion of 1799. The British considered Graaff-Reinet to be still a centre of jacobinism and indeed, since many frontier Boers still eagerly awaited the return of the Batvian Republic, it was a volcano waiting to erupt.[20] Because the rebels had drawn on the support of Khoikhoi clans and Xhosa tribesmen, there were many of these people now living in town. Van der Kemp, who was eager to convert the multitudes now in his midst, proceeded to instruct the Khoikhoi in the community's church. The reaction was immediate: Boers ran in to wipe clean the pews after the departure of the Khoikhoi congregation. Neither Van der Kemp nor the community could give way on their theological views about the propriety of allowing non-christians in the 'house of God'. Because the colonial officials delayed getting involved, the incident put the town on the brink of another rebellion.

The incident is important for our purposes because it marks the beginning of what would become a full-fledged assault on non-interventionist policies of the British administration in the colony by a civilian organization. This would have notable consequences for the development of colonial policy at the Cape. Conflicting theological views between the D.R.C. and the L.M.S. forced the administration to consider new ways of handling such civilian disputes. The incident itself was Van der Kemp's first experience with British justice in action. The district commander, Maynier, had wanted to avoid violence and therefore reasoned with the Boers by disallowing the Khoikhoi further use of the church. On this occasion, Maynier had demonstrated that the British administration was reluctant to interfere in theological matters, but, if need be, the administration would side with Boer interests for the sake of maintaining peace. It is important to remember that the British administration was not particularly committed to the missionary movement; indeed, missionaries were only allowed to reside at the Cape at the discretion of the governor.[21] British

---

19 School of Oriental and African Studies, London, L.M.S., Incoming 1/3/A: Thomas Haweis to the South African Missionary Society, Mar. 1800.

20 Graaff-Reinet was to be the site of the first signs of an Afrikaner nationalist consciousness in a rebellion of 1816. The execution of the rebels by British commanders at Slagter's Nek would cement Afrikaner nationalism. See Noël Mostert, *Frontiers. The Epic of South Africa's Creation and the Tragedy of the Xhosa People* (New York, 1992), p. 403.

21 Elizabeth Elbourne, '"To Colonise the Mind": Evangelical Missionaries in Britain and the Eastern Cape, 1790–1837', University of Oxford D.Phil., 1992; Jane Sales, *Mission Stations and the Coloured Communities of the Eastern Cape 1800–1852* (Cape Town, 1975).

evangelicals in England had not yet succeeded in making missions a priority at Westminster.

The slavery issue was now a matter of concern for the L.M.S. at the Cape. The kind of hostility that Van der Kemp experienced at Graaff-Reinet became more frequent as he more completely involved himself on the frontier in the religious education of the slaves and the Khoikhoi. His involvement was increasingly of a political nature, particularly as he continued to confront the Boers' theological beliefs and caused similar reactions as those demonstrated at Graaff-Reinet. This political activism in subsequent years brought him into conflict with the administration that was intent on defending the Boers. These problems were not kept self-contained, but instead were exported to the frontier, where Van der Kemp founded his mission in the environs of Boer farmers who either sought to create distance between themselves and the British or who sought the advantages of the open veld for their cattle. Over the course of several years, Van der Kemp and his L.M.S. colleagues made their presence on the frontier a position of strength against the policies of the colonial administration which also had a tremendous impact on the administration's relationship with the frontier.

By the second British occupation in 1805, Van der Kemp and several other L.M.S. missionaries established a station on the eastern frontier accompanied by 77 Khoikhoi from Graaff-Reinet.[22] Bethelsdorp had begun during the Batvian rule under Governor Janssens when the Netherlands were still at war with the British. It was during this period of Batvian rule that ordinances were passed making the D.R.C. the state church while granting equal rights to members of all other religious bodies.[23] Although a mission was established, the Dutch governor was strictly opposed to missionaries on the frontier because of the prospect of tensions between the British missionary society and Boer farmers. Janssens was also concerned that the L.M.S. missionaries would try to alienate the Khoikhoi from the Dutch government and discourage the Khoikhoi from enlisting in the Dutch army. Janssens therefore required that all missionaries going to the frontier have permission from the Cape administration.

For all intents and purposes, Bethelsdorp was from the outset politically implicated in frontier affairs because it harboured Khoikhoi captains who were known to have been involved in frontier conflicts.[24] Among the Boers, it gained the reputation of being a place of refuge for criminals. The missionaries themselves opposed Janssens' use of the Khoikhoi in the military because it disrupted the mission as well as the lives of those forced to serve. Van der Kemp had also begun to attack the administration for its labour policies. Janssens later commented that missionaries should be banned because 'they are politically unreliable. It is unfair to expect of a

22 J. S. Marais, *Maynier and the First Boer Republic* (Cape Town, 1962), p. 137.
23 Theal, *History of South Africa from 1795 to 1872*, I, 154.
24 Elizabeth Elbourne, 'Early Khoisan Uses of Mission Christianity', *Kronos*, XIX (1992), 19.

Governor to protect and favour people who undermine the minds of the inhabitants and turn them into enemies of the state.'[25] By the liberation of the Cape by Sir David Baird in 1805, the British would note that Bethelsdorp had been well on its way to being a controversial establishment under the Batvian Republic.

However, a new missionary epoch was unfolding in England. The first Anglican missionary, Henry Martyn, had accompanied Colonel Baird on his way to India. The Bible and the flag were becoming acceptable icons of British imperial expansion.[26] Martyn's declaration of the prospect of missions at the Cape reveal the new attitude toward empire emerging at the end of the Napoleonic wars: 'that the capture of the Cape might be ordered to the advancement of Christ's kingdom; and that England, while she sent the thunder of her arms to the distant regions of the globe ... might show herself to be great indeed, by sending forth the ministers of the Church to diffuse the Gospel of peace'.[27]

While evangelicals in London were united in their efforts to get the missionary movement underway, there was not yet a formal policy of toleration for dissenters. Thus 'Bible and flag' still reflected the church and state alliance of previous centuries. The military establishment had further become suspicious of dissenters following the mutiny at Vellore, India, in 1806.[28] Mission opponents used the mutiny to attack the baptist missionaries at Serampore for their circulation of religious tracts.[29] According to reports, Indians in the Madras army had heard rumours that the East India Company was going to make them all christians to which they were overtly opposed.[30] Company officials used the event to renew their commitment to full toleration of Indian customs and rites. Much to the disappointment of the evangelical Clapham sect, the mutiny had delayed the discussion of missions to India until 1813.[31]

The new Cape administrations of the Napoleonic era, therefore, shared the attitude of the Company servants that missionaries were all jacobin fanatics. Moreover, the correspondence of the Batvian rulers was critical of Bethelsdorp as Janssens' above cited remarks before the Asiatic council demonstrate. Van der Kemp had now become deeply committed to the slave community at the Cape not least because of his marriage to a slave girl in 1806. Cape Town society and the Boers on the frontier were equally shocked by the union and brought upon the Bethelsdorp establishment, a torrent of criticism about unethical methods used by the L.M.S. to

---

25 Cited in Enklaar, *Van der Kemp*, p. 161.
26 Brian Stanley, *The Bible and the Flag. Protestant Missions and British Imperialism in the Nineteenth and Twentieth Centuries* (Leicester, 1990), p. 63.
27 B. D. Martyn, *Memoir of the Rev. Henry Martyn* (1819), pp. 161–8.
28 Bayly, *Imperial Meridian*, pp. 138, 171, 173.
29 P. J. Marshall, *Problems of Empire. Britain and India 1757–1813* (1968), pp. 189–90; E. Daniel Potts, *British Baptist Missionaries in India 1793–1837* (Cambridge, 1967), pp. 177–8.
30 *Parliamentary Papers*, VIII (1812–13), pp. 493–7: court of directors of the East India Company to the governor and council of Fort St George, 29 May 1807.
31 Ernest Marshall Howse, *Saints in Politics. The 'Clapham Sect' and the Growth of Freedom* (1971), p. 82.

educate the 'heathen'.[32] The hostility of the colonists toward the establishment presented a problem for the British who, realizing that the colony had grown since 1803, were resolute in their belief that the missionaries had to be kept under control.[33]

The administration of the Cape had become more complicated with the abolition of the slave trade by parliament in 1807. The abolitionists at Bethelsdorp were overjoyed by the news. The Dutch, on the other hand, interpreted the ruling as a British plot to destroy their livelihoods. The Dutch farmers complained that the loss of their slave labour would create a huge labour shortage.[34] As a compromise to the Dutch colonists, the administration passed new legislation in 1809 which aimed to prevent a potential shortage and at the same time resolve the problem of Khoikhoi vagrancy in the towns.[35] The Khoikhoi therefore became the new labour source for the colony, sparking a new controversy with the missionaries who saw this apprenticeship system, as it was called, as the equivalent of the old system of slavery. Over the next 20 years, the administration and the missionaries had their horns locked over this issue.

More grave still for the administration, the missionaries turned to the British public. Beginning in 1808, the L.M.S. missionaries at Bethelsdorp kept their home society abreast of the atrocities allegedly committed by the Boers against their Khoikhoi employees. The L.M.S. made the reports public knowledge in their monthly, the *Evangelical Magazine*. This publicity in England meant that Cape affairs could no longer be treated in isolation by colonial officials. So concerned were the local authorities about these reports circulating in missionary publications that James Read, Van der Kemp's associate at Bethelsdorp, was called before the *Landdrost* of Uitenhage to explain his letters to the L.M.S.[36] According to the authorities, only one view was being represented by these accounts. The accounts themselves had a tremendous impact on the abolitionists in London who in turn exploited their 'imaginings' of the Boers in order to bring the Cape administration to heal over its lack of conformity to perceived notions of British justice.[37] William Wilberforce in a response to Read's letters to the L.M.S. in London passionately called for the execution of a few Boers in order to avenge the treatment of the Khoikhoi.[38] With the help of the lobby in London, the missionaries managed to persuade the administration to bring law to the frontier in the form of the 'black circuit', which would punish Boers guilty of maltreatment of their Khoikhoi employees. The court was to be the first victory of the L.M.S.

32 Elbourne, ' "To Colonise the Mind" ', p. 154.
33 G. E. Cory, *The Rise of South Africa* (6 vols., 1910), I, 142.
34 The Dutch also feared a general slave uprising. Robert Ross, *Cape of Torments. Slavery and Resistance in South Africa* (1983), p. 96.
35 Cory, *Rise of South Africa*, I, 201.
36 Enklaar, *Van der Kemp*, pp. 181–3.
37 Mostert, *Frontiers*, p. 544.
38 S.O.A.S., L.M.S. Home Office, Incoming, 2/5/B.

For the most part, however, the introduction of the circuit court proved to be only partly effective. It had little support from Sir John Cradock's administration, for example, because the administration was unforgiving of the L.M.S.'s meddling in colonial affairs. Many judges on the circuit court believed that Khoikhoi claims were exaggerated with the help of the missionaries at Bethelsdorp so that their judgments still came down on the side of the Dutch 'baas'. The ineffectiveness of the court to alter the condition of Khoikhoi apprentices demonstrated that the system of administration at the Cape had not changed to meet the needs of the frontier. The population on the frontier was growing, bringing a greater number of Boers into the proximity of the once isolated mission stations. Two opposing world views were continuously clashing and destabilising the eastern frontier. As we shall see, the next decade would force the incumbent governor, Lord Charles Somerset, to secure the frontier, only he too could not have predicted the problems that would arise from the arrival of the most controversial missionary of the nineteenth century, Dr John Philip.[39]

Between 1814 and 1828, the Somerset administration pursued a policy of anglicization of Cape Town. The frontier was not yet within reach of this programme, although the administration encouraged the settlement of English colonists in the border regions in the hope that they would provide some protection for the colony from the Xhosa as well as eventually assimilate the Boer farmers.[40] Despite these plans to assimilate the Boers, the administration continued to side with the Dutch in disputes with the L.M.S. missionaries. Consequently, the administration inadvertently fostered divisions between the two groups at the peril of the stability of the frontier. By placing the L.M.S. mission at the heart of such conflicts on the frontier, the society became even more politically involved particularly as its reputation at home and its future at the Cape were at stake. The issue of Khoikhoi labour continued to draw support from the public at home even though it complicated matters for the missionaries in their immediate European circles. Because of this public support, the colonial administration was considerably weakened and Somerset was recalled in 1828 on charges of maladministration.

Thus far, the colonial officials at the Cape had been slow to change the existing colonial apparatus left by the V.O.C.[41] In part this had to do with the fact that the colonial office had not yet made a firm commitment to a permanent acquisition. Consequently, the military establishment was still small and depended on the V.O.C.'s bureaucratic infrastructure. The arrival of Charles Somerset in 1814 would begin to change all that as would the Congress of Vienna. Somerset, an ex-M.P. with a sinecure military command, managed the colony as a military despot and a British,

39   Andrew Ross, *Dr John Philip (1775–1851). Missions, Race and Politics in South Africa* (Aberdeen, 1986).
40   Mostert, *Frontiers*, p. 543.
41   *Ibid.*, p. 557.

even English, patriot.[42] Unlike his predecessors, he was committed to making the Cape a British colony. In Somerset, we see the Bible at the service of the flag; the Church of England was now employed to undertake Somerset's reordering of the empire. Having come from England, Somerset knew that the colonial office had agreed to sponsor missions in India in 1813 and, in time, the other colonies. Moreover, he was well aware of the political power of the evangelical lobby in England after its successful conquest of the monopoly of the East India Company over India. Despite this experience, he was a staunch anglican who, during his administration, opposed all forms of dissent.[43]

The plan of anglicization was such that the Boers would be assimilated, albeit gradually, and the dissenters would be outnumbered by anglicans and even disappear with the D.R.C. Somerset refused to tolerate methodism which he considered to be dangerous to central administration and he threatened all dissenters with expulsion from the colony should they come within two inches of the military establishment.[44] Thus Cape Town was gradually remodelled to reflect the character of the British conquerors while the frontier became the bastion for missionaries from all sects with orders from Somerset to preach to the 'heathen' and to no other group.[45] Not surprisingly then, the number of Europeans crossing colonial boundaries and disturbing Xhosa communities increased the number of conflicts between colonists and the Xhosa which required military assistance.[46] It is during this 13 year administration, then, that the problem of the frontier would nearly consume the colony. Moreover, it is during this administration that we see the question of toleration in its many different shades of meaning shaping the political and social dynamics of the Cape.

Somerset's scheme to enhance and promote the anglican church had little success among the Dutch. The Dutch community, like the French Canadians, adhered to their own religious faith in order to ward off any attempts to assimilate them.[47] In all of this, it would be unfair to regard Somerset as blatantly hostile to the D.R.C. Rather, he sought primarily to weaken its influence in Cape society. He persuaded Britons to

42 R. G. Thorne, *The House of Commons 1790–1820* (5 vols., 1986), IV, 222–3; Bayly, *Imperial Meridian*, p. 205.

43 See conversations with Henry Reeve, in Alexis de Tocqueville, *Voyages en Angleterre et en Irlande* (Paris, 1967), pp. 128–9.

44 S.O.A.S., Wesleyan Methodist Missionary Society, South Africa, General Correspondence, 299: John McKenny to the W.M.M.S., Cape Town, Sept. 1814.

45 The British military establishment in Canada had the same policy toward the Six Nations Indians on the grounds that methodism would compromise Indian loyalty to the British crown. Robert S. Allen, *His Majesty's Indian Allies. British Indian Policy in the Defence of Canada, 1774–1815* (Toronto, 1992).

46 Clifton C. Crais, *White Supremacy, Black Resistance. The Making of the Colonial Order in the Eastern Cape* (Cambridge, 1992).

47 T. R. P. Louis-M. Régis, 'La religion et la philosophie au Canada français', in *Canadian Dualism. Studies of French-English Relations*, ed. Mason Wade (Toronto, 1960), pp. 56–77.

consider joining the D.R.C. so that it would eventually become an English-speaking institution.[48] As in Quebec, the administration also opted to promote assimilation of the local population through education. In 1818, Somerset met with the clergy, chief justice and English clergymen in order to discuss a plan to educate adult slaves as well as children. Predictably, the Dutch community opposed any suggestion that their slaves should be educated. As an alternative measure, the idea that British settlement at the Cape was the only means of 'enlightening' the Dutch about the evils of the system of slavery was making its way around anglican circles in Cape Town.[49] In 1820, the first group of British settlers arrived near Port Elizabeth at Algoa Bay.

While the importation of British settlers seemed to be the most promising means of assimilating the Dutch, Somerset had hoped that the colonization of the frontier would create a buffer zone between the Cape colony and the Xhosa communities on its borders. Frequent conflicts between Xhosa and the Boers had made the frontier unstable as both groups fought over the pasture lands for their cattle. Somerset may have sent dissenters to the frontier, but he did so while trying to exert some central authority over the administration of the frontier districts. He did so by bringing mission stations such as Bethelsdorp under more strict government control. The rumoured deterioration of Bethelsdorp at the hands of the alleged adulterous and morally unsound missionary James Read gave Somerset the suitable justification for doing so.[50] The Boers' claim that Bethelsdorp since the days of Van der Kemp was a place of refuge for notorious Khoikhoi captains responsible for many of the frontier conflicts in this period was accepted as dogma by Somerset who blamed the station for fostering ill will between the missionaries and the Boers.[51]

As Somerset was making some headway against the Bethelsdorp missionaries, the L.M.S. in London sent out Dr John Philip on a mission to repair the image of the society at the Cape. Somerset was initially impressed with Philip's straightforward approach and expressed his wish to the colonial secretary, Bathurst, that Philip would have success in changing the missions.[52] What Somerset was not prepared for was the high profile of Philip's mission and the kind of publicity it would receive in Britain. Philip's success at improving the image of the L.M.S. would leave Somerset without a convenient scapegoat for the administration's dilatory handling of the frontier.

48 Trapido, *Van Riebeck Day and the New Jerusalem*, p. 32. See also S.O.A.S., L.M.S., Incoming 7/4/D and L.M.S., 7/5/C.
49 Lambeth Palace Library, Howley Papers, Fulham Papers, Papers on India, Africa, Australia, North America, 1813–1827, vol. 1, f. 390: Sir Jahleel Brenton to Rev. Lancelot Lee, Simon's Bay, 24 June 1818.
50 Read had been found with a Khoikhoi mistress and was subsequently waiting for the home society's decision about his future as a missionary. The L.M.S. image at the Cape was suffering under the weight of the rumours.
51 Cory, *Rise of South Africa*, I, 296–300.
52 Cited in Mostert, *Frontiers*, p. 513.

Philip was originally very critical of what he saw at Bethelsdorp. However, it did not take long after his arrival in 1819 for Philip to spot the inconsistencies of the administration's frontier policy at the hands of Henry Somerset, Charles Somerset's eldest son, who had been put in charge of the frontier. Moreover, the alienation of the station by the administration had itself contributed to the station's decried deterioration. His conclusion was that the settlement needed to become more self-reliant, and, in order to do so, it needed to improve its technology. Philip was particularly eager to put the press to work so that the station could print its own materials.[53] On this issue, Philip learned that Somerset censured all printing from independent presses. Censure of the press at the Cape had enabled colonial officials to avert opposition.[54]

Philip also noted that the decline of Bethelsdorp was related to the administration's endorsement of harsh labour laws for the Khoikhoi. Because the Khoikhoi were employed for weeks at a time in the construction of roads miles from the station, the missionaries were finding it difficult to convert their flock. The problem of forced labour was delaying and in many cases, impeding, the evangelization of Africa. Similarly, Philip considered the apprenticeship system to be responsible for the general deplorable condition of the Boers. According to Philip, the frontier Boers were no more advanced in civilisation than the Khoikhoi.[55]

Philip's early reforms coincided with the arrival of the British settlers in 1820, only some 30 miles from Bethelsdorp. As a third voice to be added to Cape society, the settlers would change the nature of the debate concerning the problems of the frontier. On arrival, the settlers set themselves apart from the Boers, viewing them critically in keeping with the negative image of them which the settlers had inherited.[56] It was not long after the first settlement that the settlers came to resent the administration for having misled them about the safety of the frontier. The Xhosa had been quick to recognize the threat of this new invasion of Europeans on their pasture lands which they protected by raiding settler cattle. The condition of the frontier worsened as both groups retaliated by stealing each other's cattle. The settlers, who had been critical of the Boers for their treatment of the Khoikhoi, found themselves defining their own community identity in stark contrast to that of their enemy, the Xhosa.[57] Mounting hostility between Xhosa and British settlers required the tireless attention of the British administration. And, once again, the settlement at Bethelsdorp would once again be resented by frontier colonists, British and Dutch alike, for its amicable relations with the Xhosa beyond the colonial boundaries. Philip

53 Bethelsdorp had its own press in 1818 on the agreement that everything was to be approved by the government. S.O.A.S., L.M.S., 6/4/A. See also L.M.S., 5/1/F – 5/3/D.
54 W. Bird, *State of the Cape of Good Hope in 1822* (Africana Collectanea, XIX, Cape Town, 1966), p. 58.
55 Mostert, *Frontiers*, p. 526.
56 Thomas Pringle, *Narrative of a Residence in South Africa* (1835), p. 58.
57 Andrew Bank, 'Liberals and their Enemies: Racial Ideology at the Cape of Good Hope, 1820–1850', University of Cambridge Ph.D., 1995.

found himself trying to curb the effects of rumours that missionaries had been illegally selling guns to the enemy.[58]

Like Van der Kemp, Philip was fascinated by the Xhosa and saw the conversion of the Xhosa as the doorway to the rest of Africa.[59] Since his arrival, he had been trying to get the permission of the administration for missionary access to the Xhosa beyond the colony. On this issue, Philip did not exclude the methodists. The rejection of his proposals by the colonial government did not discourage him. Instead, he threatened the government that he would use his influence and write directly to the colonial secretary, Bathurst, and, failing that, he would call upon the aid of the British public. He added to his threat that he would inform his sources that Secretary Bird, who was the provisional governor while Somerset was on leave in England, was a Roman catholic.[60]

This fascination with the Xhosa, however, would get Philip in trouble with the British settlers. They resented his meddling in frontier matters, a sentiment that would be channelled through the community's newspaper, the *Grahamstown Journal*. In the early 1820s, the colonial administration took its own action against Philip's threats. Somerset criticized Philip to Bathurst claiming that Philip was responsible for many of the frontier difficulties. The colonial office was beginning to reconsider the wisdom of having Philip remain in the colony.[61] Reports from anglican clergy also confirmed that Philip's mission had become political rather than religious.[62]

Without waiting for government sanction of Philip's proposal to take the mission to the Xhosa (the policy of a closed frontier was particularly dear to Somerset), Philip began making his own views known to the home society. Wilberforce took a special interest in Philip's claim that the Xhosa were the key to Africa's salvation and therefore began investigating the question between 1822 and 1824.[63] Philip's discovery of letters sent by the *Landdrost* of Uitenhage to James Read also confirmed that Read's accounts of abuses of the Khoikhoi had not been exaggerated all these years. With this concrete evidence to substantiate Read's claims, Philip began to mobilize his forces against the administration. He had the evidence that he needed to exonerate the L.M.S. mission from a decade of misrepresentation by colonial officials.[64]

58 Ross, *Dr John Philip*, p. 44.
59 Enklaar, *Van der Kemp*, pp. 86–109; Ross, *Dr John Philip*.
60 Mostert, *Frontiers*, pp. 551–2.
61 *Ibid.*, p. 583.
62 The bishop of London received complaints that Philip was a dangerous member of society or a 'violent political character'. The government was becoming aware of the difficulty of independent preachers. Lambeth Palace Lib., Howley Papers, Fulham Papers, f. 445: Rev. Hough to bishop of London, Cape Town, 26 July 1824.
63 S.O.A.S., L.M.S., Home Office, Incoming, 4/1/B and 4/2/A.
64 Mostert, *Frontiers*, pp. 553–5.

Philip left for England in 1826 where he began his campaigning to vindicate the society by using the Khoikhoi issue. Upon his return, however, he discovered that his support had waned on account of the negative reports against him coming from South Africa.[65] Thomas Fowell Buxton, the president of the Anti-Slavery Society, who became convinced that the question of the aboriginal people was within the objectives of his society, gave Philip the backing he needed. With Buxton's en-couragement, Philip published his *Researches in South Africa* in 1828 which laid out in detail his criticism of the British administration as well as the Dutch and British settlers' treatment of the aborigines. The publication was well received by the abolitionist public in Britain and began talk of reform of the Cape laws by the colonial office. Before news of Philip's *Researches* reached the Cape, the more liberal administration under Major-General Sir Richard Bourke remodelled the constitutional, judicial and administrative systems in the Cape Colony in 1828. The most significant of these reforms was Ordinance 50, passed in 1829, which made the Khoikhoi freemen, entitled to all the privileges offered to other subjects of the British crown.[66] Buxton later remarked that this important legislation had passed in silence because Westminster had been so absorbed on the question of catholic emancipation.[67]

Neither Philip's *Researches* nor Ordinance 50 passed in silence at the Cape. The revocation of former Dutch laws placed the Boer way of life once again under threat of assimilation and precipitated the great trek.[68] The British settlers had also been affected by the new law, many of them now relying on cheap Khoikhoi labour on their farms. The new piece of legislation confirmed that the colonial administration was prepared to desert them on the issue of the Khoikhoi despite their own suffering since their arrival on the frontier. Perhaps more infuriating still was Philip's suggestion that the settlers were no different from the Boers.[69] Philip's criticism of the British settlers' use of the commando system to retrieve lost cattle from the Xhosa was accepted by the public in Britain. The alienation of the British settlers from the British public, and indeed from the Cape administration, combined to foster community independence that was similar to the Boers own developing sense of community self-reliance, and even an eastern Cape separatism that would become more apparent in the 1840s.[70]

What conclusions can we draw from our examination of the complexities of the issue of toleration in the South African context? Let us quickly review the many themes discussed throughout this paper. Toleration was in practice the toleration of

---

65 Ross, *Dr John Philip*, p. 36.
66 Elizabeth Elbourne, 'Freedom at Issue: Vagrancy Legislation and the Meaning of Freedom in Britain and the Cape Colony, 1799 to 1842', *Slavery and Abolition*, xv (1994), 114–50.
67 Mostert, *Frontiers*, pp. 586–9.
68 J. S. Marais, *The Cape Coloured People, 1652–1937* (Johannesburg, 1957), p. 160.
69 W. M. MacMillan, *The Cape Coloured Question* (1927), p. 172.
70 Bank, 'Liberals and their Enemies', p. 353.

Dutch institutions by the British. As in India and Quebec, the British used existing institutions for convenience as much as for maintaining the security of colonial possession. The British found it easy to accommodate the Dutch because they were protestants. Where the problem lay was in the difference of theological views. Anglicans as a minority, largely in charge of the British military corps, were less inclined to engage the D.R.C. on its theology. The L.M.S., however, although calvinist, differed fundamentally from the D.R.C. on the issue of justification by faith alone.[71] To the missionaries in the field such as Van der Kemp and Philip and to English evangelicals such as Wilberforce, slavery prevented the individual from obtaining salvation through self-reflection. According to the evangelical creed, all human beings were entitled to salvation. The D.R.C. had strict codes of conduct for the elect Dutch, which excluded non-christians from taking part as Van der Kemp's experience in Graaff-Reinet in 1802 demonstrated. It is more than likely that the Cape officials were unaware of the subtleties of the theological arguments being used by both parties which may account for their initial ambivalence about handling such civilian disputes. For the consumption of the British public these theological differences on slavery would be distilled into the image of the Boers as a primitive and backward people. This formula would not only cast the Dutch into a lower social strata at the Cape, but it would eventually bring down other Dutch institutions such as Dutch customary law, which was to be replaced by British codes of justice in the 1830s.

British dissenters also found the path to toleration a rather bumpy one at best: colonial officers did all they could to exclude them from the empire-building process. The colonial administration was primarily concerned with the transformation of the city in this empire-building process. Particularly important to this enterprise was the building of anglican churches which represented British ethnicity. In the nineteenth century, Cape Town was transformed into a lovely Victorian port. On the vital route between India and Britain, it became one of the main centres of trade.[72] The city itself reflected the pride of British civilization against the backdrop of an otherwise untamed African landscape. Despite attempts to exclude the dissenters from this construction of 'Britishness' in South Africa, missionaries none the less made themselves a powerful force in frontier politics, which in the end, made the frontier a primary concern for the colonial administration throughout the nineteenth century.

The L.M.S. was empowered by its command of frontier affairs, particularly as it could relay first hand information back to the London public through their press. Despite the efforts made by successive administrations to discredit the society, the L.M.S. became skilled at circumventing the administration by using the missionary society's press in England. Consequently, although dissenters in England were still

---

71 Elbourne, 'Early Khoisan Uses of Mission Christianity', p. 8.

72 Vivian Bickford-Smith, *Ethnic Pride and Racial Prejudice in Victorian Cape Town. Group Identity and Social Practice, 1875–1902* (Cambridge, 1995), pp. 10–13.

fighting to obtain full toleration, the rising stature of the L.M.S. earned by its activities in South Africa raised the profile of dissent in British society.[73] The L.M.S. provided through the establishment of museums and the creative use of propaganda much of the popular culture of empire. L.M.S. reports encouraged mission expansion by appealing to British nationalism and Britain's civilizing mission, and in doing so, transformed the tastes of the imperial public.[74] Philip pioneered the art of manipulating these tastes with his *Researches*, a collection of stories of the savagery of the Boers and the British settlers toward the aboriginal people. Later propaganda taken from the correspondence of missionaries such as Robert Moffet and David Livingstone would propagate the image of missionary heroes combatting the hostile African environment to bring civilization and christianity to the 'heathen'. Philip's hostile frontier in 1828, however, was not made dangerous by the Africans or the wildlife but by its state of lawlessness because of unruly European frontiersmen and a weak colonial administration.

The quest for religious freedom within the expanding empire began with the missionary assault on what was taken to be a deficient African culture. There had been no Burkean debate about the preservation of African customs and traditions in the eighteenth century as there had been on India largely because there had been no African proto-anthropological research to match the orientalist research of Sir William Jones, who had stimulated an interest in the east that was not only commercial but academic. Unlike the orientalists, European observers did not attribute to the indigenous people of the west and southern Africa any organized religion nor any of the markers of civilization that had characterized the ancient civilizations of Egypt or Asia. This perceived deficiency led evangelicals to believe that Africa waited for the light of christianity in order to illumine its path toward civilization.

British intervention in Africa, unlike in India, had been largely the result of the popular opposition to the slave trade during the late eighteenth century. The abolitionists institutionalized the African victim who needed to be brought under the paternal care of the christian world and to be protected under British laws. The success of the abolitionist movement had depended on a popularized sympathy for the condition of Africa rather than an orientalist-like fascination with differences in culture. This was most certainly true of Philip's contention that the condition of the Khoikhoi under the labour laws at the Cape, which gave them no legal recourse against abusive employers, was no better than the condition of slavery. Philip's account of the failures of the colonial administration in South Africa enabled missionary societies to continue to argue that interventionism to ameliorate the condition of the African was warranted according to British notions of justice. The

---

73 William Law Mathieson, *British Slavery and its Abolition 1823–1838* (New York, 1967), p. 197.
74 John L. and Jean Comaroff, *Of Revelation and Revolution. Christianity, Colonialism and Consciousness in South Africa* (2 vols., Chicago, 1991–7), I.

end result was a line of argument that missionaries used to put pressure on the administration to become more involved in quarrels between farmers and indigenous peoples on the frontier rather than to allow these matters to resolve themselves. As the administration tightened its control of the frontier, the eighteenth-century policy of non-intervention was being replaced by the colonialism of the nineteenth century. The question of the condition of the Khoikhoi as with the question of religious toleration had an impact on the emerging British liberalism that was behind the many parliamentary reforms of the 1830s.

The sudden distancing of the British administration from its former policy of toleration at the Cape, whether of the Dutch Reformed Church or existing institutions and laws, may be partly responsible for much of the anti-British sentiment that provoked the great trek of 1835. Somerset's anglicization of Dutch institutions had already caused some apprehension within the Dutch community of Cape Town. The dissenting missionaries accomplished much the same thing on the frontier; Philip's *Researches* had added to the community's general discontent with the British. The missionary movement had widened the gap and even exaggerated the cultural differences between the two linguistic groups. The Dutch language newspaper *Zuid Afrikaan* was one of many defences against the anglicizing onslaught. These differences are best depicted by the editor of *Zuid Afrikaan* who observed of the politics at the Cape since the second British occupation in what he called the four 'humbugs':

> Wy beginnen met FREE-PRESS **humbug**,-INDEPENDENT NEWSPAPER **humbug**, MISSIONARY **humbug**, en vooral (want dit is de paramount of non plus ultra van alle **humbugs**) de PHILIPISH-**humbug**. Vestigt, vooreest uwe geheele aandacht op deze vier voorname **humbugs**.[75]

It has been the purpose of this paper to show that toleration was the thread used by colonial administrations to tie the innovations of the eighteenth century to the changing circumstances of the nineteenth century. Toleration at the Cape began as a practical accommodation for defensive reasons, then created the conditions for assimilation and finally provoked a resurgence of ethnic defiance. Missionary attempts at christianization on the frontier met with success; this success had two contradictory outcomes. It created conflict with the Dutch (and later the British settlers), forcing the administration to abandon its tolerant, i.e. non-interventionist policy; its chosen means of pacifying the Dutch was assimilation, which provoked more hostility and failed. The British settlers of the 1820s became more like the Dutch, resenting the elevation of the Khoikhoi. There emerged a kind of common independent anti-metropolitan frontier outlook in both the Dutch and the British of the frontier. The other outcome of the success of the L.M.S. was the strengthening of reformist opinion in Britain against the Cape administration, and all such colonial administrations as in India (first with respect to the Company) which did not operate according

---

[75] *Zuid Afrikaan*, 16, 23 Sept. 1830, cited in Trapido, *Van Riebeck Day and the New Jerusalem*, p. 43.

to the emerging high ideals of British justice. These ideals put pressure on colonial governments (to a point) making it more difficult for them to deal with problems on the ground in the usual bureaucratic, military manner. The African story undermined the toleration of the Cape Dutch without successfully establishing an alternative to toleration in its own case. As a result the aboriginal peoples were neither assimilated nor valued in their own culture and allowed to evolve on their own.

Finally, the South African case reveals that the canvassing for reform of colonial government began in the colony itself rather than in the metropolis, as in Quebec, before shaping the way British liberals came to interpret conflicts between colonists and aboriginal people. Unlike Philip Lawson, I have accented the dialogue on toleration in the colonial situation. Lawson's great offering to the debate on empire, however, was his recognition that 'contemporary observers and commentators fully recognised the critical domestic ramifications of an expansionist policy that resulted in the governance of alien peoples and their cultures'.[76] It is this great awareness on the part of the Hanoverians that made the governance of the Cape colony a thorny problem in its own right. Indeed, the imperial public grasped 'the nettle of toleration' in a period of tremendous political change.[77]

76 Lawson, *Imperial Challenge*, p. 1.
77 *Ibid.*, p. 151.

17

A Working Peer Making Aristocracy Work:
The Third Lord Calthorpe*

DAVID CANNADINE

The period of British history from the loss of the American colonies until the passing of the Great Reform Act is one about which historians will surely never agree. It was once fashionable to stress the importance of change, disruption and modernity: the making of the working class, the rise of the middle class, the ups and downs of the industrial revolution, the unprecedented population growth and urbanization, and the widespread popular discontent.[1] But in recent years there has been a shift of emphasis, as some scholars now stress continuity and tradition rather than change and innovation, while others explore the conservative imperatives and implications of the changes which *did* occur.[2] One aspect of this, which Philip Lawson's work did so much to illuminate, was the consolidation and expansion of an increasingly militaristic and authoritarian empire: consolidated in Canada and Ireland, expanded in India and

---

* The two chief archive sources on which this study relies are the Calthorpe family papers in the Hampshire Record Office, Winchester (hereafter H.R.O., Cal. MS), and the Edgbaston Estate papers in the Calthorpe Edgbaston Estate office (hereafter E.E.O., MS). I have also consulted the Harrowby papers at Sandon Hall in Staffordshire (hereafter Harrowby MS), the Peel papers in the British Library, and the Local Collection at the Birmingham Reference Library (hereafter B.R.L., MS). I am most grateful to the late Brigadier Sir Richard Anstruther-Gough-Calthorpe and the late Lord Harrowby for permission to let me consult their archival collections, and to Professor Derek Beales, Dr Peter Mathias and Professor Lawrence Stone for their comments on earlier versions of this essay. Thanks also to the History of Parliament Trust, for generously allowing me to see draft biographies of the Hon. Arthur Gough-Calthorpe and the Hon. Frederick Gough-Calthorpe (the copyright of the biographies remains with the Trust). My title is shamelessly (but appreciatively) appropriated from A. Adonis, *Making Aristocracy Work. The Peerage and the Political System in Britain, 1884–1914* (Oxford, 1993).

1 This interpretation can be found in many books written a generation ago. For some of the most distinguished and influential examples, see H. J. Perkin, *The Origins of Modern English Society, 1780–1880* (1969); E. P. Thompson, *The Making of the English Working Class* (Harmondsworth, 1968); E. J. Hobsbawm, *Industry and Empire* (1968); A. Briggs, *The Age of Improvement, 1783–1867* (1959).

2 N. F. R. Crafts, *British Economic Growth During the Industrial Revolution* (Oxford, 1985); J. A. Cannon, *Aristocratic Century. The Peerage in Eighteenth-Century England* (Cambridge, 1984); J. C. D. Clark, *English Society, 1688–1832. Ideology, Social Structure and Political Practice During the Ancien Regime* (Cambridge, 1985); L. Stone and J. C. F. Stone, *An Open Elite? England 1540–1889* (Oxford, 1984).

South Africa, and everywhere characterized by a growth in proconsular pomp and circumstance.[3] Another was the resurgence of the aristocracy: as the promoters and beneficiaries of the industrial revolution, and as the rejuvenated governing *élite* of the British nation and empire.[4]

This essay addresses the second of these developments by investigating the life of George, third Lord Calthorpe, an aristocrat who mattered in his day, but who has been forgotten by posterity. He was both the embodiment and the beneficiary of two eighteenth-century trends: the possibilities of upward social mobility, especially for those born in comfortable circumstances, and the demographic crisis by which so many landowning families were afflicted, not always to their disadvantage. His paternal grandfather was Sir Richard Gough, the younger son of a Staffordshire country gentleman, who went into business, made a fortune in the far eastern trade, was knighted in 1715 and retired two years later, having purchased the manor of Edgbaston on the outskirts of Birmingham for £20,400. Sir Richard's eldest son, Henry Gough, was created a baronet by George II, and consolidated his position by marrying, in 1742, the heiress Barbara Calthorpe, who came from an ancient landed family in Norfolk.[5] Their son, Sir Henry Gough-Calthorpe, who combined his father's name with that of his mother, was ennobled by the younger Pitt in 1796, as the first Baron Calthorpe. He died two years later, and his eldest son Charles only survived as the second Lord Calthorpe for nine years. On his death in 1807, the title passed to his younger brother George, who had been born in 1787, and who was at the time of his succession an undergraduate at St John's College, Cambridge.[6]

The third lord's inheritance was adequate, if not fabulous. From the Gough side, the most important item was the Edgbaston estate, an agricultural property on which nine building leases had been granted between 1786 and 1796. There were also 23 acres, adjacent to Gray's Inn Road in London, which had been bought by Sir Richard Gough in 1706, and the pocket borough of Bramber in Sussex, for which Sir Richard and both Sir Henrys had sat during the eighteenth century and which, during the third Lord Calthorpe's public life, would have as one of its representatives his younger

---

3 C. A. Bayly, *Imperial Meridian. The British Empire and the World, 1780–1830* (1989); P. Lawson, *The Imperial Challenge. Quebec and Britain in the Age of the American Revolution* (Montreal, 1989); E. H. Gould, 'American Independence and Britain's Counter Revolution', *Past and Present*, 154 (1997), 107–41.

4 M. W. McCahill, *Order and Equipoise. The Peerage and the House of Lords, 1783–1806* (1978); *idem*, 'Peers, Patronage and the Industrial Revolution, 1760–1800', *Journal of British Studies*, XVI (1976), 84–107; P. Jenkins, *The Making of a Ruling Class. The Glamorgan Gentry, 1640–1790* (Cambridge, 1983); L. J. Colley, *Britons. Forging the Nation, 1707–1837* (1992), pp. 147–236; D. Cannadine, *Aspects of Aristocracy. Grandeur and Decline in Modern Britain* (1994), pp. 9–36.

5 For the Goughs' ancestry, see S. Shaw, *The History and Antiquities of Staffordshire* (2 vols., 1798–1801), II, 188–90. For the Calthorpes, see C. W. C. Calthrop, *Notes on the Families of Calthorpe and Calthrop in the Counties of Norfolk and Lincolnshire* (1905), *passim*. For the purchase of Edgbaston, see E.E.O., MS: release of the manor of Edgbaston in the county of Warwick, 16 Apr. 1717; B.R.L., MS 252037: conveyance deed, 10 July 1717.

6 J. A. Venn, *Alumni Cantabrigiensis, Part II, 1752–1900* (6 vols., Cambridge, 1940–51), I, 492.

brothers Arthur (1825–6) and Frederick (1826–31).[7] The more extensive Calthorpe
properties included a house and lands at Elvetham in Hampshire, the Pakenham estate
and a mansion at Ampton in Suffolk, and the historic family holdings on the north
Norfolk coast. There was also a half share in the pocket borough of Hindon in
Wiltshire, which would be represented by Frederick (1818–26) and Arthur
(1826–30), and a town house in Grosvenor Square. This inheritance provided the
third Lord Calthorpe with a gross income of £15,000 a year, and a disposable income
of two thirds that amount.[8] It formed the foundation for a varied and useful life: as
a rural and urban landlord; as an evangelical and philanthropist; and as a hereditary
legislator of liberal and well-informed views.

I

As befitted the unsystematic manner in which they had been acquired, by purchase
and inheritance, the estates which Lord Calthorpe inherited consisted of relatively
small parcels of land, none larger than 2,000 acres, scattered in five counties, along
with houses of varying size at Ampton, Elvetham and Edgbaston. During his tenure
of the title, the third lord was an attentive and innovative landowner, eager to
improve and enhance his inheritance. But there were limits to what he could achieve.
For much of the 1810s and 1820s, agriculture was in a depressed state, and he was
obliged to make extensive abatements of rentals in Norfolk, Suffolk and Hampshire.[9]
But the land he owned on the rapidly-expanding urban frontiers of London and
Birmingham offered much more positive prospects. In 1814, Calthorpe obtained a
private act of parliament, which enabled him to grant 99 year building leases on his
Gray's Inn Road estate, and also gave him powers to set up commissioners to pave,
light, cleanse and regulate the streets. In practice, this meant that most of the
development costs were thrown on the lessee, Thomas Cubitt, then at the beginning
of his Olympian career as a master builder. In two 'takes', one of 1815 and the other
of 1823, he assumed effective responsibility, agreeing not only to construct the
houses, but also to level the land, make the roads and lay the sewers. Calthorpe was

7 *The Survey of London*, XXIV, *The Parish of St Pancras*, pt. IV (1952), p. 57; R. Sedgwick, *The
   House of Commons, 1715–1754* (2 vols., 1970), I, 333; II, 73; Sir L. Namier and J. Brooke, *The
   House of Commons, 1754–1790* (3 vols., 1964), I, 390; II, 522; R. Thorne, *The House of Commons,
   1790–1820* (5 vols., 1986), II, 391–2; IV, 43; F. O'Gorman, *Voters, Patrons, and Parties. The
   Unreformed Electoral System of Hanoverian England, 1734–1832* (Oxford, 1989), pp. 32–3.
8 Sedgwick, *House of Commons, 1715-1754*, I, 347; Namier and Brooke, *House of Commons,
   1754–1790*, I, 415–16; Thorne, *House of Commons, 1790–1820*, II, 421; O'Gorman, *Voters,
   Patrons, and Parties*, pp. 29–30; H.R.O., Cal. MS, Box 35: rents received for George, Lord
   Calthorpe from Michaelmas 1809 to Michaelmas 1810; D. Cannadine, *Lords and Landlords. The
   Aristocracy and the Towns, 1774–1967* (Leicester, 1980), pp. 124–5.
9 Cannadine, *Lords and Landlords*, pp. 124–7, 136–8.

happily spared these expenses, and by the 1830 was drawing an annual income of £2,500 from the estate.[10]

But it was the Edgbaston property which offered much greater opportunities for development as a high-class habitation for the professional, financial and industrial *élite* of Birmingham. It originally amounted to 1,700 acres, but by the 1820s it had been rounded out by judicious acquisitions to more than 2,000 acres. Situated scarcely a mile from the centre of the city, on the western side, with rolling and well-wooded country, it was the ideal place for the new rich of the industrial revolution to make their suburban homes. The handful of building leases granted during the late 1780s and early 1790s had been a portent of things to come, as had the clauses which Sir Henry Gough-Calthorpe inserted in the Birmingham and Worcester Canal Act of 1791, prohibiting the construction of factories, workshops or warehouses alongside the canal where it passed through Edgbaston.[11] In 1811, John Harris, Calthorpe's agent, drew up a more systematic scheme of improvement, a 'general and well-considered plan', which proposed the laying out of wide roads, so as to make 'an immense amount' of land available for development. By granting building leases for large houses, on stringent terms prohibiting any business or manufacture, the aim was to ensure that a high social tone was established and maintained.[12]

Lord Calthorpe agreed, and during the next 40 years the estate was developed in precisely this way, with the landlord assuming a much greater responsibility than at Gray's Inn. Wide, spacious, tree-lined roads were laid out, many named after members of the family: Calthorpe, Gough, George, Frederick, Arthur. Land and money were given for St George's Church in 1833, and for local charities anxious for clean air and sylvan surroundings: the Deaf and Dumb Asylum in 1814, the Botanical and Horticultural Society in 1830 and the General Institution for the Blind in 1851. Despite the post-Waterloo depression, and another serious downturn during the late 1820s and early 1830s, the total number of building leases granted rose from nine in 1810 to 342 by 1845, and there were other indications of similar progress. The population of Edgbaston parish more than tripled between 1810 and 1831, and Lord Calthorpe's gross rents increased from £5,233 in 1810 to £11,673 in 1845.[13] 'As a whole', Harris wrote to his employer in 1823, 'the estate bids fair both in beauty and value to exceed anything of the kind in the kingdom.' This was scarcely an

10 H.R.O., Cal. MS, Box 29: T. Cubitt's proposals and comments by James Spiller, 13 Aug. 1822; H. Hobhouse, *Thomas Cubitt. Master Builder* (1971), pp. 20–35.
11 Cannadine, *Lords and Landlords*, pp. 87–92.
12 H.R.O., Cal. MS, Box 35: John Harris, observations for Lord Calthorpe's correction, 1811; F/C/157: Harris to Calthorpe, 14 June 1813.
13 For a fuller account, see Cannadine, *Lords and Landlords*, pp. 95–9, 148.

exaggeration. Before long, Edgbaston was being described as the 'Belgravia of Birmingham'.[14]

The sustained and successful development of Edgbaston did more than provide Lord Calthorpe with a growing income: by virtue of its location, on the edge of Birmingham, it gave him close links with the new urban and industrial world, and they were links he was eager to exploit. For he was always 'anxious to learn the state of public feeling on questions of importance', and he persistently demanded to know about the fluctuations in trade and the condition of the people in the town. 'When next you write', he instructed John Harris, 'be so good as to let me hear of the state of the crops in your neighbourhood, and whether there is any improvement in the prosperity of the manufacturers.' Harris's detailed replies give a vivid account of economic, social and political life in early nineteenth-century Birmingham.[15] Here is the gloomy picture in March 1820:

> Many publicans with whom I have conversed agree that the consumption of Malt Liquor has been very much diminished during the present year, and they assign the rate of diminution at about one third part of the usual consumption. The butchers also agree in opinion as to the decrease in the quantities of butchers' meat consumed, which is in about the same proportion...
>
> The American trade is certainly very bad and must so remain until another year, as the time is past for receiving orders. Those factors whose connections are *entirely* in the home trade do not complain. Indeed, they are doing well, as they are enabled to purchase from the manufacturer at a very reduced price.
>
> But the labouring mechanic is suffering from low wages and a want of regular employment. Calculating in money and loss of time, the mechanic can scarcely earn three fifths of what he has been accustomed to obtain.[16]

In September the same year, Harris reported that 'the cause of the Queen [Caroline] has been losing ground very fast in public opinion'.[17]

Two years later, prospects had improved: trade was booming, and the public had quietened down after the excitement of the Queen's trial:

> With regard to trade here, it is certainly considerable and done with very sufficient profit. Tradesmen's bills are discounted at the banks in much greater abundance than has been the case for several years past. Phipson's pin manufactory is in full work, and they have orders in hand sufficient for two months to come ...

---

14 *Gentleman's Magazine*, XCV, pt. I (1825), 393; T. Anderton, *A Tale of One City* (Birmingham, 1900), ch. 8; J. B. Redfern, 'Elite Suburbians: Early Victorian Edgbaston', *Local Historian*, XV (1981), 79–85; L. Davidoff and C. Hall, *Family Fortunes. Men and Women of the English Middle Class, 1780–1850* (1987), pp. 368–9.

15 H.R.O., Cal. MS F/C/243: Harris to Calthorpe, 27 Aug. 1820; E.E.O., MS Box 5: Calthorpe to Harris, 10 July 1826. For a more extended discussion of this correspondence, with lengthier extracts from it, see D. Cannadine, 'Economy, Society and Parliamentary Reform: Birmingham Evidence and Westminster Reaction', *Bulletin of the Institute of Historical Research*, LII (1979), 187–99.

16 H.R.O., Cal. MS F/C/226: Harris to Calthorpe, 28 Mar. 1820.

17 *Ibid.*, F/C/247: Harris to Calthorpe, 7 Sept. 1820.

I have received the same account from many others which, with the bustle of our streets and the quietness of our population as respects political affairs, are certain indicators of general prosperity.[18]

But by August 1824, the workers were beginning to demand an increased share of these enlarged profits:

Within the last three or four weeks there has been a general turn out of workmen in this town for an increase of wages, and they have succeeded in every instance in obtaining an increase of about ten per cent upon their former wages.

The manufacturers are in considerable alarm on this account, as they state it will injure the foreign trade, the profits of which are calculated at the lowest prices; but having on hand a considerable quantity of orders, they are obliged to comply with their workmen's terms.[19]

Then in December 1825 came financial crisis and popular panic:

There seems a general disposition amongst prudent persons to withdraw, as soon as they decently can, their balances from the hands of the bankers, and it is doubtful if the confidence which existed a few months since will ever be restored... I fear the business of the town will this winter proceed very heavily.[20]

By July 1826, the prospect was slightly improved:

With respect to the state of trade at Birmingham, the accounts given by different persons are exceedingly contradictory. But the foreign trade I apprehend is generally very bad. Some branches, however, of the home trade are still in full employment. Taking a summary of the information which has been given, it would seem to appear that, dividing the trade of the town into four parts: one part is in full work or nearly so; another, two thirds; a third part about a half; and a fourth not in one third of full employment.[21]

But his letters for 1827 described in similar detail a further period of poor trade, tight credit and shorter working hours.

Calthorpe's detailed knowledge of Birmingham affairs was supplemented by information culled from other quarters. He attended public lectures on subjects ranging from anatomy to astronomy.[22] He read Adam Smith's *The Wealth of Nations*, Burke's *Thoughts and Details on Scarcity*, and the principal works on free trade and the corn laws by Chambers, Jacob and Whitmore.[23] He inquired about the county gaol

18   E.E.O., MS Box 1: Harris to Calthorpe, 6 Apr. 1822.
19   H.R.O., Cal. MS Box 35: Harris to Calthorpe, 17 Aug. 1824.
20   *Ibid.*: Harris to Calthorpe, 28 Dec. 1825.
21   *Ibid.*, F/C/969: Harris to Calthorpe, July 1826.
22   *Ibid.*, Box 30: Calthorpe's engagement book for 1826: entries for 14, 25, 28 Feb., 14 Mar. In June 1829 he unsuccessfully moved the second reading of the Anatomy Bill, which would have made more bodies available for scientific research: Hansard, *Parl. Debs.*, new ser., XXI (1829), cols. 1746-7.
23   For evidence of Calthorpe's wide reading, see E.E.O., MS Box 9: Lord Sidmouth to Calthorpe, 24 Aug. 1813; Box 5: Calthorpe to Harris, 4 Nov. 1826; Box 1: Harris to Calthorpe, 24 Nov. 1826; Box 5: Calthorpe to Harris, 30 Nov. 1826; Box 5: Calthorpe to Harris, 13 Mar. 1828. The pamphlets referred to in these letters include: E. Burke, *Thoughts and Details on Scarcity* (1800); W. Jacob, *Considerations on the Protection Required by British Agriculture* (1814); *idem, An Inquiry into the*

at Salisbury, the house of correction at Devizes, and the poor rate at Bury St Edmunds. He went aboard the prison hulks at Sheerness, and was an 'eye witness of the shocking and revolting abuses' which occurred in London mad houses. And Harris's letters from Birmingham were not confined to the state of trade and business. He produced detailed reports on the local workhouse and grammar school, and when he went further afield, he was able to provide Lord Calthorpe with more information about the state of agriculture – as in July 1826, when he sent a seven page letter, examining nine counties, crop by crop.[24]

II

The third Lord Calthorpe was not only a rich man, a rural and urban landlord, with close knowledge of life in industrial Birmingham. He was also a devout christian: a well-connected Evangelical and an active philanthropist. He saw his chief task as the promotion of 'the moral welfare of the state', and the prime agent of this 'glorious work of reformation' was the established church, the 'chief guardian of great and important truths', which he admired for the 'purity' of its doctrines and the 'strictness' of its faith.[25] These views were partly the consequence of his friendship with William Wilberforce which he inherited from his father and elder brother. The two families were distantly related through Barbara Spooner, whom Wilberforce married in 1797, and whose mother was the first Lord Calthorpe's sister. The first lord was associated with Wilberforce in founding the Society for Bettering the Conditions and Increasing the Comforts of the Poor in 1796, and following his death soon after, Wilberforce acted as a spiritual guide to the infant second lord, advising him on personal conduct and public speaking.[26]

When the third lord succeeded, their friendship flowered. Wilberforce and his family were frequent visitors to Ampton and Grosvenor Square. 'I feel a sort of *craving*', he wrote in 1815, 'to spend a few days with so beloved and so kind a friend under the shade of his own fig tree.' Eight years later, he urged Calthorpe to tell him 'unreservedly what you may think wrong either in the conduct of my children or in our treatment of them'. John Harris advised Wilberforce on the business affairs of his

---

Causes of Agricultural Distress (1816); A. H. Chambers, *Thoughts on the Resumption of Cash Payments* (1819); W. W. Whitmore, *A Letter on the Present State and Future Prospects of Agriculture* (1822); *idem, A Letter to the Electors of Bridgnorth upon the Corn Laws* (1826).

24 E.E.O., MS Box 9: Lord Sidmouth to Calthorpe, 24 Aug. 1813; Box 1: pocketbook report on Birmingham Workhouse (16 pages) and Free Grammar School (8 pages); H.R.O., Cal. MS F/C/174: J. Barton to Calthorpe, 11 Apr. 1815; F/C/278: Sidmouth to Calthorpe, 17 July 1821; F/C/781: H. Estwurt to Calthorpe, 28 Nov. 1823; Box 35: Harris to Calthorpe, 17 Aug. 1824; F/C/969: Harris to Calthorpe, July 1826; Hansard, *Parl. Debs.*, new ser., XIX (1828), col. 199.

25 Hansard, *Parl. Debs.*, new ser., II (1820), col. 739; XI (1824), col. 85; XVIII (1828), col. 1606; H.R.O., Cal. MS F/C/1242: Calthorpe to Lord Liverpool, n.d. [c. 1820].

26 F. K. Brown, *Fathers of the Victorians* (Cambridge, 1961), p. 88; *The Private Papers of William Wilberforce*, ed. A. M. Wilberforce (1897), pp. 102–5: Lord Calthorpe to Wilberforce, 2 Sept. 1801.

son, Calthorpe was godfather to his friend's first grandchild, and they shared with each other the most intimate family news.[27] When Wilberforce gave up his demanding Yorkshire constituency in 1812, it was to Calthorpe's pocket borough at Bramber that he gratefully removed. His retirement from public life in 1825 did nothing to lessen their friendship, as is evidenced by one of his last letters: 'My dear friend, may God bless and prosper you, especially in the most important particulars. Oh what cause for thankfulness have you for having been called to the knowledge and feeling of salvation through the Redeemer. May you grow in grace more and more.' Not surprisingly, Calthorpe was among those from both houses of parliament who signed the letter to the Wilberforce family urging that he be buried in Westminster Abbey.[28]

These links of family and friendship with Wilberforce naturally drew a pious man like Calthorpe into the larger world of early nineteenth-century evangelicalism. He became the 'frequent companion and chaperon' of Thomas Chalmers, the Scottish preacher and writer, who was especially concerned by the condition and suffering of the labouring poor, and by the threat that urban poverty presented to the established order, and who was very much the intellectual powerhouse of the evangelical movement.[29] He corresponded with Hannah More, Thomas Fowell Buxton, the young Baptist Noel and Zachary Macaulay – the latter receiving on one occasion 'two magnificent parcels of game'. In January 1815, Calthorpe was among the chief mourners at Henry Thornton's funeral, and a year later was one of those who greeted the now-orphaned Marianne on her return to Clapham after her long tour to recover from the sudden death of both her parents.[30] But along with Wilberforce, Calthorpe's closest evangelical friendship was with Joseph John Gurney of Earlham, the Quaker and a fellow Norfolk landowner. They first met in Norwich in 1816, and despite their doctrinal differences, a close friendship soon developed, Gurney addressing Calthorpe as 'my dear and noble friend at Ampton', and reciprocating at Earlham his London and Suffolk hospitality.[31]

---

27 E.E.O., MS Box 5: Calthorpe to Harris, 18 Nov. 1828; H.R.O., Cal. MS F/C/63: Wilberforce to Calthorpe, 22 Aug. 1815; F/C/110: Wilberforce to Calthorpe, 24 Jan. 1822; F/C/90: Wilberforce to Calthorpe, 8 Aug. 1823; F/C/91: Wilberforce to Calthorpe, 23 Aug. 1823.

28 R. I. and S. Wilberforce, *The Life of William Wilberforce* (5 vols., 1838), IV, 61–2; V, 356–7, 373–4; R. Coupland, *Wilberforce. A Narrative* (Oxford, 1923), p. 374.

29 J. McCaffrey, 'Thomas Chalmers and Social Change', *Scottish Historical Review*, LX (1981), 32–60; A. J. B. Hilton, *The Age of Atonement. The Influence of Evangelicalism on Social and Economic Thought, 1795–1865* (Oxford, 1988), pp. 55–63.

30 H.R.O., Cal. MS F/C/1004: Macaulay to Calthorpe, 14 Oct. 1826; F/C/660: Noel to Calthorpe, 19 May 1823; F/C/684: Noel to Calthorpe, 13 June 1823; E. M. Forster, *Marianne Thornton. A Domestic Biography, 1797–1887* (1956), p. 98.

31 H.R.O., Cal. MS F/C/218B: Gurney to Calthorpe, 4 Mar. 1820; F/C/925: Gurney to Calthorpe, 15 Nov. 1825; F/C/994: Gurney to Calthorpe, 25 Sept. 1826; *Memoirs of Joseph John Gurney. With Selections from his Journal and Correspondence*, ed. J. B. Braithwaite (2 vols., 1854), I, 109, 233, 264, 288, 307; D. Swift, *Joseph John Gurney. Banker, Reformer and Quaker* (Middletown, Ct., 1962), pp. 120–1.

For all their saintliness, the evangelicals were a clubbable coterie, and Calthorpe was very much part of it. At Ampton, the Gurneys and Wilberforces were especially welcome. In Birmingham, he was at the centre of an expanding evangelical network, which included Bishop Henry Ryder, who was translated from Gloucester to Lichfield in 1824, and his relative William Spooner, who was appointed archdeacon of Coventry three years later. From February until June or July, the parliamentary session drew Calthorpe to London, where his like-minded, high-minded guests included not only Wilberforce, Macaulay, Buxton and the Gurneys, but also Lord Teignmouth, the Babingtons, Charles Simeon, Lord Hervey and Viscount Sandon.[32] Together, they dined, gossiped and laid their plans. 'Yesterday', wrote Lord Teignmouth, 'I dined with Lord Calthorpe, where I met the Bishop of Worcester, Mr Simeon and Mr Macaulay, and I passed a very agreeable evening.' 'We are to have a select party tomorrow at Lord Calthorpe's', Macaulay informed Wilberforce three years later, 'purposely to talk over slavery. If, therefore, you are drawn to town, you will know where the conspirators are assembled.'[33]

As a man who 'in heart and religion went with the Missionary cause', Calthorpe was closely involved with the running of many of the great evangelical societies which had been founded in the days of his youth, with their headquarters in London, and branches all over the country. He was patron of one, president of three (including the Benevolent Loan Society), vice-president of 24 (including the Church Missionary Society), and governor of four (including Christ's Hospital and the British Lying-In Hospital).[34] But he was more than just a figurehead: he was also an active participant in their day-to-day affairs. When resident in East Anglia, he shared with the Gurneys the task of chairing the local Bible Society meetings at Norwich, Acle and Ipswich. When visiting Birmingham, he attended the Birmingham Church Missionary Society, the Warwickshire Bible Society and the Birmingham Bible Society, as well as looking in on the charities located on his Edgbaston estate. And in London, he was one of the busiest of the evangelicals, attending meetings, sitting on committees and making speeches to such organizations as the British and Foreign Bible Society and the Anti-Slavery Society.[35]

Calthorpe was also a generous financial supporter of these institutions, and of many other good causes. His bank book for the years following 1808 shows extensive

32 H.R.O., Cal. MS Box 30: Calthorpe's engagement books for 1823, 1825, 1826, 1830. For Bishop Ryder, see W. J. Baker, 'Henry Ryder of Gloucester, 1815–1824: England's First Evangelical Bishop', *Transactions of the Bristol and Gloucestershire Archaeological Society*, LXXXIX (1970), 130–44; Davidoff and Hall, *Family Fortunes*, p. 84.

33 Wilberforce and Wilberforce, *Wilberforce*, v, 166; Lord Teignmouth, *Memoir of the Life and Correspondence of John, Lord Teignmouth* (2 vols., 1843), II, 371.

34 C. Hole, *Early History of the Church Missionary Society* (1896), pp. 585–6; Brown, *Fathers of the Victorians*, pp. 329–40, 357.

35 H.R.O., Cal. MS Box 30: Calthorpe's engagement books for 1823, 1825, 1826 and 1830; F/C/194: Gurney to Calthorpe, 10 Nov. 1815; F/C/490: Gurney to Calthorpe, 7 Sept. 1822; *The Christian Observer*, XIX (1820), 422; *The Anti-Slavery Monthly Reporter*, I (1827), 2–3.

outgoings for charitable purposes, with items such as 'Middlesex Hospital, £100', 'Irish Education Society, £120', and 'Christ's Hospital, £400'. These were initial purchases of shares in institutions of which he subsequently became an officer and a regular subscriber. Altogether, his London subscription list extended to 46 societies, which was twice as many as Zachary Macaulay, Lord Teignmouth and Lord Harrowby, and was exceeded among individual evangelicals only by Sir Thomas Baring, the bishop of Durham, Lord Bexley and William Wilberforce himself.[36] Calthorpe also subscribed generously to the churches and charities on his Edgbaston estate and more broadly in Birmingham, Hampshire, Suffolk and Norfolk. It is difficult to arrive at a comprehensive total for his giving, but a figure substantially in excess of £500 a year in the 1820s might not be too wide of the mark.[37]

Like all noblemen, Calthorpe also received a constant stream of begging letters, from the poor, or from the better-educated writing on their behalf. Widows, orphans and the sick; destitute government employees, out-of-work servants and indebted artisans; doctors, teachers and soldiers: all wrote, seeking money, custom or a job. It is impossible to know to how many he responded, with a letter or a gift. But about half contain references to his previous 'kind support', his 'bounty', his 'benevolence', his 'former kindness' and his 'handsome assistance'.[38] Many letters began by referring to 'the long-established connection that exists between your lordship's name and everything that is benevolent, humane and condescending', and there are specific acknowledgments: for six guineas, for religious tracts, for a loan of £21, for a 'remittance', for letters of introduction. And there were other private acts of goodness: letters to the home secretary, Robert Peel, about reprieves to convicts; the employment of the poor on his lands at Acle in the winter of 1826; and the buildings of roads at Edgbaston in the winter of 1817–18, which 'furnished employment for many poor persons during the last months who otherwise might have received parochial assistance'.[39]

---

36 H.R.O., Cal. MS Box 30: Hoares' Bank account book, 1808–14; Brown, *Fathers of the Victorians*, pp. 354–8.
37 Cannadine, *Lords and Landlords*, pp. 148–9; H.R.O., Cal. MS F/C/1207: subscriptions paid to charitable institutions, 14 Feb. to 6 June 1829.
38 H.R.O., Cal. MS F/C/228: M. Willett to Calthorpe, 30 Mar. 1820; F/C/707: J. Caulfield to Calthorpe, 13 Aug. 1821; F/C/417: S. Hyde to Calthorpe, 29 Nov. 1821; F/C/595: T. Ellis to Calthorpe, 12 Feb. 1823; F/C/598: S. Fitzgerald to Calthorpe, 16 Feb. 1823; F/C/803: G. Buttle to Calthorpe, 18 Feb. 1824; F/C/916: H. Pengree to Calthorpe, 3 Oct. 1825; F/C/1075: H. Reeves to Calthorpe, 23 Dec. 1827; F/C/1112: J. Locke to Calthorpe, 4 Feb. 1828; F/C/1113: W. Phelps to Calthorpe, 6 June 1828; F/C/1150: W. Rees to Calthorpe, 29 May 1828; F/C/1152: E. Evans to Calthorpe, 13 June 1828; F/C/1201: A. Jones to Calthorpe, 23 July 1829.
39 *Ibid.*, F/C/233: E. Hewlett to Calthorpe, 11 Apr. 1820; F/C/377: A. De Bathyn to Calthorpe, 1 Nov. 1821; F/C/216: W. Beebe to Calthorpe, 17 Feb. 1820; F/C/1023: E. Sidney to Calthorpe, 20 Dec. 1826; Box 30: W. Beebe to Calthorpe, 21 Feb. 1827; F/C/982: L. Manton to Calthorpe, 23 Aug. 1826; F/C/1152: E. Evans to Calthorpe, 13 June 1828; F/C/1150: W. Rees to Calthorpe, 29 May 1828; F/C/1007: D. MacNamara to Calthorpe, 4 Oct. 1826; B.L., Add. MS (Peel Papers) 40367, f. 112: Peel to Calthorpe, 26 July 1824; 40369, f. 18: Calthorpe to Peel, 6 Oct. 1824; 40369, f. 19: Peel to Calthorpe, 11 Oct. 1824; E.E.O., MS Box 1: Harris to the Hon. F. Gough-Calthorpe, May 1818.

Calthorpe's charitable, philanthropic and evangelical endeavours might best be seen as arising from religious impulse, social concern, prudent estate management, detailed knowledge of contemporary conditions and anxiety about the stability of society in which he wanted to see 'loyalty and respect to rank' maintained. He believed Queen Caroline to have been guilty of 'gross and degrading familiarities', but he voted against the Bill of Pains and Penalties because the proceedings in parliament had had a 'mischevious effect on public morals', by enlisting 'the warm and generous feelings of the community on the side of licentiousness'.[40] And as he explained to Lord Liverpool, he opposed the practice of allowing prostitutes on board royal navy ships when in port, partly because the sailors were already 'sunk into the lowest depths of evil and personal depravity and degredation', and partly because it would expose them to 'a degree of moral contagion as depraving as that of the lowest brothel'. The well-being of every community, Calthorpe insisted, was 'intimately concerned with the general state of its morality'. 'Surely', he concluded, 'it is high time to awake to a sense of the dangers that beset us?' For him, as for many evangelicals, the 'glorious work of reformation' was not only a moral and religious crusade; it was also an attempt to safeguard the established order.[41]

III

But although he had much in common with government men like Peel and Liverpool, Calthorpe was so liberal a tory in politics that, according to *The Complete Peerage*, 'he was a Whig for many years'.[42] His first recorded partisan speech in the Lords, in May 1816, was in favour of Lord Grosvenor's motion to retrench and reduce patronage, and in February 1822 he supported Lord Suffield's advocacy of retrenchment and parliamentary reform. During the remainder of the decade, he constantly voted or spoke on the side of Grey, Brougham, Fitzwilliam and Devonshire. Between June 1823 and May 1828, he spoke four times in favour of easing the marriage laws for dissenters and three times in support of amendments to

---

40 Hansard, *Parl. Debs.*, new ser., III (1820), cols. 1671–75; H.R.O., Cal. MS F/C/247: Harris to Calthorpe, 7 Sept. 1820.
41 H.R.O., Cal. MS F/C/1242: Calthorpe to Lord Liverpool, n.d. [c. 1820]. The Evangelicals' respect for the established order is well documented: see Perkin, *Origins of Modern English Society*, p. 282, and the references cited there.
42 Hilton, *Age of Atonement*, p. 61, describes him as a 'supporter' of the liberal tories. But cf. G. E. Cockayne, *The Complete Peerage*, ed. V. Gibbs (new edn., 13 vols., 1910–40), II, 491. For the certainties and uncertainties of party alignments in this period, see P. Fraser, 'Party Voting in the House of Commons, 1812–27', *English Historical Review*, XCVIII (1983), 763–84; F. O'Gorman, 'Party Politics in the Early Nineteenth Century (1812–32)', *English Historical Review*, CII (1987), 63–84. For the links between Evangelicals and whigs see A. D. Kriegel, 'A Convergence of Ethics: Saints and Whigs in British Antislavery', *Journal of British Studies*, XXVI (1987), 423–50.

the game laws.[43] In June 1822 he backed the unsuccessful second reading of the Catholic Peers Bill, in June 1823 he supported Devonshire's motion on the state of Ireland, in May 1825 he was in favour of the unsuccessful second reading of the Catholic Relief Bill, and he voted for catholic emancipation itself in 1829. This voting pattern during the decade and a half in which he was most active politically represents adherence to those policies on which the whigs most easily agreed during the 1820s.[44]

As befitted someone who had made a thorough study of the question by reading most of the contemporary pamphlets, and who knew about the conditions of the urban working classes at first hand, Calthorpe also advocated free trade and change in the corn laws. In May 1820, when Lord Lansdowne moved for a committee to inquire into the means of improving and extending the foreign trade of the country, he urged that 'the principles of free trade were of the utmost consequence', and that while it might be unattainable in the present circumstances, the task of the government ought to be 'to approximate to it'.[45] Three years later, in a debate on the Spitalfields weavers, he opposed the insertion of amendments which would restrict the free play of market forces and negate 'the best principles of political economy' on which the bill had originally been framed. And he went on to hope that ministers 'would not be deterred' from pursuing, 'with regard to other branches of our trade', that 'liberal policy' which he believed was 'calculated to give a stronger impulse to the manufacturers and commerce of the country'. There were later interventions to the same effect. In April 1825, Calthorpe presented and supported a petition from the Birmingham Chamber of Commerce, in favour of a revision of the corn laws, and in the following year he twice urged that 'ministers ought not to procrastinate' in taking such a step towards a 'wise policy ... with respect to commerce'.[46]

Like all whigs, Calthorpe believed in the sanctity of public opinion, and whenever he stood up in the Lords to argue a particular case, he invariably invoked 'that faithful guide', 'the public wish', 'the opinions and feelings of the people', or 'the general feelings which existed in every part of the country'. In his view, the essence of government was 'to act in unison with public opinion', and to defer to 'the wishes of the community'.[47] Of course, and again like most whigs, Calthorpe took the greatest care to define 'public opinion'. He did not mean the lower orders, the people whose

43 Hansard, *Parl. Debs.*, [1st ser.], XXXIV (1816), col. 819; *Parl. Debs.*, new ser., VI (1822), cols. 452–4; IX (1823), cols. 971–2; XI (1824), cols. 84–6, 1201; XIII (1825), cols. 452, 1031; XVII (1827), cols. 1417–18; XIX (1828), col. 288; XXV (1830), col. 1290.

44 *Ibid.*, new. ser., VII (1822), cols. 1262–4; IX (1823), col. 1072; XIII (1825), col. 768; A. Mitchell, *The Whigs in Opposition, 1815–1830* (Oxford, 1967), pp. 11–17; D. E. D. Beales, *The Political Parties of Nineteenth-Century Britain* (1971), p. 10.

45 D. Southgate, *The Passing of the Whigs, 1832–1886* (1962), pp. 99–100; Hansard, *Parl. Debs.*, new. ser., I (1820), col. 599.

46 Hansard, *Parl. Debs.*, new ser., IX (1823), col. 1534; XIII (1825), col. 149; XV (1826), cols. 39, 293–4.

47 Mitchell, *Whigs in Opposition*, pp. 9–10; Hansard, *Parl. Debs.*, new ser., III (1820), col. 1676; IV (1821), col. 360; VI (1822), cols. 452–3; XII (1825), cols. 1361–2; XIV (1826), col. 1145.

begging letters he received, who were 'not so enlightened or so ready to form just views on great national questions as other classes of the community'. By 'public opinion' he meant those whose wealth and respectability were such that they could form responsible judgments on major issues: 'persons of property and independence', 'the well-educated and well-informed part of the community', 'the manufacturing classes [and] the clergy of the country', and 'Dissenters who, from their education and rank in life, were best qualified to form an accurate opinion'.[48]

For Calthorpe, this nationwide middle class was no vaguely imagined sociological community or rhetorical construction. Whenever he invoked 'those great manufacturing or commercial towns, the inhabitants of which were rapidly increasing in wealth, and growing still faster in knowledge and liberality', he was generalizing on the basis of his detailed knowledge of the bourgeoisie of Birmingham.[49] He described them in the Lords as 'men not in the habit of coming to hasty decisions on any subject', as 'highly respectable persons, who would not come forward with frivolous complaints', as people 'incapable of putting their names to any facts of which they did not know the reality'. On one occasion, he enumerated them even more precisely: they were magistrates, clergymen, bankers, dissenting ministers, doctors, barristers and 'a great number of the most respectable merchants and inhabitants of Birmingham'.[50] He knew what (and who) he was talking about: for these were precisely the sort of prosperous, respectable people who were living, in increasing numbers, on his own Edgbaston estate.

Like Viscount Milton in Sheffield, Calthorpe's landed links with Birmingham enabled him to keep his fingers on 'the pulse of middle class opinion'.[51] But he not only knew it and respected it: he also articulated it, by presenting and endorsing petitions from the Birmingham bourgeoisie in the house of lords. Their views were generally as liberal as his, and many of his speeches on the great issues of the day – on retrenchment, parliamentary reform, the repeal of the corn laws, or catholic emancipation – were delivered in support of their petitions. This meant that during the late 1810s and 1820s, Calthorpe was one of the essential conduits of communication between unrepresented Birmingham and Westminster. Between 1820 and 1831, he presented 14 petitions: against slavery, requesting revision of the corn laws, in favour of catholic emancipation, and also for parliamentary reform. Birmingham may have had no M.P.s of its own, but thanks to Calthorpe's proprietorial connexion with

48 Hansard, *Parl. Debs.*, new ser., VI (1822), cols. 452–3; XIII (1825), col. 63; XIV (1826), col. 1146; XV (1826), col. 39; XX (1829), col. 937.
49 *Ibid.*, XII (1825), col. 1362. Cf. D. Wahrman, *Imagining the Middle Class. The Political Representation of Class in Britain, c.1780–1840* (Cambridge, 1995), pp. 302–3 n. 7.
50 Hansard, *Parl. Debs.*, new ser., I (1820), col. 388; IV (1821), col. 360; XIV (1826), col. 1146; XX (1829), col. 938.
51 D. Spring, 'Earl Fitzwilliam and the Corn Laws', *American Historical Review*, LIX (1954), 302; E. A. Smith, *Whig Principles and Party Politics. Earl Fitzwilliam and the Whig Party, 1748–1833* (Manchester, 1975), pp. 363-67.

the town, he was able to act as one of its 'virtual' representatives, and in this endeavour he was also supported by his two younger brothers in the Commons, whose voting patterns generally reflected his.[52]

The constant theme of Calthorpe's speeches in the upper house was that the legislature should listen to, and respond to, those people who possessed independence, intelligence and property. He advocated parliamentary reform because 'their lordships were sinking in the estimation of the public' and because 'there was not such a confidence in the intentions of parliament as their lordships must wish to see prevail'. He sought to bring about 'a regular corn trade' so as to 'reduce the price of bread and promote commerce'.[53] He 'preferred soothing and conciliatory measures to those which were in their operation vexatious and oppressive'. These words were uttered in a debate on Ireland: but they accurately summarized his general views. 'Nothing could be more injurious to her than to place herself in opposition to liberal ideas.' This was his opinion about the established church: but it was also his feeling about parliament. Throughout the 1820s, Calthorpe repeatedly insisted there must be moderate reform, to respond to and incorporate the respectable middle classes.[54]

By the end of that decade, and with the portentous exception of catholic emancipation, no such reform had materialized. In 1829, there was a savage downturn in the economy, as industrial and agricultural depression coincided, popular discontent reached unprecedented heights, and political unions were organized to agitate for parliamentary reform. Indeed, they originated in Birmingham itself, where the union between the middle classes, whom Calthorpe so admired, and the working classes, whose unreliability he feared, was especially strong.[55] As a result, he found himself in a position which was as difficult as it was well informed, as awkward as it was well meaning. Throughout the country, he saw an alliance between the middle and working classes in favour of sweeping parliamentary reform, while inside Westminster he witnessed the replacement of Wellington's government (which would countenance no reform) by Grey's (which seemed determined to give in to the sort of unsound public opinion he disliked). What was he to do?

52 Information from the History of Parliament Trust; Cannadine, *Lords and Landlords*, pp. 149–50; P. Langford, 'Property and "Virtual Representation" in Eighteenth-Century England', *Historical Journal*, XXXI (1988), 83–115. The success with which the town was 'virtually represented' in both houses of parliament may help explain this remark in the *Birmingham Journal* in October 1829: 'The advantage of sending representatives is merely theoretical, and is surely attended with disorder.' (Quoted in M. Brock, *The Great Reform Act* (1973), p. 44.)

53 Hansard, *Parl. Debs.*, new ser., VI (1822), col. 453; X (1824), col. 831; E.E.O., MS Box 1: Harris to Calthorpe, 24 Nov. 1826.

54 Hansard, *Parl. Debs.*, new ser., XII (1825), col. 944; XIII (1825), col. 1031; XV (1826), cols. 293–4.

55 A. Briggs, 'The Background of the Parliamentary Reform Movement in Three English Cities (1830–32), *Cambridge Historical Journal*, X (1952), 298–300; *idem*, *Victorian Cities* (Harmondsworth, 1968), pp. 186–7; Brock, *Great Reform Act*, pp. 59–61.

IV

He was not sure, and he changed his mind, opposing the second version of the
Reform Bill in October 1831, when it reached the Lords, but voting for the third bill
in April 1832. He became, in short, a 'waverer'. Why did he behave in this much-
criticized way? As a 'born reformer' who advocated 'the restriction of voting within
certain not very extended limits', he was confronted by the choice of no reform
(which he opposed) and sweeping reform (ditto).[56] This made it hard for him to take
a consistent position, as he zigged and zagged between one unpalatable view and
another. In July 1830, an East Retford Disfranchisement Bill was proposed, and
Calthorpe supported it, taking the opportunity to defend the Birmingham Political
Union on the grounds that it was 'the consequence of the town wanting representation'. As long as places like Birmingham were without M.P.s, he argued, it was
inevitable that such organizations would come into being 'to obtain that share in the
representation which they ought to have'. As late as February 1831, he supported
reform because 'the progress of public opinion on the subject ... had been such that
it would no longer be safe to withhold it'. At almost the same time, he was entrusted
with the Birmingham petition in favour of reform, signed by those whose opinions he
was always eager to convey and represent: 'most of the clergy, ... the bankers and
manufacturers' of the town.[57]

On 1 March Lord John Russell introduced the Reform Bill into the house of
commons. Like many others, Calthorpe was appalled by its boldness. He described
it to Harris as 'too sweeping or at all events precipitate', and argued that in bringing
forward such a drastic measure, the ministers had 'formed a wrong estimate of what
is really public opinion on the subject'. With the exception of annual or triennial
parliaments and the ballot, they had 'mixed themselves up with the radical reformers',
and they had 'departed from the prudent, protecting and practical independent
character which ought to mark the proceedings of all governments'. But he was also
troubled that his reaction was not entirely disinterested, since the bill, if passed, would
abolish the rotten boroughs of Hindon and Bramber. Ever since he took his seat in
the Lords, he explained to Harris, he had been resolved 'never to suffer my own
borough patronage to deter me from reform that might seem wise and moderate'. But
he did 'not know in what degree my possession of that influence may warp my
judgement when a scheme of reform including the abolition of it is proposed'. And

56 A. S. Turberville, *The House of Lords in the Age of Reform, 1784–1837* (1958), p. 290; J. A.
    Cannon, *Parliamentary Reform, 1640–1832* (Cambridge, 1973), p. 233. In *Complete Peerage*, II,
    491, he was described as 'of mean aspect, ridiculously egotistical, self-sufficient, and manifestly a
    trimmer'. E.E.O., MS Box 5: Calthorpe to Harris, 3 Nov. 1827; Box 1: Calthorpe to Harris, 2 Mar.
    1831, enclosure.
57 Hansard, *Parl. Debs.*, new ser., XXV (1830), col. 1290; *ibid.*, 3rd ser., II (1831), col. 548; E.E.O.,
    MS Box 1: Calthorpe to Harris, 2 Mar. 1831.

it was also clear that if he did oppose the scheme, he would be lumped 'with the opponents of all reform', which was not his true position.[58]

His one hope was that the Birmingham middle classes would be equally appalled, and withdraw their petition. Accordingly, Calthorpe urged Harris to find out 'the sentiments of the bankers and manufacturers' who had signed it. But his reply brought no comfort. It was true, Harris reported, that 'when they signed the petition, they had no expectation whatever that a change so great and important in its effects upon the representation of the country would have been tried'. But, he went on, 'from all I can hear, the great majority of the persons whose petition is committed to your lordship's care are entirely satisfied with the measure of reform as prepared by the government'.[59] This made things no easier for him. On 10 March 1831, Calthorpe rose in the Lords to present the petition on behalf of 'the magistrates, clergy, merchants and manufacturers of Birmingham' whom he scrupulously reported to be 'decidedly favourable' to the ministers' scheme. But he added that he 'was not prepared to accede to so extensive a change', the greatest since 1688, because it was too sweeping a measure to be passed in a single session, and 'more time ought to be allowed for consideration'. Until and unless it was, Calthorpe concluded, he would be unable to support the government.[60]

During the next few months, this remained his position. In the highly-charged atmosphere in which parliament was debating the bill, he told Harris, 'the idea of deciding upon such a plan in a few weeks seems monstrous'. 'It was a measure', he told their lordships, 'requiring the most patient attention and the greatest care ... and this measure, it appeared, had received neither.' He deeply regretted that it 'should have been propounded to the people when in a state of excitement', which meant 'they were prevented from forming a cool opinion on the subject'. He hoped the bill would 'lie over for another session', so that tempers could moderate, and it might be debated in a more calm and considered way.[61] But while this was a responsible view, it was not practical politics in the increasingly uncertain atmosphere of 1831. In April, the first bill was defeated in the Commons, and there was a general election which greatly increased the number of supporters for the measure in the lower House, and put more pressure on members of the upper House to give way to the mood of the moment. But Calthorpe stood firm. When the reintroduced Reform Bill made its way successfully from the Commons to the Lords in the autumn, he gave his proxy to the duke of Wellington, who used it against the second reading in the early hours of 8 October.[62]

58 E.E.O., MS Box 1: Calthorpe to Harris, 2 Mar. 1831.
59 *Ibid.*, Box 1: Calthorpe to Harris, 2 Mar. 1831; Harris to Calthorpe, 4 Mar. 1831.
60 Hansard, *Parl. Debs.*, 3rd ser., III (1831), cols. 326–7.
61 E.E.O., MS Box 4: Calthorpe to Harris, 5 Mar. 1831; Hansard, *Parl. Debs.*, 3rd ser., III (1831), cols. 1470–1; *Three Nineteenth-Century Diaries*, ed. A. Aspinall (1952), p. 80.
62 Hansard, *Parl. Debs.*, 3rd ser., VIII (1831), col. 342; *Three Nineteenth-Century Diaries*, ed. Aspinall, p. 134.

Since Wellington had stood out against most of the policies which Calthorpe had supported during the 1820s, this cannot have been an altogether easy decision for a 'born reformer' to make. In any case, by early 1832 it was clear that the third version of the Reform Bill, which had been reintroduced into the Commons and passed, would soon reach the upper House. At the same time, Lords Harrowby and Wharncliffe began their attempt to win over enough moderate opponents to ensure it would pass its second reading in the Lords without the need to create any new peers. Once it reached the committee stage, they reasoned, there would be ample opportunity to prune it of its most extreme features. This was the policy of 'qualified support' for which they now sought to gain adherents, and Calthorpe was an obvious target. He and Harrowby were fellow evangelicals and Grosvenor Square neighbours.[63] In late January 1832, Calthorpe received Harrowby's letter, outlining waverer policy. 'The reasoning contained in the paper', he replied, 'seems to me quite conclusive in favour of the course of qualified support of the reform bill.' It was, he felt, 'the best practicable mode of limiting its evils and also of supporting the authority and efficiency of both of the Houses of Parliament'. Illness prevented him from taking any further active part in reform politics. But on the second reading in the Lords in April 1832, Harrowby cast his friend's proxy in favour of the bill.[64] This was not the end of the Reform Bill crisis; but it was the end of Calthorpe's part in it.

Although he appeared to have behaved equivocally and indecisively, Calthorpe's conduct was consistent with his beliefs. He may have wavered in his voting pattern, but he remained firmly convinced of the need to let the middle classes into the vote, and to keep the working classes out. He was equally anxious to ensure that any important measure of reform should be carefully considered and responsibly debated by both the public and the legislature. His difficulty was that between 1830 and 1832, he was being asked to support or to oppose an extreme measure, and to do so with unseemly haste. In the early stages, his concern to limit the franchise and his hostility to rushed and intemperate legislation were so strong that they over-rode his reformist instincts and his abiding support for the Birmingham middle class, whose claims to the vote he regarded as unassailable. But once it became clear that they supported the bill, and that some measure of reform was inevitable, he accepted the policy of 'qualified support' as the best means of implementing it – though even then, he told Harrowby he would have preferred to have raised the £10 voting qualification in large towns.[65] It was an untidy record: but it was neither irresponsible nor dishonourable.

63 Brock, *Great Reform Act*, pp. 272–3; R. Colby, *Mayfair. A Town Within London* (1966), pp. 51–5.
64 Harrowby MS, XIX – 13.9: Calthorpe to Harrowby, 6 Feb. 1832; *The Greville Memoirs*, ed. L. Strachey and R. Fulford (7 vols., 1938), II, 244–5, 253; Hansard, *Parl. Debs.*, 3rd ser., XII (1832), col. 456.
65 Harrowby MS, XIX – 13.19: Calthorpe to Harrowby, 4 May 1832.

V

The passing of the Great Reform Act marked the end of Lord Calthorpe's public career. His two rotten boroughs were duly abolished, and his younger brothers made no effort to find alternative constituencies.[66] He himself made no further speeches in the Lords, rarely took part in divisions and generally inclined towards the Conservatives. But he continued to believe in free trade: in 1839 he made a rare visit to the upper House to support Fitzwilliam's motion for the repeal of the corn laws, and voted for repeal itself seven years later.[67] In philanthropy, we catch a brief, later glimpse of him in June 1840, at a meeting in Exeter Hall of the African Civilization Society, but by then most of the Clapham sect were dead: Charles Elliott in 1832, Wilberforce and Hannah More in 1833, Lord Teignmouth in 1834, Thomas Babington in 1837 and Zachary Macaulay in 1838. In Birmingham, as at Westminster, Calthorpe moved to the right, supporting the Loyal and Constitutional Association, and the Edgbaston estate became a focus for the 'conservative interest' in the town. He still subscribed to local charities, but after 1832, he was no longer the peer who 'virtually represented' the liberal middle classes in the Lords, but the landlord who lived off Birmingham ground rents. So low-profiled were his later years that his death at Lyons in 1851 went virtually un-noticed in the British press.[68]

A generation ago, Michael Brock rightly noted that the 'most obvious characteristic' of the waverers over the Reform Bill was 'their political insignificance', and no case has been advanced here that Lord Calthorpe should be rehabilitated as a major figure in the history of early nineteenth-century Britain.[69] But two things can be said about him by way of conclusion. The first is that he was, by a substantial margin, the most important figure produced by his family in 200 years: an improving and innovative landlord, an evangelical and philanthropist, and a public figure who counted in his day. The second is that his activities, though never of the front rank, bear emphatic witness to the many influential ways in which the aristocracy intersected with British life during the two decades before the passing of the Great Reform Act. Thus regarded, Lord Calthorpe is a case-study in 'aristocratic resurgence', albeit a minor one. But this was not, in his time, how his greatest friend saw things. 'You are the man', William Wilberforce wrote to him in 1820, 'in whose

---

66 O'Gorman, *Voters, Patrons, and Parties*, pp. 30, 33. The Hon. Arthur Gough-Calthorpe retired from Hindon at the dissolution in July 1830, partly on the grounds of ill-health. The Hon. Frederick Gough-Calthorpe was removed by his elder brother as M.P. for Bramber having voted *for* the second reading of Reform Bill in the Commons on 23 March 1831, and was replaced by an anti-reformer in the general election of April that year. (Information kindly supplied by the History of Parliament Trust.)

67 *Complete Peerage*, II, 491; Southgate, *Passing of the Whigs*, p. 105 n. 2; Hansard, *Parl. Debs.*, 3rd ser., LXXXVI (1846), col. 1406.

68 *The Memoirs of Sir T. F. Buxton*, ed. C. Buxton (1848), p. 514; Cannadine, *Lords and Landlords*, pp. 150–2; *The Times*, 3 Oct. 1851; *Complete Peerage*, II, 491.

69 Brock, *Great Reform Act*, p. 276.

judgement and conscience I should be disposed more implicitly to acquiesce than in those of almost anyone living.' This tribute – like the man himself – should not be forgotten.[70]

70 H.R.O., Cal. MS F/C/71: Wilberforce to Calthorpe, 15 Feb. 1820. For the notion of 'aristocratic resurgence' see R. R. Palmer, *The Age of Democratic Revolution. A Political History of Europe and America, 1760–1800* (2 vols., 1959–64), I, 286, 308–17; II, 459–64.

Index